RELIGION AND CULTURE SERIES

Joseph Husslein, S.J., Ph.D., General Editor

THE WHOLE CHRIST

The Whole Christ

*The Historical Development
of the Doctrine of the
Mystical Body
in Scripture and Tradition*

><

Emile Mersch, S.J.
*Professor of Sacred Theology at the
Facultés Notre-Dame de la Paix, Namur*

Translated by
John R. Kelly, S.J.

THE BRUCE PUBLISHING COMPANY
MILWAUKEE

Imprimi potest: PETER A. BROOKS, S.J., Praep. Prov. Missourianae
Nihil obstat: H. B. RIES, Censor librorum
Imprimatur: ✠ SAMUEL A. STRITCH, Archiepiscopus Milwaukiensis
March 2, 1938

Translated from
Le Corps Mystique Du Christ
(Museum Lessianum, Louvain)
Second French edition, 1936

Preface by the General Editor

THE TITLE given this book in its presentation to the English-speaking world is borrowed from St. Augustine. Other titles might have been the Mystical Body of Christ, or still better, the Mystical Christ. But there is a conciseness, simplicity, and intelligibility in the phrase of St. Augustine, the Whole Christ, which it would be difficult to match by any other term. Above all it is exact and tangible.

It perfectly phrases what Christ Himself expressed in one brief word when on the road to Damascus He challenged the prostrate Saul with the warning question: "Why persecutest thou *Me*?" The impassible Saviour, victor over death, and the suffering Christians dragged to prison by Saul, are here referred to by Christ as constituting together one man, "Me," who is, therefore, the Whole Christ. In that mystic unity, Christ, the Incarnate Word, is the Head, we are the members. As for His sake the members suffer persecution He suffers in them, and on the contrary, as He is the Incarnate God they in turn are divinized through their union with Him, "ye are gods."

What here takes place can be briefly described. Included in this "Me" of Christ, this Whole Christ, Christians are united with their Saviour God in a mysterious union; through that same union they are, as co-members, most intimately united also with each other; and finally through their union with Christ as the second Person of the Triune God they are united with the Godhead, with the Most Blessed Trinity. We here touch upon the mountain heights of revealed religion where they pierce into the heavens far beyond our earthly ken.

But let us hear St. Augustine himself explain this truth of the Whole Christ, the Mystical Christ, in words so simple that they might serve as a child's lesson at its mother's knee. He writes:

[vii]

What is the Church? She is the body of Christ. Join to it the Head, and you have one man: the head and the body make up one man. Who is the Head? He who was born of the Virgin Mary. . . . And what is the body? It is His Spouse, that is, the Church. . . . The Father willed that these two, the God Christ and the Church, should be one man.

All men are one man in Christ, and the unity of Christians constitutes but one man.

Let us rejoice and give thanks. Not only are we become Christians, but we are become Christ. My brothers, do you understand the grace of God that is given us? Wonder, rejoice, for we are Christ! If He is the Head, and we are the members, then together He and we are *the whole man*.

When the Head and the members are despised, then the *Whole Christ* is despised, for the *Whole Christ,* Head and body, is that just man against whom deceitful lips speak.[1]

But the Whole Christ does not merely include all the just who have been born into the world since the coming of Christ. It embraces, in the words of St. Augustine, "the whole race of saints, from Abel down to all those who will ever be born and will believe in Christ until the end of the world, for all belong to one city. This city is the body of Christ. . . . *This is the whole Christ: Christ united with the Church.*"

The masterpiece by Father Mersch, here made accessible to the general reader and rendered more attractive to him by numerous wise adaptations involving no changes in the text itself, offers us a historic presentation of the nature, development, and application of the doctrine under consideration. With such finality is this work accomplished that an authoritative critic in *Thought* remarks of the book that it seems to him assured of immortality, as one of those indispensable works that become classics. The translation, we need but say, is worthy of the original.

Coming now to the author's method of treatment, we first behold the adumbration of the doctrine of the Mystical Christ in the Old Testament. We are then shown its revelation in the New, particularly the gradual unfolding of it in St. Paul even as the rosebud opens petal by petal, while in St.

---

[1] These and subsequent quotations from St. Augustine are selected from Part III, Chapter IV, of this book.

John we have a still more definite exposition indicating how the Mystical Christ who incorporates all the faithful in Himself, is the same "Jesus of Nazareth whose deeds and words are recorded by the Synoptics." With the period of Revelation closed, at the death of the last of the Apostles, we pass beyond the Scripture limits to the great Doctors and Fathers of the East and West, whence we are borne along upon the steady flowing stream of time to the Middle Ages, and so on to our own day when this doctrine has become our special heritage.

We are indeed the heirs of all the ages, and so we can turn with satisfaction to this book which has for its particular purpose to make us comprehend what each successive period has contributed to mankind's fuller and richer knowledge of this sublime subject. Ours, as the latest comers, is the accumulated treasure of the centuries.

Naturally, there is still a further purpose to be served by our reading of this volume. The doctrine of our common incorporation into Christ, our divinization as members of the Incarnate Word, the mystery of our life as Christians united with Christ our Head and knit together with each other as cell to cell and joint to joint in one body, in brief, "the mystery of Christ in us," must be made operative in the world today, must become a mighty motive power in the civil, social, and economic life of our age no less than in our religious devotions. In it we possess the divinely given means whereby, joined to our human endeavor, we should be aided most powerfully in the world-embracing task of solving our social questions, of ending our unhappy wars, and of creating the only possible millenium of which this earth is capable. With this doctrine, too, as we are repeatedly told, every other dogma of our Holy Faith is connected, "giving each truth a new meaning for the interior life and a new lesson to guide the actions, thoughts, and affections of men." Nothing, therefore, could be of higher practical value than our complete immersion in this important truth.

Jubilantly, with that same thought in mind, St. Augustine bursts forth into a paean of joy as he realizes all the vast possibilities here placed in the hands of Christians for the transformation of the world after the Heart of Christ:

> O ye, O thou, O ye many who are one!
> O man, O unity!
> What good work art thou doing upon earth?
> What good work thou wilt perform in the Church!

JOSEPH HUSSLEIN, S.J., PH.D.
General Editor, Religion and Culture Series

St. Louis University,
February 27, 1938

Translator's Preface

TO THOSE who are acquainted with the recent theological developments on the subject of the Mystical Body, Father Mersch needs no introduction. *Le Corps Mystique du Christ,* the first edition of which appeared in 1933, has won universal admiration, and seems destined to remain, for many years at least, a standard book of reference for the scholar and the theologian.

However, the work is by no means intended solely for these. It also aims to give the educated Catholic an appreciation of the very important place which the doctrine of the Mystical Body has ever occupied in Christian teaching, and to show how the inspired writers and the greatest exponents of Christian thought have turned instinctively to the reality of the Mystical Body as the central bond of unity, whether in supernatural life, in faith, or in action.

"We preach Christ," was the boast of the Apostles: one Christ, who is both the only Way and they that follow the way; one Christ, who is both the Truth to be believed and they that believe it; one Christ, who is both the divine Life and they that live this life. This one Christ, this Mystical Christ, is the whole Christ, Head and members: Jesus of Nazareth, plus the Mystical Body which He has taken to Himself from among men.

Father Mersch has succeeded admirably in showing, by means of an abundance of well-chosen quotations, how the Apostles preached this one Christ, and how the Fathers and Doctors of the Church and the theologians have carried on, systematized, and explained the apostolic preaching, which describes Christ as living again, suffering again, dying again, and rising again from the dead, in and with His Body, which is the Church.

It is in order to make this preaching and this living voice

[xi]

of Tradition accessible to the English-speaking faithful that the present translation has been undertaken. The specialist and the scholar will not depend upon a translation; they will continue to consult the French original. Hence, in order to reduce the size of the book and to make it less forbidding to the lay reader, the long critical and exegetical notes and the exhaustive references and bibliographies have been omitted, together with all appendices. The occasional Latin and Greek phrases which remain in the text may be passed over without misgiving, since the substance of the quotation will always be found, in English, in the immediate context.

It has also been necessary to omit the splendid preface contributed by Father Lebreton. The analytical table of contents has been greatly reduced. However, the detailed summaries have been retained at the beginning of each chapter, to serve as guides to the reader. Of the index of proper names, only the names of those writers have been retained and incorporated into the general alphabetical index who are actually mentioned or quoted in the translation.

With a few exceptions, which are clearly indicated in the notes, texts of the Old Testament are cited according to the familiar Douay version (D.V.), but the New Testament is quoted according to the more modern and more readable, though unofficial Westminster version (W.V.). The translation of passages from the works of the Fathers is based, whenever possible, upon the Greek or Latin texts as contained in Migne's *Patrology* (P.G., P.L.), with occasional references to the Vienna *Corpus of Latin Ecclesiastical Writers* (C.V.), and to the Berlin *Corpus of Greek Christian Writers of the First Three Centuries* (C.B.). Other sources are indicated in the notes.

A word of caution may not be out of place for readers who are not familiar with the general outlines of the doctrine of the Mystical Body. As is evident from the subtitle, the book does not propose to give a complete, systematic explanation of the doctrine as such, but rather to point out how, in Scripture and in Tradition, the various elements of the doctrine were expressed, haltingly at first and in isolated passages, and how in time they were gradually gathered to-

[xii]

gether into a more or less unified system. In order to see and understand more clearly the method of development which is followed in the work, the uninitiated reader will do well, first to study the Introduction rather carefully, and then to turn immediately to the final chapter, where, in a few clear pages, the author sums up the results of his researches and shows briefly how almost every point of Christian teaching has been linked up by the Fathers and the Scholastics with the truth of the Mystical Body.

I take this occasion to acknowledge my indebtedness, first of all to Father Mersch himself, and to many others, for valuable assistance and advice in preparing the translation.

May a better knowledge of "the mystery of Christ in us" unite all of us more closely to the God who was made man in order that men might be made divine in Him.

JOHN R. KELLY, S.J.

Contents

PART ONE

THE DOCTRINE OF THE MYSTICAL BODY IN SACRED SCRIPTURE

PART TWO

THE DOCTRINE OF THE MYSTICAL BODY IN THE GREEK FATHERS

[xv]

CONTENTS

PART THREE

THE DOCTRINE OF THE MYSTICAL BODY IN WESTERN TRADITION

[xvi]

INTRODUCTION

Introduction

WE PROPOSE to study in these pages what St. Paul, in his Epistle to the Colossians, calls "the mystery of Christ in us."[1] It is our desire to make this mystery better known by assembling, in the best order we may, the marvelous things that Scripture and Tradition have said of it.

However, these marvelous sayings are so numerous and of so many different kinds that in order to give the necessary unity to the inventory that is to follow, a preliminary general outline is almost indispensable. Naturally, this can be no more than a résumé, which the entire work must serve to explain and to justify.

The "mystery" is before all else a prodigy of unity. God has raised to a supernatural perfection the natural unity that exists between men. Henceforth they are one, but one in Christ, one with a unity so sublime that they are as little able to attain it by their unaided efforts as they are to comprehend it by their unaided reason.

This unity affects our being from every point of view. It unites us with ourselves; it unites us with one another; it unites us each and all together with God; it unites us each and all together with Christ. Thus, by a kind of multiplication of itself, so to speak, it adapts itself to our multiplicity and enfolds us, just as we are, into its own oneness.

In the first place, it unites us with Christ. This is the principle of all the rest; it is from the Saviour that all supernatural unity comes to men, just as it is from Him that they have their whole supernatural life. And what is life but a particular mode of unity? For us, from the supernatural standpoint, to exist means to be in Christ. To have life in the eyes of God, to have a dignity, a hope, an eternity,

---

[1] Col. 1:27. The meaning of the phrase is discussed later, Part I, ch. 5.

is also to be in Christ. To perform salutary works, to know, to hope, to love, is again and always to be in Christ.

He is the Head, we are the members; He is the Vine, we the branches; He is Life in its source, and we are animated by that life; He is Unity, and we many are one in Him who is One. Between Him and ourselves all is common. The excellences that He possesses are extended even to us; in Him they exist in their plenitude, whereas they come to us by participation. But even within us they are vibrant with the beating of His own Heart. All that He is, all that He has done, even His least action, is a cause of our most interior life. His purity, His justice, His holiness "flow into" us, as theologians say; they become our own, because He has become our own; and thus we are made holy, just, and pure before God, but solely because of Him and in Him. His birth and His life, His death and His resurrection — especially His death and resurrection — are also our own, since He is ours; they are prolonged in a mysterious way, by the sacraments and by grace, in our regeneration, in our death to sin, in our elevation to glory.

As His excellences pass into men and transfigure them, so do their miseries pass into Him and are there consumed. In Him, by His Blood and by His Cross, sin has been destroyed; and the consequences of sin — sufferings, humiliations, and death — become a means of expiation, a source of life and of joy. Briefly, in Him and in Him alone is the restoration and the ennobling of man. Freed from his hideousness, transformed into the likeness of Christ, man can draw near to God.

Secondly, the "mystery" unites us with God. This union we have in Christ, and only in Christ; since He is God and since we are in Him, in Him we are made divine; since He is the Son and we are in Him, we are sons of adoption in Him; since He possesses the Spirit and we are in Him, in Him we have the Spirit. The grace whereby His humanity becomes the humanity of the Word of Life is the same grace that enables our human nature, in Him and in Him alone, to possess life within itself. The justification that makes us intrinsically holy is the prolongation in the members of the action of the Triune God, whereby the body and blood of our

Head was made the body and blood of the Holy of holies at the moment of the Incarnation.

This grace that comes to us from Him is as universal as it is sublime. It confers the new life upon all His members, but all receive it in Him alone. Therefore, since it produces in Him the supernatural life of all, it likewise produces in Him the unity of all.

Thirdly, the "mystery" unites all men together in Christ. Since in God's eyes all men have life only by reason of their attachment to the one Saviour, it follows that all men have a common life, flowing from the same principle that gives each one his individual life. Hence, men are catholic and universal; they are men of the Church and of the universe, and intrinsically so. Each is perfected by all the others in what is most interior to himself, that is, in this Christ from whom he has life; each has his personal life and holiness, his good works and his merits, but he possesses them in common with all other men; they are truly his own, but at the same time truly theirs.

One and the same holiness flows in all of humanity: each has this holiness as his own and each is intrinsically holy, because each of Christ's members is truly alive; and each possesses this holiness through union with all the others, by communion with all the saints, living and dead, because all live in one and the same Christ. Thus is mankind united with itself in Christ.

Finally, the "mystery" unites each man with himself. It is a deepening of the interior life, a deification that affects the very substance of each one's inmost self. At the same time it imposes an obligation to rise above self; it establishes a new, purer, supernatural code of morality; it calls for a Christian holiness, for a Christian chastity, and above all for a Christian charity. In Christ we must live for God and for our brethren, since we are to live with them in Christ.

The "mystery," then, is a miracle of goodness on God's part, while on our part it is a miracle of transformation, of life, of holiness, and especially of unity. No formula suffices to tell us what it is; the résumé that we have given is sadly deficient, and the pages that follow will not succeed in expressing the full reality. In order to represent it with any degree of completeness, we should have to review the entire field of Christian doctrine and point out how that doctrine is speaking, always and everywhere, of the union with God that binds all men together in Christ.

For it is precisely in explaining what Christianity is that the Fathers explain this union of men with Christ. Thus, for instance, it is in their teaching on the unity and necessity of the Church that they speak of our incorporation with Christ in the Church, and it is when they treat of the consubstantiality of the Son with the Father that they formulate a doctrine of the divinization which men receive as members of the Incarnate Word. As a matter of fact, this doctrine of divinization is often presupposed instead of being treated *ex professo*. Naturally enough, such occasional fragments of doctrine are not always easy to recognize. The general outline that we have given will render the task less difficult.

Essentially, therefore, the "mystery" is a miracle of unity. As to the precise nature of this unity, however, there is a variety of opinions. We shall first mention certain false views, in order not to be obliged to return to them later on.

To begin with, one would ill understand this unity, or to be more exact, he would not understand it at all, were he to imagine that the faithful are really and absolutely Christ Himself, or, if we may be pardoned the expression, that they are fragments or emanations of Christ. This would be a kind of pantheism, or rather, "panchristism," quite as contradictory as it is naïve, and fraught with the most absurd consequences. Severe though the judgment be, it is very true: *corruptio optimi pessima,* it is the perversion of the noblest truths that is most regrettable. We know to what egotistical pride, to what obstinacy in the queerest notions, and even to what perversion illuminism can lead: disdain for human actions, which, since they are not the actions of the Saviour, are considered to be worthless; or a proud esteem of those same human actions, because they are judged to be the very actions of Christ; lowering Christ to a purely human level, or exalting man to Christ's own level; in short, a total disregard of what is most essential to Christianity — all these can result from the exaggerated ideas to which we refer. The destination shows how false was the direction taken at the point of departure.

It is another, though less serious mistake, to rely more on imagination and sentiment than on reason and faith in a matter of such importance. Some, for example, absolutely insist on picturing the Mystical Body to themselves, by means of an image that they consider to be a perfect representation of the reality. Certainly we need images; we cannot think without phantasms, and Scripture provides many of them in connection with the doctrine of the Mystical Body. The error lies in mistaking the image for a definition and in thinking that just because they are able to conceive some huge ethereal and invisible organism or a kind of living atmosphere in which men's souls are somehow fused one into the other, they therefore possess a perfect knowledge of the mystery of the Head and members. It goes without saying that whoever allows himself to be so misled by his imagination is exposing himself to all kinds of absurdities.

It has been necessary in every age to put the faithful on their guard against false mysticism, and in our day the warning is, to say the least, as indispensable as ever. It is quite useless to describe all the forms which the illusion takes, but the reader can see how the doctrine of the Mystical Body might well serve it as a mask. The angel of darkness has ever been wont to disguise himself as an angel of light.

Moreover, the very name adds strength to the temptation. In certain minds the term *Mystical Body* gives rise to ideas of complicated piety, of sentimentalism, of spiritual ambition, and excites aspirations to extraordinary, ecstatic, sometimes morbid states. Perhaps this is the very reason why many view the doctrine with suspicious eyes.

Unfortunately, such prudent suspicions are not the only difficulty to be overcome. Among those of the faithful who are less enlightened, less well instructed, or whose good sense is less alert, the doctrine of the Mystical Body, like all other truths, is apt to be ill understood.

Some might think, for instance, that it dispenses men from all effort, and that from the moment one is made a member of Christ by baptism, there is no further need for asceticism and mortification. Why should one have to keep watch over his thoughts and actions? Why should he try to correct his faults? Why make any effort in prayer, why urge the soul to meditation and to acts of love? One's aim should be to forget self, whereas these traditional tactics of spirituality succeed only in burdening the soul with itself. We have but to be absorbed in Christ and to experience a certain tenderness at the thought — pardon the expression — that we are being dissolved in Him. This emotional persuasion would be a profitable substitute for particular examinations of conscience and for penitential practices.

Holy Scripture and Tradition show only too clearly how false and how narrow such views are, as we shall have occasion to prove in the pages that follow. Just as the life of Christ in the faithful and the life of the faithful in Christ are the sum and substance of our religion, so, too, do they sum up all the precepts of Christian asceticism. The mystery omits none of these precepts, but as we shall see, it repeats them all, giving each a fuller and deeper meaning; its demands are even more exacting, but at the same time they are more acceptable.

It is not our purpose in these pages to refute false ideas of the Mystical Body or wrong ways of representing our unity in Christ. We wish only to seek out the truth. Yet truth itself is the best antidote for error, *verum index sui et falsi.*

Now that we have indicated certain false notions of the Mystical Body, what is the correct view? The answer is that there are two; both good, and both orthodox.

The first is characterized by its realism and its mysticism. We present it here in brief outline. Its great and guiding principle is to take the full and complete meaning of the Scriptural and patristic statements. According to this view, men have a true union with Christ, a real and ontological union; He is really and truly in them and we are in Him;

we are really and truly one in Him as He is one with the Father. That this union be hard to explain is of small moment; is it to be regretted that God should have given us a union with His Son that transcends our own limited views? That it can be misunderstood is also certain; such is the case with all truths. But that does not make it less real. The important thing is to explain oneself clearly and prudently when speaking of it. That some should hesitate to call it a "physical" union is easy to understand; the very term appears to reduce it to the categories of the merely natural order. That one should refuse to accept the words "Mystical Body" and "members and Head" as the statement of a thesis whence all possible consequences can be drawn — nothing could be wiser; these metaphors, for such they are, merely indicate a unity that transcends the biological realities from which they are taken. It is best to retain the traditional name and call it a "mystical" union. However, it must be clearly understood that this term is by no means synonymous with "nebulous" or "semi-real." On the contrary, it signifies something which in plenitude and reality surpasses the things of nature and the positive concepts that our reason can elaborate.

The second view does not go so far. The union which it describes, though real, is more tenuous; it is a reality of the moral order. The reason for this restraint is certainly not to be found in the texts of Scripture and the Fathers, for these are as forceful as possible. It is due rather to the desire, very laudable in itself, not to multiply the mysteries of faith beyond what is absolutely necessary. According to this view, all can be explained by the fact of our resemblance to Christ and our absolute and manifold dependence upon Him. The Lord is the model of all our virtues, the principle of all our hopes, the expiation of all our sins, the source of all our supernatural life. He is the exemplary and meritorious cause of our justification, and in a certain sense even its final and efficient cause. He is our Emmanuel, our Master, our guide, our friend, our brother; in fine, He is our all, and before God we are nothing except with Him and through Him. In a word, we are joined to Him by all the bonds that can attach one man to another; and here these bonds are far more numerous and far more powerful. All this is quite sufficient to justify Scripture and Tradition in teaching that with Him we make up one body, a Mystical Body.

The Church has never decided between these two views. Each has its good points, if only that it acts as a check upon the other. The second has the advantage of greater clearness; it is easier to explain and to understand. The first, at least to our way of thinking, is richer in doctrine, better founded in Scripture and the Fathers, more in conformity with the analogy of the faith. If its message is more mysterious, this element of mystery is not so much an added difficulty as a transcendent truth that helps us to understand the other truths a little better.

In other words, our own choice has already been made. In the pages that follow we shall speak in terms of the first explanation; we leave it to the reader to judge, from the evidence, whether we are right or wrong. However, we have no intention of combating, or even of discussing the other view. The mystery of Christ is a mystery of union, and one should not employ, as arguments against his brother, texts that treat only of charity and mutual understanding. Theology can be militant at times; it should be so when opposing those, who, openly or not, consciously or not, are enemies of revelation. But here there are no adversaries. All are jealous of the same orthodoxy, all are equally intent upon the search for the same truth, and all wish to make the search together if possible.

As a matter of fact, this search is difficult enough in the present instance, without encumbering ourselves with controversy. Not without reason has this unity been commonly styled "mystical," mysterious; not without cause is it bound up with all the dogmas of our faith, even with those that are most obscure. To understand this unity, we must understand the nature of the Incarnation which has brought it to our earth, the nature of the divine life whence this unity flows, the nature of justification of which it is one aspect, the nature of original sin of which it is the reparation, the nature of the Eucharist of which it is the supernatural effect (*res et effectus proprius*); in a word, we must understand the whole of Christian doctrine. It would be absurd to lay claim to perfect knowledge of the mystery here on earth. Only in the rays of the Eternal Light, "on that day" spoken of by Jesus in the Gospel of St. John (14:20), shall we know how Christ is in the Father, and we in Him, and He in us. Meanwhile we must rest content with the half light of this world, a light that may be increased by study and reflection, a light that is most fruitful and most desirable, but always imperfect.

When, through Scripture and the Fathers, God speaks to us of this unity of grace, He does so by means of comparisons and suggestive, but rather imprecise expressions, much more frequently than by means of rigorous definitions and systematic expositions. The formulas ever retain a certain vagueness; in them reason seeks vainly for the clear and well-defined concepts that are its delight. If this is so, certainly it is all for the best. Since God has a more perfect knowledge than we have, both of the mystery which He reveals and of the poor intelligences to which He reveals it, He must also know better than we do what means are best suited to give us some insight into these transcendent realities. He speaks to us of the mystery as He spoke of it to the Jews of old: *prout poterant audire;* He adapts His teaching to our powers of comprehension.

In our task of gathering and repeating His message we wish to be guided by one sole purpose, a purpose that we hope to maintain religiously: we wish to repeat the message exactly as it is. The prime duty of one who would record another's thought, or even his own thought, is not to be clear, but to be faithful and true to the model. The ideas of Pelagius on the subject of grace are easier to understand than those of Augustine, but are they for that reason more true? When there is question of sublime realities, and particularly of supernatural realities, may not the very clearness of an explanation be a sign that the real difficulty, the real marvel, has been suppressed?

All data are good so long as they come from God. So we shall take them all: vague when they are vague, clear when they are clear, incomplete when they are incomplete. We shall try to add nothing, not even incidental clearness, and to suppress nothing, not even what to our clouded vision appears to be an excrudescence or obscurity. Out of veneration for the truth and out of respect for the reader, we shall, of course, do all in our power to be precise and easy to follow; but we pray God that we may betray neither the truth nor all of us who have no other need but truth.

The difficulty of a subject is no excuse for neglecting its study. On the contrary, it is at the obscure points that greater light is needed. Some may tell us: "Do not speak of such things; you are apt to be misunderstood." Detestable advice! Do men come to an understanding by keeping their thoughts to themselves? Or are there truths in our religion that are dangerous, truths that must be avoided, truths that by their very nature are capable of engendering only false notions and vain discussions?

God who has revealed all, has made His revelation full of grace and truth. If certain points are richer in applications and in interest, they must be in some sense more essential to the truth revealed, since they tell us more expressly of Him who is Truth and of the manner in which He wills to dwell in men. One of these points, or we may even say the first of these points is the doctrine of the Mystical Body. Hence we should expect to find in it a greater abundance of the light of Life and of true consolation.

For how can we believe that God, who is the Light and who wills to shine in our souls, should not have placed in this truth all the light that we need to understand it, since it is precisely the explanation of that gift which He has made to men of His most pure and most glorious Word?

The important thing, to our mind, is to seek and desire no other light but that which He offers, to resign ourselves cheerfully to the shadows that He wills to leave, to take all the indications that He furnishes, confident that they will explain each other and that as the phrases of the message are gradually assembled, each will prove to be the best commentary for the others when all shall have been brought together to form one complete whole.

Guided by God's providence, Christian teaching has been in a state of uninterrupted growth since the beginning. During the whole of the old dispensation and even during the early years of the new, it was constantly being enriched by the addition of new truths, of new revelations that served to complete and explain the others. The death of the last Apostle terminated this development by external addition; but now we see the beginning, or rather the continuation of another development, which consists in a fuller understanding and in a more perfect expression of what has been revealed. It is no longer revelation that grows, but man who grows in the comprehension of revelation.

We shall have occasion to study this twofold progress in every page of our work. For the present we wish to say just one thing about this growth, in order to avoid any misconceptions. It is, before all else, the work of God. Not of God alone, for in it God makes use of secondary causes and the reason of men. But God and God alone remains the source of truth; He and He alone reveals; He and He alone watches over the deposit of faith, to assure and guarantee its perpetual identity.

The study of a subject so complex and so sublime is a tremendous task. Needless to say, we do not expect to be able to accomplish it fully, even with respect to the point of doctrine that will occupy our attention. Our aim is simply to consider some of its aspects, to assemble a series of *studies,* each of which is distinct from the others. Each will be devoted to a particular stage of the doctrinal development. In our opinion, which may be wrong, these are the principal stages, or at least include most of the principal stages; hence the entire work will contain a general outline of the history of the development.

Naturally, we have arranged our studies according to the chronological order: first come those that refer to the Scriptures, then those that deal with Tradition. In the study of Tradition, we have treated first the Greek Fathers, then the Fathers and ecclesiastical writers of the Western Church. This division of East and West, which was necessary for a clear and logical development, forced us to depart from the chronological order. However, this departure is very slight;

[13]

as far as our subject is concerned, Western tradition as a whole may be considered as the exact continuation of the teaching of the East.

While we have not found all the interesting texts for the early centuries and up to the time of St. Augustine, we think we have discovered at least most of the important ones. For more recent periods, we cannot claim a like thoroughness; the number of authors and works which would have had to be consulted grew constantly greater as we advanced. All that we have been able to do is to uncover a few portions of one of the paths which Tradition followed on its way to us. To trace all of its itineraries would have been impossible.

Something similar must be said for our studies as a whole. Even where we think that we have located the most important landmarks, we should not venture to trace the path that connects them. The documents are too rare and their indications too incidental. From the little information that history offers, it is frequently difficult, not to say impossible, to determine all the explicit teaching of a particular Father on this point, to discover from whom and in what manner God willed that he should receive this teaching, to discern the influences whereby God led him to present it from such an angle and with emphasis on this or that particular aspect. Hence it would be rash to attempt to follow the development of the doctrine in all its continuity from a purely historical viewpoint; too often the path is lost in the darkness.

This, evidently, is a further motive for giving our full attention to the points that appear more clearly, to take note, at these more advantageous moments, of the differences and the nuances that the doctrine presents, and to pick out whatever may serve to throw light upon possible influences or relations that may have existed between the various authors.

Above all, it is an additional motive for considering the fact that there is a logical order corresponding to this historical order, and that the ideas which are differently expressed in different ages are intrinsically connected with each other. Is there any reason why Providence should not have made use of this order as well as of the first? In order that one writer

[14]

may be said to continue the teaching of another, need he have had the intention of so doing, or need he even have known about the other? Must we say that the history of Christian doctrine has no unity either in itself or in the Spirit of God, but only in the minds of the men who expound it?

Hence the reader must keep in view the special object of our work. We have called it *Studies in historical theology.* It is not a question of studying the history of an ordinary doctrine, such as men might have elaborated and enriched in their own way, building it up piece by piece at various intervals, groping, correcting, changing. There is question here of a truth that is ever the same, which an infinite Wisdom, ever the same, allows to penetrate gradually into the souls of men by means of a manifestation that continues through the ages, ever more complete, yet ever the same; the while His goodness, ever the same, gives clearer vision to their intelligences.

Certainly there is no reason to prescind from this unfailing identity and this perpetual continuity. On the contrary, we rely upon it to justify our method of comparing the various texts which we deem important, of making them explain each other, and of supplementing what may be left only partially developed in one or other passage by means of the light that is afforded by all the texts taken together; lastly, we rely upon it to show that despite the time and the distance that separate their authors, these texts are all expressions of one and the same truth and that all have a part in one and the same infusion of this truth into the souls of men.

We have made it a point to give many quotations, not only because contact with the sources is all-important from the standpoint of history, but especially because the texts adduced are the words of Scripture and the Fathers, and for that reason possess a very particular theological value. They are the very expressions that God has willed. May we not believe that as such they will serve to bring light and understanding, and that in them God Himself speaks more directly to us?

Some of our citations may appear quite colorless, almost

[15]

alien to our subject. We do not deny this possibility. Nevertheless, we beg the reader not to pass them by without asking himself whether they do not throw light upon some other text, and without reflecting that the "mystery" has many different aspects and that between these different aspects there exist many points of contact.

It is possible, indeed certain, that the multiplication of quotations has involved many repetitions. The Scriptures return often to the same thoughts, and the Fathers frequently emphasize the same aspects of the doctrine of the Mystical Body. If we were to avoid repeating the same ideas, we should have to present the Bible and Tradition otherwise than as they actually are. The reader will understand our anxiety not to overlook any element of so precious a gift of God.

Furthermore, let us remember that for the study of an object so sublime, the resources of human reason are not enough; in things divine, the mind of man is not in its own element, and it is not the part of man to judge the message. Rather is it the part of the message to judge him. Here, much more truly than in other matters, there is need for respect, for reserve, and for humility. Suffice it to say that we submit all that follows, not only to the authority of those who speak in God's name, as is quite evident, but also to the judgment of all those who, living of the life of Christ, have competence in the knowledge of these interior realities: *et in servis suis iudicet Christus.*

Yet precisely because the resources of human intelligence are so inadequate, there is all the greater need to employ them to the full. The most scrupulous objectivity must be maintained more strictly in the treatment of religious truths than anywhere else; the more divine the truth, the more reverently must it be handled. Hence we shall endeavor to be as accurate and as faithful as possible. It would be folly and a profanation to make texts so sublime express anything different than what they actually say, or to make them emphasize something that is not stressed either in the texts themselves or in other texts that come to us from the same transcendent source. Undoubtedly historical theology

[16]

can be history only insofar as it is theology, that is, insofar as it treats its subject in the one way which befits that subject and is capable of making it intelligible: humbly, reverently, remembering that He who speaks is the same who teaches in all the other documents of the faith. But conversely, it will be theology only insofar as it is history, that is, only insofar as it aims at all the rigor and precision possible, with the conviction that the message, just as God has given it, is worth infinitely more than anything which mere human reason might substitute, even for prudence' sake, in its place.

PART ONE

⋈

The Doctrine

of the Mystical Body

in

Sacred Scripture

Chapter I

The Mystical Body Prefigured in the Old Testament

><

I. *How to study the Old Testament:* It is explained by the New. The Epistle to the Ephesians tells us that in the creation God willed to effect a union of all men with Himself in Christ, who is the second, the true Adam. The Epistle to the Galatians teaches that the entire Old Covenant was in reality made with Christ and the members of Christ. Hence the Mystical Body begins with the Old Testament. The true seed of Abraham.

II. *The Old Testament.* From the very outset the Mystical Body is represented as a work of unity.

1. *Unity of the Hebrews among themselves:* they are one whole, one living being, one spouse, one man, whom God cherishes with a great love.

2. *Unity of the Hebrews with God:* God dwells in Israel; Israel is a manifestation of God in the world; Israel's cause is the cause of Yahweh; in Israel is reflected the holiness of Yahweh; so that, as we learn from the New Testament, all Israel is a figure of Jesus Christ.

I

THE INCORPORATION of mankind in Christ is, before all else, a work of unity: unity of all men with God, unity of all men among themselves, and this unity is brought about by the union of all men with Christ. It is under this aspect of unity that the Mystical Body appears in its very origins and in the first documents that speak of it.*

These documents are the most ancient books of Scripture, the writings of the Old Testament. We shall begin our study with them. However, the Scripture itself warns us that in order clearly to understand the Old Testament, we need the light shed upon it by the New. *Novum in vetere latet, vetus*

---

* Footnotes and Biblical citations of the several chapters will be found conveniently grouped together, beginning on page 585.

in novo patet, as theologians say, "the new is hidden in the old, the old is revealed in the new."

We shall, therefore, follow this detour, or rather, this only way; it will give us a comprehensive view of our horizons. Nor is it long; in order to determine the proper point of view, we need but read and reflect upon two passages of St. Paul which furnish the theological introduction to our study of the Old Testament.

The first of these passages is the prologue of the Epistle to the Ephesians; we learn that from the creation of the world, that is, from the moment that God's plan concerning the finite was put into operation, there was already question of the Mystical Body.

The Apostle may have been thinking of certain errors which were being propagated in Asia Minor, and which, with their genealogies of angels and of eons, and their precepts respecting the use of material creatures, doubtless embodied a doctrine on the origin of the physical world, or creation. At all events, in writing to these churches, Paul considers it necessary to explain at once the Christian concept of creation.

As far as we can judge, he places himself at the *instans rationis* when God foresaw original sin, and he tells us what was then God's will concerning our race. Now, insists Paul, what God willed was not to create a purely natural human-kind in a profane world, but to raise up a race of men that should be blessed, chosen and beloved in Christ; in other words, a race that should be incorporated into the Mystical Body.

The manner of being, therefore, that God willed for man was an *esse in Christo,* an existence in Christ. Human ontology, viewed in its origins, was in reality a supernatural ontology, an ontology of members destined to be joined together in a body: we have existence in order that we may become members of the Saviour.

Thus, even the creation of the world speaks to us of grace; it speaks of a union with God which is offered to us; it speaks of Christ, Head and Body. Filled with wonder at this spectacle, Paul opens his Epistle with a song of thanksgiving.

Paul, an apostle of Christ Jesus by the will of God, to the saints that are at Ephesus, the faithful in Christ Jesus: grace to you and peace from God our Father and the Lord Jesus Christ.

And the hymn breaks forth immediately:

Blessed be the God and Father of our Lord Jesus Christ, who hath blessed us with every spiritual blessing on high in Christ. Yea, in Him He singled us out before the foundation of the world, that we might be holy and blameless in His sight. In love He predestinated us to be adopted as His sons through Jesus Christ, according to the good pleasure of His will.[1]

Creation is for Paul so intrinsically Christian that he returns again to this loving design, conceived by God before the foundation of the world. For from the very beginning Christ is the term and center of all; all things were created in Him, and all subsist in Him.

The role of Christ, and the concept of the Mystical Body that follows from it, are at once cosmological and ecclesiological. That which makes Christ the first-born of every creature, explains Paul, likewise makes Him Head of the whole Church; He is the supernatural unity of all creation, as He is the unity of the supernatural work which was God's purpose in creation. We shall frequently meet with these two concepts in the course of our study; hence the need of drawing attention thus early to their close solidarity.

Here, we are at the very foundations of the doctrine. What the first verse of Genesis is for a religious understanding of the universe: "In the beginning God created heaven and earth"; and what the prologue of St. John's Gospel is for an understanding of the Word: "in the beginning was the Word" — these opening lines of the Epistle to the Ephesians are for the doctrine of our elevation to the supernatural order and our incorporation into Christ. They tell us that God, who in the beginning made all things, loved us, at the beginning of all His graces, in the Word, who was in the beginning.

Just as in God there is a pre-existence of Christ in relation to the Incarnation and creation, so there is in Christ a pre-existence of the Mystical Body in relation to all things that are created: the two are inseparable. So, too, as soon as the unity of the Christians begins to appear in the Old Testament, and still more when it reaches its consummation at the end of time, that unity does not so much rise from earth as it descends from heaven, where, in a certain sense, it is realized in advance. In the Apocalypse, St. John sees it coming down from heaven: it 'is the new Jerusalem that comes, adorned as a bride; and this heavenly Jerusalem, St. Paul assures us, is our Mother. As the streams that flow upon the earth have their prime source in the clouds of heaven, so the Church, by which we live here below, has her beginning in the glory of eternity, in Jesus Christ.

After the eternal decrees — if we may employ the term *after* for what is eternal — after these decrees, came the fulfillment. God created man, and Adam was the preparation and the figure of the Man-God who was to come.

This point merits special attention. The parallel of the two Adams was already pointed out by St. Paul, and the idea was destined to become familiar to Tradition. As a matter of fact, it is expressed by the simple representation of the skull at the foot of nearly every crucifix.

It is important to note that in this parallel the Christ who is compared with Adam is not an isolated individual, but one who possesses within Himself the life of regenerated humanity; in other words, it is the Mystical Christ. The comparison signifies, therefore, that the inclusion of men in their first father was the prototype and the figure of their incorporation in the one Saviour.

Adam forfeited the divine gift both for himself and for us. But this defection had been foreseen, and God's plan continued to work itself out in spite of us, as it were. However, in our race, henceforth laden with sin, the full realization of the divine plan would come but slowly, amid sufferings which our nature would not have known but for sin.

This realization of the design of God is related in the books of the Old Testament. But, we must repeat: even here the message can be read clearly only in the light of the New Testament. Once more Paul is God's interpreter.

[24]

We find the explanation in the Epistle to the Galatians. Certain Jews had come into the young Church, and were sowing the seeds of alarm. They maintained that the promises made by God in the Old Law were for the Jews alone, and that Christians were excluded unless they submitted to circumcision.

As if God were not already thinking both of His Son who was to come upon the earth and of those whom He would make members of His Son, when He made the Old Covenant! To reassure the Christians, the Mystical Body of Christ, Paul shows that they were already referred to in the Old Testament.

> The Scripture foresaw that it was through faith that God would justify the Gentiles and foretold to Abraham, "in thee shall all the nations be blessed." And so they that are of faith are blessed with faithful Abraham.

This point required more conclusive proof. Note Paul's argument:

> Brethren, I speak in human terms. Still, when a man's will hath been ratified, no one maketh it void or addeth thereto. Now the promises were spoken to Abraham "and to his seed." It saith not, "and to his seeds," as though there were many, but as of one, "and to his seed"; which seed is Christ.[2]

The will or testament to which St. Paul alludes does not consist exclusively in the compact which God had made with Abraham; it appears to embrace all the promises given by Yahweh to His people. In other words, it is the entire Old Testament. In fact, it was the whole of the Old Testament that constituted Israel's greatness; hence it would seem that the Jewish zealots were using the entire Old Testament as an argument against the Christians. And it was the Old Testament as a whole that had to be explained. Accordingly it is to be thought that Paul is considering here the entire Old Testament in its most solemn moment; namely, in the promises made to Abraham.

This whole testament, he explains, is meant for the Christians, for they are the true seed of Abraham. God made the covenant primarily with Christ, and they are united with

[25]

Christ. Is not Christ the term toward which the whole Law is directed, and to which it leads the souls of men, by its prophecies as well as by its precepts?

In the Epistle to the Galatians, the Apostle proves this point with a rapidity that one would be tempted to call presumptuous, did not the very abruptness of the argument point to an intuition from the Holy Spirit who inspired the writer.

The seed of Abraham, Paul declares, is designated by a word, σπέρμα, which the Scripture consistently employs in the singular. Therefore this seed can include but one man; and this one man can be none other than Christ. Hence it is with Christ, and with Him alone, that the covenant was made.

But, one may object, the fact that a certain word is used always in the singular merely proves that here we have to deal with a peculiar Hebrew idiom. Granted; but God, who created language together with all other things, may very well speak to us, if He so wills, even by means of grammar and the dictionary. If He tells us that He was thinking of a certain thing — no matter how stupendous that thing may be — and if He chooses in addressing us to use one word rather than another, and even supervises the formation of that particular word, He knows it, and we know it too, because He tells us about it. Or must we say that the history of words has the right to remain a totally profane subject?

However, the Apostle does not dwell upon his argument, but passes immediately to its consequence. If the sole heir of the promises is Christ, then we, too, are that heir, since we are in Christ.

These words are full of doctrinal significance, and we shall have occasion to return to them when we consider St. Paul's own teaching on the Mystical Body. All the Christians, he says, have put on Christ; they are taken up together in Him; in a mystical sense, they are He. Therefore the promises were made to them, as they were made to Him. But they and He, they in Him, make up the Mystical Body. Consequently, it is to the Mystical Body that the whole of the Old Testament leads.

This is a thought dear to the Apostle, and one that Tradition has been careful not to lose. As creation is "Christian," so is the Old Testament "Christian." The Mystical Body had its beginning in Abel, even in Adam, and all the pages of the ancient alliance tell us how, little by little, it was formed.

This is a principle that must be insisted upon from the outset: the Old Testament in its entirety is concerned with Christ alone, and with us in Christ.

Were we dealing with an ordinary book, such a principle would, of course, be unacceptable; for how can one hope to find the meaning intended by one author, in another author who wrote centuries later? The case of the word *seed*, σπέρμα, is striking; have we any right to look for the explanation of a particular term in a work that appeared some two thousand years after that term was used?

Certainly not. But the Scripture is no ordinary book. It is inspired; that is to say, it has but one principal author, and, when need arises, this author is always able to complete and explain His meaning; and further, He remains forever in His Church, to interpret His own meaning.

Now it is precisely the fact of inspiration that gives the Scripture its value for us, and makes it competent to speak of a subject so mysterious as is that of Christ living in us by grace. Therefore we take the Scripture, and we intend to study the Scripture, together with the rays of light which it provides in order to make its meaning clear. Indeed, without this help, it would be unintelligible.

II. § 1

Now, with the aid of those rays of light which we have discovered, it remains for us to see how the Old Testament actually does speak of Christ, and how it represents that union which even then God was preparing to establish between man and Himself in His well-beloved Son.

Alas, we must confess at once that despite these helps, our findings amount to very little. To exploit the treasures of the Old Testament would require an intimate knowledge of those ancient times, a knowledge very difficult to attain in our day, when scholars are still deep in research, and a knowledge, too, which we do not claim to possess. Such a task would also demand much labor and meditation, which we have preferred to devote to the New Testament. *Vetus in novo patet*, "the old is revealed in the new." Here, research is more easy and more fruitful; whatever indications we might with great difficulty have gleaned from the Law and the Prophets, we find more clearly and more completely expressed in the New Testament.

Hence a brief outline will suffice. Nevertheless, some such outline is necessary, since, in God's plan, the Law and the Prophets are an introduction to the Gospel. We can better understand the nature of the union which Christians have with one another and with God in Christ, if we first consider how this union was prepared.

Now, the preparation for this union, or rather, its commencement, is the union that God established through the Old Covenant; first among His faithful, the children of Abraham, and then between Himself and all of them. It is of this twofold union that we shall now speak.

First, then, we have to consider the union of the faithful among themselves. At the beginning, the Scripture shows us, those who believe form but one family. If, later on, they are to become a people, this people must, nevertheless, remain united round the same hearth, as it were. In the eyes of God they are one, one whole, a single inheritance, a single field. Again, they are one living organism, one vineyard, according to the Scriptural metaphor.

> Let me sing for my Loved One
> The song of my Loved One concerning His vineyard.
> My Loved One had a vineyard
> On a fertile hill.
> . . . He expected it to yield grapes,
> But it yielded wildlings.
> . . . The vineyard of Yahweh of hosts is the house of Israel,
> And the men of Judah are His cherished plantation.[3]

The figure of the vineyard is frequent and traditional. It has even passed from the Old Testament into the New. For us today Israel is the vineyard of Yahweh, the vineyard that failed to bring forth fruit, the vineyard to which God sent His Son in vain; no, not in vain, because He was done to death. And today, the Church, the new Israel, considers herself as the vineyard.

Israel, says the Scripture again, is the flock of Yahweh:

As cattle going down to the valley,
So did the spirit of the Lord lead them.[4]

The whole people is a sheep that God loves, a little worm on which He has taken pity. Still more frequently, Israel is but a single person. Together, the children of Israel are the bride of Yahweh; they are the spouse whom He has chosen and adorned with His gifts.

As the bridegroom rejoices over the bride,
So shall thy God rejoice over thee.[5]

Thus saith the Lord of hosts: "I am jealous for Sion with a great jealousy, and with a great indignation am I jealous for her."[6]

The prophet Ezechiel is bid to deliver this message from Yahweh to Jerusalem:

Thy father was an Amorrhite, and thy mother a Cethite. . . . Thou wast cast out upon the face of the earth, in the abjection of thy soul, in the day that thou wast born. . . . And I passed by thee, and saw thee. . . . I caused thee to multiply as the bud of the field: and thou didst increase and grow great, and . . . wast made exceeding beautiful.[7]

And the allegory continues: God adorns His bride; but she is faithless. Jerusalem abandons Yahweh; she forgets the love of her youth, and gives herself over to the idols of the nations. So Yahweh forsakes her, punishes her, and delivers her up to desolation and to ruin. But His wrath endures only for a time: He returns to recall His spouse, forever.

For a small moment have I forsaken thee,
But with great mercies will I gather thee.
In a moment of indignation have I hid My face a little while
    from thee,
But with everlasting kindness have I had mercy on thee,
Said the Lord thy Redeemer.[8]

As He had sworn to Noe, Yahweh swears a second time:

So have I sworn not to be angry with thee,

[29]

And not to rebuke thee.
For the mountains shall be moved,
And the hills shall tremble;
But My mercy shall not depart from thee,
And the covenant of My peace shall not be moved:
Said the Lord that hath mercy on thee.[9]

This divine assurance has ever been the joy of devout souls, first among the Jews, then among Christians; they have loved to meditate on the Canticle of Canticles especially, where God declares His tender affection for humanity, for the Church, for every soul, and where, in authentic and inspired language, humanity itself describes the intimate union which it enjoys with its God:

Let him kiss me with the kiss of his mouth. . . .

As the lily among thorns, so is my love among the daughters. . . .

The voice of my Beloved! Behold he cometh leaping upon the
    mountains. . . .
Come from Libanus, my spouse, come from Libanus, come. . . .
Thou hast wounded my heart, my sister, my spouse!
Thou hast wounded my heart with one of thy eyes.[10]

Even for Christians, who have some idea of how dearly God has loved the world, these verses continue to be a stirring revelation of how intense is the love of the Lord and how ardent is His desire to be near His creature, and to be one with it.

Elsewhere the people is considered as a widow, or again as a fruitful mother who bears Yahweh many children. We recall the magnificent apostrophe of Isaias:

Arise, be enlightened, O Jerusalem: for thy light is come,
And the glory of the Lord is risen upon thee. . . .
Lift up thy eyes round about, and see:
All these are gathered together, they are come to thee:
Thy sons shall come from afar,
And thy daughters shall rise up at thy side.[11]

Often, too, the Scripture describes the chosen people as forming but one man, one elect of Yahweh, a servant. God tells him:

Thou Israel, art My servant,
Jacob whom I have chosen,
The seed of Abraham My friend:
In whom I have taken thee from the ends of the earth,
And from the remote parts thereof have called thee,
And said to thee: Thou art My servant.
I have chosen thee, and have not cast thee away.
Fear not, for I am with thee:
Turn not aside, for I am thy God.
... Behold all that fight against thee
Shall be confounded and ashamed;
They shall be as nothing,
And the men shall perish that strive against thee.
... For I am the Lord thy God,
Who take thee by the hand,
And say to thee: Fear not,
I have helped thee.
Fear not, thou worm of Jacob,
You that are dead of Israel:
I have helped thee, saith the Lord,
And thy Redeemer the Holy One of Israel.[12]

To Yahweh, all the Israelites together are a son. At times
the name "son" is reserved to the king, as the official
representative of the people. But often it is the people,
considered as a whole, that is the son of Yahweh; Israel is the
well beloved, the nursling, the first-born, the favorite son, and
even the pampered child of God. Yahweh's love for Him is as
tender as that of a father for his son. Consider, for instance,
the message which Moses is to deliver to the king of Egypt;
the son of Pharaoh will be the hostage for God's own son, who
is Israel:

Thou shalt say to him: Thus saith the Lord: Israel is My
son, My first-born. I have said to thee: Let My son go, that
he may serve Me, and thou wouldst not let him go: behold I
will kill thy son, thy first-born.[13]

This son is often rebellious. But so great is God's love
that He cannot bring Himself to deal severely with him for
long. God always pardons, He always forgets. He leads all
the Israelites back from the exile into which they had been
banished for their sins.

Behold ... a great company of them returning hither.

[31]

They shall come with weeping:
And I will bring them back in mercy:
And I will bring them through the torrents of waters in a right
 way,
And they shall not stumble in it:
For I am a father to Israel,
And Ephraim is My first-born![14]

When God hears "Ephraim groaning in exile," He feels constrained to recall him:

Surely Ephraim is an honorable son to Me,
Surely he is a tender child:
For since I spoke of him,
I will still remember him.
Therefore are My bowels troubled for him:
Pitying I will pity him, saith the Lord.[15]

Such is the unity of the people that prefigures the Church. It forms but one, one whole, one living being, a single man.

§ 2

Most perfect, too, is the union of this people with God. We shall now turn our attention to this second phase. It, too, is a commencement and a figure of that union which we have, as members of the Mystical Body, with God. We have already had to speak of it, in order to show how closely the whole people is joined together by the grace of God.

The whole people is the tabernacle of Yahweh. Yahweh dwells therein, so that the Hebrews are, as it were, a manifestation of Yahweh upon earth. When the Gentiles see them triumph over their enemies, they will know that God is in Israel.

Yahweh is one with His people, and He considers the outrages of which "His son" is the object, as an offense against Himself. In times of persecution, the Jews pray Yahweh to remember that their interests are His own: "Arise, O God," they cry, "judge Thy own cause."[16] And Yahweh answers:

Behold I will judge thy cause,
And I will take vengeance for thee.[17]

Israel's cause is indeed the cause of Yahweh, and he that

[32]

lays hand on Israel, wounds Him in the apple of His eye. This Edom and Moab will one day come to realize: by insulting Israel, they insult God Himself. He will come to take up the challenge; He will enter into judgment with the nations on behalf of His own people and His inheritance. Then they shall see that He, Yahweh, has heard the taunts that were uttered against the mountains of Israel, and they shall understand that in so doing they were defying Yahweh Himself.

> Because Moab and Seir have said:
> Behold the house of Juda is like all other nations:
> Therefore behold I will open the shoulder of Moab.[18]

When He avenges His people, it is His own honor that Yahweh will restore:

> For I have spoken it, saith the Lord God.
> And I will send a fire on Magog,
> And on them that dwell confidently in the islands:
> And they shall know that I am the Lord.
> And I will make My holy name known
> In the midst of My people Israel,
> And My holy name shall be profaned no more;
> And the Gentiles shall know that I am the Lord, the Holy one
> of Israel.
> ... Now will I bring back the captivity of Jacob,
> And will have mercy on all the house of Israel:
> And I will be jealous for My holy name.[19]

This solidarity is not to be something purely extrinsic. Israel has more than an alliance with Yahweh; Israel is like unto Yahweh, because he is His son and because a son is like unto his father. As Yahweh is a God different from all others, or rather, as He is the only God, and holy God, so too Israel is a nation apart, a holy nation. This the Law reiterates unceasingly:

> I am the Lord your God: be holy because I am holy. Defile not your souls by any creeping thing, that moveth upon the earth. For I am the Lord, who brought you out of the land of Egypt, that I might be your God. You shall be holy, because I am holy.[20]

This holiness refers primarily to the absence of any juridical

[33]

defect, but according to the teaching of both the Law and the Prophets, it also means holiness of soul.

Moreover, by this holiness the whole people becomes an image and a figure of the Holy One of God that is to come. As St. Paul and constant Tradition affirm, the Old Covenant in its entirety is an immense symbol, and the virtues that adorn it, the precepts it contains, even the deeds it records, have the mission to prefigure Christ and those that are Christ's.

To search out and to develop this symbolism of the Old Testament would be a long process; we must be content with having mentioned its existence. It explains that the entire Old Law is the beginning of a plan, of a reality, of a mystery, and that this mystery is Christ, coming to live in His own.

Of this we have given some indication; little enough, it is true. Much more might have been said. However, all that we could say would seem but little. For, were one to consider the Old Testament independently and to judge from outward appearances only, might he not say that the ideal of unity which it expresses — union with God, union of all the Hebrews among themselves — differs very little from the ideal of unity to which every people aspires?

But this is precisely the point we wish to stress: the Old Testament cannot be taken alone. It is but the beginning of a message, and only the remainder of the message can give that beginning its true significance.

Chapter II

The Synoptic Gospels: The "Kingdom" and the Mystical Body

➤◄

I. The doctrine of the Mystical Body is revealed only gradually in the writings of the New Testament. There is no reason to exclude the possibility of doctrinal progress; the latter may either be explicitly recorded or merely suggested.

II. *The Synoptics* mark the transition from the Old Testament to the New. The nature of the Synoptics. Each presents the Mystical Body in its own way:

1. *St. Mark* suggests it by his manner of telling the story of Jesus' life. The Gospel has its center, its résumé, and its explanation in the death of Christ and in the beginning of a fuller human life of Christ, which is the life of Christ in the Mystical Body. The Church as the fullness of Christ.

2. *St. Matthew* speaks of the Mystical Body when he describes the preaching of the Kingdom. The Kingdom according to the expectations of the Jews; according to Jesus' teaching. It is represented by Matthew as something very closely united with the person of Jesus. The progressive stages of the revelation of the Kingdom correspond to the stages of Jesus' public ministry. The Kingdom has its own life, its "mystery." Again, it is intimately united with God and with Christ. Jesus will remain in it with His own for all time; He will be in their prayers, in the decisions of the Church, ever teaching the faithful and receiving as done to Himself whatever is done to the least of His brethren. Christ's unity with us is a prolongation of His own unity with God. The most striking text is that of the Last Judgment. The second coming, according to the Synoptics; according to St. John. Conclusion.

3. *St. Luke.* The Gospel of St. Luke is an introduction to the Acts of the Apostles; the latter contains Luke's teaching on the subject of the Mystical Body.

[35]

I

WHAT WAS present in the Old Testament only in embryo is fully developed in the New. An examination of the latter will therefore disclose the same alliance, the same promises, and the same pledges that we have seen in the Old Testament. But here the pledges are being fulfilled, the promises are being put into execution, and finally, the alliance between God and men becomes the very person of the Man-God.

However, the fulfillment is like the announcement. God knows no fevered haste; what He gives, He gives gradually, and the revelation of the gift, like the gift itself, proceeds slowly and calmly.

It will be complete in the time of Paul and of John. Not till then will God fully give and explain to men the divine unity He has in store for them. Before that time, the Acts of the Apostles represent that union taking up its abode in mankind. Earlier still, the Synoptic Gospels provide a kind of transition. They describe how the concept of a brilliant and triumphant Kingdom, appearing in a blaze of glory, which the Old Testament was apt to suggest to many Jews, was transformed into the true and Christian concept of an interior and hidden, as well as visible and empirical, Kingdom — the concept of a supernatural and mystical Kingdom, whose King comes within us, and comes to die for us. These, in our opinion, are the principal stages of the revelation; the chapters of our study of the New Testament are arranged accordingly.

There is no reason why one should not be able to find a doctrinal development even in the books of the New Testament. Whether such development be an addition to revelation itself, or whether it consist merely in a better understanding and a clearer exposition of this revelation, makes little difference. For our subject, it is unnecessary to make such a distinction. However, this much is certain: both kinds of development were possible. For, until the death of the last Apostle, revelation was capable of receiving new truths, and the Apostles themselves could have continued to grow in the comprehension of their message throughout their whole life, without any new revelation. Indeed, should we not say that this latter must have been the case? To suppose the contrary; namely, that they at once appreciated fully every aspect of the transcendent truth, and to suppose that they should immediately have found adequate and exact terms in which to express its immeasurable richness, is to postulate a profusion of psychological miracles such as God is not wont to perform. The marvel of Christianity is that God seeks the society and the co-operation of men. Is it likely that He should have dealt otherwise with those whom He Himself chose to be the first witnesses of His condescension, or that, by force of prodigies, He should have prevented them from concurring, in their imperfect way — they have no other — in His work?

Of course, He would assist them, but by directing, not by supplanting their efforts. He would aid their thoughts and reflections, not to make them more sluggish or more passive, but to give them greater ardor. Must we assume that He exempted them from all groping and from all hesitation? In that case, their effort would not have been a human effort. Is it not more natural to suppose that, without dispensing them from our processes of comprehension and of investigation, He watched over them more carefully, rendered them more clear-sighted and more prudent, to the end that the weakness inherent in our nature might introduce no inexact or doubtful element into the treasure that they bore in fragile vessels? Thus, being men, they could have made progress after the manner of men. And their progress was no less assured and divine; for He who, through them, was communicating Himself to men, He who was revealing, inspiring them, and assisting them, was always God and God alone.

Let us continue. Whatever form this progress may have taken, God could have willed to reveal the fact of its occurrence by means of His Scripture. If He willed to tell us in the Holy Books about the tunics that Dorcas was making, and of the wine that Timothy was to take, why should He not have wished to inform us of a matter far more important and far more instructive with regard to His economy of revelation: how the light of His truth has by little and little penetrated our mists, and how, little by little, men's souls have opened to its rays?

Furthermore, as there was nothing to prevent His giving us this information, so there was nothing to prevent His giving it in the manner He preferred. Not only could He do so by explicit declarations, which we should merely have had to read; but He could also have given it in words of hidden meaning, by way of indications that must be sought out and interpreted. He alone is judge, and the best way is the one He chooses.

Can one find, in either of these processes, anything unworthy of His Holy Scripture? On the contrary, have we not always believed that the Bible could contain, and actually does abound in hidden meanings, and that everything in the Scripture, even the choice and position of words, every jot and tittle, is full of significance? Is it for us to decide, according to our own *a priori* views on literary types and on the Providence of God, just how an inspired book ought to be written? It is as God has willed it, and that is enough. God has moved the human author to write this particular book; He has assisted him in the course of the writing, to insure its being exactly as He wished it; He has approved the book when completed, and, by the medium of the Church, He has given it to us as His own authentic work. Now, if this book contains indications that can be discerned and understood only after careful scrutiny, all that we can say is that they are as truly inspired as the rest of the book, and therefore deserve to be studied with equal respect. Were these indications explicitly recognized and intended by the human author? We should hesitate to say that this were necessary. In every human writing, a thousand things betray themselves without the author's knowledge. Why need an inspired writer have a consciousness so clear and so little human, of all that in one way or another is attested in his book? If he may not have seen so far ahead, at least God did; and it is God, after all, who is the principal author.

Whether or not Scripture actually does contain such indications, we can determine only by examining Scripture itself. We shall now undertake this investigation.

II

The books of Scripture which we shall now consider are those with which the New Testament opens — the Synoptic Gospels. These, of course, are not the first in date among the inspired writings; the Epistles of St. James and of St. Jude, as well as most of St. Paul's letters, were written several years earlier. Nevertheless, the events recorded by the Gospels are anterior to the exhortations and instructions that make up the Epistles, and the accounts from which they are drawn must have existed from the earliest beginnings of Christian teaching in a form, either oral or written, somewhat similar to that which they have in the Gospels.

Generally speaking, the Synoptics have little to say on the subject of the Mystical Body. The fact is not hard to understand. The Gospels are not a methodical exposition of the Master's doctrine, any more than they are a complete biography of Jesus Christ. They are the testimony rendered to Christ by the witnesses of Christ; in other words, they are a collection of facts, the purpose of which is to make known who Christ is and what it means to belong to Christ, and also to introduce the messengers sent by Christ with the commission to preach Christ to the world.

For the messengers of Christianity had to present their credentials, and these credentials were not in them, but in the Master. They were merely His witnesses. Their task was to make the Master known, to give their hearers and readers the same direct, living contact that had attracted and won their own hearts. This they did untiringly in the course of their missions, on the Roman roads, in the privacy of friendly homes, in the calm or the uproar of the synagogues. In the brief but expressive phrase of the Acts, they told τὰ περὶ Ἰησοῦ,[1] a collection of facts concerning Jesus. At first, it is likely that these details were chosen somewhat at random from among their recollections; soon, however, through frequent repetition, they took on a certain order. Doctrinal instruction was joined with the narration of events in this happy message that they were announcing. Primarily, though, the whole was a kind of portrait, intended to depict, as a very living personality, Him who still continued to be the one Master, and who was thus personally introducing His message and His messengers.

Gradually, depending upon the audience, the viewpoint of each Apostle, and the inspiration of the Holy Spirit, the choice of details began to vary; emphasis was placed upon one or other aspect of Christ's personality, and the accounts began to present differences of nuance and of interests. Thus were formed our first three Gospels. Each has its own individuality, but all remain basically the same: the testimony rendered to Jesus by His witnesses.

This special formation of the Gospels explains the manner in which they speak of the Mystical Body. They do not treat of it directly; directly they speak only of Christ. But the Christ they describe is not a Christ imprisoned within the narrow limits of His brief appearance on the stage of this world; He is a Christ who, in His very historical life, is also mystical. Yet each of the Evangelists teaches this truth in a different way.

§ 1

We shall consider first the Gospel of St. Mark, which is the record of Peter's preaching. Here the very plan of the narrative, the central theme, the progression of events, the choice of details, and the conclusion speak to us of the mystical life of Christ.

Surprising as the statement may at first appear, it is strictly true. Despite his plain and popular manner of speech, despite the impression he gives of a simple, direct working-man, despite his characteristic way of representing Christ just as He appeared outwardly in real life — despite all this Mark testifies, in a very forceful manner, to the Christ who abides within, in the mystery of the soul.

Or rather, we should not say *despite,* but *through* and *in* all these characteristics. Mark's testimony is an integral part of the Gospel story; it is the story, as circumstantiated and lived; it is the very meaning of the story.

As we shall have occasion to see more and more clearly in the course of these pages, it is precisely through his most distinctive and most personal qualities that each of the inspired writers speaks of the Mystical Body. We shall learn, too, that the doctrine of the Mystical Body is not something set apart from the most commonplace realities of Christian life: it is our own prosaic human nature that God has united to Himself in His Son. Lastly, we shall discover that Christian truth is something more than an abstraction that can be expressed in the form of theorems and theses. Before all else, that truth is Jesus Christ, and Jesus Christ teaches it not only by His words, but simply by being Himself.

Therefore it is not in the least surprising that in order to understand His message, Mark should have been content to contemplate His person and His way of acting and reacting. This does not show that the author has abandoned the scientific method or that he has forgotten the purpose which he had set for himself, or even that he is aiming at a more psychological or more concrete treatment of his subject; it betrays merely his desire to seek Christian truth in its first manifestation and in its plenitude: in the person and life of the Master.

Theology differs from other sciences in that it deals with a doctrine which, besides being a fact, is also a person. Its proper and scientific method must therefore include contemplation of the person as well as reflection on the fact. Hence, even as a science, theology must examine the Gospel narrative primarily as a narrative; in other words, the theologian must live the story over again; he must lose himself in it and make it his own; he must reflect upon the presuppositions that are implied in it and upon the meaning that it is intended to convey; he must be able to discern the tacit testimony which it contains and which is, as it were, its soul and its life.

The task is a delicate one, indeed, for there is little opportunity here to apply philological and dialectic methods of control. This is not a question of textual criticism or of

[41]

evaluating syllogisms; it is a question of reconstructing historical facts in one's own mind and soul, and of keeping
silence in order to hear them speak for themselves. We grant
that such a method necessarily remains somewhat subjective
and conjectural, and great care must be exercised lest personal
preference be mistaken for the language of the facts, and
lest mere probabilities be accepted as established truths.

Yes, the task is difficult, but it is necessary. The Gospel
history, precisely in its quality as history, is one of the
principal theological sources; nay, it is *the* great source.
No theology can be truly scientific and truly theological
unless it remains in perpetual contact with, and in the
constant meditation and contemplation of this written source.

The first feature which we note in the Gospel of St. Mark
as having a special bearing on our subject is the central
theme. Everything in the account converges toward the death
of Jesus. The same is true, though in a less striking degree,
of the other Synoptic Gospels, which follow the same general
plan as Mark's, and of the Gospel of St. John. Not only is
the death of Jesus recounted in much greater detail than any
other part of His public or hidden life,[2] but the narrative
is centered from the very beginning upon the tragedy of
Calvary. This death marks the disappearance of the historical
Jesus; yet it appears to be the principal part of the story.
One would say that the author has only one purpose in
mind: to explain exactly why the Saviour, the subject of
the story, is no longer on the scene.

This trait is particularly noticeable in St. Mark. The first
detailed episode of the Gospel indicates that a struggle is
to come; two groups are forming, with Jesus and His disciples on one side, and His enemies on the other. Of the latter
little is said as yet, except that they compare unfavorably
with Jesus. But this is precisely the source of all the trouble:
wounded self-love changes so quickly into jealousy and
hostility! The events that follow represent the opening
skirmish of what is later to become a battle to the death.
Privately at first, and without making any protest, the
Pharisees criticize the conduct of the Master who forgives
sins; soon they began to find fault openly, first with the

Apostles, then with Jesus Himself on the subject of fasting and of violating the Sabbath. When offering His defense Jesus indicates, even at this early stage, what His final and decisive action will be: He speaks of His mission and of His power, but He makes an especial point of the plan of salvation whereby His death is to become the source of life.

His death? Yes, for the subject is introduced without delay. Immediately after the events to which we have just referred, comes the account of the cure of the man with the withered hand. The same two parties face each other again: Jesus and the watchful Pharisees. The latter observe the presence of the unfortunate cripple: an excellent bait to attract the Master's sympathy. Will He dare to heal the man publicly on the Sabbath? As if in answer Jesus goes straight to carry out this act of mercy: He performs the miracle, saving this life at the risk of His own. "And the Pharisees," continues the Gospel, "went out and straightway took counsel with the Herodians against Him, how they might destroy Him."[3] Now the plot of the story is evident. All that precedes has served to convey this one idea: Jesus is come in order to die, and the story of His life will consist in showing how He comes to that end. Such is "the beginning of the Gospel of Jesus Christ, Son of God."[4]

In the other Synoptics, which reproduce the general outline of St. Mark's Gospel, there are signs, less evident however, of a like orientation. Thus in the Gospel of St. Matthew we may recall the opposition of Herod which is aroused at once, and the massacre of the Innocents which follows closely upon the birth of Jesus. In St. Luke's Gospel the same final tragedy is foreshadowed in the prophecy uttered by Simeon on the occasion of Jesus' first appearance in the temple, and in the attempt made upon His life when He began to preach at Nazareth. The latter passage is particularly suggestive, and may be compared with the first two chapters of St. Mark. In Luke's Gospel the incident introduces Jesus' public ministry, and it is without question a presage of the Passion. Jesus declares that the text of Isaias which He has just read refers to Himself, and that it describes His mission: to teach, to heal, to console. The Jews, His own countrymen, make answer by attempting to do what they would one day accomplish in Jerusalem: they cast Him out of the city and drag Him up a mountain, to put Him to death — the entire story of Calvary!

"And His own received Him not"; the prologue of St. John's Gospel expresses exactly the same thought: Jesus has come in order to die. Through all His heralds, all His evangelists, in the opening pages of Jesus' story, God turns our eyes to the Cross.

We are not surprised at this, for we have been familiar with the story since childhood. Yet it is all so strange! Our authors set out to tell the story of a life, and immediately they focus all attention upon a death; they intend to reveal a person, and what they tell us only seems to hide Him from our eyes; they begin a narrative, and then develop it as if the interest were to begin only after the ending should have been reached. This narrative is designed to accredit the preaching of the Apostles; yet it insists from the outset upon the defeat of Him who sends them forth. This is the Gospel, the good tidings, that is to bring life to the world; yet it opens with a saddening prophecy and summarizes its entire message in a death. Such an orientation given to such a history, so soon and with such emphasis, cannot but appear paradoxical as soon as one begins to reflect upon it.

But the paradox vanishes and all becomes clear when interpreted in the light of the Mystical Body. Christ has a twofold life on earth: one visible and historical, the other invisible and mystical; the first is the preparation for the second, and the second is the prolongation of the first. In the second, which is His mysterious existence in the depths of souls, Christ is far more active, far more truly alive than ever He was in the days when He walked and preached in Judea. Therefore it is quite natural and in keeping with the supernatural economy of God's plan that His life should be represented in the Gospel as already directed toward His death, since His death is the climax of His life. Are we not justified in saying that the sacred text demands some such commentary, and that this is God's way of suggesting the doctrine of the Mystical Body?

[44]

In the light of the doctrine, Christ's death, far from marking His departure from this world of ours, is seen rather to effect a more profound penetration of Jesus into the souls of men. Jesus will continue to belong mystically to this earth; He will continue to act, to suffer, to affect its history, but in a new way: His history will no longer be separate from that of the world; He will become, in the hearts of humanity, the very life of history.

Hence, when God, by means of His inspired writers, reveals the history of Christ in its true light, we can understand why He gives such prominence to an event which, though it terminates the narrative, is itself such a magnificent new beginning.

What we have just said of the central theme round which the Gospel story turns may be repeated with equal truth of its content; for this too points to the doctrine of the Mystical Body as the key to its meaning.

Let us therefore examine the principal lines of this content as they are presented by St. Mark, who enjoys the reputation of being the most objective, the most empirical, the most positive of the Evangelists. Once more, if we read attentively, the Saviour's visible life allows us to see something of the invisible prolongation of that life which constitutes the plenitude of His human reality. We have already observed in the opening episodes of the narrative that Jesus is doomed to death. But now what is He going to do? Will He be too quick for His enemies? Will He proclaim the good tidings far and wide, to so many of the people that it will be too late to suppress it? Will He kindle the flame which He has brought upon the earth in so many localities that it cannot be extinguished? No! "What you hear in secret: *Quod in aure auditis.*" He now proceeds even more silently; instead of extending the scope of His activity, He limits it; instead of diffusing it, He deepens it.

It is true that He continues to preach to the multitudes, but usually He does so in parables. It is likewise true that when He meets an audience that is better able to understand

[45]

Him, He does not refuse to instruct them. But to the Apostles alone is granted the complete explanation.

One coincidence is so clearly marked in St. Mark and St. Luke that it seems to have been a reality of fact and to have been intended by Jesus: it was immediately after the meeting which we have mentioned as taking place between the Pharisees and the Herodians, that the apostolic college was definitively established; the assembly that determined upon Jesus' death thus stands out in opposition to the Church in which Jesus will live again for all time.

No new choice is made. Jesus had chosen them from the beginning, and now He merely binds them more closely to Himself: again we notice how His life is pursuing its own course even when His enemies appear to be forcing His hand.

So, during long months Jesus now devotes Himself to His disciples. Under the spell of His miracles, under the influence of His words, under the gradual penetration of long months of intimacy with Him, their slowness of perception begins to yield bit by bit: they begin to sense the mystery that He bears in His soul.

For, to read the Gospel, it would appear that He did not choose to reveal this divine secret to them in words: He willed that His whole being should manifest it; it was by living with Him that, with God's help, they were to become aware of what lay within Him.

At last there came a day when Jesus saw that their hearts were ready. He was walking with the twelve near Caesarea Philippi. Abruptly He turns to them and asks a question: "Whom do men say that I am?" And Peter answers: "Thou art the Christ, the Son of the living God."[5]

This confession of Peter is one of the high points, the very climax, we should say, of the public life. Jesus had come to establish in the world the faith that worketh by charity, and here at last He has found one who makes open profession of that faith. But, says Holy Scripture, it is Christ Himself who by faith comes to dwell in our hearts.

Doubtless others had believed ere this; unquestionably the Apostles had long been living in the state of grace; and certainly years before a creature who was blessed among all women possessed a wonderful faith: "Blessed art thou who hast believed,"[6] it is written of the Virgin. But all this had taken place in the secret fastnesses of souls. Now this interior mystery has come to be expressed exteriorly. But by faith, we repeat, Christ abides in us. From this moment forward, therefore, He will dwell in us, not merely in the secret of souls, but in a visible organism, in a *magisterium,* and He will be enabled thus to carry on His work mystically in a visible manner. He has laid the first stone, the foundation stone of the Church as the Mystical Body.

This is as it were the Saviour's second birth. At His first birth some thirty years before, He had taken His visible flesh, in a moment's time, from the Virgin most pure. Now He is taking the visible element for His Mystical Body, by a process that will continue for a long time, as long as our human nature remains on earth, not from the Immaculate Virgin, but from sinful humanity. Both are works of God: it is His power that comes upon us, and it is the Father in Heaven who assists and who makes known the mystery. To the faith of Mary at the Annunciation, God made answer by effecting the Incarnation of the Word; to the faith of Peter near the city of Tiberius, the Word makes answer by instituting the Church.

The acts of Jesus are perpetual. From the beginning of the public life He had cast His lot with Peter and had made no secret of the fact. During His early preaching we see Him spend the night at Peter's home and perform miracles there; very soon Peter comes to look on Jesus as his own. This was not to cease, nor will it ever cease. Now, in the midst of the public life, Jesus comes to Peter once more, but in a new manner: He comes, not into Peter's house, but into his soul; not in order to work a few miracles, but in order to lead all men.

To Peter's self-surrender Jesus makes answer by giving Himself in return. To Peter's act of complete faith Jesus makes answer by an act of confidence, of self-abandonment, of faith, that is just as complete. Peter may now look upon Jesus, more than ever before, as his very own; Peter shall be the rock sustaining the whole Church; Peter shall hold

[47]

the keys; he shall bind and loose; and Peter is given to understand that God ratifies in heaven every judicial sentence that he, Peter, shall pronounce on earth.

What does Christ gain by all this? What can He do now that He could not do before? There is only this difference: Peter can do nothing except by Christ, and in Peter it is Christ alone who can do all things.

For this Church that has just been begun in Peter is still Christ, the mystical Christ. The Church is Christ, and for us at least, she is Christ in a more perfect sense than was the historical Christ; for she is Christ inasmuch as He forms one Body with us. And, if it is true that Christ came upon earth for us, may we not say that Christ is most truly Himself under that aspect in which He contributes most to our advantage? Thus we possess a new testimony to the doctrine of the Mystical Body, expressed by the Gospel narrative in its own way.

But let us proceed. If Peter's profession of faith marks a high point in the Gospel story, it likewise divides that story into two parts. Since Christ has begun to live within His own, it is no longer necessary for Him to live at their side; since it is in the Church and in Peter that He will henceforth be all things for them, He must pass into the Church. He may now quit the external scene of history and enter into the source of history, into the souls of humanity.

Hence the promises which He now makes to the Apostles conclude with the prediction of His coming departure. This is the *Noli me tangere* of the Synoptics: Why should we try to keep Him before our eyes, when He desires to enter into us? As the Gospels clearly indicate, it was at this moment that Jesus began to teach them, saying that the Son of man would be rejected, tortured, slain.

After Peter's confession, one might have expected that He would now take especial pains to sow the seeds of truth in these souls which He saw at last opening to receive it; that He would now retire to some quiet place and there, in secret, confide to His Apostles as much of His teaching as possible.

[48]

But no; He wills instead to implant Himself in their souls, for is He not the fountain of truth?

There was still time, of course, in which to teach them, and undoubtedly He did tell them many things during the few months that still remained. But to judge from the slowness of heart that they manifested during His very last days, they certainly could not have understood all. For truths so sublime mere words are so inadequate!

At all events God saw to it that little of what was said in these discourses should be recorded in the Scriptures. But what the Scripture does repeat unceasingly from this time forward is that Jesus is here in order to die. Time and again the fearful prophecy recurs: the Christ must die. Henceforth death is the only possible outcome.

But this is not all. If Christ is come into us, and if He is also come to die, then it is a life of pain, the life of the Cross, that He is come to implant in our souls. The prediction of His death must in consequence go hand in hand with an exhortation to self-denial. And, as a matter of fact, the two points are associated by all three of the Synoptics: when Jesus foretold His Passion for the first time, He predicted that sufferings and contradictions would fall to the lot of His members. Never before had Jesus spoken in this fashion in the Gospel of St. Mark. The same is true of St. Luke, and even in St. Matthew, as it would be a simple but long task to prove, these words convey an entirely new meaning. From now on, however, the thought is frequently expressed in all three of the Gospels; one may say that it is at least implicit in all of Jesus' teaching during this last period.

Soon, when the Passion has come very nigh, the prediction of suffering and persecution grows clearer and more vivid, as may be seen in the eschatological discourse. We shall consider this prophecy at the end of the chapter; for the present let us note merely that it is the final lesson which Jesus gives to show how truly the fate of the Mystical Body is one with the fate of Christ: Jesus must die, and we must die with Him. What else can this mean, except that we are part of Him?

We next turn to consider Christ's death. The doctrine of the Mystical Body, we saw, helps us to understand its early mention and its prominence in the general scheme of the Gospel narrative: now it brings out the full significance of the relation that exists between Christ's death and His life.

It is now the last week, the week during which the Paschal Lamb is to be sacrificed. Jesus goes up to Jerusalem. All things are accomplished.

But on the night before He was to die, He instituted the sacrament and the sacrifice of the Eucharist, thus making us the gift of His life, which was so soon to be taken from Him, and coming to live in His faithful disciples before the Jews should put an end to that life in Him. The communion of the Cenacle, joined with the oblation of the Cross, brings out the twofold aspect of His death. His visible existence ends with the act that establishes the sacrament of His mystical existence, and in order that the continuity of the two might not be broken, the latter takes place before the first. What He gives us is His immolated Body; the sacramental and mystical immolation of His Body precedes the historical immolation. Thus the rite whereby He communicates Himself as the living source of life, and the act whereby He lays down His life constitute in reality but one complete act: each time that the Mass is offered, the sacrifice of Calvary is present anew.

He dies, and yet He dies not. For through the Eucharist, which is His death, His death is prolonged in every Mass; the Mass is prolonged in every sacramental and spiritual communion, and these communions are prolonged in the whole of the Christ-life, interior and exterior. Thereby His death becomes the source of all supernatural activity; hence His death is His life, His true human life in its fullness and in its universality. So we can understand why it occupies the chief place, or rather why it fills the entire authentic account of His existence.

As water falling upon the dry earth remains visible for a few moments on the surface, shimmering and clear, and is then absorbed to become vegetation and fertility in the soil, freshness in the leaves, and strength in the branches, so Christ appears for a brief time on the face of our earth and then vanishes. He need remain visible only long enough to prepare for His departure, since that departure will be His entrance into the very depths of life.

If then His historical life is but a preparation for a much more expansive life, for a mystical life, it can rightly appear as a preparation, rapid and unfinished. This is the last point to be noted. Here we must introduce thoughts of a more general nature, which have to do not with a particular chapter or verse of the Gospel, but with general characteristics both of the inspired text and of the life of Christ as recounted therein.

The first of these characteristics is this: Jesus' life appears to be a total failure when it is considered without reference to the Mystical Body in which it is continued.

Think of it! God Himself becomes flesh for the salvation of men; long years He labors in order to wean them from sin and to draw them to Himself; upon this work He lavishes His prayers, His preaching, His miracles. And what is the result? A few disciples, fearful and hesitant; a handful of faithful souls who follow Him to the Cross are women; multitudes who, though enthusiastic at times, are ever inconstant, and desert Him when He turns to serious matters. How far He is from attaining His goal: the conferring of baptism on every creature, the conversion of the whole world! No, it is not He, but the Church that has fulfilled His work and continues to fulfill it. He left the world in defeat.

The doctrine of the Mystical Body shows how superficial such views are: He did not leave in defeat, because in reality He did not leave at all. What the Church has accomplished, He has accomplished, but He has done so in her; the work is all the more wonderful, all the more divine by reason of the fact that He was able to bring it about, delicate and pure though it is, by means of our awkward and unclean hands. Having thus proved itself to be more truly divine and more truly human, the work only appears to better advantage as the work of the Man-God. Again we see how the doctrine of the Mystical Body is implicitly contained in the account of the apostolic life of Jesus.

Something similar may be said of Jesus' teaching as it is recorded in the Gospels. Jesus is Eternal Wisdom, the Light that enlighteneth every man; He came to dispel our darkness. Yet what does He leave after Him at His death? Almost nothing: some sermons, a few parables, a few intimate discourses. An unparalleled heritage this is, overflowing with meaning and possessing an eternal appeal. But He has left nothing that approaches a complete exposition or a systematic expression of doctrine. His lessons are fragmentary, and they are not understood even by His Apostles. After His death, centuries will elapse before Christian dogmas receive a rigorous definition, and who can number all the controversies that will arise? Could He not have expressed Himself clearly? Could He not have spared His followers so many painful disputes, so many heresies, so many schisms, so much toil? Is it after all true that not He but the Church has had to make the synthesis, the summary, the catechism of His doctrine?

Again our answer must be in the negative, for what the Church is to do, He will do; He alone will do it in her. He is, in her as in Himself, the sole Master, but He has two ways of teaching. First He speaks to men from without, as He stands at their side; then He addresses them from within, as He abides in the conscience of each one and in an infallible human *magisterium*. If we consider his first teaching alone, it appears incomplete, precisely because it is not alone. It is only a beginning, the beginning of a lesson that is to continue to the end of time; far from being incomplete, it possesses a superabundant fullness. The whole of Tradition, in which it is to be continued, will show how rich and how significant were His least words, just as His words will in turn bring out all the life, the holiness, and the sweetness that are contained in the least theological thesis.

Thus if we review all the actions of His mortal life, all that He did, whether by way of precept, by way of example, or by way of expiation, we always find the same incompleteness in the same fullness: incompleteness when we consider in His life only the thirty years; fullness, when in His life we behold the single seed whence all life and all supernatural activity has sprung.

In narrating such a life, God can afford to be brief. He who makes the best use of all for the good of His children can be content with sketchy accounts that repeat each other, even though there be material present to fill whole libraries.

And yet, is not the knowledge of that life the most important thing in the world for us? Where can we see what we ought to be in Him and how we ought to act in Him, unless we see it in Him?

True enough. Yet, precisely because He is the life of men, we can contemplate His life elsewhere than in the pages of the Gospel. His work is not a mere monument of what He was; it is the continued existence, unto the consummation of the world, of all that He is. Everything in that work speaks of Him alone, for it exists in Him alone. Yet that work is a reality that is coexistent with every soul; it is in close contact with every soul; it is interior to every soul; it takes a hundred different forms, a thousand changing aspects. Now we see one, now another, yet all point to Him alone if we will only use our eyes. The history of the Church, the lives of the saints, the story of our own soul, the spectacle of Christian charity, of the needs of men, of liturgical ceremonies, the meditation of Christian asceticism, the contemplation of Christian dogmas — all this must supply the deficiencies of the Gospel, or rather, it must bring out all the hidden meaning of the narratives that at first reading appear so sketchy. The Gospel is like a seed: from without it seems tiny, but within lies hidden a limitless power of life and growth. Thus it is with the slightest action of Christ: The light of life that flows from Him into the Church reveals Him as the builder of the entire future. However, His visible sphere of activity remains limited: a beginning need not be presented otherwise than as a beginning; to tell a story well, it is not necessary to exhaust the subject in the introduction.

Once more, therefore, the doctrine of the whole Christ, of the mystical Christ, is suggested as the sole possible explana-

[53]

tion of Jesus' life, even as viewed historically, that is, if we consider it as having a limited existence in time. How else can one conceive that God should descend to our earth in so ineffable a manner, and that this stupendous action of His should have no greater effect than a few years' sojourn here? Thirty years, and of these so many hidden years! What is that in comparison with the thousands of years of our human history?

Is it possible to conceive that the Eternal should put forth as it were all His power and all His love, that He should overcome all obstacles and span all distances, in order to produce a result so fleeting? Why should He appear at all — if we may be excused for speaking so — if He is going to leave before He is even seen?

Unquestionably this momentary contact, this passing touch infinitely surpasses anything that we could have hoped for. But is it so great as to exhaust His divine munificence and to satisfy what He Himself calls an everlasting love? Will He, whose gifts are without repentance, be so eager, after He has once given us Himself, to retract His divine gift?

How truly all this demands an explanation! Yet how clear it all becomes once the explanation is given! He did not take back His gift from us, just as His life did not end completely: all that is in Him has been in a state of growth, like the path of the just of which the Scriptures speak. His life and His gift to men were first promised and prepared during the time of the Old Testament; they were realized in their plenitude during the days of His mortal life in His theandric person; lastly, from that plenitude they have flowed into men during all these centuries of human history. And all this makes up one Christ, who is the same as the Christ of yesterday, the Christ of today, and the Christ of all days; all this makes up one man, who reaches to every part of the terrestrial globe and who continues to grow in each succeeding century, *unus homo diffusus toto orbe terrarum et succrescens per volumina saeculorum.*[7] After the historical Body of Christ had been born and had grown to man's estate, then the Mystical Body was born and began to grow. The death of the first inaugurated the second, and still continues to inaugurate it, since the sacrifice of the Cross, continued in the Mass, is the unfailing source which sends forth, from the one Christ, the immense unity of Christianity.

As the two lives are fused into one, so are their respective histories interwoven, and we must think of the second life and history in order to see the first in all its truth and in all its intelligibility.

Hence we may say that by the way in which He disposed His life, as well as by the way in which He led the Synoptics, especially St. Mark, to record that life, Jesus gives the faithful to understand that His historical life is but a preparation and an introduction to another life, which is His mystical life.

This, of course, remains as yet only a probable hypothesis, but we shall see it confirmed by the remainder of the present study, and, through a singular but real coincidence, by the consideration of St. John's Gospel in particular.

Jesus, therefore, reveals His union with the faithful, not in words merely, but also in the very order of the events of His life. This, by the way, is a truth often repeated by the Fathers: His every action is a lesson for us, *etiam factum Verbi, verbum nobis est.*[8] If this holds true for His least action, what may we not say of His entire life, the sum total of all His actions? Is it an exaggeration to think that His life constitutes His entire teaching, and that it expresses in its own manner the whole mystery of Christianity, the mystery of God giving Himself to men in Jesus Christ, the mystery of the Mystical Christ?

§ 2

The truth which Jesus thus revealed in His manner of acting, living, and dying, He also taught in explicit statements. It is to these sources that we shall now turn.

But first it is to be noted that these are not isolated expressions, without relation either among themselves or to Him by whom they are uttered. On the contrary, we shall see that they are all interdependent, and this because they all refer to a single reality, which in turn is itself intimately connected with the Saviour as His prolongation and as His plenitude. Hence we may say that the explicit doctrine of the Mystical Body as found in the Synoptics is exactly what the life of Jesus, as told in the same Synoptics, leads us to expect.

This single reality which is so intimately associated with the Saviour and to which His teaching of the Mystical Body refers, is the Kingdom: "the Kingdom of heaven," or "the Kingdom of God."

We do not mean that the Kingdom is in every respect identical with the Mystical Body. But as we shall see, the Mystical Body is one of the elements which give unity to this many-sided concept; it is even the most intimate, the most essential, and the most mysterious of these elements, and it is the center, the explanation, and the supreme realization of all the others.

The announcement of the Kingdom is bound up with the prophecies and with the entire economy of the Old Testament. When Jesus preached His Kingdom, each of His hearers recognized in it the ancient hopes of Israel, and while He took care to rectify their ideas and to elevate their desires to a higher plane, He did not disclaim the heritage. It is well to note that He Himself made of His doctrine on the Kingdom — and, we may venture to comment, the doctrine of the Mystical Body — the continuation of the pages of the Old Testament.

At that time, the prayers and aspirations of the Jews were haunted by the thought of the Kingdom. They were familiar with the Holy Books, and in their dreams of the promised Messias, they did not conceive Him as coming alone. At His side, as inseparable from Him as His shadow and prolongation, they envisioned with enthusiasm the messianic Kingdom that He was to establish. The Kingdom of God, the Kingdom of Israel and of the Son of David, the Day of the Messias, the Day of Joy — all these concepts were intermingled in their minds. Naturally enough, not everyone interpreted the oracles of the Prophets with the same sincerity or in the same way; each understood them in accordance with his own interior hopes. All, however, associated the Messias with something else — something that to them was often more brilliant and more glorious than the Messias Himself — that was to be the exaltation of the children of Israel through Him.

In this expectation not all was false; far from it. But too often, all was understood in a material sense. Consequently, in preaching the Kingdom, Jesus had to modify these desires in a certain degree. Instead of a kingdom of this world, He had to turn their thoughts to a heavenly and spiritual Kingdom, in which, to be sure, the glory of the Messias would always shed its brilliance upon those who believed in Him, but where this glory would be more than a transient splendor; where it would be the communication of a supernatural dignity and of an eternal life: the communication of His own life to the members of His Mystical Body.

Thus the notion of the Mystical Body, which had remained vague in the Old Testament, is completed and made definite. By showing who the Messias really is, a Messias much humbler, but likewise far more glorious than was expected, the Gospels show at the same time the nature of the Kingdom that He brings: much more hidden, but far more wondrous than was thought, since it is, in part, the Mystical Body of that Messias.

Indeed, as we saw in the Synoptic Gospels, the preaching of the Kingdom holds a central position in Jesus' teaching. Furthermore, the Kingdom is shown so united with Jesus, and possessing such solidarity with Him, that the principal divisions that may be noted in the public life of Christ also mark the principal aspects under which the Kingdom is presented.

Jesus' Gospel is the Gospel of the Kingdom:

> After John had been delivered up, Jesus came into Galilee preaching the gospel of God and saying, "The fullness of time is come and the Kingdom of God is nigh; repent, and believe in the gospel."[9]

He preached "the Gospel of the Kingdom," says St. Matthew; according to St. Luke, "He preached the Kingdom of God." Later, when He sends the disciples on their mission,

Jesus Himself condenses into one brief formula what they are to teach: "Say that the Kingdom of God is nigh upon you."[10]

Such, it seems, was the tenor of Jesus' early preaching. He presents Himself to the world as God's envoy, and at the same time introduces the Kingdom of God that He has come to establish.

But this simple, open style of instruction could not continue for long. Opposition is soon aroused. Jesus has to hide, in order to avoid the Scribes and the Pharisees; He remains aloof, in desert places, and devotes His attention chiefly to His Apostles. At the same time, the preaching of the Kingdom is done less openly; as a rule, the Kingdom is now described to the multitudes only under the veil of parables. But to the disciples, to whom He manifests Himself, the Master also discloses the mystery of the Kingdom.

At last, as a result of these conversations with Jesus, the Apostles begin to understand. One day Peter, the first among them, receives light from God and sees clearly; he confesses that He is the Christ, "the Son of the living God," and Jesus answers with the promise of the keys of the Kingdom.

At once, as we have already seen, a profound change takes place in the manner in which Jesus speaks of Himself and of the Kingdom. He tells them that He is going to His death; He will be delivered to the Gentiles and crucified; then, on the third day, He will rise again. And the Kingdom, too, is about to enter into a period of tribulation; they will have to renounce everything, all the dreams of Israel, all human ambitions; they must bear the cross and mount the hill of Calvary; they must abandon all if they will be with Him. In short, for Jesus as for the Kingdom, a catastrophe is imminent. Certain of the disciples there present will not taste death before the coming of the Kingdom.

In the Synoptics, and particularly in St. Mark, there is an evident parallel between the manifestation of the King and that of the Kingdom. One feels that an intimate union must exist between these two realities.

Let us consider the Kingdom in itself. In Jesus' own words, repeated by all three of the Synoptics, the Kingdom is a "mystery." We shall see what this mystery is. In the first place, it possesses a marvelous solidarity; it is like a flock whose unity is assured by the shepherd. The sheep do not wander at will, and if one goes astray, the shepherd follows it, and brings it back rejoicing. Sometimes the Kingdom is likened to a living thing, or to a plant.

Like a living thing, it has its principle of growth hidden within itself. At first small and insignificant, it develops under the influence of the energy that comes from within. It is like to leaven, or a seed.

> And He said: "Thus is the kingdom of God, as when a man casteth seed upon the earth — night and day he sleepeth and riseth, and the seed is shooting up and growing, he knoweth not how. Of itself the earth beareth the crop — first the blade, then the ear, then the full-formed grain in the ear. But when the crop is ripe, straightway he sendeth for the sickle, for the harvest is ready."
>
> And He said: "To what are we to liken the kingdom of God, or in what parable to set it forth? It is like to a mustard seed, which when sown upon the earth is the least of all the seeds upon the earth; yet when it is sown it springeth up and becometh greater than all the herbs, and putteth forth great branches, so that the birds of the air can dwell beneath the shade thereof."[11]

Since it is life, a very mystery of life, the Kingdom is also a union and a mystery of union. Just as a living thing draws its parts together unto itself, so the Kingdom will enfold its constituents in so close an embrace that they shall be as one. Their meekness will know no bounds, their kindness toward their brethren will be modeled upon Christ's; their readiness to forgive will be untiring, and their love for one another perpetual, unconditional, generous. Like the Master, they too will be the light of the world, but through Him. It is not a moral theology of contracts, of rivalries, of distinctions that Jesus is proclaiming, but a moral theology of union. Each one will have his own goods, of course; but above all, let each be disposed to give. That, we may say, is the great lesson of the Sermon on the Mount. True, Jesus laid down other precepts on this occasion, and His teaching is not confined to this discourse; but here as everywhere, the ground upon which all must rest, is union and love. Often does He repeat this:

> But I tell you, love your enemies and pray for them that persecute you, that ye may become yourselves children of your Father who is in the heavens; for He maketh His sun to rise upon the evil and the good, and He raineth upon the just and the unjust.
> Ye, therefore, shall be perfect, even as your heavenly Father is perfect.[12]

It is brotherly love, then, but a love that comes from God. Jesus makes it a matter of divine worship, of religion.

> If therefore thou be offering thy gift at the altar, and there remember that thy brother hath something against thee, leave there thy gift before the altar, and go first and be reconciled to thy brother, and then come and offer thy gift.[13]

It is the condition required for entrance into the Kingdom of God; our justice must abound, and overflow in the form of charity. This is the price God places upon His favors: Give, and He shall give to you; forgive your debtors, and He shall forgive your own debts; grant pardon, and He shall pardon you.

Peace with God, union with God. This is a second grace that those of the Kingdom shall receive, and this grace is more important and more characteristic than the first.

The little flock to which God was pleased to give the Kingdom, is the object of a special Providence. God, who clothes in glory the lilies of the field, knows its needs, and He will provide for them: to them that seek first the Kingdom of God and His justice, all else shall be given besides.

The same thought is contained, in one form or other, in a series of parables which later tradition even considered as symbols of the Eucharist, the sacrament of perfect union; and certainly Jesus' insight was no less clear. The parables of the marriage feast, of the seed, of the lost sheep brought back on the shoulders of the Good Shepherd, all deserve to be studied from this point of view. However, this would require a long commentary, which does not appear until later.

Hence we think it best to leave the parables aside, and to dwell instead on a few words that are clear in themselves. They are to be found chiefly in the Gospel according to St. Matthew.

The passage which sums up the entire Gospel from the standpoint of the doctrine of the Mystical Body is that which serves as the conclusion of the narrative. The words are perhaps the last which Jesus uttered before His ascension. His last act, which consisted in a blessing, was to impart all His power to the Church. More than that: He Himself passes into the Church.

> All power in heaven and on earth hath been given Me. Go ye, therefore, make disciples of all the nations, baptizing them in the name of the Father and of the Son and of the Holy Spirit; teaching them to observe all that I have commanded you.
> And behold, I am with you all days, unto the consummation of the world.[14]

He is with them all days, according to the Vulgate translation. When Yahweh sent forth His prophets of old, He employed the same phrase to signify His solidarity with them. Now, when Jesus is about to send forth the Church, He takes the place of God and unites Himself with her. He bestows upon her all His powers and all His rights: the right to teach, to command, to sanctify. And the explanation of this supernatural power comes at the end: the Church can do whatever Christ can do, because Christ is within her. It is He who, through her, continues to exercise all power.

If this were an isolated text, one would doubtless be rash to see in it such a depth of meaning. But it is by no means isolated; on the contrary, it is rather the final résumé of a teaching which is expressed in several different passages of the Gospel and then repeated in its entirety, so to speak, in a long discourse of the Master.

This discourse, which is found in the eighteenth chapter, is so full of instruction concerning the Church that it might be called the "ecclesiological" discourse, just as St. Matthew is considered the most "ecclesiological" of the Evangelists. Probably Matthew wrote for the benefit of Jewish-Christian

[61]

communities, to whom it was necessary to prove that the Church of Christ was the true House of God.

Now, the discourse contains the greater part of Matthew's teaching on the subject of the Mystical Body. Once more we see that it is by means of the most characteristic features of its books that Scripture speaks of the Mystical Body.

There is a special significance in the very circumstances which lead up to the discourse. Jesus was wont often to speak of the Kingdom, and the subject had become the occasion of petty rivalries among the Twelve; each one wished to have the best place for himself. One day, in the course of an apostolic journey, the depths of hearts were revealed, and along the way the Apostles disputed their claims to the first place. Upon their return home, Jesus asked them what they had been so hotly debating on the road. Silence was their only answer. Then the Master called a child to Him, and taking it in His arms, He spoke to them of the Kingdom, of peace, of humility, and especially of the unity that should inspire their every action.

And He called unto Him a little child and set it in their midst and said, "Amen I say to you, unless ye turn again and become like little children, ye shall not enter the kingdom of the heavens. Whosoever therefore shall humble himself as this little child, he is the greatest in the kingdom of the heavens. And whosoever receiveth one such little child in My name, receiveth Me.

"But whosoever shall scandalize one of these little ones that believe in Me, it were profitable for him that a great millstone were hung around his neck and he were drowned in the depth of the sea. Woe to the world because of scandals! For it must needs be that scandal come; yet woe to that man through whom the scandal cometh!

"See that ye despise not one of these little ones; for I say to you, their angels in the heavens always behold the face of My Father who is in the heavens. For the Son of man hath come to save that which was lost.

"What think ye? If a man have a hundred sheep and one of them stray, will he not leave the ninety-nine upon the mountains and go in search of the one gone astray? And if it befall that he find it, amen I say to you, he rejoiceth over it more than over the ninety-nine that went not astray. Even so it is not the will of your Father in the heavens that one of these little ones perish.

[62]

"But if thy brother sin, go, show him his fault, between thee and him alone. If he listen to thee, thou hast gained thy brother. But if he listen not, take with thee one or two others, that in the mouth of two or three witnesses every word be established. And if he will not hear them, tell the church. But if he will not hear even the church, let him be to thee as the heathen and the publican.

"Amen I say to you, whatsoever ye shall bind upon earth shall be bound in heaven; and whatsoever ye shall loose upon earth shall be loosed in heaven. Amen again I say to you, if two of you agree on earth about anything for which they ask, it shall be done for them by My Father in the heavens. For where two or three are gathered together in My name, there am I in the midst of them."

Then Peter came to Him and said, "Lord, how often shall my brother sin against me and I forgive him? Up to seven times?" Jesus saith to him, "Nay, I say to thee, not up to seven times but up to seventy times seven.

"Therefore is the kingdom of heaven like to a king who wished to make up his accounts with his servants.

"And when he began to make them up, there was brought to him one who owed ten thousand talents; and whereas he had not wherewith to pay, his lord commanded him to be sold with his wife and his children and all that he had, and payment to be made. The servant, therefore, falling down prostrated himself before him, saying, 'Have patience with me, and I will pay thee all.' And the lord of that servant was moved with compassion and released him and forgave him the debt.

"But upon going out, that servant found one of his fellow-servants who owed him a hundred shillings; and he seized him and throttled him, saying, 'Pay what thou owest.' His fellow-servant, therefore, fell down and besought him, saying, 'Have patience with me, and I will pay thee.' But he would not, but went and cast him into prison until he should pay what was owing.

"His fellow-servants, therefore, seeing what had befallen, were deeply grieved; and they went and explained to their lord all that had befallen. Then his lord sent for him and saith to him, 'Thou wicked servant, all that debt I forgave thee because thou besoughtest me; shouldst not thou also have had pity on thy fellow-servant, even as myself had pity on thee?' And his lord, being angry, delivered him to the torturers until he should pay all that was owing.

"So also shall My heavenly Father do to you, if ye forgive not each his brother from your hearts."[15]

In general, the chapter is an instruction on the Kingdom

and the Church; it is introduced by a dispute relating to the Kingdom, and in several places it speaks explicitly of the Kingdom. But, as we shall see, it deals at the same time with that mystery of unity which is the Mystical Body. What is said upon this subject is presented as an instruction on the prayer of the Church (vv. 19, 20); as an instruction on the power of the Church (vv. 15–22); as an instruction on the dignity of a Christian (vv. 2–7; 10–14; 23–34). Let us consider these parts successively.

We shall begin with the instruction on prayer. When His brethren assemble to pray, the Lord will be in their midst. They need not search far, nor call Him; their very union will make Him present. Jesus explains that the Father Himself will see Him in them, and it is for this reason, that He who can never be deceived, will hear His children's prayer:

> Amen I say to you, if two of you agree on earth about anything for which they ask, it shall be done for them by My Father in the heavens. For [note the word, *for*] where two or three are gathered together in My name, there am I in the midst of them.[16]

So, when the Church prays, she prays in Christ, and her prayer implies His prayer. This teaching is even more forcefully expressed in the words of Jesus recorded by St. John: We must abide in Him, and He in us, as the branches abide in the vine; then we shall obtain all that we ask.

Secondly, the passage contains an instruction on the power of the Church. The Church that governs and commands is united to the one Master by the same bond which unites the Church that prays with the one Priest. Whatever the Church shall bind upon earth, declares our Lord, shall be bound in Heaven, and whatever she shall loose, shall be loosed in heaven. Jesus had already given the same assurance to Simon Peter in the same Gospel.

> I will give thee the keys of the kingdom of the heavens; and whatsoever thou shalt bind upon earth shall be bound in the heavens, and whatsoever thou shalt loose upon earth shall be loosed in the heavens.[17]

St. Luke records similar, but perhaps even stronger words

addressed to the seventy-two disciples. The passage concludes the discourse that sends them upon their mission. Jesus bids them go and announce the coming of the Kingdom. Men are to know that this Kingdom and its ambassadors are closely united to the King: those who receive them and those who reject them will be receiving or rejecting the Lord Himself.

> He that heareth you, heareth Me; and he that rejecteth you, rejecteth Me; and he that rejecteth Me, rejecteth Him who sent Me.[18]

When they speak, it is not their own words that will be heard. Again, as St. Matthew mentions in another context, the *magisterium* is not a mere multitude of pastors: in them all, there is only Christ.

> Be not ye called "Rabbi," for one is your Master, and all ye are brethren. And call ye "father" no man upon earth, for one only is your Father, who is in heaven.
> Neither be ye called "leaders," for one only is your Leader: the Christ.[19]

But we must note that it is not the teaching Church alone that derives humility and dignity from its union with Christ. By the same union, all the faithful are changed and transfigured. This is the third point to be considered in this passage of St. Matthew: the instruction on the dignity of the faithful in Christ.

> Whosoever receiveth one such little child in My name, receiveth Me.[20]

Let us carefully study the sentence. It marks one of Christ's most familiar traits. Directly and naturally, as it were, He takes the place of all His brethren, particularly of the most humble. Repeatedly in the Gospel does Jesus speak of this substitution that is so dear to His heart. He returns to the same thought in St. Matthew, at the close of the discourse on the apostolate:

> He that receiveth you, receiveth Me; and he that receiveth Me, receiveth Him who sent Me. He that receiveth a prophet because he is a prophet, shall receive the reward of a prophet; and he that receiveth a just man because he is a just man, shall receive the reward of a just man. And whosoever shall

[65]

give one of these little ones but a cup of cold water to drink because he is a disciple, amen I say to you, he shall not lose his reward.[21]

Mark and Luke record the same declaration:

> Whosoever receiveth one such little child in My name, receiveth Me; and whosoever receiveth Me, receiveth, not Me, but Him who sent Me.
> Whosoever receiveth this little child in My name, receiveth Me; and whosoever receiveth Me, receiveth Him who sent Me.[22]

The element common to these three passages is most significant. It is a sort of gradation: first, there is the union of Christ with the Father, and then the union of the Son with the faithful. And the two unions are so closely bound together that the one leads to the other: to receive a Christian is to receive Christ, and to receive Christ is to receive the Father.

This view of the economy of redemption is developed in the Epistles of Paul and especially in John's Gospel, and we shall meet it again when we study those writings. But it is expressed more than once in the Synoptics. Thus, Jesus declares that God's pardon comes to us by the same gradation.

> Forgive us our trespasses, as we forgive those who trespass against us.

Such is the petition which the Master prescribes in the Lord's Prayer. For, as He explains:

> If ye forgive men their transgressions, your heavenly Father will likewise forgive you; but if ye forgive not men their transgressions, neither will your Father forgive you your transgressions.[23]

The authority that the Apostles received from Christ follows the same order:

> All power in heaven and on earth hath been given Me. Go ye, therefore, make disciples of all the nations.
> He that rejecteth Me, rejecteth Him who sent Me.[24]

In a word, all salvation comes through unity; and the bond of all unity is Christ.

[66]

To conclude, there remains one last text of St. Matthew. It repeats the instructions which we have already met, but, under the circumstances, it is so important a commentary of all Christ's preaching of the Kingdom that it must be studied separately. It gives the final word of the doctrine of the Synoptics on this subject.

After the confession of Peter, as we have said, the preaching of the Kingdom becomes catastrophic and "eschatological"; the day of the Lord will be attended by calamities so great that it turns Jesus' thoughts to the Last Day. Hence, for the exegete, there arises the difficult question of eschatology in the New Testament. Happily, however, we do not have to find a complete solution to this problem, but merely to note what may be said from the viewpoint of our union in Jesus Christ.

Jesus Himself gives this partial answer in the closing passage of His last discourse, where He explains in somewhat fuller detail what the coming of the Kingdom will be. For here, too, there is still question of the coming of the Kingdom. In this passage, cosmic disturbances pass to the background; we no longer see external calamities, and the context speaks only of moral dispositions, of watchfulness and of fidelity. The coming itself is summed up in an apparition of Christ, but of Christ declaring His mystical identity with His brethren.

> But when the Son of Man cometh in His glory, and all the angels with Him, then shall He sit upon the throne of His glory, and all the nations shall be gathered together before Him. And He shall separate men one from another, as the shepherd doth separate the sheep from the goats; and He shall place the sheep on His right hand, but the goats on His left.
> Then shall the King say to those on His right, "Come, ye blessed of My Father, inherit the kingdom prepared for you from the foundation of the world. For I was hungry and ye gave Me to eat, thirsty and ye gave Me to drink: I was a stranger and ye brought Me within, naked and ye clothed Me: I was sick and ye visited Me, in prison and ye came unto Me." Then shall the just answer him, saying, "Lord, when did we see Thee hungry and did feed Thee, or thirsty and did give Thee to drink? When did we see Thee a stranger and did bring Thee within, or naked and did clothe Thee? When did

we see Thee sick or in prison and did come unto Thee?" And the King answering shall say to them, "Amen I say to you, inasmuch as ye did it to one of the least of these My brethren, ye did it to Me."

Then shall He say likewise to those on His left: "Depart from Me, ye cursed, into the everlasting fire, which was prepared for the devil and his angels. For I was hungry and ye gave Me not to eat, thirsty and ye gave Me not to drink: I was a stranger and ye brought Me not within, naked and ye clothed Me not: sick and in prison, and ye visited Me not." Then shall they likewise answer, saying, "Lord, when did we see Thee hungry or thirsty or a stranger or naked or sick or in prison, and did not administer to Thee?" Then shall He answer them, saying, "Amen I say to you, inasmuch as ye did it not to one of these least, neither did ye do it to Me."

And these shall depart unto everlasting punishment, but the just unto everlasting life.[25]

Thus shall end the history of the world, with a solemn affirmation of mystical identity. Since Jesus is the epitome of that entire history, He is able to speak exclusively of Himself, as if He alone had lived in the multitude of men.

Evidently, He is not denying the other truths of faith; He is simply taking them for granted. For an alms to possess so great a value, men must first be raised to the supernatural order; they must be united to the whole Trinity, by grace and by the Sacraments, in the Church. The dogmas of justification, of ecclesiology, of Christology, are here supposed. But they are only supposed; for the moment, Jesus takes only such aspects of these truths as directly affect Himself — Himself and us. To love Him in men is everything. Nor shall we add further comment.

His final and glorious coming will render testimony to another coming, which is secret and perpetual; it will be, so to speak, the sudden glorification and the manifestation of the latter. His coming before the world will simply attest the fact that all this time He has been present in men's souls and in the Church. Is not this what He means when He declares in the same Gospel of St. Matthew: "Behold, I am with you all days, unto the consummation of the world"? Yes, He will truly be with men, unto the last day of humanity.

The inspired text places this capital passage at the end of the last recorded discourse of the Master. It is a kind of transition from the doctrine preserved for us by the Holy Ghost in the Synoptics to that which He has given us in St. John.

In St. John, as we shall see later on, the "end," the Kingdom of God, is the real Kingdom, and it has its beginning on this earth. Christ abides in us, and we in Him, and He gives us eternal life; death and judgment, therefore, are realities of the past. The light has already risen, never to be extinguished.

But John is not the only one to recall this concept of the Kingdom; we need not go far to find it in the Synoptics as well. However, in the latter it is less conspicuous, and for a reason we can understand. They were written at a much earlier date, at a time when the Church was tearing herself away from the Synagogue, and consequently, at a period when the Apostles were suffering most keenly from the separation. Furthermore, what the Synoptics describe is the first impression which the Master's teaching made upon the Apostles. Now, if we consider His teaching on the relations of the Kingdom with Israel, that first impression must have been painful indeed. It meant breaking with their past and renouncing their privileges as Jews; it meant a real death. So we can understand how, after this first shock, they should have been particularly impressed by those words of the Master which pictured the coming of the Kingdom as a catastrophe, and which compared it with the end of all things. God willed that this initial impression should be revealed to us, and, in the Synoptic Gospels, we find it given considerable prominence — a prominence, however, that must not be exaggerated.

But this is far from being the only impression that they record. In addition to all the other indications concerning the Kingdom that may be gleaned from the first three Gospels, and which are assembled by theologians in the treatise on the Church, one can discern in the background, but in clear outline, and occasionally even in the foreground, the affirmation that this Kingdom is a "mystery," a mystery of interior

[69]

life. The Master will always be with His disciples, even after He shall have disappeared from their sight. He will be present through them; He will be present in them. God Himself will see Him praying and forgiving in the Church. The faithful, too, will find Him speaking to them when the Church teaches, and alas, spurned when the Church is rejected. In this Church, each Christian will be united to Him: whosoever receives any one of them, receives Him; and whatever is done to the least of His brethren, to any one among men, is in reality done to Christ.

In a mere cursory reading, the Kingdom described by the Synoptics is a reality so rich in contrasting aspects that in it one is tempted to see several entirely different realities. At times it appears to be the interior justification of the soul; again, it is a visible and external organization; sometimes, a heavenly reality that we shall behold only when the world is no more; or again, it is an earthly, everyday reality that is already existing; now we see it as a thing that meets us almost on our own level, and now as a lofty peak that only the violent can scale; sometimes it is the Church militant, sometimes the Church triumphant.

However, upon closer investigation, these contrasting realities converge and fuse into one, just as, at the proper distance, the varied tints of a painting blend into a single image. As Père de Grandmaison very aptly remarks: The expression, "the Kingdom of God," varies in form, but it "always brings us back to the same reality, to the same vast plan of mercy and grace: God uniting Himself with His human creatures by the bond of mutual, and ultimately eternal, love. This is truly an unique gift, but virtually incalculable: both because it is wrought into as many shapes as there are individual destinies, and because, socially, its manifestations, though closely connected, are distributed with very unequal intensity."[26] And a little further on the same author concludes the chapter devoted to the Kingdom of God with the following declaration: "Thus we may justly say that the Kingdom of God is Jesus, known, tasted, and possessed. St. Paul says in the same sense: 'for me, to live is Christ.' "[27]

Such, too, is our conclusion. The Kingdom is indeed rich in contrasts, but it forms one whole. Its most essential, most interior, and most mysterious aspect, the aspect that was perhaps the most jealously reserved for the Master's private conversations with His Apostles, is none other than God's taking possession of man and giving Himself to man in the Mystical Body of the Man-God, wherein He unites mankind to Himself.

§ 3

It would seem only proper to devote a special study to the third Gospel, as we have done for the first two. But this is out of the question. For, when the Gospel of St. Luke is considered as a unit in itself, it contains very little that can be properly called its own on the subject of the Mystical Body; all the important points which it touches upon have already been considered in connection with the other Synoptics. It is true that in speaking of the Kingdom and of the Mystical Body which is in process of formation, Luke insists more than the others do on certain aspects of this supernatural reality, such as its interior and hidden character and the universality that destines it for all men, and very particularly for little ones and for sinners. But these few details do not offer sufficient material for a separate development.

This circumstance should cause no surprise. When taken alone, St. Luke's Gospel contains little of its own on the subject of the Mystical Body for the simple reason that it was not intended to be taken alone. The author himself describes it as a beginning, as "a first account" ($\pi\rho\hat{\omega}\tau o s$ $\lambda\acute{o}\gamma o s$),[28] to be explained and completed by a sequel or second account ($\delta\epsilon\acute{u}\tau\epsilon\rho o s$ $\lambda\acute{o}\gamma o s$), which is the Acts of the Apostles; that there is a real continuity is attested by many indications in both parts of the complete work.

However, we shall see that the master idea which establishes this continuity and which directs the plan of the entire work, is an implicit affirmation of the doctrine of the Mystical Body.

The purpose of the twofold work, as we know, is to show the universal character of the salvation brought by Christ. The Gospel lets us see this universality in its source, by show-

[71]

ing how totally and how supernaturally human are these "good tidings" and the Master who announces them; the Acts let us see it in its realization, by describing how these good tidings of salvation are carried to the whole world. The distinctive note of St. Luke's doctrine of the Mystical Body is its emphasis on the catholicity, the universality of that Body. It was left for the faithful companion of Paul to proclaim, in the language of actual facts, how in His Body, which is the Church, Christ is exactly what He is in Himself, in His Body of flesh: the mystical Christ, like the historical Christ, is destined for the whole world; His is a life universally human. The same Spirit who led the Saviour, in the days of His mortal life, to preach the Gospel to the poor, to the captives, to the blind, leads Him even now in the days of His mystical life in the Church, to take possession of, and to unite in Himself the poor human world that has wandered far from light and life.

The path which the Spirit follows in accomplishing this twofold mission corresponds exactly with the plan followed by St. Luke in his complete work, which gives a twofold description of the mystical Christ, except that in the two books the steps are arranged in inverse order. The Gospel relates how the word of salvation starts out from Galilee and how, by way of Judea and Samaria, it comes to Jerusalem; the Acts tell how the same word goes forth from Jerusalem, passing through Judea and Samaria, to reach the ends of the earth.

Hence the scene in Jerusalem, with which the Gospel closes, is not the end of the story; it is a turning point, a new beginning: the mortal life of Christ ends only to initiate the flow of His mystical life. This truth had already been indicated by St. Mark as the only logical answer to the riddle of Jesus' earthly existence, every detail of which pointed inexorably to His death. St. Luke follows the same procedure in his Gospel, but in the Acts he shows how the same truth is expressed in the actuality of history; in other words, he relates how the life of Jesus has accomplished the salvation of the world through the preaching of the Gospel.

[72]

The angel announced to Mary, says St. Luke in the beginning of his Gospel which is his "first account," that the Son who was to be born of her should inherit the throne of David, that He should reign forever over the house of Jacob, and that His Kingdom should have no end. Yet, according to the Gospel Jesus did not occupy the throne of David at all; instead, He died on the Cross in the city of David and saw the apparent defeat of His whole work. True enough, continue the Acts, which are the "second account," but, in this city of David, Jesus is born again; He lives again in the Church, to grow and expand with the Church to the utmost limits of the earth.

Consequently the third Gospel is a kind of introduction; it is the story of the sowing of a seed. This fact lends new significance to certain of its distinctive features. For instance, St. Luke is more inclined than are the other Synoptics to represent the Kingdom as a hidden, interior, tiny reality, and he refers to this Kingdom more insistently than the others do in recounting the events that took place when Jesus instituted the Eucharist and when He went forth to die for His own. A seed is such a little thing, but what hidden energy it possesses! And Jesus' gift of Himself to His faithful was the sowing of the seed of the Kingdom upon this earth.

But more especially, the fact that the Gospel of St. Luke is an introduction and a beginning shows us that in order to understand clearly his teaching on the subject of the Mystical Body, we must look for that teaching primarily in the Acts: it is only by seeing the harvest that we can discover all that is contained in the seed.

Hence, in order to study St. Luke and his doctrine properly, we must go to the Acts of the Apostles; we must also examine the Gospel, of course, but we must do so in the light of the commentary that is given in the Acts.

It was the mission of St. Matthew, we may say, to present the doctrine of the Kingdom at greater length; it remained for St. Luke to show what the Kingdom is, and how it is the mystical continuation of Christ.

[73]

Chapter III

The Acts of the Apostles, the Coming of the Kingdom and of the Church, the Body of Christ

><

I. In the Acts of the Apostles, we see the Kingdom taking form in reality, and manifesting its inner mystery, the mystery of Christ, living mystically in His faithful.

II. The Church, the Mystical Body, is born as Christ was born; the promise of the effusion of the Holy Ghost is very like the promise of the Incarnation. The Church, like Christ, is born *de Spiritu Sancto*. Like Christ, she is guided by the Spirit. Christ appears in her, and particularly at the *death of Stephen* — a death closely resembling that of Christ.

III. So, too, at the *conversion of Paul*, He appears in the persecuted Christians. "I am Jesus, whom thou dost persecute." This was an objective vision; was there an interior vision as well? Christ declares that He is in the Church teaching as truly as in the Church suffering. "Saul, Saul, why dost thou persecute Me?"

I

THE PREACHING of the Kingdom that Jesus had inaugurated is carried on in His name by the Church. This is the story related in the Acts. Here we see the Church in the process of its formation, but at the same time we may say that there is still question only of the coming of the Kingdom.

From the very opening words, the narrative suggests this idea. St. Luke tells us that after His passion Jesus showed Himself to His disciples, appearing during forty days and speaking to them of the Kingdom of God. At the beginning, then, there is question of the Kingdom. The same is true

[74]

of the end, for in the closing lines we are told that Paul
lived in a hired lodging, receiving all who came to visit him,
proclaiming the Kingdom of God and teaching about the
Lord Jesus, boldly and unhindered.[1] Always, then, there is
question of the Kingdom, and the Kingdom is always placed
in the same proximity to and the same union with the person
of Jesus.

As we should expect from this setting, the book has much
to say of Christ and of His Kingdom, and of the union of
the two; that is, of the Mystical Body. On this point, indeed,
the teaching of the Acts is the exact prolongation of the
doctrine of the Synoptics.

In general, as we have seen in the preceding chapter, the
teaching of the Synoptics may be summed up as follows:
Jesus will return, and will remain with His own forever.
He will be in the *magisterium* in order to teach and to
govern; He will be in the faithful in order to live and suffer
in them.

The Acts contain the same doctrine, but no longer expressed
in words alone; it is actually being accomplished.

Jesus will return. It is precisely for this reason that He
leaves them, so that He may return in a closer, more inward
presence. It is thus that He Himself announces His
departure, His Ascension, in the Acts of the Apostles. The
disciples have just asked Him, now that He is about to
return to the Father, whether the hour has at last arrived
for the restoration of the Kingdom of Israel.

Jesus' answer is twofold. Concerning the Kingdom of
Israel of which they ask, He utters a few evasive words:
it is not for them to know the times and the seasons which
the Father has appointed by His own authority. But He
immediately begins to speak, clearly and positively this time,
of something else that shall come from heaven, and which
is very near — a mere matter of days — and which shall
establish the Kingdom of God in the souls of men and in
the world. And what a Kingdom that will be!

> Ye shall be baptized with the Holy Spirit, not many
> days hence.
> Ye shall receive power from the coming of the Holy Spirit

upon you, and ye shall be My witnesses in Jerusalem, and in all Judea and Samaria, and unto the end of the earth.[2]

Or, as the same St. Luke says in his Gospel:

And behold, I send forth upon you the promise of My Father. But do ye bide in the city, until ye be clothed with power from on high.[3]

These are solemn words; they close one inspired work, the third Gospel, and begin another, the Acts of the Apostles. At the same time, the remarkable similarity of the two texts brings out the continuity that exists between the two narratives. This is a point of capital importance for the Gospel, and therefore for the history of Christ. The Gospel is the record of "what Jesus began to do and to teach"[4] up to the time of His Ascension; the Acts tell us what He continued to do and to teach after His Ascension in the Church, through the Holy Ghost. In both, therefore, there is question only of the life of Christ: first of His historical life, and then of His mystical life in the Church.

II

Indeed, it is a new life that Jesus is now beginning, and one cannot fail to be impressed by the great resemblance between the promises we have just read and the promises with which the life of Jesus opens in the Gospel.

In the sixth month after the conception of the Precursor, the Angel Gabriel was sent from God into a city of Galilee called Nazareth, to a Virgin espoused to a man, and who was named Mary, to tell her that she should conceive and bring forth a son, and that this son should be the Son of the Most High, and it came to pass that the Virgin asked the angel how this wondrous thing could be.

And the angel answered and said to her:

"The Holy Spirit shall come upon thee, and the might of the Most High shall overshadow thee. Therefore the Holy One to be begotten shall be called Son of God."[5]

We see the points that are common to the two announcements. In each there is mention of an effusion, an effusion of the Holy Ghost; there is question of power from on high, of a power that shall enter into, and even cover up our weakness, a power that shall cause something superhuman and divine to rise in our humanity. The first announcement, that of the Incarnation, was made by an angel; the second, that of Pentecost, was made by Christ Himself.

We have quoted Christ's promise as it is recorded by St. Luke. We should add that it is also to be found in the Gospel of St. John. Throughout the discourse that follows the Last Supper, Jesus keeps telling the Apostles that He is going away, but that His going will be a return. It is good for them that He should go, for He must go in order that the Spirit may come. Here again, we see Christ's departure connected with the coming of the Spirit. In both accounts, too, it is stated that the coming of the Spirit will give the Apostles an understanding of Christ's doctrine and will make them victorious over the world. What relation this coming of the Spirit bears to His own return, Jesus does not say expressly, but from what He reveals during the discourse about His return and about the unity that He will give His brethren in Himself, it may be inferred that the effusion of the Spirit will have its part in the formation of the Mystical Body. However, we shall make no further use at present of these texts of St. John, since we are reserving the study of the Fourth Gospel until later.

Let us return to the book of the Acts. Ten days have elapsed since the Ascension. All the disciples are gathered in the Cenacle with Mary, the Mother of Jesus, and with the holy women. The narrative continues:

> There came a noise from heaven, as of the rushing of a blast of wind, which filled the whole house where they were seated. And there appeared to them tongues, as though of fire, which parted and sat upon every one of them. And they were all filled with the Holy Spirit.[6]

Thus was born the Church, the Mystical Body. By a special disposition of Providence, Mary was present. Is it an exaggeration to see, in this simple remark of the inspired book, an allusion to the part taken by the Mother of God

[77]

in every expansion of the divine life? As the Head was born physically *de Spiritu Sancto ex Maria Virgine,* so the "Body" is born mystically by the operation of the Spirit and by the mediation of Mary.

In this promise of the Spirit we may note a further resemblance which exists between the "baptism" of Pentecost and that baptism with which Jesus began His public life. The body, like its Head, shall make its entrance into the history of this world under the influence of the Holy Spirit.[7]

Born as Christ was born, the Church lives as He lived. Her unity is very early attested by extraordinary signs. Above all, a principle of superior life is operating within her. The Holy Spirit, so the Acts tell us, is directing and leading the Church as He led Jesus. After His baptism at the hands of John, says the Gospel of St. Luke,

> Jesus, being full of the Holy Ghost, returned from the Jordan, and was led by the Spirit into the desert.[8]

It is the Spirit who guides the Church, who directs her apostolate and makes it fruitful; He it is who guides her preachers, leads the way for them and points out other paths. He suggests the words they are to speak, gives force to the testimony that they render to the Resurrection, and fills them with wisdom and truth.

The Church is conscious of this Spirit who animates her. She possesses Him and gives Him to men; she explains His meaning and speaks in His name. The phrase she uses to express this certitude is at once naïve and daring: "It hath seemed good to the Holy Spirit and to ourselves,"[9] in the decree of the Apostles and priests at the Council of Jerusalem. The Holy Spirit and themselves — twelve fishermen and a few priests of the Church of Jerusalem! They could not have affirmed more boldly what was to be the great conviction of every Council; namely, that the Church and the Holy Ghost are inseparable.

Thanks to this supernatural assistance, the government of the Church is no mere administration. These men are the vicars, the continuers of Jesus. It is He who by their means teaches and rules the faithful, just as it is He who through them heals the sick. When Peter is about to cure the lame man at the Beautiful Gate of the Temple, so certain is he of Christ's presence within him that he can say: "Silver and gold have I none, but what I have, that I give thee; in the name of Jesus Christ of Nazareth, walk." And he cures Aeneas, for eight years a victim of palsy, with the words: "Aeneas, Jesus Christ doth heal thee."[10] In the words of Bossuet, "it is Jesus Christ who animates everything in the nascent Church."[11]

In everyday life, this assistance is concealed beneath the ordinary course of events. But in decisive moments, particularly in times of persecution, it becomes visible. Jesus had promised to be always with His brethren; and He keeps His word. The Acts relate two instances of this kind, in two events that are closely related in themselves: the stoning of Stephen and the conversion of Saul.

Stephen's death was like the death of Jesus, insofar as the death of a man can be like the death of a God. Like Christ, he was immolated outside the gates of the city, charged by false witnesses with having spoken against the Temple and the Law. The same declaration that had brought sentence of death upon the Master unchained the hatred of the Jews against Stephen. Jesus had said: "Ye shall see the Son of Man coming upon the clouds of heaven," and all cried out, "He is worthy of death." Stephen said: "Behold, I see the heavens opened, and the Son of Man standing on the right hand of God."[12] Then the Jews cried out with a loud voice, and stopped their ears, and all rushed upon him. And, dragging him out of the city, they stoned him. There is a striking resemblance, even in the wording of the narrative, between these two supreme confessions. And the resemblance continues to the end. The deacon dies like Jesus Christ, praying for his executioners and commending his spirit to God.

> While they were stoning Stephen, he prayed and said, "Lord Jesus, receive my spirit." And falling upon his knees, he cried out with a loud voice, "Lord, lay not this sin to their charge." And after saying this he fell asleep.[13]

Stephen died, his eyes fixed upon the vision of Christ. But so closely did he at that moment resemble the Master, that he himself presented the same vision; Christ had died a second death, so to speak, in a member of His Mystical Body. When the deacon said, "I see the heavens opened, and Jesus at the right hand of His Father," the Jews refused to hear of this second coming of the Son of Man; but now it was accomplished in the very act of rage by which they had silenced the voice that heralded His return.

III

Now Saul, the Acts inform us, had approved the murder of Stephen, and had watched the garments of the executioners. So he was a witness of the scene; later, he expected to forget it. Perhaps he smiled at Stephen's prayer for his executioners, and gave it no further thought. Nevertheless, at that moment he had been marked out for Christ. He went on his way, ravaging the Church, breaking into private dwellings to lay hold of men and women and to cast them into prison. But he was merely drawing nearer to the hour when, to quote Paul's own words, God would lay hold of him. On the road to Damascus, Christ had laid an ambush for him in broad daylight. A light from heaven shone about him.

He heard a voice saying to him, "Saul, Saul, why dost thou persecute Me?"
But he said, "Who art Thou, Lord?"
And He said, "I am Jesus, whom thou dost persecute."[14]

The words are clear, like the flash that blinded Paul, and as direct as a blow. There is no commentary, no attenuation. Paul bore a grievance against the Church, and he was persecuting these men and women who placed all their hope in a certain Jesus; his hand was already lifted to seize them. But lo! They are no longer only themselves, but Christ! Another has taken their place, and, rising among them, or rather, within them, confronts Saul: "Saul, Saul, why dost thou persecute Me?"
The word is as old as Revelation itself. God long before

had united Himself with the prophets and with His people in the Old Testament; to strike them was as grave an offense as to wound Him in the apple of His eye. But that union had been as yet only a moral union, or better, the beginning and the symbol of a physical union. In the New Testament, God follows up the same declaration, but with greater precision: whatever is done to the least of His brethren, is done to Him. Here we have a real and ontological solidarity. Immediately it passes into act. Within five or six years after His death on Calvary, Jesus declares that it is accomplished, and He who had held His peace before His own executioners, cries out when He is attacked in the person of His faithful: "Saul, Saul, why dost thou persecute Me?"

For this Jesus who appears is a persecuted and suffering Jesus; it is the Jesus of the Passion and the Cross. He has gained the victory, to be sure, and it is as victor that He now speaks; but the victory is not so complete as to dispense His followers from the heat of the combat. Even Paul, as he was soon to learn, would attain union with this perpetual Redeemer only at the cost of great sufferings and at the risk of his life.

Did Jesus speak to Paul only from within His brethren? Or did He also manifest Himself to Paul interiorly, at the same time that He appeared to Saul in the Church, or shortly after? The account of the conversion as given in the Epistle to the Galatians would seem to suggest as much:

> Ye have heard of my former life in Judaism — how that I persecuted the Church of God exceedingly and ravaged it, and in Judaism went beyond many of my age from among my people in my earnest zeal for the traditions of my fathers. But when He who set me apart from my mother's womb and called me by His grace was pleased to reveal His Son in me, that I might preach Him among the gentiles, at once without taking counsel with flesh and blood, etc. . . . .[15]

"God was pleased," says St. Paul, "to reveal His Son *in me*" (ἐν ἐμοί). What does he mean? We gather from the context that Paul's primary object is to prove that he has received a personal manifestation of the Risen Christ, that therefore he is as much an Apostle as the others, and like

[81]

them appointed to preach the Gospel. The emphasis is upon the word *reveal*. But, says the Epistle, this revelation took place in Paul (ἐν ἐμοί). Does this mean merely that Paul had truly received the message and understood it, that he was preaching it correctly to the Christians, and that the latter could learn it by listening to his words? Or is the Apostle endeavoring to show that the light was interior as well; that Christ, who had manifested Himself to him in the Church, had likewise shed His light within Paul's soul, to help him grasp the meaning of the external vision, and to give him strength and courage to make it known? To tell the truth, we cannot decide the question; the passage is too brief, and the context too indefinite. But if we consider the natural meaning of the words, and reflect upon the similar and very clear text that follows shortly after: "It is no longer I that live, but Christ that liveth in me" (ἐν ἐμοί),[16] and if we recall how often Paul refers to the interior presence of Christ in the soul, it seems highly probable that the Apostle is here speaking of a vision whose object was interior, and assuring us that at that moment he recognized Christ within himself.

Was this occasion the same as that of the external vision, or did it occur shortly after — at his baptism, perhaps — or must it be put at a later date among the other visions with which Paul was favored? This question, too, must be left unanswered. In any event, as we shall see, Paul speaks of baptism as an entrance into the Mystical Christ, and his conviction of the Saviour's presence within him can be found in the earliest of his epistles.

Let us return now to the road to Damascus. The sudden apparition of the Saviour has not yet yielded quite all the instruction that it contains for us. The vision, we saw, was objective, with a compelling, almost brutal objectivity. Paul surrenders, and, in a burst of light, Christ takes possession of his soul. To compensate for the loss of his bodily eyes, the Apostle has gained other eyes, to see Christ united with the Church.

Immediately the dialogue continues. In Paul's own words,

I said, "What am I to do, Lord?"
And the Lord said to me, "Arise and go into Damascus, and

[82]

there thou shalt be told about all things which are appointed for thee to do."[17]

There is still the same swift brevity, the same sharpness of detail, and there is still the same substitution. Thus far, Christ had revealed Himself in His brethren. It is I, He says, who am persecuted when they are persecuted. Now, however, He effaces Himself, and where He was, the Church appears, to speak in His name. It is she who will tell Paul, not what she thinks and what she wills, but who that Christ is who has just appeared, and what she is in Him. There is, as it were, a twofold and mutual interiority: so truly do the Bridegroom and the Bride possess all things in common, that in the Church the future Apostle beholds Christ, and in the voice of the Church, he hears Christ.

Who knows whether this consideration may not lead to a complete explanation of one of the peculiarities in the various accounts of Paul's conversion? The third time that the book of the Acts narrates the apparition, it places on Christ's lips words which elsewhere are attributed to Ananias. A mere oratorical simplification, some may think; in the presence of Agrippa and Bernice, who are led to listen through curiosity, Paul does not wish to overburden his discourse. This may no doubt have been the reason, but perhaps, too, it may be due to the mysterious profoundness of the Scriptures, and an implicit lesson given by the inspired author. In the eyes of Paul, and in very truth, what the Church says through her minister is also, and truly, what Christ Himself, the Mystical Christ, says.

The Head and the members are one; therefore, since he has been conquered by the Saviour, the Apostle of the nations now belongs to the Christians.

"Saul, Saul, why dost thou persecute Me?" The words remain ever engraved in his memory. Willingly does he repeat the story of his conversion. In the several accounts, as it happens, the details may vary; but the central point always remains unchanged. Everything turns upon Christ's words, and each time these are reproduced without change: "Saoul, Saoul, why dost thou persecute Me?" The Saviour, that day, had aimed at his heart, and the shaft remained.

"Saoul." It has been remarked that everywhere else the Acts of the Apostles say "Saul." But here, Paul's name is given its Aramaic form. Jesus had addressed Paul directly, in the language that was the mother tongue of them both. And Saul never forgot the voice of the Shepherd who calleth His sheep by name.

Chapter IV

St. Paul — 1. The Mystical Christ in Paul's Preaching

➤◄

I. *The preaching of Paul.* Its importance for the doctrine of the Mystical Christ; its dependence on the vision of Damascus. II. *Christ in this preaching.* He is the same living, real personality here as in the Gospels. III. 1. *The Mystical Christ in this preaching.* 2. He is its center. The so-called "Paulinism" is built round this truth; the latter is the basis of Paul's doctrinal and moral teaching; it is the résumé of what Paul himself terms his "gospel," or more often, the "mystery." 3. The *"mystery."* Paul expresses it more and more clearly as time goes on. At first, he merely mentions it in passing; later on, he introduces it in a series of thoughts in the Epistle to the Corinthians; he presents it several times in outline form, and once, in the Epistle to the Romans, he even gives it a separate treatment. Finally, he expounds it fully in the Christological Epistles. IV. *Doctrinal progress* made by Paul. It is to be explained not by profane influences, but, according to the Apostle's own testimony, by reference to the Old Testament and to his visions. Was there a doctrinal progress in Paul's own life? This is probable, but we have only a few indications of such a development. Hence, it is best to group the ideas according to the logical order.

I

ALL THAT we have thus far seen, rich in instruction though it be, is as yet only an introduction. We saw in the Old Testament that God was preparing a union of all men in Himself; the Synoptics showed Christ founding the Kingdom in order to effect that union; in the Acts we learned that the Kingdom was being set up on earth, and that the union thus established is to endure to the end of time. But as to the intimate nature of this union and of this Kingdom, God has until now spoken only in very summary fashion.

This He tells us in the Epistles of St. Paul, and, in a somewhat different way, in the writings of St. John.

We shall first consider the Epistles of St. Paul.[1] They are not something entirely new in the doctrine of the Mystical Body; they are simply its continuation. We have just seen, in studying the Acts, that Paul had received the revelation of Christ living in the Church. Now he transmits this revelation to the Church.

Many were the visions granted to the Apostle, but he speaks of them merely in passing. The single exception is Christ's appearance on the road to Damascus; this he describes repeatedly, and in great detail. Indeed, it is this vision that furnishes the true explanation of his work and of his writings. Whether he refers to it explicitly or whether he is speaking merely of revelation in general, he seems always to be thinking of this one when he wishes to explain his knowledge of Christ.

It was this vision that made him an Apostle, an official witness of the risen and living Christ; it gave him his message, with the peculiarities it presents; it is always at the heart of his preaching, so that it may be called the whole of his preaching. In his instructions as well as in his controversies the Apostle is simply paraphrasing Christ's own words: "I am Jesus, whom thou dost persecute."[2] As he was called to the apostolate by a manifestation of the Mystical Christ, so he becomes the Apostle of this Mystical Christ.

II

His doctrine is the same as that of the other Apostles; he was schooled in the usual *catechesis*, having learned the truths of Christianity from one of the most respected Christians of Damascus. He himself tells us that he was in perfect agreement with the Twelve, whom he calls the pillars of the Church.

Like the Christ of the Gospels, his Christ is a truly living personality, not a hazy abstraction; He is positively and unquestionably real; He speaks with authority, and conquers his man with a mere word. He is a real being of flesh and blood. His life was passed on this earth, like our own. Paul is familiar with the events of that life, and dwells untiringly on the Passion and the Cross.

And Christ's Passion is no mere speculative truth. In it Paul senses an ardent love that is seeking him out personally. "He loved me, and He delivered Himself for me."[3] And the heart of the Apostle is transpierced by those loving eyes that are fixed upon his soul; henceforth a most personal attachment exists between Paul and the One "who has loved him,"[4] as he calls Jesus.

To "this Man," to this Man-God whose ardent affection and ineffable goodness he has come to know, Paul has vowed a violent love. He loves Him with all the stubbornness and all the exclusiveness that characterizes his whole nature. He serves this Master above and against all others. He never ceases to think of Him, to speak of Him; he is pursued, obsessed, by His name. He quotes Jesus, repeats His words, in season and out of season, for though his heart be brimming over with Christ, yet he cannot sate his hunger. His is an "ecstatic love," says Cornelius à Lapide, "a love that snatches and carries Paul out of himself, and into the object of his love."[5]

III. § 1

We must go even further. There is more here than a preference, more than an obsession. It is a presence. Not only is Paul in love with Christ; he possesses Christ. His Christ is not simply a man who has died and happens to find himself alive again; He is a Man who gives life to all other men.

This doctrine of the Mystical Christ takes on an entirely new emphasis in the Apostle's writings; it gives his Epistles their individuality, and we may say with St. John Chrysostom that in all his writings, Paul is intent upon one thing: to show the faithful that they possess all things in common with Christ. Paul's teaching, "Paulinism," is frequently summed up in a series of theses, or better, of oppositions: the Gospel as opposed to Judaism, grace as opposed to sin, and finally our justification as opposed to any previous merit on our part.

[87]

Now, the objection may be raised that not one of these oppositions speaks, explicitly at any rate, of the Mystical Body.

This is certainly true, as long as we view them from the exterior only. But let us reflect a moment. Their very structure testifies that under this form they are merely incidental. Had it not been for human pride and the machinations of the Judaizers, Paul would never have adopted an attitude of defense in his teaching. The controversy that he takes up betrays an ardent love, not for the adversaries whom he attacks, but for the truth he is defending. And this truth is precisely our incorporation in Christ.

If the Gospel is greater than the Law, it is because it alone gives us true life, in Christ; if grace is contrasted with sin, it is because it alone frees us from all baseness and all iniquity by renewing us in the Saviour; finally, if justification precludes all previous merit, it is because it makes us members of the Incarnate Son, and because no effort of our own can make us worthy of a life so sublime. Thus, it is always the same error that Paul is combating on every side and under varied forms, and his refutation in each instance is an act of faith and love in the new life that is given us in Christ.

True, Paul defends this one doctrine with virulence; but his very virulence, in its own way, renders testimony to the same truth. Each figure of dualism, of opposition, of struggle, to which the Apostle has recourse, is certainly a reflection of his ardent temperament and of the contradictions that harass him. But do they not likewise remind one of Paul's own combat, of that first combat which made him an Apostle? On the road to Damascus — for thither we must ever return — the Gospel rose up before him, so to speak, and struck down the man of the Law; the light of grace burst upon his soul and put to rout sin and its allies; and Paul was inundated by a love that all too plainly excluded the very thought of pre-existing merit. In this dramatic conversion lies the seed of all of Paulinism, controversial as well as positive. For both to grow, all that is needed is that contradictors appear and that Paul's life continue.

Hence let us leave aside the outer shell of controversy, and take a closer view of the fruit within. The doctrine of our incorporation in Christ is at the heart of Paul's teaching. It appears everywhere, even in letters to very recent converts; it is repeated at every instant, with a superabundance of comparisons and forms of expression. It is used in the explanation of many points of Christian doctrine as well as for the inculcation of moral precepts. Like a living seed, its roots have penetrated the Apostle's entire thought, gathering and grouping everything together. As Bossuet declares, "Whoever would delete the passages in which Paul proposes this doctrine, would not only weaken his invincible arguments, but would even suppress the greater part of his divine Epistles."[6]

§ 2

The Apostle himself takes care to point out the position which the doctrine holds in his teaching. It is around it that he makes his synthesis, by incomplete efforts at first, but later in a full development.

We shall begin with the uncertain attempts. However, in order to appreciate their significance, we must keep the final result in mind. This we shall briefly indicate at present, and return to it when the chronological order of the Epistles brings it up again later on. We find the complete expression in the exposition of the "mystery," which is the object of the Christological Epistles. Let us consider, for example, a few verses of the Epistle to the Ephesians.

I, Paul, the prisoner of Christ Jesus on behalf of you the gentiles . . . for ye have surely heard of the gracious commission of God given me in your regard, how by revelation the mystery was made known to me, as I have written in brief above. By reading that ye can perceive my insight into this mystery of Christ, which was not made known to other generations of the sons of men, as now it hath been made known to His holy apostles and prophets in the Spirit — that in Christ Jesus through the gospel the gentiles are coheirs and concorporate and comparticipant in the promise.

Of that gospel I was made a minister by the free grace of God, given me by the operation of His power. Unto me, the least of all saints, hath been given this same grace, to preach to the gentiles the unsearchable riches of Christ, and to make clear what is the dispensation touching the mystery which from ages hath been hidden in God the Creator of all.[7]

The passage will suffice; besides, it is supported by the entire series of the Epistles of the captivity. It tells us that all of Paul's preaching is summed up in the "mystery," and that this mystery consists in the incorporation into Christ of the pagans as well as of the Jews. According to Père Prat, the "mystery" is the plan conceived by God from all eternity but revealed only in the Gospel, to save all men without distinction of race by identifying them all with His well-beloved Son in the unity of the Mystical Body.[8] All men without exception are called in Christ Jesus to be saints, and this divine bounty, this grace, this mystery, expresses at once all that Paul teaches and all that constitutes our justice; it is Paul's entire Gospel, which is the Gospel of Jesus Christ.

Nor is this mystery, as presented in the Epistles of the captivity, the abrupt manifestation of something whose existence was until then unsuspected. Paul was certain, enthusiastically certain, of the truth from the beginning of his ministry. But discussions with alarmists who saw the end of the world at hand, controversies with zealots of the Law, and all the opposition that met him at every turn during the early years of his preaching, left him neither time nor leisure to prepare a complete, systematic treatment of the subject. Moreover, as yet he did not have at his command the words, images, and comparisons with which to express it; he had not as yet been able to organize his thoughts, and it may be that he had not yet considered giving a full and complete exposition. Such a systematic development presupposes a long psychological and logical labor of preparation, and God is not wont to do this work for men, even in the case of the inspired writers whom He has chosen to announce His message. This is the work that He uses as His instrument; it is this He initiates, directs, assists, and ratifies in the Scriptures. Hence, as a general rule, He would scarcely begin by suppressing it.

Nor is it necessary that the human author of the sacred

text be fully conscious of this labor. Through the instrumentality of man, God produces greater effects than man is aware of. When truth, particularly divine truth, is once received in the human heart, it lives and develops by its own powers, with the energy it has from God; and God watches over His truth far more jealously than does the man who has received it.

Now, what the author does not necessarily perceive in an explicit way in his own mind, will not find expression in his book in a manner that is immediately perceptible either. Hence this psychological and divinely directed development of the revealed truth may appear, not in the form of clear statements, but rather by way of indications or certain series of indications that only a careful scrutiny will bring to light. It is like an underground stream that flows unseen, and whose existence would never be suspected, except that an occasional resurgence, the dampness of the soil and the abundance of vegetation betray its presence.

Such, it seems to us, is the expression of the mystery in the early Epistles. One would think it absent, but it is in process of formation. A more careful investigation detects traces of it in a few isolated phrases, or even in a series of connected ideas. These traces, it is true, are scarcely visible, and at times may prove a source of annoyance to the commentator, if he fails to see to what they are leading; but they become eloquent, when they are interpreted in the light of the finished formula.

No one can deny that alongside the general theme of a work there also exist secondary themes. Pure, dry unity or dull monotony can exist only where rhetoric is misunderstood. The real man has a soul; he thinks with all that soul, and if he is eloquent, he expresses himself with all his soul. All his memories, all his reflections, all his interests, in a word, his entire being reacts as a unit when he is deeply moved. There is unity of direction and of inspiration, but accompanying this is a full, rich harmony, the response of an unsuspected multitude of sympathetic reactions that modify the whole, yet blend into a single state of soul. Such is the secret, the incommunicable secret of living eloquence. It is in this that the profuse beauty of Paul's Epistles consists; when he speaks of Jesus, the whole man struggles for expression, and particularly what is deepest in his heart and least capable of expression. Who can analyze the ardor of this soul, all intent upon the pursuit of a single object? Certainly the Apostle makes no effort to do so; he thinks neither of a synoptic plan nor of desirable pruning. One thought leads to similar thoughts; at times a series of related ideas is introduced by way of digression from the principal theme. But the whole is a perfect unit, for it is the voice of a single soul, completely filled with a single love.

Why should God not make use of all this in speaking to us? He is the sole principal author of the Scriptures; He alone can speak to us in this fashion. If all this is found in the Scriptures, God has willed it so, although the human author may not have adverted to its presence. It is all inspired, and as such it should be carefully studied. The task of assembling these indications is an important one, for they permit us to touch the very chords that vibrated in the heart of Paul when he spoke of Jesus, and they give us an inkling of the discreet and gentle manner in which God enlightened the mind of His Apostle. But it is likewise a delicate task, for the indications we must seek are imponderable; it would even be impossible, if the author himself had not marked the path, and if his later writings did not point out the direction that his thoughts had taken from the beginning.

This is the task we wish to perform here; we wish to see how, under God's inspiration, Paul makes the doctrine of the "mystery" the central theme of his preaching.

§ 3

The first passage to be noted is an isolated but very early verse, hidden away in the First Epistle to the Thessalonians. The author places it among the moral counsels which usually make up the second part of his letters. Here, it seems rather out of place, but it takes on real meaning when compared with the Epistle to the Ephesians.

Rejoice always, pray without ceasing,

[92]

In everything give thanks; for this is God's will toward you in Christ Jesus.

Quench not the Spirit, spurn not prophesyings; but test all things, hold fast the good, keep yourselves from every form of evil.

May the God of peace Himself sanctify you through and through, and may your spirit and soul and body be preserved whole without blame against the coming of our Lord Jesus Christ.[9]

The verse to be singled out is the act of thanksgiving because of God's will in our regard in Jesus Christ. Not that the passage is not a moral counsel; it is one. But when it is compared with other texts, it also becomes a statement of the "mystery." It is incomplete, of course, and somewhat confusing, because of its presence in a different development; but it breaks the continuity of the whole by a kind of distinct personality. It is more vague than the rest; it is crowded into a reference to the Trinity: God, Jesus, the Spirit; it is accompanied by a blessing; it seems to sum up the whole economy of salvation, and to give us, by itself, the reason for joy without end.

Next, we shall take an example of a series of thoughts parallel to the principal theme and connected by the idea of the "mystery." It is to be found in the First Epistle to the Corinthians, written four or five years later than the text we have just read. Here we see a more precise expression of the ineffable reality.

We know under what circumstances the letter was written. Paul was in Asia Minor when he learned that the Church of Corinth, which he had founded a short time previously, was in a ferment of discord. The neophytes had been visited by Apollo and, it would appear, by certain Jewish Christians as well. Upon contact with these men, the flock soon began to divide into opposing factions. One of these claimed the eloquent philosopher Apollo for its head, and made wisdom its boast. Another party, probably organized by some of the Jewish Christians, took the name of Cephas. Others, who remained more or less faithful to the Apostle Paul, swore by his name. Finally, a fourth group, more presumptuous or more fanatical than the rest, called themselves Christ's. Further division had been caused by disputes over moral problems and ritual observances. Such was the turbulent community to which the Apostle addresses his letter.

For our immediate subject, we need consider one only of these many circumstances. It appears that one or more of the troublesome factions at Corinth laid claim to a deeper, more philosophical view of Christianity than was Paul's. At all events, the Apostle's Gospel was too banal and too simple for the taste of certain "intellectuals."

This criticism did not leave the Saint indifferent. He could not let it be said that his preaching, the authentic Christianity, was a doctrine lacking in depth. It, too, has its wisdom, a sublime wisdom, as he is going to prove. Among the many cares that occupied Paul's mind at the thought of Corinth, there is one that has a special interest for us. This is his anxiety to bring out all the hidden meaning, the wondrous "mystery" of the Gospel.

Furthermore, Paul shows that the mystery is a marvel of unity. All this wrangling has impaired the harmony of the Christian community. They who set up factions after the manner of men do not understand that they are all one in Christ. Therefore, in opposition to their narrow exclusivism Paul explains the wonderful mystery of unity.

Let us read the Epistle; one sees at once what is uppermost in Paul's mind, for the opening verses are full of it.

> I give thanks at all times for you (cf. Eph. 1:3,16), because of the grace of God (Eph. 1:6,7) bestowed on you in Christ Jesus (Eph. 1:6; 2:13), by reason that in Him you have been enriched in everything (Eph. 1:7,8), in all utterance and all knowledge (Eph. 1:3,8) . . . God is trustworthy, through whom you have been called (Eph. 1:3,4,5) into the fellowship of His Son, Jesus Christ our Lord (Eph. 1: *passim*).[10]

The resemblance between this passage and the Epistle to the Ephesians is quite evident. We have indicated, in parentheses, those phrases of the first chapter of that Epistle which bear such a resemblance. The parallels are numerous; both texts are acts of thanksgiving to God, and both present the same explanation of the election of the faithful in Christ.

But Paul does not pursue the exposition of the mystery further. Distracted by the thought of the divisions in the Corinthian Church, he begins vigorously to reprimand the factious members. He preaches unity, but is not that the same as preaching the mystery? The rebuke then leads to the declaration that he is sent, not to baptize, but to preach — and not to preach the speech of "wisdom," but the "folly" of the Crucified. The mention of "wisdom" reminds him of the reproaches that have been made against his Gospel, and immediately he is again intent upon showing its sublimity. It does appear to be folly, he explains; and such it is, for the world. But in God's eyes it is wisdom, a wisdom too ineffable to be understood by worldlings. Indeed, he continues, the doctrine that he preaches by God's command is something inconceivable: God has chosen even the lowliest things in the world; He has chosen all of us in Christ, that we may be holy in Christ by participation in the holiness of Christ.

> The base things of the world, aye, the things that are despised, the things that are not, God hath chosen, so as to bring to nought the things that are, lest any flesh should vaunt itself in the face of God.
> It is from Him (Eph. 1:3 sq.) that you have your being in Christ Jesus (Eph. 1:3,4,6 sq.), in that He hath become to us wisdom God-imparted (Eph. 1:8), yea, and justness (Eph. 1:5) and sanctification (Eph. 1:4) and redemption (Eph. 1:4,7,14).[11]

The last verse resembles the opening lines of the Epistle. Both passages contain a résumé of the mystery as it is later described to the Ephesians. Here again we have indicated the many points of resemblance that exist between the present text and the first chapter of the Epistle to the Ephesians. We have before us a brief exposition of the "mystery"; only the name is wanting.

And the name itself appears a few verses further on. There is still question of "wisdom"; Paul is still repeating that his preaching is wisdom. But, he adds, he does not share this wisdom with everyone who comes. It is an instruction reserved to the perfect; it consists in a "mystery," formerly hidden, but now revealed by the Spirit. And it concerns an eternal predestination of God, choosing us for glory:

> Yet among the [spiritually] mature, we do speak of a wisdom, a wisdom, indeed, not of this world, nor of the rulers of this world, who are tottering to their fall. Rather, we speak of the wisdom of God [embodied] in a mystery, that hidden wisdom which God devised before the ages unto our glory.[12]

The similarity of this passage with the two preceding texts is visible, and its resemblance to the Epistle to the Ephesians is unmistakable. A mystery hidden, then revealed, bearing upon our glorification, and upon the ineffable sanctification that God effects within us: all these points are a preparation for the Epistle to the Ephesians.

This wisdom, continues Paul, is understood only by those who have "the sense," the spirit, of Christ.[13] Others, and particularly fomenters of discord, can comprehend nought of it. Then, absorbed once more by the thought of factions and disunion, the Apostle returns to the subject of union, and then passes to other moral counsels. From this point forward, he loses sight of the mystery. It does not return again in the course of the Epistle, except in a few scattered verses.

However, from the indications we have gathered, we can see that the thought is becoming organized in his mind. The psychological process, we repeat, is directed by the Holy Ghost, who thus prepares His messenger. And since these indications are in a canonical book, they, like the rest of the Scripture, are inspired, but only as indications.

Nor does the Spirit allow this process to cease. Soon the references to the "mystery" reappear, more complete than before. Paul is no longer content to mention it in passing or to leave it implicit in a series of related developments; now it receives a brief exposition of its own which, as may be seen in the Epistle to the Romans, written about a year later, appears to form a unit by itself.

As a matter of fact, several passages of the Epistle deserve to be quoted because of their resemblance to the general tone and doctrine of the Epistle to the Ephesians. Thus, as soon as Paul begins to develop the general topic of his entire letter, justification, he refers to the latter as the "mystery."

> But now the justness of God hath been manifested quite apart from the Law, though witnessed to by the Law and the prophets — the justness of God through faith in Jesus Christ, for all who believe. There is no distinction; all have sinned, and need the glory of God. By His grace they are justified freely, through the redemption which is in Christ Jesus; whom God hath set forth a propitiation by His blood, to have effect through faith, unto the showing forth of His justness. For through the patience of God the sins of times gone by are to be passed over, unto the showing forth of His justness at the present time — just Himself, He will also justify him that is of faith in Jesus.[14]

The thought of redemption in Christ (cf. Eph. 1:3,4,5,6), by His blood (1:7), the idea of election (1:4), of glory (1:6, 12,14), of purification and justness (1:4,7), of redemption foretold in ancient times (1:4), and now revealed (1:13,14, 16), the idea especially of the universal vocation of pagans and of Jews in Christ (*passim*), in fine, all the thoughts of the passage are elements that together constitute the "mystery."

The same mystery receives emphatic mention elsewhere in the same letter, as in certain passages of the sixth, seventh, and eighth chapters. We shall cite a few that figure prominently: each one is either the conclusion or the beginning of a development, and they sum up brief expositions of doctrine.

> The wages of sin is death, but the gift of God life everlasting in Christ Jesus our Lord.[15]
> There is now no condemnation, therefore, for those in Christ Jesus.[16]
> [Nothing] shall be able to separate us from the love of God in Christ Jesus our Lord.[17]

But the characteristic passage is the last conclusion of the letter — for it has several conclusions, as if the Apostle could not make up his mind to break off. At last he seems to have remembered what he still had to say, and takes pen in hand to trace at the foot of the Epistle the few autograph lines

[97]

that served as signature. In these he sums up what he has dictated, just as the Epistle itself sums up the doctrine of the Great Epistles. And this résumé is an exposition of the "mystery."

> Now to Him who is able (Eph. 1:5,8) to establish you (1 Cor. 1:6) in my gospel and in the preaching about Jesus Christ (1 Cor. 1:6), in accordance with His revelation (1 Cor. 1:7; Eph. 1:9 and *passim*) of that mystery (1 Cor. 2:6; Eph. *passim*), which in ages past was kept secret (1 Cor. 2:7; Eph. *passim*), but hath now been made manifest, and through the writings of the prophets hath by command of the everlasting God been made known to all the nations (Eph. *passim*), unto obedience of faith — to the only wise God be glory through Jesus Christ forever and ever. Amen.[18]

In this passage we have noted in parentheses the references that indicate its place in the development of the doctrine. It both sums up the explanation of the mystery given in the rest of the Epistle, and introduces the Epistle to the Ephesians. It seems like a tiny sprout, ready to leave the grain, and grow.

And it has ample time to grow. Here intervene the four or five years of St. Paul's life that are related in the closing chapters of the Acts. They were eventful years, marked by riots, plots, and intrigues. The Apostle, imprisoned and interrogated, several times narrowly escaping death, passed from prison to prison while waiting to be sent to the tribunal of Caesar. His imprisonment, however, was often mild enough; he was treated with consideration, and so this troublous period could be a time for reflection. It was to end at Rome, where for two years Paul lived in a rented house, under guard, but free to preach the Gospel as much as he pleased. After the stormy times through which he had passed, this was at least a comparative peace; he now had an opportunity to put in writing the fruits of his reflections and the message which the Spirit wished to reveal through him.

This message we possess in the Epistles of the captivity. Their formulas are so enlightening that we have already been led to quote two long passages from them. The reader will allow us to repeat a few verses of a passage to which we have already referred. Under the inspiration of the Holy

Spirit, Paul here develops his doctrine in a song of gladness. Thus had Jesus been wont to speak of the wonders that God had so long kept hidden from the proud, but now permitted the little ones to see; for such was His good pleasure.

Blessed be the God and Father of our Lord Jesus Christ, who hath blessed us with every spiritual blessing on high in Christ. . . .
In Him we have redemption through His blood,
    the forgiveness of our transgressions,
    according to the riches of His grace.
For God hath given us abundance thereof,
    together with full wisdom and discernment,
    in that He hath made known to us
    the secret of His purpose according to His good pleasure.
It was the purpose of His good pleasure in Him —
    a dispensation to be realized in the fullness of time —
    to bring all things to a head in Christ,
    both the things in the heavens and the things upon the earth.[19]

The following chapters will enable us to make a detailed study of this merciful design and of this union of all things in Jesus Christ. At present let us note merely how joyously and how emphatically Paul declares that this incorporation is at once the eternal plan of God and the epitome of his entire Gospel. For a long time, perhaps, the Apostle has been seeking for this expression of the mystery. Even with the assistance of grace, the search was not easy. Now he has found it, and his soul is filled with gladness and understanding.

The whole of Christianity unfolds before his eyes, and he sees that everything points to Christ: there is only Christ, who mystically embraces in Himself all the faithful, and all their grace, and all their knowledge, and all their hope.

It is true that Paul introduces a certain number of juridical terms into these considerations. Christ has paid our ransom; God considers Him as answering for us all; juridically, He sees us all in Christ, and, in Him, He pardons us all. But this is not all; mere legal fictions alone cannot account for the decisions of the God of truth. Nor does Paul stop here. When he wishes to show the ultimate reason for these merciful substitutions and for these inclusions of grace, he returns to the mystery, to Christ, who is all in all. Truly and mysteriously, Christ contains us all. Now everything becomes clear: this is the reason why, in Him, we cease to be sinners, and why, in Him, we become pleasing to God.

IV

This the Apostle expresses more clearly than anyone had done before him; or rather, God expresses it more clearly by means of the Apostle. Here, then, there has been a development in the Christian teaching concerning the Mystical Body. Very naturally the question arises: How is this development to be explained?

Of the various schools of philosophy that flourished at the time when the doctrine of the Mystical Body made its appearance in the Greco-Roman world, there are two which on first sight at least bear a certain resemblance to that doctrine. The first is the school of the Stoics, who described the world as a single living being, a kind of immense body consisting of men as its members. The second is the Platonist school, which likewise considered the world as a single organism possessed of a soul and a life of its own, adding however that the true reality, the foundation of the universe, is a world of Ideas, a world of intelligible unities.

It is quite possible that these speculative developments concerning natural unity may have been of some assistance in the process of conceiving and of expressing the supernatural unity of men, and that they may at the same time have impeded the process by threatening to falsify the true concept of that unity. It is certain, for instance, that those Fathers of the Church who were Platonists have spoken more forcefully than others of the unity of men in Christ. The supernatural order, which concerns the destiny of revelation as well as the sanctification of souls, is not simply superimposed upon the natural order; it takes the natural order, and adapts its elements to its own purposes.

Historical criticism, particularly of the Rationalist variety, has tried very hard to connect Paul's doctrine with Stoic philosophy. For, according to Harnack, it is Paul, and Paul's teaching on incorporation in Christ, that constitutes the great problem. As a matter of fact, the critics have looked everywhere: they speak of the infiltration of mystery cults, of the influence of a certain religious syncretism, consisting of diverse and little known elements which were gaining favor among the masses at that particular period. And now we have Freud, to explain everything by psychoanalysis!

Unquestionably natural factors may have exerted a certain general influence on the progress of the doctrine; in His work God deigns to make use of everything that is human. Why should He reject human philosophies?

In the present instance, however, we are left completely in the dark. The resemblances become much less striking when they are studied at close range, and Paul never refers to any such sources. On the contrary, first as a fanatical Pharisee, and afterwards as a thoroughgoing Christian, he shuns the wisdom of the world, which he considers a dangerous thing. When he indicates his sources — and he does indicate them — he speaks of something entirely different: his visions and the inspired Books of the Old Testament.

What he preaches is the Kingdom of God, the Kingdom promised to Israel and brought by Jesus, the ancient alliance, of which the patriarchs and even the whole Law were a figure, and which has now been revealed. According to Paul, the Gospel has sprung from the ancient Jewish root, and the Mystical Body is the true seed of Abraham.

The only new factor is that he, Paul, has received a fuller understanding of the ancient promises and of their fulfillment in Christ. He neither assigns nor suspects any other cause of the doctrinal progress which is being effected through him. Nor shall we search further.

One final question remains. Is this doctrinal progress, of which Paul is the instrument, also taking place within Paul himself? Did he learn all this and understand all this at once, or did he come gradually to his knowledge of Jesus?

To answer this question is impossible. Despite the Acts of the Apostles and the Epistles, we have too few documents. At times there does appear to be a development of thought

[101]

on certain points, or at least one of expression. We have just noted an example of this in the wording of the "mystery," and we shall have occasion to point out others later on. But that is all.

Hence, in the chapters that follow, we shall confine ourselves to the logical order of ideas. However, we shall call attention to any signs of chronological development that may appear.

Chapter V

St. Paul — 2. Christ in Us, We in Christ

⊁⊰

I. Christ is in us. He is in Paul; He is in each one of us. He is the principle of all good within us. And we are in Christ. *In Christo;* the expression is very frequent in St. Paul: the Church is in Christ; the Christian, and the life of the Christian, are in Christ.

II. The meaning of the phrase: the wide sense, the technical sense. The latter meaning, which is almost always present, is that of a mystical inclusion in Christ. The proof is found in the Epistle to the Ephesians and in Paul's doctrine on baptism. Baptism clothes us with Christ; it makes Christ our life. Like the formula "in Christ" is the phrase "in the Spirit." Christ is life-giving spirit. The formula *"in Christo"* signifies something dynamic, not static; it signifies a life, like the similar formula, "Christ is in us." The two are interchangeable, and signify union with the same higher life, union with a living organism.

I

WE MUST now examine in greater detail the nature of the mystery which Paul is proclaiming. The first thing he says of it, is that it consists in a certain presence of Christ within us, and of ourselves in Christ. The expression appears in the opening line of his first Epistle:

Paul and Silvanus and Timothy,
To the Church of the Thessalonians in God the Father and the Lord Jesus Christ:
Grace to you, and peace.[1]

Even thus early, the phrase presents its full meaning, as may be seen from a comparison with the headings of the other Epistles. There is question of a certain mystical inclusion of the Church in Christ. The expression remains a

[103]

favorite with Paul to the last, and at the time of the Christological Epistles, it becomes dearer still. In these, he declares that it sums up his thought, and that the mystery, which is his whole Gospel, is simply Christ in us.

Paul speaks of this interior treasure in every possible way. First, he himself is convinced of Christ's presence in his soul. What matter if his strength declines and his forces are spent? Christ is within him, and strengthens him in Himself. Christ is in his preaching, to give it His truth; He is in his words, to give them His authority; in his decisions, to give them efficacy; in his soul, to continue there His Passion; in his heart, to love the faithful. Paul loves his neophytes, as God will testify, in the heart of Jesus Christ. So, when they receive Paul, it is Christ that they receive; and to imitate Paul is to imitate the Lord.

Paul, as it were, has given place to Christ within him. Since God has manifested Christ in his soul, Paul himself has passed to the background. He still lives, it is true; but no! It is no longer he that lives, but Christ that lives in Him. Christ is in him, like a new soul, and, whether Paul preaches or prays or suffers, it is not so much he who does these things, as Christ who does them in Paul.

Like Paul, the faithful too possess Christ within them. Paul sees them as temples in which Christ dwells. Since that day, when he saw Christ in the Church which he was persecuting, it seems that he can no longer look into the eyes of a Christian without meeting there the gaze of Christ.

This he repeats to his converts. By faith, they possess the Lord who abides in their hearts. Christ works in them, acts in them, and lives in them and whoever sins against them sins against Christ. If Paul spends himself day and night for their souls, it is that he may see Christ grow in them. They have within them the spirit of Christ, the wisdom of Christ, the peace of Christ, and they must needs be total strangers to themselves, not to know that they have Christ in their hearts:

> Make trial of your own selves, whether ye be in the faith; prove your own selves. Or is it that ye know not yourselves — even that Jesus Christ is in you? Unless indeed ye be reprobate![2]

[104]

Outwardly perhaps, Christians may have no distinguishing mark, yet they bear within their souls a mystery of greatness.

Christ is in His own, and this indwelling, like love, is mutual. They too are in Christ. While the phrase "Christ in us" is frequent in St. Paul, the expression "in Christ," that corresponds to it, is more frequent still.

Ἐν Χριστῷ: "in Christ." St. Paul repeats the formula over and over again, one hundred sixty-four times in the few of his writings that have come down to us. In certain passages he reiterates it unceasingly. The expression must have been upon his lips at every moment, as was the precept of love on the lips of John. Hearing him speak thus, Paul's disciples must have learned the habit from him, as a passage from the Epistle to the Romans seems to indicate.

The letter ends, like many others, with a series of salutations. Paul and the disciples who are with him greet the brethren they know at Rome. We can readily picture the scene. The Apostle has just finished dictating; about him Timothy, and Lucius, and Sosipater, and the others with him at Corinth, claim their place at the end of the letter, to send their fraternal greeting. Tertius, the secretary, writes from dictation:

> Greet ye Prisca and Aquila, my fellow-workers in Christ Jesus. . . . Greet ye Ampliatus, my beloved in the Lord. . . . Greet ye Tryphaena and Tryphosa, who labor in the Lord. . . .
> Timothy my fellow-worker greeteth you, and Lucius and Jason and Sosipater, my kinsmen.[3]

The disciples have given their message. And, while the Apostle is endeavoring to recall whether there is anyone else to name, Tertius quickly slips in his own greeting:

> I, Tertius, who have written this epistle, greet you in the Lord.[4]

It is not a long salutation, and the dictation is immediately resumed. But the few words of this Christian of the first generation have a special significance. He has spoken like the Apostle: "I greet you," he says, *"in Christ."*

[105]

Not only is the phrase "in Christ" of frequent occurrence under Paul's pen, but it is employed in a great variety of contexts. The whole Church, he declares, is in Christ, and the individual churches are also in Christ. Like the Church, the faithful, too, are in Christ. They live in Him; they are holy in Him; in Him they have their virtues, their qualities, their functions, their sorrows, their joys, their glory. Their ways are in Christ, in the strength and grace that are given in Him; in the faith, hope, and charity that are in Him, they advance to the salvation, redemption, and vivification that are in Him. For them, all is in Him, and whether they are being born, or whether they live, or whether they labor, or whether they die, they may say with St. Augustine, *"ab uno eodemque Christo non recedimus:* we remain always in Christ."[5]

II

The faithful, therefore, are in Christ. But what does Paul mean by this expression? The Apostle does not always employ the term in the same sense. In some passages it seems to signify no more than "Christian," or, "in a Christian way." Thus, at the end of his letters, when Paul speaks of his fellow-workers in the Lord, of Apelles, "approved in Christ," and of Rufus, "elect in Christ," we should render his thought accurately if we are to consider the expression, "in Christ," as equivalent to the adjective "Christian," which is missing from his vocabulary.

In a number of other places, the phrase has not a definite, fixed meaning. It is used to convey the idea that Christ is the cause, the mediator, the intercessor, the exemplar of a grace; it signifies that the thing spoken of is in Christ as in its cause, its source, its prototype or intermediary, but does not explain how this thing is in Him. In these cases, the expression would be made more precise by some such paraphrase as: "like Christ," "with Christ," "through Christ," "for Christ," "because of Christ." Some commentators have even adopted this method of explanation as a habit or principle. In their commentaries, they always replace the rather vague words, "in Christ," by one or other of the clearer formulas we have just indicated. In this we see a laudable, but somewhat indiscreet eagerness to add clearness to the text.

The danger is that in always substituting some other phrase for "in Christ," one is apt to lose sight of the primitive and natural sense of the expression. For, in this formula, it is scarcely probable that "in" should never, or almost never mean "within."

In order to determine the exact sense, it seems best to consult first the passage in which the phrase most often occurs. Here, the Apostle seems particularly pleased with it, and besides, the multiplication of examples makes it easy to determine his meaning. Here we have the best chance of finding, in all their clearness and purity, the lessons that God gives us through His inspired author.

Our search need not be long; the expression is repeated at frequent intervals throughout the first chapter of the letter to the Ephesians, and its general meaning is very clear. As we have already remarked, the passage is a hymn in honor of the "mystery," that is, in praise of God who unites us all in Christ.

> Blessed be the God and Father of our Lord Jesus Christ, who hath blessed us . . . in Christ. Yea, in Him He singled us out before the foundation of the world . . . [by the] grace wherewith He hath made us gracious in the Well-beloved. In Him we have redemption through His blood, the forgiveness of our transgressions. . . . It was the purpose of His good pleasure . . . to bring all things to a head in Christ. . . . In Him we also have come to have our portion, having been predestined . . . as having been the first to hope in Christ. In Him are ye too, who have heard the word of truth, the glad tidings of your salvation. For ye have believed therein, and have been sealed with the Holy Spirit of the promise.[6]

In these lines the expression "in Christ," or its equivalents, occur several times, and the meaning is obvious. There is question of a supernatural inclusion in the Saviour; all mankind, and even the whole universe, is summed up and included, as it were, in Him. Only in Him does God see it and bless it. But God sees things as they are. Hence Paul

[107]

means that by the operation of grace we are truly plunged, truly incorporated into Christ. This real and mystical inwardness is the full sense, the technical sense, so to speak, of the formula *"in Christo."*[7]

On the other hand, it does not always present this full meaning. Quite often, as we have said, it means merely "Christian," or "in a Christian way." But, as we should expect, the words retain something of their natural signification even here, and the sequence of ideas will always appear more clearly, if in translating we remember that to be a Christian is to be, in a mysterious way, in Christ.

We may seek further light on this same expression in what Paul says of baptism. Let us take, for instance, a passage of the Epistle to the Romans:

> Know ye not, that as many of us as were baptized unto Christ Jesus [i.e., baptized in order to be immersed in Christ], we were baptized unto His death [i.e., baptized in order to be immersed in His death]? We were buried therefore with Him through this baptism unto death, that as Christ was raised from the dead through the glory of the Father, so we also should walk in newness of life. For if we have become with Him [*lit.*, if we have been grafted upon Him] in likeness of His death, why, then, we shall also be in likeness of His resurrection.[8]

The Apostle, or rather the Holy Spirit, who speaks to us through the Apostle, wishes clearness at any cost: four times and more in these few lines he repeats that we are included in Christ. We are baptized in Christ; we are baptized in the death of Christ; we are buried in His death; we are grafted upon Him by our likeness to His death. In another passage Paul declares that at baptism Christ covers us like a garment.

> All of you who were baptized into Christ, have put on Christ.[9]

"You have put on Christ." One could not hope for greater clearness. Christ, then, becomes our environment and our atmosphere; He becomes, so to speak, "the element in which we live, the form that envelops us."[10]

This supernatural clothing, as Paul points out in other

passages, demands of us a new manner of life. Our actions, our views, our sentiments must reproduce those of Christ. However, this resemblance and this imitation are simply a necessary, but of themselves very superficial result of a change that is more profound. "To put on Christ" means not only to be inspired by Him after the fashion of an actor who "plays a character well," but, as is very clearly shown in the above passage of the Epistle to the Romans, it means to enter into a new life, and a new manner of existence.

From this point of view, a comparison with another similar expression is instructive. Paul frequently speaks of being and acting "in the Spirit." He uses the term in the same context, and apparently in the same sense in which he employs the formula "in Christ."

The role of the Holy Spirit in the Mystical Body will be considered in a later chapter. All that need be noted at present is that for Paul the Spirit is an internal principle of life and sanctification, a principle of the interior spiritual life. To be in the Spirit means to be in the "act" of the supernatural life; consequently, to be in Christ means the same: to be supernaturally "in act."

This does not mean, of course, that Paul's Christ is a fugitive or nebulous reality, for we know how truly living He is, but rather that His life is so intense as to overflow into us.

Thus, He is our "spirit."[11] Indeed, the use of the word *spirit* is not restricted to the Third Person of the Blessed Trinity and to the immaterial part of our being. For Paul, it expresses what is more subtle and more mysterious than the realities of everyday experience; it denotes a mystical reality, we should say.

It should be added that the new life we receive in Christ is an active thing, and one that makes us active. And it must also be noted that neither the phrase "to possess Christ," nor the expression "to be in Christ," implies sleep or repose. There is no question of being absorbed into an atmosphere that is inert, but of being lifted up and carried into an ardent life. Christ is action, Christ is the force that raises the world to higher things: to be in Him means to share in an activity that is immense; to possess Him is to possess in one's soul a constant incentive to action.

To conclude, then, the two expressions, "to possess Christ," and "to be in Christ," are synonymous, though they evoke images that are at first sight incompatible. But let us now leave images aside.

The Apostle employs both expressions to render the same thoughts. He passes from one to the other in the same context, and does so as if there were no change in meaning. Thus, in the Epistle to the Romans, he declares that we are in Christ, and a little further on in the same chapter, that Christ is in us. After assuring the Corinthians that he is speaking in Christ, he goes on, a few verses later, to say that Christ is speaking in him. He had already expressed himself in the same way in the Second Epistle to the Thessalonians: may God make you worthy of your vocation, he writes,

> that the name of our Lord Jesus may be glorified in you, and you in Him, through the grace of our God and the Lord Jesus Christ.[12]

So, for Paul, the thought to be expressed remains fundamentally the same, and the two phrases are equivalent in meaning. The thought is that of a mystical life, of a single organism, which constitutes the atmosphere in which the faithful are united and given life, but which is at the same time a source of energy and activity within each individual.

Chapter VI

St. Paul — 3. The "Body" of Christ

⊱⊰

I. Paul makes use of various images in order to represent the single organism which men form in Christ. The figure of the "Body."

II. *The Great Epistles* show the gradual formation of the metaphor. In these early Epistles the "Body" is mentioned only in passing. It occurs thrice in the First Epistle to the Corinthians: first, in connection with purity; secondly, in connection with the Eucharist and the meats offered to idols; in the third and most complete reference the figure is used twice in connection with charity. This latter twofold reference is combined into one in the Epistle to the Romans. The general meaning of the expression in the Great Epistles is this: we are all one in Christ.

III. *The Epistles of the captivity* present the complete expression, with a slightly different meaning. The best text is found in the Epistle to the Ephesians, where the application of the figure is explained by successive steps. God recapitulates all in Christ, and though Christ is present in the Church, He nevertheless remains superior to her and imparts to the Church, which is His Body, the power to grow. The Church as the fullness of Christ.

IV. *Comparison of the two formulas.* The second formula is more complete and more definite. In the first, Christ appears to be the soul of the Body; in the second, He seems to be the Head. Yet the two are in substantial agreement. Paul makes his metaphors express what he wishes to say. The points of divergence are due to differences of circumstances and of particular needs, but the meaning is identical.

V. *The source of the Headship.* Christ's death and resurrection manifest His Headship and even actuate it, so to speak, but they are not its cause. Christ is Head in His human nature, but only because He is God.

I

VARIOUS figures are employed by the Apostle to describe the one living organism that the faithful form in Christ.

[111]

Now he represents it as a woman, the only spouse of Christ, now as a plant, or as an olive tree; at times it is a single edifice which appears to have life, for it is seen to grow and to develop itself. But these figures have no special prominence in the writings of Paul.

The contrary is true of another metaphor, that of the human body, which is used to represent the same union. This figure, which is very frequent and very expressive in St. Paul, had previously been little used in the Scriptures, and with the exception of the Stoic philosophy, especially in the popular form, it had remained rare in profane writings.

St. Paul employs it often. It is the figure which he most frequently uses to designate the unity of the Christian community. It is found even in the Great Epistles, although it attains its full development only in the Epistles of the captivity. In order to follow the Apostle's thought, we shall study the metaphor of the "body," first in the earlier Epistles, and then in the later group.

II

It is in the earliest of the Great Epistles, the First to the Corinthians, that we find most frequent mention of the "body." Here it occurs three times. The references are usually brief and always incidental. Paul speaks of the "body" only to explain or demonstrate some other point; but he does so without explanation, as if it were something already known. Hence the idea must have been quite familiar to the Christians. Otherwise, since the Apostle is so careful to present to his neophytes only such nourishment as they can bear, he would have added the instruction necessary for the understanding of so sublime a doctrine.

The first mention is in the sixth chapter. Grave abuses were beginning to creep into the community. Paul wished to set things in order and to point out the sinfulness of such conduct.

> Know you not that your bodies are members of Christ? Am I then to take the members of Christ and make them members of a harlot? God forbid! Or know you not that he that

cleaveth to a harlot is one body [with her]? "The two," it is said, "shall become one flesh." But he that cleaveth to the Lord is one spirit [with Him]. Flee from impurity.[1]

Our bodies, then, are Christ's members; any profanation of them is a sacrilege. To make this point clear, Paul institutes a comparison between the union of a man and woman in sin, and the unity which Christ forms with His brethren. The sinner becomes one body with his accomplice; he that loves God becomes one spirit with Him.

"One spirit," says the Apostle. This is not the expression that one would expect; the entire context should have led him to say one "body." But he has just used the word in connection with sin, and it seems he dare not now apply it to things that are holy. In any event, God who inspired the Scriptures did not will that it should appear in such a context.

However, the phrase which is thus held back, so to speak, at the last moment, soon makes its appearance. We find it a few chapters further on, once more in connection with some other subject.

This time it is a case of conscience, concerning meats that have been offered to idols. Paul explains that these meats can defile no one so long as they are eaten in good faith. But he warns the faithful that to participate in the ritual repast that accompanies the sacrifices, and in which such foods are served, is real apostasy.

Therefore, my beloved, flee from idolatry. I speak as to men of understanding; judge for yourselves what I say. The cup of blessing which we bless, is it not fellowship in the blood of Christ? The bread which we break, is it not fellowship in the body of Christ? We many are one bread, one body, for we all partake of the one bread. Consider Israel according to the flesh: have not they who eat the sacrifices fellowship with the altar? What then do I mean? That the idol offering is anything? Or that the idol is anything? No; but that what the gentiles sacrifice, they sacrifice to devils and not to God; and I would not have you enter the fellowship of devils. You cannot drink the cup of the Lord and the cup of the devils; you cannot partake of the table of the Lord and of the table of devils.[2]

Here again, the argument rests upon a comparison between

[113]

a sinful union on the one hand, and on the other, a union of salvation. These exclude each other, explains Paul; one cannot at the same time associate with devils and have part with Christ.

Still, these two unions are very different. After all, the idols are nothing, and the meats that are offered to them can unite one to nothing; it is all a lie and a diabolical deception. But our union with Christ is something real. It is accomplished by the mysterious bread that gives us communion with the Body of Christ, and which unites all the communicants into one body: "We are one body, for we all partake of the one bread."

"One body." Is Paul thinking of the unity of a religious assembly, of a society, of the "body" of communicants? Or, when he goes on to point out that on the one hand all is error, and on the other, all is truth, does he mean to say that Christian unity, and it alone, is real, and that, nourished by one and the same life, the faithful make up but one organism? The latter is the conclusion that the Apostle's ordinary thought and customary vocabulary would seem to imply. But, taken alone, the inspired text is not as clear as we should wish, and so it seems that God did not will it to possess this clearness. We should say that here again, because of the proximity to sinful realities, the doctrine of the Mystical Body is unable to develop freely.

Once this undesirable association disappears, however, the doctrine will be unfolded. We have not long to wait, for in the twelfth chapter, where the author gives a eulogy of charity, the supernatural truth finds the atmosphere that it needs.

The new Corinthian converts, turbulent even in their fervor, were eager for extraordinary graces. Everyone desired miraculous powers and the gift of tongues. Paul recalls them to humility. Each one, he says, should keep his own place, and be content with the office and the graces he has received, just as in the body each member is satisfied with its position and performs its duties for the benefit of all.

Now there are varieties of gifts, but the same Spirit. . . .
To one through the Spirit is granted utterance of wisdom; to

another utterance of knowledge, according to the same Spirit; to another faith, in the same Spirit; and to another, gifts of healings, [still] in the one Spirit; and to another, workings of miracles, to another, prophecy, to another, discernings of spirits, to another, [divers] kinds of tongues, and to another, the interpretation of tongues. But all these are the work of one and the same Spirit, who apportioneth severally to each as He will.

For as the body is one and hath many members, and all the members of the body, many as they are, form one body, so also [it is with] Christ.

For in one Spirit all we, whether Jews or Greeks, whether slaves or free, were baptized into one body; and were all given to drink of one Spirit.

Now the body is not one member, but many. If the foot say, "Because I am not a hand, I am not of the body," not for all that doth it cease to be of the body.

In the body, all is unity and mutual assistance. The members serve one another.

That there may be no schism in the body, but that the members may have a common care for each other. And if one member suffereth, all the members suffer therewith; if a member be honored, all the members rejoice therewith.

Now you are [together] the body of Christ, and severally His members. And God hath appointed sundry in the Church, first apostles, secondly prophets, thirdly teachers; then [there are] miracles, then gifts of healing, aptitudes to succor [or] to govern, [and] divers kinds of tongues. Are all apostles? Are all prophets? Are all teachers? . . .[3]

So, according to the Apostle, there exists in the Church the same diversity of functions as in a living body. Hence he concludes that there is also the same unity. And he continues the Epistle with the praises of charity.

The whole of this long passage is nothing else than a description of the Mystical Body. The Christian community is one body; it has but one life-giving breath, it is animated by the one Spirit. Whoever enters the Church becomes part of a unity that already exists, just as a grafted branch becomes part of the living tree. So, too, in this one body all is common. The holiness of one member becomes the glory of all; all suffer from the pain of one; all rejoice at the happiness of each one. Even while they each perform their particular functions, the members live for all, and the services thus rendered by each member to each of the other members, seal the union of the whole. Consequently, instead of complaining against those who are more privileged, the Corinthians should rather have rejoiced. For all derive benefit from whatever one member possesses, and the very inequality of graces that is necessary for the existence of an organized body, tends to draw together all the members into the same living unity, and therefore, into the same essential dignity.

The unity of the members with Christ is still more intimate than their union among themselves, since the former is the cause of the latter. The entire body, says St. Paul, is the body of Christ, or, to translate more literally, it is "a body of Christ":

> You are [together] body of Christ, and severally His members.

Or again, as he says a few verses earlier:

> As the body is one and hath many members, and all the members of the body, many as they are, form one body, so also [it is with] Christ.[4]

Here we have two similar formulas, that would complete each other if they were joined by the same context. We need only bring them together in order to have the full expression.

This is done by the Apostle himself, or rather, by God who inspires the Scripture, in the Epistle to the Romans. The passage is exactly parallel to the one we have just read. Again the mention is incidental; again there is question of charity, and of the too frequent failings of jealousy and pride.

> I say to each one among you, not to think more of himself than he ought to think, but to be sober in thought, each according to the measure of faith which God hath assigned him. For as in our one body we have many members, and all the members have not the same function, even so we many are one body in Christ, and members each of the other. But we have gifts which vary according to the grace that hath been given us, whether of prophecy, to be used according to the proportion of our faith; or of ministry, in ministering, etc.[5]

Mark the formula that forms the center of the passage:

As in our one body we have many members, and all the members have not the same function, even so we many are one body in Christ, and members each of the other.

The exposition is a combination, so to speak, of the two expressions we met in the Epistle to the Corinthians; it includes the beginning of the one, and the conclusion of the other. The whole sentence forms the synthesis of Paul's teaching as it is given in the Epistles of that period. In general, this teaching may be summed up as follows: All the faithful, united together, are one; they are one whole; they are one body.

"A body of Christ" (σῶμα Χριστοῦ). The figure is not yet as precise as might be desired; at least it has not yet been rendered familiar and definite by frequent use. For Paul employs the word *body* (σῶμα), without the article: *a* body of Christ, a kind of body of Christ, we might add by way of explanation.

Of this body, Christ is the principle of unity. He gives life and cohesion to the whole; He is the person that possesses the whole body, and that is, in a certain sense, its "Ego." But, for more complete information on this body, we must study the Epistles of the captivity.

III

In the Epistles of the captivity, the doctrine of the Mystical Body has attained a much fuller development. The Apostle no longer restricts himself to mere casual reference. Here the "mystery," that is to say, this wonderful "body," becomes the central thought which he means to develop for its own sake, and which God teaches us through him.

He enters into his subject in the very opening lines of the letter to the Ephesians. He gives thanks to God for having chosen us all and loved us all in Christ, for having "recapitulated" us all in the Son. The term *recapitulate* (ἀνακεφαλαιώσασθαι), still lacks definiteness, but the context makes its meaning clear. However, that one may grasp the explanation, divine light is necessary.

[I pray that God] may grant you the Spirit of wisdom and

[117]

revelation unto the full knowledge of Himself, and enlighten
the eyes of your heart to know what is the hope of His calling, what the treasures of the glory of His inheritance among
the saints, what the surpassing greatness of His power toward
us that believe, [displayed] in the working of the might of
His strength.[6]

When the eyes of their hearts are illumined by God, the
faithful can see:

> With that same strength He hath wrought in Christ, raising
> Him from the dead, and seating Him at His right hand in the
> heavenly places, above every principality and power and virtue
> and domination, above every name that is named not only in
> this world, but also in that which is to come.
> And He hath subjected all things beneath His [Christ's]
> feet, and hath given Him for supreme Head to the Church,
> which is His Body, the fullness of Him who is fulfilled in all
> [or, according to the translation of Père Prat: Who gives
> Himself His fullness, i.e., by making men His members].[7]

Now we have the metaphor in full detail. Regenerated
humanity appears in God's eyes as one body. Of this Body,
Christ is the Head. He imparts to His whole Body the power
to grow, and in this Body appear all the forces of sanctification that belong to the Head.

The figure is complete. But even yet it does not tell all.
So Paul takes up the subject again in the fourth chapter.
His purpose is still to convince the faithful that a diversity
of graces, far from being a source of division and jealousy
in their "body," should rather contribute to its unity.

> He that descended [into the lower parts of the earth], the
> same [Christ] is also He that ascended above all the heavens,
> that He might fill all things [with His presence].
> And Himself gave some as apostles, some as prophets, some
> as evangelists, some as shepherds and teachers, for the perfect-
> ing of the saints in the work of the ministry, unto the build-
> ing up of the Body of Christ, till we all attain to the unity of
> the faith and of the full knowledge of the Son of God, to the
> perfect man, to the full measure of the stature of Christ. Thus
> we shall be no longer children, nor tossed on the waves and
> carried around by every wind of doctrine, through the trickery
> of men crafty in devising error. Rather we shall hold the truth
> in charity, and grow in all things into Him who is the head,
> Christ.

> From Him the whole body, welded and compacted together
> throughout every joint of the system, part working in harmony
> with part — [from Him] the body deriveth its increase, unto
> the building up of itself in charity.[8]

The description is certainly overburdened. Paul could not
finish the sentence until he had put into it all that clamored
for expression in his soul. Phrase follows phrase, repeating,
completing, complicating the thought. The entire passage is
involved and hard to understand. Nevertheless, the general
sense, the only one that interests us, is immediately evident.
Christ is the Head. By mysterious influences, He imparts
force and life to the whole body, to the entire Church. United
and bound together by Him, the members interchange their
blood, their energies, their assistance. And, by the life-giving
virtue of the Head, the whole body has within itself its own
principle of development and of growth. Hence, the body
lives; it lives truly, and it effects its own development. Paul
insists upon this interior life: the body, he says, increases
the body, unto its own upbuilding. He could scarcely repeat
himself more. But the idea is even more complex; and the
text goes on to say that the principle of this growth which
the body takes on, is not the body itself, but the Head. As
Paul says, it is from Christ, by the assistance of Christ that
the body derives its growth and builds itself up.

The Epistle to the Colossians had already expressed the
same thought, but in a sentence that is less involved. Take
care, it insists, not to be like those unhappy ones who will
not act or believe except according to their own liking,

> not holding fast by the head. For from this [which is Christ]
> the whole body, nourished and knit together by means of the
> joints and ligaments, doth grow with a growth that is of God.[9]

The same role of Head is attributed to Christ in another
passage of the Epistle to the Ephesians. Here, however, the
image is twofold. Paul is now speaking, not only of the body
and its members, but also of the bridegroom and the bride.
He mingles the two comparisons, explaining and complicating the one by the other. But the very confusion of images
adds force to the lesson of unity, by showing how far this

living unity transcends all the representations that could be given of it.

> Wives, [be subject] to your husbands as to the Lord, because the husband is the head of the wife, as Christ too is Head of the Church, Himself being the Saviour of the Body. Well, then, as the Church is subject to Christ, so also should wives be to their husbands in everything. Husbands, love your wives, as Christ also loved the Church and gave Himself up for her sake, that He might sanctify her, purifying her in the bath of water by means of the word, and that He might present her to Himself a glorious Church, not having spot or wrinkle or any such thing, but holy and without blemish.
> Even thus ought husbands to love their wives as their own bodies. He that loveth his own wife loveth himself. Surely no man ever hated his own flesh, nay, he doth nourish and cherish it, even as Christ the Church; because we are members of His body. "For this shall a man leave father and mother, and shall cleave to his wife, and the two shall come to be one flesh" (Gen. 2:24). The mystery here is great — I mean in reference to Christ and to the Church.[10]

So Christ is the Head, the Church is His Body, and she is "the same flesh" with Him. And this union is the mystery, the mystery that Paul is proclaiming in this letter, and which God is revealing to the Christians through the preaching of Paul, a mystery so sublime that it confers a mysterious and sacred character upon that union which is only its imitation, the union of husband and wife.

Still other passages in the same Christological Epistles represent Christ as the Head.

> As then ye have received Christ Jesus the Lord, so walk in Him, rooted and built up in Him, and established in the faith according as ye were taught, abounding in thanksgiving. See to it that there be no man making you his spoil by force of his philosophy and deceitful fancies, following the traditions of men, following the elements of the world, and not following Christ. For in Him dwelleth all the fullness of the Godhead corporally: and ye are filled [therewith] in Him who is the head of every principality and power. In Him again it is that ye were circumcised with a circumcision not wrought with hands, the stripping off of your fleshly body, in the circumcision which is of Christ.[11]

These lines add little to the knowledge of "the body and

the Head" that we have gleaned from the first passages we studied. The same may be said of some other texts which we now cite:

> He hath reconciled both [Jew and gentile] in one body to God through the cross.[12]
> [Be] careful to keep the unity of the Spirit in the bond of peace: one body and one Spirit, as also ye were called in one hope, that of your calling: one Lord, one faith, one baptism.[13]
> I make up in my flesh what is lacking to the sufferings of Christ, on behalf of His body, which is the Church.[14]
> Put on charity, the bond, that is, of perfection. And in your hearts let the peace of Christ stand supreme, whereunto also ye are called as [members of] one body; and be grateful.[15]

Though these last passages have not much to say about the Head, they do tell us something about the body, which is the Church.

We must now say a few words concerning this body. The Church, especially as described in the Epistles of the captivity, is the fulfillment, the fullness ($\pi\lambda\acute{\eta}\rho\omega\mu\alpha$) of Christ, as Paul repeats. She is in the same relation to Christ as a building to its foundations, as the stem to the root, as the organism to the life that animates it. The Church continues Christ; she expresses Him; she develops all the powers of sanctification that are His. Without her, Christ would be incomplete, like a head without a body. The expression is strong; but the Apostle says it over and over again: without the faithful, Christ has not His fullness.

This fullness, it is true, adds nothing new to Christ. As we have already seen, the body derives its growth entirely from Him, and it is His merits, His grace, and His holiness that are the life and the activity of His faithful. He is the cause and the origin in all; it is from Him that grace and strength descend upon the whole Church, and God sees us and blesses us only for His sake, in Him, and through Him. But He had to have this supernatural expansion, in order that the eyes of all might contemplate the plenitude that was not manifest in His individual existence.

IV

The figure of the Mystical Body is more fully developed in the Epistles of the captivity than in the earlier Epistles. In the latter Paul spoke only of a body composed of many members. Now he mentions the special role of the Head, the prolongation, if we may so speak, of the Head in the body, and the vital interchange that takes place between the members.

Now, too, the "body" appears as a more concrete reality. In the earlier Epistles, as we have noted, its outline was less clear; the Apostle spoke of it somewhat vaguely, as "body of Christ," without the article. Now he calls it "the body of Christ," using the article. This, of course, is a slight modification, but it may indicate that the image has now become more distinct in his mind, and that, by a more frequent use of the figure, Paul himself has naturally come to look upon it as something very definite.

To this modification we must add another, which, like the first, introduces no change in the thought expressed. In the Great Epistles, Christ appeared to be within the whole body. He was, in a certain sense, its "Ego"; He was the source of concord and of unity between all the members, adapting each to the others in Himself, like the soul or vital principle. Now, in the Christological Epistles, Christ appears primarily as superior to any body. He is the Head, says Paul — the word did not appear in the earlier letters — and it is especially from above that He imparts life and unity to the entire organism. In his commentary on the Epistle to the Galatians, Cornelius à Lapide formulates well the difference between the two images: "The expression, 'ye are Christ's,' may be rendered thus: 'ye are the members of which He is the Head,' or 'ye are the Mystical Body, of which He is the soul.' "[16]

Though much has been said about this difference, it is merely a question of vocabulary. The thought has not changed. In the early Epistles, the role of Head is attributed to Christ; only the word is absent. Even thus early Paul declares that He is the foundation of the entire edifice; He is the first-fruits; it is He who distributes grace, and it is by Him that salvation comes to us. Hence, far from being lost in the multitude of the faithful whom He joins in Himself, the personality of Christ ever stands out clearly defined and transcendent, since it is like the supreme Unity, from which all else has unity.

On the other hand, for all its novelty, the figure of the "Head" as formulated in the Epistles of the captivity, does not by any means exclude the role which the great Epistles ascribe to Christ. Even when raised up above the whole organism, He nevertheless remains within it. He animates and gives life to the whole; and though this whole constitutes His growth and His fullness, yet it comes entirely from Him. In its entirety, too, it had to be present in Him first of all — *eminenter et causative,* as the Scholastics would say. His superiority as Head corresponds, therefore, in every way to the superiority that characterizes the soul, when it gives life to the entire living being.

For the rest, it matters little to Paul whether such be exactly the function of the head in an organism. He is no slave to the figures he employs; he makes them say what must be said, though he should have to force them a bit as he goes along. In another passage treating of the same subject, have we not seen him take two figures that are almost irreconcilable, "to be in Christ," and "to possess Christ," and combine them without even appearing to notice the difficulty? So it is with the figure of the head. It must tell us that although Christ is in every respect superior to the whole organism, He is nonetheless present everywhere within that organism, animating it with His power. And this is what the figure actually does express. That it seem a trifle forced does not concern him in the least.

Moreover, the time had come, in the Epistles of the captivity, to emphasize the pre-eminence of Christ. In the days of the earlier Epistles, there was question only of the Church. The Judaizers had wished to subordinate her to Judaism, and Paul had to show that she possessed a divine life, that she was a body animated by Christ. Now, the method of attack has changed: visionaries are striking at Christ and at His divinity. So, it is Christ's divinity that Paul emphasizes. He insists upon the superiority that puts the Head above the body, without at the same time separating the one from the other.

But whatever be the figure used, the doctrine remains identical. Whether he exalts the Church, as in the Great Epistles, or whether he exalts Christ, as in the Epistles of the captivity, Paul is always repeating the same affirmation: the Church is united with Christ, and she is His Mystical Body.

V

In almost all the texts which treat of Christ's function as Head, that function is very closely associated with His death on Calvary and with His resurrection.

> And [Christ] Himself is the Head of the body, the Church: it is He who is the beginning, the first-born from the dead. . . . It hath pleased the Father . . . through Him to reconcile all things to Himself . . . making peace through the blood of His cross.[17]

By one and the same act, so to speak, Christ is both "Head of the Church and the Saviour of His Body," as St. Paul explains to the Ephesians.[18] He is Head of all in the sense that:

> along with Him ye were buried in baptism: along with Him also ye had your resurrection through your faith in the power of God, who hath raised Him up from the dead.[19]

Since this Head attaches all the members closely to Himself, all have died in His death and all are risen in His resurrection. God's great work in the world, which is to incorporate all men in Christ, was accomplished through the events of Good Friday and of Easter morning. Paul marvels at the tremendous power of God's operation in us.

> With that same strength He hath wrought in Christ, raising Him from the dead. . . . He hath subjected all things beneath His feet, and hath given Him for supreme Head to the Church.[20]

There is union and continuity between Christ's death and

resurrection on the one hand, and His universal power of vivification on the other. It is by making all men partakers of the Blood which He shed and of His life-giving Body that He gathers them all together, through the Eucharist, into a single organism. His death and resurrection make Him the second Adam; by their means He has opened the door through which all humanity is to enter; by their means He has begun in Himself the divine alchemy that is to transform the whole race of men. Therefore it is by their means that He is able to incorporate into Himself this multitude of sinful humanity; it is by their means that He has become Head of all the members of His body.

Once more we repeat: the doctrine of the mystical Christ does not tend to obscure the history of the concrete Christ: on the contrary, it presupposes and integrates that history. The events that took place at Jerusalem during the week of the Pasch belong also to the theoretical teaching which explains how the divine life continues to flow, always and everywhere, into humanity. Though these events belong to the past as far as their material execution is concerned, yet in their supernatural efficacy they continue to be the principle that acts in all human events; nay, they are become in a sense the one and perpetual event of human history.

But they possess this mystical universality only because Christ Himself is universal and mystical; *operari sequitur esse*, we might say in Scholastic phraseology. Jesus' actions, and above all, His last actions, have this universal effect precisely because they are the actions of Jesus; simply by being His actions, they have the same universal and irresistible power which He possesses by being the Man-God.

In vain will one search for a text in which St. Paul states or implies that God conferred the Headship on Christ only after the resurrection. On the contrary, the Headship is mentioned many times without any reference whatever to the resurrection. When there is question of the latter, as is often the case, the resurrection and death of the Saviour are represented merely as the means whereby the Christ-life enters into the souls of men or whereby the souls of men come in contact with the Christ-life; it is repre-

[125]

sented as the model of the transformation which God wills to bring about in the faithful, or as a motive which the faithful have to act for God; above all, it is represented as the external revelation and manifestation of the marvelous expansion and universal efficacy of a power that was present in Christ from the beginning. Indeed, the resurrection is frequently treated as an element which, however important, has not yet been assigned to a definite place in Paul's teaching of the Mystical Body.

We may say in general that the resurrection does not enter, at least primarily, into the doctrine of the "mystery" and of the life *in Christo,* whether we consider the descriptions of the complex organism which is the Mystical Body or the expressions in which Paul tells us that this organism is so truly one as to constitute a single man, one Christ.

Hence, in spite of its great importance, it remains something secondary. The essential, ultimate, and complete explanation of the resurrection, of its mystical efficacy, and of all that is mystical in the Saviour, lies in the fact that the Saviour is God. This is why Paul's teaching can be strictly theocentric without being any less Christocentric: for if Christ is the center of all in man, God is the center of all in Christ.

> In Him dwelleth all the fullness of the Godhead corporally: and ye are filled therewith in Him.[21]

What more could we ask? Christ Himself, the supreme gift, is the final explanation:

> He is the image of the unseen God. . . . And Himself is prior to all, and in Him all things hold together.
> He again is the Head of the Body, the Church. . . .
> For in Him it hath pleased the Father that all the fullness should dwell.[22]

All these "fullnesses" are linked together, and each one of them lives by reason of its attachment to the one that precedes. Since Christ possesses in Himself the fullness of the divinity, He also possesses in Himself the fullness of all supernatural human life; hence we, too, are filled in Him, filled with all the fullness of God. There is only Christ: He

[126]

is the first, the first in all; He is all, all in all; for He is God.
He is God, and we are sons of God:

> For ye are all through your faith sons of God in Christ Jesus. . . .
> Ye are all one person in Christ Jesus.[23]

This divinization that is given in Christ will be treated
later on; what we shall say then will continue the explanation which we have begun here. For the present only one
point is to be noted; namely, that just as it was God who
willed to recapitulate all things in Christ, so, too, it is God
who effects this recapitulation of all things in Christ. To
anticipate the terms of later theology, we may say that if
the Saviour is Head through His humanity and in His
humanity, He is such only by reason of the divinity.

Chapter VII

St. Paul — 4. Secondary Formulas of the "Mystery"

⸝ ⊱⊰

I. Various expressions other than that of the Head and members which are used to denote the "mystery":

1. Verbs compounded with σύν, "with." Their meaning, origin, peculiar uses; their relation to the idea that the Church is the *pleroma* of Christ.

2. *Asceticism and the Mystical Body.* The charity and purity that befit the members of Christ; suffering in Christ, resurrection in Christ. Christ our life, a life ever new, a divine life.

3. *The new creation;* a general and complete renewal.

II. *The Mystical Christ.* The Christians are one in Christ: a new man, a perfect man, one Christ. To divide the Church is to divide Christ; a body of many members; such is Christ. Between Christians worldly distinctions no longer exist; in them there is now only Christ. The Apostle's very style is reminiscent of the vision which took place on the road to Damascus.

III. *The "mystery" and divinization.* Since the Head is God, and since He is Head by reason of His divinity, the members are deified; they become light, life, and glory. They are united with the Father, and are His sons by adoption. They possess the Spirit, who acts in the faithful and in the Church, and who is "their Spirit," but not in the same sense that Christ is their Head. Through Christ they are united with the entire Trinity.

IV. *Conclusion.* The doctrine of the Mystical Body in Paul's writings presents many different aspects, but all combine to express this one truth: in Christ, all Christians are one body, one Mystical Christ. In this teaching Paul simply transmits to the Church what he has learned from the Saviour.

I. § 1

IT IS often thought that Paul scarcely ever treats of the "mystery" without using the figure of the Head and members.

This is by no means the case. In the present chapter we shall consider certain other expressions of the same truth which are perhaps less evident at first sight, but which are certainly no less forceful.

In the first place, certain verbs compounded with σύν merit our attention. These are peculiar verbs, and they express a thought that is unique; they tell us what Christ does in His capacity as Head of a body, or what is done by the faithful in their capacity as members of that Body. For the Mystical Body must needs manifest its unity by its manner of acting: since we are the Body of Christ, Christ has lived and died and is risen with us, and we with Him. Now, for Paul, who is always somewhat in a hurry, the ideal is to express all these concepts at one and the same time. Naturally, he is at a loss for words. For who ever had such a message to announce? So he has to coin the words, and this explains the presence, in the Apostle's vocabulary, of verbs, overburdened with meaning. These express the deeds and the sufferings of Christ, but Paul prefixes the preposition σύν, "with." Thus, the reader understands that he must keep two things in mind: the acts of Christ and our own, and he must think of them as one. The expression may not be elegant, perhaps; but Paul is little interested in Attic idiom! His concern is with the excessive charity of Christ; this he must exalt in its fullness.

The verbs occur for the first time in the Epistle to the Galatians. Until then, when he spoke of our solidarity with the Saviour, Paul was content with the ordinary modes of expression, which are still present, in considerable number, at the beginning of this Epistle. However, in the face of the obstacles that are being raised against him, Paul's thoughts turn particularly to the Cross of the Saviour. In the second chapter, he synthesizes the two ideas:

> I died to the Law through the Law in order that I might live to God. With Christ I am nailed to the cross; it is no longer I that live, but Christ that liveth in me. So far as I live now in the flesh, I live by faith in the Son of God, who loved me and delivered Himself for me.[1]

Χριστῷ συνεσταύρωμαι, with Christ I am nailed to the Cross,

or literally, I am "con-crucified-with" Christ. "Christ died upon the Cross," declares Paul, "and I died upon it too. This Cross has caused me to die to the Law and to the life I once led; this death has given me a new life, the only life by which I truly live. We therefore died together, and by His crucifixion I have been crucified."

"I am con-crucified with Christ." The expression, which thus makes its first appearance in the Epistle to the Galatians, was not to remain alone. The Holy Spirit, who, perhaps by a long psychological process, had led the Apostle to discover the phrase, also makes him repeat it often: we have died with Christ, and we are buried with Him, in order that we may rise with Him; we are vivified with Him and exalted with Him, that we may sit with Him at the right hand of the Father.

Paul uses these verbs in speaking of the death, resurrection, and glory of the Saviour, but not to designate Christ's existence or the ordinary acts of His public life. When he is concerned with these latter topics, at most he employs analogous adjectives, as, for example, when he says that we are "conformable with Christ."[2] But such expressions are not characteristic, and they remain the exception. We may say in general that this mystical community of action does not exist for Paul except in connection with the suffering and glorious life of Christ.

This, we think, is easily explained. It is in His suffering and glorious life that Christ is, so to speak, most mystical. For then it is that He deposits His life within us; it is then that He redeems us in order to make us members of His Body, and institutes the sacrament by which He nourishes us with Himself. Moreover, did not Christ Himself reserve these supreme moments for His most complete confidences concerning the work of union that He was going to accomplish?

These verbs do not ordinarily stand alone, but come in groups, most commonly in groups of three.

If we have "died-with" Him, we shall also "live-with" Him: If we endure, we shall also "reign-with" Him.[3]

In Christ Jesus through the gospel the gentiles are "coheirs" and "concorporate" and "comparticipant" in the promise.[4]

[We are] "joint-heirs-with" Christ — if, that is, we "suffer-with" Him, that we may also be "glorified-with" Him.[5]

Ye were "buried-with" Him in baptism; ye had also your "resurrection-with" Him through your faith.[6]

Obviously, there must be a reason for this insistence: The Spirit, who inspires Paul, wishes to arrest our attention. And, as a matter of fact, the thought which these verbs express is one of the great concepts of the Pauline doctrine of the Mystical Body. They signify that Christ's actions and sufferings are prolonged and consummated in the actions of the Christians, and that only in this way do they attain their totality and their *pleroma*. Yes, their *pleroma*. The verbs compounded with σύν express, in the order of supernatural activity, what is expressed in the order of being and of reality by the doctrine, so dear to Paul, that the Church is the continuation, the fullness, the *pleroma*, of the Saviour. Thus God, the Creator of all things, can make use of all, even of the structure of our words, for our instruction.

§ 2

Since the life of Christ is prolonged in ours, our lives must appear as the continuation of His own. Hence there is a special asceticism for the members of the Mystical Body; from their incorporation in the Lord, this asceticism deduces the rules that should govern their conduct.

These rules we have already seen, and for the sake of brevity we shall merely summarize them here. Says Paul, or rather, through Paul, the Spirit of Christ declares: Christians must love one another, since they are members of the same body. They must remain pure, out of respect for their bodies, which are the members of the Saviour. They should be truthful in their dealings with one another, for they are members one of the other. Their life is a "communion";[7] they must live in union with men, with their brethren, rejoicing with those that are glad, mourning with those that mourn, for they are all one in Christ. They must live in union with

[131]

the Saviour and learn to suffer with Him, for it is by their union with His sufferings that they are saved. Just as Christ receives the complement, the *pleroma* of His own life in their lives, so in their sufferings He receives the consummation and the *pleroma* of His Passion: "I make up in my flesh what is lacking to the sufferings of Christ, on behalf of His body, which is the Church."[8]

For Christians, therefore, suffering is one of the duties of their state of life. Nay, they are already dead, and their life is hidden with Christ in God. By baptism they are buried with Christ and raised up with Christ. By His victory over death they are born anew to a higher life. This transformation of their being shows forth the mystical fullness of the Saviour's resurrection, just as their death to sin manifests the mystical universality that was contained in His death.

This view of the history of the Mystical Body as the continuation of the history of Christ is familiar to the Apostle; in an earlier chapter we saw that it was likewise familiar to his faithful companion Luke, the author of the Acts. It would serve, if necessary, as the center of a general exposition of the Pauline doctrine of the Mystical Body from the standpoint of the growth of that body.

According to Paul, then, the faithful are no longer of this world, just as Christ Himself is no longer of this world. The things of earth are worthless in their eyes, and only the things of heaven possess value. By all that they are, by all that they do, whether they live or whether they die, whether they eat or whether they breathe, they are Christ's.

"They are Christ's," Χριστοῦ εἶναι.[9] This phrase expresses, not some vague relationship of the Christian with Christ, but a new, profound manner of being, more profound than their natural being. They are Christ's because they are of His body: in themselves, they are no longer merely themselves. Hence they should experience in their souls, not so much their own impressions as the sentiments of the Saviour Himself:

Let that mind be in you, which was also in Christ Jesus.[10]
For our part, we have the mind of Christ.[11]

[132]

For them, Christ is all things: He is their hope, their wisdom, their redemption; when they die, they shall fall asleep in Him, and as long as they live, their life, their very act of living, is Christ.

> With me, to live is Christ, and to die is gain.[12]
> When Christ, our life, shall appear, then also shall ye appear with Him in glory.[13]

§ 3

Such a transfiguration is a tremendous change. Death is a little thing by comparison, and even creation is only a beginning. This emphatic declaration appears for the first time in the second Epistle to the Corinthians. The passage does not treat directly of the Mystical Body, but the thought of the body seems to be presupposed throughout. Directly, the Apostle is simply defending his Gospel; but the excellence of that Gospel lies precisely in the fact that it is Christ's own work. Christ is hidden within it; Christ grows within it; in it, Christ wills to transform all things. No force can prevent so vigorous an expansion.

> The charity of Christ constraineth us, since we judge thus, that one died for all — therefore all had died — and that He died for all that they who live may no longer live to themselves, but to Him who died for them and was raised from the dead.
> So that ourselves henceforward know no man according to the flesh. Nay, even if we have had knowledge of Christ according to the flesh, yet now we have such knowledge of Him no longer [or, we wish now to have knowledge only of the Christ who reneweth the spirit].
> If, then, any man be in Christ, he is a new creature: the former things have passed away: behold all things are made new!
> But all things are of God, who hath reconciled us to Himself through Christ and hath given to us the ministry of reconciliation; God, as it were, was reconciling the world to Himself in Christ, by not reckoning against men their transgressions, and by the word of reconciliation wherewith He had entrusted us. On Christ's behalf, then, we are ambassadors, God as it were exhorting through us; we beseech you for Christ's sake, be reconciled to God![14]

"If, then, any man be in Christ, he is a new creature. The

former things have passed away: behold, all things are made new." One cannot fail to have remarked this triumphant assertion. Of what concern are a few petty adversaries? A new life is rising in mankind; the Creator is at work. Who can arrest these all-powerful energies?

The same thought recurs in the Epistle to the Galatians. There, too, adversaries wished to destroy the work that had been accomplished. But there will be a reckoning. At the close of the Epistle, Paul warns them that God will not be thwarted.

> As for me, Heaven forbid that I should make boast of aught save the cross of our Lord Jesus Christ, whereby the world is crucified to me, and I to the world [the former state of things has been done away with, and the ancient distinction between Jews and gentiles no longer exists]. For neither circumcision is aught, nor uncircumcision, but a new creature.[15]

The life of grace, he tells us elsewhere, is as gratuitous a gift as was creation.

> By grace ye are saved, through faith; and that not of your-selves, it is the gift of God . . . lest any should boast. For we are His handiwork, created in Christ Jesus for good works, which God hath prepared beforehand that therein we may walk.[16]

This divine handiwork, this second creation, is so far-reaching that, through man, it affects nature itself; the whole universe groans in agony and hope. The birth of this new world suggests to Paul's mind the new light that shone forth upon the nascent world. But the situation is far better now than it was at the beginning.

> It is the God who said, "Out of darkness shall shine light," that hath shone in our hearts, unto the illuminating knowl-edge of the glory of God, in the person of Christ.[17]

The light of the first day was a mere creature, but the Light that now shines within us is God, the eternal Light.

II

For the second time, therefore, the faithful have experienced the touch of the Creator's hands. Humanity is beginning anew: there is a new Adam; there is a new race, and this new race is so united that it forms but one man, a new man, one perfect and complete man.

This gives us all that still remains to be said, and we shall see how characteristically and realistically these affirmations of the Apostle complete his doctrine of the Mystical Body. Not only do the Christians form one "body"; they even form but one man, as Paul declares in answer to those who exalt the Law and consider the Gentile converts far inferior to the Jews.

In Him is neither Jew nor Greek, neither slave nor free, neither male nor female;
For ye are all one person in Christ Jesus.[18]

"One person," εἶς; the word is used, not in the neuter, as if there were question of a thing, of some vague concord or abstract entity, but in the masculine, since there is question of a person, a mystical person. The Apostle takes up the thought again, in the Epistle to the Ephesians, and explains who this one person is.

Wherefore remember that aforetime ye, the gentiles according to the flesh — ye that are styled "uncircumcision" by that which is styled "circumcision," [a circumcision] done with hands in the flesh — remember that ye were at that time Christless, alienated from the commonwealth of Israel and strangers to the covenants of the promise, without hope and without God in the world.

But now in Christ Jesus ye that were once far off are brought near through the blood of Christ. For He is our peace, He that hath made both [Jew and gentile] one, [ἕν, one thing], and hath broken down the dividing barrier, the [sign of] enmity. He hath brought to nought in His flesh the law of commandments framed in decrees, that in Himself He might create of the two one new man, and make peace and reconcile both in one body to God through the cross, slaying their enmity in His own death.

And so He came and brought glad tidings of peace to you that were afar off and of peace to them that were near: because through Him we both have access in one Spirit to the Father. Therefore ye are no longer strangers and foreigners, but ye are fellow-citizens of the saints and members of the household of God.[19]

[135]

Three times does the Apostle repeat the same thought in similar terms in these verses. The statement is at first somewhat vague; you who were once strangers, God has made one, ἕν, one single thing. Then it becomes more precise: Christ has united you all, by creating you in Himself, in such a way as to make of you all one single new man, εἰς ἕνα καινὸν ἄνθρωπον. Finally the statement is taken up again, this time in familiar terms: By His Cross, Christ has reconciled you in one body.

One thing, one man, one body. In this triple affirmation, the second is the formula which we wish especially to study at present. It states, but in more explicit terms, the thought we have just seen expressed in the Epistle to the Galatians; namely, that the faithful make up one single person — one new man. Moreover, the two accompanying expressions are its commentary: this new man is something unique; he is the Mystical Body of Christ.

Paul speaks of this new man in other passages. We see that he is a collective reality; he is formed by the union of Jews and Gentiles. Nevertheless, though he is a collective being, he perfects those qualities that are most personal to those who are his members. He brings them nearer to God, makes them more like to the Father, more holy, more charitable, and more upright. In fine, he makes them more new, in the candor of an innocence and a sweetness that are always youthful.

Despite this twofold aspect of collectivism and individuality, the new man is one. Like the "body" of Christ, with which he is often identified, he constitutes a single reality. He is even more truly one than ordinary individuals are, for he is one with the unity of the Master. He is one in Christ's blood, one by Christ's Cross; in him Christ does away with the distinctions that so easily arise between personalities so narrow as we are of ourselves.

A little later in the same Epistle to the Ephesians, Paul again speaks of this mystical man. This time, however, he calls this supernatural organism, not merely a new man, but a perfect man.

He that descended [into the lower parts of the earth], the

[136]

same is also He that ascended above all the heavens, that He might fill all things. And Himself gave some as apostles, some as prophets, some as evangelists, some as shepherds and teachers, for the perfecting of the saints in the work of ministry, unto the building up of the body of Christ, till we all attain to the unity of the faith and of the full knowledge of the Son of God, to the perfect man, to the full measure of the stature of Christ. Thus we shall be no longer children. . . .[20]

Like the new man, this perfect man is also a collective reality. For, like the new man, he is composed of all of us together, and, again like the new man, he explains what the body of Christ is.

One man, one new man, a perfect man. All these phrases are powerful descriptions of the unity of the Church. But this is not enough; we have not yet heard the Apostle's strongest expression. The faithful? Why, he assures us, they are Christ Himself!

Paul ventures to employ the expression for the first time quite early in his teaching, in the first Epistle to the Corinthians. We recall that factious groups had caused a division in that Church.

Now I exhort you, brethren, by the name of our Lord Jesus Christ, all to speak the same thing, thus ending the divisions among you, and to become fully united in the one mind and judgment. For it hath been made clear to me concerning you, my brethren, by those of Chloe's household, that there are quarrels among you. This is what I mean — each of you saith, "I am for Paul," [or] "I am for Apollos," [or] "I am for Cephas," [or] "I am for Christ."
Is Christ divided?
Was Paul crucified for you? Or was it in Paul's name that you were baptized?[21]

Divisus est Christus? "Is Christ divided?" One can feel all the pent-up indignation in the words. Don't you see, cries the Apostle, that in destroying the unity of the Church, you are dismembering Christ?

Divisus est Christus? The expression is so true that it has become classic. The Church, who is qualified to interpret the Scriptures even when she gives no formal definition, has

[137]

found in these words the phrase that stigmatizes schism: the sin of those who withdraw from her unity consists in the fact that by so doing they tear the Saviour asunder.

Divisus est Christus? Of course, other translations are possible; for instance: "Is Christ's Church subject to such divisions?" Or again "Does Christ belong to rival factions?" Or finally, we might say, with many moderns: "Is Christ cut up into pieces, so that each Christian possesses a different part of Christ?" In our opinion, however, these versions do not convey the full force of the text, for the reason that they either speak only of the Church, the Body of Christ, or of Christ without reference to His Body. But the context of the passage is arranged differently. The preceding sentences do not speak of different doctrines or of heresies, but of factions and of division; hence there is clearly question of the Church. On the other hand, it is equally evident that this verse and those that follow have reference to Christ. Consequently, in order to keep the full sense of the phrase, it must be borne in mind that there is question of Christ Himself, and yet that this same Christ is the Church. The subject of the development, therefore, is the Mystical Christ, and the Apostle gives warning that to attack the unity of the Church is to dismember Christ Himself.

That such is in truth the meaning intended by Paul and by the Spirit, is clearly brought out, we think, by other passages of a like structure. Let us consider, for example, another verse of the same Epistle. While the context is not exactly the same, it is quite similar. Here there is question, not indeed of factions, but of different kinds of graces. Alas, such is man's nature that these differences were arousing jealousy, and jealousy always leads to disunion. To this spirit of division and of rivalry, Paul opposes the same doctrine of unity. There is indeed, he says, a great variety of spiritual gifts, but we must understand that variety well. It is produced by one and the same Spirit; it is for the good of the whole, and consequently it is for the cohesion and the unity of the whole:

As the body is one and hath many members, and all the

[138]

members of the Body, many as they are, form one body, so also [it is with] Christ.[22]

Again we find the same tone of authority, and again, there is question in the beginning of a plurality, a multiplicity of members. The author, we feel, is going to liken this organism to the union of all the faithful, to the Church. But no; the sacred text goes further: "so also it is with Christ." The faithful are not merely in Christ, nor are they simply one in Christ; they are Christ Himself, the one Christ, the Mystical Christ.

This is a startling identification, and again it is not a phrase that escapes Paul in a moment of abstraction. He returns to it, and repeats it almost in the same words, in the Epistle to the Colossians.

> Lie not to one another. Strip off the old man with his practices, and put on the new, that is being renewed to fuller knowledge after the image of his Creator. Herein there is not gentile and Jew, circumcision and uncircumcision, barbarian, Scythian, slave, freeman, but Christ is all and in all.[23]

Here we find again the same abrupt, forceful manner of speech. Paul seems to lose patience with these near-sighted ones who can see the Church only as a multitude, with no profound unity. Is such blindness possible? No! Look carefully at these many different Christians. They are no longer a mere crowd: the unity of Christ has penetrated them and united them. They are one; they are the Body of Christ; they are Christ. And Paul rejects those expressions that emphasize the multiple aspect of the Church: he wills to hear no more of different categories of Christians; there is now only Christ, who is all in all.

In these vigorous affirmations, everything is significant, even to the structure of the sentence. This development, which tells of the Church and of the multitude that she embraces, and in which the outward aspect of things is suddenly lost; this unexpected mention of Christ, who, without warning, is substituted for the rest and assumes that multitude into Himself; and the sentence which at first referred only to the faithful, and now, at the end, speaks

[139]

only of Christ — this development, thus followed up and then broken off, reproduces, in the Apostle's own style, the lightning-like apparition that one day had struck him down and had placed him in the presence of the Lord. Paul, who until that moment had seen in the Church merely a sect of men and women, apostates from the synagogue, and who had thought only of hunting down this multitude, suddenly found himself facing a single person: Christ had taken the place of His brethren.

This startling revelation left its mark on Paul's teaching, and even upon his manner of thinking and writing. In certain turns of his sentences, we see Christ suddenly appear, and take up His brethren in Himself, like the fierce eagle that comes to shelter her little ones from danger beneath her wings.

III

Thanks be to God! The gift that He makes to men in Christ is even more ineffable! United with Christ, living in Christ, the faithful are the body and the fullness of Christ; they are Christs. And being united in Christ, they are united in God.

> For in Him [Christ] dwelleth all the fullness of the God-head corporally: and ye are filled therewith in Him who is the Head of every principality and power.[24]

This is the most astounding mystery of all. Christ is God; hence to be one with Him means necessarily to be one with God. Thus St. Paul's teaching on incorporation in Christ includes a doctrine on the divinization of men in Christ. It is this doctrine that fully explains the "mystery" and shows how that mystery, which has eternity for its source, like-wise has eternity as its term; it is this doctrine that accounts for the supreme, the most sublime, and the most essential qualities of Christ's "body"; in fine, it is this doctrine that constitutes the best and the most clearly formulated part of the "Gospel" of St. Paul.

True enough, St. John expresses the same doctrine with even greater forcefulness. But like the Synoptics before him,

Paul also has made it a part of his teaching. One cannot interpret his message fully or show the Mystical Body as he describes it without reference to these sublime perspectives. Therefore we shall consider them with him as our guide. However, to avoid needless repetition of what has been said in the foregoing pages or of what will be said when we treat the fourth Gospel, we shall make our study rather brief.

We have seen that even in His capacity as Head of the Church, Christ is God. Nay, it is precisely in His Headship and in His communication of supernatural life that His divinity appears most strikingly. Paul loves to emphasize the Saviour's divinity in just this way, by extolling His mystical function as Head.

> He is the image of the unseen God, first-born before every creature. For in Him were created all things in heaven and on earth, things seen and things unseen, whether Thrones or Dominations or Principalities or Powers — all creation is through Him and unto Him. And Himself is prior to all, and in Him all things hold together. He again is the Head of the body, the Church: it is He who is the beginning, the first-born from the dead, that so among all He Himself may stand first. For in Him it hath pleased the Father that all the fullness should dwell.[25]

It is clear that according to the Apostle Christ's primacy as Head is the continuation of His primacy as Word, and that these two prerogatives of excellence mutually explain each other, "that so among all He Himself may stand first." Hence it is in God that all Christians are incorporated, and the dignity, the excellence which belongs to them as members of Christ cannot exist without a dignity and an excellence that they receive by reason of the fact that in this Head they are united to God.

We must remember, too, that according to Paul incorporation in Christ is the "mystery," and that this mystery is the act whereby God in His mercy unites all men to Himself and deifies them all in His well-beloved Son: incorporation in Christ and divinization are therefore inseparable. This is indicated clearly enough by the passages which we have quoted in our fourth chapter on the subject of the mystery. To recall the memory of these texts we need repeat only one of the most important, taken from the opening lines of the Epistle to the Ephesians:

> Blessed be the God and Father of our Lord Jesus Christ, who hath blessed us with every spiritual blessing on high in Christ. Yea, in Him He singled us out before the foundation of the world, that we might be holy and blameless in His sight. In love He predestined us to be adopted as His Sons through Jesus Christ, according to the good pleasure of His will, unto the praise of the glory of His grace, wherewith He hath made us gracious in the Well-beloved. In Him we have redemption through His blood, the forgiveness of our transgressions, according to the riches of His grace.
>
> For God hath given us abundance thereof, together with full wisdom and discernment, in that He hath made known to us the secret of His purpose according to His good pleasure. It was the purpose of His good pleasure in Him — a dispensation to be realized in the fullness of time — to bring all things to a head in Christ, both the things in the heavens and the things upon the earth.[26]

Hence by being Christ's we are God's; it is God who unites the world to Himself in Christ. Men have a new manner of existence: they were once darkness, and now they are become light; but it is in the Lord that they are light. They are sons of the day, children of light, and their existence is described as an ever-increasing brightness and glory.

As they are light, so, too, are they life, for Christ is the Light of life; they were once dead, but now, in the Saviour, they are alive.

> Ye have died, and your life is hidden with Christ in God. When Christ, our life, shall appear, then also shall ye appear with Him in glory.[27]

They are alive, and with what a life! Their life is the life of Christ; it is life in Christ, holy and pure; above all, it is an eternal life, the life of God.

> Christ liveth His life to God. Even thus do ye reckon yourselves to be dead to sin, but living to God in Christ Jesus.[28]

They are therefore wholly alive, in glory. They are already enthroned with Christ on the right hand of the Father in the highest heavens, and though they still have many things to pray for, their first duty is to give thanks at all times for all things:

> And in your hearts let the peace of Christ stand supreme, whereunto also ye are called as one body; and be grateful.[29]
> Sing and make melody with your heart to the Lord, giving thanks always for all things in the name of our Lord Jesus Christ to God the Father.[30]

For the Father, in giving His Son to the faithful, has indeed given them all things, and He will continue to give them all things. Between the Only-begotten and them an astounding intercommunication takes place: their miseries are consumed in Him, and His glory ennobles their insignificance. Something undreamed of, something superhuman, something divine is being wrought in their souls: they have entered into the Eternal, and the things of heaven are now their element; they are become worthy objects of the divine good pleasure, they are holy and immaculate before God, and even the commonplaces of their everyday life are made sublime.

> Whatsoever ye do in word or in work, do all in the name of the Lord Jesus, giving thanks to God the Father through Him.[31]

Since Christ is the Son, and they are His members, they, too, are sons, sons of adoption, and are predestined to be made conformable to the image of the only Son. At their baptism they have put on Christ; with Him they all form but one Christ; with Him and in Him they are all children of God, and hence heirs of all that the Father gives to His Only-begotten.

In the presence of the Father their attitude will be that of children, their confidence will be like that of children; their holiness and their interior manner of life will be like that of children. So sublime and so glorious is the dignity which they bear still hidden within them that all nature eagerly awaits the day when it shall be revealed. The reader will recall the magnificent prosopopoeia of the Epistle to the Romans:

> Yea, creation with eager straining awaiteth the manifestation of the children of God. For creation was made subject to vanity — not of its own will, but by reason of him who sub-

[143]

jected it — yet with hope that creation itself shall be freed from its slavery to corruption unto the freedom of the glory of the children of God. For we know that all creation doth groan and travail together to this hour.[32]

Thus the grace of adoption penetrates even to the depths of the universe: it confers a new manner of existence upon the whole world, that vast body wherein all humanity lives.

As a matter of fact, if we examine St. Paul's reasoning closely, Christians are not sons of adoption so much as members of the Son Himself; the grace they have received is not a favor complete in itself, wholly separated from the eternal generation. It is but one aspect of incorporation in this Eternal Son who has become incarnate; it is, if we may use the expression, incorporation into His sonship. There is, and there can be only one Son. But, declares the Apostle, all Christians are so united in this Son that together with Him they are but one, *unus,* one Christ, and one son.

For ye are all through your faith sons of God in Christ Jesus. For all of you who were baptized into Christ, have put on Christ. In Him is neither Jew nor Greek, neither slave nor free, neither male nor female; for ye are all one person in Christ Jesus. And if ye are Christ's, then are ye the seed of Abraham, and heirs by promise. . . .

When the fullness of time came, God sent forth His Son, born of a woman, born under the law, to ransom them that were under the law, that we might enter upon our adoption as sons. And because ye are sons, God hath sent forth the Spirit of His Son into our hearts, crying, "Abba, Father!" Wherefore thou art no longer a slave, but a son; and if a son, an heir also by the act of God.[33]

There is only one Son, but in this one Son is included the multitude of poor sinful men; and in Him they, too, are sons, sons by participation in His sonship. This participation is their adoption.

As proof of this, Paul cites the fact that they all have the Spirit within them. Their adoption in Christ is as much a reality for them as is their possession of the Spirit in the same Christ. God has saved them

by the laver of regeneration, and renovation of the Holy

Ghost, whom He hath poured forth upon us abundantly, through Jesus Christ our Saviour.[34]

They are all filled with this Spirit; He is given to them, He abides in them, they are His temple, and the love of God is poured forth in them by this Spirit who is given to them. The Kingdom, this divine gift brought by Christ, is for them justice, peace, and joy in the Holy Spirit.

The Holy Spirit is their interior principle of life, strength, charity, holiness, joy; He it is who guides them, who renews them, who gives them assurance of their resurrection and of the glory that awaits them; He it is who infuses into their minds the discernment and the wisdom that befit Christians; He it is who has united them to Christ in baptism, who seals their souls with the sign of salvation, who daily draws from their hearts prayers that ascend straight to God; He it is who makes them address the Most High Himself as "Father."

Hence they must reverence both their interior Guest and their very selves, for they are sanctified by His presence. They must take care not to give Him pain or to drive Him from their souls. If they were to lose Him, they would no longer be Christ's and therefore they would no longer even be themselves.

Just as the Spirit forms Christ in each individual, so, too, He forms Christ in the whole Body which is the Church: these are but two different aspects of one and the same divine operation. As Paul explains at some length to the Corinthians, it is the Spirit who gives to each his proper grace and who, in the name of the whole Trinity, adapts it to the entire organism which is the Church:

> Now there are varieties of gifts, but the same Spirit. And there are varieties of ministrations, and the same Lord. And there are varieties of workings, but the same God, who worketh all things in all. But to each is given the manifestation of the Spirit for the general profit.
>
> To one through the Spirit is granted utterance of wisdom; to another utterance of knowledge, according to the same Spirit; to another faith, in the same Spirit; and to another, gifts of healings, still in the one Spirit; and to another, work-

ings of miracles, to another, prophecy, to another, discernings of spirits, to another, [divers] kinds of tongues, and to another, the interpretation of tongues. But all these are the work of one and the same Spirit, who apportioneth severally to each as He will.

For as the body is one and hath many members, and all the members of the body, many as they are, form one body, so also is it with Christ.

For in one Spirit all we, whether Jews or Greeks, whether slaves or free, were baptized into one body; and all were given to drink of one Spirit.[35]

Thus, in the Mystical Body, the Third Person of the Holy Trinity is the principle of adaptation and of concord: He directs the Church's ministry and preaching and unites the "body" to God even as He unites it to itself.

> Be careful to keep the unity of the Spirit in the bond of peace. [There is but] one body and one Spirit.[36]

The Christian community, therefore, is one in the Spirit as it is one in Christ; it is a participation (κοινωνία) of the Spirit, as it is a participation (κοινωνία) of the Son of God. For the Spirit is the Spirit of the Son, the Spirit of Christ; wherefore He must also be the Spirit of the sons of adoption, the Spirit of adoption, the Spirit of the Mystical Body.

Here, however, we must note a point that is of importance for the theology of the Mystical Body. While the Apostle repeats insistently that the Spirit does everything in the Mystical Body and in its members, and while he even seems to say that the Spirit *is* everything in the body, yet he never says that the body or the members are in any way a prolongation of the Spirit or that they are, in a mystical sense, the Spirit. According to his constant teaching, regenerated humanity has this relation only with Christ and, in Christ, with the Son.

Herein lies the chief distinction which St. Paul draws between the union of the Spirit with us and the union of Christ with us. Never does he say, as others have said or at least seem to say, that the Spirit is now united with holy souls and with the Church in somewhat the same manner as the Word is united with the human nature of Christ, and that the present era or the era to come is the era of the Spirit, as the Old Testament was the era of the Father and the New Testament the era of the Son.

For St. Paul, there is only Christ; but, as we have seen, this Christ is one with the Church and with the faithful. Since they are mystically Christ, the faithful possess all that He possesses; in Him and in Him alone they are what He is, as it is in Him and in Him alone that they are what they are.

There is only Christ. But in Him is all fullness: all the fullness of the divinity substantially, and all the fullness of humanity mystically. Hence, in Him and in Him alone, the whole of humanity has access to the whole of the divinity, and the supernatural society of men is united with the divine society of the three Persons who are but one God.

> Ye were at that time Christless, alienated from the commonwealth of Israel and strangers to the covenants of the promise, without hope and without God in the world.
> But now in Christ Jesus ye that were once far off are brought near through the blood of Christ. . . . He came and brought glad tidings of peace to you that were afar off and of peace to them that were near: because through Him we both have access in one Spirit to the Father.
> Therefore ye are no longer strangers and foreigners, but ye are fellow-citizens of the saints and members of the household of God.[37]

In the mind of the Apostle, this relation of the members of Christ with the whole Trinity is so close that most of the texts which seem to allude to the three divine Persons also speak of the Mystical Body and of the members of that body. Several of these texts have already been quoted, but we shall here add a few more. The names of the divine Persons are italicized to indicate the references to the Trinity:

> [There is but] one body and one *Spirit,* as also ye were called in one hope, that of your calling: one *Lord,* one faith, one baptism: one *God and Father* of all.[38]
> For as many as are led by the *Spirit of God,* these are the sons of *God.* For ye have not received the spirit of slavery, to be once more in fear, but ye have received the spirit of adoption, whereby we cry, *"Abba, Father!"* The *Spirit* Himself

[147]

beareth witness with our spirit that we are the children of *God*.

And if children, heirs also: heirs of *God*, and joint heirs with *Christ* — if, that is, we suffer with Him, that with Him we may also be glorified.[39]

I bend my knees to the *Father* . . . that He grant you to be strengthened powerfully through His *Spirit* . . . that *Christ* may dwell in your hearts through faith.[40]

He that is warrant for us and for you unto *Christ*, who also hath anointed us, is *God;* He, too, hath sealed us and given us the earnest of *His Spirit* in our hearts.[41]

In *Christ* you also are built together into a habitation of *God* in the *Spirit*.[42]

The *Spirit of God* dwelleth in you. But if any man hath not the *Spirit of Christ*, that man is not of *Christ*. And if *Christ* be in you . . . your spirit is life by reason of justness. And if the *Spirit of Him who raised Jesus from the dead* dwelleth in you, then *He who raised Christ Jesus from the dead* will also bring to life your mortal bodies through His *Spirit* who dwelleth within you.[43]

Your bodies are members of *Christ*. . . . He that cleaveth to the *Lord* is one spirit with Him. . . . Know you not that your body is the temple of the *Holy Spirit* who is within you, whom you have from *God?*[44]

The grace of *our Lord Jesus Christ* and the charity of *God* and the fellowship of the *Holy Spirit* be with you all.[45]

Not all of these passages are equally significant. But they are so numerous that they leave no room for doubt. According to the doctrine of the Apostle, the sanctification of Christians in Christ is a real deification, a deification through union with the inner life of God, through union with the Trinity itself.

Nevertheless, despite its intrinsic importance, this deification is not the most prominent element of Paul's doctrine. What he teaches with the greatest forcefulness is the means through which God gives us this divinization. This is the union of grace, whereby all Christians are made one Christ.

IV

In the foregoing pages we have touched upon the principal statements of St. Paul concerning our incorporation with

Christ. We have seen that they take on a great variety of forms. First, frequent mention is made of the presence and life of the Mystical Christ within us, and of our own in Him. Then, there is the statement, likewise of frequent occurrence, that in Christ we all form a single living body, which is the body of Christ. Again, the life of Christ is declared to be inseparable from our own, and therefore we must express His sentiments and His virtues in our conduct. According to St. Paul, we are completely changed, entirely new, wholly deified; together we constitute a new creature: one man, a new man, a perfect man, one Christ, and, in the sense which we have just explained, one son.

Of these statements, the most vigorous is not the declaration that we are the body of Christ; for all its energy, it does not designate so intimate a union as do the brief sentences in which Paul declares that, in Christ, we are *unus*, one mystical person, one Mystical Christ.

These affirmations of oneness with Christ figure in the most varied contexts. At times Paul uses them to inculcate charity, or chastity, or peace; now he employs them to help us understand what the Church and Christianity are; again he has recourse to them in order to explain to the faithful the nature of their life as regenerated men and as children of God; upon it he bases his arguments against those who claim to find grounds for hope in themselves or in the Law; in fine, he uses them to give a brief summary of God's plan regarding the world, and of the entire economy of salvation.

But, despite their variety and their adaptation to different contexts, they always express the same reality. Paul varies the phrasing and the development only that he may better exhaust the full meaning of this central truth; and, in their very variety, the expressions that he employs possess features in common. It will not be disrespectful for us to call attention to these features, to assemble them, and with them to try to formulate the fundamental expression of the "mystery" that is the theme of all these many forms, and which God so insistently repeats to us in the sacred text.

This general expression, we think, would be as follows: Οἱ πάντες (or, οἱ πολλοί), ἐν τῷ Χριστῷ, εἰς or ἓν σῶμα, or εἰς ἄνθρωπος, or εἶς Χριστός: all of us, in Christ, are one body, one man, one Mystical Christ.

Paul carries this announcement to the whole world. It has been engraved upon his heart by Christ Himself. He can always hear Christ repeating: "I am Jesus whom thou dost persecute: I am Christ in the Church."

From that day forward he has a message to deliver, and in his preaching we can hear the voice that ever echoes in his soul. He preaches only what he has learned. He goes about, repeating the central mystery of Christianity: Christ in us. He preaches it on every occasion and in every circumstance, in season and out of season, in sentences as energetic as his soul, as tempestuous as his life, and as overburdened with meaning as his Gospel overflows with love. And occasionally, in these hurried and ardent sentences, like lightning flashes, appear brief mentions of Christ, of the Mystical Christ — reminders of the sudden apparition that made Paul an Apostle.

And today, when we read his Epistles, we come into contact with the impulse he received. The conviction and the motive that urge him on and which he communicates to others, do not proceed from him. He is but the intermediary. In his hasty sentences that bring us suddenly face to face with Christ; in his emphatic declarations that Christ is in us, that He suffers in us, lives in us; that He is one with us and we are one in Him; in the Apostle's voice, stirred and still vibrant with the mystery that he preaches, it is not Paul we hear. As he tells the Corinthians, we have proof of Christ who speaks in him.

Chapter VIII

St. John — 1. Sources of John's Teaching.
The Apocalypse

><

I. Introduction. The Gospel of St. John. It completes the teaching of the Synoptics, especially on the subject of the Mystical Body.

II. *The Apocalypse.* It indicates one of the sources whence John drew his doctrine of the Mystical Body. We study the Apocalypse only from this viewpoint. It heralds a "return"; in each of its four parts, but particularly in the last, it describes this return: Christ unites Himself with His own. John's vision may be compared with that of Paul on the road to Damascus; its influence on John's Gospel.

III. *Interior contemplation.* That this may have been a further source of John's teaching is indicated by the Apostle's meditative temperament and his interest in the things of the spirit. Signs of the psychological process whereby God brings him to realize that the Christ who lived in Judea is the same Christ that lives in us.

IV. *The special purpose of John's Gospel,* as stated at the end of the Gospel, at the beginning and end of the first Epistle, and in the prologue of the Gospel, is to show that Christ is God and that we are vivified in Him, and that therefore the very fact of the Incarnation affects all men. Conclusion.

I

THE APOSTOLIC age is drawing to its close. It has been years now, thirty or forty perhaps, since the last Epistles and the Synoptic Gospels were written. Peter, Paul, and the others who saw the Lord, have gone to contemplate Him in heaven. John alone, as if he were destined not to die, is still living at Patmos, and later, it would seem, at Ephesus; but

[151]

he is a very old man, and he, too, is about to pass from the scene.

It was at this period that the writings of the beloved disciple were addressed to the Christians: his Apocalypse, his Gospel, his Epistles; one last message of the Spirit who inspires, and the final touch given to revelation. The great Christian dogmas of the Trinity, of the Incarnation, of justification, attain their final Scriptural expression, while the function of the Church, the nature of the "coming" of Christ, and the essence of the Christ-life are more clearly defined.

At the same time, new light is shed upon the doctrine of our union with Christ. This light comes even in the greater clearness given to the other points of faith, for John makes this truth the focal point of Christian doctrine.

In the Old Testament, we recall, God had foretold the union which He planned to form with men. How Christ accomplished this union is shown in the Synoptic Gospels, and Paul tells us in what it consists. There now remains only the task of synthesizing the two aspects, of explaining that the unity of which the Apostle speaks, the Mystical Christ who incorporates all the faithful in Himself, is none other than that Jesus of Nazareth whose deeds and words are recorded by the Synoptics. This synthesis is furnished us by the beloved disciple; such, in the logical order, is the position of his teaching on the subject of the Mystical Body.

Hence, as we cannot too often repeat, this teaching is not something new; it is merely a continuation. The other Evangelists had already reported Jesus' assurance that He Himself, who will come to judge the living and the dead, is the same who lives in the lowliest Christian and receives as done to Himself whatever is done to them. John, however, has been commissioned to give this assurance with greater emphasis. His writings, the last in date of the inspired books, were to continue what the others had begun, give the finishing touches to the whole, and set the final seal upon the system.

Destined as he was to be the instrument of God in so great a doctrinal development, the Apostle John had need of special preparation. Two phases of this preparation we know:

one is related by John himself, and the other we can infer from his writings.

II

The first was the vision of Patmos, recorded in the Apocalypse. In great part, of course, the Apocalypse is a sealed book. It is an extremely delicate task to distinguish what is positive affirmation from that which should be attributed simply to the nature and style of the work. It is more difficult still, in the visions that are described, to pick out the truths that God wished to transmit to the Church.

Fortunately, we have only one point to consider; namely, what the Apostle has to say of our union with Christ. No long search is necessary in order to find this teaching; it is everywhere. Had not Jesus Himself, in the prophecies that He uttered concerning the end of the world, and which have been styled the "Apocalypse of the Synoptics," already affirmed His mystical presence within the Christians?

> The King answering shall say to them, "Amen I say to you, inasmuch as ye did it to one of the least of these My brethren, ye did it to Me."[1]

The Apocalypse, which the Holy Spirit inspired John to write, repeats exactly the same message. After a few introductory verses containing the heading and the initial doxology, the announcement follows:

> Behold, He cometh with the clouds, and every eye shall see Him, even they who pierced Him, and all the tribes of the earth shall wail because of Him. Yea, Amen!
> "I am the Alpha and the Omega," saith the Lord God, "who is and who was and who is to come, the Almighty One."[2]

And the book closes with the same affirmation. Jesus tells John not to seal his book, because the time is near at hand, and He will come to accomplish all things. For He is the first and the last, the beginning and the end: it is He who encompasses all things. This promise should inspire a great hope:

> And the Spirit and the Spouse say, "Come!" And let him

[153]

that heareth say, "Come!" And let him that thirsteth come!
Let him that willeth take the water of life freely!

The statement is clear, and is immediately repeated:

He who testifieth these things, saith, "Yea, I come quickly!"
Amen. Come, Lord Jesus!
The grace of the Lord Jesus be with the saints.[3]

Thus, in the concluding lines as well as in the opening
verses, the Apocalypse directs the minds of its readers toward
a return of Jesus. To be more precise, this return is announced
to the faithful who are suffering persecution, to those who
are "copartners in Jesus, in the tribulation, and in the kingdom, and in the patience."[4] To these is Jesus coming, to
assure them that He is present, and that He comes in all
their afflictions.

As we might expect from such a setting, the whole book
speaks of Jesus' return, of a hidden coming, which occurs
particularly when the Christians are suffering, and which will
be made manifest in heaven, at the moment when their
sufferings will have produced their effect.

In fact, the message is to be found scattered throughout
the book, not so evident when there is question of struggle
and of trials, but clear when the recompense is mentioned.
Of the former references we shall say nothing, except that
they represent the sufferings that they describe, and the
triumph of which they allow us a glimpse, as bringing us
nearer to Christ.

We may dwell a bit on the latter references, for they
possess some interesting features. The victory which they
promise and paint for us, is a communion with God and
with Christ. It is the new Jerusalem, the holy city, in which
mankind shall henceforth be one in God:

And I beheld a new heaven and a new earth; for the first
heaven and the first earth were departed. . . .
And I saw the holy city, the new Jerusalem, coming down
out of heaven from God, prepared as a bride adorned for her
husband.
And I heard a loud voice from the throne, saying, "Behold
the dwelling of God with men, and He shall dwell with them:
. . . and God Himself shall be with them.
"And He shall wipe away every tear from their eyes, and

death shall be no more, neither shall mourning or wailing or pain be any more, because the first things are passed away." And He who sitteth upon the throne said, "behold, I make all things new."[5]

It is, as Paul had already said, a new creation. In this transfigured world, God dwells with men, and Christ's greatness passes into His own. He is their temple:

I saw no sanctuary therein, for the Lord God almighty is the sanctuary thereof, and the Lamb.[6]

And the Lamb is their light:

The city hath no need of the sun or of the moon to shine upon it, for the glory of God enlighteneth it, and the lamp thereof is the Lamb.[7]

And the Lamb provides the living water that they drink, and the fruit of life that they eat:

And he showed me a river of the water of life, clear as crystal, issuing forth from the throne of God and of the Lamb. . . .
On either side of the river was the tree of life, which beareth fruit twelve times, yielding every month its own fruit.[8]

With these visions, the Apocalypse closes. Thus will the heavens reveal in glory that union with Christ which began upon earth in pain. And the entire Apocalypse may once more be summed up, we think, in the phrase with which the book opens and ends: "He cometh." In the trials of this life, that which takes place is a coming: the coming of Christ in His brethren.

So, in order that the faithful may understand the true meaning of history, which seems so profane and at times so scandalous, Jesus reveals the meaning of events, of all events, to John first, and, through John, He reveals it to them. The great prophecy embraces all ages, those of the beginning and those to come; and though it may be difficult and at times even absurd to try to read there a prediction of the political revolutions that appear so formidable in our eyes, but in eternity's balance are so trivial, we nevertheless have the right to seek the eternal meaning, the only true meaning, of the

[155]

entire course of history. Through all, and, says the prophecy, more especially in times of persecution than at other times, "He cometh." The sorrows of the first century, like those of today and those of tomorrow, but prepare and veil a return. Lest their patience fail, Jesus Himself, through John, gives to the Churches an assurance of this coming: "Behold, in all that cometh, it is I who come."

It was in similar terms that Christ had already spoken to Paul, showing him that He who is persecuted and who comes to the aid of His faithful in the Church, is Himself. This word of the Saviour was the starting point and the source, so to speak, of the Apostle's entire teaching.

The very same idea is found at the source of the teaching of St. John. Christ, the faithful witness, ever gives the same testimony: at the close of the Apostolic age, no less than at the beginning, He assures the persecuted Church that He is with her all days.

In this way, the Apocalypse is the introduction to the Fourth Gospel. Of course, we also find many differences between these two books. As the one is tumultuous and colorful, so the other is calm, and as it were, all interior. The author of the first is the son of thunder; the other is written by the disciple whom Jesus loved.

But both are from the same John. The Apocalypse supplies the prelude for the teaching which the Gospel is to give concerning the Word and the Incarnation. At times it even anticipates the tone of the Gospel. From this point of view, its beginning and conclusion are characteristic. Let us read, for example, a few lines of one of the messages to the Churches:

> Whomso I love, I rebuke and chastise; be earnest therefore, and repent.
> Behold, I stand at the door and knock. If any man hear My voice and open the door, I will come in to him, and I will sup with him, and he with Me.
> As for him that conquereth, I will give him to sit with Me upon My throne, as I Myself conquered, and sat down with My Father upon His throne.
> He that hath an ear, let him hear what the Spirit saith to the churches![9]

[156]

These, however, are merely comparisons of detail. There is another point of far greater importance, where the resemblance between the two works is more clearly marked. This is the manner in which John regards Christ. In the next few chapters, we shall see that for the Evangelist, the Saviour is exactly the same Saviour who is described in the Apocalypse: a Christ who comes to live in men.

In this sense, the Apocalypse is a source for the Fourth Gospel. This does not necessarily imply that the visions it recounts, or other visions, furnished John with hitherto unpublished information concerning Jesus' life or doctrine; but it did help him to understand what the Saviour had said in the course of His mortal life, and it made him see more clearly how even then Christ was already the life of the Church. John relates nothing that the Twelve had not seen and heard as well as he. But with the special instruction he had received from God, and with the visions of Patmos and the grace of inspiration to aid his memory, John possessed a better understanding of what all had witnessed.

III

It seems that this external vision did not remain alone, but was accompanied, preceded, or followed by an interior illumination. It would be well to say a word here of this second means which God appears to have used to prepare the sacred author for his task. Thus had Providence dealt with Paul, a little more than half a century before: at the time of his objective vision on the road to Damascus, or a little later, Paul was favored with a further grace that enabled him to see Christ interiorly. So, too, in the case of John: God, who had granted him the lightning-like visions of Patmos and had also given him to behold the sweet and humble appearance of the Master in Judea, now gave him the interior grace to understand how these two manifestations explained each other, and how the Christ he had contemplated in former days was the same who ever lives in the Church and suffers in the Church.

Did this grace consist in an extraordinary illumination, in

[157]

interior visions or words, or in the certainty of grace and of faith? We do not know; God has deigned to leave us only indications of the paths by which He led John. Fortunately, however, these indications are quite numerous.

Let us note, first of all, that the Apostle had abundant time. He wrote sixty or seventy years after the events had taken place — a long time to live with one's memories. Besides, his was a nature both ardent and contemplative: his soul was sensitive to emotion and given to profound reflection. His manner of thinking, as mirrored in his writings, is to come and go, and return over the same idea, to take it up again in successive waves, as it were, in order better to penetrate its meaning and to develop it further. In the Apocalypse, for instance, there is one theme, among others, that he repeats incessantly: Christ is coming. In the Gospel and in the Epistles, there are certain thoughts — those of light, life, charity, faith — that are mentioned time and time again, and frequently one within the other. His very sentences advance by beginning anew. Yet, despite this continual repetition, there is no disorder; all is calm and clear, and the lines fit into one another to form one whole.

As a final indication, this contemplative is concerned with a very special object. His object is Christ, but a Christ who declares that He abides in the souls of men, and that these souls abide in Him. He even promises — and this significant detail is carefully recorded — that there will come a day when the disciples shall know that He is in the Father, and they in Him, and He in them; when they shall see Him, for He shall manifest Himself to them.

Did John see the dawn of this promised day, even here below? It is a mere supposition, of course; but for our subject, the faintest glimmering of light has its value.

Time has accomplished its work of sifting and of simplification; in this soul, occupied by a single thought and a single love, memories have assembled and become organized. Together, in a harmonious grouping of all details, they present, in general, a single picture. And the Christ who dwells in the souls of men could not permit this work to go on unaided. The psychological process is guided by the grace of inspiration and divine assistance, and perhaps, too, in a degree that we cannot measure, by the light of revelation; so that when finished, it is the work of God in the mind of John, and much more truly God's work than John's reflections. In this way, the Saviour once more manifests Himself to the disciple whom He loved; this time, not before his eyes alone, but within his soul; not to teach him anything new, but to help him to understand more clearly what he had heard and seen at the beginning.

The first manifestation took place one evening on the banks of the Jordan. John never forgot the details: Jesus had passed by, the Baptist had pointed Him out as the salvation of the world, and two disciples, John and Andrew, followed the Master without a word. The latter turned and said to them: "Come."

They went therefore and saw where He abode,
And they abode with Him that day;
It was about the tenth hour.[10]

The second occurred during the long vigil that followed Pentecost. We know not the day, nor the hour, nor the place; perhaps it lasted for a long time. Was it an extraordinary vision or certainty of faith? Did it consist in a sudden unveiling or in a gradual penetration? We know not. Did it occur before the vision of Patmos, or at the same time, or later? Here, too, John is silent; but he wrote his Gospel.

IV

The Gospel itself tells us what thoughts filled its author's mind. John is not unaware of this preoccupation; when he writes, he has a thesis, and he formulates that thesis as often as he can. Since it is thus stated in the inspired account, this thesis is as truly inspired as the rest. God willed that it be communicated to us, lest, in reading the sacred text, we should fail to comprehend all that He wished to teach us by its means.

Now John's thesis, the purpose of his Gospel, is to teach us who the Master is in Himself, and what He is for us:

[159]

it is written that we may believe that Jesus is the Son of God, that we are in Him, and that, in Him, we have life. In a sense, the thesis is twofold, but its two aspects are intimately related. It is because He is God that Christ is able to give us life, and it is by belief in His divinity that we receive His life within us. In the supernatural order, we cannot be separated from Him. This is the same message that was announced in the Apocalypse.

The author states this purpose in the conclusion of his Gospel:

> Many other signs also did Jesus in the sight of the disciples, that are not written in this book.
> But these are written, that ye may believe that Jesus is the Christ, the Son of God,
> And that believing, ye may have life in His name.[11]

He has a twofold purpose, then: to show that Jesus is the son of God, and to inspire the Christians with faith; and the two aims are really one, for to possess eternal life through Jesus, and in His name, it is enough to believe that He is the Son.

John's first Epistle, which is closely related to the Gospel, repeats the same statement with insistence in its concluding lines. The passage deals with the testimony that God renders to the Son.

> And this is the witness, that God hath given us everlasting life; and this life is in his Son. He that hath the Son, hath the life; he that hath not the Son of God, hath not the life.

And John emphasizes his declaration:

> These things I have written to you, even to you that believe in the name of the Son of God, in order that ye may know that ye have everlasting life. . . .
> And we know that the Son of God is come, and hath given us understanding to know Him that is true, and we are in Him that is true, even in His Son Jesus Christ.
> He is the true God and everlasting life.
> Little children, keep yourselves from idols.[12]

Still we see the same double purpose: to show that Christ is God and eternal life, and that in this Christ, or in the name of this Christ, which means the same thing, we have eternal life and are united with God. Here, even more than in the first passage, it is clear that the two purposes are one; for it is in explaining how Christ is life, that we are made to see how He is our life.

The opening verses of the Epistle express precisely the same thought, except that now John is speaking more explicitly of the union (κοινωνία), that joins us in Christ, and, through Christ, with God. The reader is familiar with this magnificent passage, which is so like the prologue of the Gospel:

> That which was from the beginning, that which we have heard, that which we have seen with our eyes, that which we beheld, and our hands handled, in regard of the Word of Life —and the Life was manifested, and we have seen and bear witness and declare to you that everlasting Life which was in the Father and was manifested to us — that which we have seen and heard we declare to you also, in order that ye may have fellowship with us. And our fellowship is with the Father and with His Son Jesus Christ. And these things we write in order that our joy may be full.[13]

So John intends to write what he has seen with his own eyes: the manifestation of eternal life that has trod this earth. But, while this is his principal object, it is not his only one. John is thinking also of the faithful, and his purpose is to lead them all, by means of his narrative, to a communion that will unite them both with one another and with the Father and the Son.

The prologue of the Epistle brings us to the prologue of the Gospel. The latter contains the same twofold declaration, with new indications, and with a more intimate unity and blending, so to speak, of the various concepts. Hence we must study the passage more carefully.

Let us first consider the explicit indications. In beginning his work, the Evangelist states his purpose. He will speak of the Word made flesh; that is, of the Word inasmuch as He is one with His human nature. But he will also speak of men, for the terms that John uses to designate the Saviour are those which best describe His expansion over our entire race. He is called Life, Light, Son; this Life, John tells us, is the light of mankind; this Light illumines all souls, and this Sonship gives us the power to become children of God. Particularly significant from this point of view are the closing words of the prologue: The word is full of grace and truth, and this fullness, this grace, and this truth are destined to flow into us.

> [He is] full of grace and truth.
> For of His fullness we have all received, and grace on grace; for the Law was given through Moses, grace and truth came through Jesus Christ.[14]

Again and always, John has only one chief purpose, but this purpose extends to a second: to speak of the God Christ, and, in speaking of Him, to speak of us who, in Him, are animated with a divine life.

The very structure of the prologue gives the same teaching. The Incarnation figures here as an individual, but by no means an isolated event. Like the Word and the Sacred Humanity, the Incarnation concerns all men. In fact, John establishes this universal perspective at the very outset. We behold, not a finite being in presence of the Infinite, but the whole of creation, all that was made (ἐγένετο), in presence of the Creator who possesses the perfection of all being: (ἦν). In the beginning, this most perfect Being alone existed. Thus, in the solemn words with which the Gospel opens:

> In the beginning was (ἦν) the Word, and the Word was (ἦν) with God, and the Word was (ἦν) God. He was (ἦν) in the beginning with God.

Then, in strong contrast, we behold the created world:

> All things were made (ἐγένετο) through Him, and without Him was made (ἐγένετο) nothing that hath been made (γέγονεν).[15]

Now Providence turns toward this changing Being that It has produced; the Word, who was (ἦν), draws near to what has been made (ἐγένετο), and makes it ready:

> In Him was (ἦν) life, and the life was (ἦν) the light of men;

[162]

and the light shineth in the darkness, and the darkness hath not overcome it.

There was a man sent from God, whose name was John; he came for witness, to witness concerning the light, that all might believe through him. He was not (οὐκ ἦν) the light, but was to witness concerning the light.

But this is only a preparation. The Light itself, the Light which "is," has yet to come.

It was (ἦν) the true light, which enlighteneth every man that cometh into the world. He was (ἦν) in the world and the world was made (ἐγένετο) through Him, and the world knew Him not. He came to what was His and His own received Him not. But to as many as received Him He gave power to become (γενέσθαι) children of God, to them that believed in His name, that were begotten not of blood, nor of the will of the flesh, nor of the will of man, but of God.[16]

The reconciliation is complete: in the Word, finite beings have power to become children of God; that which "is" has shared itself with what "was made." And in how marvelous a manner we shall see:

And the Word was made flesh (σὰρξ ἐγένετο).

The two realities are united, which of themselves were separated by an infinite distance: the Word, "who was," has come down among "what was made."

And dwelt amongst us (καὶ ἐσκήνωσεν ἐν ἡμῖν).[17]

"And dwelt amongst us"; not that the Evangelist is referring to the indwelling of the Word in our souls. He simply wishes to show how Jesus Christ appeared in visible form, and how he, John, is His eyewitness. But the affirmation has been given its direction, in a manner of speaking: the entire context goes to emphasize that the one Incarnation is a union of God with all creation, a communion (κοινωνία) without bounds.

In fact, once the statement is placed at the center of this limitless perspective, it is linked by John with all that surrounds it. The doctrine expressed in the prologue is continued in the preaching of John the Baptist, and, at the moment when Jesus enters upon the scene, it is continued in the concrete events of the general history of mankind.

Such is the testimony of the beloved disciple, considered in the light of all the passages in which he explains its purpose.

The Synoptics had already depicted Jesus, chiefly as He appeared from without. But the Holy Spirit did not consider this sufficient for us. So He raised up John; He prepared, enlightened, assisted him to make us see Christ as He is in Himself, and also as He makes us live in Him: Christ in Himself and Christ in the faithful; Christ living a life of mysterious intensity, and at the same time a life wondrously real. And John wrote his Gospel, that we might know that Jesus is the Son of God, and that in Him we have life.

Chapter IX

St. John—2. Jesus, Our Life

⨯

I. *Christ according to St. John.* He is a living, real Christ, and at the same time He is the life of His faithful. How Christ is presented in all the Gospels.
II. *Christ is Life.* The life we receive in baptism. The incident of Nicodemus. We must be born anew. This life is nourished by the Eucharist. The discourse at Capharnaum. The Incarnation and the Eucharist; Jesus, who is Life itself, imparts that life to His own.
III. *Christ is Life and Light.* Faith and life in Christ. God is Light; so, too, is Christ. The Light foretold; then it manifests itself: "I am the Light of Life." The light is within us, enabling us to see. The incident of the man born blind. The Light also gives life. The parable of the Good Shepherd.
IV. *Christ united with His own.* The discourse after the Last Supper: union with Christ, a union that makes us divine. He abides in us and we in Him. The meaning of the expression; it refers especially to the humanity of Christ. Comparison with St. Paul. A mutual indwelling, in the same living organism. The Vine, glimpsed by the prophets, is realized perfectly in Christ.

I

CERTAIN modern critics find that the Christ of St. John is not a living Christ. The reason is that they view Him through a metaphysical theorem. In reality, when the Evangelist wrote, his soul was still aflame with the Truth which he had contemplated and his body still thrilled from its contact with the Word of Life.

His Man-God is supremely alive. We see Him weary; we sense His indignation; we can even feel the tears welling to His eyes. His actions are clear cut and significant, His attitude firm and uncompromising; when He speaks, His words are brief and to the point; and He has a way all His own of directing a conversation: "Go, call thy husband,"[1] He says to the Samaritan woman; and to Nicodemus: "Art thou the teacher of Israel, and understandest not these things?"[2]; and to the multitude: "Why seek ye to put Me to death?"[3] We feel the very throbbing of His heart in words of infinite tenderness: "Little children, a little while only I am with you. . . . No longer do I call you servants . . . but friends, for all things that I have heard from My Father, I have made known to you."[4] The Synoptics record a greater number of concrete incidents, but they have not left us as many words that are so sublime and so living. Throughout the Fourth Gospel we are put in contact with the very interior of Jesus, with His life, with His "Ego."

However, this "Ego" is not one of those narrow, ever hateful personalities of which Pascal speaks. Rendered imposing by the very qualities that make it invading, it takes its rightful place within every man. This is the marvel, and for some, the mystery and the scandal of the "Johannine" Gospel. This Jesus, whose history it traces, whose actions and psychology it portrays with perfect clearness, is at the same time and without contradiction, a mystical reality. That is, while He is supremely alive in Himself, He is also living within us. It is precisely in those passages where he speaks most of Jesus, of His life and of His excellence, that John has most to say of His union with men and of the dignity that comes to men by reason of His presence within them.

The facts of Jesus' life that are best circumstantiated, the most concrete, the most historical, blend either into His own teaching on the life of the faithful in Himself or into explanations which the Apostle furnishes on the same subject. Between the event and the doctrine, as between the doctrine and John's authentic commentary of that doctrine, there is no clearly indicated break. The reason is easy to find: John's purpose is precisely to show that in reality there is no such complete break; that the events, the acts of Christ, are continued in our faith and there attain their *pleroma;* that the doctrines proposed by the Master have their inseparable prolongation and their consummation in the preaching of the Church; in fine, that the Head and the body are not two, but one.

Evidently, only the Word of Life could have a history so rich in instruction for us, since only the term of the Supreme Intelligence could possess such a fullness of light for our intelligence. Evidently, too, only the Holy Spirit could be the principal author of such a history, which, without ceasing to be concrete and rigorously historical, is at the same time a perpetual doctrine, a doctrine of the eternal life led by Christ, and by which the faithful live in Christ.

Thus, throughout the Gospel, *facta Verbi verba sunt :*[5] Christ teaches by His very actions. The incident of the man born blind, for instance, is accompanied by an instruction on the Light that enlightens men's souls. Moreover, the narrative and the doctrine blend together into one, not by a pedagogical trick of the writer, but by reason of the significance of the event itself. Similarly, too, in the case of the raising of Lazarus from the dead; in the inspired book, and hence also in reality, the incident is bound up with a doctrine on the resurrection. The same can be seen everywhere in the Gospel; we might add that even where the sacred writer does not combine the two so explicitly, the lesson that concerns us and the words that tell us of our life are one with the history of the Word of Life, by whom and in whom we live.

Nor is this manner of teaching Christ peculiar to John alone; the other Evangelists also make use of it, and in the very picture which they draw of the life of Christ they bring in the Mystical Body of this Christ as a background, as an explanation suggested by the rest of the picture.

Our second chapter was an effort to make this clear. St. Mark's narration is such that the life of Christ seems incomplete and unintelligible unless we recognize in it the starting point and introduction here below of a life which is universal and mystical. St. Matthew, in recording the preaching of Christ and the promise of the Kingdom, teaches that the Church is simply Christ, continuing in the faithful His own presence, His activity, His teaching and all His functions. Lastly, St. Luke presents his Gospel as the preface and the first part of what is to be, in the Acts of the Apostles, the history of the infant Church, as if to say that the complete work, in its two parts, is the portrait of the one Christ, the whole Christ, but considered in two different stages: first Christ in His mortal life, then in His mystical life, the two making up but one complete Christ.

Each of the three Evangelists gives testimony to the Mystical Christ by that which is most personal to and most characteristic of himself: St. Mark by his direct and vivid style, St. Matthew by his doctrine of the Kingdom, his sermons, his ecclesiology, and St. Luke by his twofold narrative. And so it is with St. John. Of all the Evangelists, he is the most inclined to spirituality, to the interior life, to meditation, and to theology, and his teaching on the subject of the Mystical Christ reflects this special turn of mind. While he repeats and develops the same lessons that are contained in the other Gospels, he does so in a more interior, more meditative, more theological way. But he does not divorce this teaching from the life of Jesus. The authentic Christ, the only authentic Christ, the Christ whom God has willed to present to the faithful in all the Gospels, is a Christ living in the hearts of His own.

Nowhere in all the sacred writings is there question of Christ as an individual wholly cut off from other individuals and completely self-contained. And it is well to remember here that there was no reference to such a Christ in the preaching of St. Paul. The reader will recall that Paul the Apostle, like John, Mark, Matthew, and Luke, sees no discontinuity between the historical life of Christ and His mystical life. For him as for them, the two lives are one, and it was precisely in order to describe this miracle of unity that he coined those peculiar verbs compounded with σύν, which say at once that Christ died, is risen, and in glory, and that in Him, by the same act as it were, we too have died, are risen, and are glorified with Him.

The same thought which Paul expressed with so little respect for idiom is now formulated in turn by John, but in calm, recollected sentences, for the mystery has come nearer to us. And because it is nearer, it is now more clearly understood. Its grandeur appears in fuller light; there is no longer question merely of Jesus' last moments, of His Passion and of His life of glory, but of His entire life and of Himself. All that is His reflects the same richness: if we examine the Gospel carefully, we shall see in it the whole Church, living by Him and in Him.

Thus the very style of the Gospel is an implicit but powerful testimony to the Mystical Christ; the Spirit who inspires it all is able to speak to us through its every detail. However, the same testimony is given with far greater force by the Gospel's content, and to this we must now direct our attention.

II

As the Gospel proceeds, this testimony becomes more precise, but without ceasing to be the same testimony. From beginning to end, it seems to us, there is question of the life that is given us in the Incarnation. But by the successive new beginnings that characterize John's style, he comes to explain more and more fully how we are animated by that life. In the prologue and also in the opening lines of the first Epistle, the author has already indicated the order that he will follow. He intends to prove that the Word is our life, that He is likewise our light, and that He communicates His divine glory and His Sonship to us, in Himself. This series of thoughts returns again in the Gospel. In the early chapters the principal, though not exclusive, theme is the eternal life which is coming to fill our souls; then, particularly from the eighth chapter on, John adds that this life is light, and that by living this life our minds are opened to God. At the end he returns once more to these thoughts, especially to that of life, with new emphasis, but noting, too, as the entire book meanwhile has told us, that this life is eternal life, and that, being communicated to us, it makes us all children of God in Christ.

This arrangement, of course, is only secondary. Primarily, the order indicated in the prologue marks the stages in the struggle between Life and death, between Light and darkness.

[169]

But, working as it were beneath the principal plan, this secondary plan develops successively the different aspects of this new life that comes to snatch us from death. That this was John's explicit intention, we should not venture to say. But what does that matter? If it is present, it is because the Spirit that inspires willed it so. What better reason could be desired? Is this order rigorously followed out by the author? Certainly not. John's is no analytic mind, that advances without either anticipating or repeating itself. He links everything together, but his thought nevertheless moves forward with a sure, even methodical pace. We see no better order to follow in outlining his doctrine than this secondary plan: Christ the Life, Christ the Light, Christ uniting His own in Himself, as He, the Son, is united with the Father.

In the first place, the Gospel hastens to tell us that Jesus is Life, and that by believing in Him we have eternal life. Then, after the first two chapters, which may be considered as an introduction, in which Jesus makes Himself known to various persons and under different aspects, there follow two events and two discourses, all related to the same subject. These are the meeting with Nicodemus and the reflections that follow it, and the testimony of John the Baptist, likewise followed by reflections. They occupy the entire third chapter, and treat of baptism, that is, our entry into the true life.

Everyone is familiar with the brisk account of the interview with Nicodemus, one of the "rulers" among the Jews. Upright but fearful, it would appear, and very much concerned with "what people would say," this Sanhedrite came to Jesus by night. It was springtime, and the air was filled with the perfume of early blossoms. The setting is precise, and living details give the episode a realistic background. Soon, but without abandoning this solid support, we shall penetrate into the ineffable, under the guidance of John or rather, of the Holy Spirit.

Nicodemus, courteous and fond of discussion, greets Jesus as a rabbi, but as a rabbi sent from God:

Rabbi, we know that Thou art a teacher come from God;

for no one can do these signs which Thou dost unless God be with him.

Jesus at once leads him to sublime heights:

Amen, Amen, I say to thee, unless a man be born from above, he cannot see the kingdom of God.[6]

Here we are at the heart of the mystery. This is no time for discussion, or for attempts to improve things that are outmoded. There is question of a new life, the only life that is really worth while. But in order to live, we must be born again:

Unless a man be born of water and spirit, he cannot enter into the kingdom of God. That which is born of the flesh is flesh; and that which is born of the Spirit is spirit.

A new order of reality is being established; like its origins, it too is a mystery:

The wind bloweth whither it listeth, and thou hearest the sound thereof, but knowest not whence it cometh or whither it goeth; so it is with everyone that is born of the Spirit.[7]

One can hear the whisper of the spring breeze. But it comes from unsuspected sources and passes on to unknown regions; of its action we can know only what we experience in the little corner where we are. But this very real breeze is also a symbol; it represents a life whose immensity transcends even space and time. Into this life we are plunged at our rebirth, and all we know of it is the tiny spot where we are grafted onto eternity. It is to this thought that Jesus is leading:

. . . that whosoever believeth in Him [the Son of Man], may have everlasting life.
For God so loved the world that He gave His only-begotten Son, that whosoever believeth in Him may not perish, but may have everlasting life.

We have passed beyond the perspectives of this world. No longer is there a death to come, nor judgment.

He that believeth in Him [the Son] is not judged; he that believeth not is already judged, because he hath not believed in the name of the only-begotten Son of God.

[171]

Now herein is the judgment, that whereas the light is come into the world, men loved the darkness rather than the light; for their works were evil. . . .

He that believeth in the Son, hath everlasting life.[8]

Thus, we see, the entire third chapter speaks of the first coming of this life within us, that is, of baptism.

The two chapters that follow have not the same importance for our subject. They relate various incidents, instructions, and miracles. However, their two main passages, those, namely, that possess the greatest doctrinal significance, contain a few verses that we must mention. These are the incidents of the Samaritan woman and of the paralytic healed at the pool of Bethsaida. At Jacob's well, Christ declares that we must ask Him for the living water that quenches one's thirst forever, and which becomes in the soul a fountain, flowing unto eternal life. He likewise declares, in the case of the sick man whom He has cured, that He is the absolute Master of life.

As the Father raiseth the dead and giveth them life, so also the Son giveth life to whom He will.

For neither doth the Father judge any man, but He hath given all the judgment to the Son. . . .

Amen, amen, I say to you, he that heareth My word, and believeth Him that sent Me, hath everlasting life, and cometh not unto judgment; but he hath passed out of death into life.[9]

Now we come to the sixth chapter, which, like the second and third, speaks only of life. However, there is no longer question of its first effusion, but of its preservation and growth. It is the discourse on the Eucharist, that follows up the instruction on baptism.

Here again, the account presents all the concreteness of historical fact. Bread was needed, and Philip estimated that they should have to buy more than two hundred shillings worth, if each person were to receive even a small portion. Yet Jesus feeds them all: five thousand men sit down on the grassy slope and eat of the miraculous food. Then comes the stormy night on the lake and the calm that followed Jesus' command, the arrival at Capharnaum, and finally the return of the multitude, who had likewise crossed the Sea of

Tiberias. Again, the setting is very real: sails and ropes, the waves of the sea, and the bread given to these fisherfolk. But all this is to prepare the way for a doctrine. Jesus is going to elevate all this from an earthly to a heavenly plane. The episode continues without a break, and everything takes on a meaning, its full 'meaning, from its contact with the Word. The perishable bread which these people have received, is nothing; the only true food is that which abides, which has value for eternal life, and which the Son of Man gives.

> Amen, amen, I say to you, Moses gave you not the bread from heaven, but my Father giveth you the true bread from heaven. For the bread of God is that which cometh down from heaven, and giveth life to the world. . . .
> I am the bread of life; he that cometh to Me shall never hunger, and he that believeth in Me shall never thirst. . . .
> For this is the will of My Father, that everyone who beholdeth the Son and believeth in Him have everlasting life, and that I raise him up on the last day.[10]

Jesus is the perfect Bread, for He has life in abundance, enough to give life to all His brethren. Hence, in order to understand all that He is, we must see Him in the Eucharist, in the act of giving Himself to us. The instruction continues, with emphasis on this last point, and still without losing touch with reality. The thought of the manna which their fathers had eaten, serves as the point of departure:

> Your fathers ate the manna in the desert, and they died; this is the bread come down from heaven, that a man may eat thereof and not die.
> I am the living bread come down from heaven. If anyone eat of this bread, he shall live forever; and the bread which I will give is My flesh, for the life of the world. . . .
> Amen, amen, I say to you, unless ye eat the flesh of the Son of Man and drink His blood, ye have not life in you. He that eateth My flesh and drinketh My blood hath everlasting life; and I will raise him up on the last day. . . . He that eateth My flesh and drinketh My blood abideth in Me, and I in him. . . .
> This is the bread come down from heaven: not as the fathers ate and died: he that eateth this bread shall live forever.[11]

Jesus spoke these words in the course of an instruction

given in the synagogue at Capharnaum. He tells the Jews who He is: a man of flesh and bone, but also the Son of God and the life of men. And all this is one. The Eucharist is inseparable from His Incarnation; the two are so intimately associated that He speaks of both at the same time, and commentators find it no easy task to distinguish between what relates to the hypostatic union and what has reference to the Blessed Sacrament. Such is the life that Jesus gives His faithful: it is Himself; He becomes their food, causing them to live by Him, as He lives by the Father.

These verses are brimful of meaning, which was to be brought to light, as we shall see, by Tradition. For the present, we shall be content to interpret the text with the help of certain ideas that John proposes elsewhere.

The faithful, he says — and we assume that he means those who eat this Bread — have within them one greater than they; a kind of divine seed (*semen Dei*)[12] has been sown in their hearts; hence they are in embryo, so to speak, and their true dignity is so hidden that in all the greatest and most beautiful gifts that they have received, they are objects of faith even to themselves.

III

Hence, in order that they may fully know themselves, they need a new light. Indeed, from the seventh chapter on, while He is still speaking of life, Jesus insists upon the truth and light that faith will give to those who are united with Him. As the account of His miracles and actions continues, the mystical teaching unfolds.

Faith, light, truth. As we know, faith is one of the great thoughts, nay, even the purpose, of the Fourth Gospel, since it was written in order that men might believe that Jesus is God and that they have life in Him. Moreover, faith is the necessary condition for that life; without it, one cannot possess eternal life, and with it, by simply accepting Jesus' words, the sheep of the fold will receive life. "Whosoever liveth and believeth in Me," says Jesus, "he shall never die; he shall have the light of life," or, as it is phrased in the prologue of the Gospel, he shall have "the life that is the light."[13]

In the first Epistle, the divinity is the Light. Hence, to be with God is to be in the light, in eternal light; and it is charity, especially fraternal charity, that brings us into this radiant atmosphere. But in the Gospel, strictly speaking, Christ is the Light. A magnificent text in the seventh chapter prepares us for this declaration. It was during the Feast of Tabernacles, and a great multitude was present in the Temple. On the last, and most solemn day,

> Jesus stood forth and cried aloud, saying, "If any man thirst, let him come to Me, and let him drink. Whoso believeth in Me, as the Scripture saith, 'Out of his belly shall flow rivers of living water.' "
> This He said of the Spirit, which they were to receive who believed in Him. For there was not as yet the Spirit, because Jesus was not yet glorified.[14]

Since Jesus had not yet died for us, the effusion of the Spirit had not as yet taken place. But this fact does not affect what He is in Himself. Also during the same Feast of Tabernacles,

> Again therefore Jesus spoke to them, saying, "I am the light of the world. He that followeth Me shall not walk at all in the darkness; but shall have the light of life."[15]

The same statement is repeated several times in the Gospel. Thus, at the close of His ministry, He says:

> I am come as light (ἐγὼ φῶς) into the world, that whoso believeth in Me may not abide in darkness.[16]

Between the two statements just quoted, are included all the chapters of the Gospel from the discourse on the Eucharist to the Passion. The Lord affirms that He is the Light. Now, this light is not primarily the brightness that is shed upon the object, but that which illumines the eye itself. For the Hebrews, the eye was the cause of light within us; it was both light and a torch, and it is according to these concepts that Jesus expresses Himself.

The story of the man born blind, which serves as a center

[175]

for this teaching, is characteristic. Here Jesus shows that He is the Light, because He enables our eyes to illumine us fully. We have already alluded to these pages. They are a simple, realistic statement of fact, but symbolic as well, for in them the Word takes part. Everything follows His movements, but everything, too, is focused in a certain direction. Thus, in heaven, we shall understand all history as a progress toward Christ. In the opening lines Jesus calls Himself the Light:

> We must work the works of Him who sent Me, while it is day; the night cometh, when no man can work. As long as I am in the world, I am light to the world.[17]

Then He made clay with spittle and anointed the blind man's eyes — always there is the same union of our prosaic world with the eternal splendors — and the blind man saw. He saw, but the stupendous miracle only exasperated the Pharisees and Scribes, who were so accustomed to their half-light. They rebelled; they would not believe, while the blind man gave testimony to the Light that had made him see, and so merited still clearer vision: he believed.

> And Jesus said, "For judgment have I come into this world, that they who see may not see, and they who see may become blind."[18]

Thus do the concrete reality and the revelation of Christ unfold as one; guiding the narrative is the same Spirit who guided the Saviour in the days of His mortal existence.

So Jesus is Light, and His very acts prove that He is a light which must penetrate us, to make us lightsome too.

> Jesus therefore said to them, "Yet a little while the light is among you. Walk whilst ye still have the light, that the darkness overtake you not; and he that walketh in the darkness knoweth not whither he goeth. Whilst ye have the light, believe in the light, that ye may become sons of light."[19]

This light is no cold phosphorescence. As we have seen, John represents it as life, as the light of life. Furthermore, in speaking of this subject, the Evangelist, who is fond of expressing at one and the same time all that is dear to his heart, begins once more to speak of life; not by tumultuous comparisons, as Paul would do, but in his own way, by gradual transitions. Or rather, for we must always return to the first cause, the inspiring Spirit who used Paul to show, in spite of appearances, how close a bond exists between these supernatural realities, now employs John, to show how natural this union is.

Moreover, Jesus Himself has pointed out the connection. On the day He healed the man born blind, He saw Calvary's ransom already nigh, and He wished to prepare the minds of the Twelve for the hours when the light would be no longer with them. This He does, especially in the discourse on the Good Shepherd, given in the tenth chapter. The discourse is closely bound up with the incident of the man born blind. The priests of Israel had cast the man out of the synagogue, which was, so to speak, their fold. Jesus receives him into His own fold, among the sheep that believe in Him, and who through their faith live by Him.

> The sheep hear His [the Good Shepherd's] voice; and He calleth His own sheep by name, and leadeth them forth. When He hath brought forth all His own, He goeth before them, and the sheep follow Him, because they know His voice.[20]

So, from Him who is Light, the sheep receive light. So, too, from Him who is Life, do they receive life. For, not only is the flock joined to the Shepherd by the fact that it follows in His footsteps, but it is one with Him through the very flow of life by which it lives. For the Good Shepherd gives His life for His sheep, and He gives life to His sheep; and the day of payment approaches, when He will immolate Himself for His own.

> I came that they may have life, and have it abundantly.
> And I lay down My life for the sheep.
> My sheep hear My voice, and I know them, and they follow Me,
> And I give them life everlasting.[21]

Indeed, the catastrophe is nigh at hand. After this discourse, Jesus retires beyond the Jordan. Hither messengers come to inform Him of Lazarus' illness, and from here He sets out to raise His friend from the dead, and thereby to prove that He is the resurrection and the life.

> I am the resurrection and the life;

[177]

He that believeth in Me, even if he die, shall live, and whosoever liveth and believeth in Me, he shall never die.[22]

And the resurrection of Lazarus is the miracle that determines the Sanhedrin to put the Saviour to death.

IV

But this death will be for the life of the world, as Jesus explains in a long conversation with His Apostles on Holy Thursday evening. It is then that He tells them the meaning of the disasters that are about to come upon His work. Defeat, or at least apparent defeat, is very near. But it will be the beginning of the true victory; at the tragic but happy hour that is to take Him from the sight of His faithful and bring on His death, Jesus will come to dwell in their souls and bring them life.

The discourse contains some important instruction concerning that life, to which we shall return in the following chapter. Our present study embraces only one phase of this instruction; namely, that this life comes to us through union with the Saviour, by His indwelling within us, and ours in Him, and by our attachment to Him who, in the words of the Gospel, is the Vine.

Christ abides in us, and we in Him. John has a particular fondness for the word *abide*, μένειν. Perhaps it is a habit that he learned from the Master, for in the Gospel the expression is always placed on the lips of Jesus. In the "Johannine" writings the phrase is often combined with another very similar expression that helps us to determine its meaning. The Father, says the Gospel, abides in the Son, and the Son in the Father. Here there is question of the perfection of inwardness, of the consubstantiality that makes the Divine Persons interior to one another, by what theologians call "circumincession."

Our indwelling in Christ is to be understood in an analogous sense; it, too, is an ineffable inwardness, bearing a remote resemblance to circumincession. This meaning is clearly implied by the contexts where it is mentioned. The first, and, except for the discourse after the Last Supper, the only passage in which it occurs, is the discourse on the Eucharist.

He that eateth My flesh and drinketh My blood, abideth in Me, and I in him.[23]

The first part of the verse explains the last with complete, even realistic, clearness. Just as food becomes interior to him who eats, so Christ will become interior to the faithful, and the faithful will become interior to Him.

The other passages are quite as clear. They are all grouped in the few verses containing the allegory of the vine, which we shall quote presently. The sense is perfectly evident: There is question of the inwardness that joins together all the parts of an organism, and which imparts to each of them the life of the whole.

Let us reflect, too, upon the circumstances. The Last Supper has just ended. John does not record the institution of the Blessed Sacrament, and contents himself with a rapid allusion to this excess of love. But the order of events remains the same. When Jesus addresses His Apostles, He has just come to dwell in them, and they in Him, for the first time. What He is saying now, forms the natural continuation of the discourse on the Eucharist which we have already read; He is speaking of the same life and of the same inwardness. So truly will His disciples possess His life within them, explains the Master, that they will be exalted in God's own eyes; it will bring to their souls a purity, a fidelity, a charity, a fecundity, and a docility to the commandments of God, which will be convincing proof that they live by Christ and that Christ is living in them.

"Abide in Me, and I in you." Their inwardness with the Saviour will be truly reciprocal: they in Him, and He in them. Paul, we remember, had already expressed the thought in a similar way; in the same context, sometimes in the same verse, he would say that the faithful are in Christ, and that Christ is in the faithful. John usually expresses both ideas at once: We abide in Christ at the same time as He abides in us.

Like Paul, John synthesizes these two seemingly irreconcilable expressions in the figure of a single organism. "The Body," said Paul; John says: "The Vine."

"The Vine." . . . Long since had Yahweh spoken to His people of the vine. Isaias summed up an entire tradition when he wrote:

> The vineyard of Yahweh of hosts is the house of Israel; and the men of Judah are His cherished plantation.[24]

Such was the parable in the time of the prophets. But now, at the hour of the Last Supper and of the Cross, figures everywhere give place to reality. Now God continues, and fulfills what He had in ages past foretold.

> I am the true vine, and My Father is the husbandman. Every branch in Me that beareth not fruit, He taketh away; and every branch that beareth fruit He cleanseth, that it may bear more fruit. Ye are already clean, because of the word which I have spoken to you; abide in Me, and I in you. As the branch cannot bear fruit of itself, unless it abide in the vine; so neither can ye, unless ye abide in Me. I am the vine, ye the branches; he that abideth in Me, and I in him, the same beareth much fruit, for apart from Me ye can do nothing. If anyone abide not in Me, he is cast forth as the branch and withereth; and they gather them and cast them into the fire, and they are burned. If ye abide in Me, and My words abide in you, ask whatsoever ye will and it shall be done to you. Herein is My Father glorified, in that ye bear much fruit, and become My disciples.[25]

"I am the true Vine." The first was but a shadow; it was merely something that belonged to Yahweh. Now it is a kind of identification, a mystical identification, that is being accomplished. In His Incarnate Son, Yahweh declares: "I am the Vine." The first vine represented the people, and it does so still; there are branches that are dead, and others that should produce more abundant fruit. But now the whole vine is something more: it is Christ.

In this one Vine, the faithful abide; they are in Christ, and the life of Christ is in them. Nor is this all: in this Vine, they enjoy real activity; they actually produce fruit.

But, at the same time, and even primarily, these fruits are formed by the Vine; they would not be the fruits of the faithful, were they not, before all else, Christ's.

If they are cut off, the branches are only dry wood. But, rooted in Christ — Paul employs the same expression — the faithful are grafted onto Life. They have a hardy life, if we may venture so to speak; if one branch is cut off, others grow, and God prunes the plant in order to increase the harvest.

Its life is eternal life. By its root, which is Christ, it receives a participation in the divine life, the life of glory, the life that flows from the Father to the Son.

Chapter X

St. John—3. Our Divine Life. "That They May Be One, As We Are One"

✄

I. *Unity* in the discourse after the Last Supper. Unity with the Son, making us "children of God." Unity in the Gospel and in Christ's prayer.

II. *"One as we are one."* In Christ's prayer, all centers upon the prayer for unity, "that they may be one, as We are one." Preparation for the prayer; its expression; its explanation. It is made first for the Apostles, then for all the faithful. Once taken into this unity, we share in the glory that belongs to the Son by reason of His generation from eternity.

III. *Explanation.* This unity truly resembles that of the Trinity, and constitutes the glory of the Church; a union, not of equality, but of dependence. John's affirmations usually take this form: our supernatural privileges have their fullness in Christ, who receives them from God. Unity proceeds from Christ, and is the mark of Christ. Collective unity.

IV. *Charity.* Charity in the Gospel. God is love; love unites men to God and with each other. God loves us with the love He bears toward His Son, because the Son is in us. The term and crown of all. The divine value that Christ gives us, even in the eyes of the Father. History in the Gospels.

I

THE DISCOURSE after the Last Supper is as rich in instruction as it is overflowing with affection. In the last words of Him who is Love and Light, we have already discovered many a lesson, but a second and closer scrutiny will reveal still more. In the final sentences appear the most complete declarations, for which the others were only a preparation.

In general, one may say that the entire discourse is an

instruction on unity. Before His death, before the dispersion of the Eleven, our Lord excludes in advance everything that can lead to division. There is only union: union of the Father and the Son, union of Christ and the faithful, union of the faithful among themselves; union of charity, union of faith, union effected by the Holy Ghost, and lastly, a union like to the union of the Divine Persons. And these unions all combine and unite among themselves; the mind of the Master passes from one to the other, then returns again and again, joining and mingling them all. For in Him they all attain a perfect synthesis, and by Him they all come to the faithful. And the unity which is the principle of all the others, is His union with the Father, which is communicated by grace to the faithful. It produces them all in men: union with God, faith, charity, light, even the possession of the Holy Spirit and confidence in the Father.

He gave power to become children of God, to them that believed in His name.[1]

This was the third of the points mentioned in the Gospel prologue. After explaining that Christ is the Life which is given to every man, after showing that this Life is the Light that enables us to understand this divine effusion and the supernatural realities, John had still to point out that the very title of Sonship, which gives life to the Saviour, passes together with that Life into those who believe in Him; and that, in consequence, the Incarnation makes humanity something divine, makes it live, and makes it one. Once more, the two messages that the author of the Fourth Gospel wishes to deliver are but one. The thought is several times expressed in the Gospel.

As the Father hath life in Himself, so He hath given to the Son also to have life in Himself.[2]

That perfection of life which makes the Father the principle of all divinity, flows into the Incarnate Word, and, by making Him the Only-begotten Son, it makes Him universal Life.

As the living Father hath sent Me, and as I live because of

the Father, so he that eateth Me, he also shall live because of Me.[3]

This expansion of glory and of divinity that flows into our souls had been indicated by Christ merely in passing in the words He had previously uttered in the course of His public life, and which have also been recorded in the Synoptics. At the end, as the discourse after the Last Supper is drawing to a close, He proclaims it again, for the last time, but emphatically now. Long has He been speaking with men; now He goes to speak with the Father, and to render an account of the mission that He has fulfilled. But so truly are He and ourselves one, that in this solemn interview of the Son with the Father, there will be question almost exclusively of us.

II

The prayer is given in the seventeenth chapter. It has three parts: Christ's prayer for Himself, His prayer for His Apostles, and His prayer for the Church. But the three parts are intimately related. From the beginning of the first, Christ is speaking of the life that He imparts to every soul. Thus had He been always wont to speak.

These things spake Jesus, and lifting up His eyes to heaven, He said, "Father, the hour is come: glorify Thy Son, in order that the Son may glorify Thee: even as Thou hast given Him power over all flesh, in order that to all Thou hast given Him, He should give to them everlasting life.

"Now this is everlasting life, that they know Thee, the only true God, and Him, whom Thou hast sent, Jesus Christ. I have glorified Thee upon earth, having accomplished the work which Thou hast given Me to do; and now do Thou glorify Me, Father, with Thyself, with the glory which I had before the world was, with Thee."[4]

For Himself, then, Christ asks that He be glorified. However, this glorification consists, not only in the majesty which He had from the beginning, but also in that abundant and fruitful life which the Church is to receive through Him. Between Him and His faithful there is no separation.

[184]

Then the prayer continues: Christ speaks of His work and of the care that He has devoted to the Twelve. They have believed in Him; and by reason of their faith, their souls share in the supreme effusion of life that proceeds from the Father to the Son:

I have manifested Thy name to the men whom Thou hast given Me out of the world; Thine they were, and to Me Thou gavest them, and they have kept Thy word. Now they have known that all things whatsoever Thou hast given Me are from Thee; because the words which Thou hast given Me I have given to them, and they have received them, and they have truly known that I came forth from Thee, and have believed that Thou didst send Me.

For them I pray; not for the world do I pray, but for them whom Thou hast given Me, because they are Thine (and all things Mine are Thine, and all things Thine are Mine), and because I have been glorified in them.[5]

This preamble is a preparation. Before He formulates His prayer, Jesus shows that His disciples are ready to receive the divine munificence; all that the Father has belongs to the Son, and the Son has given all to His Apostles: His words, His doctrine, His cares.

I am no more in the world; and they are in the world, and I come to Thee. Holy Father, keep them in Thy name which Thou hast given Me, that they may be one, as We.[6]

"That they may be one." That is everything. Christ puts His chief preoccupation at the center of His prayer. He is about to go away; He will be no longer with His brethren. Hence the Father must take care of them; and all will be safe, if they have unity. The Lord makes no further request; the petitions that follow simply detail the consequences and the various aspects of this all-important gift.

While I was with them I kept them in My name which Thou hast given Me, and I guarded them, and not one of them hath perished, save the son of perdition, in order that the Scripture might be fulfilled. But now I come to Thee, and these things I speak in the world, in order that they may have My joy fulfilled in themselves. I have given them Thy word, and the world hath hated them, because they are not of the world, even as I am not of the world. I pray not that Thou

[185]

take them out of the world, but that Thou keep them from evil. They are not of the world, as I am not of the world. Hallow them in truth; Thy word is truth. As Thou hast sent Me into the world, so I also have sent them into the world. And for them do I hallow Myself, in order that they too may be hallowed in truth.[7]

In these words, again all is an effusion of unity. Like the vine and the branches, the Apostles and Christ will possess all things in common. They will bear within them, in its fullness, the joy of Christ; they will keep in their hearts the same word that He has received; they will present themselves to the world, invested with the same mission. Nor will the world's hatred be deceived; it shall persecute them just as it has persecuted Him, because, like Christ, they are strangers to the world.

Belonging to a new order of things, to a new creation, they are changed and sanctified, and the consecration that makes Christ the supreme Priest and Victim, likewise constitutes their holiness: "And for them do I hallow Myself, in . order that they, too, may be hallowed in truth."

With these words ends Jesus' prayer for the Apostles, and the prayer for the Christians begins at once. The horizon broadens; beyond the Eleven appear all those who will believe by reason of their words. For these, too, Christ prays, and He asks the same graces, in the same terms, and in the same order. Repeating and repeating again, the prayer becomes each time more insistent. Jesus, one might say, desires only this one thing — which, alas, we have destroyed, and which, in a sense, is still to come — and He wishes it with all His heart.

Not for them only do I pray, but also for those who believe in Me through their word, that they all may be one, even as Thou, Father, art in Me, and I in Thee — that they, too, may be in Us, in order that the world may believe that Thou hast sent Me. And the glory which Thou hast given Me, I have given them, that they may be one, as We are one — I in them, and Thou in Me — that they may be perfected in unity, in order that the world may know that Thou hast sent Me, and that Thou hast loved them, even as Thou hast loved Me.[8]

The introduction of this prayer is brief. The Christians

have believed as the Apostles have believed, and faith has set their feet upon the path of grace. That is enough. For them, too, Christ at once prays for unity. Three times does He ask it, *eundem sermonem dicens*, as He prayed in His agony.

Having made the prayer, He does not leave the subject: He joins to the principal request other petitions that explain and complete it: that all the faithful, united in Him, may be with Him, for they have believed; that they may share His glory; that they may be united in Him to God. At the end of His first prayer He had already asked that the Apostles might be consecrated ($\dot{\eta}\gamma\iota\alpha\sigma\mu\acute{\epsilon}\nu o\iota$) as He is consecrated ($\dot{\alpha}\gamma\iota\acute{\alpha}\zeta\omega$). The prayer for the Church ends in like manner; that they may be loved by the Father as the Father loves Him, the Son.

In these last requests, the tone of the prayer becomes more urgent. Jesus appeals, as it were, to all His rights: "Father, I will it," and, lifting His eyes to heaven, the Incarnate Son confides to His Father His dying wish:

Father, that which Thou hast given Me, I will that where I am, they may also be with Me; in order that they may behold My glory, which Thou hast given Me, because Thou didst love Me before the foundation of the world.

Just Father, indeed, the world hath not known Thee, but I have known Thee, and these have known that Thou hast sent Me; and I have made known Thy name to them, and will make it known in order that the love wherewith Thou hast loved Me may be in them, and I in them.[9]

Unity could go no further!

III

But what is this unity? "That they may be one, as We are one," says Jesus. Each time that He mentions this unity, He specifies it with the same comparison — a comparison that is intentional, one that He loves to repeat, and which occurs four times in a single page of the Gospel:

That they may be one, as We.
That they all may be one, even as Thou, Father, art in Me, and I in Thee.

> That they may be one, as We are one.
> I in them, and Thou in Me — that they may be perfected in unity.[10]

Jesus does not hesitate to repeat Himself. Indeed, His insistence was necessary, for without it, who should ever have dreamed of such a resemblance?

Not always has Tradition been so daring. As we shall see later on, the interpretation of these verses was hampered by the Arians, who appealed to the passage as a confirmation of their doctrine. They maintained that when Jesus compared His unity with the Father to our unity among ourselves, He meant to lower the former to our level, and not to elevate us to His own. Men, they contended, are one only by affection or by resemblance; consequently, it is in this sense that the Son is one with the Father. He does, indeed, bear a distant likeness to the Father, but He is not the same God. This heretical interpretation of the passage made the Fathers very circumspect; in their commentaries they are careful to limit the meaning of the words, and to note that they do not identify the unity of the Father and the Son with the unity that exists between creatures.

Granted, but exegesis has other functions than merely to determine what a text does *not* mean. Especially in passages such as this, where Christ incessantly repeats a certain truth, it is not enough simply to take precautions against possible exaggerations. This the Fathers themselves understood very well, and, as we shall see, the greatest of them, after repeating the usual warning, have made of their commentaries on this passage the most forceful pages that have ever been written on the subject of our incorporation in Christ.

And this is the direction we must follow. The Arian danger is past; today, heresy is attacking the divine character of the Church. In a sense, expediency itself is forcing exegetes to insist upon the points that Jesus emphasized most in these passages.

"One as We." Of course, no one dreams of introducing here a rigorous equality; there is no hint of any such enormity in the Gospel. To tell the truth, we are concerned

[188]

less with a resemblance than with a dependence and a participation.

St. Paul had already presented the subject in the same way; in the principal passages where he proclaims the divinity of Christ, he calls attention also to the dignity that flows from that divinity into the entire Mystical Body. This corresponds exactly with John's view. In the latter's eyes, the whole supernatural economy consists in two intimately related communications. First there is that which the Father communicates to the Incarnate Son, and then that which the Son imparts to men; a communication of nature and of grace in the eternal generation and in the Incarnation that makes Christ Jesus, and a communication of grace in the justification that makes the members of Christ.

This twofold effusion, often indicated in the Gospel, finds its perfect expression in the discourse after the Last Supper and in Christ's prayer. The perfection of all truth, all power, all life, all love, is in the Father; from the Father, it flows to the Son. Then, by participation, from the Incarnate Son it passes into us. We are His fullness, His *pleroma,* as St. Paul has said. However, like Paul, John too insists that far from our adding anything to Him, we receive from Him the very thing which appears to give Him that plenitude.

The same is to be said of unity. We are one, ἕν, one single being in Christ, as the Three Persons are ἕν, one single Being, one nature. Theirs is a living unity beyond doubt, a unity of intelligence and love, but it is also a supreme and ineffable unity, whose principle is a unity of nature and not a unity of person; from this point of view, the neuter renders the thought more accurately than the masculine would have done.

The Son enjoys an absolute unity with the Father — a unity of nature, not of person. By becoming incarnate, He communicates the likeness of this unity to men. Hence they are one among themselves in the degree in which they are united to God in Christ.

Consequently, theirs is a real unity, real with the highest degree of reality, since it is sealed by that Unity which is necessary in itself.

Nor is it only a unity of individuals with Christ. It is also

[189]

a collective unity, consisting in that union of all Christians with one another which is a participation and a representation of the union of the Divine Persons among themselves.

Up to this point the Fourth Gospel has dealt chiefly with the union of each of the faithful with Christ and with God. We have seen that each Christian possesses Christ in himself and is himself in Christ; each Christian has life in himself; each Christian possesses within himself fountains of living water and the light of life. But now, at the supreme moment, in these parting words, the mystery is seen in full perspective. There is no longer question of individuals merely, but of one whole. As He goes to His death Jesus discloses the sublime universality of the reconciliation which is to be effected through His sacrifice. They who are to be one in Him, as He is one with His Father, are all those who believe — all, without exception.

Lastly, their unity is supernatural; it is a unity of grace, a divine unity, a unity which, though wrought through the humanity of Christ, and though it incorporates all mankind into that humanity, is nevertheless a communication and a participation of God Himself, and of the Trinity. All Christians shall be made one by Unity itself; they will all be united together because they will all be in Christ, by reason of an interiority that flows from the eternal circumincession; all together they will form one and the same entity, just as the Divine Persons, by reason of their consubstantiality, are one and the same God.

Consequently, theirs is a holy unity, a unity which by its very nature raises up and makes divine; a unity that we cannot begin to understand without turning our thoughts to God. Just as we can attain full knowledge of things only through their cause, so before we can clearly understand the unity of the Church, we must know the Trinity itself through faith.

And, conversely, it is enough to possess by faith a knowledge of this participated unity, in order to grasp something of the mystery of the Three Persons. For the unity of the Church is as eloquent as that of the Trinity is mysterious.

[190]

This unity is, as it were, a sign. It can be seen, and what one discerns therein is not a mere multitude of men joined together by a wise government, but that unique effusion of love and of eternal life which, from the Father, through the Son, and in the Spirit, makes those that are Christ's, one in Christ by the power of God. Jesus makes the statement Himself:

> That they all may be one, even as Thou, Father, art in Me, and I in Thee — that they too may be in Us, in order that the world may believe that Thou hast sent Me.
> That they may be perfected in unity, in order that the world may know that Thou hast sent Me.[11]
> Hereby shall all know that ye are My disciples, if ye have love one for another.[12]

The unity of the Church will be no ordinary thing, but a sign of credibility, a note. As Jesus declares in St. Matthew, He will be in the midst of His own, when they are gathered together in His name; He who is the light will surely find a way to manifest Himself to the pure of heart.

But men will not be alone in this unity: God Himself must take it into account, and if He will love His Son unto the end, He must also cherish those whom He makes one in that Son.

> That they may be perfected in unity, in order that the world may know that Thou hast sent Me, and that Thou hast loved them, even as Thou hast loved Me.
> I have made known Thy name to them, and will make it known, in order that the love wherewith Thou hast loved Me may be in them, and I in them.[13]

To us, this last verse seems the most emphatic of the entire discourse. It places the mystery of love at the very heart, so to speak, of the mystery of unity.

IV

Charity is one of the leading thoughts of St. John's Gospel, and even more so of his first Epistle. Now, this charity is no merely natural affection. As mysterious as the God who

[191]

is its source, as supernatural as the Life of which it is the manifestation, and as transcendent as the unity that it seals, it embraces, in a marvelous way, man's every wish and act.

And, like life and light, this charity is an effusion, a participation of God through Christ. God is love. In this love He has willed the Incarnation; in this love, too, He embraces us in His Incarnate Son. And this love must reign in our souls: it is the object of a new commandment. And, so specifically Christian is it, that it is at once the precept, the imitation, and the mark of Jesus Christ.

> Hereby shall all know that ye are My disciples, if ye have love one for another.[14]
> We do know that we have passed out of death unto life, because we love the brethren.[15]

To have charity, then, is our vocation.

> Beloved, let us love one another, for love is of God, and whoso loveth is born of God, and knoweth God. He that loveth not, knoweth not God, for God is love.
> Herein hath the love of God been manifested in us, in that He hath sent His only-begotten Son into the world, in order that we might live through Him. Herein doth lie the love, not in our having loved God, but in His having loved us, and having sent His Son as a propitiation for our sins.
> Beloved, if God hath so loved us, we also ought to love one another.

This love brings God within us.

> If we love one another, God abideth in us, and His love is perfected in us. . . .
> And we have come to know and have believed the love which God hath in us. God is love, and whoso abideth in love abideth in God, and God abideth in him.[16]

On this love, Christ dwelt untiringly throughout the discourse after the Last Supper: His love for the Father, the Father's love for Him, His love for His own, and the love which His own should have for Him, the love that they should have for one another; over and over again He returns to this love, at once single and manifold, which has its center in His own person. The hour has come when sin and hate shall reach their culmination, but it is also the hour in which love exceeds all bounds: as it overflows from the heart of Christ, its name falls repeatedly from His lips: *ex abundantia cordis os loquitur.*[17]

It would seem that Christ had reserved the most urgent request of all for these last moments. At the very beginning of the discourse that request escapes Him, as it were, like a secret that has become too burdensome and can no longer be kept, just as the sorrowful prediction, "Amen, I say to you, one of you will betray Me,"[18] had been wrung from His lips a few moments before. One is the secret of a love that longs to pour itself out, and the other is the secret of a love that knows it has been betrayed. His disciples must love one another, even as He has loved them. The love which He has in His own soul is about to invade the hearts of His faithful, and they will then love one another even as He Himself had loved, as God loves.

Once more we see the term to which the doctrine of the Mystical Body leads: the mystery of love, the keystone of Christianity, begins in God, and in God, through our Lord Jesus Christ, it finds its supreme expression. And so Jesus, at the close of His discourse, brings it to divine heights. He discloses the absolute love that binds the Trinity into unity, and He Himself will take possession of all humanity in unity.

> That the love wherewith Thou hast loved Me,
> May be in them,
> And I in them.[19]

The words are few, but each carries a world of meaning. The love of the Father for the Son, which was full when the world existed not; the love that is the eternal glory possessed by the Son before creation and which will be restored to Him, and which His faithful will possess — for they shall be with Him; the love that has wrought the Incarnation and the Redemption, shall descend within us. Despite the lowliness of their nature and the insignificance of their good will, all Christians must believe that they are pursued by an everlasting love. Together, sealed in this supernatural unity, they are all objects of that love, and in no uncommon way. God is one; love is one; Christians are one. God will cherish these least among men with that necessary and infinite love that He bears to the Son: "Inasmuch as ye did it to one of the least of these My brethren, ye did it to Me."

Evidently, God does not confuse our personalities. Each is loved according to his supernatural individuality. Christ is loved as the Only-begotten Son; the Christians, as His members and as His fullness. But Christ is not divided; so, in order to love His Son unto the end, God must extend His love to the last member of the human race. "And I in them." These words explain all. In order, as it were, to force the love of the Father to enter all of humankind, Christ has entered it first.

The Father has loved first; surely the faithful cannot refuse to extend that love to others. Jesus can ask that they console all their brethren with humility and serve them with respect, for He is in them.

"And I in them." Only the unity of Christ and the Christians, the unity of the Vine and the branches, can give charity its true meaning, and enfold all these mysteries of grace in the single mystery of the Incarnation.

And now, Christ has pronounced the last words of His last discourse. He has no more to say, naught else to ask for; there remains for Him now only to accomplish His mission, and to go and give life to His brethren.

> Jesus was to die for the nation; and not for the nation only, but that He might also gather together into one the scattered children of God.[20]

In conclusion, we must repeat that the Gospels, and especially the Fourth Gospel, contain a wealth of meaning which at first might be bewildering. Let the Rationalists cry, if they will, that all this is artificial and unintelligible; it is their prejudice and narrow-mindedness that blinds them to what is beyond their understanding. But Christians have no right to be surprised. When we are dealing with the life of God Himself, with a history written under God's own inspiration, are we justified in showing astonishment when the slightest incident and the most casual word are found to be fraught with meaning, in the very concreteness of their reality? Is it strange that the briefest phrases and even words and punctuation should be filled to overflowing with doctrinal significance?

Recognition of this fact is not a rejection of history and science; rather is it the realization that history achieves its fullness in Christ, just as in Christ humanity itself has reached its fullness. Christ is a reality of experience which is one with the absolute Intelligible, and thus the actions of Christ can very well be facts of experience, without ceasing to constitute one single whole with the whole of intelligibility, while the narration of those facts, and especially their inspired narration, need not cease to be a narrative in order to become a lesson for practical life and a light to illumine the understanding. Nay, it does not even need to become a doctrine, for it is such already. In order to derive instruction on the truths of faith from this narration, there is no necessity whatever of putting aside the facts and of giving oneself over to abstract speculation; it is enough to open one's eyes and read. He whose story is being recounted is Light itself.

In Him there is nothing that the mind cannot grasp. He is Light, not by reason of some accidental quality, but by subsistence. Hence His actions can also be causes of light, not merely through some concrete aspect, by reason of a certain connection of circumstance, but by their very substance and their concrete reality.

Nor is there in all this any cause for shame: *qui me erubuerit coram hominibus. . . .* On the contrary, all this is part of our worship of God, part of our gratitude. Nay more, it is also in keeping with strict objectivity, that we should be happy and proud that our Christ and our holy Scriptures are so real.

Chapter XI

Conclusions on the Holy Scriptures

⊁⊰

I. *St. John and St. Paul.* Both have doctrines that are alike in content and in many details. But they differ in the initial vision and in the manner of presentation. John indicates rather the definitive aspect, and the theandric character of the Church. II. *The Doctrine in Holy Scripture.* It is one, but it becomes more and more explicit. The different stages. Various ways of expressing union with Christ in the New Testament: Kingdom, Mystery, Life. But all center in Christ, and the end of the message was implied in the beginning. It is God who speaks in the inspired word. III. *But Scripture is not enough.* In several books, its final word is to tell us that Christ is coming in the Church. The Christians wait, and Jesus indeed comes, and shall come forever. So, to understand the Scriptures and the Incarnation, we must study Tradition.

I

ST. JOHN'S "Gospel" has the same content as the "Gospel" of St. Paul. It is quite true that there are many differences, and these we shall indicate. But what must be noted first of all, is the perfect agreement of doctrine. Let us compare, for instance, the discourse after the Last Supper and the Epistle to the Ephesians. Despite differences in tone and literary style, the doctrine in both develops along parallel lines. In both, God's plan is described as the work of an everlasting love. God has singled us out, chosen us, from all eternity; above all, He has loved us in Christ; He has made us one in Christ, so truly one in Him and with Him that His holiness passes into us, as do His knowledge, His glory,

His joy, and the Father's love for Him. For both authors, the whole of Christianity consists in a union, an attachment, an incorporation with Christ. For Paul as well as for John, the Son alone exists and is of consequence in the sight of God. But, in this only Son, God sees all Christians, all the members of this Christ.

As we have seen, Paul presents this doctrine in formulas that may be summed up as follows: "In Christ we all form but one body, one Mystical Christ." John's teaching does not so readily lend itself to a brief résumé. Let us simply recall that it is contained almost entirely in these few propositions: "Abiding in Christ and He in us, we live by Him, as He lives by the Father; and we are one in Him, as He is one with the Father."

The two doctrines are so similar that they may be combined into one: "The Christians are one, living by the unity and by the life of Christ, which proceed from God, and in which they share by grace." This expression is all the more venerable, we think, because by eliminating what is peculiar to each Apostle, it now contains very little beyond the testimony of Christ and of the Spirit.

Alongside this fundamental resemblance may be added several traits of detail that are common to both. John and Paul each received a vision at the beginning of their preaching, and this vision had reference to our union with Christ. Both beheld the Saviour present in His brethren: the one near Damascus, the other at Patmos. For both, a supernatural unity reigns between Christ and ourselves, a unity that places Him within us and ourselves in Him, so that we are His prolongation and His fullness, and so that the Head and the members, the Vine and the branches, form one living organism, animated by the life that descends from the Father to the Incarnate Word. Both connect this central truth with numerous applications. The Eucharist is its sacred sign; and charity, patience, a complete renewal of the soul, should be its fruits.

But, however striking these resemblances may be, there are nevertheless real differences. How, indeed, could it be possible for two men endowed with such opposite temperaments, and conducted by grace along such different paths, to betray no individuality at all?

Paul, the active, uncompromising Apostle, was won over by a sudden revelation. A flash of lightning blinded him, and the word entered like a knife into his soul. "The word of God," as he tells us himself, "is living, and energizing, and keener than any two-edged sword; and penetrating even to the division of soul and spirit, of joints and marrow."[1]

In John, the beloved Apostle, no such forcible entrance was necessary. As he puts it, the word "abided" in him, and he possessed the word of God "abiding" in his soul. There, little by little, it became the light of life.

Paul was converted in the way that best suited the character of Paul. The Word of God leaped forth upon him like a robber, and in consequence there remained an element of aggressiveness and of abruptness, even in his style. John was of a different stamp, and God won him as befitted John. The truth unveiled itself within his soul, as a summer landscape rises before one's eyes at eventide. The sentences are calm; the picture is without that sharpness of outline which, in Paul's teaching, sets off the smallest detail. One would say that the lesser objects have disappeared, but the lofty summits are more majestically and more silently imposing. The meaning of the whole is more interior, more withdrawn into itself.

Such is the Fourth Gospel. At the first contact, it shows itself more simple and more interior. The sentences come and go, and begin anew, unaffected, but singularly appealing, and, like a meditation or like love, constantly insisting upon the same thoughts. The doctrine carries with it fewer applications and fewer details than does Paul's. The strenuous Apostle was endlessly drawing lessons of charity, of purity, of zeal, and of obedience; everywhere he found arguments for discussion and for the refutation of adversaries. John proceeds straight to the essentials and remains there: we must attach ourselves with all our heart to the Word of life. The rest, he knows, will come of itself.

The aspect of struggle, which the doctrine presented in St. Paul, is gone. The Word has come; it is enough. As the rising sun dispels the darkness, so, at Christ's coming, the true light is already shining, at least *de iure.* We "abide" in Jesus Christ. The word is characteristic, and it suggests definitive realities. No more uncertainty, no more hesitation, for on God's part the gift of eternal life is without repentance. We alone can forfeit it, by our sins. Sorrows indeed will come, and there will be a struggle; but these are intended, in God's plan, to put us more completely in possession of the gift that we already have, as we await the day when we shall enjoy it without the veil.

Hence the Church is no longer merely the militant body described by Paul, the Apostle who labored more than the others. She is a transcendent reality, belonging rather to heaven than to earth, a reality in which is prolonged the glory of the God-Man.

It is precisely in this respect that the chief difference of the Fourth Gospel consists. More clearly than the others it shows, in those that are Christ's, a reality of a theandric order. Just as Christ is the God-Man, so, in Him and by Him, His Mystical Body is at once human and divine. One by reason of a unity that proceeds from the unity of the Divine Persons, beloved of the Father, vivified by the Son, and sanctified by the Spirit, it is a kind of prolongation of the Incarnation, or rather, it is the Incarnation in its fullest realization, and giving dignity to all the members of the Incarnate Word.

It was not left to men, not even to those chosen by the Spirit of God as instruments in the writing of the Scripture, to give this final touch to the doctrine. Christ Himself, who is Unity, willed personally to tell men that they are one in Him, as He is one with the Father. This He said during the days of His mortal life. And the Spirit, who gives understanding, who directs the memory, and who leads men to all truth, inspired John to report these words to his brethren.

II

Thus end the Scriptures, and their concluding thought is the same as that which was outlined in their beginning. In the preceding pages we have seen, in a very rapid survey,

[199]

that the message remains ever the same. The teaching of the Fourth Gospel is what was announced in the Old Testament. Already under the Old Law, it was union that was promised, a union of all the faithful among themselves and a union of them all with God. In the New Law, what is preached is the very same union, but in its accomplishment. At first, in the Synoptic Gospels, we witness the coming of Him who makes that union in Himself, and who, on this earth of ours, is the union of the divine and the human, Jesus Christ. We see His actions, we see Him effecting this union within us. But, thus far, we can gather very little information on the real nature of this union. One might say that God willed to sink its foundations more deeply before giving us a more complete description of His work.

In fact, preceding the years of Paul's and John's writing, there intervenes the period that is described in the early chapters of the Acts. There we see the Church coming into existence; we see her being born as the body of Christ, one with His unity and living by His life. The great moments, or at least several of the great moments, of this period, and those which have exercised the most powerful influence on the spread of the Gospel throughout the world, are likewise moments in which a certain mystical identity between Christ and all the faithful is most fully realized and most clearly manifested. Pentecost, the martyrdom of St. Stephen, and Paul's conversion, show both the nature of the Church's inner life and the nature of the force that is destined to carry her to the ends of the earth. Now it seems that the gift is widely enough known for God to give an explanation of its nature. So Paul, who has just learned by revelation how real is Christ's presence within the Church, sets himself to preach this inwardness everywhere. We are in Christ, and Christ is in us; we are His body, He is our Head, and we are members one of the other; in Him we are made pure; in Him we are sanctified; in Him we are deserving of love in the sight of God and are made divine; in Him is our all, all our hope and all our dignity. Then comes John, to teach the same truth; or rather, Christ and the Spirit teach it by means of John, with even greater insistence. As John dwells more emphatically upon Christ's divinity, he likewise stresses with greater force the divinization which is given to them that are Christ's; and as he insists more energetically on the unity of the Father and the Son, so does he inculcate more powerfully the unity that is given in the Father, the Son, and the Spirit, and which makes all Christians one as the Divine Persons are one.

In His ordinary teaching to the Jews and to the Apostles, Christ embodied this message of unity in the instructions on the Kingdom. As we have seen, the Kingdom is in part, and even principally, the union of all men in Christ with God. Paul summed up the same message, but in different terms; he spoke, or rather, the Holy Spirit spoke through him, of the "mystery." Like the Kingdom, the mystery is the vocation given to all men, Gentiles included, to unite themselves to God by being incorporated with Christ. Finally, in John's Gospel, the same message is given in the preaching of Life. The life He receives from the Father, Christ causes to flow by participation into us, so that by Him, we truly live in ourselves, and are united to the Father by being united with one another in Him.

Kingdom, Mystery, Life. At first sight, the three notions seem very different. This is because the one gift is rich in contrasting aspects. The first notion, that of the Kingdom, expresses the economy of salvation in terms of the oracles of the prophets and the expectations of the multitudes. If we may venture so to speak when there is question of pages so sacred, such a method of approach was necessary in the presence of the early audiences of Palestine. Christ adopted it for His ordinary teaching; in the beginning at least, it was the method that made the greatest impression upon the Apostles, and which they themselves employed most commonly during the early years of their own preaching. This is the manner of presentation described in the Synoptics and in the Acts of the Apostles.

The second idea, the "Mystery," is already a theology, and almost controversial, contrasting as it does the immense splendor of the eternal decrees with our narrowness of vision and our exclusivism. If we may once more be excused for hazarding a hypothesis on the subject of inspired authors, it was the manner of expression best suited to the temperament of an Apostle who had to struggle more than the others, and whose mission it was to defend the infinite transcendence and mercy of the divine gift in the face of Israel's nationalism and the short-sighted wisdom of the Gentiles.

Finally, the third notion, "Life," is more psychological and at the same time more metaphysical. It shows Christianity in what is most interior to it, and also in what is most interior to us — more interior to us than we are to our very selves. This is the manner of presentation we find in the last of the inspired books, in the writings of John, the Apostle whom God seems to have trained, more than the others, to the interior life.

But we must note that while these ideas differ according to changing circumstances and a shifting of emphasis, still, when we seek the basic reality that they express, they all say the same thing. The Kingdom bespeaks an ownership, a subjection, a consecration; the Mystery tells of a hidden plan of sanctification and of unity; the Life, of a regeneration that gives us a new existence. But all this is tantamount to saying that we are incorporated into Christ. This incorporation suffices to make us children of the Kingdom, beneficiaries of the Mystery, and sons of adoption.

Now, these three ideas are an epitome of the entire New Testament. One sums up the Synoptic Gospels and the Acts, the second summarizes the Epistles of St. Paul, and the third is a résumé of the writings of St. John. And the New Testament, in turn, is the manifestation of the Old. Furthermore, these three ideas are summed up in Christ, for it is in Christ that the Kingdom is established, the Mystery revealed, and the Life communicated.

Christ, then, is the consummation and the epitome of the Scriptures, as He is the term and the whole of God's work here on earth. As the Holy Books contain but one truth, which is Christ, so they constitute but one message, which is summed up in Christ. Might we not say that the Father has but one word to address to the world by the Spirit, and that this one word is the Word that was made flesh, and in whom we are all destined to be included?

It is a single, but all-embracing message, that begins with the opening lines of Genesis and closes only with the last words of John's Gospel. Because of its unity, it forms but one announcement, a single sentence. Years, even centuries apart, sacred writers have been raised up to pronounce successive syllables of this sentence, but the thought was ever infinitely beyond the intelligence of those who uttered it, and until the very last word, its meaning was left in suspense. Human authors have lent their ministry, their docility, their research, their psychological and literary labor. But through them all, only One has spoken. To understand the sentence, we must hear it in full; but it has been uttered in full by God alone.

III

This message, spoken by God and revealed by Christ, is transcended as well by its content as by its Author. This the Scripture itself tells us: when its voice is stilled, the Christ of whom it is ever speaking and who gives it all its value, is going elsewhere, but He will not abandon it.

Probably the reader has noticed that several of the Holy Books, in closing, indicate a place outside themselves, whither Christ is going, in order to teach in the future. Thus does Jesus Himself speak in the last lines of the Gospel according to St. Matthew. He who is about to ascend to the Father, is also He who will dwell forever in the Church. Together with her who is destined to conquer all nations, it is He who is going to take possession of the human race; so that, although His mortal life is ended, He has yet another life that is just beginning. *Ecce ego vobiscum sum omnibus diebus.*

Jesus makes the same statement again, according to St. Matthew, in the last discourse of His public life. He is going away, and will return on the Last Day; and yet, He will reside, hidden, but no less truly, in each of the Christians. In them, we can still serve Him and love Him. For, whatever is done to the least of His brethren, is really done to

Him: *quamdiu fecistis uni ex his fratribus meis minimis, mihi fecistis.*

Thus again, as St. John testifies, Jesus speaks in His last conversation with the Apostles at the end of His mortal life. Before commending His spirit into His Father's hands, He makes the Church the depositary of His rights, His power, His greatness — in fine, of His entire Self, so that God, in order to love Him completely, must forever cherish our entire race: *ut dilectio qua dilexisti me, in ipsis sit, et ego in ipsis.*

As does the Master, so do the Apostles. John ends his great Epistle by proclaiming that the Christians live the life of Christ by participation. Paul closes his Epistles to the Romans, to the Corinthians, and to the Galatians, with the same thought.

Thus, the Scriptures remain consistent throughout. Like the Old Testament, the New also ends with a promise. Christ is come, certainly, but He is come that He may return in another, even better way. Truly it is good for us that He should go, because of the return that will follow.

So the Christians wait. Though they have received Christ, they still greet one another with the words: "He cometh";[2] and the last line of their Bible places on their lips a prayer of perpetual hope: "Come, Lord Jesus."[3]

And He cometh indeed. In the early days of the Christian era, we have seen Him reveal Himself to Paul, and then to John. And it is in the Church that He manifests Himself, and it is the Scripture that tells us so.

We know, too, that He will appear again at the end of time. The God who has loved us in Christ before the world was made, will once more tell us, before the world shall pass away, that it is in Christ that we have lived. Jesus will come, at the end of time, to give the complete résumé of the history of men. The summary will consist in a single declaration: He hath lived in His brethren, and all the good, and all the evil that hath been done here below, hath been done to Him. Again it is the Scripture that assures us of this presence of Christ in the Church.

Hence we see that the Holy Books always end with the same indication. Their content, their Christ, does not leave them, but passes into the Church. To separate the Scriptures from the Church would be to take them out of their context, and to rob them of both their meaning and their Author.

Consequently, it is in the Church, in the great life of Tradition, that we wish to study them. And, in order to know what they tell us about the Christ who lives in us, we must follow Christ Himself, when He comes to take up His abode in us.

PART TWO

⁕

The Doctrine of the Mystical Body in the
Greek Fathers

Introduction

WITH PAUL'S preaching of the Gospel to the Romans, the inspired history of Christian origins is brought to an abrupt close. It is the end of one epoch and the beginning of another. Having reached Rome, the Gospel has found its proper home; henceforth it is the Church that will continue the Scriptures. So, in order to remain in the school of the Holy Spirit who has spoken in the Scriptures, we must go to hear Him where He is teaching now: in the Church, the Catholic, Apostolic, and Roman Church. Thus from the Scriptures we pass directly to Tradition.

For the study of Tradition it seems best to consider the Fathers in the order of time, beginning with those of the Greek Church. The principal objection to the method is that of repetition, since each of the Fathers treats much the same doctrinal points as his predecessors, in order to supplement their teaching. But at least this order will enable us to record most of the important texts that have to do with our incorporation in Christ. And it is part of our purpose to render this service to Christian piety.

Besides, this procedure seems more theological. The Fathers are authorities in the Church, authentic witnesses of the Faith. In order to learn the doctrine as God has stated it, we must hear it from their lips.

Of course, as we said in the beginning, we do not intend to repeat all that they have said; that would be a task entirely too great, particularly for less ancient times. Nor do we propose to retrace the development of the doctrine of the Mystical Body in an exact historical order. Research in this field of history is not sufficiently advanced to enable us to detect the affinities of doctrine and the ramifications of varied influences. We shall note any indications of such influences that may appear, but our primary aim is to gather the ever-increasing

[209]

measure of grain from the hands of those whom God has appointed His faithful stewards.

Semen est verbum Dei. The word of God fell upon our earth like a seed; and a seed is made to sprout and to grow. Of this growth, which is the development of Christian doctrine, we have said a few words in the introduction to the first part of this work. But the delicacy of the subject prompts us to return to it again.

Up to the death of the last Apostle, that is to say, during the entire period covered by the Scriptures, the deposit of doctrine could be augmented by the addition of new truths. Now that the age of revelation is closed, growth can henceforth consist only in a fuller understanding and clearer expression of a deposit which itself remains unchanged. What has hitherto been known only implicitly, will now be stated explicitly; there will be a fuller appreciation of the meaning, the beauty, and the unity of what until now has been only imperfectly and dimly perceived; consequences will be drawn, the richness of the truth will be presented in detail, parts will be linked together, and a more systematic, more satisfactory exposition can be built up. But the doctrine remains ever the same; it is simply given a more precise expression.

Preposterous, some may say. How can men express God's message better than God Himself? But why not, if God speaks through men? This fact must ever be borne in mind when we speak of Tradition. True, the Church is not inspired as the Scriptures are. But she is assisted by God; and if He wills to express His message more clearly through her than He has done in the Scriptures, who will dare to say Him nay? Is He not Master of His light?

To know whether He has done this is another question, a question that cannot be answered by *a priori* reasoning, but only by examining what has actually taken place.

It would appear that He has not done so for the doctrine of the Mystical Body, at least as far as energy of expression and richness of formulas are concerned. No document of Tradition can match the inspired texts of St. Paul and St. John for fullness of meaning, impressiveness, or directness. But, while there is no need for development in vigor of expression, yet the scientific and systematic growth comes only by gradual stages. God, it seems, has reserved to men the task of shaping His message into a body of doctrine, into a theology.

This is the process that we shall consider in these pages. It is a slow and patient process. Such is the law of things human; and the God who became man, the God who has brought His light into our souls, has willed that His doctrine, too, should become something human.

Man is not completely himself unless he is constantly striving to realize himself more fully. His identity with himself consists largely in a search for himself, in a building of himself. He must grow in order to live; to remain immobile would be to grow rigid in death. Paradoxical though the expression may appear, it is perfectly true that for man the radical suppression of all change would be an absolute change, for it would mean the suppression of himself.

Within us, therefore, Christian doctrine is in a state of growth, of progress. What does this mean, except that it must grow as we grow? Not that God could not have given us the doctrine, perfect and complete, from the outset; He could, but His goodness has prompted Him rather to give us one that is perfectly suited to our being, which is not made all at once.

Man is subject to time; he is subject to progress; and to these supernatural truth is likewise subject insofar as that truth is in man. Human progress is affected by a thousand circumstances, by differences of mentality and of race, by historical events. The progress of truth will be influenced in like manner. All that happens here below, especially factors of an intellectual and affective order, systems of philosophy, different ways of thinking and feeling, even heresies — in short, all that can react upon the minds of men will affect the development of truth.

Real as these influences are, however, they can have only a secondary importance. Since they exist and since God has willed that they should exist, we shall mention them wherever we can detect their presence. But we must state very clearly, and repeat very often in the chapters which follow, that such influences do not explain the progress of the doctrine. If God has deigned to make use of these factors, they may have caused Christian teaching to develop, at a given period, in this or that particular direction, to present certain charateristics, a specific emphasis, a special nuance. But they are not and cannot be either the force that causes the advance or the special Providence that guarantees the truth and authenticity of the progress.

Christian dogma has its life and its power of growth within; it makes use of human causes, but it is not their toy. It lives because it is divine truth, because it is Christ, ever communicating Himself more and more fully as light and knowledge. It lives because, being transcendent truth expressed in human concepts, it is ever more beautiful than anything we can say of it, so that as our knowledge grows, we realize that it must still be studied more profoundly.

And, just as it possesses within itself its own principle of growth, so Christian dogma contains within itself the criterion that passes judgment upon the legitimacy of its development. The two, indeed, are one and the same: they are Christ, Christ dwelling in His brethren; that is to say, in the Church. Hence it is the Church alone that can adequately effect and definitely authenticate doctrinal progress.

With this point we close our introduction to the study of Tradition. Just as doctrinal progress comes only from Christ, so it has its force and its fullness only in Christ. But while it is true that Christ lives in all Christians, He does so only through the priesthood and the teaching Church, the *magisterium;* and the priesthood and the *magisterium* are not complete unless they include the entire episcopate and the Pope. The progress will be accomplished by the Christians: by the saints, the faithful, the theologians, etc. But it will be accomplished by all these only through union with and submission to the *magisterium;* and it will not be final until the *magisterium* shall have spoken, or rather, until Christ shall have spoken in the *magisterium.*

Chapter I

The First Witnesses. St. Ignatius of Antioch and the Unity of the Church in Christ

><

I. *The Apostolic Fathers.* St. Clement and the unity of the Church; St. Polycarp, Hermas. The *Didache* and the Eucharist. Insistence upon ecclesiastical unity.

II. *Ignatius of Antioch,* the man of unity: unity with Christ, unity of Christians among themselves. Like Christ, this unity is both visible and spiritual.

a) *Visible unity* of the Church. The bishop; the necessity of communion with the hierarchy; the beginnings of canon law.

b) *Spiritual unity,* the effect of visible unity. It is the unity of Christ, a divine unity, coming from the Holy Trinity. "That they may be one."

c) Conclusion: the Pauline complement of St. John's teaching. Tradition.

III. The *Epistle of Barnabas;* Christ and the Church foretold in the Scriptures. The *Second Epistle of Clement:* the Church pre-existent.

IV. *The Apologists.* The *Epistle to Diognetus;* a few words of St. Justin.

I

AFTER THE inspired writers, the first Christian authors are the Apostolic Fathers and the Apologists. These we shall study in the present chapter without making any distinction as yet between Greeks and Latins, for at this early period the doctrines differ but slightly.

To speak first of the more important group, the Apostolic Fathers are Christian writers of the first and early second centuries, writers whose teaching can be considered a fairly immediate echo of the preaching of the Apostles. Although somewhat indefinite, the term *Apostolic Fathers* is a convenient

[213]

title used to designate a group of authors whose works bear a certain mutual resemblance and who are themselves especially venerable by reason of their antiquity. These are the authors of the *Epistle of Barnabas* and of the *Didache*, St. Clement of Rome, St. Ignatius of Antioch, St. Polycarp, Hermas, and a few others who are either of minor importance or whose right to be ranked with the above-mentioned writers is not generally conceded.

However, they do not all treat the doctrine of the Mystical Body with equal fullness and richness. Most of them scarcely refer to it, and for these a brief mention will suffice here.

The earliest document of the Apostolic Fathers which can be dated with some certainty is the letter of St. Clement of Rome to the Church of Corinth. It was written about the year 96 or 97. It has almost nothing to say about the Mystical Body. Clement, the bishop of Rome, and a true Roman, shows himself primarily a man of government. His letter is an exhortation to order and to obedience. "All must be done according to order," he declares;[1] the phrase is a perfect summary of the letter.

Indeed the exhortation was necessary. The Church of Corinth, which seems to have been peculiarly subject to shocks and disturbances, was once again in turmoil at the end of the first century, as it had been forty years earlier in the time of Paul. Once again factious members had aroused the Christian community against its lawful pastors, and the church was on the verge of anarchy.

Against these dissensions Pope St. Clement opposes a lesson of unity, just as St. Paul had done before. But his letter is not the stirring appeal for unity that the Apostle voiced in his Epistles to the Corinthians. It is rather a just remonstrance uttered with calm. It cites as examples the excellent hierarchical order maintained in the Roman legions, and the marvelous organization of the human body. There is scarcely more than a passing reminder that schism is an attack against the body of Christ, that the factious members are tearing their own body asunder when they disrupt the unity of the Church, and that by sinning against unity, they sin against God, whose will it is to unite all Christians in Himself.

[214]

Undoubtedly this teaching includes the essential features of the doctrine of the Mystical Body: unity, unity of life, unity proceeding from God, unity by incorporation in Christ. But the emphasis is so slight that there is no reason for our dwelling upon it.

The same is also true of the letter of St. Polycarp to the Church of Philippi. The most that can be said is that it contains a few allusions to the Mystical Body.

The *Pastor* of Hermas is somewhat richer in indications. We may note, for example, that it insists upon the unity of the Church by comparing it to a single body, a single person, or again to a tower whose stones are so closely joined together that the whole seems to constitute one solid rock.

Having mentioned these writings briefly, let us now turn our attention to two other more fruitful sources of doctrine.

The first of these is the *Didache*, or *Doctrine of the Twelve Apostles*. This tiny book was discovered only sixty years ago, and its date, its origin, and even its true nature have not as yet been established with absolute certainty. At all events the work is very ancient, and informs us in considerable detail concerning the life of certain Christian communities at the end of the first century.

The *Didache* does not make explicit mention of the Mystical Body, but its teaching regarding the Eucharist is permeated with the doctrine. As St. Paul had taught so forcefully: "We many are one body, for we all partake of the one bread" (1 Cor. 10:17), so the *Didache* inculcates Catholic unity, of which the Blessed Sacrament is the efficacious sign. This doctrine of unity, though still incomplete, at times finds expression in terms of magnificent fullness and depth.

> We thank Thee, our Father, for the life and knowledge that Thou hast made known to us through Jesus, Thy Son. Glory to Thee forever.
> As this broken bread was scattered over the mountains, and was gathered together and is become one; so may Thy Church be gathered together from the ends of the earth into Thy Kingdom; for to Thee is glory and power through Jesus Christ forever.[2]
> When ye are filled, give thanks thus: "We thank Thee, holy Father, because of Thy holy name that Thou hast made to

dwell in our hearts, and because of the knowledge, and faith, and immortality that Thou hast made known to us through Jesus, Thy Son. Glory to Thee forever."[3]

O Lord, remember Thy Church, to deliver her from all evil, and to perfect her in Thy love, and gather her from the four winds, made holy, into Thy kingdom which Thou hast prepared for her. For Thine is the power and the glory forever. Let grace come, and let this world pass.[4]

These passages, like those to which we refer in the works of the other Apostolic Fathers, with the exception of the *Epistle of Barnabas* and the *Second Epistle of Clement*, present the truth of the Mystical Body in the form of a doctrine of ecclesiastical unity. The unity of the Church is most perfect, say St. Clement, St. Polycarp, and Hermas. The *Didache* specifies that this unity is effected by the very Body of Christ.

II

St. Ignatius of Antioch completes the doctrine. The unity of the Church, he tells us, is one with the unity of Christ Himself. In order to understand clearly the holy bishop's teaching, we must recall the circumstances in which it was proposed. It was during the reign of Trajan, at a time when the Church of Asia Minor was menaced from every side, by persecution without, and by fomenters of schism and discord within. Ignatius, the bishop of Antioch, had been arrested — the circumstances of his arrest are not known — and a band of soldiers, whom he calls ten leopards on account of their cruelty, were bringing him to Rome to be thrown to the beasts. At times the caravan was halted by forced delays, and bishops would come from nearby cities to salute the martyr in the name of their churches. Ignatius took advantage of these brief respites to send his last recommendations to the young churches of the surrounding country. We still possess these letters; their authenticity is beyond all criticism and we can still feel Ignatius' soul vibrant in them.

At these supreme moments, he has but one thought: unity, the unity of Christ. The word *one* (ἕν), and its compounds recur at every moment, and the appeal for unity is expressed without ceasing. For himself, Ignatius aspires to unity with

Christ; for the Churches, he prays with all his soul for the
unity that will hold the faithful together, for unity in Christ.
First of all, unity with Christ. Ignatius longs for death, or,
to bring out more clearly the relation of these phrases to the
doctrine of the Mystical Body, we should say that the member
yearns to be forever joined with the Head. Like Paul before
him, he writes his *cupio dissolvi* — to disappear and to go to
the Saviour. This is his one desire; his one fear for himself is
that some ill-advised intercession may rob him of martyrdom.

> Suffer me to be the food of the beasts, for through them I
> can possess God. I am the wheat of God, and I am ground by
> the teeth of the beasts, that I may be found the pure bread
> of Jesus Christ. . . . Then shall I be truly a disciple of Jesus
> Christ, when the world shall no longer see even my body.[5]

He wishes henceforth to be only in Christ:

> My love has been crucified, and within me there is no fire
> of desire for material things. But there is in me a water that
> lives and speaks, and says to me from within: "Come to the
> Father."[6]
> I seek Him who died for us; I desire Him who rose for us;
> the pains of birth are upon me. Suffer me, my brothers, do not
> keep me from life. . . . Let me imitate the sufferings of my
> God. If anyone has Christ within him, let him consider what
> I wish, and let him sympathize with me.[7]

And amid these burning words, the aspiration returns frequently, insistently: to reach God, to possess Christ.

Ignatius is obsessed by this desire for union, and when he
thinks of the Christian communities, almost the only blessing
he can wish them is union. He says himself that he is the man
of unity, and he raises his voice in a loud, ringing cry of warning to these young churches which he sees surrounded by
wolves, to draw close to their pastors in unity.

> I cried out, when I was among you; I spoke with a loud
> voice, the voice of God: "Heed the bishop, the priests, the
> deacons."
> Some thought that I said this because I had foreknowledge
> of certain factions. But He is my witness for whom I am bound,
> that I knew it not from human flesh. The Spirit told it to me,
> saying: "Do nothing without the bishop; watch over your
> flesh as the temple of God; love union, flee from divisions, be

ye imitators of Jesus Christ, as He also was of His Father."
I have done my part, as a man set on unity.[8]

As we shall see, this unity is the supernatural cohesion which
proceeds from Christ and makes of the entire Mystical Body
a single organism. And, as Ignatius frequently tells us, this
unity has the same two aspects, one corporal, the other spiritual, that we find in the Saviour. In this unity, as in Christ,
the corporal and the spiritual are intimately united; more
than that, they are, in this unity, only the prolongation of
what they are in Him.

In their own way, even the heretics bore witness to this
solidarity between the Head and the members. Just as they
denied the physical reality of the Body and Blood of Jesus,
and saw in the flesh of the Saviour merely an appearance —
whence their name "Docetists" — so too did they rise in
rebellion against the visible hierarchy. In the words of St.
Ignatius, they refused to recognize any corporal element either
in the historical Christ or in the Mystical Christ. Consequently, in all his letters Ignatius insists both upon the concrete reality of Christ and upon the concrete reality of Christian unity. This last is the point that interests us.

The visible unity of the Church, says St. Ignatius, is as
necessary as the visible flesh of Christ. The faithful must pray
together, round the same altar, breaking the same bread, professing the same beliefs, remaining in concord, and above all
by submitting to the same head, in order that they may be
united with the Lord. This last is the most essential. The
visible and "corporal" unity of the Church is incarnated in the
clergy, and primarily in the bishop.

> Whoever does anything without the bishop, and priests, and
> deacons, is not pure in conscience.[9]
> Let no one, without the bishop, do anything that pertains
> to the Church; let that Eucharist be considered true at which
> the bishop presides.[10]
> Take care to use one Eucharist, for the flesh of our Lord
> Jesus Christ is one, and one chalice for the union of His blood,
> one altar, as there is one bishop with the priests and the
> deacons.[11]

For the remission of sins, as for the Eucharist, one must be
in communion with the bishop. Baptism requires his inter-

[218]

vention, and even marriages are not to be celebrated without his approval. All, priests and deacons as well as the faithful, must obey him. And they must love him. In a word, the sacramental life of the community and the visible unity of the Church are centered in the bishop. Even in these early times, the relations of the bishop with his flock were determined by a set of regulations which may be termed the first draft of a canon law.

But one must hear how Ignatius promulgates this nascent canon law. It has nothing of the usual dryness of human codes; it is formulated in sentences of fervent, even exalted love. Ignatius uses no harsh or crude figures to describe the order that he requires; he speaks rather of music and of harmony, of voices blending in the unity of a single hymn. Is there not question of members that are grafted into the unity of a single body?

For the external unity of the Church is but the body and the armature of an internal unity, of a "spiritual" unity, to borrow the saint's own expression. This latter is the perfection of unity, the guardian of the Church, and the force of its prayers; it is a holy, pure, immaculate unity, or just "unity"; the word itself is eloquent enough, and like Ignatius, the Fathers also use the word absolutely, to show how this unity is to be understood and how necessary it is.

For it is the unity of Christ. The bishops who watch over it are but intermediaries; the source is in Christ and in God. This unity is made of the Christ-life that comes to us through the Eucharist; it is sealed by the blood and passion of the Saviour.

It is this unity with Christ that sanctifies the entire life of the faithful. Because of this unity, they must perform all their actions in Jesus Christ, they must consider one another only in Jesus Christ; Jesus Christ must be their faith, their hope, their charity, their life, their inseparable life, their all, and if they wish to remain chaste, their motive must be respect for the flesh of Christ.

This unity is produced in our souls by God Himself, and in an especial manner by the Holy Spirit. It bears so plainly the mark of its origin that in order to describe it more fully, Ignatius regularly mentions it in connection with the persons of the Holy Trinity.

> . . . subject to the bishop as to the grace of God, and to the clergy as to the law of Jesus Christ.[12]
> Live, then, in a divine manner; reverence one another; and let no one consider his neighbor according to the flesh, but in Jesus Christ; love one another in all things. Let there be nothing between you that can divide you, but be united with the bishop and with those who are set over you for an example and a lesson of immortality.
> As the Lord did nothing without His Father to whom He was united, neither by Himself nor through His apostles, so do ye nothing without the bishop and the priests.[13]
> Reverence the deacons as Jesus Christ, and also the bishop who represents the Father, and the priests as the assembly of God and the college of apostles.[14]
> Obey the bishop as Jesus Christ obeys the Father, and the priests as if they were the apostles. Reverence the deacons as the commandment of God.[15]

It would be easy to cite a score of similar passages. The terms of the comparison would vary, for, as can be seen from the preceding texts, while the dogma itself was fixed and established before the death of the last Apostle, definite and scientific formulas for its expression and explanation to the faithful had not yet been developed. Nevertheless, beneath the verbal differences, the same thought is ever recurring: the unity of the faithful ascends, through the bishop and through Christ, to God. First, there is the unity of the three divine Persons; then, through Christ and through the Church who possesses Christ, this divine unity establishes in the faithful an analogous, participated unity, which is the unity of the Mystical Body.

This is the operation of grace, and Jesus had already described the various steps of the process in the same way during His discourse after the Last Supper, when He asked the Father: "That they may be one in Me, as We are one" (John 17:22,23). The last letters of the martyr Ignatius, who like Christ is about to offer himself up for the Church, contain the same words and the same thoughts that Christ Himself expressed during that last discourse before He entered upon His passion.

[220]

Thus Tradition takes its place as the exact continuation of the Scriptures; Ignatius' doctrine repeats that of John. But Tradition does more than repeat; it completes the Scriptures. In the teaching of St. John, one point had been left vague and indefinite; namely, the visible aspect of the Church's unity and the role of the hierarchy. This point is explained by St. Ignatius. Yet, such is the coherence of the whole that even this completion is borrowed from other passages of Scripture which had themselves been awaiting the explanation that they receive by means of this juxtaposition. We refer to parts of the teaching of St. Paul.

Several features of the doctrine of St. Ignatius remind one of the Pauline Epistles in general. There is the same frequent mention of the "body," the same fondness for the phrase "in Christ," the same exuberance of expression; but of especial significance here is the fact that Ignatius manifests the same solicitude for ecclesiastical organization which the Apostle shows in his pastoral Epistles. In these last letters, St. Paul seems to be concerned exclusively with this organization; he feels that his own course is run, and in writing to the young bishops who are to be his successors, he hastens to instruct them in their office and duties. He appears to have forgotten his doctrine of the Mystical Body; if he refers to it at all, he does so only in passing. It has ceased to be the center to which all else is directed.

Implicitly, however, it still remains the soul of all. This Ignatius shows us when he explains what St. Paul says on the subject of the hierarchy in the light of St. John's doctrine of unity. The function of the hierarchy, he tells us, is precisely to produce and to incarnate unity; it is through the hierarchy that the union of the faithful among themselves and with Christ is established and maintained.

Thus the synthesis is reached. Nothing has been added to the revealed truth, but its cohesion becomes more evident, and its own light has become visible. The work of theology has begun.

The principal contribution which the Apostolic Fathers make to the doctrine of the Mystical Body is their teaching on the subject of unity. "That they may be one." This was the last prayer of Jesus during His mortal life, and this is the exact point at which the Church enters in. She is the prolongation of Christ; she teaches, and her teaching is the Master's teaching continued.

Certainly this unity, as inculcated by the Apostolic Fathers, is something visible and tangible, just as Christ Himself was visible and tangible. But it is more. Before all else, it is a unity of life, a mysterious, interior unity, a supernatural and divine unity, as was Christ. Such is the teaching of St. Ignatius and of the other Apostolic Fathers who treat of the same subject.

However, they do not tell us this *ex professo;* they do not devote a separate treatise or special chapter to the explanation of the unity of the Mystical Body. Unity must be within that which it unites, as the yeast must be within the dough that it leavens. So it is with the doctrine of unity in St. Ignatius and the other Apostolic Fathers. It enters so perfectly into their general teaching that one might fail to detect its presence. Apparently they speak only of avoiding schisms, and think only of peace and obedience, in fine, of ecclesiology. That is true, but the interesting point is this: the doctrine of unity forms one whole with the truths that it serves to explain.

III

We have reserved until now two documents which are rather similar in their references to the Mystical Body: the *Epistle of Barnabas* and the *Second Epistle of Clement.*

The *Epistle of Barnabas,* though its real author is not the Apostle, nevertheless dates from a very early period, probably from the beginning of the second century. It enjoyed such authority in the Church of Syria that it was numbered among the sacred books of Scripture, and is to be found immediately after these in the *Codex Sinaiticus.* It speaks with some emphasis of the union of Christ with the faithful and of the influence which Christ exercises upon the faithful by all the acts of His life. In His boundless love for them, He has made them temples, holy temples, perfect and spiritual. He has sanctified them, renewed them, created them afresh, by a total re-creation.

Take heed, that the temple of the Lord may be splendidly built.

How? Listen: it is by receiving the remission of sins and by hoping in the name [of the Lord] that we are made new, being created again from the beginning. Thus it is that God truly dwells within us, in the abode which we are.

And how is this? [Within us dwell] His word as the object of our faith, the vocation of His promise, the wisdom of His judgments, the precepts of His teaching; Himself dwells in us; He opens the door of the temple (which is the mouth [of the preachers]), to us who were enslaved to death, giving us repentance, and leads us into the incorruptible temple. For he that desires to be saved regards not the man, but Him that dwells in him and speaks in him, amazed that he has never heard or even wished to hear the words of Him who speaks by the mouth [of the preacher].

This is the spiritual temple that is being built for the Lord.[16]

So powerful and so real is this new creation that the first creation was but a type of it.

When He renewed us by the remission of sins, He gave us a new kind of being, that we should have the souls of children, as if He were creating us anew.

For it is of us that Scripture speaks, when [God] says to the Son: "Let Us make man to Our image and likeness. . . ." And when He saw how fair a creation we were, the Lord said: "Increase and multiply, and fill the earth" (Gen. 1:26,28). These words were spoken to the Son. But I shall also show thee how, faithful to His word to us, He has in these last days made a second creation. For the Lord says: "Behold, I make the last things as the first" (Cf. Matt. 19:30; 20:16).[17]

We naturally note the phrase: "It is of us that Scripture speaks when God says to the Son," etc. In this passage the author, following the lead of St. Paul, as he often does in the exegetical portion of the epistle, considers the Old Testament as directed toward Christ and toward those who are Christ's, in other words, toward the Mystical Christ. His explanations may be involved at times, but his conviction is clear. In this epistle we can observe the first beginnings in Tradition of an exegetical method which has its foundations in Scripture and which was to be often used by the Fathers — the method of interpreting the sacred text in terms of the Mystical Body. The same remark may be made concerning another work

[223]

which is generally included among the writings of the Apostolic Fathers, and which is known as the *Second Epistle of Clement*, although the document is in fact neither an epistle nor the work of St. Clement. Its date and author are unknown, and it is a homily, the oldest we possess. Like the *Epistle of Barnabas*, it, too, was ranked with the Holy Books in the Church of Syria, and is included with them in the *Codex Alexandrinus*.

Again like the *Epistle of Barnabas*, it teaches that the book of Genesis, in telling the story of the first creation, also relates the second, by which all Christians are made one with Christ in the Church. We quote an entire chapter of the "epistle":

> So, brethren, if we do the will of God our Father, we shall belong to the first Church, the spiritual Church which was created before the sun and the moon. But if we do not the Lord's will, we shall be included in the words of Scripture: "My house is become a den of robbers" (Jer. 7:11). Let us choose therefore to belong to the Church of life, that we may be saved.
>
> You are not ignorant, I think, that the living Church is "the body of Christ" (Eph. 1:22,23), for Scripture says, "God created man male and female" (Gen. 1:27); the male is Christ, the female is the Church. And the Scriptures and the Apostles affirm that the Church belongs not to the present, but has been in existence since the beginning. For she was spiritual, like our Jesus, and she has appeared in the last days in order to save us.
>
> And the Church which was spiritual has appeared in the flesh of Christ, showing us that if any of us keep the Church in the flesh without corrupting her, he will receive her in the Holy Spirit. For this flesh is the copy of the Spirit; no one who has defiled the copy shall have part in the original. This, my brethren, is what the Scripture means: Have respect for the flesh, that you may have part in the Spirit. Now, if we say that the flesh is the Church and that the spirit is Christ, then he that abuses the flesh abuses the Church; such a one shall not have part in the spirit, which is Christ.
>
> Such is the life and incorruptibility in which our flesh can have part through union with the Holy Spirit, and no man can express or tell of the things "that the Lord hath prepared" (1 Cor. 2:9) for His elect.[18]

It must be admitted that these speculations on the subject of the pre-existing Church are rather crudely expressed, and may at times appear strange. In a later day, some writers were to carry the idea to exaggerated lengths and so become heretics, while we shall meet with others in the course of our study whose attempts at explanation were not the most felicitous. But is it not clear that the truth expressed in these sentences of the epistle is the same as that taught by Paul and John from the very beginning; namely, that in the divine economy Christ and the Church were in existence previously to anything that exists now, that with Christ they make up but one Mystical Christ, and that this is the mystery prepared from the beginning, the mystery which is so great, in Christ and in the Church?[19]

It is quite true that the indications furnished by the *Second Epistle of Clement,* like those contained in the *Epistle of Barnabas,* are in themselves few and of little importance as far as the Mystical Body is concerned. But as regards the exegetical method according to which Scripture is interpreted in terms of the Mystical Body, they mark the first step in a tradition. It is especially for this reason that they are deserving of consideration.

IV

Next in order after the Apostolic Fathers should come the Apologists. These were Christians of the second or third centuries, usually men of considerable learning, who undertook to demonstrate the excellence, purity, and antiquity of the Christian religion and to answer the calumnies that were raised against it.

However, their very purpose was not apt to lead them to speak of the Mystical Body. They have scarcely anything to say in this connection beyond the affirmation of God's immensity and of His presence in all things. This last thought was dear to them, and they emphasized it all the more willingly, since it was calculated to appeal to the more virtuous and better educated of their readers. At the same time, the idea bears some analogy — we do not say more — to the doctrine of the Mystical Body. At a later date, certain Fathers of the Church make use of it to explain how the Word is united to the whole human universe through the sacred humanity which He has assumed.

The following is one of the most characteristic passages dealing with this subject. It is taken from the *Apology* which is attributed to Melito, and which has been published by Cureton. The document dates from the third century, being written shortly after the year 200, according to Rauschen.

> Therefore I counsel thee that thou shouldst know thyself, and shouldst know God. For understand how there is within thee that which is called the soul: by it the eye seeth, by it the ear heareth, by it the mouth speaketh: and how it employeth the whole body. And whensoever He pleaseth to remove the soul from the body, it falleth and goeth to decay. From this, therefore, which exists within thyself and is invisible, understand how God also moveth the whole world by His power, like the body, and that whensoever it pleaseth Him to withdraw His power, the whole world also, like the body, will fall and go to decay.[20]

It would not be too difficult to find like passages in the writings of other Apologists. But they are not striking enough to justify the multiplication of citations. We might stop here, were it not for the *Epistle to Diognetus* and the writings of St. Justin.

In the former, we must note the beautiful and powerful sentences that exalt Christian charity and the close union that binds the faithful together. These constitute an indirect and remote testimony to be added to what has been said in the preceding pages on the subject of charity and unity.

Next we must mention St. Justin. Born of pagan parents, Justin was converted about 130. Of his writings, his two *Apologies* and the *Dialogue with Trypho* are extant. This last work contains a few words that are of interest to us. Justin declares that the Lord is come to take up all things, to sum up all things in Himself. Thus, he explains, the robe which, as it is written, Jesus will wash in the blood of the grape (Gen. 49:11), "consists of those men who believe in Christ and in whom abideth the seed of the Word."[21]

While the expression is not very significant in itself, we wished to cite it on account of its resemblance to the texts already quoted from the *Epistle of Barnabas* and the *Second Epistle of Clement*.

[226]

Chapter II

St. Irenaeus and the "Recapitulation"

⊱⊰

I. *St. Irenaeus.* Irenaeus and Ignatius of Antioch. Both teach the same doctrine of the Mystical Body, but the former expresses it differently, in opposition to Gnosticism, which was the most prominent heresy of his day.

II. 1. *The "Recapitulation" in the teaching of Irenaeus.* The meaning of the term: first in general, then as applied to the Mystical Body. The theory forms the nucleus, both of Irenaeus' refutation of Gnosticism and of his own theology. It expresses our incorporation in Christ, the second Adam. It represents God taking back His creation into union with Himself; it includes the whole of the Old Testament, even Adam, and the entire ancient economy. Therefore Christ contains and really sums up all: all ages, all things, all mankind.

2. Hence the Church is His fullness. She is a visible reality, and possesses an invisible life. In her is wrought our divinization in Christ. The role of the Holy Spirit. By Him we become what Christ is. Thus the recapitulation brings all things back, through Christ, to the first principle, which is the Father.

III. *Conclusion.* Irenaeus presents a rich doctrinal synthesis, which integrates and unifies many different dogmas. But it is still too dependent upon the imagination, and it lacks accuracy of expression. Hence the doctrinal progress must continue.

IV. *Appendix.* Melito of Sardis and St. Methodius of Olympus. The doctrine of the two Adams. Various traits which appear to have been common to many writers of Asia Minor in treating of the doctrine of the Mystical Body.

I

THE EARLIEST general exposition of the doctrine of the Mystical Body is furnished by St. Irenaeus, who may be styled the first theologian. On this particular point Irenaeus belongs to the tradition of the Greek school, for this future bishop of Lyons came to Gaul as a grown man. His childhood and youth were spent in Asia Minor, at Smyrna and in the vicinity; and he received his instruction in the faith from the martyr-bishop of Smyrna, Polycarp, whose letter to the Philippians we have mentioned, and to whom Ignatius addressed one of his epistles.

After his elevation to the see of Lyons about 177, he remained faithful to his early training. Indeed, there is a striking resemblance between him and Ignatius of Antioch, for Irenaeus was to the closing years of the second century what the Syrian bishop had been to the end of the first century: the great voice of Tradition, proclaiming communion with the episcopate, that is, the unity of the Church, as the only means of escape from apostasy and error.

But, while this doctrine of ecclesiastical unity becomes for both a doctrine of the Mystical Body, each explains it in his own way. Ignatius' letters are short, breathless cries of alarm; Irenaeus, on the other hand, has left long doctrinal expositions, the work of patient erudition and systematic reflection. More comprehensive than Ignatius, though lacking the latter's power of intuition, Irenaeus embodies his ecclesiology in a general synthesis of the divine plan here below. Hence his doctrine of the Mystical Body is more complete.

In fact, heresy had forced him to adopt this course. For, like Ignatius, he, too, had to deal with heresy; with this difference, however, that during the intervening century error had grown and spread like a thicket of brambles, and could now be got rid of only by a process of complete eradication. Gnosticism, against which Irenaeus had to do battle, is the most inextricable system, or rather hodgepodge of systems, that has ever existed. Theogony and cosmogony, world history and ascetical doctrine, philosophy and science — to this confusion were added, and not without alteration, Christian truths and passages from Scripture.

To give a much simplified description of the system, we may say that its point of departure is a certain contempt for matter, and by way of consequence, also for the God who created matter, the God of the Old Testament. Our material universe is the result of a sin. In the beginning there existed a world of spiritual and divine beings called "eons," which were more or less harmoniously co-ordinated according to the various systems, and operated either in pairs or as isolated individuals. Now it chanced that one of these eons became dissatisfied with his lot and wished to rise higher. This disrupted the equilibrium of the divine spheres, and the offender was cast out.

It was of this disorder that our universe was born, the sinful work of an inferior and disgruntled god. However, by reason of its origin, particles of the Divine are scattered throughout the universe. These could not be left forever in exile; so another eon came to their rescue, and took, not a material body, of course — for matter is evil — but the appearance of a material body (hence the name "Docetism"), and descended into the world of matter. They in whom these divine particles are found will be saved, and the saviour-eon will carry them away to glory. Meanwhile, he has given them an esoteric doctrine, a *gnosis,* concerning the divine world and the means of returning thither. It is this *gnosis* that has given its name to Gnosticism. Into this general pattern, which is common to practically all Gnostic systems, each sect wove new explanations and new complications. The tangle has not been unraveled to this day!

Such were the errors that were spreading in the Rhone valley in the time of Irenaeus. To him fell the task of checking their advance, and he did not shrink from the combat. The heresy was complication itself. Nothing daunted, he set himself to unravel it with a view to its refutation. Even the Christian dogmas had not as yet received their complete and definite expression, but he did not hesitate to try his hand at a synthesis. There rose up in his young and courageous soul the ardor of Christian thought, a spirit that has no fear of error, since it knows that through Tradition it possesses the truth as a family heritage, and that through the teaching Church, which is also Tradition, truth sustains Christian thought.

Now it is at the very heart of the theology of Irenaeus, as of the teaching of Ignatius, that we find the doctrine of the Mystical Body.

II. § 1

And the heart of Irenaeus' theology is the theory of the "recapitulation." This theory traces its origins to the earliest Christian teaching, since it is merely a development of the Scriptural doctrine of the two Adams. Now, however, it becomes a theological system, in which the parallel of the two Adams is made the basis of a general exposition of the economy of salvation.

The term *recapitulate* has so many different senses that it necessarily remains somewhat indefinite. Fortunately, we need not detail all its manifold meanings; we shall be content to show what Irenaeus wishes to teach us, by its means, concerning the Mystical Body.

As a first general approximation, we may say that by the word *recapitulation* as applied to the work of Christ, Irenaeus means a sort of recommencement in the opposite direction by which God, reversing, as it were, the process whereby sin infected the earth, gathers together and reunites all creation, including matter, but especially man, in a new economy of salvation. He gathers up His entire work from the very beginning, to purify and sanctify it in His Incarnate Son, who in turn becomes for us a second stock and a second Adam. In Him, the first Adam and all his posterity are healed; the evil effects of disobedience are destroyed and as it were reversed by their contraries. Man recovers the holiness which was his at the beginning and he is divinized by union with the God from whom he came. As we see, the term presents many meanings: a résumé, a taking up of all since the beginning, a recommencement, a return to the source, restoration, reorganization, and incorporation under one Head. But these meanings are all related; in spite of their diversity they fit into one another, and even when expressed singly, each one suggests all the others.

Because of its wealth of meaning and its power of connotation, the idea of recapitulation was well fitted to serve as the center for a theology so fully developed as was that of Irenaeus. Indeed, he has recourse to this idea as well in refuting the

Gnostics as in formulating the truths of faith. He uses it to show that the heretics are wrong when they set up the New Testament in opposition to the Old, or when they maintain that matter is essentially evil. For he tells us that Christ came precisely in order to restore the entire Old Testament and all material creation in Himself, and to "recapitulate" them in His new alliance. Conversely, all of Christian doctrine, and even all of Christianity is summed up in this recapitulation that has been wrought by Christ. So certain is Irenaeus of this that he does not hesitate to insert the word into the very heart of the expositions of Christian belief which are scattered like so many brief symbols of faith throughout his works.

One such passage occurs at the beginning of the *Adversus Haereses*. When the author contrasts the marvelous unity of the faith with the multiplicity of the heretical fables for the first time, and hence at a significant moment, he uses the word to indicate the very purpose of Christianity. The passage is a profession of faith in the Trinity, followed by an exposition of the work of Redemption.

The Church, spread over the whole world even to the confines of the earth, has received from the Apostles and from their disciples faith in one God, the Father Almighty, who created heaven and earth and the sea and all that is in them; and in one Christ Jesus, the Son of God, who became incarnate for our salvation; and in the Holy Spirit, who by the prophets announced the dispositions and the comings, and the virgin birth, the passion, the resurrection from the dead, and the ascension into heaven in the flesh, of the beloved Christ Jesus our Lord, and His coming from the heavens in the glory of the Father to recapitulate all things, and to raise up all human flesh, in order that to Christ Jesus our Lord and God and Saviour and King, every knee may bend, according to the good pleasure of the unseen Father. . . . Having received this doctrine and this faith, as we have said, the Church, though spread over the whole world, keeps careful guard over them, as if she dwelt in only one house. And she believes these things [everywhere] in the same manner, as if she had but one soul and one heart, and she teaches them [everywhere] in the same way, as if she possessed but one mouth. For, though tongues differ throughout the world, yet the virtue of Tradition is one and the same. . . . As the sun, God's creature, is one and the same in the whole world, so the preaching of the truth shines everywhere and enlightens all men who wish to come to a knowledge of the truth.[1]

The *Epideixis,* or *Demonstration of the Preaching of the Gospel* contains a very similar passage. Here, too, it is in a rule of trinitarian faith that the recapitulation is mentioned.

> The second article is as follows: it is the Word of God, the Son of God, Jesus Christ our Lord, who appeared to the prophets in the form described in their oracles and according to the special disposition of the Father; [the Word] by whom all things were made; and who, in the fullness of time, to recapitulate and contain all things, became man, in order to destroy death, to manifest life and to restore union between God and man.[2]

Many other passages might be cited in which the idea of recapitulation plays the same central role in the exposition of Christian doctrine. They would not indeed prove that the word itself figured in the creed of St. Irenaeus, but merely that according to the Saint's theology the concept is a compendium of Christianity.

But we must continue. While the idea of recapitulation does not exactly coincide with that of the Mystical Body, it is very closely related to the latter. It explains how the Mystical Body is actually formed and how the salvation of the world is wrought in the Mystical Body. We may say that the idea of the Mystical Body, contained in the idea of recapitulation, constitutes the center of the theology of St. Irenaeus.

This last is the principal point to be established. We shall treat it at some length, explaining those passages which speak expressly of recapitulation by means of other passages where the idea is present, though the word itself is not mentioned. We shall see from the Saint's words how Christ purifies and divinizes the entire human race according to His own image, by taking it up wholly in Himself, in a manner that is mysterious but real.

In Christ, God the Creator has come to take up anew, in His own hands, as it were, the work of the six days. As Irenaeus often repeats, it is His own creation, τὸ ἴδιον πλάσμα, that the Word has recapitulated in Himself. He has come to us, not in His glory, but in a manner that is suited to us. At the Incarnation,

> He recapitulated in Himself the long history of men, summing up and giving us salvation, in order that we might receive again in Christ Jesus what we had lost in Adam, that is, the image and likeness of God.[3]

Longam hominum expositionem in seipso recapitulavit, in compendio nobis salutem praestans. What a magnificent image, if we may take it literally! The long development of our race is summed up in Christ, as the long stem attains its perfection in the flower, which in turn, through the mystery of the seed, contains the entire plant.

He is the second Adam, and He takes up again, "recapitulates," and saves the first Adam in Himself. His birth as well as His death reproduce, though in a quite different way, the history of Adam.

No being is neglected by grace, for all things must be taken up again and healed in Christ. As Irenaeus so wonderfully expresses it, Adam did not escape from the hands of God; even after the fall, they held him fast. Throughout the Old Testament, "The Word was ever present to the human race, until the day when He united Himself with His creature, and was made flesh";[4] it is as if He and the Holy Spirit were accustoming themselves to dwell among us, until He should come to take the lost sheep upon His shoulders.

So truly do the events of the Old Law prefigure the life of the Saviour that Christ's coming begins even with the patriarchs and the prophets. Irenaeus expresses the thought in a splendid image:

> The prophets foretold the sufferings of the martyrs. . . . And in their own persons they prefigured all these things for the love of God and for His Word. For, since they too were members of Christ, each of them in his capacity as member manifested Him whom, as prophet, he foretold. Together they are an image of the one Saviour, and foretell the events of His life. For, just as by our members the operation of the entire body is made manifest and as the figure of the whole man is shown not by one member but by all; so the prophets all pre-

figured the one Saviour, and each, in his capacity as member, foreshadowed some aspect of Christ.[5]

Jesus Christ recapitulates all the Old Testament and all the sacrifices that were offered therein. This He Himself said when He told the Jews of His generation that they would be held accountable for the blood of all the just shed on earth (Luke 11:50):

> Thus signifying that the blood of all the just and the prophets shed from the beginning would be recapitulated in Him.[6]

The Old Testament foreshadows, not Christ alone, but also the Christians, the future members of Christ.

> Just as we were prefigured and foretold [in the just of the Old Law], so are they reproduced in us, that is, in the Church, and receive the reward of their labors.[7]

For Christ, the Incarnate Word, is not subject to the same narrow limits of self as are other men. In addition to His incommunicable individuality, He possesses most intimate relationships with all. Thus, according to a view that is peculiar to our Saint, Christ passed through all the ages of a man's life in order to sanctify them all in Himself; thus, too, the events of His mortal life have a perpetual influence upon our justification. In Him, we have all been obedient unto death; in His Passion, we have all been roused from sleep, and when He ascended into heaven, we ascended with Him.

His work is one of solidarity and of unity. In dying, He traced the sign of the Cross upon all things, and, in the beautiful words uttered by one of the early Christians and recorded by Irenaeus, His two crucified arms, wide outstretched, were an appeal to union addressed to every nation.

Again, His work is one of renewal. "By fulfilling the will of His Father in us, He renews us from age unto the newness of Christ."[8] You may ask, explains the Saint:

> What, then, did the Lord bring at His coming? Know that He brought all newness, by bringing Himself, who had been foretold. For this was announced, that a Newness would come, to renew and give life to man.[9]

And His work is a universal and catholic work. In order to

sum up all things in Himself, Christ has become Head of the whole Church, and through her He continues His work of restoration in all times and in all peoples:

> Thus there is one God the Father, as we have shown, and one Christ Jesus our Lord, who comes in the entire Old Testament and recapitulates all things in Himself. But in all things He is also man, a creature of God; therefore He recapitulates man in Himself. The invisible is become visible, the incomprehensible is become comprehensible, and the impassible, passible; and the Word is become man, recapitulating all things in Himself. Thus, just as He is the first among heavenly and spiritual and invisible things, so also is He first among visible and corporal things. He takes the primacy to Himself, and by making Himself the Head of the Church, He will draw all things to Himself at the appointed time.[10]

This important passage constitutes a veritable formula of faith. The words, suggested by the first chapter of the Epistle to the Ephesians, show how the ecclesiology of St. Irenaeus is linked up with his theory of the recapitulation.

§ 2

For St. Irenaeus as for St. Ignatius, the Church is the continuation of Christ. Like the Saviour, she has a twofold character, a visible aspect and an invisible or spiritual aspect, and the two are but one.

Her visible character consists not so much in individual bishops as in the successions or genealogies of bishops. The reason is that since the days of Ignatius many years have passed, and it is now necessary to go back several generations before coming to the Apostles. The bond has been extended, but it has not been weakened in any way; it still unites the Church as closely as ever to the Saviour. Throughout his work Irenaeus insists upon this vital aspect of apostolic Tradition — upon the spiritual transfer, the communication of grace, which is effected through the episcopate. Union with the episcopal sees is necessary, he says, because it is this union that gives life. By abandoning this union,

> schismatics . . . lacerate and divide the great and glorious body of Christ, and do all in their power to kill it. . . . The true

gnosis is the doctrine of the Apostles, and the ancient organism of the church throughout the world, and the character of the Body of Christ according to the succession of the bishops to whom the Apostles entrusted each of the local churches.[11]

Since they have cut themselves off from the Church, schismatics are also cut off from the divine life. For Irenaeus cannot conceive any absolute separation of the two. Thus his ecclesiology and his theory of recapitulation, like the ecclesiology of St. Ignatius, lead to a doctrine of the deification of men.

In the "body" of Christ, the Holy Spirit continues the work that He began in Christ.

For through the prophets the Lord promised to send forth this Holy Spirit upon His servants and handmaidens, that they might prophesy. Thus the Spirit also descended upon the Son of God who had become the Son of Man, in order to become accustomed to dwell with Him in the human race, to repose in men and to abide in God's creatures, fulfilling in them the will of the Father and renewing them from age unto the newness of Christ.

Then after the Ascension, says Luke, He descended upon the Apostles with power, to bring life to all nations and to open to them the New Testament. Thus did they join together, to sing in every tongue a hymn to God, whilst the Spirit brought the scattered tribes into unity and offered the first-fruits of the nations to the Father. For the Lord had promised to send the Paraclete to unite us with God. For, just as it is impossible with dry flour to form one mass or one loaf without water, even so we many could not become one in Christ Jesus without the water that is from heaven. . . . For by baptism our bodies received that unity which is unto immortality, but our souls received it through the Spirit. . . . This is the gift that the Lord received from the Father and which He has given also to them that are united with Him, by sending His Holy Spirit upon the whole earth.[12]

The Church is the Spirit's field of activity. To her He communicates an eternal renewal and through the ages He is to her what the life-giving breath of God was to creation. "Where the Church is, there is the Spirit, and where the Spirit is, there is the Church and all grace." One cannot leave her without cutting himself off from life, and they that are not her members must die of hunger and thirst, since "they do not drink of the pure stream which flows from the body of Christ."[13]

In the Church, by Christ and by the Spirit is accomplished the divinization of the faithful. For according to Irenaeus, the Word of God became incarnate and He recapitulates us in Himself in order to make us what He is.

> The Lord has redeemed us by His Blood; He gave His soul for our souls and His flesh for our flesh, and sent forth the Spirit of the Father to bring about unity and communion between God and man. Through the Spirit He gave God to men, by His Incarnation He raised man to God, and in His coming He gave us lasting and true immortality through communion with Him. Thus all the teaching of the heretics is proven false. . . .
>
> For not in appearance only was He man, but in substance and in truth. . . . Nor would He have possessed the real flesh and blood whereby He redeemed us, had He not recapitulated in Himself the first creation of Adam. In vain therefore do the Valentinians claim that salvation does not include the flesh. . . .
>
> Wrong too are the Ebionites, who do not receive in their souls by faith the union of God and man, but persevere in the old leaven of the Law. They refuse to understand that the Holy Spirit came upon Mary and that the power of the Most High overshadowed her; and that therefore what is born of her is holy and the Son of the Most High God, the Father of all. In effecting the Incarnation, God has revealed a new birth, in order that as by our first birth we inherited death, so now by this [new] birth we might inherit life. These heretics reject the mixture of the heavenly wine; they wish only the water of this world, and do not receive the God who has come to unite Himself with them.[14]

Thus, as Irenaeus tells us in very powerful though somewhat imprecise language, recapitulation in Christ includes a communion of God and men, an infusion of divine life, a commingling of God and men in Christ.

At the creation, with His divine hands God had formed Adam to His own image, and in Adam He gave to all of us the same divine likeness. Adam lost this likeness, and we, too, have lost it in him; for we are all included in Adam. But, by the grace of God, what was thus destroyed in Adam is righted and restored, recapitulated, in Christ. "O man," writes Irenaeus,

> Since thou art the work of God, await the hand of thy Maker, who does all things for the best. . . . Offer Him a tractable and docile heart, and keep the form that He gives thee; have in thee some plasticity, lest by thy hardness thou lose the impress of His fingers. If thou keep it, thou wilt rise to perfection, for the artistry of God will hide the clay that is in thee. In thee His hands have fashioned thy substance; He will cover thee without and within with pure gold and silver, and He will so adorn thee that the King Himself will love thy beauty. . . . If therefore thou give Him what is thy own, that is, faith in Him and obedience, thou shalt receive His art, and shalt be the perfect work of God.[15]

This marvel is wrought by the second Adam.

> To believe, not only in the Father, but also in His Son, who has revealed Himself; for it is He who leads man to communion and to unity with God.[16]

This is the proper effect of the Incarnation.

> The Word made Himself like unto man, and made man like unto Himself, in order that by his likeness to the Son man might become precious in the eyes of the Father.[17]

But, for man to become thus precious in the Father's eyes, Christ must truly be the second Adam; that is to say, He must be like us in all things.

> Christ, as we have said, has united man to God. . . . For this it was necessary that the Mediator of God and men should possess the nature of both, in order to restore friendship and concord between them, to present man to God and to manifest God to man.
> For how could we share in the adoption of sons unless the Son had given us communion with the Son, and unless the Word had united Himself to us by becoming flesh? For this He came, in all ages, to restore all to communion with God.[18]

Irenaeus repeats over and over again that the false doctrines of the heretics concerning the mystery of the Incarnation and the recapitulation are in reality a denial of our elevation to the divine life.

> Those who say that He was only a man, the son of Joseph,

remain and die in the slavery of the first disobedience; they are not united to the Word of God the Father, nor do they receive freedom from the Son, according to His own words: "If the Son shall make you free, ye shall be free indeed" (John 8:36). But since they know not the Emmanuel born of the Virgin, they are deprived of His gift, which is eternal life. . . .

Some do not receive the gift of adoption, because they sneer at the pure Incarnation and birth of the Word of God. They rob man of his ascent to God and remain ungrateful to the Word of God who became incarnate for their sakes. For this is why the Word of God is man, and this is why the Son of God became the Son of Man, that man might possess the Word, receive adoption, and become the son of God.

In no other way could we receive incorruptibility and immortality except by being united with incorruptibility and immortality. But how could we be united with incorruptibility and immortality, unless incorruptibility and immortality had first become what we are, in order that what is corruptible might be absorbed by incorruptibility, and what is mortal by immortality, that so we might receive the adoption of sons?

God willed to be born, to be with us, to descend into the lower regions of the earth in order to find the lost sheep that is His own creature; He willed to ascend into heaven, to present to the Father this man that He had found, and to offer in Himself the first-fruits of man's resurrection. As the Head is risen from the dead, so the rest of the body of every man will rise again when the penalty of disobedience shall have been paid. This body will be united again by joints and sinews; it will be strengthened by a divine growth, and each member will have his own proper place in the body. There are many mansions in the Father's house, since there are many members in the body.[19]

It is in the Trinity that the perfection of all is realized. The theology of Irenaeus, like the whole of Christian truth, guides us back to the Triune God. The return of all creation to the God who made it, the restoration of man through the Spirit and through the Son to the Father; this is the term and the scope of the recapitulation.

III

Such is the doctrinal synthesis that Irenaeus has built up round the idea of the recapitulation. It is truly a vast synthesis, comprising a theory of the Redemption, of the Church, and of grace; a conception of the Saviour's life and of the Christ-life in the faithful. And all this gives us at the same time a doctrine of the Mystical Body.

As in the works of the Apostolic Fathers, so in those of Irenaeus the doctrine of the Mystical Body is not treated for its own sake, but in connection with some other truth. For the Apostolic Fathers, that other truth upon which they laid the greatest stress was the doctrine of ecclesiastical unity. This is also the truth most strongly emphasized by Irenaeus, but it is no longer a doctrine merely of ecclesiastical unity; it is rather an explanation of how salvation and union with God come to us in the Church, and how in the unity of the Church we are all united, entirely, even corporally, with one another, and how all together we are united to God in the Saviour who recapitulates all things.

Basically, it is still a doctrine of the Church, an ecclesiology; but the doctrine is growing, and little by little, with the assistance of the Holy Spirit, it is attaining its full stature. Now the Church is considered as a means established for salvation; we have an ecclesiology that is at the same time a soteriology.

In the beginning the Church had drawn only a few gems from the treasure that she possesses through Tradition. Now she displays many more. We may even say that from now on the doctrine is complete in all its essential elements. In the process of completion it may have lost the directness and energy that it had in the letters of St. Ignatius of Antioch, and certain points remain to be developed by later tradition. But there is scarcely anything to be added. We see that the antiquity and the immensity of the Mystical Body are given great emphasis: we are told that it begins with Adam and that it is intended to include all men.

Yet, despite its immensity, it is shown to be one. The just of today continue the life of the just of the Old Testament, and are sustained by their merits. This is the Communion of Saints, taking its place in the doctrine of the Mystical Body.

And it is a communion with Christ; we may even say it is a mystical communication of properties with Him. Strictly speaking, as we know, the communication of properties is that

[240]

prerogative of the Saviour according to which, under certain conditions, we may say of Him as Man what is strictly true only of His divinity, and vice versa. In the writings of Irenaeus we see this interchange extended to the entire Mystical Body. We receive in ourselves the outpouring of the glories of Christ, while He takes our infirmities into Himself, in order to destroy them.

From this there follow two mystico-physical theories: one of the Redemption and another of grace. Our faults and our debts are effaced in the Saviour by the very fact that He exists. Secondly, since He is God and since all humanity is united to Him by the very fact of His existence, all humanity is *de iure* made divine. Thus we have a mystico-physical theory of sanctifying grace and of the adoption that makes us divine.

Since by His very substance Christ is the source of grace, He is so always and in His every act. Whence follows the conception of the physical and mystical causality that all the events of His life exercise upon the sanctification of men.

So truly do we possess all things in common with Him, that from what we are it is possible to infer what He had to be, just as it is possible to see, from what He is, what we in turn are destined one day to be. Thus Irenaeus proves that Christ had to possess a real body, since human nature includes matter, and since it is human nature that had to be saved; thus, too, from the glory of the Saviour he proves the glorification to which we are called despite the material element of our nature.

The first of these arguments is a theological source which we shall often see employed by the Fathers. We may call it the "soteriological argument," since it infers what the Saviour must be from the work of salvation that He came to accomplish. The structure and presuppositions of the argument will appear more clearly later on when we see it applied more frequently and more deliberately. We wish here simply to note its first systematic appearance. As a matter of fact, it was already contained in St. Ignatius' refutation of Docetism, but since it was not as yet complete, the argument would not have been so easily recognized.

[241]

It is not true, however, that this insistence upon the mystical aspect of the Saviour leads Irenaeus to ignore the concrete personality of Jesus. On the contrary, it was the Gnostics who, like the Docetists of Ignatius' day, rejected both the concrete, real Christ and the mystical life of this same Christ in the concrete and visible Church. With the truth we need fear no such disastrous compromise. Those Fathers who are most energetic and most accurate in speaking of the Mystical Body also show most clearly that the Saviour is a distinct person, one and real and living. Indeed, does not the Mystical Body owe all its reality to the unity and life of Christ?

Nor is it true that in his effort to emphasize our union with Christ, Irenaeus overlooks what distinguishes us as individuals. No, for man is made of flesh, the flesh separates us one from the other, and Irenaeus is writing precisely to defend the place which matter occupies in the work of salvation. When man is grafted upon the true olive tree that is Christ and receives the Spirit, he retains the substance of his flesh, but the quality of his works is changed for the better; it is the real man, the man made of matter, who is fashioned anew by Christ to the image of God.

Such is the theology of our Saint in its logical sequence; the progress achieved by Christian thought in the course of a single century would be truly astounding, did we not know what force was at work.

Yes, there has been progress, but we must also admit that perfection has not yet been attained. Irenaeus' theology has its weak points, and of these we must say a word here. For we find the same weak points in his doctrine of the Mystical Body.

In the first place, it must be granted that his teaching gives wide play to the imagination. The view is magnificent: we see all the events of sacred history and all the ups and downs of the inner life of souls epitomized in Christ, while the very current of the centuries advances toward Him. But while the picture shows us something of the Mystical Body in the very process of its growth and of its victory over sin, it is not so much a scientific explanation as a vast "theory," in the etymological sense of the term. Consequently, its speculative value does not equal its power of representation.

Moreover, no clear distinction is drawn between what pertains to the humanity of Christ and what is proper to His divinity in the work of our incorporation in Him. At times Irenaeus states very expressly that it is through the body and blood and death of the Saviour, and hence, through His human nature, that man and all of material creation are reunited with God. But at other times he speaks as if the divinity itself were the intermediary uniting us to the Father, and, therefore, as if His were a divinity less distant from our misery, a less perfect divinity. This is not to say that we may accuse Irenaeus of subordinationism; he merely speaks too cautiously. Discussions and attacks, reflection and detailed examination of the entire deposit of revelation have yet to come. The particular point of doctrine in dispute is not the dignity of the Son, but the goodness and power of the God of the Old Testament. Hence the Saint is thinking principally of these. He shows that the Creator is the supreme God and that Christ leads us to Him by recapitulating our race in Himself. But since the dignity of the Son does not enter into the controversy, it does not receive the same careful attention.

Therefore progress must still be made, both as to Christian doctrine generally and as to the doctrine of the Mystical Body in particular.

IV

Before proceeding further, we wish to mention two other writers, Melito of Sardis and St. Methodius of Olympus. Melito was bishop of Sardis in Lydia when Irenaeus was bishop of Lyons. Little more is known of his biography. Of his theological lore, we know, from Eusebius, merely that it was considerable; of his writings, only a few fragments are extant. However, one of these fragments speaks of our union with Christ in a way that recalls the theory of the recapitulation.

For this reason did the Father send His Son from heaven without a body, in order that becoming incarnate in the womb

[243]

of the Virgin and being born man, He might give life to man and gather together his members that had been scattered by death. For death had divided man.

And the text goes on to speak of the mystery of the Incarnation.

. . . After our Lord was born as a man, He was judged, in order that He might give us grace; He was bound, so that He might set us free; He was taken captive, so that He might give us liberty; He suffered that He might have compassion on us; He died, so that He might give us life; and He was buried, so that He might raise us from the dead.[20]

We cite this passage, not because it speaks of the Mystical Body, but because it refers to another doctrine which is a corollary to that of the Mystical Body, and which expresses the union of the life of Christ with the life that we have as regenerated men.

After Melito, we must say something of St. Methodius of Olympus. He was bishop, apparently not of Olympus, but of Philippi, and died a martyr's death in 311. His knowledge, his fluent style, and his orthodoxy earned for him a theological authority to which such great geniuses as St. Jerome and St. Gregory of Nyssa were fond of showing homage.

Unfortunately, Methodius is less reliable on the subject of our incorporation in Christ, and his Catholic commentators consider his position untenable.

The principal passage is found in the *Banquet*, a sort of philosophical and theological discussion after the manner of Plato, in which eleven virgins in as many discourses sing the praises of virginity. The words that interest us are placed in the mouth of the third of these virgins, Thalia. The thread of the discourse has led her to speak of Adam, and at this point she outlines the theory of the two Adams. But how boldly she takes the figure for concrete reality! According to her, the first Adam was actually Christ Himself and not merely the type of Christ. The first of the eons, as she explains in a disquieting jumble of Gnosticism and subordinationism, was the archangel called "Word." At the beginning of time he united himself with Adam, and in Adam, with the whole human race.

Thus Adam was all that Christ is, since Christ is the union of man with this same Word. In Christ, as in Adam, the result, or we might even say the term and the ultimate reality of this union, is the union of the whole human race "with the pure and perfect divinity."[21] The subordinationism of the first part has disappeared, but now the Saviour's distinct personality is obscured, and the individual Incarnation appears to be merely the preliminary step toward a collective, even universal incarnation.

The remainder of this discourse, as well as the discourses of the other virgins, stress this union of the entire human race with the Word. In each of the faithful must be reproduced what took place in Christ: each must die to his former life, he must receive the Word in himself, and partake of the Spirit. The Christians are so many Christs; or rather, they are but one Christ, for the Word unites Himself with them all.

The reader will grant that the picture is nebulous; it reflects more of imagination than of an exact and critical mind. Of the two principal ideas which it represents, the first, which concerns the real identity of the two Adams, was destined not to endure. It represents merely an exaggeration of the theory of the two Adams. But there is a history connected with the second idea, which insists less upon the union of the Word with the individual humanity of Christ than it does upon the union of the Word with humanity in general. We shall find this view again, expressed by the most illustrious Fathers, such as Hilary, Gregory of Nyssa, John Chrysostom, Cyril of Alexandria. The whole point is to determine exactly what is meant by Methodius; that is, whether there is really question of a universal incarnation taking the place of the true Incarnation, or whether such expressions are to be taken as more or less happily chosen but certainly forceful affirmations of a universal divinization through the incorporation of all in Christ?

St. Methodius leaves the answer uncertain; he does not explain himself with such clearness on this point as to enable us to determine his exact meaning. We believe that the fairest and most objective procedure would be to consider the passages we have just summarized as a rather unfortunate attempt at a synthesis, and to suspend judgment as to the precise meaning of the idea in Christian Tradition until such time as we meet with more numerous indications.

So, as we have seen, St. Methodius formulates a most forceful doctrine of the Mystical Body, based upon the truth of the two Adams. And we saw that St. Irenaeus had already done the same; and perhaps also Melito of Sardis. We say perhaps, for this last point rests upon uncertain evidence. Perhaps, too, the same may be said of St. Justin, if the few lines which immediately follow a quotation from the apologist in *Adversus Haereses* and which speak explicitly of the recapitulation, are Justin's own words and not explanations added by St. Irenaeus.[22] If we add to this what we have said of St. Ignatius and of his forceful teaching concerning our union with Christ, it will be observed that with the exception of St. Methodius, whose birthplace is not known, all of these writers come from Asia Minor. Justin appears to have received his theological training at or near Ephesus; Irenaeus studied at Smyrna and Melito at Sardis, both very near Ephesus; Ignatius was bishop of Antioch, a little further away, but he must have been in close touch with the communities of Asia Minor, for we see representatives of these communities come to visit him on his arrival at Ephesus.

Moreover, this same Asia Minor, and more particularly the city of Ephesus and its environs, had received fuller instruction than other regions on the subject of our incorporation in Christ. It was from Ephesus that Paul wrote the first Epistle in which he speaks expressly of the Mystical Body; this was his First Epistle to the Corinthians. In all probability it was also from Ephesus that he wrote his Epistle to the Romans, which insists so strongly upon the parallel between the two Adams. But since the references which he makes to the Mystical Body, and even to the two Adams, are only incidental, we may not be far wrong if we suppose these references to be an echo of the Apostle's teaching in this community, which seems to have included, even at this early date, a considerable number of highly educated persons. Indeed, when five or six years later the Apostle writes to the Ephesians themselves, his letter is a long development of the "mystery," which is our incorporation in Christ. He treats the subject without lengthy explanation, as something already known. In writing to the nearby Church of Colossae, his procedure is the same. These two Epistles, both addressed to churches of Asia Minor, are the only ones that speak at length of the Mystical Body. It was in Patmos, situated at a distance of about one hundred kilometers from Ephesus, that St. John later had his vision, and it was most probably at Ephesus that he wrote his Gospel, in which he speaks so eloquently of the unity that unites us all in Christ and gives us eternal life in Him.

Again, not only the prefecture, but the whole diocese and province of Asia Minor were at this time the territory most deserving of the name "Christian," and it was here that the Church was organizing and growing most rapidly.

These indications appear to justify the assumption that one or more centers of theological studies were thriving among these early Christian communities; that in these centers the doctrine of the Mystical Body was given special prominence; that the element of that doctrine which was stressed most of all was the lesson of ecclesiastical unity (thus speak Ignatius and Irenaeus, with whom we may join Paul and John); and lastly, that in one or more of these centers the doctrine of the two Adams was commonly used to illustrate the unity of the Church and of the Mystical Body.

[247]

Chapter III

The School of Alexandria

⋊⋉

I. The first school of Alexandria. Clement and Origen. The plan we shall follow in discussing their ideas.
II. *Systematic exposition.* Incorporation with the Incarnate Word through the virtues and through the "Gnostic" life. To be wise and just is to be united with Christ as Wisdom and Justice. He Himself, as Wisdom, produces this union in the souls of men. This union seems to be a participation in Christ's divinity rather than an incorporation in His humanity. Origen's peculiar view on this point. In general, the systematic doctrine of the Mystical Body in the writings of the early Alexandrians is primarily a moral doctrine. The relation of this peculiarity with certain deficiencies of their theology, with their subordinationism, their teaching on grace, their allegorism.
III. *Some more significant texts:* Our resurrection in Christ; our continual birth in Christ; in us, Christ is subject to God; in us, He still grieves for sin. A sample of Scriptural exegesis based upon the communication of properties between the Head and members of the Mystical Body. Christ is the soul of the entire Mystical Body; this universal function helps to explain how He can be God, the Infinite itself.

I

IN THE forefront of the vast theological development that took place in the Eastern Church during the great patristic period, we must place the famous school of Alexandria, called the "Didascaleion."

The Didascaleion was founded at a very early date. We know that Pantaenus was already teaching there in 180. About the year 200, he was succeeded by Clement, who is known to history as Clement of Alexandria. Scarcely had Clement taken charge of the school when, in 202 or 203, he

[248]

was forced to flee because of the persecution of Septimius Severus, and his place was taken by Origen. Origen was then eighteen, hardly more than a boy. But he was a tireless worker, "a man of iron," Eusebius calls him, and at the same time one of the greatest minds that have adorned the history of Christian thought. In a time of bitter persecution, he and Clement undertook an epoch-making work of theology.

One may, and often must criticize or reject many of their ideas; but before their enthusiasm and their science, their limpidity of soul and their sublimity of thought, it is impossible not to experience a feeling of intense admiration and even of affection.

On their own and succeeding ages, these two men, and especially Origen, exerted an influence that was enormous. There is scarcely a thesis in theology that is not to be found in embryo in the latter's teaching.

However, much as they have done for Christian doctrine in general, they have contributed little to the doctrine of the Mystical Body. We find a few magnificent passages scattered here and there in their writings, but aside from these, what they say of the Mystical Body is not particularly impressive. Years before, the doctrine had been formulated almost as well by the Apologists, and far more forcibly by Irenaeus.

At the same time they are of sufficient importance to warrant our devoting a chapter to a summary of their teaching. For, despite its deficiencies, or rather because of its deficiencies, that teaching is instructive; but more especially, those few passages which do speak of the Mystical Body are too beautiful to omit. However, since the doctrine of the two authors is much the same, we may combine what we have to say about them into a single exposition, taking care to indicate, as we go along, the ideas that are proper to each.

The exposition is not an easy one to give. The difficulty lies in bringing the different texts on the Mystical Body into one single plan. For our part, we confess our failure to discover any key to a synthesis of the whole. Hence we must rest content with dividing their doctrine into two parts. First we shall indicate what appears to be their systematic teaching; this is related to their principal interests and constitutes a unified whole by itself. Then we shall consider certain other ideas which, though extremely interesting at times and ordinarily colored by what we have termed their systematic teaching, nevertheless betray no marked connection, as far as we can see, either with this system or with one another. This division is convenient, and while we believe that it is not unfounded, we beg the reader not to forget its arbitrary nature.

II

Both Clement and Origen admit that the primary characteristic of their system is that it is a *gnosis*. Not of course that they are Gnostics after the exaggerated fashion of the heretics mentioned in the preceding chapter; our authors are orthodox Gnostics. They wish before all else to preserve the Christian faith, the faith of all believers. But they aim at a deeper understanding of that faith, an understanding that holds out more subtle lessons for the intellect and more sublime counsels for the will. They and their disciples are to live up, not indeed to a doctrine different from that of ordinary Christians, but to a more refined, more spiritual interpretation of that same doctrine. Hence their fondness for the name "Gnostics," which means "those who really know."

With this Gnosticism is connected what we have termed their systematic concept of the Mystical Body, the concept which presents the general characteristics of their theology. The *gnosis* is an effort, in all things and at all times, to bring one's speculative and practical intelligence to resemble God and His Christ; its effect should be to unite all one's thoughts, desires, and deeds, one's whole manner of being and acting, in a tendency to do good and to practice virtue.

But this virtue is Christ Himself. As the Word of God, Christ is Justice, Holiness, Wisdom, Goodness itself; He is all that is good; He is all good; and His entire doctrine of holiness which is Christianity, is summed up in Him, no matter how profoundly or how "gnostically" that doctrine is understood. According to Clement,

> Our *gnosis* and our spiritual garden is our Saviour Himself. We are transplanted into Him, and are thus removed from our

former life onto good ground. But transplanting makes for a more abundant harvest. Therefore the Lord, into whom we are transplanted, is the true Light and the true *gnosis*.[1]

We must acknowledge that the passage is more explicit and more forceful than most of the texts in which our authors speak of the Mystical Body. But aside from this fact, it does sum up their ideas. For them, to be a "Gnostic" is to be in Christ. For to be a Gnostic means to possess virtue, self-mastery, perfection; therefore it means to possess Christ within oneself, inasmuch as Christ is virtue, interior peace, and perfection. Consequently, Gnosticism consists in a resemblance and an imitation, but not in any ordinary resemblance and imitation.

For such Platonists as the masters of the Didascaleion, the world of ideas possessed a more substantial reality than it does for us. To be in Christ because one is virtuous, meant to be enveloped in Christ in a real way, a way which, though rather hard to define, is almost concrete.

Furthermore, in this imitation Christ is not simply the model that a man reproduces in himself; He is also the Master who teaches how to make each effort of imitation.

Of this most excellent Master, the masters of the Didascaleion have spoken in splendid and touching language. He is the Master, but a Master who knows His doctrine so well that He has become identified with it; thus, when He communicates His precepts to us, His little children, He is giving Himself to us as food. His doctrine is as it were His very substance; by giving us that doctrine, He gives us life in Himself and makes us members of His Mystical Body.

Therefore this unique Master is present not only in His teaching, but also in those who hear it. By contrast with human masters who speak only from without, He is able to address the soul directly and to produce within it the understanding of His message.

Even in the material universe, the Alexandrians explain, following the lead of the Apologists, the Word of God is the inner principle of order and harmony. *A fortiori* He is the same in men's souls; *a fortiori* again, in the souls of the faithful; *a fortiori*, in fine, in the souls of the "Gnostics."

[251]

True Gnostics are His abode and His heaven; He dwells in them as Word, as Wisdom, as Perfection; He dwells in them by giving them understanding and virtue.

But when we speak of Christ as Word and as Wisdom, we consider Him in His divine nature. Hence, according to the professors of the Didascaleion, it would follow that Christ as God is Head of the Mystical Body. This is an error. For, as we shall see later on, it is in His human nature that Christ is Head of all the regenerated.

Certainly Clement and Origen do not lose sight of Christ's humanity, but it is not our purpose here to develop their entire doctrine. It will suffice for our subject to note that their system does not assign to the humanity of Christ its full and proper role in the work that gives us life through incorporation in Christ.

To give a clear idea of this system we shall allow the masters to expose their own doctrine for a few moments, before commenting further upon it.

> There is no doubt that as Word and Wisdom and all else, Christ was in Paul, since Paul asks: "Do you seek a proof of Christ that speaketh in me?" (2 Cor. 13:3, D.V.) . . . It is clear from this that Christ is in each one in proportion to his merits.[2]
>
> When St. Paul says, "live to God in Christ Jesus" (Rom. 6:11), it is just as if he said: "live to God in wisdom, in peace, in justice and sanctification," for Christ is all these. Wherefore to live to God in these virtues is to live to God in Christ Jesus. But if no one can live to God without justice, without peace, without sanctification, surely no one can live to God except in Christ Jesus.[3]
>
> Every wise man, inasmuch as he is wise, partakes of Christ, inasmuch as He is Wisdom; everyone that has power, inasmuch as he is powerful, partakes of Christ, inasmuch as He is Power. And the same is to be said of sanctification and of redemption.[4]

Each Christian, too, partakes of Christ as God.

> Since we have a Guide, let us enter upon the arduous path of virtue, that by imitating Christ to the best of our ability, we may become partakers of the divine nature. For it is written: "he that saith he believeth in Him [Christ], ought him-

self also to walk even as He walked" (1 John 2:6). He is Word
and Wisdom; if we imitate Him we shall deserve to be called
wise and reasonable men. He became all things to all men
that He might gain all men; and to the weak He became weak
that He might gain the weak (1 Cor. 9:22).[5]

And lastly, He became man, among men, to win men.

He became man, that thou mightest learn from a man how
man may become God.[6]

Evidently, the doctrine lacks neither sublimity nor inspiration, but we can also see that it does lack realism. Our union
with the Saviour is made to consist primarily in an imitation
and a resemblance, a resemblance that is very perfect, and
which includes a certain interior presence, a spiritual and
"Gnostic" interiority of Christ in us; but for all its mystery
this resemblance still continues to be a reality of the moral
order.

The Mystical Body which our authors give to the Saviour
is a reality of an intellectual and ascetical order, and we may
say without hesitation that after all it is a spirit rather than
a body. It is a kind of spiritual environment, a vital atmosphere consisting in a particular manner of thinking and of
willing; in short, it is a *gnosis*. The word *gnosis* brings us back
to the ideas that we have already described, and it is also the
best résumé of our authors' systematic doctrine on this point.

The doctrine undoubtedly lacks realism, but it must be
noted that this lack of realism is connected with the least
sure and least orthodox elements of the teaching of the Alexandrians. We have particular reference, first to their subordinationism, secondly, to their incomplete doctrine on grace,
and lastly, to their excessive fondness for allegorical exegesis.
These three defects, we think, are closely bound up with the
weak points in their doctrine of the Mystical Body.

First we shall consider their subordinationism, which is particularly noticeable in the writings of Origen. He considers the
Son far inferior to the Father, although — and here we find the
remedy for the error — He is the most perfect image of the
Father. It is this subordinationism that leads the Alexandrians
to regard the Saviour's divine nature as the intermediary be-

tween God and the world and as the Head of the Mystical Body of regenerated mankind.

Next, we must mention their theology of grace. While this theology may not perhaps be false, it is certainly incomplete. Being educators, they insist less upon our absolute need of this divine assistance than they do upon the condition, indispensable it is true, of our co-operation. Furthermore, and again perhaps because they are educators, they are inclined to regard this very assistance as a lesson that instructs, rather than as a power that lifts us to a higher plane. Not that they are Pelagians; they do not deny our helplessness. But often their expressions seem to point in the direction that Pelagius was to take later on.

This deficiency in their doctrine of grace corresponds exactly with the lack of realism that characterizes their idea of the Mystical Body. Both our justification through Christ and our incorporation in Christ appear to them, not exclusively, of course, but still principally, as a *gnosis,* a spiritual and ascetical instruction. In both, Christ is a teacher rather than Life, and Christianity is represented as being not so much an assimilation, wrought by God, of the very substance of our race unto Christ, but rather as being a vast and magnificent Didascaleion, a "university."

Often again in the course of this work we shall notice the intimate solidarity that exists between the doctrine of grace and the doctrine of our incorporation in Christ. Hence it is important to call attention here to one of the earliest manifestations of this solidarity.

Finally, we shall consider their manner of interpreting Scripture. Here again we find indications of a relationship with the doctrine of the Mystical Body. In their exegesis, as is well known, the masters of the Didascaleion introduced a great deal of allegory. They were not the originators of the practice; it was the fashion in Alexandria long before Christianity. This fashion Clement and Origen merely followed, but with what determination! The main thing, Origen declares, "is to transform the corporal Gospel into a spiritual one."[7] Read the Scriptures; but beneath the letter we must always look for moral exhortations and maxims of "gnostic" life, even if this search should require subtle exegesis. Indeed, one ought to look for little else in the Holy Books. After all, this is the only thing of importance.

> If I am come to hear the Holy Spirit's message to the human race, what matter is it to me to learn that Abraham was standing beneath a tree?[8]

As educators and as preachers, what Clement and Origen seek for are motives for the practice of virtue. On occasion, of course, they can in masterly fashion discuss the literal meaning of a text. But ordinarily this "corporal" and material sense holds little interest for them. They are constantly on the watch for opportunities to introduce moral applications and ascetical counsels; and they feel no regret that these rules for holiness should eclipse the concrete and material details which the Scriptures give us either of the life that had been as it were outlined for the Saviour in advance in the Old Testament, or of the life that He led during the days of His mortal existence.

Thus the Head is treated like the members. It is well to note this parallel. The same exaggerated allegorism that finally reduces the living, concrete Christ to a collection of moral counsels, also leads our authors to regard the most emphatic Scriptural affirmations of our incorporation in Christ as mere exhortations to a careful imitation and to a "gnostic" life. In both cases the realistic and obvious meaning is lost in a system of edifying considerations. Again and always, the Head and the Body are one.

From all that has been said, we may conclude that a tendency to minimize the ontological and mysterious aspect of our incorporation in Christ is no infallible sign that a theologian is possessed of an exceptional sureness of vision or a keener sense of orthodoxy. The doctrine of the Alexandrians is deficient precisely because it is not realistic. This remark may not be wholly useless, for as we suggested at the beginning of this chapter, may we not perhaps find a lesson for ourselves even in these deficiencies of the masters of the Didascaleion?

III

But we shall dwell no longer on these defects. It would be both unpleasant and unjust to devote a chapter to such men as Clement and Origen, and then to conclude it with reservations. So, leaving aside their systematic conception of the Mystical Body, we shall now consider some other passages that are more significant and more noteworthy. The vocabulary and manner of expression are still "Gnostic" at times, but one soon perceives that the thought they express is no longer the speculations of our authors, but their faith.

This faith is alive, enthusiastically alive and firm unto martyrdom. And they often proclaim this faith in terms that are surprisingly vigorous and perfect. Such are the expressions that we shall now quote. They fall naturally into line with the purest tradition, repeating and completing what other Fathers had already said, or formulating in advance what still others were to express more perfectly at a later time.

Thus, for example, the following lines in which Origen speaks of our resurrection in Christ remind one of Irenaeus' finest passages on the recapitulation.

> [On the last day], death shall be vanquished. Christ's resurrection after the sufferings of the cross contains the mystery of the resurrection of Christ's whole body. As the visible body of Jesus was nailed to the cross and buried, and then raised up, so the whole body of Christ's saints is nailed with Him to the cross and now no longer lives. . . . But when the resurrection of this true and complete body takes place, then the members of Christ, which now resemble dry bones, shall be united, bone to bone and joint to joint, each will have its proper place and all together they will form the perfect man, according to the full measure of the stature of Christ (Eph. 4:13). Then shall the many members be one body, since all the members will belong to the same body.[9]
>
> "God hath raised us up and seated us in Christ Jesus in the heavenly places" (Eph. 2:6). What Paul means is this: If you believe that Christ is risen from the dead, believe also that you yourselves are risen with Him; if you believe that He is seated at the right hand of the Father in heaven, believe that you too dwell no longer upon earth, but in heaven . . . and if

[256]

you believe that Christ died to sin and lives for God, do you also die to sin and live for God.[10]

This new life transports us, so to speak, into the glory of Christ. It makes us sons of God, by giving us life in the Incarnate Son.

In eternity this blessed transformation will be manifested in splendor; during this mortal life it takes place unseen. But it is as real in its beginning as it will be real in its consummation. In our every action God is continually engendering us unto eternal life in His Son.

We are begotten of the devil, so to speak, as often as we commit sin. Unhappy is he who is always being begotten of the devil. But happy is he who is always being begotten of God. For the just man is not begotten of God once only, but constantly, by his every virtuous act. To understand this more clearly, let us consider our Saviour. He was not generated by the Father in a transitory manner, but He is continually being generated. So it is with the just man. The Saviour is the reflection of the Father's glory. But the reflection is not generated by the light once and for all, and then cease to be generated; for as long as the light shines it continues to send forth its reflection. Similarly the reflection of God's glory is ever being generated. . . . So too if thou dost possess the Spirit of adoption, God begets thee in Himself by thy every deed, by thy every thought, and through this perpetual generation, at every moment thou art being born a son of God in Christ Jesus, to whom is the glory and the power forever. Amen.[11]

If it is true that at every moment the faithful are being born sons of God in Christ Jesus, it follows that at every moment they are also being born sons of Mary in Christ Jesus. This thought of the divine Maternity of the Virgin is expressed by Origen in the preface to his *Commentary on St. John.*

We must say that the Gospels are the principle (ἀπαρχή) of all the Scriptures, and that the Gospel according to St. John is the principle of all the Gospels. The profound meaning of this Gospel can be understood only by him who has reclined upon the breast of Jesus and who has received Mary from Jesus as his own Mother. . . .

For, according to those who reason rightly, if no one is Mary's son except Jesus, and if Jesus said to His Mother,

"Woman, behold thy son," instead of saying, "Behold, this one is also thy son," it is as if He had said: "Behold Jesus whom thou hast begotten." Truly, he that is perfect no longer lives, but Jesus lives in him. And since Jesus lives in him, we may say of him to Mary: "Behold thy son, Christ."[12]

Just as Christ's glory passes into us, so do our own infirmities pass into Him. Thus it can be said of Him that He is not as yet perfectly subject to the Father, but that eventually He will be so, according to the Scriptures: "When all things shall be subject to Him [the Son], then shall the Son Himself be subject [to the Father] who subjected all things to Him, that God may be all in all."[13] Origen explains that this subjection concerns the Mystical Christ. When we ourselves shall be fully subject to God, that is, when we shall have been fully and definitely incorporated in Christ, then, and not till then, will Christ be wholly subject to God in us.

This exegesis is found in a passage of the *Homilies on Leviticus*. The beginning of the passage is obscure; the author declares insistently and without qualification that even now Christ grieves over our sins and suffers because of them. So clear does the statement appear that St. Bernard and even Pierre-Daniel Huet declare that it is impossible to defend Origen's orthodoxy on this point. We believe that he may be judged more leniently. The concluding paragraph, which the author explicitly links up with the opening words, explains the sense of the entire passage: from beginning to end there is question, not of Christ as considered in Himself alone but of Christ as mystically united with men. The text is rather long, and we shall, therefore, cite only the principal parts; but we think that these few citations will suffice to show in what sense the present sufferings of Christ and His subjection to the Father are to be understood.

Origen asks how we are to explain Jesus' declaration that henceforth He will not drink of the fruit of the vine until the Kingdom of God come (Matt. 26:29). This means, he tells us, that before the coming of the Kingdom there will be a time of expiation and of suffering. That time is the present. And he continues:

Even now my Saviour mourns over my sins. My Saviour cannot rejoice as long as I remain in iniquity. . . . How can He drink the wine of joy, He who is the advocate for my sins, the while I grieve Him by sinning? . . .

He, therefore, is sad as long as we persist in doing wrong. If the Apostle mourns the fate of those who have sinned and have not done penance for their sins (2 Cor. 12:21), what shall we say of Him who is called the Son of love? . . . If the Apostle grieves for sinners and weeps over the wicked, can we believe that my Lord Jesus weeps not when He goes to the Father to offer a sacrifice of propitiation for us?[14]

This ever-sorrowing Christ is the Mystical Christ. True, Origen might have stated this more explicitly, for the passage does seem rather to refer to Christ in His individual personality. But the rest of the passage explains everything. These sins for which Christ is weeping, continues Origen, are the obstacles that prevent His work from being perfect; so long as we, His members, carry the stains of sin, so long will He Himself be deprived of the holiness that He should possess in us. Now the meaning of the passage is plain: it refers to the Mystical Body. The author develops this consideration at length, applying it to the text of St. Paul mentioned above: "Then shall the Son be subject to the Father" (1 Cor. 15:28).

Since we are all His body, and are called His members, therefore as long as some of us are not yet perfectly subject [to God], He Himself is said not to be subject. But when He shall have consummated His work, and shall have brought the whole of His creation to the highest perfection, then He shall be said to be subject in those whom He has subjected to the Father, and in whom He has fulfilled the work appointed unto Him by the Father, so that God might be all things in all men.[15]

Thus, continues Origen — and this is the most interesting passage for us — thus Jesus is not completely in glory so long as His body is not completely in glory:

He does not wish to receive His perfect glory without thee, that is, without His people who are His body and His members. For He wills to dwell as the soul in this body of His Church and in these members of His people, so that its every movement and its every work may be done according to His

[259]

will. Thus will be fulfilled in us the saying of the prophet: "I will set My tabernacle in the midst of you, and . . . I will walk among you" (Lev. 26:11,12). . . .

And thus shall we too be able to say: "It is no longer I that live, but Christ that liveth in me" (Gal. 2:20). For as the Apostle tells us, we are as yet His members and His bones only in an imperfect manner. But when these bones shall be joined together, each one to its joint, as we have said above, then of us may be understood the prophecy: "All my bones shall say: 'Lord, who is like to thee?' " (Ps. 34:10.) For all these bones speak, they sing a hymn, and they give thanks to God. . . .

Before, each of these bones was miserable, and was held down by the hand of one stronger. It had not the jointure of charity, nor the sinews of patience, nor the veins of a living spirit, nor the vigor of faith. But when He came who was sent to gather what was dispersed and to bind together what was scattered, joining bone to bone and joint to joint, He began to build the holy body of the Church.

All that I have just said, continues Origen, is outside my commentary, but it was necessary in order to explain why the high priest of the Old Law was forbidden to drink wine before entering into the tabernacle of the testimony (Lev. 10:9). The reason is that the present is a time of preparation and of penance. But once this time has passed, then will come the hour of triumph, the hour for the wine of joy and for the effusion of a new life. Origen speaks enthusiastically of this newness of life:

Then indeed He shall drink the wine, but it will be a new wine, a new wine in the new heaven, and in the new earth, and in the new man, with new men, with them that sing the new canticle. Thus you see that one cannot drink the new cup of the new wine as long as he does not put off the old man and his works.[16]

Now that we have the passage in its entirety, one may judge whether we had reason to say that from beginning to end it speaks of the Mystical Body. The closing lines are sufficient evidence; there is question throughout of the Christ who has not as yet attained in us the fullness of His growth and the measure of the perfect man. For this reason, as we are told in the opening words of the text, He is ever struggling within us against sin, while the conclusion states that He is ever making progress in us, in order that ultimately He may become wholly obedient to God. As we shall see in the course of our study, such ideas were to become familiar to Tradition.

As a matter of fact, the somewhat obscure beginning of the passage holds far less interest for us than the very clear conclusion in which we find an example of a method of exegesis that was to become traditional: Origen applies to the Mystical Body what the Scripture says of Christ in general. Christ will be subject to the Father, when we shall be subject to the Father. For such an interpretation to be valid, one must necessarily presuppose that the unity between Christ and the Christians, between the Head and the members, is so close that the Scriptures can attribute to the one that which is strictly true only of the other.

This type of exegesis we shall meet again in the works of the later Fathers, but we wished to point out that it dates from the Didascaleion of Alexandria. Origen employs it on many occasions, not only when commentating the present text of the first Epistle to the Corinthians, but also when explaining other passages.

In addition to the method of exegesis, we must note a forceful statement contained in the passage we have quoted. Christ, says Origen, acts as the soul of the entire Mystical Body; He wills to abide in the Mystical Body "so as to direct its every movement," in such wise that whatever it does may be the expression of His own thought.

This universal action of Christ's humanity, this function of sanctification that it fulfills within every man, helps us also to understand the union of that humanity with the Infinite, with the Word. Origen considers this mystical aspect of Christ so certain that he even draws from it an argument in favor of His divinity.

This he does in a passage of his work *Contra Celsum*. Although Celsus admitted with the Stoics that the wise man was the equal of the gods, he ridiculed the Christian dogma according to which the soul of Jesus is united with the Word, the first-born of every creature (Col. 1:15). Origen replies that the truths of Christianity are perfectly consistent with one another; that, according to the Scriptures the Word is united with the whole Church and hence there is no reason why it should not also be united in a particularly excellent way with the humanity of Christ. The passage, as we shall see, is a kind of profession of faith; the thought, which we must admit is expressed somewhat "gnostically," is the common belief of the Christians.

> We say, according to the divine Scriptures, that the body of Christ, animated by the Son of God, is the whole Church of God, and that the members of this whole body are the individual believers. For as the soul gives life and movement to the body, which otherwise would be inert, so the Word imparts to this whole body which is the Church, movement and power unto good; He moves each member of the Church, so that none acts without Him. All this seems quite consistent and logical. Then what is there to prevent the soul of Jesus, or rather the whole Jesus, from being united to the Word in so close and excellent a union that He should be none other than the Only-begotten and the First-born of every creature?[17]

With this text we shall conclude. Many other passages might doubtless be drawn from the works of Origen and Clement. But is it presumption on our part to believe that the few we have cited will suffice to give some idea of the rich treasures contained in their theology and of the position which, after all, the doctrine of the Mystical Body occupies in that theology?

Chapter IV

St. Athanasius. The Divinity of the Word and the Divinization of His Mystical Body

><

I. *Before Arianism.* The *Logos* in the world; the life of the Mystical Body a proof of Christ's resurrection.

II. *The struggle against Arianism.*

1. *Doctrinal exposition.* The doctrine of our divinization. The Incarnate Word is the principle of divine life in the Mystical Body. Our divinization proves His divinity, for it is His divinity that effects our divinization. Our union with the Word; our unity in the Incarnate Word. The capital text: "That they may be one."

2. *Controversy over the Arian arguments.* Exegesis based upon our divinization in the Mystical Christ. The Word is exalted in us, sanctified in us, created in us.

III. *The treatise on the Incarnation and against the Arians.* Whether it is authentic or not, it comes from the school of Athanasius. It presents the same ideas, more fully developed, and the same kind of exegesis. Christ sanctifies Himself in us, and completes in us His own Incarnation.

IV. *Conclusion.* Athanasius and the doctrine of the Mystical Body. Summary of his teaching; what he leaves unexplained; the corollaries which he draws from the doctrine.

I

ATHANASIUS was not a professor, but a bishop. As patriarch, or as he was called, "pope" of Alexandria, he was the pillar of the Church and the father of orthodoxy for forty-five years, from 328 until 373. In him lived again the souls of the great bishops whom we have already studied, the souls of an Ignatius and an Irenaeus, their jealous zeal for tradition, their ardent fearlessness in reasoning out and defending the faith, and also — since these characteristics always go hand in hand

[263]

— their profound sense of the life of Christ in the Church.

Athanasius was much more concerned with dogma than with subtleties of thought. Consequently there is no question, in his writings, of the philosophical and "Gnostic" speculations with which Christian doctrine had been enveloped and at times overburdened at the hands of Clement and Origen. He seeks only divine truth, the revealed truth, and though he is resolute in his efforts to understand its meaning, nevertheless the effort consists in a search for the truth's intrinsic light rather than in an attempt to adapt it to a metaphysical system.

Not that Athanasius rejects philosophy; on the contrary, he even praises it, but only as an auxiliary. Consider, for instance, how he speaks of the Mystical Body in his earliest work, the two discourses, *Against the Pagans* and *On the Incarnation*, written between the years 318 and 320.

> The Greek philosophers say that the world is a great body. And in this they are right. For we see that the world and its parts are sensible things. If, then, the word of God resides in this world which is a body; if He is present in each and every thing, is there anything strange or absurd in our claim that the Word is present in man?[1]
>
> Like a musician who has attuned his lyre, and by the artistic blending of low and high and medium tones produces a single melody, so the Wisdom of God, holding the universe like a lyre, adapting things heavenly to things earthly, and earthly things to heavenly, harmonizes them all, and, leading them by His will, makes one world and one world order in beauty and harmony.[2]

In these lines we recognize the conception, expressed by a master this time, according to which the Mystical Body represents not human nature only, but the entire universe. Irenaeus had already expressed the thought when he said that the Word recapitulates in Himself all of the material creation; it can be found in the Apologists as well as in the early Alexandrians, who show that since He is *Logos* and Wisdom, the Incarnate Word joins all things in unity and harmony with one another and with God. In Clement and Origen, it is true, the idea was not free from a certain subordinationism. But it is also true that to give accurate and clearly defined expression to concepts so sublime, was no simple task which could be accomplished all at once. The Spirit who assists the work of Tradition is not wont to exempt even the most docile minds from a certain amount of groping, except in those moments when the *magisterium* of the Church is acting in the fullness of its authority.

But the Holy Spirit is ever in the Church, pursuing His work of truth, and we know how vigorously Athanasius and his successors have spoken, under His influence, of the perfect equality of the Son with the Father.

The idea that the Incarnate Word is in Himself the unity and harmony not only of men, but also of the entire universe and even of material things, was to remain a favorite theme for the Fathers of the Church. The idea appealed to them first, by reason of the Platonist training in philosophy which many of the Fathers had received; secondly, it appealed to them because of its opposition to the atomism, so often immoral, of Epicurus; lastly and chiefly, because of its profound truth and because of the vast perspective that it gives concerning God's providential plan and the Mystical Body.

Athanasius in particular is so penetrated with this thought that he expresses it often. He loves to repeat that Christ is the leaven of the world; πᾶσα κτίσις, τὰ πάντα, the whole universe is the mass that He leavens and the body to which He gives life.

But our Doctor is not satisfied with this point of view, which is still too philosophical. He immediately proceeds further, to center his doctrine round the supreme theological truth, the dogma of the divinity of the Son and of the Incarnation. This he does in the second part of the *Discourse on the Incarnation* already referred to. Athanasius was but twenty-five years of age when he wrote this book, which is justly regarded as the pearl of theological treatises written in Greek. It is full of youthful freshness and ardor, but already powerful and sharply defined; one feels that the author is at home with Christian dogma, and that his whole soul is imbued with it.

The theme of the discourse is the communication of virtue, power, and sanctity, in a word, of supernatural life, which takes place between the Christians and Christ and manifests the union that exists between the Head and the members; in other words, it is the unity of the Mystical Body. According to Athanasius, this communication is so abundant and so evident that in order to believe in Christ's resurrection one need only see the vitality which the Church receives from her Head.

The whole earth, explains the Saint, is full of Christ. His doctrine reaches everywhere, silencing the oracles of the demons; everywhere magic retreats when opposed by His moral teaching. The false pagan gods change from village to village, while the Saviour alone, everywhere the same, conquers the whole world and is adored by all.

> By the mere sign of the cross are confounded all the wiles of the demons . . . and whereas the Greek philosophers, for all their many writings, have been unable to induce even a few men of neighboring countries to accept their doctrine of immortality and the practice of virtue, Christ alone by His simple, unaffected speech and by means of unlearned disciples, has succeeded in persuading multitudes of men throughout the world to despise death and to seek only after things that are immortal.[3]
>
> Let anyone come who wishes to try this experiment: in the very midst of the magic of the demons and of the oracles of hell, let him make the sign of the cross, at which the pagans smile, and let him simply pronounce the name of Christ. At once he will see the demons flee, the oracles cease, and sorcery disappear.[4]
>
> Death, too, has been conquered by the cross. . . . The disciples of Christ tread upon death as upon a corpse. . . . Even children hasten to meet it; not only men, but women too, cross swords with death. . . . All they that walk in Christ fearlessly tread death underfoot, and laugh at it as they bear witness to Christ.
>
> And if anyone doubts death's defeat, let him embrace the faith of Christ and attend His school; then he will see the weakness and the defeat of death. Thus it is that many who once refused to believe and used to laugh at us, but afterwards believed, came so to despise death as even to become martyrs of Christ.[5]

Christ's action transcends our concepts as the vast movement of succeeding waves escapes the eye. In a moment, His doctrine and His action have filled the earth, like the spreading light of the rising sun. Everywhere He has succeeded in inculcating temperance and virginity, and by His hidden power a multitude of barbarous peoples, once torn by constant warfare and cruel even to their own kindred, have been so transformed that now they think only of peace and concord. The whole development is summed up in the triumphant question:

> Who, then, is this Christ, and how great must He be, whose name and whose presence overshadow and efface all else; who alone is more powerful than all others, and who fills the entire world with His teaching?[6]

"Who is He?" The answer to which the entire contexts leads us can be only this: He is God, God in the fullest sense of the word; He is, if we may use the expression, as fully God as God can be. Yet He is not separated from us by this transcendence; on the contrary, this it is that makes Him interior to every soul, and makes Him active even in the whole universe. We stress this point because for Athanasius, as for the whole Church, it is a capital element of the doctrine of the Mystical Body. Precisely because in Himself He lives a life of transcendent perfection, the Saviour, or, as Athanasius often calls Him, "our common Saviour," is at the same time the life of the world.

> Since the Saviour produces such effects in men . . . can anyone still doubt that Christ lives, yea, that He is Life itself?[7]

Christ is Life; Life in Himself and the life of men. In these very terms St. John's Gospel had already expressed both Christ's absolute superiority and His inner presence in the soul, which constitute Him our Mystical Head. The Greek Church was to remain particularly faithful to this concept; it is in terms of life that the Greek Fathers prefer to formulate their teaching regarding our incorporation in the Saviour. They explain the communication of life from the Father to the Son, from the Son to His Sacred Humanity, then from this humanity to all men. This method we shall note in the following chapters, and even in the present chapter.

But doctrinal development and long meditation upon the revealed truth were still necessary before an adequate expression of this life and of this mystical communication of life could be found. We have just seen the beginning of this theological process in the writings of St. Athanasius, and here we too shall study its first stages. We have thus far considered only the writings of the Saint's youth. As yet there was no question of Arianism, of which he was destined to be the great adversary.

II. § 1

While the *Discourse against the Pagans* was being written, about the year 318, and in the very city of Alexandria where Athanasius was a deacon, Arius was beginning to preach his errors. These spread like wildfire, and in a very short time the heresiarch found himself at the head of a large and determined army.

As we know, his heresy was as follows: The Word may, of course, be called God, but He is not God in the same sense as the Father is God. He was created, before all other creatures indeed, but created nonetheless; therefore He was made, and made not of the substance of the Father, but out of nothing. Hence He is absolutely inferior to the Creator. It was not always true that He existed, and since He was produced by that radical change which is creation, He belongs essentially to the order of changing and destructible things, subject to imperfection. However, He has so confirmed Himself in good by the exercise of His free will, and He has received so many graces and such unparalleled excellence from the generosity of the Father that He is superior by far to all other creatures. Thus in a certain sense He can be called God; He is God not by nature, but by grace.

To prove their position, the Arians maintained that according to the Scriptures the Word was subordinate to the supreme God, even before the Incarnation. And in confirmation of their error, they quoted many texts which we shall see later in this chapter.[8]

Arianism was but ten years old when, in 328, three years after the Council of Nicaea, Athanasius was proclaimed patriarch of Alexandria. He had already shown strenuous opposition to the heresy, and during the half century of his episcopate he was to be in the thick of the combat. In admiration, Msgr. Duchesne exclaims: "It may even be said that at times Athanasius was the sole champion of the faith. But that was enough. Athanasius was opposed by the empire and the army, by the councils and the bishops; yet so long as such a man stood firm, the battle was not one-sided."[9]

In his refutation of the heretics St. Athanasius attacks both the doctrinal system of Arianism and the Scriptural arguments that were employed in its defense. To the doctrinal system his answer is a precise exposition of Christian teaching regarding the disputed points; to the Scriptural arguments he opposes a method of exegesis. We shall examine both, for both affirm our incorporation in Christ. Here again, as in his early writings, the holy Doctor makes the doctrine of the Mystical Body the center of his teaching.

St. Athanasius regards the Arian doctrinal system as primarily a theory of divinization. According to them, he tells us, the Word is not God by nature, but is made divine by the Father. He is the instrument of our salvation, the intermediary of which God makes use in creating us and in raising us to the divine adoption. Therefore like ourselves, He is God by participation, but in a much more perfect degree.

Impossible, replies the Saint. If the Word is not God in the strictest sense of the term, if He is not consubstantial with the Father, we are not deified in Him. For how can He communicate to His members something which He does not possess in its fullness?

But we are made divine, and that in Christ; we are made adoptive sons of God, and that in Christ. Therefore this Christ must be God and Son, and He must be such in all perfection.

Athanasius bases his argument upon the divinization of the Christian. This was a truth universally accepted; we have already met it in St. Paul, in the Fourth Gospel, in St. Ignatius of Antioch, and in St. Irenaeus.

From this divinization Athanasius argues to the strict divinity of the Word, not merely as one argues from an effect to its cause, but as one can infer what the Head must be if he knows what the members are.

If we had only the first line of reasoning, and if the great Doctor had been content to say simply that since Christ is the principle of our divinization He must therefore be God in all perfection, the argument would give us no conclusion concerning the doctrine of the Mystical Body. There would be only a causal relation. This is the case in Athanasius' letters to Serapion, in which he proves the divinity of the Holy Ghost, arguing that the Holy Spirit must be God, since He makes us divine. It does not follow from this that we are incorporated in the Spirit or that He deifies us by some kind of insertion in Himself. But Christ is not only the causal principle, but as it were the very vital principle of our divinization. He makes us sons, not merely by producing something within us from afar off, but by producing that something through union with Himself, by a communication that takes place from the Head to the members, by an organic, and not only efficient nexus.

We wish to call the reader's attention to this last point, for it is the demonstrative element in the quotations that follow. Its prominence is immediately noticeable. To establish the strict divinity of the Saviour, Athanasius uses the same argument with which he had proved Christ's resurrection and His divinity in general. The Saint insists upon the union of Christ with men, upon the divine life that we have in Him; this union and this life prove that He is equal to the Father, just as it proved that He is risen from the dead.

Let us now consider his doctrine of divinization; that it is a doctrine of the Mystical Body will become more and more apparent as the exposition proceeds. First, there is a divinization, and this divinization is wrought through union with Christ.

For there can be no adoption apart from the true Son, since He Himself tells us, "No one knoweth who the Father is, except the Son, and he to whom the Son may choose to reveal Him" (Luke 10:22). . . . Since then all they that are called sons and gods [by grace], whether on earth or in heaven, have received adoption and divinization through the Word, and since the Word is the Son, it is evident that all receive of Him, that He is Son before all others, nay, that He alone is true Son, He alone true God of true God.[10]

In another passage which we shall quote at some length, we

can see that the argument of St. Athanasius presupposes a most intimate union between ourselves and Christ.

> If the Son were a creature, man would remain mortal as before, since he would not be united with God. No created thing can unite other created things to God, for itself needs someone to unite it with Him. Nor can any part of creation bring salvation to that creation, for the part itself has need of salvation. For this reason God sent His own Son, who took unto Himself created flesh and became the Son of man. Now all men were condemned to death, but He who was innocent offered His own body to death for all, so that all have died through Him, all have died in Him, and the sentence of our condemnation has been fulfilled. Henceforth through Him we are all freed from sin and its curse; we are risen from the dead and shall remain forever, clothed with immortality and incorruptibility.[11]

We have all this "in Christ." The text goes on to show even more strikingly all that is given us, in this same Christ:

> When the Word became incarnate, as we have often explained, all the sting of the serpent was wholly extinguished in the flesh; its evil inclinations were extirpated, and death itself, the consequence of sin, was overcome, as the Lord Himself declares in these words: "The ruler of the world cometh, and in Me he hath nothing" (John 14:30). And, as John writes, "To this end was the Son of God manifested, that He might undo the works of the devil" (1 John 3:8). When the flesh had thus been delivered from these miseries, we were all set free and united with the Word through our kinship with His flesh. And so, since we are united with God, we are destined not to remain upon earth, but as He tells us, where He is, there we shall also be (John 14:3). . . . But that would have been impossible if the Word were a creature. For the devil, who is also a creature, could have resisted Him forever. . . . Hence truth itself proves that the Word is not a creature, but that He is rather the Creator. For he took a created and human body in order, as Creator, to renew it, to deify it in Himself, and thus to lead us all to the Kingdom of heaven in imitation of Him.

There is no dividing line drawn between the Incarnate Word and the faithful; in Him the divinity deifies the human race. And the Saint continues in the same strain:

> Union with a creature could not have made man divine.

[271]

This is a tremendous concentration of thought: the hypostatic union, the Saviour's humanity, and the divinization of the human race, all crowded into a single line. Nor is this a phrase that has escaped him in an unguarded moment, for the Saint is sparring carefully against a watchful opponent. He concludes:

> Hence it was necessary that the Son be true God. Never could man have stood in the presence of God, unless He that had taken a body were the natural and true Word of God. And, just as we should never have been freed from sin and malediction unless the flesh taken by the Word were truly human flesh — for we should have had nothing in common with a stranger — so man would never have been deified unless He that became flesh were by nature the true and proper Word of the Father. For this was the union effected, that he who is man by nature might be united with Him who by nature is God, and that thus our salvation and our deification might be lastingly assured.[12]

One finds passages so rich in doctrinal content only in the writings of the very greatest of Doctors, but in Athanasius they occur frequently. The Saint keeps a vigilant eye upon doctrine; one might even say that he foresees its future, for with one neat stroke he forestalls the two later heresies of Nestorius and Eutyches. Christ, he declares, must be true God, true man, and truly one, in order truly to unite men with God. This is the soteriological argument which we have encountered before and which will be further developed by Tradition. It is here expressed by Athanasius with telling brevity. The crux of the argument, and the truth which is either implicitly or explicitly presupposed throughout these enlightening pages, is that Christ is so truly one with us that He can communicate His divinity to us in Himself.

Such a manner of speaking explains why Athanasius has been ranked among those Fathers, mentioned when we spoke of St. Methodius, who are accused of teaching a hypostatic union of the Word not with an individual human nature, but with human nature in general. Yet this same manner of speaking, and particularly the Saint's insistence upon the transcendence of Christ, are a sufficiently clear indication of his meaning; namely, that human nature in general is united with the Word only through the intermediary of the one Man-God.

But he does not regard this one Man-God as separated from the rest of human nature. On this point everything in his writings, even the structure of his sentences, is significant. We have already noticed, and we shall have frequent occasion to notice again, that he is so accustomed to associate in his mind these two who are one, that he passes quite naturally from speaking of Christ to speak of the faithful without any line of demarcation. Grammarians may disapprove, but theologians are delighted. They see in the Saint's very style a witness to the unity of Christ and His members, a witness that is all the more revealing because it is less directly intended.

Certainly the redemption is essentially the work of the passion, of the cross, and of the Saviour's struggle against sin. This Athanasius repeats time and again, but he also considers the redemption primarily as a work of unity. The world is so truly one whole that when the Word enters into it and becomes one of our race, all things take on a new dignity. Moreover, this unity is supernaturally intensified and strengthened by the Incarnation, and thus becomes a more powerful means of diffusing the effects of the Incarnation.

> Such is God's love for men that He willed to become Father, by grace, of those whom He created. This takes place when men who are mere creatures receive in their hearts the Spirit of the Son, crying, "Abba, Father" (Gal. 4:6). These are they who on receiving the Word, receive of Him the power to become sons of God. Now, since they are but creatures, they could not become sons unless they received the Spirit of Him who is the natural and true Son of God. Therefore was the Word made flesh, to render man capable of receiving the divinity. . . . We are not sons [of God] by nature, but the Son who is within us [is such by nature]; nor is God our Father by nature, but He is the Father of the Word who is in us, in whom and by whom we cry "Abba, Father" (Rom. 8:15). And to those in whom He sees His Son, the Father says: "I have begotten you" (Ps. 2:7), and He calls them His sons.[13]

Therefore we are deified by adoption in the Incarnate Son and by union with the Word of God.

> Just as [the Word] shared our infirmities by taking a human

body, so do we, by receiving the Word, share His immortality.[14]

This, he continues, is the whole purpose of Christianity.

> The Arians pretend to be scandalized; they deem the Word inferior because it is written that He was troubled and wept (John 11:38,35). In this they seem to be totally lacking in human emotion, for they fail to understand human nature in its weaknesses. Rather should they marvel that the Word should have taken such weak flesh at all, and that He did not shield it from every attack, as He might well have done. . . . But, as I have said above, He came to suffer in the flesh, and thus to make the flesh henceforth impassible and immortal; He came, as we have often said, to take God's indignation and chastisements upon Himself, that these evils might no longer dare to molest men, but might be utterly destroyed; He came, that henceforth men might forever be the incorruptible temples of the Word. If Christ's enemies had thought of this, if they had realized the purpose for which the Church was instituted, if they had clung tightly to that purpose as to an anchor, they would never have suffered shipwreck of the faith.[15]

The same *Discourse against the Arians* contains the most striking passage on the subject of the union of all Christians with the Word in Christ. Athanasius is speaking of the weaknesses of our nature which the Word has taken upon Himself, and of the glories of the divinization that He imparts to us.

> Now that the Word has become man and made His own the ills of the flesh, because of the Word who came in the body these ills no longer molest the body, but are destroyed by Him. Men are no longer dead in their sins, but, restored to life by the power of the Word, they remain forever immortal and incorruptible. Hence when His flesh is born of Mary, the Mother of God, He Himself is said to be born who brought all other things into existence. In reality, however, it is our birth that He is taking unto Himself; no longer are we mere dust, destined to return to dust, but we are united with the Word from heaven, who will bring us into heaven. Similarly, it was not without reason that He took upon Himself the other infirmities of the body. For He willed that we should no longer be merely men, but that we should belong to the Word and partake of eternal life. Death, which was our heritage by reason of our first birth, is now no more; our birth and all the weaknesses of the flesh are transferred to the Word. We are lifted up from the earth, and the curse of sin is removed from us by Him who,

[274]

in us and for us, was made a malediction. And rightly so; for as we are all formed of dust and as we all die in Adam, so being born again of water and the Spirit, we all receive life in Christ. Our flesh is no longer earthly; for it has been made Word because of the Word of God who was made flesh for us.[16]

The flesh, the flesh of all of us, is united with the Word. To render the full meaning of the Greek, we should say that the flesh is "verbified." We see how realistically Athanasius conceives and expresses our union with the Incarnate Son. After a few lines, he continues to insist on this point:

> Since their ills have been taken over and destroyed in Him who is not subject to infirmity, men become strong and free forever, as John tells us in these words: "And ye know that He was manifested in order to take away sins, and sin is not in Him" (1 John 3:5). If this is true, no heretic can object with the question: "Why is the flesh, which is by nature mortal, restored to life? And if it is restored, why does it no longer suffer hunger and thirst and pain and death? Is it not dust? How can it be rid of what is natural to it?" If a heretic should argue thus, the flesh may reply: "Yes, I am made of dust and am by nature mortal. But I am become the flesh of the Word; He has borne my infirmities, although He was not subject to them, and I have been set free. I am no longer their slave, because of the Lord who delivered me from them. If you blame me for being set free from my natural corruptibility, take care lest by so doing you also find fault with the Word of God for having taken my state of slavery upon Himself." For as the Lord took a body and became man, so we men, being assumed by the flesh of the Word, are by Him made divine and heirs of eternal life.[17]

The conclusion explains the entire passage; until the very last sentence, one might think that "the flesh" referred to is exclusively the physical body of Christ. It is the flesh of the Word, says Athanasius, the flesh which through contact with the divinity has been delivered from its infirmities. But at the same time the Saint is thinking of the unique reality which consists of the Head united with the members, and he describes both in the same development. Of this the concluding words leave no doubt; from the beginning to the end he had all the faithful in mind, and "the flesh of the Word" signifies them all.

Therefore they are something sacred. Because of Christ, the adoration that is due to God alone must also include humanity, the Sacred Humanity of Christ and ourselves. In other words, Athanasius remains faithful to his habit of associating Christ's humanity with our own. According to the Saint, the Scripture refers to this extension of cult when it tells us that after His death Jesus was exalted by God and that He was adored by the angels.

The fact that the Lord became incarnate, that Jesus is adored, that He is believed to be the Son of God and the Revealer of the Father, shows clearly that this exaltation was not conferred upon the Word in His capacity as Word, but upon ourselves. By reason of our kinship with His body we too are become the temple of God and are made sons of God; so that the Lord may now be adored even in us, and whosoever sees us can cry, in the words of the Apostle: "God is indeed within them" (1 Cor. 14:25).[18]

Christ's body makes our own bodies precious in the eyes of God and of men; that body is of itself a kind of mute intercession, and through it Jesus says unceasingly to the Father:

"I am Thy Word, and Thou art in Me. But I am in them through My body, and by Thee man's salvation has been wrought in Me. Therefore I ask that they may be one according to the body that is in Me and according to the perfection of this body; that being united with this body and becoming one in it, they too may be made perfect; that they may all be one body and one spirit, one perfect man, as if I bore them all in Myself." For since we all partake of the same Christ and possess within us the one Lord, we all become one body.[19]

Such, continues the Saint, is the true sense of the text, "That they may be one, as We are one" (John 17:22). This unity is the unity of Christ, which embraces us all.

§ 2

Let us delay for a moment on this commentary, for it contains in embryo certain developments that we shall meet again later on. Upon this particular text of St. John, "That they may be one, as We are one," the Arians based one of their principal arguments. They concluded that the Father and the Son are one by a mere union of resemblance, since Jesus Himself compares that union with the union that binds the Christians together. But this latter can be no more than a union of resemblance. Therefore the Father and Son are no more consubstantial than we are consubstantial with one another.

"False," replies Athanasius. In the phrase "that they may be one as We are one," the word *as* does not indicate equality, but a mere likeness that may be very remote. However, he continues with a very interesting argument, it is not true that we are united merely by a resemblance and by a common nature. There is also a union of charity and of harmony. And, more important still, there is within us "something more excellent and more perfect: the Word has entered into us, since He has taken our body."[20] And the Saint continues with the passage just quoted. A little further on, he explains that we are one with a divine unity, as the Son is one with the Father.

This explanation was to be supplemented by St. Hilary and then by St. Cyril of Alexandria in their commentaries on the same verse of the Fourth Gospel. It is precisely here that they present their most fully developed teaching, the most perfect ever formulated by the Eastern Church concerning our incorporation in Christ.

This is not the only text that was disputed and won back by Athanasius from the Arians. The latter had seized upon many others, upon all that appeared to subordinate the Word or Christ to the Father; texts that refer to the humiliations Christ endured during His Passion, those that speak of His obedience to the Father, those that declare that Wisdom was created by God in the beginning of His works.

Athanasius disarms the heretics. Far from favoring the Arian heresy, he says, these texts inculcate Christian truth; not indeed that particular truth which the heterodox deny, but another, which is the doctrine of our intimate union with the Saviour. They apply not to Christ's divinity, but to the humanity that He has taken: in other words, they apply to His Sacred Humanity and our own; so close is the bond which attaches us to Him, that these texts apply to both together.

This answer may seem strange. Modern exegetes find it simpler to consider only the Sacred Humanity of Jesus and to apply to it all the imperfections that are attributed to the Saviour. But they are not Athanasius. Undoubtedly the great doctor knew quite as well as they that the simple distinction between the two natures of the one Christ would suffice. At times even he is content to give this distinction, but such occasions are rather rare. He usually prefers a richer and more complex explanation. Everywhere he sees the Saviour united with His own, and he is reluctant to separate what God Himself has joined together.

Evidently, if Athanasius had but seldom had recourse to such a method of exegesis, or if he were the only Father to employ it, we might regard it merely as a controversial tactic and hesitate to draw any conclusion from it. But as we shall see in the course of our studies, this method of interpretation is traditional in the Church; hence it will not be rash of us to regard it as a witness of Christian belief. For this reason we must study the method more closely. Athanasius uses it deliberately, in virtue of the following principle:

> What is written of the Saviour in a human way should be referred to the common race of men. For He has taken our body and borne our human weakness.[21]

Indeed, Athanasius refers the passages of which we speak much more to the human race than to Christ's individual human nature. Thus his controversy against the Arians becomes a long discourse on the Mystical Body. The argument occupies ten chapters in the first *Discourse against the Arians,* where he discusses the text of St. Paul: "Christ humbled Himself by obedience unto death. . . . Wherefore God hath exalted Him and hath bestowed on Him the name which is above every name" (Phil. 2:9). This exaltation of Christ was the Arian's delight: since the Word was still capable of further glorification, He was not of Himself superior to all things from the beginning. The conclusion is false, retorts Athanasius; for this exaltation concerns only the Saviour's human nature and ourselves.

> The eternal Word, the image of the Father, took the form of a slave, and as man, suffered death in His flesh for our sake, in order that He might offer Himself to the Father for us by

death. Therefore it is also as man, because of us and for us, that He is said to be exalted. Just as by His death we have all died in Christ, so shall we be exalted in this same Christ, when, after our resurrection from the dead, we shall ascend into heaven, "whither, as Forerunner, Jesus hath entered on our behalf" (Hebr. 6:20). He hath not entered into . . . a mere type of the true, but into heaven itself, "to appear now before the face of God on our behalf" (Hebr. 9:24). But if Christ, who was always Lord and Creator of the heavens, has now entered into heaven for our sake, then for our sake is it written that He is exalted. Again it is written that He who sanctifies all men hallows Himself for us in the sight of the Father. Surely this does not mean that the Word Himself must become more holy, but that He sanctifies us all in Himself. We must take the present text in the same sense. "God hath exalted Him," not to raise Him to greater perfection, for He is the Most High, but that He may become our justice and that we may be exalted in Him and enter the gates of heaven which He has reopened to us. They who stand guard at the gates say: "Lift up your gates, O ye princes, and be ye lifted up, O eternal gates: and the King of glory shall enter in" (Ps. 23:7). The text does not mean that the gates had until now been closed to Him who was the Lord and Maker of all things; but this too is written on behalf of us, to whom the gates of Paradise had been closed. Therefore, because of the flesh He bore, it is written of Him in human fashion, "Lift up your gates and He will enter in," as if a man were entering. On the other hand, since the Word is God, He is called in divine fashion the King of glory. This our exaltation was foretold by the Holy Spirit in the words of the eighty-eighth psalm: "And in thy justice they shall be exalted, for thou art the glory of their strength" (Ps. 88:17,18). Since the Son is Justice, He has no need of exaltation, but it is we who are exalted in justice, which is Himself.[22]

Here we shall cite a few lines referring to one of the texts mentioned in the above passage: "And for them I hallow Myself, in order that they too may be hallowed in truth" (John 17:18).

In these words He shows that it is not He who is sanctified but that it is He who doth sanctify. For He is not hallowed by another, but He hallows Himself, that we may be hallowed in truth. Now, he that sanctifieth Himself is the Lord of sanctification. It is as if He said: "I, the Word of the Father, having become man, give Myself the Spirit; in that Spirit I hallow Myself as man, in order that henceforth all men may be hal-

[279]

lowed in Me who am the Truth; for it is written, Thy Word is truth" (John 17:17).

But, if He sanctifies Himself for our sake, and did so when He became man, it is clear that the Holy Spirit, in descending upon Christ at the Jordan, really descended upon us, because Christ bore our body. Nor was this done for the advantage of the Word, but that we might be made holy, that we might share His anointing, and that it might be said of us: "Know you not that you are the temple of God, and that the Spirit of God dwelleth in you?" (1 Cor. 3:16.) So, when the Lord was purified as man in the Jordan, it is we who were purified in Him and by Him, and when He received the Spirit, it is we who received the Spirit.[23]

Therefore when the Scripture is speaking of the Word or of Wisdom, it may say that He is "created" (ἔκτισε),[24] but in reality such terms apply only to His human nature and to us.

Now if He did not come upon earth for His own sake, but for ours, then He was not created in Himself, but in us. And if He was not created in Himself, but in us, then He is not Himself a creature, but is speaking in the name of the flesh that He has taken. That this is the meaning of the Scriptures we learn from the Apostle, who writes to the Ephesians: "He hath broken down the dividing barrier . . . that in Himself He might create of the two [Jews and Gentiles] one new man, and make peace" (Eph. 2:4). If the two are created in Him, and if they are in His body, it may be said in a certain sense that He is created, since He bears both in Himself. For He has united creatures in Himself and He lives in them, becoming a creature like themselves. . . . Just as He is said to be weak, because He has taken our weaknesses upon Himself, although, since He is the power of God, He is not weak; and as He was made sin and malediction for us, though He had not sinned, because He bore our sins and our malediction; so, when He creates us in Himself, He can say "God created Me," although He is not a creature.

But if the Word is a creature, as the Arians say, and if it is of Himself that He says, "The Lord created Me," then surely He was not created for our sake. But if He was not created for our sake, we are not created in Him. And if we are not created in Him, then He is not within us, but outside of us; He is only a teacher from whom we receive instruction.[25]

To such a thought Athanasius will not listen. A Christ who is only a professor of religion and ethics like the masters of the Didascaleion, ceases to be Christ. Either Christ is our life and our resurrection or we are the most miserable of men. Hence Arianism, which denies this truth, is the worst of errors. Athanasius continues:

> If this is true, if Christ is only a master who teaches us from without, then sin holds sway in the flesh as much as before and it has not been driven out. But this the Apostle denies when he tells us: "We are his handiwork, created in Christ Jesus" (Eph. 2:10). If then we are created in Christ, it is not He that is created, but we are created in Him, and the word "created" is used because of us. For although the Word was the Creator, yet because of our weakness He deigned to use the language of creatures. Hence the term "created" does not apply to Him as Word, but to us who are created in Him.[26]

III

For Athanasius this method of exegesis is not a second choice, but the ideal; none other was to his way of thinking more "ecclesiastical." The more he reflects on it, the better he likes it, as we see from the last of his doctrinal works, the treatise *On the Incarnation and against the Arians,* if we may assume that the work is authentic.

There are indeed strong reasons for doubting its authenticity. But as we shall soon see, these arguments are not necessarily conclusive. In any case, for the point of doctrine that interests us, the work is a perfect continuation of the Saint's chief writings, particularly of his *Discourses against the Arians.* If Athanasius was not its author, he was certainly its inspiration, for he is everywhere in the work. We find the same method of refuting the same adversaries, and the same habit of speaking in the same breath of Christ and of the Christians. This last is a more significant indication, since it is a more unmistakable revelation of the author's mentality. The only difference is that the refutation is more fully developed and that weightier arguments are adduced in support of the textual exegesis. This progress may be accounted for by attributing the work, as the Maurists suggest, to the Saint's last years, years of greater tranquillity which gave him more leisure to breathe and to think. It seems to us that this hypothesis would solve some of the objections raised against its authenticity; it would explain the looseness of the style and the more frequent repetitions, and it would also partially account for certain modifications of formulas.

We shall, therefore, quote certain passages from the work as a complement to our study of Athanasius. In doing so, we shall be obliged to cite developments, the substance of which we have already given. At the same time, however, the identity of doctrine will be all the more evident, while from certain new features, and even from the repetitions we shall observe that the thought has become richer and more definite. First we shall take a few lines that treat of the infirmities of Christ.

> Not for His own salvation did the immortal God come, but to save us who were dead; not for Himself did He suffer, but for us, and if He took upon Himself our baseness and our poverty, it was that He might bestow on us His wealth. His Passion is our impassibility; His death is our immortality; His tears our joy, His burial our resurrection, and His baptism our sanctification. He says: "For them I hallow Myself, in order that they too may be hallowed in truth" (John 17:19). His bruises are our salvation for "by his bruises we are healed" (Isa. 53:5). His chastisement is our peace, for "the chastisement of our peace was upon Him" (*Ibid.*); that is, He was chastised for our peace. His ignominy is our glory, for in the words: "Glorify Me, Father, with Thyself, with the glory which I had before the world was, with Thee" (John 17:5), He was asking for glory on our behalf. It is we who are glorified in Him. His abasement is our ascension, as it is written: "God hath raised us up and seated us in Christ Jesus in the heavenly places, to show in the ages to come the surpassing riches of His grace through His kindness to us in Christ Jesus" (Eph. 2:6,7). His words on the cross: "Father, into Thy hands I commend My spirit" (Luke 23:46), recommend to the Father all men who receive life in Him. For they are His members and the many members form one body, which is the Church, as St. Paul writes to the Galatians: "ye are all one person in Christ Jesus" (3:28). He therefore recommends them all to the Father in Himself.[27]

Not only is the procedure the same, but the argument is based on the same principle of continuity between Christ and the faithful.

> Whatever Scripture says that the Son has received, it says because of His body; which is the first-fruits of the Church.

[282]

For "Christ is the first-fruits" (1 Cor. 15:23). When the first-fruits received the name that is above all names, then the entire mass was raised up with Him and seated with Him on His throne, according to the words: "He hath raised us up and seated us in Christ Jesus in the heavenly places." It is thus that men have received the grace to be called gods and sons of God. First the Lord raised His own body from the dead and exalted it in His own person; then He raised up the members of His body, in order that as God He might bestow on them all the graces that He has received as man.[28]

So perfect is the union of Head and members that even when the Saviour gives us life in Himself, it is Himself that He vivifies.

Therefore He gives life to Himself, He sanctifies Himself, He exalts Himself. Consequently when He says that the Father has sanctified Him, raised Him up and given Him a name which is above all names, and has given Him life, it is evident that the Father has done all this through Him. Through Him does God raise Him up, through Him God sanctifies Him, through Him does God glorify Him, and through Him does God give Him life. And when Jesus commends His spirit into the hands of His Father, He is commending Himself as man to God, in order thus to commend all men to God.[29]

Christ's whole humanity is the Church. Therefore, declares Athanasius:

When Peter said: "Let the whole house of Israel know for certain that God hath made Him both Lord and Christ, even this Jesus whom ye have crucified" (Acts 2:36), he was not speaking of the divinity, but he means that His humanity, which is the whole Church, was made Lord and Christ.[30]

To preserve the full force of this and other passages we have cited, it seems we must say that the hypostatic union does not affect our Lord alone, but that it is somehow prolonged in us, the members; that we are the prolongation of the Head, and that the hypostatic union renders us divine by reason of our continuity with the Man-God. This Athanasius repeats:

After the crucifixion, it is the Church who governs and rules in Christ; she is anointed for the kingdom of the heavens, that she may reign with Him who emptied Himself for her and who, by assuming the form of a slave, has taken her into Himself. For the Word, the Son of God, was always Lord and God. He

[283]

was not made Lord and Christ after His crucifixion, but as I have said above, it is His human nature that the divinity has made Lord and Christ.[31]

Again Athanasius reiterates, with the insistence of age: by our continuity with Christ, we are all made divine.

All the lowly things which the Scriptures tell us concerning the Lord refer to His poverty. These things are said to show us that we are enriched in Him, and not to make us blaspheme the Son of God. The Son of God became the Son of man in order that the sons of men, the sons of Adam, might be made sons of God. The Word, who was begotten of the Father in heaven in an ineffable, inexplicable, incomprehensible and eternal manner, came to this earth to be born in time of the Virgin Mary, Mother of God, in order that they who were born of earth might be born again of God, in heaven. . . . Therefore He calls Himself the Son of man, so that men may call God their heavenly Father: "Our Father, who art in heaven" (Matt. 6:9, D.V.). Just as we, the servants of God, are made sons of God, so the Lord of servants became the mortal son of His own servant Adam, in order that the mortal sons of Adam might become sons of God, as it is written: "He gave them power to become children of God" (John 1:12). The Son of God suffers death because of His father according to the flesh [i.e., Adam], so that the sons of man might have part in the life of God, because of God who is their Father according to the Spirit. He is the Son of God by nature, we by grace; He has become the son of Adam through His goodness and graciousness, while we are sons of Adam by nature. . . . He has bestowed upon us the first-fruits of the Holy Spirit, so that we may all become sons of God in imitation of the Son of God. Thus He, the true and natural Son of God, bears us all [in Himself], so that we may all bear [in ourselves] the only God.[32]

These passages are sufficient proof that the doctrine contained in the treatise *On the Incarnation and against the Arians* is identical with that expressed in those works of the Saint which we have already studied.

IV

And now, by way of conclusion, we may say that the doctrine of the Mystical Body occupies a place of prime importance in the theology of St. Athanasius. We have seen that it is very often used by the Saint to explain, to express, and to prove that particular truth in the defense of which he labored most strenuously; it is frequently used also to refute the principal arguments of his greatest adversaries, that is, in order to give an orthodox interpretation of those texts with which the Arians tried to support their heresy. So deeply had this truth penetrated into his soul that he expresses it almost unconsciously — so deeply indeed that we, too, must keep that truth in mind if we are to understand the passages in which he speaks of the Saviour and of us at one and the same time, without making any distinction between the two.

Having thus taken possession of Athanasius, the doctrine grew with him. It flowed from his pen with a clearness and a forcefulness of expression that increased in proportion as Catholic orthodoxy became, so to speak, incarnate in him. We have been able to observe this fact in the preceding pages: the works of his maturer years contain more frequent references to the doctrine than do the writings of his youth.

Thus we may say, in the words of an author who is no longer modern, but whose appreciation is no less true today than when it was written: "Athanasius had taken deep, firm root in the Church. He identified himself with her, and her past was ever present to him. He taught that Jesus Christ is interiorly united with His Church, and that in a sense He Himself is the Church."[33]

If we now pass to the content of the doctrine, the first thing we note is the fact that this truth is not developed for its own sake. A superficial reading might even give the impression that it is totally, or at least almost totally absent. The Scriptural comparisons of the body and members, of the vine and branches, are relatively rare. Almost the only expression of frequent occurrence is St. Paul's phrase: "in Christ."

As we have already remarked in speaking of Irenaeus, the truth of the Mystical Body is not always explained *ex professo* or given a separate treatment. Indeed, if we are to make our study fruitful, we must rid ourselves of a too fragmentary conception of Christian dogma. Since that dogma is one whole, the various parts of revelation are implicitly contained one within the other. And, more than other dogmas, the truth of

[285]

our incorporation in Christ, which is so rich in applications, in consequences, and in contrasting aspects, is often developed, and forcefully, too, without being explicitly mentioned.

Thus it is with Athanasius. His teaching on the Mystical Body is a doctrine of the divinization of the faithful. He explains that we are changed, raised up, adopted, and deified through the union of grace which the Incarnate Word gives us with Himself. What he says either of our justification or of the Incarnate Word, he applies also to the supernatural body which we form in the same Incarnate Word.

He was disposed to adopt this attitude, both by his philosophical mentality and by reason of his pastoral cares. We see this in his early writings, where he beholds the divinity in the effects that it produces among us; in the vitality of the Church he sees a manifestation of the life of the risen Saviour. This attitude he retains; it is even intensified and becomes more deliberate during the Arian controversy. What he ever sees, what he ever emphasizes in the life of the Church and in the life of the Christians, is the divinity, the strict divinity of the Saviour. This divinity makes us divine; the Incarnation that has produced the Man-God is an all-conquering act; it is to make us adoptive sons of God; in fine, to cite the oft-repeated words of the Fourth Gospel, since Jesus Christ is the Son, He is our Life.

But how and why He is our life, and how the Incarnation has of itself this power to unite the entire regenerated human race with God in Christ, Athanasius does not explain. On this cardinal point his work remains incomplete. The task of completion was to be accomplished chiefly by St. Hilary and by St. Cyril of Alexandria.

Still, although the theology of Athanasius on the Mystical Body is not perfect, it is extremely rich in doctrine. We can see how much of that theology is concerned with our adoption in the Saviour, our redemption through union with Him, the communication of properties from Christ to us, the dignity of our bodies and of our souls, the veneration due to the saints, the influence exercised upon us by each event of Jesus' life, the inhabitation of the Holy Ghost in our souls, and the supernatural unity of the whole Church. All this Athanasius tells us when he shows how we are deified in Christ. We have already met with practically every one of these elements of the doctrine in the works of St. Irenaeus, while in the writings of the later Fathers — or at least of those Fathers who have left us a rather fully developed teaching on the subject of the Mystical Body — we shall have occasion to see nearly all of them again. To avoid needless repetition, we shall not enumerate these elements each time they appear, for Tradition is now in complete possession of the treasure.

It is to be noted, however, that to this treasure Athanasius has added a gem, a gem discovered before him, but which he has cut and polished. We refer to the method of exegesis that is founded upon our mystical identity with the Saviour, and which our Saint employs so constantly against the Arians. It is a jewel destined to shine often in the years to come.

Chapter V

St. Hilary. Divinization by Incorporation in the Incarnate Word

><

I. *St. Hilary.* Why we place him with the Fathers of the East. His importance. Conversion and first contact with the doctrine of the Mystical Body. Other possible contacts during his exile in Asia Minor.
II. *His doctrine.* 1. All men are one; they are contained in Christ. Hilary has even been accused of conceiving the Incarnation as a hypostatic union of the Word with the entire human race.
2. Christ contains the whole "nature" of men, their whole race. This is a "sacrament," which is effected by baptism, and which places us in "the body of Christ." Thus we are "assumed" in Christ, that we may be divinized in Him.
III. *The Mystical Body and the Eucharist.* Commentary of the text: "That they may be one, as We are one." Our union is real, for it is the effect of baptism, and Christ tells us that it is real. Christ produces this unity especially in the Eucharist, where He becomes truly one with us without ceasing to be one with the Father. The Eucharist makes the Incarnation complete; that is, it makes men divine by uniting them to Christ in a unity that is ineffably real.
IV. *Conclusion.* The chief characteristic of this doctrine of the Mystical Body is realism. The alleged "collective incarnation" is simply the mystical extension of the effects of the Incarnation to all men. But whence has the Incarnation this power of expansion? Hilary does not tell us. His doctrine closes with a certain vagueness, and with some rather infelicitous expressions. Providence must still lead the dogma of the Incarnation to its perfect expression, by means of the theological development of the fifth century.

I

HILARY belongs to the Latin Church. He was born at Poitiers about 315, of pagan parents. The exact date of his conversion cannot be ascertained, but we know that in 355 he assisted as a bishop at the Council of Milan. He received his profane education in the then famous schools of Poitiers, and it was probably also at Poitiers that he studied the truths of Christianity.

Nevertheless, for the doctrine of the Mystical Body at least, his teaching is more in line with oriental tradition. He repeats the theology of St. Athanasius; whether or not he realized the fact, is not important. He even makes some notable contributions to that theology, and these contributions are precisely those that we shall see again later in the works of Cyril of Alexandria. Of this the reader may judge from the whole of the following study.

We do not know the explanation of these resemblances. One might easily conjecture certain possible influences, but that is all we can do at present. The study of Hilary's connections with Greek theology, and even of his connections with the Greek language, might lead to interesting conclusions. But the study would be a long and difficult one, and as far as we know no one has yet been tempted to undertake it.

At all events, our Saint has merited the title of "the Athanasius of the West." Not that his thought and style are those of the great Doctor; on the contrary, his writings make hard reading. But he possesses the same strength of soul coupled with the same sweetness of character; he has the same jealous love of orthodoxy; he carries on the same battles against the same enemies; he suffered the same exiles: Hilary, from Gaul to Asia Minor, and Athanasius from Alexandria to Gaul. And finally, he teaches the same energetic doctrine on the subject of the Mystical Body.

As to the manner in which he came into contact with the doctrine of the Mystical Body we have but one indication. This indication, while precious — for he gives it himself — is also very incomplete, since it deals with only one aspect of this doctrine. Besides, it is not easy of interpretation.

We have reference to an account given in the beginning of his work *De Trinitate*, which was written about 356 or 357. Here he tells the story of his conversion, which had taken place several years earlier; the exact year is unknown. The

[289]

narrative, which serves as an introduction to the book, treats of our knowledge of God, which faith alone renders sufficient and even perfect; in this way Hilary leads up to the studies on the Trinity which are contained in the volume. However, the very literary purpose of the account lessens its documentary value. There is always the possibility that these thoughts may have been suggested by his state of mind at the time of writing rather than by his actual impressions as a catechumen. This is all more likely because of Hilary's preoccupation with the theological questions upon which he is working and in which he soon becomes wholly absorbed. Moreover, the manner in which the phases of his conversion are recorded reminds one of the apologetic method outlined thirty years earlier by Athanasius in the *Discourse against the Greeks* and in the *Discourse on the Incarnation*. The reader will recall how the patriarch of Alexandria insisted upon the vitality of the Church as a proof of the divinity of Christ. The thoughts which Hilary develops follow along much the same line.

For these reasons it is difficult to determine to what extent Hilary's account is a true biographical document. However, we shall not disregard it; its tone of sincerity and conviction, as well as its place at the beginning of a treatise whose sole aim is the objective search of the whole truth do not seem to permit us to regard it as mere fiction. Its resemblance to the treatise of Athanasius may be simply a proof that the process described by the holy patriarch was at least occasionally the same as the course followed in actual life by the workings of grace.

However that may be, we shall mention the indications which the passage contains. To begin with, Hilary declares that he had always felt that to know God was the one thing necessary. To satisfy this thirst for knowledge he had turned to the systems of philosophy, but these led only to contradictions and absurdities. At last he chanced upon the Holy Books, and in them he found the truth. He was particularly impressed by what they said of the divine immensity, in virtue of which God contains all things, and by the doctrine of the Incarnation as it is taught by St. John. This doctrine, as the reader will recall, is also a doctrine of the Mystical Body; St. John explains both that Christ is the Word of God and that as His members we receive the divine life in Him.

Although the account is not very clear on the point, it would seem that at this time Hilary had already taken the decisive step; he tells us that he had found more than he had hoped for; he had been baptized, and faith had given him a new birth and a new life.

For the Word who is God became flesh, that through this Word made flesh, the flesh might attain to union with the Word who is God.[1]

For the Word has created our race anew in Himself; He has blotted out the ancient decree of condemnation.[2]

Life in Christ, divinization in Christ, a second creation in Christ. All these are ways of expressing our mystical incorporation in the Saviour. In the present passage they are not very prominent, since they record only Hilary's first contact with the doctrine.

We wish to note these expressions, unfruitful as they seem to be in indications, because they throw some faint light upon the way in which God watches over the deposit of truth and promotes its growth. In the course of these studies we shall see that ever since apostolic times Providence seems more than once to have made use of visions and inner experiences, not indeed in order to teach men any new doctrine concerning the life of Christ in the soul, but in order to aid them in understanding what the Scriptures have said upon this subject. Even in the days of the Apostles we saw that God followed a like method in directing the writers of His Scriptures. It was in a vision that He taught Paul how He is with His brethren all days, and it was probably also in a vision that He gave John a deeper understanding than the other Apostles of His life in us and ours in Him. He remains faithful to His ways; He guides Tradition in the same manner as He guided the composition of the Scriptures.

We make this remark in order to prevent a possible misunderstanding of the meaning and importance of certain visions which we shall mention in this book. None of these were given as the revelation of new truth, except, of course, those recorded in the Scriptures; their sole purpose was

[291]

to direct attention to what had been taught since the beginning.

Returning now to St. Hilary, we must note that the vision we have cited does not appear to have been the principal source of the Saint's information concerning the Mystical Body. It is highly probable that he received instruction on this point in the schools of Gaul where he studied theology. As we shall see, many texts of his *Commentary on the Gospel of St. Matthew,* which dates from this period, already betray considerable familiarity with the teaching of Tradition on the subject.

Not long afterwards, during his exile in Asia Minor, he had an opportunity to learn more of the doctrine, although we cannot accurately determine either to what extent this further study was still necessary, or how much he actually did learn at this period.

Hilary's exile dates from the early years of his episcopate. Until then he had not even heard of Arianism or of the struggle against the heresy. Now he, too, was to be thrown into the conflict. At this very time Saturninus of Arles was endeavoring, with the support of Ursacius and Valens, to win Gaul away from the side of orthodoxy. Hilary resisted him vigorously, but his courage exposed him to the imperial displeasure. In 356 he was banished by Constantius to the political diocese of Asia.

He was entering a region where the doctrine of the Mystical Body had been the subject of much study, as we remarked in the conclusion of the chapter devoted to St. Irenaeus. In this way Hilary, who was to become the soul of the opposition against Arianism, necessarily came into close contact with the doctrine. In fact, his most important passage on the Mystical Body dates from the period of his exile. As we shall see, the passage bears a striking resemblance to a long text of St. Cyril of Alexandria, who likewise had many connections with Asia Minor. These two facts seem to point to an oriental influence.

However, since it is impossible for us to distinguish what Hilary then learned from what he already knew, we shall make no distinction between the works that were written before and after his exile.

[292]

II. § 1

For St. Hilary as for St. Athanasius, there is a close solidarity of all men even in the natural order. In the supernatural order their solidarity is still more intimate. All together, they form but one body, one whole, a *universitas*. In each man we find all other men. Thus, in the paralytic who lay at the Saviour's feet all nations are present, waiting to be healed; Doeg represents all the wicked; Adam, and later Abraham, contain all men in themselves. As Hilary writes in the *Commentary on St. Matthew*:

> Every man was in Christ Jesus, and so His body, the instrument of the Word, accomplished in itself the whole mystery of our redemption.[3]
> Our Lord is transfused into the bodies of each of the faithful.[4]
> He has taken the body of each of us, and through this body He is become our closest of kin.[5]
> Thus, by reason of this body, all humanity is contained in Him. By this union of all men in Himself, He is like a city, and by our union with His flesh we are the inhabitants.[6]

There is no need of pointing out the energy of such expressions; they brought upon Hilary the same accusation that was made against St. Methodius. As early as the sixteenth century, Erasmus complains that Hilary went so far in teaching a union of the Word with the whole human race, that he lost sight of the incommunicable nature of the Incarnation. Even today, Protestant critics speak in the same strain. Nor have these expressions failed to arouse astonishment on the Catholic side. Certain writers explain them away as oratorical exaggerations, and say that Hilary and other Fathers who employ similar formulas simply meant that Christ has merited all justice for us and that our holiness bears some distant likeness to His own. This, they maintain, is sufficient reason why the Saint should speak of a universal incarnation; the Incarnation is universal, not indeed in itself, but in its effects, and those effects are quite distinct from the hypostatic union.

The answer is a good one, but it seems to sacrifice overmuch of the truth. Must we abandon ways of speaking which are so direct and which are sanctioned by so many of the Fathers, with a mere appeal to extenuating circumstances? We think not. In our opinion, these formulas contain doctrinal treasures so sublime and so delicate that years of trial and effort were necessary before they could be given satisfactory expression. One by one the Fathers take up this work, until at length one of them succeeds in putting into words what all have been trying to explain from the outset; namely, the close mystical union that exists between the Saviour's divinity and the divinization of the Christian.

In the time of St. Hilary the process was only beginning, and his formulas are far from being perfect; but no long study is needed to convince one that what the Saint is trying to express is the wonderful mystery of our incorporation in the Man-God.

§ 2

Our Saint readily admits that it is a mystery, a "sacrament" (*sacramentum*); that is, something full of meaning, transcendent meaning, something, too, that imposes an obligation upon one, by virtue of a religious and sacred necessity. It is, he says, the "sacrament" of us in Christ, or again, it is the "sacrament" of Christ in us.

These two expressions are synonymous, and have been so since the beginning of the Christian era. If need be, their meaning may be determined by comparison with other expressions of which the Saint is almost as fond, and which likewise speak of the same two correlative interiorities. Hilary loves to repeat that all men were in Jesus Christ, in Him was the nature of us all; and, at the same time, he tells us, Christ is in the nature of every man, in the nature of all flesh, by reason of the body that He has assumed.

The context leaves no possible doubt concerning the sense of the word *nature* in these expressions. Nearly always there is question, not of the comprehension of human nature, to use a philosophical expression, but of its extension. The Saint means and says that all men have become interior to the Saviour in a certain real sense. His explanations make this point decisive. The effect of this presence of the nature of us all in Christ is to enable us all to contemplate ourselves in Him, while in virtue of the Incarnation, He Himself dwells within each one of us. Or again, he tells us that the Good Shepherd has taken the lost sheep not upon His shoulders, but into His own flesh.

Among the other Fathers, we know of only one who makes use of the term *nature* (*natura* or φύσις) in the same expressions and with the same frequency. This is St. Cyril of Alexandria, who also has other points in common with St. Hilary. Here again we are unable to assign a reason for the resemblance, but the fact at least merits mention.

Perhaps a Platonist training in philosophy may partially explain why both make similar use of the word *nature* and why both consider all the individuals of a species as forming one whole. But this at least is certain, that neither Hilary nor Cyril is here drawing upon philosophical theses. Human speculation may have helped them to discover formulas, and it may have made those formulas hard for us to understand; but we cannot see that it taught them anything about the truth itself. This truth, as they present it, is a mystery, a mystery that follows from the Incarnation, and not a corollary drawn from abstract metaphysics. It is the ancient teaching of Scripture and Tradition, that Christ abides in us and we in Him.

It will be well to note that the term *natura* (or φύσις) which they use so freely does not correspond exactly to our word *nature*. It often has a vague, general meaning; to render the thought, we have found no better word than *reality* and its derivatives. Frequently it is best not to try to translate it at all. In such cases we shall use the English word "nature," but within quotation marks. We shall take care always to make the expression easily recognizable.

Let us now return to the mystery, the "sacrament" of which Hilary speaks so often: the mystery of our nature in Christ, and of Christ abiding in us all.

The Saint explains that this mutual penetration takes place for the first time in baptism. Did not he himself experience this at the moment of his own baptism? By being born again of water and the Holy Spirit,

> We are reconciled in the body of His flesh. Therefore by union with the flesh that He has assumed, we are in Christ. This is God's mystery, hidden in God for ages and generations and now revealed to His saints, that in Christ we are coheirs, concorporate and comparticipants in the promise of God (Eph. 3:5,6). By union with His flesh, all enter into Christ. . . . He will transform their baseness into the glory of His flesh, on condition that they resist their passions, purify themselves of their stains in the sacrament of the new birth, and remember that henceforth they bear not their own flesh, but Christ's.[7]

> He renews us unto a new life; He transforms us into a new man, by placing us in the body of His flesh. For He is the Church; by the mystery of His body, He contains her wholly within Himself.[8]

At our death the change will be made manifest in a wondrous way. This the Saint explains when he compares the body of Christ with a holy mountain, where we shall find our rest.

> His holy mountain is the body which He has taken of man. . . . Upon this mountain is built a city that cannot be hid, for as the Apostle says: "Other foundation no man can lay, but that which is laid, which is Christ Jesus" (1 Cor. 3:12, D.V.). Since, then, they that are Christ's have been chosen by God in the body of Christ before the creation of the world; since the Church is the body of Christ, and Christ is the foundation of our edifice and the city built upon the mountain, the question now arises: "Who can rest upon this mountain?"

The answer is that upon it we ourselves shall enjoy lasting peace after death.

> All our hope of repose is in the body of Christ, and since it is upon this mountain that we are to rest, then this mountain can only be the body which He has taken of us. Before He took it, He was already God; in it, He is still God, and by it He transforms the infirmities of our body unto the image of His own glorious body, provided that on our part we crucify the vices of our body to His Cross, so that we may rise in His body. It is to this body that we shall ascend, after our sojourn in the Church [militant during our mortal life]; in it shall we repose in the glory of God.[9]

The passage requires explanation. In the preface to his edition of St. Hilary's works, Dom Coustant expresses clearly the

idea which the Saint is trying to propose.[10] The glorification of
the elect is considered in two stages; first, while awaiting the
final judgment, the souls separated from their own bodies are
united to the body of Christ, which is already risen. This the
Saint calls the Kingdom of Christ. Then, after the general
resurrection and when they are reunited with their bodies,
the souls will enjoy the glory of heaven directly. And this he
calls the Kingdom of God.

To what extent these ideas express a profound conviction of
St. Hilary is hard to say; neither his works nor Tradition
supply the necessary context. He may simply have considered
this a convenient way of representing and expressing what he
had to say. At least we may remark in passing that the passage
gives evidence of the supereminent role reserved to Christ's individual human nature by this same Hilary who is accused of
disregarding that individuality.

There is no need to push our investigation further; the
Saint's doctrine of the Mystical Body is independent of these
eschatological views. For him our incorporation with Christ
is just as real, if less manifest, during our life on earth as it
will be after death.

> Being made man of the Virgin, He took in Himself the
> "reality" of the flesh. Thus the whole human race is united and
> sanctified in Him. And, as all are restored in Him through the
> body which He willed to take, so too does He take up His
> abode in all spiritually.[11]

> He had no need of becoming man, for it was He that made
> man. But we had need that God should become flesh and dwell
> in us, that is, that He should assume one body of flesh and
> thus dwell within all flesh. His abasement is our nobility, His
> ignominy is our glory; since He is God in the flesh, we are
> renewed from the flesh unto God.[12]

So, as our Saint is fond of saying, we are "assumed" in Him;
the mystery, the "sacrament" consists in our "assumption" in
Christ. He expresses this thought several times in the long
passage on the Incarnation which opens the ninth book of the
treatise *De Trinitate*. The extracts we shall cite illustrate the
sure sense of orthodoxy which enabled Hilary, like Athanasius,
to condemn the heresies of Nestorius and Eutyches years
before their appearance. We may likewise observe how, like

[297]

Athanasius, Hilary makes scarcely any distinction between what is true of Christ and what is true of the Christians. For Hilary as for Athanasius, what is essential is the continuity that joins the Head and the members, causes the glories of the Head to pass into the members, and effects the collective divinization of human nature by virtue of the singular union of the Word with the Saviour's humanity. First we give a few introductory texts. "Nestorius and Eutyches, beware!"[13] warns the editor, Dom Coustant.

> All those of our common faith should be well instructed, in order that as the confession of that faith gives us eternity of life, so it may also give us an understanding of eternity.
> He is ignorant, totally ignorant of his own life, who does not know that Christ Jesus is both true God and true man. It is equally dangerous to deny in Christ Jesus either the spiritual element that makes Him God or the flesh of our body.

"The flesh of our body." The formula is well chosen to show the relation of the Incarnation to the human race. As the author says further on:

> This mystery is not for God, but for us. God gains nothing by our "assumption" [i.e., by taking us into Himself], but His voluntary abasement is our exaltation. God loses none of His divinity, while man is enabled to become God.

"Man is enabled to become God." Of what man is Hilary speaking? Does he mean the physical humanity of Jesus, or the entire Mystical Body? He does not tell us explicitly, but he at once goes on to insist upon the communion that unites us to the Saviour:

> God, the Only-begotten Son, is born man of the Virgin, so that He may raise man, in Himself, to the dignity of God.[14]
> God is therefore born that we may be taken up [lit., for our "assumption"] into God; He suffers to restore us to innocence; He dies to expiate our sins. Thus the human nature of each of us is in God, and our infirmities and sufferings are united with God.[15]

Plainly, Hilary means that that union with the Word, which is possessed by Christ in all plenitude, is somehow extended to us by participation. This the Saint tells us immediately, when he explains the following text of St. Paul's Epistle to the

Colossians: "In Him dwelleth all the fullness of the Godhead corporally, and ye are filled [therewith] in Him, who is the head of every principality and power" (Col. 2:9,10).

After declaring that the fullness of the divinity is corporally present in Christ, the Apostle at once goes on to speak of the mystery of our "assumption." He tells us "Ye are filled in Him." For, just as the fullness of the divinity is present in Him, so we too are filled in Him. Nor does Paul say merely, "Ye are filled," but "Ye are filled in Him," because whether we are already regenerated or whether we have yet to be re-generated by the hope of our faith unto eternal life, we all abide now in the body of Christ. Later on we shall be filled, no longer in Him but in ourselves, on that day when, as the Apostle tells us, "He will transform the body of our lowliness, that it may be one with the body of His glory" (Phil. 3:21).[16]

Such is the mystery of His "nature" [of what He really is] and of our "assumption" [still the same continuity]; it is the fullness of the divinity dwelling in Him and our being filled in Him by reason of His human birth.[17]

Our resurrection will manifest our exaltation. Then it will be clearly seen that Christ unites our whole "nature" to the divine immortality; that Christ has taken the "nature" of all flesh, and by thus becoming the true Vine He contains in Himself the whole race of branches, and makes us sons of God as He was made the Son of man; that all can enter and that each has entered into the body of God and into His Kingdom by virtue of the Incarnation. For by becoming flesh, the Word assumed the "nature" of the entire human race.

III

As we see, not only does the Saviour's physical body occupy a pre-eminent position, but it also has a necessary function in this Mystical Body. It is through Christ's individual human nature that human nature in general is united in God. And this is true not only in the life to come, but in this life and always.

St. Hilary explains this point in his most remarkable passage concerning the Mystical Body. He is speaking of the prayer of Christ recorded by St. John: "That they may be one, Father, as We are one." In our study of St. Athanasius we have already seen what an uproar the Arians made about this text,

[299]

and the consequent importance, from the standpoint of the doctrine of the Mystical Body, of the commentaries given by the Fathers.

St. Hilary's commentary is more complete than that of Athanasius. It possesses many additional features which closely resemble those we shall see in St. Cyril of Alexandria. Both bring the Eucharist into the commentary; both show that the sacramental Body communicates to us unity in God and in Christ; both declare repeatedly that this unity wrought by Christ is real. It is, declares Hilary, *unitas naturalis;* ἔνωσις φυσική, insists Cyril.

St. Hilary places his commentary at the beginning of the eighth book of the treatise *De Trinitate.* He introduces his subject with a vigorous attack against the proselytizing heretics, who are more zealous in spreading error than are the Catholics in the defense of the truth. As an instance of their impiety and trickery, he cites their interpretation of the text in question. In the unity of the Father and Son they admit only a union of wills, not a unity of substance. The sole argument they give is that the unity which binds us together, and to which Christ compares His own unity with the Father, is just such a unity, a mere unity of charity. Scripture itself suggests this interpretation, the heretics assure us, since it clearly ascribes the unity of the faithful to the fact that "they have one heart and one soul" (Acts 4:32, D.V.). Hilary retorts with some heat:

> One must be quite insane not to know God. And, since Christ is Wisdom, he must be bereft of wisdom who does not know Christ.[18]

The thought of a mere moral unity, whether among the faithful or among the Divine Persons, seems to him frankly absurd. According to the Arians the faithful are one because they have but one heart and one soul. But, pursues our Saint, the truth is that this unity of wills has its source in the unity of faith, and the unity of faith is a "natural" (we should say "real") unity. For it consists in that new, unique life which we receive at baptism: it comes from that eternal reality which is present in us by the operation of grace. This profound unity of life is alone capable of producing unanimity of heart and soul. "Let us hear no more of a mere union of wills in those who are one in the 'reality' of one and the same regeneration."[19]

We are neither preaching any new doctrine of our own nor corrupting the meaning of words in order to deceive our hearers with lying fictions. . . . The Apostle himself teaches that the unity of the faithful proceeds from the "nature" of the sacraments. "All of you who were baptized into Christ, have put on Christ. There is neither Jew nor Greek. . . . Ye are all one person in Christ Jesus" (Gal. 3:27,28). Can we attribute this unity, which exists amid so great a diversity of nationalities, of circumstances, and of sexes, to a mere agreement of wills, and not rather to the unity of the sacrament, to this baptism which is the same for all and which clothes us all in one and the same Christ? What has mere unanimity to do here? We are one because we have all been clothed with the one Christ in the "reality" of one and the same baptism.[20]

Thus the argument, by which the heretics thought to defend their interpretation, is turned against them. Now Hilary comes to the text itself: "That they may be one, as We are one." No one with the slightest understanding of this passage, says our Saint, could interpret it as the Arians do.

Why do you talk of unanimity, of unity of soul and heart resulting from an agreement of wills? If the Lord had intended to make us one in this manner, He should rather have worded His prayer thus: "Father, as We will the same thing, so may they too will the same thing, that by this unanimity we may all be one."

Is He, who is the Word, ignorant of the meaning of words? Or is He, who is Truth, unable to speak the truth? Can He who is Wisdom have uttered meaningless words? Or is He, who is Power, so impotent that He could not say what He meant? No! He has expressed the mysteries of the Gospel in words that are true and exact. He was addressing not only our intellects but our faith as well, when He said: "That they all may be one, even as Thou, Father, art in Me, and I in Thee; that they too may be one in Us" (John 17:21). First He prays for them, "That they may all be one." Then He points to the divine unity as the model of their unity, saying: "As Thou, Father, art in Me, and I in Thee, that they too may be in Us." As the Father is in the Son, and the Son in the Father, so all should be one in the Father and the Son according to the example of this unity.[21]

The Saint proceeds to show that so far is this unity from

[301]

being merely a union of wills, that it is a sign of Christ's divinity; it is not the simple result of our own good dispositions, but a grace coming from God. It is the glory that Christ has received of the Father and which He extends to us; it is the communication of His divinity to men. These are daring words, as Hilary admits, but they are deserving of our faith; to hope for such a thing would be folly, but not to believe in it is blasphemy. All the faithful are "assumed by the glory of the Son, unto unity with the glory of the Father."[22]

But we have already spoken of this divinization, says the Saint (and, since we, too, have already treated the subject elsewhere, we shall not dwell upon it here). What we must now examine, continues Hilary, are the means by which that divinization is communicated to us. As he explains in several splendid pages which we shall quote at length, this means is the Eucharist.

> I shall now ask a few questions of those who admit only this union of wills between the Father and the Son. Is Christ within us today by agreement of wills, or by the truth of His "nature"? Since the Word has truly become flesh, and since in the Lord's Supper we truly receive the flesh of the Word, how can anyone say that He does not abide "really" in us? For by becoming man He has taken to Himself for all time the "reality" of our flesh and has united both the "reality" of His flesh and the "reality" of His divinity in the Sacrament of His flesh which we receive. This is why we are all one: the Father is in Christ and Christ is in us. Therefore whoever denies that the Father is "really" in Christ must first deny either that he himself is "really" in Christ or that Christ is "really" in him. For that which makes us one in the Father and the Son is the fact that the Father is in Christ and Christ is in us. Since, therefore, Christ has taken the flesh of our body, and since He is truly a man born of Mary, and since beneath the sacred species we truly partake of the flesh of His body (and are thus made one, since the Father is in Him and He is in us), how can there be question of a mere union of wills? The "reality" of His presence within us in the Eucharist and of our "assumption" in Him through the Incarnation prove how perfect is our unity with the Father.[23]

Therefore Christ is united with the Christians for two reasons: He has taken them all into Himself by His Incarnation and He comes into them all in the Eucharist. True, these two mystical interiorities are not on the same level. The first, which proceeds from the Incarnation, is the indispensable principle of the other. The second is simply the application to all men, the full realization, of the first. It is by coming into us in the Eucharist that Christ enables us to live that divine life which, by means of the Incarnation, He has brought to every man. Let us hear the Saint continue his exposition of these marvels of Eucharistic theology. We could not imagine a more intimate union, he explains.

> Christ Himself tells us how truly we are in Him by the communion of His body and blood, when He says: "The world beholdeth Me no more; but ye behold Me, because I live and ye shall live. In that day ye shall know that I am in the Father, and ye in Me, and I in you" (John 14:19,20). If He meant a mere union of wills, why did He thus indicate the steps by which this unity is to become perfect? What He means is that He is in the Father by the "reality" of His divinity, that we are in Him by His corporal birth, and that He is in us by the mystery of the Eucharist. This is the perfect unity that we have through the Mediator: He contains us in Himself and at the same time He abides in the Father; and while He abides in the Father, He abides in us. Thus we attain unity with the Father, for He is "really" in the Father, we are "really" in Him, and He is "really" in us.[24]
>
> Christ tells us how "natural" [real] is this unity in us when He says: "He that eateth My flesh and drinketh My blood, abideth in Me and I in him" (John 6:57). No one will be in Christ unless Christ be in him, and Christ will take ["assume"] into Himself the flesh of none save those who have partaken of His own flesh. He teaches us the mystery of this perfect union in the words: "As the living Father hath sent Me, and I live by the Father; so he that eateth Me, the same also shall live by Me" (John 6:58, D.V.). So He lives by the Father, and we live by Him in the same way as He lives by the Father. . . . If then we men live "naturally" by Him, that is, by possessing within us the "reality" of His flesh, how is it possible that in His divinity He should not possess the Father "naturally" in Himself, since He lives by the Father?[25]

The Saint concludes with a reference to the question that led to this exegetical discussion.

> We have mentioned this matter because lying heretics use the analogy of our own union with God as a proof that the

[303]

unity of the Father and the Son is a mere unity of wills. As if we were united to the Son, and by the Son to the Father by no other bond than our obedience and our readiness to serve, and as if this "natural" communion through the sacrament of His Body and Blood had nothing to do with it! On the contrary, the glory of the Son that is given us, the presence of the Son in us by His flesh, and our inseparable and corporal union in Him, all show that we must preach the mystery of a true and "natural" unity.[26]

IV

Here we have Hilary's own summary of his teaching on the Mystical Body. Having now presented it in its entirety, we can examine some of its characteristics. The dominant trait, we may say, is realism. For Hilary it is literally true that all the faithful are one, really one, in Christ, and that in Him they receive a new, divine life, the life which the Incarnation has given in all its plenitude to the human nature of the Saviour.

It is this realism that inspires so many forceful expressions. Christ contains in Himself all the "reality (*natura*) of our race," and "we ourselves are all contained in Christ." It is this realism, too, that leads the Saint to compare our unity in Christ with the consubstantial unity of the Divine Persons and to regard the mystical presence of the Saviour in the souls of men and His sacramental presence in the Eucharist as equally real.

Hilary's doctrine, like that of St. Athanasius, is essentially a doctrine of our divinization, with this difference that it is more developed than Athanasius' teaching and tends to become also a doctrine of the Incarnation. However, it does not quite attain that goal.

According to Hilary, our union with Christ and with one another is closely related to the union of the Son with the Father; we are all taken up, all assumed, all made divine in the body taken by the Word.

And the Saint points out the means whereby this assumption is accomplished; this means is the Eucharist, the union of our souls with the flesh of Christ.

Thus his is a more vigorous expression of the very clear

doctrine of Athanasius that we are incorporated not directly into Christ's divinity, but into His humanity.

But the Saviour's human nature has this power by virtue of His divinity. The man Christ makes us divine because He is God. Thus our divinization is explained by the Incarnation.

Hence the one transcendent Incarnation has as its consequence a certain collective and mystical incarnation, and the two not only do not exclude each other, but the second is simply the radiation of the first. This is Hilary's true teaching concerning this particular point in which he has been accused of error. He does not deny the one Man-God; on the contrary, he never ceases to profess Him. Some few passages there are which, if removed from their context, might seem to imply something else, but even they render the same testimony when they are restored to their proper place in the whole of his teaching. All these passages have appeared in this chapter; the reader can judge of their meaning.

But how does this union with the divinity enable the humanity of Christ to contain us all mystically? What gives the Incarnation this universal and unseen prolongation? The bishop of Poitiers does not tell us. It would seem that he has some inkling of the answer, but he halts at this point, hesitant and uncertain.

He knows very well in what direction the answer must be sought; he knows that everything is to be explained by a certain exaltation, by an "amelioration" produced through the hypostatic union in the humanity of the Word. But he himself does no more than venture a few hazardous steps toward a solution. One might say that he lets imagination supply for doctrine in order to represent the excellence of the Saviour. He pictures the humanity of Christ as superior in essence, formed of some heavenly matter by reason of His virgin birth and the part taken by God and by the Son Himself in His conception. Hilary considered the sacred humanity to be by nature independent of the laws of nature, not subject to fatigue or sorrow or death. To walk upon the water, to heal the sick by a mere touch were not extraordinary effects, but rather its normal manner of acting. If it suffered, if it ceased to live, the sole reason is that it so willed.

[305]

However, we must add that Hilary does not connect these privileges of Christ with his doctrine of the Mystical Body. It is just as well, else the doctrine would be compromised by association with so suspicious an element. For it cannot be denied that these privileges bear an unpleasant resemblance to Docetism. A human nature so superhuman would not be perfectly consubstantial with us; we should at times be afraid of finding in it only the appearance of a body. Certainly such a fear is unfounded. Our Saint declares too plainly and too often that the Saviour is perfectly human, to permit any doubt. But it is nevertheless true that upon this essential point his doctrine remains incomplete. The guiding Spirit has not as yet led Tradition to the discovery of adequate formulas.

Moreover, the truth of our incorporation in Christ is too intimately bound up with Christology to reach its final expression until the period in which the Christological dogma should receive the most careful attention. This period came only after the Arian controversy, in which Hilary was so deeply engrossed. We must, therefore, wait until the fifth century before we can find a sufficiently complete systematic exposition of our incorporation in Christ.

God guides Tradition with a patient and long-suffering hand. With one act, though after a long preparation, He had given us the whole truth by giving us His Son. But when there is question of bringing men to grasp fully the splendor of His message, He could not proceed so rapidly, unless He were to dispense with our co-operation or to do us violence, so to speak. This in His goodness He refuses to do. Before men can appreciate all the light that came to them when they received Him who is Light; before they can express to one another the full significance of the words they heard when they received the Word of God, time — much time — is necessary, even though we have God's assistance.

Chapter VI

St. Gregory Nazianzen and St. Gregory of Nyssa

><

I. The Cappadocians. St. Basil has little to say of the Mystical Body.
II. *St. Gregory Nazianzen.* His theology and the interior life. His doctrine of the Mystical Body and the interior life. "A mystery in us"; "my" Christ; Christ is united with us in all things; verbs compounded with σύν. The events of His life are taking place in us today; they affect our entire existence. He is still active in the Christian feasts. He makes "me" God by bearing "me" wholly within Himself.
III. *The Soteriological argument* used in the refutation of Apollinarism. "What is not assumed is not saved."
IV. *St. Gregory of Nyssa* argues in the same manner. Christ has taken the lost sheep in Himself. The soteriological argument also used by St. Damasus; it is traditional, and it presupposes the unity of the Mystical Body.
V. *Exegesis based upon our incorporation in Christ.* "The Son will be subject to the Father." This means that we, His members, will be obedient. All the virtues of the members come from the Head, and in the members they still belong to the Head.
VI. Gregory of Nyssa and the divinization of all humanity in Christ.

I

AFTER Athanasius and Hilary, the next forward step in the development of the doctrine is taken by St. Cyril of Alexandria. We know of no intermediary stage, as far as the essential elements of the doctrine of the Mystical Body are concerned. However, for certain secondary points, for applications and consequences of the doctrine, several other Fathers of the intervening period are of considerable importance. We shall devote a few chapters to their teaching.

First to claim attention are the great Cappadocians: Basil

and the two Gregorys. Of their number Basil the Great should be considered first, but unfortunately the bishop of Caesarea has very little to say of our incorporation in Christ. When he describes the Christ-life to the faithful and to his monks Basil stresses the ascetical effort that is required to imitate Christ rather than the mysterious transformation that makes us members of the Saviour. Therefore we shall pass at once to the school of his friend, Gregory Nazianzen.

II

Gregory was about a year older than Basil. He made his studies with Basil at Caesarea of Palestine and at Athens; later, in 372, he was consecrated at Nazianzus by Basil and became the latter's suffragan as bishop of Sasima. Then, in 380, after his friend's death he was promoted to the see of Constantinople, resigning shortly afterwards in the face of a storm of opposition. He died in 389 or 390 near his native city, Nazianzus.

Gregory was neither a man of action like Basil nor a bold speculative like Gregory of Nyssa. He was a delicate, even timid soul, it would appear, and of the three Cappadocians he was the most "interior." "To Myself," is the inscription of several of his little poems as well as of some of his homilies. The title illustrates one of his characteristic traits: his habit of seeking, in Christian truth, for what touches the personal life.

Yet he is no vague sentimentalist; his thought is clear and forcefully expressed. His keenness and clearness was acknowledged even by the ancients, who called him "the Theologian" because he seemed so much at home in things divine.

These two characteristics, insistence upon the interior life and intellectual vigor and force of expression, are to be seen in his doctrine of the Mystical Body.

First, his interest in the interior life. For Gregory, it is not the Christian in general and in the abstract, but each Christian in particular, who is incorporated into Christ; it is each Christian in his most personal life; in a word, it is himself, his own Ego.

"What is this new mystery in me?" he asks, in the oration delivered at his brother's funeral.[1] This exclamation, which he uses to introduce an exposition of our divinization in Christ, may serve as an introduction to his entire doctrine of the Mystical Body.

The scene is laid in the church of Caesarea; the orator has been giving expression to his memories, recalling the image of the departed and old family intimacies. But little by little his soul begins to vibrate in its wonted manner and he allows it to speak. The discourse becomes a meditation on the vanity of passing things. More and more, as the sights of earth fade, the light of eternity glows with ever greater brilliance. Grief is slowly transformed into hope, even into assurance, for we bear this eternal life within our mortal bodies even here below. It is this contrast that constitutes the Christian.

> What is this new mystery in me? I am little and great, lowly and exalted, mortal and immortal. I am one of these with the world, the other with God; one with the flesh, the other with the spirit.

And he is all this in Christ.

> I must be buried with Christ; I must rise with Christ; I must be a coheir with Christ; I must become a son of God; I must become God.
> See whither the progress of our discourse has carried us. I should almost thank the misfortune that has suggested these thoughts and which has instilled into me a greater longing for the resurrection and for the life to come.
> This is what the great mystery means for us — the mystery of God become incarnate and poor for us. He is come to raise up the flesh, to save His image, and to restore man. He is come to make us all one in Christ, in Him who came perfectly into us in order to give us all that He is. Now there is neither male nor female, neither barbarian nor Scythian, neither bond nor free; for these are distinctions of the flesh. We now bear within us only the divine image according to which we were created, and which we must impress upon ourselves, that we may be recognized by it alone.

A mystery within us, an event of the interior life; this, for Gregory is the supernatural. Christ — "my Christ," he says lovingly — is the constant companion of his soul. To live is to act with Him. *To act-with*. In order to express this incessant communion of operation the Saint makes free use of the verbs compounded with σύν (with), which the Apostle had coined for the same purpose. It is true that his sentences have not the same burning energy as Paul's, but they nevertheless throw a new light upon an old truth. Over and over again our Saint repeats that the events of Christ's life remain always in us, and that the Christian feasts are not mere commemorations.

> What feasts I find in each of Christ's mysteries! Their one purpose and scope is my perfection, my restoration, my return to the innocence of the first Adam. . . .
> Celebrate then the Nativity that has freed thee from the bonds of thy nativity; honor that little town of Bethlehem that has brought thee to paradise; adore the crib through which, when you were bereft of reason, you were fed by the Word. . . .
> Run with the star; in company with the Magi offer thy gifts: gold, frankincense, and myrrh to the King, the God, and the Man who died for thee. With the shepherds sing the praises of God, with the angels chant a hymn, and join in song with the archangels. . . .
> As Christ's disciple, walk blameless through all the years and virtues of His life. Be purified and be circumcised. . . . Teach in the temple; drive out the buyers and sellers; be stoned, if need be. Thou shalt escape the stones, and like God thou shalt pass through their midst, for the word cannot be stoned. . . . Thy silence will inspire greater respect than the long speeches of other men.[2]

The author continues the enumeration at great length. Here as elsewhere he reviews the whole of Christ's life, in order to show in it the model of our life. And he concludes:

> Finally, be crucified-with Christ, be put-to-death-with Him, be buried-with Him, in order to rise-with Him, to be glorified-with Him, and to reign-with Him.[3]

At His baptism Christ immerses the old Adam completely in the purifying waters. When He comes forth from the stream, He raises up the whole world in Himself and He sees the reopening of the heavens that Adam had closed to himself and to his race.

Christ's miracles are still taking place today; they are being renewed in our souls. We are the Canaanite whom He heals, and Lazarus whom He raises from the dead. When we receive the Word we possess in our souls all the cures that He wrought. The fact that He has lived sanctifies our existence:

> In truth, He willed to sleep, in order to bless our sleep; He willed to be weary, in order to sanctify our weariness; He willed to weep, in order to give merit to our tears.[4]

As the prophet Eliseus had stretched his body at full length upon the corpse of the Sunamite boy in order to restore it to life, so Christ extends over us all His acts and His merits in order to save us.

> He has laid wood against wood, and hands against hands: His generously extended hands against those that reach out with greed; His nail-pierced hands against those that are fallen in discouragement; His hands that embrace the whole world against the hand that brought about Adam's banishment from Paradise.[5]

Thus the passion of Christ is taking place today. He is still suffering daily, in the sense that His sufferings are still operative in us, and are constantly being renewed by sinners.

> See what sufferings the Word endures even now! Some honor His divinity, but others despise His human nature.[6]

He keeps on, ever uniting Himself more and more with the lives of men. Thus the great Christian feasts are more than simple commemorations of past events; they are the celebration of a reality that is present. Christmas, for instance, is not a mere reminder that Christ was born in a distant past; it tells us that His birth continues within us even now. And, pursues the Saint,

> Even now the angels are rejoicing, the shepherds are startled by the blinding light; even now the star is coming from the East toward the great and inaccessible Light. Even now the Magi kneel to offer their gifts.[7]

And so with Easter. Even now we have the Resurrection:

> Yesterday I hung on the Cross with Christ; today I am glorified with Him; yesterday I was dying with Him, today I am brought to life with Him; yesterday I was buried with Him, today I rise with Him.

[311]

Let us become like Christ, since Christ also became like us. Let us become gods for Him, since He became man for us.[8]

"Let us become gods." Always the doctrine of the Mystical Christ is bound up with a doctrine of divinization. The Man-God, the heavenly leaven, transforms us into Himself.

St. Gregory Nazianzen expresses this divinization, as he does everything else, in his own characteristic way, that is, in relation with the interior life. "He has made me God. His work is to make me a son of God, to make me God," we heard him say in the funeral oration at Caesarea.

Even now, as man, Christ makes intercession for my salvation, for He still possesses the body which He assumed in order to make me God by virtue of His Incarnation.[9]

This Gregory says to his faithful, for this same divinization will be personal to each of them. Speaking to the catechumens whom he is about to baptize, he tells them to believe that:

Christ is wholly man and wholly God, for the sake of man who had wholly fallen, in order to save thee wholly. . . . He became man for thee as truly as thou oughtest to become God through Him.[10]

This the Saint repeats in the explanation of a famous text which we shall encounter again in the works of St. Gregory of Nyssa: "The Son will be subject to the Father." Between Christ and the Christians, he explains, there is a personal communication, an interchange of the human and the divine.

In the form of a slave, He came down to join His fellow slaves, and took a form that was not His own.

He bears me wholly within Himself, with my weaknesses, in order to consume in Himself what is evil, as fire consumes wax or as the sun absorbs the earth's vapors, and that by this union I may share all His goods.[11]

Hence the Incarnation is not simply an event that has given us Christ and renewed the face of the earth, but it is also an event of our interior life. It reaches within us to the depths of our inmost selves. By becoming incarnate the Word makes "me" God.

While all this undoubtedly betrays an intense interest in the personal life and reveals a soul that lives inwardly with Christ by faith, it also gives evidence of a keen and vigorous mind capable of expressing treasures of doctrine in brief, concise phrases. "He makes me God; what feasts I find in every event of His life; what a wondrous mystery in my interior life!"

III

We find the same keenness of thought in the following texts. They have to do with the controversy against Apollinaris, of whom we must say a few words by way of introduction. Apollinaris was bishop of Laodicea in Syria from 361 until 392. He had at first been a defender of the Catholic faith, but so fiercely did he oppose those theologians who exaggerated the dualism, the distinction of natures in Christ, that he finally went to the opposite extreme. In order to explain better how the divine and human natures made only one Christ, Apollinaris taught that the human nature was incomplete. Otherwise, he argued, when it is joined with the divine nature, which is necessarily complete, there would be two complete beings in Christ, which of course is false. Moreover, he pursued, if the human nature were complete it would make Christ capable of committing sin, a defect which is necessarily present in human nature but cannot be in Him. Therefore His human nature must be incomplete. It lacked the νοῦς, that superior part of the soul which is the seat of personality, liberty, and the power to commit sin. The divinity took the place of this νοῦς, and by means of this substitution it entered into and united itself perfectly with the human nature. Therefore Christ was wholly one, but by the mutilation of one of His natures.

It was against this heresy, and probably in the year 382, that Gregory wrote his two *Letters to Cledonius*. In a short time these letters, particularly the first, became famous, and they were cited as decisive documents by the Councils of Ephesus and of Chalcedon. In one of the letters Gregory writes:

> He that places his hope in a man without a mind, is himself a fool and unworthy of salvation. For what is not assumed [by Christ] is not saved; that alone is saved which is united with God.[12]

[313]

"What is not assumed is not saved." To render the full force of the original Greek, we should say "the nonassumed is nonsaved." This directness and brevity have made the phrase an axiom among theologians.

The Saint does not leave the statement stand alone and isolated. He returns to the thought in the same letter, to refute one of the arguments of Apollinaris. The heresiarch maintained that Christ's human nature could not possess a mind (νοῦς), since the mind is sinful and accursed. The Saint retorts in triumph:

> But what of our flesh? Did it escape the curse? Then either take it away [from the Saviour] because of sin, or else give Him a spiritual soul for our salvation. If the least noble part of our being was assumed, that it might be sanctified by the Incarnation, why was not the more noble part assumed, that it too might be sanctified by the Incarnation? O wise men, if our clay has been leavened and is become a new paste, is the image of God within us not leavened, or united to God or deified by the divinity?[13]

The supposition is impossible:

> Because of our sinful flesh, Christ had need of flesh; because of our soul He had need of a soul. Similarly, because of our mind it was necessary that He have a mind. Indeed, was it not the mind that sinned in Adam, and sinned even before the body? . . . It had therefore greater need of salvation. But whatever needed salvation, was assumed. Therefore the mind was assumed.[14]

A few years later we find the same line of argumentation in the writings of another Cappadocian, St. Gregory of Nyssa.

IV

Gregory, the future bishop of Nyssa, was born about 355; he was about five years younger than his brother, Basil. In 371 he was raised by the latter to the episcopal dignity, against his own inclinations, as was the case with Gregory Nazianzen. He died a few years after Gregory, about 394. Of the three Cappadocians he was the most given to speculation and to science.

[314]

As we have remarked, he, too, wrote against Apollinarism. Four years or more after the Theologian had written his *Letters to Cledonius*, Gregory of Nyssa composed the *Antirrheticus contra Apollinarem*. This is the most important of the ancient works written against the heresy, and by reason of its abundant quotations it is one of our principal sources of information regarding the doctrinal system of Apollinaris. The following passage illustrates his manner of expressing the arguments of St. Gregory Nazianzen:

> Let no one accuse us of seeing two Christs or two Lords in the one Saviour. But God the Son, who is God by nature, Lord of the universe, King of all creation, the Maker of all that exists and the Restorer of what has fallen, has not only not deprived our fallen nature of communion with Him, but in His great bounty He has deigned even to receive it again into life. But He is Life. Therefore, at the end of centuries, when our wickedness had reached its height, then in order that the remedy might be applied to all that was diseased, He united [lit., "mingled"] Himself[15] with our lowly human nature, He assumed man in Himself and Himself became man. He explains this to His disciples: "Ye in Me, and I in you" (John 14:20). By this union He made man what He Himself was. He was the Most High; lowly man was now elevated. For He who was the Most High had no need of being elevated. The Word was already Christ and Lord. But that which is assumed becomes Christ and Lord.[16]

Our restoration cannot be complete until our whole being is united to God in the Saviour:

> Who does not know the divine mystery, to wit, that the Author of our salvation has taken up the lost sheep? We are that sheep, we men who by our sins have wandered away from the hundred good sheep. He takes upon His shoulders the whole sheep, for she had not been lost only in part, but wholly. Therefore, He carries her back whole to the flock. The Good Shepherd does not carry only the skin, as Apollinaris would have it, having no care for what is within. He carries her upon His shoulders [lit., *in* His shoulders]; i.e., in His divinity. Being thus assumed, she becomes one with Him; in this way He wills to seek and to save what was lost. Having found the sheep that He sought, He took her upon His shoulders. She did not move by her own powers that had led her astray, but she was supported by the divinity. . . . Having therefore taken the sheep upon Himself, the Shepherd became one with her. And so

[315]

He can speak to His sheep with the voice of the sheep. How indeed could our human weakness understand a divine voice? So He speaks as a man, or as a sheep, if we may use the expression, saying: "My sheep hear My voice" (John 10:27). And the Shepherd who has taken the sheep upon His shoulders and who speaks to us through the sheep, is both sheep and shepherd; He is the sheep in the nature that He has assumed, and Shepherd in the nature by which He has assumed it.[17]

Everything in the passage, the substance as well as the form, is the very voice of Tradition. The figure which the Saint uses is the Scriptural parable of the lost sheep, already dear to St. Irenaeus. The thought is an application of the doctrine, likewise Scriptural and familiar to Tradition, of the two Adams. It had already been used by St. Ignatius in refuting the Gnostics and by St. Irenaeus in developing his theory of the recapitulation.

The argument itself we have pointed out in the works of practically all the Fathers that we have studied. Ignatius of Antioch, Irenaeus, Athanasius unhesitatingly conclude, from what we are, to what Christ must be.

The two Gregorys, as we may well imagine, were not the only ones to employ the argument in the controversy against Apollinaris. Athanasius had employed it, and Pope St. Damasus (366–384) had already made use of it, very probably before Gregory Nazianzen. In the synodal letter of a council held in Rome, at a date which cannot be accurately determined, he says:

> If God had assumed an imperfect human nature, the gift of God would be incomplete, and our salvation too would be incomplete. For the whole man would not be saved.[18]

For, continues the Pope, the whole man had perished; in particular the "mind" the νοῦς, which Apollinaris refused to admit in Christ, had sinned more than the rest.

> How then can one imagine that at the end of time there should be no need for that to be saved which had sinned before all the rest? But we, who know that we are saved wholly and completely, confess according to the faith of the Catholic Church, that the perfect God has assumed the perfect man.[19]

[316]

The same argument is expressed by St. Cyril of Alexandria. In short, we may say that this manner of thinking is traditional in the Church.

Now that we have met the argument a sufficient number of times we may reflect upon what it presupposes. For it has a presupposition. That we may conclude from what the faithful are to what the Saviour is, salvation must be a matter of mystical solidarity between ourselves and Him; we must be able to say in truth that men are saved only in virtue of their incorporation in the Saviour.

In any other hypothesis, and in particular if Christ were simply a substitute who accumulates merits for others, why was it strictly necessary that He should be of the same nature as ourselves? For instance, the Word could have accumulated merits quite as immense and quite as applicable to us if He had assumed an angelic nature. True, the application of these merits would then have been somewhat more arbitrary, but that would have added only a little extrinsicism to the divine plan. After all, God could just as well have decided to make this other creature the juridical head of our race, in somewhat the same manner as Christ is Head of the angels, although He is not of the same nature as they.

Undoubtedly this could have been. But the Fathers do not teach such a mere juridical transfer. As we have already noted in speaking of St. Athanasius' doctrine of the divinization, the idea underlying their argument is that of a vital nexus. When they argue, they consider the supernatural organism to be a reality that is one; so truly one that we can know the nature of one of its extremities by studying the other extremity, so truly one that we may know the Head by examining what the members are. But again such an argument necessarily presupposes that there is a single organism, in other words, that the Mystical Body is a reality.

Of course, the affirmation is implicit. The Fathers do not formulate this presupposition; it may even be that they are not always clearly conscious of it. But what does that matter? For that very reason it is a more significant witness to their mentality and to the spirit of Christian doctrine.

[317]

V

Certain other passages of St. Gregory of Nyssa deserve mention here. Of these the most important is a short controversial treatise, devoted to the text: "Then shall the Son Himself be subject to [the Father] who subjected all things to Him" (1 Cor. 15:28).

We have already spoken of this text and of the joy it gave to the Arians. We are informed by Theodoret of Cyrus, who wrote some decades later, that the words were ever on their lips. We have recorded Origen's interpretation and his declaration that this future submission of Christ is the obedience that will be rendered to God by men, the members of Christ, after they shall have been completely united with the Saviour.

St. Gregory of Nyssa gives exactly the same explanation, but he develops it at greater length, so that to our knowledge, his treatise is the most important extant example of this type of exegesis.

At the outset the bishop of Nyssa remarks that the term *subjection* has several different meanings in Scripture and that the question is to determine which of these senses is demanded by the context. Here, he tells us, the Apostle Paul is speaking of the adoption that we receive through Christ and which makes us all children of God. This to his mind is sufficient indication that the subjection of which the Apostle speaks is the filial obedience that we are all bound to render to God in Christ. And, he pursues, there is no other truth which St. Paul inculcates so forcefully as our incorporation in Christ and the consequent interchange of dignity and infirmity that takes place from Him to us and from us to Him. When, therefore, we are subject to God, we may say that Christ also is subject to God; for He is subject to God in us.

> Since by participation we are joined to the one body of Christ, we all become one body, His own. When we shall have all become perfect, then His whole body will be subject to the life-giving power [of God]. The submission of this body is called the submission of the Son Himself, since He is united [lit., "mingled"] with His body, which is the Church.[20]

[318]

This is the argument in brief form. The Saint returns and develops the thought; we have all things, he tells us, in common with Christ.

Since He is in all, He takes into Himself all who are united with Him by the participation of His body; He makes them all members of His body, in such wise that the many members are but one body. Having thus united us with Himself and Himself with us, and having become one with us in all things, He makes His own all that is ours. But the greatest of all our goods is submission to God, which brings all creation into harmony. Then every knee shall bend in heaven, on earth, and under the earth, and every tongue shall confess that Jesus Christ is Lord (Phil. 2:10). Thus all creation becomes one body, all are grafted one upon the other, and Christ speaks of the submission of His body to the Father as His own submission.[21]

The perspective has become immense. It is the universe itself that pays its obedience to God in Christ. We may note in passing that this expansive view is customary with St. Gregory. For him all creation is included in the unity that Christ brings to the faithful. The obedience which the universe and men render to God in Christ is attributed to Christ, just as we attribute to our souls what applies only to our bodies. Does not the Gospel tell us that the rich man stood before his well-filled barns, saying: "Soul, take thy rest; eat, drink, make merry" (Luke 12:19). Notice, says the Saint, how

he attributes to his soul the satisfaction of his body. In like manner the submission to God of the body, which is the Church, is attributed to Him who dwells in the body. . . .

The Lord is Life; through Him, says the Apostle, His whole body will have access to the Father, when He shall hand over the Kingdom to our God and Father. His body, as we have often said, is the whole of humankind, to which He has united Himself. It is in this sense that Paul often calls the Lord the Mediator of God and men (1 Tim. 2:5). For He who is in the Father, and who came into men, carries out His function of mediator by uniting all men in Himself and thereby uniting them with the Father, as He says in the Gospel, addressing the Father: "that they may be one in Us, even as Thou, Father, art in Me and I in Thee" (John 17:21). These words clearly show that He produces our union with the Father in Himself, by uniting us with Himself, who is in the Father.[22]

Whatever good we do comes to us through Him; it is His before it becomes our own. It is Christ who produces in us our good thoughts and our good deeds, and they must be attributed primarily to Him.

The Saint now continues an argument which he had formulated in the same words a few pages earlier. All good works, he says, are but different forms of one and the same obedience to God. Like all good works this obedience and subjection come to us from Christ; before they are in us, they are in Him as in their principle. Therefore the Scripture is right in ascribing them to Him.

> If we are united with God by our submission, we must attribute that very submission to Him who lives in us.[23]

Examples of this type of exegesis are very frequent, though less fully developed, at the period of which we speak. They may be found in St. Gregory Nazianzen, St. Nilus of Sinai, Didymus of Alexandria, St. Cyril of Alexandria, and elsewhere. We shall have occasion to return to this point later on in our study.

VI

In addition to the exegesis that we have just read, we must also mention a number of passages in which St. Gregory of Nyssa insists very forcefully on our mystical identification with Christ. Bearing as they do a rather striking resemblance to certain texts of St. Methodius and of St. Hilary, already cited, they have also drawn a like accusation. Protestant critics maintain that our Saint is one of those Fathers who taught rather a collective than an individual Incarnation. We shall see the absurdity of this claim.

The most incriminating passages occur in the *Great Catechesis,* which is a kind of résumé of Christian teaching. In it the Saint expresses the thought, already formulated by Athanasius and Origen, that one can very well conceive the union of the divine and the human in Christ if he begins with the thought of the intimate presence of God in all things. God pours Himself out, as it were, and flows into all that exists.

[320]

This shows, pursues the Saint, that He can also "unite Himself with what is proper to us," as He does in Christ, in order to deliver us from death and destroy our infirmities. Just as fire takes away all impurities from gold and communicates its own brilliance to the metal, so the Incarnation infuses the resurrection and eternal life into our whole race.

Since it was necessary that our whole nature be raised up from the dead, God reached out His hand to us, so to speak; He looked upon the corpse that we were; He even drew so near to death as to unite Himself with mortality. Thus did He give to human nature the principle of the resurrection in His own body; thus did He raise up the whole man in Himself. For the flesh He had assumed came from no other source than our race, and by the resurrection that flesh was welded to the divinity. In our body, whatever is experienced by one of the senses is felt in the whole organism. Similarly, as if all human nature were a single living being, the resurrection of one of its members extends through the entire body, and because of the continuity and unity of our nature, it passes from a part to the whole body.[24]

The exact meaning of the passage is not hard to determine. Far from being a denial of the transcendent individuality of the Man-God, it makes that individuality the one principle of our divinization. Yet this universal divinization is placed in very close relationship with Christ's divinity. St. Gregory begins with the contemplation of the inner activity which the divinity exercises in all things; in this activity he sees the first beginnings of the Incarnation. Hence he conceives the Incarnation, too, as a work that affects the universe. But in this universal activity, Christ remains just as personal as God, notwithstanding His presence in all things, remains transcendent. However, we must call attention to a feature that more closely concerns the theory of the Mystical Body: according to Gregory, the intimate union which enables Christ to purify us all in Himself, is analogous to the union of all things with God.

But to look for anything else is vain; in St. Gregory as in the other Fathers, the so-called denial of an individual Incarnation is nothing else than an affirmation of the incorporation of us all in the Incarnate Word. For him as for the others, Platonist philosophy may have furnished a systematic method and facilitated the conceptual expression of the truth. But we do not see that it exerted any influence upon the teaching itself. All that our Saint says, all that he means to say, all that he strives to understand as fully as possible, is the eternal wisdom of God, manifested in the mystery of which Paul had spoken long before and which Christ had brought to our earth. In the transmission of this ancient message through the centuries, human philosophy has been merely an external agent, scarcely more than an epiphenomenon.

Whence the Incarnation has this power of expansion and this universal power of divinization is not explained, as far as we can judge, by either of the Gregorys. Progress has still to be made, in order to explain the riches of the truth, which, though it was contained in revelation and already formulated in Scripture, did not as yet present any semblance of a system.

Chapter VII

St. John Chrysostom, Doctor of the Eucharist and of Almsgiving

><

I. *St. John Chrysostom* was trained by reading St. Paul. We quote a few passages in which he develops themes familiar to the Apostle.

II. *The Eucharist.* Here the Saint brings out the ardent love of Christ, and the intimate union that He wishes to have with us in this sacrament. He wills to possess us, to give Himself to us; He desires not only to be near us and with us, but in us, one with us. "The flesh that He has taken is thy own." The Incarnation, universal in its effects.

III. *Almsgiving.* The doctrine of the Mystical Body and its practical applications. We can still harbor Christ, and in doing so we can gain more merit than could those who harbored Him during His mortal life. The contrast between Christ, living in misery in the poor, and the pampered life of Christians. We must first succor Christ in His members before we honor Him in the adornment of churches. Christ's supplication in the poor. Almsgiving and the Eucharist; the religious and solemn significance of almsgiving.

I

MANY AUTHORS should be named here: St. Cyril of Jerusalem for instance, and St. Epiphanius of Salamis. But these make no notable contribution on the subject of the Mystical Body. We should likewise consider the great exegetes of the school of Antioch, such as Theodore of Mopsuestia and Theodoret of Cyrus, who have left us a number of noteworthy passages explaining the principal texts of Holy Writ that treat of our incorporation in Christ. Into these explanations has passed something of the energy and realism of the Scriptures.

However, quotations would simply be a repetition of what we have already seen in studying the Scriptures themselves.

Hence we shall not delay upon them. The only representative of the school of Antioch who must occupy our attention for a time is St. John Chrysostom. In point of fact, the Saint is rather a doctor of the Church than a representative of the school of Antioch.

Born at Antioch in 344, he was ordained priest in 381, and won immediate renown as a preacher. In 397 he was called to the see of Constantinople, where he remained for ten years, ten years of zealous labor.

There is no break in the line of Tradition. John Chrysostom is a worthy successor of Ignatius, Irenaeus, Athanasius, and Hilary. Their fight was for doctrine; his is a struggle for Christian morals. But the combat is the same: he shows the same courage in the service of the same ideal; he meets with the same hostility and the same persecutions; he suffers the same banishments, and he finally dies in exile, in 407, while being carried off to Pityus, in the Caucasus.

He appears to have received his training, in theology as well as in oratory, chiefly from the study of Scripture rather than from human masters. Particularly does his soul bear the mark of St. Paul. At such a school, he was in an excellent position to study our incorporation in Christ.

Indeed, John was impressed by the Apostle's vigorous inculcation of this truth. He remarks how Paul is always on the alert for the strongest and most decisive expressions; how he shrinks from no formula, even though it may make his audience shudder, and how his constant thought is to show that Christians have all things in common with the Saviour. John Chrysostom so admired this insistence that he could not refrain from imitating it. Let us see, for instance, how he makes his own the full force of Pauline passages. "Ye are all through your faith sons of God," writes the Apostle to the Galatians (3:26).

> Behold, how great is the power of faith, and how the Apostle reveals that power as he writes! He had already pointed out that faith makes us sons of Abraham: "Know, then, that they that are of faith, they are the sons of Abraham" (Gal. 3:7).

[324]

Now he shows that they are sons of God as well: "Ye are all through your faith sons of God in Christ Jesus." By faith, not by the law. Then, since this is so great and wonderful a thing, he explains the mode of adoption. "All of you who were baptized into Christ, have put on Christ" (3:27). Why does he not say, "All of you who were baptized into Christ, are born of God"? For this is what he ought to say, in order to show that they are sons. But Paul wishes to state this truth in a manner far more striking. For if Christ is the Son of God, and if you have put on Christ, then since you have the Son within you and are assimilated unto Him, you are of the same family and likeness as He.

"In Him is neither Jew nor Greek, neither slave nor free, neither male nor female; for ye are all one person in Christ Jesus" (3:28). What an insatiable soul! He has just said, "Ye are all become sons of God by faith." But he does not stop at this; he wishes to say more, to express more clearly the intimacy of our union with Christ. Even after he has said, "Ye have put on Christ," he is not satisfied with the phrase; he explains it, and in doing so describes a closer union still: "Ye are all one person in Christ Jesus." All of you have but one form, one likeness, which is Christ's. Could one find a more astounding declaration? He who before was but a Greek, or a Jew, or a slave, now bears the likeness, not of an angel or archangel, but of the Lord of all things; in his own person he is the image of Christ.[1]

As we see, the disciple has appropriated his master's thought and style, with this difference, that the rushing torrent of the Pauline epistles is become a river, but a river which even on the plain retains the momentum that it has gained in its descent from the mountains. It has its undercurrents and its breakers; like a succession of waves, it returns again and again to the same thought, drawing itself up and concentrating its force, as if to dislodge the obstacles that bar its progress. This method of development by progressive repetition, we may remark in passing, is characteristic of our Saint, as it is characteristic of all effective eloquence.

To cite all the passages in which Chrysostom interprets the Apostle with the same forcefulness and with the same happy choice of expression would involve too long a reiteration of ideas that we have already analyzed in our study of the Epistles of St. Paul.

II

We shall restrict our study to those developments that exemplify the Saint's teaching on the Eucharist and on almsgiving, selecting by preference passages that are less frequently quoted.

On the subject of our union with Christ in the Eucharist the holy bishop utters cries of impassioned eloquence that have never been surpassed. Other Fathers have shown more clearly the theological significance of the sacrament of unity: St. Hilary, for instance, as we have seen, and St. Cyril of Alexandria and St. Augustine. But none has expressed the meaning of this communion in language so profoundly human and so moving.

We must study this wonderful sacrament; we must learn the purpose of its institution and the effects which it produces. We are one body, says the Scripture, and "members of His flesh and of His bones" (Eph. 5:30, D.V.). Let the initiated follow me.

He wishes that we become His body, not through charity alone but that we be actually "mingled" with His own flesh. This union is accomplished by means of the food which he has given us as proof of His love for us. Therefore He has "mingled" Himself with us, He has implanted His body in us, that we may be one, as a body united with its head. What ardent love this manifests! . . .

All this has Christ done, to bring us into closer friendship with Himself and to show His love for us. To those who yearned for Him He has not only appeared, but He has given Himself in the flesh, to be touched, to be eaten, to be broken by our teeth,[2] to be "mingled" with us, and thus to satisfy every desire.[3]

Christ is insatiable; He wishes this union to be as intimate as possible. Listen to St. John Chrysostom's description of the divine love that encompasses us and breaks down all barriers.

Not only did He shed His blood, but He gives it to all of us as drink. "If, therefore, you love blood," He begs us, "go not to the altars of idols, which are covered with the blood of beasts, but redden My altar with My own blood." What could be more wonderful? What, I ask, could be more lovable?

This is what a lover does. When he sees his beloved interested in something else and forgetful of him, he makes gifts of his own goods, to turn the beloved away from those other things. Lovers make presents of money, of robes, of their possessions. But of their blood? Never. Yet Christ has proved His tenderness and His burning love for us even by His blood. In the old Law, which was less perfect, God reserved blood to Himself, because it was being offered to idols and because He wished to win His people away from idols. That was already proof of ineffable love. But here He establishes a more august and more magnificent liturgy; the very sacrifice is changed, and instead of immolating animals, He bids us sacrifice Himself.

"The bread which we break, is it not communion in the body of Christ?" (1 Cor. 10:16.) Why does Paul not say "participation" [i.e., the reception of a part]? Because he meant something more, and wished to show the closeness of the union. When we communicate we do not simply receive a part, but we are united with Christ. For just as this body is united with Christ, so by this bread we are all united with Him.

Why does Paul add, "which we break"? This breaking we see in the Eucharist, but not on the cross; there, on the contrary, "not a bone of Him shall be broken" (Num. 9:12). What He did not suffer on the cross He permits for thy sake in the Host, and lets Himself be broken that we may all be filled.

Paul had just said "communion in the body of Christ." But the communicant is distinct from that of which he communicates. Yet even this distinction, slight as it may seem, Paul excludes. For, after saying "communion in the body," he still seeks something more intimate, and continues: "we many are one bread, one body, for we all partake of the one bread." Why, he says, why speak any longer of communion? We are this very body. For what is the bread? It is the body of Christ. And what do the communicants become? The body of Christ. Not many bodies, but one body. For as the bread consists of many grains, so united that they are no longer distinguishable, and as they still subsist, though their individuality is no longer apparent to the eye because of their intimate union, so are we united one with the other and with Christ. You do not eat of one body and your neighbor eat of a different body, but we all eat of the same. And so Paul adds: "We all partake of the one bread." If therefore by eating of the same body we all become that body, why do we not manifest to one another the same charity, and become one in this respect as well?[4]

Such is Christ's love. Let us, therefore, not complain either of our bodily weakness or of the instability of our free will, for it is these that enable us to unite ourselves to the Lord.

See, my beloved friends, how we are honored! And yet some foolish and thoughtless men will ask: "Why are we free and masters of our actions?" But all these actions which we have mentioned, all these acts in which we can imitate God, would be impossible for us without free will.

God tells us: "I command the angels, and so dost thou, through the first-fruits [Christ]. I am seated on the royal throne, and so art thou, through the first-fruits. He hath raised us up with Him, as it is written, and seated us with Him at the right hand of the Father. The cherubim and seraphim, the whole host of heaven, principalities, powers, thrones, and dominations adore thee because of the first-fruits. Accuse not the body that is so honored, and before which the very incorporeal Virtues tremble.

But what am I saying? It is not only by these honors that I manifest My love, but also by My passion. For thee I was covered with spittle and buffeted, I stripped Myself of My glory, I left My Father and came to thee, to thee who didst hate Me, who didst flee Me, who didst not wish even to hear My name. I followed thee, I ran after thee; I caught hold of thee, and embraced thee. "Eat Me," I said, "and drink Me. . . . It is not enough that I should possess thy first-fruits [the physical body of Christ] in heaven; that does not satisfy My love. I come once more to the earth, not only to "mingle" Myself with thee, but to entwine Myself in thee. I am eaten, I am broken into pieces, that this fusion, this union, may be more intimate. When other things are united, each remains distinct in itself; but I weave Myself into thee. I want nothing to come between us; I wish the two to become one."[5]

Underlying this and the preceding text we recognize that view of the Incarnation that we have encountered so frequently, according to which the union of the Word with the Saviour's human nature is considered as a grace calculated to divinize the entire human race. This conception figures more prominently in a long passage of the eighty-third homily on St. Matthew, in which St. John Chrysostom exhorts his hearers to the fervent reception of Holy Communion.

How many people there are nowadays who say, "I should like to see His person, His features, His robes, His sandals." But you do see Him, you touch Him, you eat Him. You would like to see His robes; He gives you Himself, not to be seen merely, but to be touched and eaten, and to be possessed within you. Let no one therefore approach [this sacrament] with coldness or indifference, but let all approach with love, fervor, and recollection. For if the Jews ate the pasch standing, staff in hand, and in haste, how much more ought we to be alert! They were going to leave Egypt for Palestine, and therefore they were attired for a journey. But you are about to ascend from earth to heaven.

As the speaker enlarges upon the sublimity of the Eucharist, his exhortation to fervor becomes more urgent.

Think how indignant you feel toward the traitor and those who crucified Him. But take care lest you too be guilty of the body and blood of Christ. They slew His Sacred Body, and you, in return for so many benefits, receive that Body into a soul that is defiled.

He was not satisfied to become man, to be beaten and to be made a sacrifice; He even "mingles" Himself with us, not only through faith, but in all reality; He makes us His body.

How pure then ought he be who partakes of this sacrifice! Purer than the sun's rays should be the hands that touch this flesh, the mouth that is filled with this spiritual fire, and the tongue that is reddened with this precious blood! Consider the honor that is done you, and the table that is offered you. We eat Him at whose sight the angels tremble and on whose glory they cannot gaze without fear. We are "mingled" with Him and become the one body and the one flesh of Christ.

"Who shall declare the powers of the Lord? Who shall set forth all His praises?" (Ps. 105:2.) What shepherd ever fed his sheep with his own members? Did I say shepherd? Why, do not even mothers, after the pains of childbirth, give their children to others to nurse? But Christ did not do as they. He nourishes us with His own blood, and attaches us to Himself in every way. Lo, He is born of our very substance! But, you will object, this does not concern us all. On the contrary, it does concern us all. For if He has come to our nature, He has come to us all; and if He has come to all, He has also come to each one. But why, then, you ask, do not all profit by His coming? Surely this is not by any fault of His; it is the fault of those who refuse to receive Him. For by this sacrament He "mingles" Himself with each of the faithful; He Himself nourishes those whom He has begotten, thus giving another proof that the flesh that He has taken is thy own.[6]

"The flesh that He has taken is thy own." The Saint's doctrine is realistic throughout. Christ's flesh comes truly into

[329]

us; our lips, he says, with a force of expression that requires explanation, our lips are reddened with His blood, and our flesh becomes truly the flesh of Christ. At Communion the Word enters into all of us, as He had entered into one at the Incarnation. All blends into a single perspective, with the Incarnation ever as its center. But Chrysostom has not explained how the single, individual Incarnation can yet have a collective and mystical prolongation.

III

The Saint's preaching does not ordinarily remain on these theological and dogmatic heights. He is before all else a moralist, and his primary aim is to form his hearers to Christian living and to virtue. Even when he speaks of the Eucharist, what he emphasizes is not so much the mystery that is taking place as the dispositions of purity, holiness, and especially of respect requisite in those who assist or communicate.

The same is true in general of his treatment of the doctrine of the Mystical Body; his developments most often deal with its practical applications. Hence, in order to learn his mind regarding the doctrine, we should examine what he says of these applications, on the subject of peace, charity, patience, chastity, and especially of almsgiving — all based upon our incorporation in Christ.

Never has almsgiving been so urgently and so constantly recommended or so closely associated with our incorporation in Christ. To this doctor of charity the strongest argument is ever the mystical identity of the poor with Christ; persistently and sharply does he remind his hearers of the Saviour's words: "Inasmuch as ye did it to one of the least of these My brethren, ye did it to Me" (Matt. 25:40).

Do you see the courage of the holy women, their love for Christ, the generosity with which they spend their treasures and risk their lives? We men ought to imitate these women; let us not abandon Jesus in His hour of need. They gave so generously of their goods at the risk of their lives, for His dead body. But we refuse to feed Him when He is hungry, to clothe Him when He is naked; when He asks an alms of us, we pass Him by. Oh, no doubt, if you were to see Christ Himself you would each give lavishly. But this man is Christ; He tells us: "It is I." Why then do you not give Him all you have? For even now you still hear Him say, "Ye do it to Me." Whether you give to Him or to this beggar matters not, and what you do is no less noble than the deed of the holy women in ministering to Him then. Nay, your act is even more noble. No, be not shocked! To feed the Lord when He is visibly present, and when the very sight of Him would move a heart of stone, is not as meritorious as to care for the poor, the lame and the deformed because of His words. For in the first instance, His appearance and the majesty of His presence makes us feel generous. But here the reward of charity is due solely to your good will.[7] Besides, it is a proof of greater love for Christ to lavish every attention upon a fellow servant simply because of His words.

The appeal becomes more and more passionate:

He it is whom we despise in the poor; hence the enormity of the crime. Thus, when Paul persecuted Christ's brethren, he was persecuting Christ Himself. Wherefore He says: "Why dost thou persecute Me?" (Acts 9:4.) Let us then be so disposed in giving alms as if we were giving to Christ. For His words are more trustworthy than the evidence of our eyes. So when you see a poor man, remember the command He has given us to feed Him. Even though it be not Christ that we see, still, beneath these appearances it is really He who begs and receives. Do you blush at my saying that Christ begs? Blush rather with shame when He begs and you give not. That is shameful and that deserves punishment. For that He should beg of us is owing to His goodness, and we ought to rejoice at it. But if we do not give, we are guilty of cruelty. If now you do not believe that when you ignore one of the poor faithful, it is Christ Himself that you ignore, you will believe it when you are summoned to appear before Him, and hear Him say: "Inasmuch as ye did it not to one of these least, neither did ye do it to Me" (Matt. 25:45).[8]

It is better to give to the poor than to contribute to the church.

What is the use of loading Christ's table with vessels of gold, if He Himself is dying of hunger? First satisfy His hunger; then adorn His table with what remains. . . . Tell me, if you saw a man in need of even the most necessary food and if you should leave him standing there, in order to set the table with dishes of gold [but no food], would he be thankful to you? Would he not rather be angry? Or again, if you saw him clothed in rags and shivering with cold, but without giving any thought to his raiment, you were to erect columns of gold, telling him that all this was in his honor, would he not think you were mocking him and treating him with the utmost contempt?

But consider well that this is the way you treat Christ when He goes about as a pilgrim, a homeless vagabond, and when instead of taking Him in, you embellish the floors and walls and capitals of columns, and suspend lamps from silver chains, but refuse even to visit Him when He is in chains. I am not saying this to criticize the use of such ornaments; we must attend to both, but to Christ first![9]

Blows so direct naturally aroused virtuous indignation. This, however, could not deter the Saint from his efforts to shake the complacency of the too economical rich:

All this leaves us unmoved; so ungrateful are we that we deck out our servants, our mules and our horses with trappings of gold, and despise our Lord who goes naked and begging from door to door and who stands with outstretched hand at the street corner. Nay, often we look at Him with distrust. Yet it is for our sake that He submits to these miseries. Willingly does He hunger that He may feed thee; He goes naked to give thee the robe of immortality. But you will give Him nothing of your own. Of your robes, some are being eaten by the moths; the rest, locked away in chests, are but useless worry to you. Meanwhile He that has given you all this, and everything else beside, goes naked![10]

This is Chrysostom's usual procedure, to bring out the violent contrast between the sumptuous life of Christians and the poverty of Christ. He describes the magnificent raiment, the lavish use of gold and silk even in the matter of footwear; then abruptly: "Shall I present to you Christ hungry, Christ naked, Christ everywhere chained in prison?"[11] At times the contrast almost breaks one's heart:

Your very dog is gorged with food, while Christ faints from hunger![12]

And even when he speaks more mildly, the comparison is still a painful one:

Perhaps you say to yourself: "If I were asked to receive Paul as my guest, I should do so with all my heart." Lo, you may have Paul's Master as your guest, if you so wish. For He tells us: "Whosoever receiveth one such little child, receiveth Me" (Matt. 18:5). The humbler this brother is, the more truly do we receive Christ in him. For he that receives a great personage often does so through vainglory; but he that receives a little one, acts purely for Christ. . . .

Keep, then, a refuge for Christ. Say, "this is Christ's room; this house is reserved for Him." No matter how humble it be, He will not despise it; for He goes about naked and a stranger, and has not even a roof. Don't be cruel and inhuman; you who are so careful of your temporal goods, be not cold toward spiritual things. Entrust this task to your most faithful servant; have him bring in the lame, the beggars and the homeless. This I say to move you to shame. Such a guest ought to be lodged upstairs in the best apartment. If you will not do this, at least receive him downstairs, even though it be in the servant's quarters or in the stable.

You are indignant, perhaps? But what if you do not even this much?[13]

We might easily multiply such citations, for the Saint does not scruple to repeat himself. He is haunted by the picture of the homeless Christ begging at the gates of the palatial homes of the Christians; like remorse, he harries the consciences of his hearers with this thought. Let us listen for example to the following appeal taken from the fifteenth homily on the Epistle to the Romans:

The Father has delivered up His own Son, but thou wilt not give even a bit of bread to Him who was delivered up and immolated for thee. For thy sake the Father did not spare Him, though He was His own true Son; thou dost spurn Him when He is fainting from hunger, though everything you have belongs to Him. What could be more despicable? He was delivered up for thee. He was immolated for thee, He goes hungry for thee; He wills that to give should be to your own advantage, but even so you give not. What stone could be more unfeeling than the hearts which remain diabolically cold in the face of such appealing proofs of love?

He was not content merely to endure the cross and death; He willed to become a poor pilgrim, a beggar; He willed to be naked, to be cast into prison and to be subject to infirmities, in order that these at least might move thy heart. "If thou wilt give Me no return for the sufferings I endured for thy sake," He says, "then take pity on My poverty. If thou wilt not pity My poverty, let My infirmity and My chains stir thee

[333]

to compassion. If all this still leaves thee unmoved, at least grant My petition because it is such a little thing I beg. I ask thee for nothing costly, but for bread, a roof, and words of comfort. If you are even yet hostile, at least be stimulated by the thought of the Kingdom of heaven and the rewards I have promised. Has even this no appeal for thee? Then show at least a natural compassion when thou seest Me naked, and remember the nakedness I endured for thee on the cross. . . . I was bound for thee, and I am still bound for thee, in order that, stirred either by My former bonds or by those I bear today, thou mayest be minded to show Me some mercy. I suffered hunger for thee then, and I suffer it now for thee; I was thirsty as I hung on the cross, and I still thirst in the poor, thus to draw thee to Myself and to make thee merciful for thy own salvation. Wherefore after having bestowed a thousand favors upon thee, I ask thee some return. I do so, not as demanding the repayment of a debt, but that I may crown thy generosity, and that in exchange for such little things, I may give thee the Kingdom.

"I do not say, 'deliver Me from poverty' or 'give Me riches,' although I did become poor for thee. I ask only for bread, for clothing, and for some little relief from My hunger. If I am cast into prison, I do not ask that thou break My bonds and set Me free; I ask only that thou come and see Me who am in chains for thee. This favor will be enough for Me, and for it alone will I give thee heaven. True, I have delivered thee from the heaviest of chains. That makes no difference; it is enough that thou shouldst visit Me in My prison. I might even crown thee without that, but I wish to become thy debtor, so that thou mayest wear the crown with assurance. This is why, though I could feed Myself, I go begging; this is why I stand with outstretched hand at thy door. I wish to be fed by thee, for I love thee ardently. Like all who love, I am happy to be at thy table. I am proud to be there, and I shall proclaim thee before the whole world: 'Behold him who fed Me.' "

When someone gives us food we are ashamed and hide ourselves. But because of His glowing love for us, He proclaims our deeds with great praise; even though we be silent, He is not ashamed to say that we clothed Him when He was naked and that we fed Him when He was hungry.[14]

Accents such as these remain one of the glories of Christian oratory; they compelled the applause of the faithful of that day, and even now we are moved by their vehement defense of the eminent dignity of the poor in the Church. For Chrysostom almsgiving is more than mere beneficence; it is an act of faith, of charity, of religion; it puts us in the presence of the Saviour.

Therefore alms should be given with recollection; for can we show too much reverence in holding the cup from which Christ drinks? It must be done worshipfully; for nothing is better suited to prolong the effects of the Eucharist than a visit paid to Christ in His little ones.

In the holy doctor's eyes the unfortunates standing in the public square present an august spectacle; they remind him of the majesty of an altar made ready for the sacrifice. Indeed, they are more venerable:

> This altar is composed of the very members of Christ, and the Lord's body becomes an altar for thee. Venerate it; for upon it, in the flesh, thou dost offer sacrifice to the Lord. This altar is greater than the altar in this church, and hence far greater than the altar of the Old Testament.
>
> Do not protest! This stone altar is august because of the Victim that rests upon it; but the altar of almsgiving is more so because it is made of this very Victim. The former is august because, though made of stone, it is sanctified by contact with the body of Christ; the latter, because it is the body of Christ. Therefore, my brother, it is more venerable than the altar beside which thou art standing.
>
> What is Aaron when compared with this? What are the crown, the bells, the Holy of holies? But why speak of the altar of the Old Law when the altar of almsgiving is so sublime in comparison with our own altar here? Thou dost honor this altar because it receives the body of Christ. But the other, which is the body of Christ, you treat with ignominy and you look on indifferently while it perishes.
>
> This altar you can see everywhere, in the streets and in the market place, and at any hour you may offer sacrifice thereon; for it too is a place of sacrifice. And, as the priest standing at the altar brings down the Spirit, so you too bring down the Spirit, like the oil which was poured out in abundance [upon the altar of the Old Law].[15]

We shall now bring our study of St. John Chrysostom to a close. It is plain that for him, as for the other Fathers, Christ is everything in Christianity. Let us listen to his own words:

> Christ does not possess grace by way of participation, but He is the very source, the very root of all good things: He is

Life itself, Light itself, Truth itself. He does not keep these abundant gifts to Himself, but extends them to all others; yet after He has done so, He is still filled with them. He is still no poorer as a result of His generosity; despite the fact that He is constantly giving away and communicating His goods to all, He possesses the same plenitude. . . . If we take a drop of water from the sea, the sea is diminished, tiny though the loss may be. But with this source the case is quite different; no matter how much we draw from it, it is as abundant as before.[16]

Thus all comes through Him, and only through Him: it is in Him, in the open wound of His sacred side, that men are united among themselves and with God, and the entire multitude of the saved is none other than the "body" of the Saviour.

To sum up, Chrysostom's doctrine of the Mystical Body is less systematic than that of Athanasius and Hilary, but it is no less forceful. He is more a preacher than a theologian, and he bears witness to the Mystical Christ in his own way, with the style and emphasis proper to the pulpit.

However, it must not be imagined that we have to do here with mere oratorical developments, or with the pleasure that an orator may experience in returning to a theme that offers opportunity for striking antitheses. Such might possibly be the case were John Chrysostom the only one to speak in this manner. But the truth is that what he says is also what all the Fathers say. He contributes his style and the sweeping movement of his eloquence, but the voice that speaks within him is the voice of pure Tradition.

Chapter VIII

St. Cyril of Alexandria. The Incarnation and the Mystical Body

><

I. *The doctrinal synthesis of the Greek Church:* the doctrine of the Mystical Body in its relation to the dogma of the Incarnation.

II. *The very fact of the Incarnation makes Christ's humanity the "Head" of a Mystical Body.* Its union with Life makes it life-giving; it is the instrument of the Word in raising the dead, in giving light, and in the work of sanctification; it contains our supernatural life. A comparison of St. Cyril's teaching with that of St. Hilary.

III. *The Eucharist is the "act" of this all vivifying humanity;* therefore it is the sacrament of the Mystical Body. Connection with the preceding. The body of Christ produces in us what the Word effects in His humanity; it transforms, vivifies, deifies us. Thus, through the Eucharist Christ unites us, in Himself, with God and with one another. "That they may be one"; one with the unity of Christ, a unity that is physical, permanent, spiritual, and corporal. Union with God.

IV. 1. *The life thus communicated to us is divine.*

2. The mystical and collective prolongation of the Incarnation. "Christ bears us all in Himself"; "our nature is in Him." "Christ unites us to God in Himself"; He offers us to God. Through Christ, the Word abides in us; in the Only-begotten Son, we become sons of adoption. The role of the Holy Spirit; return to the Trinity.

V. *Conclusion.* Collective Incarnation? The doctrine of St. Cyril; its unity, continuity, and realism. Its principal points; its place in the life of Christian dogma.

VI. *Appendix.* Pseudo-Dionysius, St. Maximus the Confessor, St. Anastasius of Antioch, St. Anastasius of Sinai, St. John Damascene.

I

ST. CYRIL of Alexandria brings the doctrine of the Mystical Body to the highest perfection that it attains in oriental tradition. His teaching includes all the elements that we have considered, and presents them in such a manner that each point helps to complete the others.

This synthesis, in our opinion at least, is the work of Cyril only in a restricted sense. In the preceding pages we saw that it was being attempted by others. Nevertheless it owes its real title to Cyril.

No better man could have been found to introduce the synthesis. Cyril was born at Alexandria — the exact year of his birth is not known — and succeeded his uncle Theophilus as patriarch of that city in 412. The year 429 marked the beginning of his controversy against Nestorius. He died on June 4, 444. With Athanasius and Augustine he ranks as one of the three great lights of the Church. Popes, Councils, and Fathers have praised his authority to the skies. So it is always: When there is question of our union with His Son, God teaches us through the greatest of His Doctors.

Nor is this all. The holy patriarch was chosen by Providence to formulate and defend the dogma of the Incarnation. But the doctrine of the Mystical Body is an essential element of this exposition. Again, therefore, we find the doctrine at the very heart of Tradition.

Hitherto, with Athanasius and Hilary the doctrine of the Mystical Body had been developed chiefly in terms of the dogma of the Trinity, as a doctrine of our divinization. Now its progress is linked up with the development of the dogma of the Incarnation. There still remains perfect continuity with the preceding stages; there is still question of the Incarnate Word, who communicates His dignity to us by uniting us in Himself to His Father. But attention is now directed more exclusively to this Incarnate Word; emphasis is placed upon His interior constitution, so to speak, and upon that property which enables Him to contain us all mystically and to make us divine. Athanasius and Hilary aimed primarily to show that it was to God that we were united in Christ; St. Cyril stresses rather the union itself which joins us to eternal life.

[338]

II

In Christian Tradition Cyril is the Doctor of the Incarnation. Long before the Nestorian controversy, we see him insisting upon the dogma of Christology, and, faithful to the Alexandrian tradition, emphasizing the oneness of Christ. He cannot repeat often enough that in the Saviour the humanity and the divinity, or, according to his habitual phrase, "the flesh and the Word," are one with a real, intimate unity, with a unity that is "physical," he tells us in language that requires some explanation. The controversy against the dualism of Nestorius intensifies his interest in this point; expressions which up to that time had seemed satisfactory both to the earlier Fathers and to himself now appear insufficient. No longer, for instance, does he countenance the use of such terms as the "inhabitation" of the Word in the flesh, or "contact," or even "union." He must have *unity*. The Word has not only taken flesh, but *become* flesh, so perfectly that to consider His humanity apart from the divinity is to represent it otherwise than as it is.

This unity, of course, introduces no change in the divine nature, nor does the humanity cease to be perfectly like to us. As we shall see shortly, the latter is simply ameliorated. And it is here that the outlines of Cyril's doctrine of the Mystical Body begin to appear.

Christ's humanity, insists our Saint, is one with the Word. But, he continues, the Word is Life, incorruptible, eternal, subsistent Life. Therefore the flesh and blood of the Word are the flesh and blood of Life. Therefore they are capable of giving life. In consequence, they contain the supernatural life of humanity, as a spring contains the water which flows from it. We are contained in Christ and we are vivified in Him, and this vital unity which takes us up and incorporates us in Him constitutes the entire Mystical Body under one Head.

Let us listen as the Saint develops the various points and consequences of this teaching in a passage of one of his early works, the *Commentaries on St. John*. The essential elements of the doctrine are present, but the inaccuracy of certain

Christological formulas indicate that the commentary ante-
dates the Nestorian controversies.

> If the nature of the flesh is considered by itself, it is evi-
> dently not life-giving. No created thing has the power to vivify;
> on the contrary, itself has need of a life-giving principle. But
> if we study carefully the mystery of the Incarnation, we shall
> see who it is that inhabits[1] this flesh. Then, if we are not to
> blaspheme the Holy Spirit, we shall believe that the flesh can
> give life, despite the fact that of itself the flesh profiteth noth-
> ing. Once it is united to the life-giving Word, it is become
> wholly life-giving, since it is raised to the power of the Word.
> The flesh does not bring the Word down to its own level; for
> the divinity can in no wise be diminished. Of itself the flesh is
> incapable of imparting life; it can do so only because it has
> within itself the life-giving Word and because it exercises all
> the power of the Word. It is the body of Life itself, not that
> of an ordinary man. Of the latter it may justly be said that
> "the flesh profiteth nothing" (John 6:64). The flesh of Paul,
> for instance, or of Peter could not produce this effect in us,
> but only the flesh of our Saviour, Christ, "in whom dwelleth
> all the fullness of the God-head corporally" (Col. 2:9). For
> if honey can communicate its perfection to foods that are not
> naturally sweet, and if it can transform into its own nature
> whatsoever is mingled with it, it is not absurd to say that the
> life-giving nature of the Word could not raise to His own per-
> fection the body in which He dwells? Of all other men it is
> true that "the flesh profiteth nothing"; of Christ alone it is
> not true, since in His flesh dwells Life, that, is, the Only-
> begotten Son.[2]

Again and again the holy patriarch recalls this same principle:

> The Word Himself makes His body life-giving, since He gives
> it His own power. How this is done we can neither fully under-
> stand nor clearly explain. We must venerate the mystery in
> silence and in the faith that surpasses understanding.[3]

Christ's humanity is thereby given the power to perform
miracles; to convince us of this, God remits sin and raises the
dead only by its means.

> Thus we notice that even when He raises the dead to life
> the Saviour is not content to act in a divine manner only, by
> a mere word or command. He allows His flesh to co-operate with
> Him, so to speak, in this marvelous work, in order to prove that

[340]

it possesses life-giving power and that it is one with Him. For it is His very own flesh, and not that of someone else. When He restored to life the daughter of the president of the synagogue with the words, "Maiden, I say to thee, arise!" (Mark 5:41), He took the child by the hand, as it is written. He gave her life, as God, by an all-powerful command; but also by contact with His sacred flesh, to show that one and the same power was operating in both.[4] Again, coming to the city of Naim, where the widow's only son was being carried forth, He touched the bier and said: "Young man, I say to thee, arise!" (Luke 7:13-17.) Thus not only does He give to His command that power to raise men from the dead, but, in order to show that His body is life-giving, as we have already said, He touches the dead, and through His flesh sends life back again into the corpse.[5]

Not only does the Saviour's humanity vivify, but it also gives light. Speaking of the man born blind, Cyril writes:

Just as we believe that Christ's body is life-giving because it is the temple of the Word of the living God . . . so do we declare that it produces light. For it is the body of Him who by nature and in truth is the Light. . . . Thus He anoints with spittle [the eyes of the man born blind], to show that His body can generate light by the slightest touch. For it is, as we have said, the body of the true Light.[6]

Similarly, the incidents of Christ's life possess the power to sanctify:

He was scourged unjustly, to deliver us from the chastisement that we justly deserved; He endured mockery and blows, in order that we might be able to resist Satan and to escape the sin that we had incurred through [Adam's] fall. For we believe, and with reason, that all Christ's sufferings took place because of us and for us, and that they have the power to turn aside and destroy the evils which we deserve because of sin. Just as it was enough to free all from death, that He who knew not death should offer His own flesh to death (since the one Christ died for all), so in like manner we must say that in order to deliver all from stripes and ignominy, it is enough that our Lord has endured them for us.[7]

St. Cyril effects a synthesis which enables him to state, with new force, the general principle already familiar to Tradition, that the humanity of Christ assumes our infirmities and our death, in order that we may receive eternal life in that humanity, which is united with Life. Whatever it possesses, passes into us; the events of its existence are the common patrimony of humankind. Often Scripture itself speaks without making any distinction between that humanity and ourselves, in order to show clearly that Christ's work will not be finished until He shall have made us by grace what He is by nature.

We have already encountered similar ideas in the writings of St. Hilary. The bishop of Poitiers likewise emphasized strongly the glories conferred upon the Saviour's humanity by virtue of its union with the Word. But he was still feeling his way along dangerous paths. In his day the revealed truth had not yet been examined with such thoroughness as to enable one to furnish rigorously exact formulas for the more subtle points; and although the Holy Spirit assists the work of Tradition, He does not will to dispense the Fathers from all exertion or to smooth over every difficulty, but merely to direct their efforts and to prevent their making any change in the faith.

Thus St. Hilary considers the privileges of the Saviour as an elevation of His human nature, which he knows to be truly human; that it is human in a particularly excellent manner he also sees, but not so clearly, and his explanations on this point are less sound. According to him, the humanity of Jesus had a natural power to perform miracles and to escape death; in other words — this is the weak point — it was not perfectly like our human nature.

But for St. Cyril the days of hesitation are at an end. Not that we have arrived at perfection; for can there ever be perfection where God deigns to admit our human co-operation? Later we shall have the opportunity to point out where Scholastic theology renders the revealed truth with still greater accuracy. Nevertheless this is one of the high points; the dogmatic formula of Ephesus is ready in Cyril's writings. In particular, while he puts the privileges of the Sacred Humanity in strong relief, he does not view them as attributes superadded to our nature or as a sort of complication arising indepehdently of the Incarnation. They are present in the humanity of Jesus simply as the effect of its union with the

Word of Life. Thus both doctrinal formulas and theological explanation come to correspond more and more exactly with the data of revelation.

III

The effects which the humanity of Christ produced by a visible activity during its mortal existence it now produces invisibly, but no less truly, in the Eucharist. Theologians consider St. Cyril's Eucharistic teaching to be one of the most complete. Also, for there is ever the same coincidence, it is one of those which are most intimately connected with the truth of the Mystical Body.

> If mere contact with the sacred flesh [of Jesus] gives life to a dead body, should we not experience effects still more wonderful when we receive the sacred "eulogy" [Eucharist]? Surely it must completely transform those who receive it into its own perfection, that is, into immortality. Be not surprised at this; do not ask how it is possible. Think rather how water which, though cold by nature, seems to forget its nature when it is set upon the fire, and takes on the victorious energy of the fire. It is the same with us. Corruptible as we are in the flesh, we lose our own weakness by this "mingling" [with the "eulogy"], and we are transformed into what is proper to the "eulogy," that is, into life.[8]

What took place at the Incarnation happens once more in Communion. Just as the Word, by uniting Himself with the flesh, elevated it to His own likeness and made it capable of imparting life, so, though of course in a lesser degree, when the flesh of Christ enters within us it transforms us into its own image and gives us life. The two operations are similar, or rather, the second operation is the continuation of the first, and the diffusion of the same life. Thus the Saint employs the same terms and the same comparisons for both. Like the Incarnation, the Eucharist too is likened to a fire that invades a cold object and changes it to hot. Elsewhere he likens it to a spark that is buried in straw in order to preserve the fire, and which consumes all; it is like the leaven, hidden in the dough, which transforms the whole mass:

"A little leaven," says St. Paul, "leaveneth all the dough"

[343]

(1 Cor. 5:6). In like manner a tiny "eulogy" leavens our whole body and fills it with its own power. Thus Christ passes into us and we in turn pass into Him. And may we not truly say that the leaven is in the whole mass, and conversely, that the whole mass is absorbed by the leaven?[9]

So certain is this power of the Eucharist that our Saint uses it as an argument to refute Nestorius. When the heresiarch declares that the flesh of Christ is not the flesh of the Word he can no longer admit that the Eucharist gives life; he destroys the whole economy of salvation:

> Whosoever does not confess that the flesh of the Lord is life-giving and that it is the proper flesh of the Word who proceeds from the Father; or if he says that it is like the flesh of another and united with the Word in honor merely, because it is the habitation of God; and if he does not say rather that it is life-giving, as we have said, since it is become the proper flesh of the Word who can give life to all: let him be anathema.[10]

The holy doctor explains this condemnation on three different occasions, each time with evident reference to the Eucharist. Elsewhere, still intent upon refuting Nestorius, he writes:

> We eat the proper flesh of the Word, which, because it is the flesh of Him who lives by the Father, is become life-giving.
> Just as that body is life-giving which the Word made His own by an inconceivable and ineffable union, so we who partake of His sacred flesh and blood are wholly vivified. For the Word abides in us, both divinely by the Holy Spirit and humanly by His sacred flesh and His precious blood. . . .
> By becoming partakers of the Spirit we are united with the Saviour of all and with one another. We become concorporal too: "We many are one body, for we all partake of the one bread" (1 Cor. 10:17). The body of Christ within us binds us into unity, since it is in no way divided.[11]

The exposition closes with a kind of profession of faith:

> We believe that the Word of God, by uniting Himself in an ineffable and mysterious union with a body born of the Virgin and animated by a rational soul, has made this body life-giving, since the Word, being God, is Life Itself. His purpose was to make us partake of Himself in a manner both spiritual

and corporal, to make us victorious over corruption and to destroy the law of sin that reigned in our members.[12]

IV. § 1

This unity that comes to us in the Eucharist is described by the holy doctor in pages that are unsurpassed for depth and vigor of thought. He explains the text of St. John's Gospel in which Christ asks that His disciples may be one as He is one with the Father. As we have seen, the Arians had appropriated this text, and the Fathers, especially Athanasius and Hilary had given important developments concerning the unity of the faithful in Christ in order to explain it clearly. Cyril does the same thing. Whether he intended it or not, his exegesis falls directly into the line of Tradition after that of Athanasius and Hilary. It completes both of the latter interpretations by developing the work of the Holy Spirit in our union with Christ, and by repeatedly insisting that the unity of the Mystical Body is produced by the very unity of Christ, the unity of His body of flesh. This is to our knowledge the most complete passage that the Eastern Church has left us on the subject of our incorporation in the Saviour.

The heretics maintain, explains Cyril, that the union of the Son and the Father is like that which exists among ourselves; to wit, a union of resemblance and agreement of wills; in short, a moral union. But, continues the Saint, bringing in the doctrine of the Mystical Body, is it true that we are bound together only by a moral union? Does not the sacred text itself tell us of something more, of a real, "physical" union? And Cyril develops the thought in passages which, though long and charged with repetitions, as is his wont, are so rich in doctrine that we must quote them at some length.

> Therefore the only Son of God, who is in the very substance of the Father and who in His nature wholly possesses the Father, was made flesh according to the Scriptures; He has as it were "mingled" Himself with our nature through an ineffable union with a body taken from this earth. Thus He who is God by nature is become in truth a heavenly man, not a "God-bearer" only, as some would have it who do not understand this sublime mystery; but He is God and man in one

[345]

and the same [person]. Thus He united in Himself two natures which of themselves were separated by infinity, and enabled man to communicate and partake of the divine nature. For the communion of the Spirit has come even to us; the Spirit has taken up His abode in us also. This [inhabitation of the Spirit] began in Christ and was realized in Him first. For when He became like to us, that is, when He became man, He was anointed and consecrated, although as God, proceeding from the Father, He Himself by His own Spirit sanctified the temple of His flesh and all things that He had created, accordingly as each was to be sanctified. Therefore the mystery that took place in Christ was the beginning and the means of our participation in the Spirit and of our union with God.[13]

Here we see the Incarnation of the Word and our incorporation with Christ explained in their continuity. Let us now see the relation of the Eucharist to these two mysteries.

In His Wisdom and in accordance with the counsels of the Father, the Only-begotten Son has found a means of bringing and welding us into unity with God and with one another, although by reason of our souls and bodies we are each distinct personalities.

Through one body, which is His own, He blesses, by a mysterious communion, those who believe in Him, and He makes them concorporal with Himself and with one another.

Who can now separate them or deprive them of their "physical" union? They have been bound together into unity with Christ by means of His one holy body. For if we all eat of the one bread we all become one body, since there can be no division in Christ. For this reason is the Church called the body of Christ, and we severally His members, according to the teaching of St. Paul (Eph. 5:23,ss.). Since we are all united with the one Christ through His sacred body, and since we all receive Him who is one and indivisible into our own bodies, we ought to look upon our members as belonging to Him rather than to ourselves.[14]

Hence the unity of the Mystical Body is the unity of the Saviour Himself, communicated to the faithful. Therefore it is real, "physical," indestructible, and made by God, just as the unity of the Man-God is real, indestructible, and made by God. In none of his developments does the Saint appear to limit the union which the Eucharist gives us with Christ to the few short moments that the Sacred Species remain within us. One would even say that here as in the mystery of the Incarnation, the terms of union, contact, inhabitation, are not strong enough, and that we must say *unity*, not a hypostatic unity, of course, but nevertheless real. Again, like the unity of the two natures in Christ, this unity of us in Christ is a divine work that can come only from the Holy Spirit and from the Trinity. This our Saint explains in the passage which immediately follows the one just quoted:

> Since we all receive within us the one Spirit, who is the Holy Ghost, we are "mingled," so to speak, both with one another and with God. For, although we are distinct one from the other, and the Spirit of the Father and of the Son dwells in each one individually, yet this Spirit is one and indivisible. Therefore He joins our many distinct spirits into unity and somehow makes them one spirit in Himself. Just as the power of the sacred flesh makes concorporal those who receive it, so, in my opinion the one indivisible Spirit who dwells in all, brings all into a spiritual unity. Therefore St. Paul exhorts us: "bearing with one another in charity, [be] careful to keep the unity of the Spirit in the bond of peace: one body and one spirit, as also ye were called in one hope, that of your calling: one Lord, one faith, one baptism: one God and Father of all, who is above all and throughout all and in all" (Eph. 4:3–6). And truly, if the one Spirit abides in all of us, then the one Father of all will be God within us, and through His Son He will bring into unity one with the other and with Himself those who participate of the Spirit.[15]

This part which the Holy Ghost takes in our incorporation with Christ is of the highest importance and is stressed insistently by our Saint. However, a fuller explanation of this operation of the Spirit and of His relation to the effects of the Eucharist would involve theological considerations not directly in line with our present purpose. Hence we shall not enter into the subject; we merely wish to note how the passage brings out the transcendent and supernatural aspect of our union with the Saviour. The Saint concludes as follows:

> We are all one, in the Father and in the Son and in the Holy Ghost. We are one, I say, by identity of nature (for it is well to repeat what has already been said), by our training in piety, by communion in the sacred flesh of Christ, and by partaking of the one Holy Spirit, as we have said.[16]

These statements, clear and insistent though they are, do not

[347]

yet fully satisfy Cyril. In the following chapter he returns to the same subject from another angle, which enables him to repeat the entire doctrine. Through the Eucharist, he continues, not only does Christ unite us among ourselves, but He unites us also to God.

> Christ comes into us corporally as man, "mingling" and uniting Himself with us through the mystery of the "eulogy"; but as God He comes spiritually, by the power and charity of His Spirit, who comes into us to infuse a new life in us and to make us partakers of His divine nature. Thus we see that the bond of our union with God the Father is Christ; as man He unites us with Himself, and as God He unites us to God, for He remains truly in the Father. Our nature, subject as it is to corruption, could not attain to incorruption unless the nature that is superior to all corruption and change had come down to us, raised our fallen nature to its own perfection, detached us from the condition of created things through communion and a "mingling" with itself, and transformed into its own likeness us, who are not such by nature. We are perfected in unity with God the Father through our Mediator Jesus Christ. For when we receive within us, corporally and spiritually, the true Son who is substantially united with the Father, as I was just saying, we have the glory of participating and communicating in the divine nature.[17]

Thus, the doctrine of the Eucharist, like that of the Incarnation, leads to a doctrine of the deification of men. This point we shall now consider in greater detail.

§ 2

So far Cyril has told us that the proper result of the Incarnation is to vivify the human race. And, he continues, since the life that it communicates is the divine Life itself, its ultimate effect is to produce in each soul a participation and an analogy, distant if you will, of itself. Thus in St. Cyril as in other Fathers we once more find the thought that we have already met so often, of a mystical and collective prolongation of the Incarnation. And, like the earlier Fathers, Cyril, too, has been accused of being so intent upon the union of the Word with all men as to lose sight of what is incommunicable in the hypostatic union. Now that the doctrine of the Incarnation has been explained in its entirety, the time has come to dispel this ancient grievance.

We shall examine the passages which have brought this accusation upon the Saint. They are ordinarily centered round two expressions, which were already employed by St. Hilary: "Christ bears us all in Himself," and "all human nature is in Christ." For Cyril as for Hilary the two formulas have the same meaning. The term *nature,* which appears in the second formula, refers not so much to the constitutive elements of each man as to the totality of the human race. The Saint makes this point quite clear when he says that by this assumption of "our nature" in Christ we are all restored, all crucified, all victors over death, all risen from the dead, all adopted by the Father.

We have already seen, and it will be more evident from the texts which follow, that in these formulas Cyril refers rather to our justification than to the Incarnation; or rather, that he views the Incarnation as prolonged in our justification, and speaks of the Saviour's relations with men rather than of His relations with the Father.

But of special interest to us is the fact that our Saint thus combines in a single system two different concepts of our justification, both of which are ways of regarding the Mystical Body. The first is the doctrine of the two Adams, according to which we are all contained in Christ as we were all contained in our first parent, and being thus in Christ, we are holy before God, on condition, of course, that our actions be in conformity with this union. The second is the doctrine of vivification. Sin has deprived us of life and of immortality. But the Word is Life, superabundant and perfect Life. By possessing Him within us, we are all regenerated.

We have frequently met these two doctrines separately; some few times we could see them converging and about to unite. But we believe that St. Cyril was the first to effect the synthesis. He shows that Christ is the second Adam, the second stock that includes our whole race; this is the first concept. He establishes this first point by showing that Christ is Life, that He is Life in such fullness as to contain within Himself as in its source, the life of all humanity, and that in

[349]

consequence He has the power to impart life to every soul. This is the second view, the doctrine of vivification.

Let us read, for instance, the following passage:

> The Scriptures tell us that the Word who was God, begotten of God from all eternity, is begotten today (Ps. 2:7). What does this mean except that He willed to confer on us the adoption of sons? For the whole of humanity was in Christ as man. In like manner, although He already possesses the Spirit, the Son is said to receive the Spirit, so that we may all receive the Spirit in Him. This is why He assumes the posterity of Abraham, as it is written, and becomes like to His brethren in all things. The Only-begotten Son does not receive the Spirit for Himself; for the Spirit belongs to Him, is in Him, and [proceeds] from Him. But [He receives the Spirit] because, having become man, He contained our whole nature in Himself, in order to repair and restore it wholly. . . .
>
> Let us see why the Scriptures call Christ the second Adam. The reason is that the human race was created and then was by disobedience corrupted in the first Adam, while in the second, who is Christ, it has as it were a new beginning and is raised to a new life and to immortality. "If any man be in Christ, he is a new creature," as St. Paul tells us (2 Cor. 5:17). The Spirit of renewal, the Holy Ghost, the principle of eternal life, was given to us when Christ was glorified, that is, after His resurrection, and when, after having broken the bonds of death, He rose superior to all corruption and lived again, possessing our whole nature in Himself, as man and as one of ourselves.[18]

Therefore it is by His humanity that Christ contains our whole nature, that is, all regenerated men, and by right, all men. Our Saint repeats this incessantly; it is by becoming man, it is because He is the first-fruits of our race that Christ bears us in Himself, in His body. He is like the first-fruits that of old were offered to God in token of the whole harvest.

> The only Son became man, and He who is Life penetrated as it were into our nature. Thus He put an end to the rule of death and destroyed the leaven of corruption that was within us, since the divine nature is wholly exempt from all inclination to evil and since He bore us in Himself by means of His flesh. For we were all in Him as man, that He might mortify the members which were on earth, that is, the passions of the flesh; that He might destroy the law of sin which held sway in our members, and also sanctify our nature; that He might

become our model and guide in the path of virtue, and communicate to us a pure knowledge both of the truth to be known and of the good to be practiced. All these benefits Christ obtained for us by becoming man. For it was necessary that human nature be raised to the highest perfection.[19]

Hence there is still question not of the Incarnation as such, but of its consequences. This the holy doctor tells us again, in his commentary on the verse of St. John (John 1:14): "And the Word was made flesh, and dwelt amongst us" (or, according to the Greek text, "dwelt *in* us.")

"The Word dwelt in us." These words reveal a most profound mystery. We were all in Christ, and the common person of humanity is formed anew in Him. Therefore is He called the second Adam because He communicates to our whole nature all the blessings of happiness and glory, just as the first Adam brought down upon us the curse of corruption and ignominy.

Through One, then, the Word has taken up His abode in all and since this One is constituted the Son of God in power according to the spirit of holiness, He communicates His dignity to the whole of humanity. And so because of one of us, the saying applies also to us: "I have said: you are gods, and all of you the sons of the Most High" (Ps. 81:6).

In Christ, therefore, the slave is truly set free; he is elevated to mystical unity with Him who took the form of a slave. Thus, too, are we raised up, in imitation of this unique exemplar, by reason of our kinship with Him according to the flesh. Why did He not take the nature of the angels? Why did He come into the race of Abraham? Why should He become like to His brothers in all things by becoming true man? Is it not evident to everyone that He did not choose the condition of a slave to gain any advantage for Himself, but to give Himself to us, to enrich us by His poverty, to raise us up, because of our resemblance to Him, to His own ineffable perfection and to make us Gods and sons of God by faith? He has dwelt in us who is the Son of God by nature, so that in His Spirit we cry: "Abba, Father" (Rom. 8:15). And in the unique temple that He has assumed for us and from our race, the Word dwells in all, in order that having us all in Himself, He may reconcile us all in one body to His Father, as St. Paul tells us (Eph. 2:16).[20]

Hence, while the hypostatic union, by making Christ the supreme Life, removes Him to an infinite distance from us, yet at the same time it unites Him with us by making Him our life. Since His divinity enables Him to contain us all in Himself, He communicates His glory to us in Himself. Such is the universal consequence of the one Incarnation. Cyril insists:

> Remember well this profound and great mystery, and keep in your heart the true canon of the divine truths. You hear how the Word, the Only-begotten Son of God, has been made like to us, in order that we too may become like to Him, as far as this is possible for our nature and as far as the plan of our supernatural renewal will permit. He lowered Himself in order to raise, to His own dignity, that which is base by nature; though by nature He is God and Son, He took the form of a slave, that He might transform those who are slaves by nature into the glory of adoption according to His likeness. He is become like unto us, that is, He is become man, that we in turn may be made like Him, that is, Gods and sons; and He takes our infirmities in Himself as His own, that He may give us His glories in exchange.[21]

We find the same teaching in the following passage, where, true to the tradition of the great doctors, St. Cyril insists but little upon the distinction between Christ and ourselves, in order to bring out more effectively the continuity that attaches the members to the Head:

> ✓ Christ is at once the only Son and the first-born Son. He is only Son as God; He is the first-born through the salutary union which He established between Himself and us by becoming man. By this union, in Him and through Him we are made sons of God both by nature and by grace. By nature we are sons in Him and in Him alone; through Him and in the Spirit, we are sons by participation and by grace. Therefore just as Christ in His humanity is called and is the proper Son of God, because that humanity is united with the Word according to the economy of salvation, so too because of this union with the flesh, the Word properly is and is called the first-born of many brethren.[22]

Therefore, by virtue of the Incarnation Christ is the Mediator, the mediator of divine life. From Him proceeds all adoptive sonship, as all fatherhood derives from the Father.

> The Son enables us to become that which by nature is proper to Him alone. He lets us share it, to prove His love for men and His charity for the world. . . . By participating in Him

through the Spirit, we are sealed as it were with His image and the likeness of the Father.[23]

Like the Incarnation, so the mystical prolongation of the Incarnation within us is to be attributed to the Holy Ghost.

> The Spirit by His power of sanctification conforms us perfectly to Christ. For He is, so to speak, the form [i.e., the perfect likeness] of Christ our Saviour, and by His very person, He impresses upon us the divine image.[24]

Concerning this presence and operation of the Holy Spirit in the souls of the just, the Saint makes some emphatic statements whose exact meaning is even today the object of discussion. There is no need for us to enter into the debate. Whether or not St. Cyril regarded the action of the Holy Spirit in the just as proper and personal to the Third Person, he certainly maintained that this action makes us truly divine and that it unites us, in Christ, to the entire Trinity. All that we wish to consider here is the phrase "in Christ."

> We are justified in Christ, and we attain unity with Him by the participation of the Spirit, in the good pleasure of the Father.[25]

Just as everything comes from the Father, through the Son, in the Spirit, so all returns in the Spirit, through the Son, to the Father.

> The Spirit is the perfect image of the substance of the Son, as Paul writes: "Those whom He hath foreknown, them He hath predestined to bear a nature in the image of His Son's" (Rom. 8:29). He makes those in whom He abides like to the Father's image, which is the Son. And so all things are brought back by the Son to Him from whom He proceeds, that is to the Father, through the Spirit.[26]

The entire tenth chapter of his eleventh book on St. John, from which this passage is taken, is a development of the same thought.

> Our return to the Father is effected through Christ our Saviour only by means of the participation and the sanctification of the Spirit. The Spirit it is who elevates us to the Son and so unites us to God. When we receive the Spirit we become sharers and partakers of the divine nature. But we receive the Spirit through the Son, and in the Son we receive the Father.[27]

[353]

V

Such is St. Cyril's doctrine concerning the divinization of all men in the Incarnate Word. Now that we have seen it in its ensemble we can judge for ourselves whether he loses sight, even for an instant, of the one hypostatic union. Nothing of the sort; Cyril sees nothing but that union. But he does see it in its full mystical extension.

For indeed there is a collective aspect of the Incarnation. This universality, however, is only the result, in a sense the natural result of what is unique and incommunicable in the Incarnation. The Saviour's human nature must be united perfectly with Life, if it is to infuse into all men a divine life that will enable them to have part with the Man-God. In order to speak of a union of God with all men or, if the expression may be permitted, of a collective incarnation, it is no more necessary to deny the true, one and individual Incarnation than it is necessary to destroy the foundation in order to erect a building.

Christian doctrine does not have to sacrifice one dogma for another, and nothing is more simple than the progress of truth toward its full expression under the guiding hand of Him who is the fullness of Truth.

Of this the doctrinal synthesis of St. Cyril is a splendid example. Perhaps, now that we have quoted the principal passages embodying this synthesis, it may be well to indicate the general outline and to show its unity. In the following explanation our purpose is not to add anything, but simply to systematize the Saint's teaching in terms of the doctrine that we are studying.

In this synthesis, there is unbroken progression; each element refers us back to the Incarnation, but the Incarnation itself is given its full extension, and embraces the whole human race.

To begin with, we have a single principle; namely, the Christological dogma that Christ's humanity is one with the Word of Life. Then a single consequence, which has a twofold aspect: since it is the body and blood of Life itself, that humanity is life-giving; therefore it possesses both an unparalleled excellence and a function that is universal. Now let these truths unfold, and we have the Saint's doctrine on the Eucharist, on the deification of men, and on the mystical aspect of Christ; in short, we have his doctrine of the Mystical Body in all its realism and all its richness.

Yes, realism. For as truly as the Word of Life became flesh and as truly as His humanity has thereby become the life of men, so truly are we vivified by incorporation with Him. Here the very Incarnation is at stake, and our Saint cannot find language strong enough to condemn those who would reduce our unity in Christ to a collection of mere moral relationships. On the other hand he is also at a loss for words emphatic enough in praise of this unity. Often he calls it a "physical" unity, a union according to the flesh, a union certainly mysterious, but real, just as real as must be our attachment to the Vine, just as real as must be our incorporation into His body.

The Eucharist is the most perfect means of effecting this insertion. In this sacrament Christ comes to take us, to change us, to vivify us by uniting us all in Himself, to one another, and to God. Here again it is the Incarnation that is at stake; and in order to understand what the Word has done to the humanity that He has taken, we must accept the theology of the Blessed Sacrament in its entirety. Since He is Life, He has made His humanity life-giving, absolutely and universally life-giving; we see it as it is only when we see it in its act of universal vivification.

For we must remember that it is as man that Christ is the life of men, Mediator, and Head of the Mystical Body. St. Cyril's teaching is very clear on this point. This again is only another aspect of the Incarnation; for Christ assumed human nature precisely in order that it might be the salvation of the human race. Of itself, and wherever it is, human nature possesses a certain universal character. In Christ, on account of the divinity, it has this character in a transcendent manner. The principle of all life is eternal Life, and the hypostatic union is the sole explanation of the supernatural life that is in Christ, or as the Schoolmen say, of His grace.

This same hypostatic union causes to flow into our human

nature the life that it imparts to the humanity of Christ. Once
the Three Persons of the Holy Trinity have wrought the Incarnation, it is enough; without further divine intervention,
the reserves of life are already stored up, so superabundant,
so perfectly human, that they are capable of vivifying the
whole human race.

Now, when all obstacles shall have been removed and when
Christ's death shall have conquered sin, these reserves extend
over the entire universe. And this, not through our own efforts,
not simply because of our community of nature with Christ,
but because of the Incarnate Word, because of the union of
our nature with God in Him, because of the union which
joins His humanity with us and joins us all together through
the immensity of His supernatural life.

Thus it is His personality, His subsistence, that makes
Christ's human nature "mystical"; His union with the Word
of Life explains His union with us; and His Headship, far
from being a superadded privilege, is part of His essential
glory.

Christ, however, is no less truly personal or less real or less
alive for being "mystical." On the contrary, it is the very intensity of His personal life that makes Him the universal
principle of supernatural life. Nor, on the other hand, do the
faithful lose any of their individuality by reason of their elevation to a higher life. Long before the Council of Trent,
Cyril points out that grace sanctifies each one personally; our
life simply becomes more abundant, more perfect, and consequently more personal and more immanent, by being made
divine in Christ.

Hence there is no question in St. Cyril — or for that matter,
anywhere in the doctrine of the Mystical Body — of a nebulous theory that would suppress every distinction, deprive
Christ of His supreme dignity, and men of their individuality
and confuse them all in a vague, indeterminate kind of life.
Nor is there any question of attributing to the Saviour a
nature half divine and half human, with an immensity all its
own, midway between divine omnipresence and human limitations. Monophysites may indeed speak thus, for they have lost
sight of Christ's strict consubstantiality with men; but despite

some few less felicitous phrases, Cyril has nothing in common with Monophysitism. His Christ is true God and true man and truly one.

However, just as Christ is "mystical" simply because He is Christ, so, too, according to St. Cyril the Incarnation is "mystical" simply because it is the Incarnation. By this we mean that in the Saint's eyes, by its pure and simple union with the Word, the Saviour's humanity is placed in a special order and possesses at the same time such an abundance of supernatural life that only the divinization of the entire human race can adequately manifest its plenitude. Though complete, totally complete in itself from the indivisible moment of the Man-God's conception, the Incarnation is still not complete from every point of view. Or, to speak more accurately, it was already in that instant so complete that the religious history of mankind can do no more than unfold its glorious mysteries.

In order, therefore, to say what Christ is, and what the Incarnation is, we must speak of the faithful. Thus the same theological process that has led the Christological dogma to a definitive expression has likewise perfected the doctrine of the Mystical Body. The teaching of St. Cyril was not a sudden, individual discovery, but the climax of a long and laborious search in which many of the Fathers have co-operated; or rather, it was the growth of a seed over which God had been keeping careful watch since the beginning.

For just as our thoughts are not something inert, but live by the life of our souls, so, too, Christian truths do not remain a dead letter in the Church, for they are impregnated with the life of Christ, who is both Life and Truth.

We have been able in the course of this study to discern the successive stages of this development. Even in the time of St. Ignatius of Antioch several elements of the doctrine of the Mystical Body had already taken definite form, and were centered round the doctrine of ecclesiastical unity. Later, St. Irenaeus built up a similar synthesis in terms of the theory of the two Adams and the system of the recapitulation.

The decisive orientation appears with St. Athanasius. The idea of life is emphasized more and more, and one by one the other points of doctrine are organized round this concept.

[357]

When St. Cyril teaches that the life of the Church is none other than the communication to the Christian of that supernatural fullness of life which the hypostatic union had given to Christ, the second Adam, he is merely completing a process that has been going on for centuries.

This growth is more truly God's work than it is the work of men. We may well imagine that even those who contributed to it were often unaware of the part that they were taking. Again, it is frequently impossible at present to discover whether one author was dependent upon, or influenced by the teaching of the others. Nay, who can even determine whether an explanation that we regard as the work of a particular Father, is not merely a repetition of what had been said by many others before him in the anonymity of Christian preaching?

But what matters our inability to distinguish clearly the work of men as long as the work is God's own? In the progress of Christian truth it is Christian truth itself that is active, and grows and lives. He who is Truth and who has deigned to dwell in us is also He who is Life, and who lives in His truth. It is by His interior influence, by His guidance at times unperceived, and by His light which enables men to see without letting itself be seen, that Christians have grown in the truth.

Ultimately there is only Christ, only the Incarnation. The statement is simply a summary of this part of our study. The Church's whole life and her marvelous harmony of doctrine, all have their sole source in the life and unity of the Saviour. To have the whole Christ is to have the whole of Christianity, just as the complete Incarnation is the expression of the whole of Christian doctrine.

VI

The authors who followed Cyril in the Greek Church have contributed little that is of importance when compared with this theology. Hence we shall confine ourselves to the mention of a few names and some brief quotations. First, the Pseudo-Dionysius and St. Maximus the Confessor give us some vigorous passages concerning our divinization in Christ. Then there is St. Anastasius, patriarch of Antioch, who lived in the middle of the sixth century, half a century after the Pseudo-Dionysius. Anastasius was a friend of Pope St. Gregory and the defender of the faith against Justinian. Of his extant writings we possess a very interesting passage which expresses the soteriological argument with new force:

> God bore in Himself everything that we are. He assumed our entire race in one individual, and thus He became the first-fruits of our nature.
> For He willed to restore wholly that which was fallen. But our whole race was fallen. Therefore He "mingled" Himself with the whole Adam; He who is Life "mingled" Himself with the dead Adam to save him. He penetrated wholly into him whom He had united with Himself, as the soul would do in a great body, animating it completely and communicating life to it throughout, in a perceptible fashion. For this reason is the human race called "the body of Christ, and severally His members" (1 Cor. 12:27), since Christ is present equally in all, yet abides in each one individually.[28]

About a century later, another Anastasius, a monk and abbot of a monastery of Sinai and, therefore, styled the "Sinaite," deserves mention. In addition to a sample of the method of exegesis based upon our incorporation in Christ, to which we have often referred, we also find in his writings certain historical data concerning this method. Anastasius traces it to St. Paul, and among its earliest defenders he names Papias, Pantaenus, Clement of Alexandria, Irenaeus, Cyril of Alexandria, Ammonius, the two Gregorys of Cappadocia, and Philo.

A few years later we find the theory of this method expressed by St. John Damascene. John, who was born at Damascus toward the end of the seventh century and died in 749, is the author of a general exposition of Christian faith, which soon became and continued to be the classic expression of Christian truth for the Greek Church. Therefore his work is of great theological importance, and from it we should have liked to draw long passages on the Mystical Body.

Unfortunately we have found very little on this subject. For the most part, his explanations bear on points that had been treated explicitly and *ex professo* by the earlier Fathers, and also on points that were contested by the heterodox of his time. But the truth of our incorporation in Christ is not one of these; if it is explained or attacked, it is always in connection with some other truth. Hence John has very little to say about the Mystical Body. We have found only a few indications scattered through his works. These indications we shall group together here.

In the first place the doctor of Damascus is careful to note that the Saviour's human nature, despite its universal function, is not a universal nature. This precision was necessary, and it had to be expressed with force, in order to exclude absurd ideas which the Platonist concept of nature might have introduced into Christian tradition, had not God been watching over the deposit of faith.

Yet, while it is thus a very individual and very concrete human nature (a point of which, as we have seen, Christian teaching has never lost sight), nevertheless the Saviour's human nature has an activity, and in a certain sense an extension that are universal. In it the whole of human nature has been raised up and exalted, just as in it our race has been assumed with all its infirmities, in order to be purified and set free.

Thus, remarks the Saint, the Scriptures can attribute to Christ lowly and humble things that are true only of ourselves; for does He not contain us in Himself? In two different passages the Saint gives us the theory of this manner of speech. The first time, he is explaining Christ's words: "My God, My God, why hast Thou forsaken Me?" (Matt. 27:46); then, in another long passage he explains the various ways in which theology permits us to speak of Christ. On this point, he tells us, we must distinguish what was proper to the Saviour, first, before the Incarnation; secondly, in the Incarnation itself; thirdly, after the Incarnation had taken place; and lastly, after His resurrection. And in all these we must further distinguish what is proper to Him according to His human nature and what is proper to Him according to His divine nature. The particular mode of predication that interests us is that which considers Christ's humanity after the hypostatic union, and then after the Resurrection. On such occasions, explains the Damascene, Christ puts Himself in our place and speaks in our person. It is we who were under the power of sin and under the curse, on account of our indocility and disobedience; it is we who were forsaken by God; and yet He speaks of the punishment that He Himself receives. Let us see how the Saint expresses the thought in the first of these passages.

We must understand that there are two kinds of appropriation. One is physical and essential, while the other is personal and according to dispositions. The first, which is physical and essential, is the one which led God, in His love for us, to assume our nature and all the elements of that nature, to become a natural and true man and to experience all that is proper to our nature. The other appropriation, which is personal and according to dispositions, is had when one impersonates another by his dispositions, that is, by his mercy or his love, and when in the other's stead he utters words which do not apply to himself. The latter was used by the Lord when He appropriated to Himself our curse and our dereliction and other things which are not natural [to Him]. These things were not in Him, but He was impersonating us, and placing Himself among us. It is in this sense that He is said to become a curse on our behalf (Gal. 3:13).[29]

What is true of our misery and weakness may also be applied to the prayers that we say when we are weak and miserable. When Christ prayed, it was not that He needed to raise His spirit to God or to ask for things that were required; He was Himself God. But He spoke in our name and expressed in Himself what we should do, that He might be our model in all things.

Indeed, the Incarnation has made Him so like us that we can judge what He is by simply reflecting upon what we ourselves are. We have often seen this method of reasoning in the Fathers. And the Saint of Damascus has borrowed it from them, for when he employs it he usually cites St. Gregory the Theologian and the latter's famous maxim: "What is not assumed is not saved."

St. Gregory himself had used the argument against Apollinaris. After him it was adapted to the controversies with the Aphthardocetists and the Monotheletes. The former held that even before the Resurrection Christ's humanity was absolutely incorruptible and impassible by reason of the hypostatic union, and only apparently subject to infirmity. The Monotheletes, on the other hand, claimed that the humanity of Christ had no will or activity of its own, but was moved by the divinity, and that therefore Christ possessed but one will. These points may be variously understood, but it is not necessary to enter into distinctions here.

Leontius of Byzantium (485–543) had on several occasions employed the soteriological argument against the Aphthardocetists, and St. Sophronius of Jerusalem (about 560–638) had recourse to it against the Monotheletes; it had been used by the Lateran Council under Pope St. Martin in 649, and later on by Pope St. Agatho in his famous dogmatic epistle. But these cases had been of rare occurrence and the argument was not made prominent; it was indeed retained, but was kept in the background. For the most part the refutation of heresy consisted in maintaining that since according to the definition of Chalcedon, Christ had two natures, He must likewise have two modes of operation and two distinct wills.

While retaining this last consideration, St. John Damascene insists much more upon the soteriological argument than others had done. We quote the following, not from his great work, the *Fount of Knowledge,* but from a short treatise composed in answer to the Monotheletes. We choose this passage because it is the most complete. Moreover it bears a strong, and at times even literal resemblance to the *Fount of Knowledge.*

> He assumed all that was sick in order to heal it wholly. For what is not assumed is not saved, but whatever is assumed, even though it may have fallen, that is saved.
> But what had fallen, and what was diseased first, if not the mind and its rational appetite which is the will? Therefore this had to be cured, since sin is precisely a malady of the will. Therefore if He had not taken a rational and spiritual soul together with its free will, He would not have healed the sickness of human nature.
> It was for this that He assumed a human will; but He did not assume sin, for sin is not His work. Therefore, in order to drive far from our souls the malady of sin which had been sown in them by the enemy, He assumed a soul and the free will proper to it. But sin He did not [assume]. Similarly, in

order to deliver the body from corruption and from the bondage of sin, He assumed a body.

He assumed even the penalty that was our due because of the first sin, in order to pay our debt for us and to deliver us from condemnation.[30]

The passage is an adaptation of the soteriological argument to the controversy with the Monotheletes. We find here also a thought, timidly expressed, that we shall see again in the works of the Scholastics; namely, that Christ has assumed the consequences of sin in order to transform them in Himself into a remedy for sin.

According to St. John Damascene Christ takes possession of us, consumes our misery in Himself, and imparts His dignity to us, principally by means of two sacraments, baptism and the Eucharist. Of the first he tells us, though as yet without any great emphasis, that at the Saviour's baptism the old Adam was buried in the water, and that at our baptism we die with Christ in order to rise with Him to a new life. And, pursues the Saint, baptism is as necessary for every man as was the death of Christ.

Our union with Christ reaches its consummation in the Eucharist. This sacrament makes us His body, and since all share the same incorporation, it puts us in communion with one another and unites us all together. This, he declares, is the reason why we must have absolutely nothing to do with the sacraments of the heretics; any other course of action would expose us to condemnation with them.

> For if this sacrament gives us union with Christ and with one another, then we are united in every way to those who receive it with us.[31]

Strong as the expression is, it receives from St. John Damascene neither comment nor explanation, and adds nothing to what had been said by those Fathers whom we have already studied. The same remark may be made of the Saint's writings; he gathers and organizes the teaching of previous generations into a general exposition. By so doing, he does throw some light upon the doctrine, but he contributes little new explanation.

We shall conclude our study of the Greek Fathers with the

summary that he has given us of their theology. Much indeed might be found in the works of authors who wrote after his time, or in the writings of others who lived during the periods that we have considered. Our studies have no claim to be exhaustive. However, we have the impression, unfounded perhaps, that they include the most important developments of the doctrine.

PART THREE

✄

The Doctrine of the Mystical Body in Western Tradition

Introduction

NOT UNTIL the age of Augustine does the Latin Church present a doctrine of the Mystical Body that is comparable, for development and originality, with that of the East.

By this we do not mean, of course, that no one had written anything of importance on the subject before Augustine. On the contrary, as we have already seen, not a few Latin writers had spoken of our incorporation in Christ in no uncertain terms, while some of their number were the first to indicate certain secondary aspects and consequences of the doctrine. The texts of St. Hilary, for instance, and of Popes St. Damasus and St. Martin, which we have cited, and those of St. Cyprian which we shall see in the following chapter, prove that however much the Latins may have been dependent upon oriental theology, they were never satisfied with a mere repetition of what others had said before them.

Yet for all their individuality the Western authors previous to Augustine betray so great a resemblance to and so real a dependence upon the Greeks that it is possible to study their teaching in conjunction with that of the Eastern writers. Thus, in Part Two of our studies, we saw that the first Christian authors of the West, St. Clement of Rome and Hermas of Rome, could be grouped with the Apostolic Fathers of the East; as yet they required no separate treatment.

From this time forward, however, on the subject of the Mystical Body as well as on other points of sacred theology, the Western teaching begins to take on a more specifically Latin character, which is a special and profound interest in moral problems and in rules of conduct. As we shall see in the course of the present study, this interest was to remain a distinctive feature of the occidental doctrine of the Mystical Body.

[367]

Naturally, this statement is intended only as a preliminary general indication, subject to correction and completion in the light of the whole of our studies. We have to evaluate a vast development of thought, a development to which contributions have been made not only by many different human minds, but also and chiefly by the Divine Truth itself. To sum up such a development with the bald assertion that the doctrine of the West is practical, while that of the East is speculative, would be extremely simple, but it would also be both inaccurate and naïve. The Greek Fathers, too, insist upon the moral consequences of our incorporation in Christ, and upon the fervor, charity, and purity that befit our dignity as deified men, while on the other hand, the Latin Fathers also devote themselves to purely speculative considerations on this truth.

We mean simply that there are certain preferences and tendencies which are more natural to some minds than to others, and that God deigns to admit such human factors as these in His work. As we shall see, the Latin theology of the Mystical Body was built up principally in connection with a question of a practical nature: the question of grace. Undoubtedly the subject possesses a vast doctrinal and speculative significance, but the problem that it presents is primarily one of life and of action: What are we, in the supernatural order, and how are we to act in that order? This initial question puts the entire doctrine in a different light, and tends to transform it into a code of Christian life, into a doctrine of the spiritual life.

Another general statement which may be added, subject to similar reservations and likewise to be taken as a preliminary and tentative grouping of ideas, is that the two schools follow along precisely the same lines in proposing the doctrine, but approach it from opposite directions. The Fathers of the East begin with the first principle: God and the Trinity. First they show us the Father, who communicates eternal life to the Son; then the Son becomes incarnate and communicates eternal life to His humanity; finally this humanity, now endowed with the power to give life, communicates that life to the entire human race. Thus the Eastern doctrine is synthetic, peculiarly suited to a speculative development.

On the other hand, the Fathers of the West are more inclined to adopt the analytic method. What interests them is a problem that has arisen close to them, nay within their very souls: the problem of Christian life and action, the problem of grace and free will. For its solution they go to the source of grace and of Christian life; they go to Christ, who, by incorporating men in Himself, unites them with God and endows them with supernatural activity.

Yet despite the difference of method, the two streams of development present a real continuity. In the first place, there is continuity in the order of time: the one begins as the other ends. Cyril of Alexandria, whom we studied last among the Greek Fathers and whose works are a summary and synthesis of the teaching of the Greek Church, was a contemporary of Augustine, who in turn was destined to become the master of the ecclesiastical writers of the Latin world. Cyril was patriarch of Alexandria from 412 until 440, and Augustine was bishop of Hippo from 396 until 430.

That there is a historical continuity corresponding to this chronological continuity, we are not in a position to say. For while the East unquestionably exercised great influence upon Western theology, it is impossible to distinguish all the factors that may have affected the development of the doctrine of the Mystical Body. This lack of information is regrettable, perhaps, but it is no great misfortune. After all, our ignorance of the relations that may have existed between various authors, and the fact that we cannot determine whether or not St. Augustine was acquainted with the theology of St. Cyril, become matters of minor importance when we remember that there is one invisible Master, uniting them all and binding them all together: this one Master is God, who teaches in His Church.

Besides the question of chronological and historical continuity, there is yet a third: logical continuity. For, in point of fact, the ideas expressed by Western tradition are an exact continuation of the teaching of the East.

In general, the Greek Fathers tell how the divine life comes from God, in Christ, to men; but they do not say how that life vivifies men. This is precisely the point which is brought out by the Western theologians. The doctrine develops as one whole, although when viewed separately, the individual contributions may appear somewhat fragmentary and disconnected.

We hope that this general conspectus will be of some assistance to the reader in understanding the studies which follow. These in turn will help to correct the necessarily simplistic and *a priori* nature of these opening remarks.

We shall begin our study with a brief glance at African theology. For it was the Church of Africa that gave Augustine his training in the faith, and it was there, too, that he taught. But even before Augustine, the Church of Africa had already given to the world two great theologians, two stars of quite unequal glory: Tertullian and Cyprian. These we must consider first.

Chapter I

Tertullian and St. Cyprian

>-<

I. *Tertullian*. Doctrinal deficiencies of his ecclesiology and of his doctrine of the Mystical Body; a few striking passages.

II. *St. Cyprian*. Like St. Ignatius of Antioch, Cyprian is an ardent champion of ecclesiastical unity.

1. *Invisible unity*. His own personal experience at the time of his conversion. This unity is catholic; it is necessary; the "sacrament of unity." It is the unity of Christ, divine unity: "Christ bears us all in Himself." Therefore our prayers should voice His interests, which are catholic interests. The Eucharist is the sacrament that makes us all live in the Saviour.

2. This unity is *visibly* represented in the bishop, union with whom is a necessary means for attaining union with God. A summary of the Saint's sound doctrine.

III. *The weak point*. Cyprian fails to bring out the catholic aspect of ecclesiastical unity: there is no "bishop of bishops," but a mere unanimity among shepherds. The same criticism may be applied to his doctrine of the Mystical Body, whose supreme unity is at times made to appear as a purely moral bond.

I

OF TERTULLIAN there is little that we can say. Born at Carthage about 160, and becoming a Christian about 195, he fell away from the Church in 213 and died a few years later. The exact year of his death is not known, but St. Jerome states that he lived to a very advanced age.

The most remarkable feature of his doctrine of the Mystical Body is a lacuna, an omission, which, discernible even in his Catholic writings, grows more pronounced in his later works, and eventually becomes his heresy. He was inclined either not to see, or at least to give but scant attention to the external, visible, and concrete character, in virtue of which the Church,

as the Mystical Body of the Saviour, is the prolongation of
the visible and historical Christ.

Another strange tendency led him to conceive the inner, invisible spirit of the Church as something akin to the spiritual
tension that characterizes certain conventicles of *illuminati;*
he regarded it as an unhealthy condition rather than as the
immense vitality whereby the regenerated universe is transformed into one single organism in Christ.

These are deficiencies, of course. But need we add that they
do not represent the whole of his theology? In striking contrast, and as witness to a soul profoundly, enthusiastically
Christian, Tertullian has left us some beautiful passages on
the life of the Church which are at the same time concerned
with the Mystical Body. Although these texts do not constitute a unified theory, at least they do contain, and at times
vigorously express, certain elements of such a theory.

The Church, he assures us, is essentially one; she is the
mother of us all; and she is the body, the "spiritual body,"
of Christ. In her every soul is gathered up — one feels tempted
to say "recapitulated" — just as in Adam every soul was
caught up by sin. The Christian possesses Christ within him,
and in Christ he is united with God.

One passage in particular, composed prior to the beginnings
of his apostasy, expresses the idea of Christ's presence in the
faithful in such beautiful language that it deserves to be
quoted here. The words are drawn from an exhortation to
public penance. This is an unpleasant exercise, the author
admits, but there is nothing to fear. For, he explains,

> we perform it in the presence of our brethren and fellow-ser-
> vants of God, all of whom have the same hopes and fears, the
> same joys, sorrows, and sufferings as thyself, since all have
> received the same spirit from the same Lord and Father. Why
> dost thou look upon them as different from thyself? Why
> fearest thou them that have experienced the same failings, as
> if they should laugh at thine? The body cannot take pleasure
> in the pain of one of its members; the whole body must needs
> suffer with it, and seek a remedy. When two Christians are
> united, there is the Church; and the Church is Christ. There-
> fore when thou dost cast thyself at the knees of thy brethren,
> it is Christ whom thou dost embrace; it is Christ to whom thou

[372]

dost pray. In like manner, when they lament over thee, it is Christ that mourns, Christ who prays to the Father for thee. Any favor which the Son asks is readily granted.[1]

The brisk style is typical of Tertullian, but the spiritual note, which is not usual with the apologist, may perhaps be an echo of the familiar Christian preaching of the time, rather than the fruit of the writer's own reflections. In that case, the passage is all the more precious as a witness of Christian thought.

However, we mention these few texts of Tertullian not for their intrinsic importance so much, but because they lead up to the more sublime passages of St. Cyprian and St. Augustine concerning the Church and the Mystical Body.

II. § 1

Cyprian, like Tertullian, was the son of pagan parents; he was past forty at the time of his conversion, which took place about the year 245. In 248 or 249 he became bishop of Carthage, and died a martyr's death during the persecution of Decius, in 258.

Cyprian might be compared with the greatest of the Fathers, but in our opinion he most resembles St. Ignatius of Antioch. Both were bishops, both primates — if we may employ the title — both martyrs; both have the same keen appreciation of and the same insight into spiritual things, and both manifest the same zeal for unity.

To be sure, each expresses these thoughts in his own way: the Syrian bishop speaks in breathless, staccato phrases; Cyprian writes with the calm brevity of the executive. The latter's concern is with practical admonitions that apply to the complexity of real life; thus from the very outset the Latin mentality brings its own peculiar genius into the field of theology, for God rejects no human factor in the building up of the body of Christ.

But though the tone is different, the doctrine remains the same. For both, union with the Church is union with Christ, and like the unity of Christ of which it is the mystical prolongation, the unity of the Church presents two aspects, one visible, the other invisible, which are absolutely inseparable.

First of all, according to St. Cyprian, the invisible unity of the Church is the unity of a single life. It extends throughout the whole Church, yet everywhere remains one and indivisible, because it is always one in its source, which is Christ.

It would appear that our Saint had been favored with a certain vision, partial no doubt, of this interior reality at the time of his conversion. He had hesitated for a long time before taking the decisive step, through fear of the obligations that he would have to assume. But at the moment of his baptism God gave him to see something of the new force and life that is given to Christians.

> When the waters of regeneration had washed away the stains of my past life, a light shone, serene and pure, within my purified breast; I breathed within me the spirit that comes from heaven, and my second birth made of me a new man. In some marvelous way my doubts vanished on the instant: what had been incomprehensible became evident, what had been obscure was made clear. I now had the power to do what before had seemed difficult. By these signs I came to see that the faults to which my carnal birth had enslaved me proceeded from what was earthly in me, and that the life which the Holy Spirit now communicated to me was from God.[2]

It is a new life, an ardent life, a rich, abundant life, as Cyprian tells us a little further on:

> The Spirit pours Itself out generously: no levee can block Its path, no restraining wall can hinder Its expansion. It wells forth unceasingly; It overflows, inundates all. Let us but thirst, and open wide our hearts: they will be flooded with graces in proportion to the capacity we make in them.[3]

From the present text alone, this effusion of life might appear to affect only the individual soul. But a flow so abundant cannot be confined to individuals; it must extend to the whole. And even in the individual soul it still belongs to the whole. It can continue to live only on condition that it be united with the vast catholic life stream.

Becoming bishop four years after his baptism, Cyprian soon found occasion to formulate this appeal for unity. It is the theme of his entire treatise *De catholica ecclesiae unitate,* which was read in 251 at the Council of Carthage.

The Church is one, yet such is her fertility that she becomes a multitude, as the rays of the sun are many, yet the light is one; and as the branches of a tree are many, yet their strength, founded in a firm root, is one; or as streamlets that flow from a single source may divide and spread with the volume of water that they receive, yet lose not their unity of origin. Take away one of the sun's rays: the light is too truly one to suffer any division; break a branch from the tree, and it can no longer produce fruit; cut off the stream from its source, and it ceases to flow.

In like manner the Church, flooded with the Lord's light, sheds her rays over the whole earth. Yet, though diffused everywhere, the light remains one, nor does the body lose aught of its unity. She extends her wondrously fruitful branches over the entire world, and her generous streams flow far and wide. But there is only one head and one source, one mother, rich and fruitful in her children. We are born of her, we are nourished with her milk, we are animated with her spirit.[4]

The picture is the same as that of Cyprian's earlier vision, but richer now and broader in its scope. The flow of life that animates each soul has become vast as the universe. But it still remains one, and though it reaches to the ends of the earth, its force is in no wise diminished. According to the Saint, the unity existing at the source is maintained in the entire flow, so that, to leave the image and to return to the reality that it represents, the whole Catholic world is everywhere one with the unity of Christ.

This inner unity is as necessary as it is boundless, and for the same reason: it is the unity of Christ. In order to live and to be united with God, one must be in the Church. On this point the Saint speaks most firmly:

He cannot have God as his Father who has not the Church as his mother. If it was possible for anyone to escape the Deluge outside the Ark, then perhaps may one escape death outside the Church. . . .

The Lord says: "I and the Father are one" (John 10:30), and of the Father and the Son and the Holy Ghost it is written: "These Three are one" (1 John 5:7). Is it conceivable that this unity, established by God's own power and sealed by the heavenly mysteries, can be broken or destroyed by the conflict of wills within the Church? He who keeps not this unity does not keep God's law; he keeps not the faith of the

Father and of the Son; he possesses neither life nor salvation. This "sacrament" of unity, this indissoluble bond of concord, was prefigured by the tunic of our Lord Jesus Christ, which, according to the Scriptures, was not divided or rent in any way.[5]

The term "sacrament of unity," which figures in the last paragraph, occurs rather frequently in the writings of St. Cyprian. It is instructive, too, indicating as it does that this necessary and world-embracing unity is also something secret and invisible: a mystery of life, a mysterious life.

In the time of St. Cyprian, as we know, the word *sacrament* did not have the technical sense which it possesses now. For him it signified a military oath, an obligation or necessity, something sacred and secret, an abstruse and sublime doctrine. Hence the phrase "sacrament of unity" connotes the necessity and obligation of being in unity. Yet this primary meaning does not exclude the others: this necessity possesses a religious character, and it is based upon sacred and mysterious reasons. It is the unity prefigured in the Old Testament by the Ark and symbolized in the New by the Saviour's tunic. Lastly, this unity is something essential and necessary, proceeding from the very unity of God.

For, according to St. Cyprian, this unity is something very special, something living, a vital thing. Unity in the Church is the unity of Christ, the unity of the Lord, absolute unity; it is unity itself; or, as St. Cyprian says, after St. Ignatius and before St. Augustine, it is just "unity." It is the divine unity, the unity of God, the unity of the Father and the Son and the Holy Ghost. Through Christ there exists a continuity of unity, so to speak, between the Triune God and ourselves.

> God is one, and Christ is one, and the Church is one, and the faith is one; and the Christian people are one, held firmly together by the bond of concord in the solidarity of a single body.[6]

If we exclude the rather colorless word *concord*, the passage is extremely powerful. Nor is it an isolated expression. Like St. Ignatius of Antioch, Cyprian takes delight in showing how the successive stages of this unity correspond to the steps traced by the divine Life itself as it came down to effect our divinization.

This divine life and unity come to us through our mystical inclusion in the Saviour. Often does St. Cyprian repeat: "Christ bore us all in Himself." The expression is very striking, and it was destined to become dear to Tradition. We have already met it in the Greek Fathers: St. Athanasius, St. Hilary, and St. Cyril of Alexandria. But these writers lived long after our Saint. It is possible, of course, that the phrase had been employed by others in the East even before their time, particularly since it simply brings out one aspect of the ancient Scriptural doctrine of the two Adams.[7] On this point we have no evidence; and as far as we can judge, it was in the West, and in the writings of Cyprian, that the expression appeared for the first time.

When the Saint makes use of the phrase, he does not deem any commentary necessary; he rather treats it as something clear and familiar enough to help explain the rest. Thus, in his explanation of the Lord's Prayer, he uses it to illustrate his teaching on the Christian duty of praying for all the brethren. Christ, he tells us, bears us all in Himself; by that very fact He obliges us to entertain catholic interests:

> Above all, the Doctor of peace and the Master of unity did not wish us to pray apart and each one for himself alone.
> When a man prays he should not pray for himself only. For we do not say, "My Father, who art in heaven," "Give me this day my daily bread." . . .
> Ours is a common and public prayer, and when we pray, it is not for an individual but for the whole people, for we are one with the whole people. The God of peace and the Master of concord, who taught us unity, willed that as He bore us all in one, so each of us should pray for all.[8]

When we pray in this manner, the prayer that rises from our lips is the prayer of the Saviour Himself.

> We pray as God, our Master, has taught us, and we draw near to Him in the prayer of Christ. May the Father recognize His Son's words in our supplications, and may He that abides in our hearts be also upon our lips.[9]

Thus, as He bears us in Himself, so do we bear Him within us. St. Paul had already spoken of this mutual interiority. The expressions "We in Christ," and "Christ in us," he had employed indiscriminately in referring to the mystery of the supernatural life.

Nowhere does this compenetration appear so strikingly as in the Sacrament of Life. The Christ of the Eucharist who comes to us as food, bears us all in Himself in order to give us life. The very species beneath which He conceals Himself are themselves a figure and a symbol of this unity:

> The very sacraments of the Lord illustrate how firmly and how indissolubly Christian unanimity is sealed by charity. For when the Lord tells us that this bread, formed by the union of many grains, is His Body, He signifies that the whole Christian people which He bears in Himself, is one. And when He says that the wine, pressed from many grapes to form a single liquid, is His Blood, He again signifies that our flock is one through the union of many together.[10]

Of the terms *unanimity* and *charity* that appear in the opening sentence, we shall have occasion to speak again later in the present chapter. But let us note the realism of the remainder of the passage: the Lord unites us all in Himself as the grains of wheat are united in the bread. The same thought appears in a passage of Cyprian's famous letter to Caecilius, in which the symbolism of the Eucharist is developed at greater length:

> Since Christ bore all of us in Himself, as He also bore our sins, we see that the water represents the people and the wine represents the Blood of Christ. When the water is mingled with the wine in the chalice, the people are united to Christ, and the multitude of the faithful is attached and joined to Him in whom they believe. So perfectly are the water and wine united in the cup of the Lord that they cannot be separated. In like manner the Church, that is, the multitude of the faithful united in the Church and persevering in the faith, can never be separated from Christ. She will ever adhere to Him with an undivided love. For this reason it is not lawful to offer either water alone or wine alone in the cup of the sacrifice. For if wine only is offered, Christ's Blood would be present without us; if only water, then the people are without Christ. . . . And, as the cup of the Lord is neither water alone nor wine alone, but a mixture of the two, so too neither flour alone nor water alone can become the Body of Christ. The two must be mixed together, they must adhere together in one firm loaf. Thus we see that the sacrament itself symbolizes the unity of the Chris-

tian people. As many grains are gathered and ground and kneaded together to form one bread, let us realize that we too are one body in Christ, the heavenly Bread, to whom we are joined and united.[11]

This Eucharistic doctrine does not match the teaching of St. Hilary or of St. Cyril for theological depth. Whether he is speaking of the dogma of the Eucharist or of the Blessed Sacrament itself, Cyprian is concerned chiefly with what is external and capable of representation. For that reason his teaching remains incomplete. Later on, after it has been taken up by St. Augustine and the Scholastics and incorporated into a broader synthesis, the doctrine of Cyprian helps to portray the Eucharist as the Sacrament of unity. Then these passages become the classic explanation of how the very appearances of bread and wine are symbolic of the change which Christ effects within us, and indicate the reason why He is present.

Before dismissing this particular point, let us note two other figures used by the Saint to illustrate this same life-giving inclusion in Christ: we are in Him, that is, in the unity of the Church, as the tree is in the root whence it derives all its sap, or again, as the unborn child is in its mother's womb, the only place in which it can live.

Such is the sacrament of unity, the mystery of that necessary and all-embracing life which constitutes the invisible element in the unity of the Church.

§ 2

However, this same unity possesses another element, visible and external, which consists in union with the same head and in obedience to the bishop. Cyprian is one of the most outspoken defenders of the rights of the bishop in the Christian community. Yet we need only hear him speak in order to perceive that episcopal authority is totally different from any merely human domination, and that it is but another aspect of our union with Life.

The lesson, alas, was sadly needed. At this time — the middle of the third century — the Church of Africa, already sorely tried by the Decian persecution, was being divided by schism. Certain misguided priests, together with a number of "confessors of the faith" whose heads had been turned by all the honor paid them on account of their past sufferings, had refused obedience to the bishop. One of these hotheads, Florentius, had the effrontery to write to Cyprian, denouncing his claims to authority. That bishop's vigorous rebuke expresses a doctrine of the Church's visible unity. We quote the principal sentences:

> Even though a whole multitude of stubborn and proud men abandon her, the Church does not abandon Christ. The Church is the faithful united with the priest, the flock gathered close to its shepherd. Therefore you must understand that there is a bishop in the Church and that the Church is in the bishop. Whoever is not with the bishop is not in the Church. Vain is the security of those that are not at peace with the priests of God, but think that they can remain in the Church by means of secret and private assemblies. The Church is one and catholic, and she cannot be torn asunder or divided; she remains one, united by that bond whereby her priests are joined together.[12]

Then, to lend added emphasis to his doctrine, the Saint concludes with this solemn attestation:

> You have my letter, and I have yours. On Judgment Day, both will be read before the tribunal of Christ.

Cyprian clearly regards the episcopate as the firm bond of the Church. The unity of the shepherd constitutes the unity of the fold, since the former is but a reflection and communication of the higher, invisible unity of God and of Christ.

> God is one, Christ is one, and the Church is one. There is but one episcopal authority (*cathedra*), which the Lord built upon the rock. No other altar may be set up, and no new priesthood may be established, except the one altar and the one priesthood.[13]

Here again the unity of the bishop is represented as the bond linking the unity of the Church with the divine unity. Apart from the bishop there can be no security, as Ignatius had already said before him. Cyprian writes to Jubaianus:

> It is we who by God's permission give drink to His thirsting people; it is we who determine the flow of living water.[14]

[380]

Here ends the more reliable part of our Saint's teaching concerning the Church and the Mystical Body. To sum up, we may say that he views the Church as a body, animated by a life that is one, mysterious, and divine; a body to which we must be united in visible communion, if we wish to be united with Christ and with God.

III

Thus, in concert with the rest of Tradition, Cyprian declares that the unity of the Church and of the Mystical Body is attained through the bishops. However, the inevitable question arises: "What bond is it that unites the bishops together?"

The same question occurred to Cyprian, for he saw very clearly that the bishops have to be united. The episcopate, he tells us, is a function that is one and essentially catholic. Though it is exercised by the individual bishop over a limited territory, it is nevertheless universal by its very nature. The true supernatural reality is the whole Church, and each bishop will be held partially accountable for the whole Church. Even while, under normal conditions at least, he is to attend simply to his own diocese, his interests should be boundless; he must share a common care and a common responsibility with all other shepherds of souls.

> We are many shepherds, but we all feed one flock. We must gather up and care for all the sheep that Christ has redeemed by His Blood and Passion. We must not permit our afflicted and suppliant brethren to be cruelly neglected or trodden down by proud and presumptuous men.[15]

Yes, the Saint realized clearly that episcopal authority is one before it is divided among the shepherds, and that even when divided, it still remains radically one; were a bishop to withdraw from the others, he would by that very act lose his authority and his power to unite the Church in his person.

Yet for all his insistence upon the internal unity of the episcopate, Cyprian does not see its external unity quite so well. In case of a division among the bishops themselves, how can one know which is the side of unity? To this burning question he supplies no definite answer. He speaks of concord, of prudent unanimity, of peace; but although he admits the need for visible unity within the Church, he fails to recognize the corresponding need for visible unity among the bishops.

True, the bishop of Rome is the first of the shepherds, just as Peter was the first of the Apostles. But he is not "bishop of the bishops." He enjoys the privilege of occupying a more honorable See and of governing the most illustrious and most apostolic of the churches. Moreover, whoever is united with the bishop of Rome need never doubt that he is in communion with the whole Catholic Church. For, the Saint notes, things always manifest their essential character most clearly where they have attained their fullest realization. Thus in Peter, who was the first of the Apostles, and in the Church of Peter, which is the mother of so many churches, one sees more clearly than elsewhere the necessity for all to be united with the bishop, with all the bishops, and particularly with the bishop of Rome, in order to be united with Christ.

The many and sometimes strikingly vigorous expressions which Cyprian uses to exalt the power of Peter and the See of Rome do not necessarily mean any more than this, if they are taken in their context. The most significant of such passages merely point — but how emphatically! — to the further step which the inner logic of Cyprian's teaching demanded.

Circumstances were in part accountable for this silence and incompleteness. Especially during the closing years of his life, Cyprian was preoccupied with the dispute concerning the validity of heretical baptism. Since the Pope was defending the orthodox view against him, it is not to be wondered at that he should not be inclined just then to emphasize the rights of the bishop of Rome. Again, the domestic troubles of his own diocese naturally focused his attention upon the unity that should prevail in each Church rather than upon the union of the churches among themselves. At all events, the fact remains that he speaks less positively and less accurately of this supreme and ultimate unity.

It is interesting to note a corresponding inconsistency in his doctrine of the Mystical Body. We have called attention to two instances of this, and others might be indicated. Our

Saint begins with bold strokes to portray our incorporation in Christ; then he hesitates abruptly, using the blunt end of the stylus, so to speak, to finish what he had begun with the point. He speaks of the divine unity that makes us all one in the Saviour, and we feel that he is about to stress the reality of this union and of the new life that is given us in the body of Christ; but the vigorous realism of the thought diminishes as he proceeds, until at the end Cyprian seems to be thinking of nothing more than an intense mutual love, a common submission to the same pastors, a moral unanimity.

Unanimitas, harmony, agreement of wills. The word is frequently used by Cyprian to describe the unity of the Mystical Body. One may find the term weak, and weak it is. But he could find none better to characterize the supreme unity of the Church, the final bond that unites all the bishops and all the churches into one.

It may be disconcerting to find such deficiencies in the doctrine of so great a saint, theologian, and bishop as Cyprian. But the God who guides Tradition did not see fit that men should find adequate formulas for the entire deposit of revelation all at once. Where He deigns to admit our human co-operation, time and effort and patient search must be expected.

Chapter II

St. Augustine — 1. Augustine and the Donatist Schism

><

I. *Introduction*. The importance of Augustine's teaching in general, and of his doctrine of the Mystical Body in particular; the latter owed its early beginnings partially to external influences, but chiefly to an interior experience. The *Confessions*. A yearning love for Truth; an interior revelation of God, of the Mystical Christ, of the Church.

II. *St. Augustine and Donatism*. Division of the Saint's writings into three periods: (*a*) The controversy against the Donatists; (*b*) The controversy against Pelagius; (*c*) Positive preaching to the faithful.

III. *Donatism*. The origin of the sect; its fanaticism. In combating the heresy Augustine continues and completes the ecclesiology of St. Cyprian. He teaches a doctrine of unity, a vast unity that embraces all men, even sinners, and all virtue, even that which appears to flourish outside the Church. This unity is vast because it proceeds from Christ and possesses His life and His holiness. Consequently it is wholly independent of the meanness and baseness of men. This view of the Mystical Body compared with that proposed in the dispute against Pelagius.

I

AFTER Tertullian and Cyprian it is Augustine who continues the forward progress of Tradition. He was born at Tagaste in 354, and received baptism in 387; he became bishop of Hippo in 396, and died there on August 28, 430, while the city was being besieged by the Vandals.

Augustine is perhaps the greatest of the Church's Doctors, and he is one of the most outspoken on the subject of our incorporation in Christ. He was a genius of rare versatility and

[384]

brilliance: a true African and a true Roman, yet the first of the moderns; a great character, as fitted to lead men as he was ready to spend himself for them; best of all, a soul whose only love was Truth, a soul that reveals itself perfectly and entirely in his writings, yet without a trace of ostentation. In short, Augustine stands out as one of mankind's greatest glories.

Like his personality and like his theology in general, his doctrine of the Mystical Body is rich and full of contrasting elements. Therefore it will demand a rather long study and many quotations.

In order not to overlook any feature of that doctrine, we must go back to its earliest beginnings. However, the reader need not be alarmed, for we are not undertaking to solve a problem of philology, but the problem of a soul. At present we shall simply try to study the soul of Augustine and God's operation therein, in order to find an explanation of certain distinctive traits of his doctrine of the Mystical Body.

Both in the doctrine itself and in Augustine's manner of proposing it, great prominence is given to interior realities, such as the life of Christ within the soul, and the union, likewise interior, of each soul with all other souls and with the Church. For this reason it is very useful to know the psychology of this man's soul if we are to understand clearly his concept of the things of the soul.

It seems that God had equipped the soul of Augustine expressly for the perception of such realities. The word "within" (*intus*) is constantly on his lips: we must seek within, we must turn our eyes within, everything is within. For him, thought consists not so much in the association of concepts as in a search for Truth within oneself: his whole soul, the very depths of his soul, reach out for that Truth; he divines it, he recognizes it, as much perhaps by the answering chord that it strikes in his inmost being as by those expressions of Truth which he is able to discover outside himself. In order, therefore, to understand the doctrine, we must understand the man. The *Confessions*, in which he relates his own life story, will ever remain the best introduction to his writings.

This, then, is the first source that we shall consult. What

do the *Confessions* tell us of the manner in which our Saint was led to understand the Scriptural teaching on the subject of Christ's mystical presence in the soul?

The earliest indication to be noted is the very style of the *Confessions*. Augustine describes his life in a long conversation with God, in a hymn of praise to Him whose inner melody fills his soul with silent joy. He lives with God, but without the suggestion of effort or strain. For this was he created. His heart, more than other hearts, was made to find no repose, no satisfaction until it should rest in God. Thus, even as a prodigal, while keeping far aloof from the one thing necessary, he experienced a painful void in his soul, the yearning of his entire being for Him without whom we cannot live. He tells us that this hunger for Truth caused him intense suffering and pain.

Let us note in passing how gently the hand of divine Providence guided the future Doctor of the Church. It was primarily as Truth, as Light, that God attracted him.

O Truth, Truth, how intensely did the marrow of my soul even then sigh after Thee![1]

This prayer rises from every fiber of his soul, and in this prayer are contained in embryo all the future workings of divine Truth within him. For, though he knew it not, the painful void was a preparation. As yet he did not recognize the divine Guest whose approach had wrung this cry from his soul. He was still seeking outside himself, in creatures, for the beauty that is ever old and ever new, and which all the while was present within.

At last God revealed Himself by means of a simple natural cause. Augustine had just quitted Africa, in 383, already disgusted with Manichaeism, when by some chance, or — as he was later assured by Simplicianus, the priest and saint who had baptized St. Ambrose — by a special Providence, he came upon certain Neo-Platonist books. Here he read the following bit of advice: to discover light and truth, one must look beyond the senses and sense images, and enter into himself. The young man obeyed.

Thus counseled to return to myself, I entered into my innermost soul, by Thy guidance. This I was able to do because Thou hadst become my helper. I entered, and with new eyes that were superior to those of my mind, I saw an unchangeable Light. It was not the ordinary light that is visible to the eyes of the body, nor was it simply a greater light of the same nature made to shine much more brilliantly and to fill all things with its immensity. No, it was not that, but something different, very different. It was not above my mind in the same manner that oil rises above water or as the heavens are above the earth. It was above me because it had made me, and I was beneath it because I was made by it. He knows this Light who knows Truth, and who knows it, knows Eternity. It is known to Love. O eternal Truth, and true Love, and lovable Eternity! Thou art my God. I sigh after Thee day and night. When first I came to know Thee, Thou didst raise me up, to show me how many things were still unknown to me and how incapable I was as yet of knowing them. Thou didst shine brightly within me, and didst show me the limitations of my own vision; and I trembled with love and fear. I saw that I was far from Thee, on an entirely different plane, and Thy voice came to me as if from above: "I am the food of the great; grow, and thou shalt eat Me. Thou wilt not change Me into thyself, like the food of thy flesh; thou wilt be transformed into Me."[2]

Augustine's own description is ample evidence that his experience had nothing in common with the semimetaphysical, semimystical intuitions which were in vogue among the Neo-Platonists of the period.

The reason is that he had entered into this experience not merely with the mind of a philosopher, but with a soul long since sealed by Christ with an impression so profound that nothing could efface it. He had not just now found God; he had rediscovered Him, and by the light that broke in upon his darkness he found himself in the presence, not of a pure Idea or of the *bonum in se,* but of the God of the Christians, who spoke to men in the Saviour.

God willed to establish a more intimate union still. It was in a garden at Milan that He came, to cast out the old man and to take up His abode in the soul of Augustine. The incident is so well known that we need simply remark, without dwelling upon details — Augustine himself does not enlarge upon these — that the words of St. Paul which finally opened his soul to the light refer to the Mystical Body:

[387]

Let us walk honorably, not in revelry and drunkenness, not in chambering and wantonness, not in strife and jealousy.

But put ye on the Lord Jesus Christ, and take no thought for the flesh, to fulfill the lusts thereof.[3]

"Put ye on the Lord Jesus Christ." In the immediate context these words have no very evident connection with the Mystical Christ. But if we compare them with similar passages and interpret them in terms of the Apostle's general teaching, the meaning is clear. There is question of a mystical incorporation in Christ; we are to adopt His way of thinking and acting, and to allow His spirit to pervade our souls.

Augustine does not indicate whether he perceived this signification of the passage, either at the time or later on. We mention the point solely for its objective interest. In any case, as soon as he read the words, the miracle of grace took place: he put on Jesus Christ. "A light of security filled my heart, dispelling all the darkness of doubt."[4]

Into this soul, whither He had, so to speak, forced an entrance, Christ continues to pour Himself. This divine action our Saint was to experience again a few days after his conversion. Forced by the pain in his chest and impelled, too, by a desire to spend a few days in recollection before making the final step, he resigned his chair of rhetoric, which he called his "business in speech," and retired with a few friends to Cassiciacum. The sacrifice cost him dearly, but he found something far better:

Christ Jesus, how sweet it suddenly became, to be without the sweetness that we find in trifles! I used to dread their loss, but now it was a joy to give them up. For Thou didst cast them from me, Thou the true and supreme Sweetness; Thou didst cast them out, and didst enter in their place, sweeter than any sweetness, but not for flesh and blood; brighter than any light, but more interior than any secret; more sublime than any honor, but not for the proud.[5]

Thus he began to live another life, a "living life,"[6] he calls it, for it was full of God. God and he, God in him; to Augustine naught else mattered.

The little we have said will suffice to give the reader a view, or rather a glimpse of the beginning of God's dealings with

Augustine. This preparation of the soul and these experiences are not, of course, new elements to be added to Tradition. The growth of revealed truth does not come from any external source, however holy that source may be. At most these experiences are but a means which God uses to help men to a clearer realization and to a more accurate expression of the ancient, invariable treasure of revelation. It is our understanding of that treasure which must grow.

Were it our purpose to touch upon every point, we should here consider certain other texts of the *Confessions* which indicate the function of the Church in bringing about the union of each individual soul with Christ. But these texts are neither very numerous nor very significant. Hence we shall not delay on them, especially since the later works of Augustine furnish data far more abundant on the same subject.

II

Augustine received the sacrament of baptism the night before Easter, April 24, 387. Returning to Africa in the autumn of the following year, he landed at Carthage, where he planned to lead a life of retirement in the company of some friends, devoting his time to prayer, meditation, and study.

A Christian philosopher's paradise! But it was destined to be short-lived. In 391 the faithful of Hippo insisted on having him as their priest. Reluctantly he acceded to their demands and was ordained, succeeding Valerius as bishop of that city in June or July, 395.

Grave troubles were in store for Augustine. The thirty-five years of his episcopate were to be disturbed by several heresies, particularly by Donatism and Pelagianism. The former had reached its greatest strength about the end of the fourth century; the other began later, but rapidly attained a like violence. Augustine was obliged to combat these foes in addition to his duties of protecting the faithful and of teaching them the principles and practice of Christian living.

Whatever his personal preferences may have been, our Saint did not shirk the task imposed upon him. He devoted himself wholeheartedly to his flock and to the defense of the truth.

[389]

His fame soon became known abroad, and with its diffusion came the additional burden of answering the letters that arrived from all points, asking for advice.

It was in the midst of this life of intense ecclesiastical activity that Augustine's doctrine of the Mystical Body developed and grew to maturity. It became the center of his preaching and teaching, and a favorite weapon against the heresies of Donatus and Pelagius.

Augustine and Donatism, Augustine and Pelagianism, and Augustine in his sermons to the people: such will be the outline of our study. It will enable us to bring out the full significance and richness of the Saint's teaching.

In expounding the doctrine of the Mystical Body against the Donatists, Augustine continues the work of St. Cyprian; in his anti-Pelagian writings he prepares the way for the teaching of the Schoolmen and of modern theologians on grace and the Mystical Body. But in his sermons to the people it is his soul that speaks; nowhere else is his teaching so faithful a reflection of his personality or so eloquent a testimony to the truth.

Augustine and the past, Augustine and the future, Augustine and himself. This division seems most natural and most convenient; it would be perfect, except for one defect, always regrettable where Augustine is concerned: the mere fact that it is a division.

III

He had entered the lists against the Donatists as early as 393. In 421 the battle was still in progress, though the efforts of the imperial police had greatly moderated its violence.

Here was no ordinary foe. Of all the outbursts of fanaticism that occurred in this turbulent land of Africa, Donatism was the worst. Its adherents were actually bent on excommunicating the whole world, charging that all the priests and bishops of Christendom had lost their powers. The trouble had begun in 311, according to the Donatists, when Bishop Felix of Aptonga consecrated Caecilianus as bishop of Carthage. This consecration was irregular, they alleged, because Felix was a *"traditor,"* i.e., he was said to have surrendered the books of the Scriptures to the pagans during the persecution of Diocletian. The Catholics denied the charge, and were even able to prove the contrary from official records, but all their efforts were in vain. Not only had the Church of Carthage been contaminated by this unworthy pastor and by those who had succeeded him, but all the churches in the world had disgraced themselves by remaining in communion with the culprits. The entire clergy was cut off from God and deprived of holiness, and hence could not validly administer the sacraments. Africa alone, and in all Africa the Donatists alone, constituted the pure and glorious Body of Christ!

This inflexible attitude appealed to fanatical minds, while violence, the bigot's favorite weapon, overcame the hesitancy of many others. Although the heresy was scarcely eighty years old in Augustine's time, it already boasted a complete hierarchy of bishops and had enlisted an army of cutthroat propagandists.

St. Cyprian's doctrine of ecclesiastical unity and of the Mystical Body had prepared the ground for the struggle against these adversaries. But on the essential point, which the present situation rendered more important than ever, his doctrine was vague and indefinite. It was very clear in speaking of the unity of the local church with its bishops, less precise on the unity that binds all the bishops together, and had nothing whatever to say of the criterion whereby one might determine which of two rival bishops or groups of bishops belonged to the true unity of Christ. Such a weapon was useless in the face of the Donatist schism. The logic of history as well as the logic of Cyprian's own teaching called for further correction and completion. This task, begun by Optatus of Mileve, was continued by Augustine, who enters at this point into the development of the African tradition.

It would be out of the question to review every detail of the controversy. We are interested only in those considerations that tell us something about the Mystical Body. These do not appear prominent at first sight, but on closer study they prove to be numerous and rich in doctrinal significance. Augustine's defense against Donatism is essentially a doctrine of the unity of the Church, but here too, as we observed in the case of St. Ignatius of Antioch, St. Irenaeus, and St. Cyprian, the doctrine of unity very soon becomes a doctrine of the Mystical Body. In one of his sermons, which happens to be interesting from many points of view, our Saint remarks:

> Before the [Donatist] schism, the unity of Christ was not explained so thoroughly as nowadays.[7]

Augustine very particularly sets out to conquer the schism by preaching unity. He never tires of recounting the glories of unity as they had already been indicated by the Fathers, or of calling attention to new ones. Again and again he repeats that this unity is as vast as the world, that it is one as Christ is one, broad enough and human enough to include a multitude of sinners, yet so divine and so pure that it can remain undefiled within them and can sanctify them in itself. And the reason he gives is always the same: it is the unity of Christ, the unity and the life of Christ communicated to men.

The qualities he stresses most are the extent, the catholicity of Unity. To understand this insistence we need but recall the narrow views of the schismatics. He loves to repeat that Scripture everywhere teaches this universalism. On almost every page it speaks of Christ and the Church, of the Head and Body, of these two who have but one history and who fill the whole earth. To those that have broken away from her, the Church can say:

> O brothers, scattered children, lost sheep, broken branches, why do you speak evil of me? Why do you not acknowledge me? "Search ye the Scriptures, because in them ye think to have everlasting life; and these are they that bear witness of me" (John 5:39). What our Head said to the Jews, His body tells you now: "Ye shall seek me, and shall not find me" (John 7:34). Why? Because you search not the Scriptures which give testimony of me.[8]

The Saint goes on to recall certain passages in which reference is made both to the glorified Christ and to the Church which is to bring Christ to all the world. Let us quote a few lines:

> There you have a testimony concerning the Head, which

also concerns the body. Here is another, referring to both the Head and body in one short sentence. Speaking of Christ's resurrection, the Psalm says: "Be Thou exalted, O God, above the heavens"; and immediately it proceeds to speak of the body: "And Thy glory above all the earth" (Ps. 56:6).[9]

Everywhere Augustine finds this view of the Church as the body of Christ, the prolongation of Christ throughout the entire world. And he observes that our Lord expressed Himself in the same fashion.

> Let us hear His own words, spoken both of Himself as the Head and of His body, which is the Church. Do not our heads speak in the name of our bodies? First He speaks of the Head. He has risen from the dead . . . and He tells His disciples: "Thus it is written: that the Christ should suffer, and should rise from the dead on the third day." This concerns the Head. Now He speaks of the body: "and that in His name should be preached repentance unto forgiveness of sins unto all the nations, beginning from Jerusalem" (Luke 24:46,47).[10]

The Church, that "holy mother" and "virgin mother" of whom Augustine delights to speak, is for him no mere legal fiction. The Church is Christ, inasmuch as He is present in all places and bears all humanity in Himself. Hence, in the Church that is His body, He does not contain only the just and the good. For, as Augustine often reminds us, on the Lord's threshing floor there is chaff as well as wheat, and the mixture will remain until the final winnowing, which is the Last Judgment. Meanwhile the good grain must bear with the encumbering straw and live in unity with it.

The extremists who insist on severing relations with all sinners can succeed only in bringing universal condemnation upon themselves. *Securus iudicat orbis terrarum*.[11] By rejecting the Church's catholicity, African exclusivism has pronounced its own death sentence.

Unity, on the contrary, the unity of the body of Christ, is vast as the earth. Is it not written that the field of the Lord is the world, and that the harvest will come, not in the days of Donatus, but at the end of the world? And Augustine ever chants the praises of this universal unity, the sole unity that is truly Christian, the sole unity that is secure. He calls it the unity of all nations, the unity of Christ, the unity of Christ's

[393]

body; it is a true and perfect unity, a sweet and steadfast unity; a unity of charity. It is visible communion with all Christendom. In fine, he calls it simply "Unity," to indicate how highly he values this one characteristic note of the Church. For it is the external sign of the one, necessary life which the Saviour communicates to His body. Outside Unity there can be only death, for he who is not in unity is not in Christ. Apart from Unity, charity is false, the martyr dies in vain, and miracles are a deception. It is better to be a finger united with the body than to be an eye that is cast off from the body.

Yet this rigor of principle does not degenerate into harsh exclusivism. On the contrary, Augustine's doctrine is all-inclusive precisely because it is so uncompromising. The unity that he preaches is no cold abstraction, but the embrace of a single love that seeks union; it is but one immense life, the life of the Mystical Christ that is offered to every soul. But alas, this generous offer is spurned by great numbers of men. Hence it is that in the divine predestination, that is, in truth, many seem to belong to Christ who in reality are not His, while on the other hand many do not appear to be His, and yet really do belong to Him. One finds upright and holy souls in the ranks of the schismatics, while among the faithful there are, alas, a multitude of sinners.

But here the Saint scores a triumph, when he points out that in the last analysis whatever is good is Catholic. A sect possesses no salutary power except that which it has stolen from Unity, and if good works are possible within its fold these must be attributed to the hidden bond that still unites its adherents with the parent stem. If one finds a bunch of grapes hanging from a thorny bush he is not deceived; he gathers the grapes, carefully avoiding the thorns, but he knows from what source the fruit has come.

So it is with Unity. She is the root of all that is good. And all this good is so truly her own that she can never be reconciled to its loss. In her name, and with unflagging charity, Augustine voices heart-rending appeals to the sectaries, and even her most bitter foes he insists upon addressing as brothers.

[394]

Come, brothers, please, and be engrafted on the vine;
We grieve to see you lying there, cut off from what is thine.[12]

These words he wrote at the time of his entrance into the dispute. Later on, at the critical moment during the synod of 411, Augustine carried the generosity of his appeal to the point of heroism. At his suggestion the Catholic bishops offered their collective resignation in the event that the imperial arbiter should decide in favor of the Donatists, and promised, in case a contrary decision were given, to share the honors and duties of their sees with any bishops who should be willing to return to unity. For, he explains:

We must make them realize what great love prompts the Catholic root to seek out the broken branch.[13]

"Come back, come back!" Everything within them is a reminder that they belong to the Church. The very form that the severed branch has kept, and the few leaves still visible upon it plainly indicate the sole root from which it can draw life.

Let them but return, and they shall find their true home in unity. For the ultimate reason Augustine gives why Unity is vast, all-embracing, and necessary is the fact that it is the very unity of the life of Christ; it is living, Christian unity.

This Augustine repeats over and over, not only in controversy with the Donatists, but also in his instruction to the faithful. Of his sermons we shall speak in the following chapter, but one can readily see how effective the argument would prove against the destroyers of Unity. It is Unity that sanctifies us and saves us; Unity alone can truly pray; Unity alone can be pleasing to God. For Unity is the body of Christ; it is Christ.[14]

This, too, is precisely the reason why schism is so wrong. It has divided Christ, though even the Jews dared not break a bone of Him; it has dismembered Christ, while even His executioners respected His tunic; it has reduced Him to the limits of a tiny sect, though Satan himself was not bold enough to hurl Him down from the pinnacle of the temple. The very accusations which they pronounce against the great Church prove that they have torn themselves away from the Saviour.

They speak only of the supposed crimes committed by the Catholic episcopate and of the innocence of their own bishops. Is not this ample evidence that their hope is founded upon men and that they no longer live solely by their attachment to the Lord? Again, when they attack the validity of the sacraments among Catholics, are they not thereby denying Christ Himself and His efficacious action in men's souls?

The Catholics, on the other hand, regard the Church simply as the mystical prolongation of Christ. For them there is but one Mediator, who is holy enough to communicate His holiness even by means of unworthy ministers, and near enough to all Christendom to be the immediate source of holiness in every soul. His sacraments, be they received from Peter or Paul or Judas, always possess the same virtue, since, no matter whose hand confers them, He that operates through them is ever Jesus Christ.

Ultimately, in the whole Church there is only Christ, Christ the Head and members. The hierarchy is nothing and the unity of the Church is nothing, apart from the Lord who continues to unite His own in Himself. Dignity of function and personal insignificance: these constitute the charter of the Catholic episcopate, a charter that guarantees the security of the faithful everywhere. Augustine is fond of repeating to his flock this consequence of our incorporation in Christ, for he had in him no trace of that spirit of intolerance which, masquerading under the cloak of piety, and denying the sublime dignity of the priestly office on account of the sins of men who hold that office, is the mother of discord and the fomenter of schism.

> My brothers, I have often told you this, but I wish to emphasize it again: It matters not what we are. You are safe, for you have God as your Father and His Church as your mother.[15]

The one principle, the one source, the one Head whence all Christian life derives, is Christ. This formula, which was often on the lips of our Saint, we may take as a résumé of the controversy against Donatism. It is because the Church is the body of Christ, it is because she is holy with the holiness of Christ, that she is able to extend the Christ-life over the whole earth and to contain all the good of this world without suffering contamination either from the sins of her members or from the unworthiness of her ministers. In short, we may observe by way of conclusion that the ecclesiology which constitutes St. Augustine's reply to Donatism is in part, like the teaching of St. Cyprian, a doctrine of the Mystical Body, but expressed now in a more systematic form.

Still, how does that flow of grace take place, by which the holiness of the Head is communicated to the members? And what is this immense, unique life that makes all Christendom a single organism, a single catholic man? Augustine was to develop these logical complements of the doctrine later, in the course of his controversy against Pelagius and in his sermons to the people. We shall now accompany him to these new fields of action.

Chapter III

St. Augustine — 2. Augustine and Pelagianism

>-<

I. *The Pelagian controversy.* Pelagianism is a kind of Christianity, minus the two dogmas of solidarity in evil (original sin) and of solidarity in good (grace). In refuting the heresy Augustine represents Christianity as a grouping of all mankind into two "masses," into two men, who are the two Adams. Our solidarity in evil is founded upon original sin and its consequences in all men, while our solidarity in good rests upon the Redemption and the Mystical Body, a new birth and an ever-growing life that is the continuation in us of the life of Christ. "The same grace that makes Christ the Son of God, makes Christians the children of God." The Incarnation is the prototype of grace, and explains the properties of grace.

II. *Augustine's teaching compared with that of St. Cyril of Alexandria.* Despite the difference of circumstances, there are certain similarities, since the unifying principle is the same in both doctrines. Cyril's, however, is the more complete, because it begins with the first principle, which is the Incarnation. In the Pelagian dispute Augustine's teaching suffers from an over-emphasis of the members and of their sad plight, while not enough attention is given to the Head. Hence doctrinal progress is still necessary.

I

IN 412, before the Donatist controversy had run its course, another began which was to prove no less bitter. This was the Pelagian controversy. Equally violent and even more cunning, the new foe clothed his errors in equivocal terms and kept constantly changing his formulas. He would abandon one false position, only to take up the defense of the next, and seized upon the slightest inaccuracy of expression on the Catholic side as an occasion for a virulent offensive. Such tactics may well have exhausted the strength of Augustine, but they could not wear out his patience. In 430, when the holy Doctor was at the height of his fame, death found him, pen in hand, composing a line-by-line refutation of a book, written by a young Pelagian named Julian of Eclanum, in which Augustine himself was made the butt of much personal abuse.

The Saint answers his new adversaries as he had the Donatists, with a doctrine which is in part, indeed largely, a doctrine of the Mystical Body. However, this fact is even less immediately evident here than it was in the dispute with the African separatists. Some reflection is necessary in order to appreciate the significant position which the Mystical Body occupies in Augustine's reply.

We shall endeavor to indicate that position in the pages that follow. For this reason our exposition of the controversy may appear partial and biased to some of our readers, but we feel that such an impression will not persist. We ask that two points be kept in mind: first, that we are investigating one particular aspect of Tradition; and secondly, as the next chapter will prove, that Augustine is very well acquainted with the doctrine of the Mystical Body. Hence it is not unlikely that he should adopt it as his favorite weapon against the Pelagians.

Quite naturally, there is now a change of emphasis; our Saint does not stress exactly the same points as he did in controversy with the Donatists. The object of the attack has shifted from the visible hierarchy and its powers to the invisible life of grace in the Church and in the faithful. Consequently the tactics of the defense must also change. No longer is Augustine called upon to vindicate the part taken by the hierarchy in our incorporation into Christ; instead he must explain what that incorporation is, the nature of the new powers that it confers upon us, and how God brings about these wondrous effects.

Pelagianism, it seems to us, may be described as an adaptation of Christian faith and asceticism to the individualism of the Stoics. It consists essentially in the thesis that it is within the power of every man, alone and unaided, to live up to all his obligations. Pelagius maintains that each man is the principal, and in a sense the only cause of his moral dignity. For has not every man liberty? And does not this liberty give him the power to act in conformity with the whole law, because he wills it and solely because he wills it? Otherwise, argues the heresiarch, one is forced to admit that the divine precepts are impossible of observance and that God has created a depraved human nature. The idea of an original sin which is transmitted by generation and which renders man incapable of doing good is, according to Pelagius, unthinkable. Such a doctrine is a denial of God's justice; nay, it even makes Him accountable for our sins. To say that concupiscence is something wrong, something reprehensible, when it is so intimately bound up with our flesh and is the very origin of our race, would mean that God's own work is a temptation and an evil. Granted that Adam may have done us some harm; but that harm can be no more than the evil influence of bad example. Whoever imitates Adam's fault has only himself to blame. Besides, the evil effects of that first bad example have been destroyed by the good example and the teaching of Christ. Christ has done yet more for us; He has merited the remission of our personal sins and an aid that enables us to observe the commandments with greater facility.

As time went on the system grew more and more subtle, but there is no need to consider all its successive phases. We have already seen the point that is essential to our purpose: Pelagianism is Christianity minus two mysteries, both of which are in great part mysteries of solidarity. Gone is the mystery of human helplessness and of the divine assistance that is ever necessary for us, members who can do nothing without the Head. Gone is the mystery of our fall, and of the sin that we all bear who have sinned in Adam. Gone, in a word, is the mystery of solidarity in sin and in death, and the corresponding mystery of solidarity in good and in life.

To this system of clear and distinct ideas Augustine opposes all the mystery of the economy of salvation; to this individualism in which every man is sufficient unto himself, he opposes Christianity as an immense tableau in which are made to figure prominently all the common bonds that do and must unite our individual personalities with Christ and with one another. Hence the whole doctrine of grace, of which he is the Doctor, becomes a doctrine of solidarity and of union. It is from this point of view that we shall study his teaching.

For Augustine the great struggle that is taking place in the world is a matter not of individuals, but of two groups, two "masses," each vast as the earth. Thus it is that against Pelagius as against the exclusivism of the African sectaries, his doctrine is a defense of universalism. In God's eyes the human race is not a horde of isolated individuals. It is a multitude, but that multitude forms two cities, two kingdoms, two bodies. Augustine's teaching on this point may be summed up in his famous phrase: "There are two loves, and they have built two cities."[1] On the one hand stand covetousness and concupiscence; on the other, charity and true love. The entire history of mankind is determined and divided into two streams by obedience to these two forces. The good and the bad, the wheat and the chaff may seem hopelessly jumbled to our eyes of flesh, but in reality they are as distinct and as far apart as if each belonged to an entirely different order.

Augustine goes even further: all humanity is not merely two cities, but two men:

> In the history of two men, of whom the one lost us in himself by doing his own will rather than that of his Maker, whilst the other saved us in Himself by doing not His own will, but that of Him who sent Him — in the history of these two men, I say, properly consists the whole of Christian faith.[2]

The words are simply a restatement of the traditional doctrine of the two Adams, but one can already observe how that doctrine receives a personal touch at the hands of Augustine.

Let us consider the first man as our Saint represents him to us. Adam, he tells us, is all humanity. All men are Adam, and Adam is all men. In Adam all are guilty of disobedience, and he is in them all, constituting them sinners. For in the last analysis it is from him that they have their life, a life therefore that is defiled in its origin, defiled anew by reason of the concupiscence through which it is transmitted, defiled in fine by the sins that they themselves have committed in yielding to that concupiscence. Hence from their very birth, nay by reason of their birth, men have been made unworthy of eternal happiness, in Adam, their first father.

[401]

So firm a hold has this sin taken on human nature that even the divine remedy of baptism does not deliver us from all its consequences. Concupiscence remains until death, making each man a temptation unto himself.

No man can observe the commandments unless he have a wholly gratuitous assistance from God, and so weakened are we that even with this help we cannot avoid all venial sins. Augustine likens all humanity to a huge invalid, stretched helpless over the entire face of the earth.

But God has taken pity on the invalid. He determined to remedy this solidarity in sin by means of another work opposed to the first. This, too, is to be a work of solidarity, but of solidarity in good. Therefore in His absolutely gratuitous bounty He has chosen from among this cursed and condemned mass of men, a certain number of "elect," in order to form another mass, the holy and immaculate mass of the predestined. But this new mass, as described by Augustine, is nothing else than the Mystical Body of the Saviour as viewed from within.

We enter into this mass, explains the Saint, through baptism, for it is by baptism that we are incorporated into the Saviour. The essential effect of baptism is precisely to confer upon men a new existence and to introduce them into a new order of things, so that they are freed by a second birth from the evils which they contracted in their first birth. And like the first, this new birth is the beginning of a life that is meant to develop and to increase. The new man must grow in us, but as long as he is here below that growth will be a constant struggle. He must ever be on the alert to turn the movements of concupiscence to his spiritual advantage; he must pray unceasingly for the divine assistance that is absolutely necessary for the performance of good acts; he must ever and always ask God's forgiveness for his faults, since, because of the weakness of his human nature, faults he will always have. All these acts are possible only through grace and through Christ. As Augustine loves to repeat, the branches can do nothing without the Vine, and whatever strength the members possess must come to them from the body.

When he speaks of these truths our Saint's favorite Scriptural texts are references to the Mystical Body. They are the words of Jesus recorded by St. John: "Apart from Me ye can do nothing,"[3] and the statement of St. Paul: "The charity of God is poured forth in our hearts through the Holy Spirit who hath been given us."[4] In the first text we are taught that the branches must needs be sterile apart from the tree; in the second, that our efforts will be vain unless they be transformed by a new energy. In short, both passages tell us of that mutual interiority wherein the life of the whole is communicated to the parts and the parts are assumed to the life of the whole; both tell us of the unique and necessary organism of grace which is the Mystical Body.

The Christ-life is characterized by the same incompleteness and dependence as are the members in relation to the whole organism. In order to appreciate its essential dependence, adherence, and beauty, we must study this life as it flows from the Head and thence into the body. In other words, the best way to understand the nature of grace is to study Christ. Augustine had already given expression to the same thought in his writings against the Donatists. These men who despised the Church were reminded that Christ is the principle, the source, and the Head of all Christian life, and that in consequence of its origin, this life can have nothing in common with the sins of the faithful or of their bishops. Now the Saint develops the same idea further: our incorporation in the Saviour serves not only to establish the indefectible sanctity of the Church, but all the chief attributes of Christian holiness and grace as well. The argument is treated most fully in two of his last works, *De praedestinatione sanctorum* and *De dono perseverantiae,* both of which were written in 428 or 429. While these writings were directed against the semi-Pelagians rather than against the Pelagians strictly so called, they nevertheless emphasize the same aspects of the doctrine of grace. In particular, the quotations which we shall give touch precisely the same points that Augustine stressed against Pelagius. In the work *De praedestinatione sanctorum* the Saint writes:

> Great light is thrown upon the question of predestination and grace if we consider the Saviour Himself, the Mediator of

God and men, the man Christ Jesus (1 Tim. 2:5). For how could the human nature that is in Him point to any previous merits, whether of good works or of faith, that should entitle it to such a dignity? Answer me this question: in what way did this man deserve to be elevated to personal unity with the Word who is co-eternal with the Father, and to become the Only-begotten Son of God? Did any good action of His precede the union? What had He done, or what had He believed, or what had He asked, that God should so exalt Him? Was it not rather because of the Word and because of His assumption by the Word that this man began to be the only Son of God as soon as He began to exist?[5]

These wholly gratuitous gifts, which made Christ the Son of God, were the beginnings of the grace that makes men Christians:

> All these wonderful privileges, and whatever else may be rightly said of Christ, human nature, that is to say, our nature, has received in Him, without any previous merit on His part. . . . For whatever He is or has, He is and has through grace.[6]

Let us briefly consider the argument which the Saint proposes in these and the following passages. First he reasons *a fortiori:* if grace was not merited in Christ, then still less can it be merited in the faithful. But the argumentation possesses a particular interest for us in that it also proceeds *a pari* or *a continuo,* so to speak. For Augustine presupposes, and even states explicitly that grace is a single life animating a single organism; that from the Head which is the plenitude of grace, it flows into this organism and into the members, each of which receives its proper share; and that even in its fullest expansion this life is exactly the same as in the source, since the entire expansion remains in the unity of the one Mystical Christ.

As we see, the demonstration resembles the soteriological argument that we have so often noticed. The ideas are the same, but arranged in inverse order. In the soteriological argument we conclude what the Head must be by considering what the members are; here St. Augustine argues in the same manner, but from the Head to the members. However, both methods bear the same testimony to our incorporation in

Christ, for both are based upon the vital continuity and real unity that exist between Head and members.

Let us now listen as Augustine proceeds with his argument. Having shown that all the dignity of the Saviour's human nature is a free grace of God, he immediately goes on to say that its power to communicate supernatural life is likewise a grace.

Let us therefore understand that our Head is the very source of grace; from Him grace flows into all His members, according to the capacity of each.

Every man who receives the faith is made a Christian by the very same grace whereby this man, from the first moment of his existence, was constituted Christ. We are born again of the same Spirit by whose power he was born; we receive the remission of our sins from the same Spirit who preserved him from sin of any kind.

Unquestionably God knew all these things before He brought them to pass. But this is precisely what we mean by the predestination of saints, which is nowhere more clearly exemplified than in the Holy of Holies Himself. Can anyone who rightly understands the Scripture deny this? We are told that the very Lord of glory was predestined, if He is considered as a man raised to the dignity of the Son of God. The Apostle of the Gentiles exclaims in the opening verses of his epistle [to the Romans]: "Paul, a servant of Jesus Christ, called to be an apostle, separated unto the gospel of God, which He had promised before by His prophets in the holy scriptures, concerning His Son, who was made to Him of the seed of David according to the flesh, who was predestinated the Son of God in power according to the spirit of sanctification, by the resurrection of our Lord Jesus Christ from the dead" (Rom. 1:1-4, D.V.). Jesus therefore was predestined, in order that He who was to be the Son of David according to the flesh should also be the Son of God in power according to the spirit of sanctification, because He was born of the Holy Spirit and the Virgin Mary. Thus was accomplished the ineffable assumption of man by the Word of God, so that being at once Son of God and Son of man, the same person is truly and properly called the Son of man by reason of the human nature that has been assumed, and the Son of God on account of the Only-begotten God by whom it was assumed. Hence there are not four, but only three Persons in God.

God had predestined this elevation of human nature to the highest possible dignity, just as the divinity could stoop no lower than it did in assuming human nature with the weaknesses of the flesh and in submitting even to the death of the Cross.

Now, just as this one man was predestined to be our Head, so we many are predestined to be His members. Here let all human merits be silent, for they perished in Adam; let only God's grace reign, which reigns through Christ our Lord, the only Son of God and only Lord.

If one can find in our Head any merit prior to His ineffable generation, then may he hope to find some merits in us, His members, prior to the regeneration of the individual man. But His generation was not a reward; that He should be born of the Spirit and of the Virgin, free from any taint of sin, was a pure gift. And it is the same for us: to be born again of water and the Spirit is not a recompense for any good we have done, but a free gift. True it is that faith leads us to the waters of regeneration; yet we cannot conclude from this that we have been the first to give, and that we receive regeneration as our reward. For He that gave us the Christ in whom we believe has likewise given us our faith in Christ. He who made the man Jesus to be the author and finisher of faith is Himself the source and perfection of men's faith in Jesus.[7]

We know from Augustine's own testimony that even while he was writing these lines in which grace and the Mystical Body appear as one, he had the intention of returning and completing the development in the companion treatise, *De dono perseverantiae*. There he writes:

We have no more illustrious example of predestination than the Mediator Himself. The Christian who desires to understand this mystery has only to look upon the Saviour: in Him he shall find himself.[8]

An example, indeed. But the likeness is more than accidental. So perfect is the resemblance in the present instance that it is possible to draw this astounding conclusion: to see Christ is to see oneself! Then, in order to explain clearly what grace is, the Saint restates the dogma of Christology in a series of definite formulas which exclude one by one all the major heresies. It is thus that we discover the nature of that life which flows from the Head into the members. Summing up, he tells us that while Christ is perfect God and perfect man in an indivisible unity of person, yet this union of the two natures does not in any way compromise the integrity of either. Then he goes on to explain what the members are, from what we know concerning the Head:

> Therefore, of the seed of David God formed this just Man, who through no previous merit of His will, was never unjust, and the same God has transformed unjust men into just without previous merit of their wills, so that He should be the Head and they His members. God so made this Man, without any previous merits on His part, as to need pardon for no sin, whether of origin or of voluntary commission; and those that believe in this Man, God has so made that He can pardon them all their sins. In fine, He who made it impossible for this Man ever to have an evil will has also changed into good will the evil will that existed in His members. Hence God has predestined both Him and ourselves. For in making Him our Head and us His body, it was not our antecedent merits that God regarded from all eternity, but His own future works.
>
> If they who read this understand, let them give thanks to God. If they understand not, let them ask Him to teach them interiorly, "out of whose mouth cometh prudence and knowledge" (Prov. 2:6).[9]

"The same grace that makes Christ the Son of God makes Christians the children of God." The beginnings of this formula, which may be said to sum up the several passages we have quoted, may be seen in those writings of Augustine that date from the first Pelagian disputes, or even much earlier. We may call it one of the high points, one of the first principles, of the doctrine of grace which the Saint proposes against the heretics. It is by no means the only argument that he employs, but it does serve to make them all more striking. Never is such light thrown upon the essence and properties of grace, and never does one realize so clearly that grace consists in a supernatural elevation of our being, that it is gratuitous and necessary for salvation, that it destroys sin and sanctifies the soul, as when one sees in it the prolongation of the Incarnation.

At the same time, this admirable formula of grace is also a formula of the Mystical Body. It represents the Mystical Body as the organism whose life is grace, or in other words, as the organism which is animated supernaturally by the prolongation of the Incarnation. First, by reason of the hypostatic union, unparalleled grace is conferred upon the individual human nature of Christ. Then this holiness is communicated from the Head to the members. There takes place, as it were, a kind of progressive extension of the hypostatic union to all the faithful. Hence, while the supernatural life is personal to each individual member, it nevertheless continues to be, even within each one, the property of Christ and of the whole body.

Thus in the controversy against Pelagius Augustine introduces the doctrine of grace, the divinity of Christ, and the divinization of the Christian in order to define the Mystical Body. In his synthesis each of these truths continues and completes the rest, just as in the actuality of the divine plan the realities that underlie these truths are each continued and completed in the others, and unite to bring about one single work of salvation, one gift of God in Christ.

II

We found a very similar theology of the Christ-life in the writings of St. Cyril of Alexandria. Cyril lived in the same period, having been made patriarch of Alexandria in 412, the year in which Augustine entered the controversy against Pelagius. Cyril's doctrine is more complete and more systematic than the teaching of Augustine, but in essentials the two coincide. Both conceive the Incarnation as a reality which by its very nature, so to speak, affects the whole human race: the mere fact that Christ's humanity is united with the Word renders that humanity the source of supernatural life for the regeneration of all mankind.

Cyril's immediate object was, of course, quite different from that of Augustine. The former's whole purpose was to defend the unity of Christ against Nestorius. But all the Christian dogmas are very intimately linked together, and the relation between the dogma of grace and the dogma of the Incarnation is the closest of all. Both express the same necessity for union of God and man in the work of salvation: the dogma of Christology is concerned with the union of the human and divine natures which is necessary in order to give us our

Saviour, whereas the dogma of grace treats of that union of human effort with divine grace which is necessary for every salutary act.

Thus, guided by the same Spirit in quest of the same truth, yet each intent upon the development of his own doctrine, the Doctor of the Incarnation and the Doctor of Grace~unite in a common teaching, which represents Christianity as the Incarnation, extended by means of grace to the whole "body" of Christ.

But since each has arrived at this doctrine by a different route, each presents it from a different point of view and with unequal perfection. Bent on proving that the man Christ is truly one with the Word, St. Cyril deduces His title as Head of the Church from the dignity and excellence which is communicated to the Sacred Humanity by virtue of the hypostatic union. Christ's humanity is the very flesh of Life, he explains; therefore it must be life-giving. Therefore it possesses with itself, and is the source of the life of all the faithful. The Incarnation is the ultimate principle that accounts both for our incorporation in Christ and for the power which enables the humanity of Christ to incorporate us in itself.

Augustine, on the other hand, scarcely touches this particular point of Christology and of the doctrine of the Mystical Body. The Pelagian controversy was not of such a nature as to direct his attention first to the Head of that body and thus lead him to study the divine plan from its very beginning. Yet this is the only method that will permit a full, detailed view of that plan. Our Saint succeeds in explaining a great deal, it is true. He makes it quite clear that the very fact of the Incarnation makes Christ the Head of the Christians. But he fails to take the final step; he does not say how and why the hypostatic union endows the Saviour's humanity with such supreme perfection. This phase of the doctrine was to be left for further development at the hands of medieval and modern theologians.

It is important to note the need for doctrinal progress on the point in question, particularly because at this period a certain deficiency begins to make its appearance in Augustine's teaching, alongside other elements of the highest value. The guilty party is Pelagius, for it was his vaunting of man's sufficiency that led our Saint to insist so vehemently upon our helplessness. A reaction was necessary, beyond a doubt, but the occasion and the need were but momentary.

Of course, we must always speak of our helplessness; else we should not be speaking about ourselves. Christianity is a religion of pardoned sinners, and if one chooses to ignore the fact of sin he cannot hope to understand the essentials of its teaching. The marks of sin are too profoundly graven, first in our human weakness and then in the wounds of Christ. No one has expressed this truth better than Augustine. Nay, does it not even seem that Providence had arranged or permitted everything in his life — his contact with Manichaeism, the falls of his youth, his hesitation, his resistance to grace — in order precisely to prepare him to champion the place of sinners in the Church and the place of sin in the Christian, against the subtle pride of Donatists and Pelagians? When he speaks of our weakness and misery, of the divine assistance without which we must die, or of the humble prayer without which our efforts are doomed to sterility, his words are so clear and so decisive that to become dogmas of faith they needed only the solemn approbation of the Church.

But is it not fair to add that on occasion he also speaks very severely about our weakness and misery? True, he repeats over and over that evil is only a privation, a thing that should never have been and which one day will no longer be; but does he not extend beyond due measure the limits and the effects of this privation? Must we really believe that every human heart is so perverted that without grace it can do naught but evil? Unfortunately, it will be necessary, in a later chapter, to say something about Calvinism and Jansenism. It is chiefly for this reason that we feel called upon to make certain reservations now concerning the doctrine of Augustine. The bishop of Ypres had only to tear certain passages of Augustine out of their context and force their meaning by means of a clever grouping of texts, in order to build up a complete exposition of a pessimistic and harsh dualist heresy.

It is scarcely necessary to observe that our Saint is quite

innocent of such exaggerated views. If one should wish to
know to what extent a writer can distort the meaning of
another and yet do little more than quote the latter's own
words, let him choose at random and read a few pages, first of
Augustine and then of Jansenius' *Augustinus*.

However, we must also bear in mind the fact that the
Church has never accepted every detail of the doctrine of the
bishop of Hippo. She draws a distinction between Augustine
as the Doctor of Grace and witness of the faith, and Augustine as a private theologian whose teaching she herself has the
right and duty to correct and complete.

Such, in our opinion, is the case for the passages of which we
speak. When the Saint is insisting upon man's perversity or
the fewness of the good, when he describes the Mystical Body
as an organism which is indeed immense, but pitifully small
in comparison with the vast multitude of the wicked, or again
as an organism burdened by sin and its consequences rather
than transfigured by grace and its salutary effects, his words
no longer convey to us the pure voice of Tradition. They are
no longer a witness to the wonderful things that God can do
with such miserable beings as ourselves. Rather are they the
lasting and humble recollection of the years during which he
resisted the call of grace and begot Adeodatus; they are likewise a reaction against the narrow pride of consciences less
candid and less human than his own.

We hope that we have made our meaning clear. Not for
anything in the world do we wish to dim the glory of Augustine. Few other saints so compel admiration and love. But
perfection is not of this world; as Augustine himself was wont
to repeat, truth is more beautiful than anything he could say
of it. The few reservations that we have made do not affect
any essential part of his magnificent theory of the Mystical
Body. They concern only a particular point of an accessory
nature, which casts a certain shadow over his teaching; but
we can easily prescind from the shadow without disturbing the
solid truth of the whole. Moreover, this shadow is to be found
only in the Pelagian dispute: only the heretics are to blame
for its presence. Elsewhere it vanishes, and all is lightsome.

Chapter IV

St. Augustine — 3. Sermons to the People

⊁⊰

I. 1. *Augustine's sermons:* their doctrinal importance; they reveal the Saint's true self and contain a very powerful, very psychological, and very realistic doctrine of the Mystical Body. Favorite themes, with some examples.

2. Often such passages are suggested by Scriptural texts, and seem to conform to a fixed plan. Possible influences: St. Ambrose, Ticonius. How Augustine came to know and apply the latter's *Seven Rules;* the limited influence of the *Rules.*

II. *An exegetical principle: Duo in voce una.* In the Scriptures, Christ and the Church speak as one. Christ speaks for us, particularly when there is question of our infirmities — a lesson to the Pelagians.

III. *Applications:* 1. *Prayer:* Christ prays in us. We must pray with Him; catholic prayer.

2. *Suffering:* In us Christ suffers a prolongation of His Passion; catholic expiation. Christ's sacrifice continued in the Mass and the Eucharist. A realistic and mystical theory of the Blessed Sacrament.

3. *Holiness:* Christ's holiness is our holiness; it gives us new life, new strength, and real sanctity despite our frailty.

4. *Unity in Christ:* In ourselves we are many, but in Christ we are one. One man: even when He is taken with us, Christ is still one. One Son, one Shepherd. "For them do I hallow Myself," says our Lord, "for they are Myself."

5. *Divinization* of the faithful; of the Church.

6. *Charity:* God loves us all in Christ. Charity must be catholic, in order that the whole Christ may love Himself.

IV. *Conclusion.* The theory is very psychological and very realistic. The Mystical Body is shown to possess its own inner life. The most prominent feature of Augustine's doctrine of the Mystical Body is its insistence upon this inner life, which he explains more clearly than any other writer had done before him.

I. § 1

WHILE there may be some dispute concerning Augustine's title to the highest rank in the metaphysics of dogma, he has no equal in explaining the interior and psychological aspect of our faith. Neither abstract exposition nor reasoned controversy were suited to bring out the best that was in him. The battle against heresy was waged, so to speak, on the outskirts of dogma. Being on the defensive, Catholic writers were forced to state the truth in terms of the enemy's attack and in language that he would readily understand. Under such unfavorable conditions, the principal thing — the thing that is all-important when there is question of a truth so central, both to the Christian religion and to the soul of Augustine, as the truth of the Mystical Body — must necessarily remain unsaid.

But when he can allow his soul to speak, in the living and secure intimacy of Christian assemblies, Augustine describes the intimate union of Christ and the Church in accents that well from his inmost being, such accents of love as others will never find. We now come to listen to this voice of his soul, and we must listen with even greater attention than before. For, as the bishop teaching his flock, he is now in a truer sense acting as the witness of Tradition; he is the Father of the Church, explaining his most "ecclesiastical" and at the same time his most personal doctrine.

The Augustine of the *Confessions,* the Augustine whose heart God had endowed with so keen a perception of the life of the God-Truth in men's souls, the Augustine who in the heat of debate was at times hidden from view by the controversialist, we now find once more, but even greater than before. In the early days of his life as a Christian it was only for himself and for a few friends that he sought the interior bread and the inner light. Now this individualism, which was legitimate enough but narrow in outlook, has been broadened; his pastoral duties and his discussions against Donatist and Pelagian exclusivism have rendered his soul more universal, more catholic. He has become truly and completely the churchman, and his first care is for the union between Christ

[413]

and all Christendom; this is the truth he meditates, and the theme he preaches to the faithful.

And he preaches it untiringly. He repeats again and again, on countless occasions, that Christ and the Church are one and the same thing, one soul, one man, one person, one just man, one Christ, one Son of God. Hence the whole Christ is not the Saviour alone, but the Head plus the members, Christ united with the Church. The members of Christ are one with Him: He is they and they are He. All are gathered together into this unity, and in God's eyes they are but one well-beloved Son.

At times such statements are uttered in passing; like the Alleluias of the Paschal liturgy, they are the sudden outburst of a joy that can no longer be restrained. At other times our Saint develops the thought at length, leisurely, as if to taste its sweetness. Let us listen to some examples:

What is the Church? She is the body of Christ. Join to it the Head, and you have one man: the head and the body make up one man. Who is the Head? He who was born of the Virgin Mary. . . . And what is His body? It is His Spouse, that is, the Church. . . . The Father willed that these two, the God Christ and the Church, should be one man.[1]

All men are one man in Christ, and the unity of the Christians constitutes but one man.[2]

And this man is all men, and all men are this man; for all are one, since Christ is one.[3]

Augustine feels this one man present and living in the Christian assemblies, and addresses him in these words:

O body of Christ, holy Church.[4] . . . O people of God; O body of Christ, O noble traveler! Thou art not of earth, but from above.[5]

What is thy hope, O body of Christ? O Christ, Thou art seated in heaven at the right hand of the Father, but Thou dost still suffer on earth in Thy members.[6]

O ye, O thou, O ye many who are one![7]

O man, O unity, what art thou doing upon earth? What good works thou wilt perform in the Church![8]

This one man is the whole Christ, Head and body.

When by faith Christ begins to abide in the inner man, and

[414]

when by prayer He takes possession of the faithful soul, He becomes the whole Christ, Head and body, and of many He becomes one.[9]

Our Lord Jesus Christ, like a whole and perfect man, is Head and body. . . . His body is the Church, not simply the Church that is in this particular place, but both the Church that is here and the Church which extends over the whole earth; not simply the Church that is living today, but the whole race of saints, from Abel down to all those who will ever be born and will believe in Christ until the end of the world, for all belong to one city. This city is the body of Christ. . . . This is the whole Christ: Christ united with the Church.[10]

So close is this union that it makes us Christ Himself, the Mystical Christ. Augustine exults with joy as he teaches this mystery to his faithful.

Let us rejoice and give thanks. Not only are we become Christians, but we are become Christ. My brothers, do you understand the grace of God that is given us? Wonder, rejoice, for we are made Christ! If He is the Head, and we the members, then together He and we are the whole man. . . .

This would be foolish pride on our part, were it not a gift of His bounty.

But this is what He promised by the mouth of the Apostle: "You are the body of Christ, and severally His members" (1 Cor. 12:27).[11]

All this is a reality. He is as truly within us as He truly walked the roads of Judea. Nay, He is even more truly within us, inasmuch as faith is more perfect than evidence, and as grace is more perfect than nature.

Had He deigned always to remain visibly present among us . . . we should prefer the eyes of the flesh to the eyes of the heart. But He, knowing which are the more perfect, has withdrawn Himself from the eyes of the flesh, in order to arouse faith in the eyes of the heart. For it is a greater thing to believe in Christ than to see Him always bodily present. . . . When we believe, He is present to the eyes of the spirit. . . . Let no one regret His ascension into heaven as if He had abandoned us. He is with us, if we believe; His presence within thee is more real than if He were to stand beside thee, before thy very eyes. If thou believest, He is within. If thou wert to receive Christ as a guest in thy room, He would be with thee. Behold, thou dost receive Him in thy heart, and He is not with thee?[12]

[415]

These few texts will provide a preliminary view of Augustine's teaching. Now we must consider this teaching in greater detail.

§ 2

Usually it is in the explanation of Holy Scripture that Augustine introduces such passages as we have cited above. When verses occur that attribute infirmity to Christ, he explains that in reality there is question only of the members of Christ, since Christ and His members are one.

Many of the more lengthy developments of this kind seem to be built up according to a fixed pattern. First comes the text containing the difficulty, then the declaration that the meaning becomes clear as soon as one accepts the principle of the mystical identity of Christ and the Church; finally, proofs are given to establish this identity. The proofs are frequently drawn from the words addressed to Paul on the road to Damascus. If Christ and the Church were not one person, argues the Saint, never could the Saviour have said to the persecutor of the Church: "Saul, Saul, why dost thou persecute Me?"[13]

Augustine has left us many such passages, centered round the words that converted the Apostle. Who can say whether their very recurrence is not an indication, a revelation of the influence exerted upon Augustine's soul and upon Augustine's theology by the memory of his own conversion, which, like Paul's, was accompanied by an interior revelation of Christ?

At all events, it would be a mistake to regard these passages as mere conventional forms. No doubt they lose some of their vividness by force of repetition, and become somewhat monotonous when, as in the present study, one wishes to give many quotations. But the holy Doctor is ever stressing their importance. He unhesitatingly includes them either in solemn formulas or in brief summaries of the faith. The repetition is done deliberately, since, as he tells us, no other method of interpreting Scripture is more "ecclesiastical" or more traditional.

Athanasius had already expressed himself in the same terms.

This method of exegesis had been in use at each stage of Tradition, but it was to be brought to its full development in the Latin Church, and, we may say, in the universal Church, by Augustine.

Our Saint himself certainly received it from Tradition: perhaps from St. Ambrose or St. Cyprian, for it was used by both; or perhaps from the method commonly accepted at the time for the interpretation of Scripture, particularly of the Psalms. By a remarkable though perhaps fortuitous coincidence, this seems to have been at that period the most usual manner of explaining the Psalter, and we find that Augustine used it most often, and probably for the first time, in his *Enarrationes in psalmos.*

Augustine himself gives us no information on this matter of literary dependence. The only source which he mentions are the writings of a certain Ticonius, of whom we must say a few words here. Ticonius was a peculiar individual. Though a Donatist, he was less bitter than the others; he was fair-minded enough to acknowledge publicly the justice of the Catholic claims on certain points, and was finally excommunicated by his own co-religionists. Even then, however, he remained in schism, and in his place of retirement wrote several famous treatises. One of these was the *Book of the Seven Rules,* which will occupy our attention for a few moments.

The *Seven Rules* are seven exegetical methods, seven keys, by means of which, the author asserts, one can determine the meaning of the most difficult passages of Scripture. The first, entitled *Of the Lord and of His Body,* is the method of which we have been speaking. Ticonius observes that the Scriptures refer to Christ and to the faithful indiscriminately. It is left for the exegete to distinguish the two. Then he cites numerous instances of this complication of thought in the Holy Books, and illustrates how the distinction is to be made. For example, Christ tells us in the Gospel that the Son of man will return very soon. In reality there is question here of the birth of the Church; in the same breath and without distinction, the Saviour speaks of Himself and of His "body." Ticonius explains:

We may say that the whole Church is the Son of man, since the Church, that is, the children of God assembled in one body, is said to be the Son of God, one man, and even God, according to the words of the Apostle: "against all that is called God or is venerated" (2 Thess. 2:4). What is here called God, is the Church.[14]

Augustine had the *Seven Rules* in his possession at the beginning of his episcopate. It is known that during this period he wrote several letters to Aurelius, bishop of Carthage, asking his opinion of the book. Again, in the first edition of *De doctrina christiana* he breaks off at the very point where in the completed work he explains the *Rules*.

Though he gives no express approbation of the *Rules* during the next quarter century, he clearly shows himself favorably inclined toward them. They guide him in *De genesi ad litteram*, written between 400 and 415; then in 419 he cites them and makes use of them in *Quaestiones in Heptateuchum*.

At last, in 426, when he comes to complete the work *De doctrina christiana*, he takes a definite stand. Beyond a word of caution that the author is a schismatic, and a remark to the effect that the *Rules* are not quite so all-sufficient as they claim to be, he gives them his full approval. They are of great assistance, he says, in understanding Scripture. He then quotes the *Rules* and explains each in a separate chapter for the benefit of the faithful.

However, long before he came to this conclusion, and perhaps even before he heard of the *Rules*, Augustine had made use of our incorporation in Christ in order to explain obscure Scriptural texts. In *De diversis quaestionibus*, written somewhere between the years 388 and 395, and certainly before he began to have any doubts on the subject of the *Seven Rules*, he furnishes a beautiful example of this type of exegesis. Moreover, other examples, equally as numerous as in any of his later works, are to be found in the first of the sermons to which a definite date can be assigned. These are the first thirty-two *Enarrationes in Psalmos*, delivered during the early years of his episcopate, the very period of his uncertainty.

But best of all, one need only read the *Enarrationes* or any other of the Saint's writings to see how little they have in common with Ticonius' treatise. They resemble the *Rules* no more than a poem can be said to resemble a treatise of grammar. One is not simply an outgrowth of the other.

Therefore Augustine was not dependent to any appreciable degree upon the Donatist Ticonius as regards the exegesis based on the Mystical Body. At the very most Ticonius may have put him in closer touch with a tradition that had already reached him through other channels.

However, the important thing is not how the doctrine came to him, but rather it is the new note that he discovers and reveals in it. He took it as a living thing into his inner life; he meditated it; he interpreted and completed it by the study of the Scriptures. One of his chief masters was St. Paul, whose forceful words he cites so often. The same thing had previously taken place in St. John Chrysostom, that other model of Christian orators — a proof that Tradition draws its life from contact with its sources, from contact with Scripture.

II

Now let us listen to St. Augustine himself. Christ and the Church, the Head and the body: herein, he declares, consists the whole mystery of all the Scriptures. Hence the doctrine of Christ's union with the Church is an important exegetical principle:

> In order to understand the Scriptures, it is absolutely necessary to know the whole, complete Christ, that is, Head and members. For sometimes Christ speaks in the name of the Head alone . . . sometimes in the name of His body, which is the holy Church spread over the entire earth. And we are in His body . . . and we hear ourselves speaking in it, for the Apostle tells us: "We are members of His body" (Eph. 5:30). In many places does the Apostle tell us this.[15]

The Head and the body are one. Why then should they speak as if they were two? Husband and wife are one flesh. Why then should they not have but one single voice? This last expression recurs frequently:

> Christ Himself has said: "They are no longer two, but they are one flesh" (Matt. 19:6). Is it strange then, if they are one

[419]

flesh, that they should have one tongue and should say the same words, since they are one flesh, Head and body? Let us therefore hear them as one. But let us listen to the Head speaking as Head, and to the body speaking as the body. We do not separate the two realities, but two different dignities; for the Head saves, and the body is saved. . . . The Head is there to purify from sin, and the body to confess its sins. Yet there is only one voice, and we are not told whether it is the Head that speaks, or the body. We make the distinction when we hear, but He speaks as one. . . . Nevertheless, when you hear the body speak, do not separate it from the Head; and when you hear the voice of the Head, do not take away the body. For "they are no longer two, but they are one flesh."[16]

Such is the infinite mercy of our God.

In order to hold converse with us and to comfort us whom He sees justly condemned to eat bread in the sweat of our brow, the Lord our God deigns to address us from within, to show that He not only created us, but that He abides in us.[17]

If we say that the words of the Psalm which we have heard and sung are our words, it is to be feared that we are mistaken, for they are rather the words of the Spirit of God than our own. But if we say that they are not our words, then we are surely wrong. For such lament can come only from those in misery.[18]

It is wrong, even under the pretext of safeguarding the holiness of Christ, to say that these words of confession and self-abasement have nothing to do with Him. Augustine warns the Donatists that their apparent piety is in truth a sacrilege:

What has the Church done to thee, that thou shouldst wish to decapitate her? Thou wouldst take away her Head, and believe in the Head alone, despising the body. Vain is thy service, and false thy devotion to the Head. For to sever it from the body is an injury to both Head and body.[19]

The Scriptures mark no distinction between the Saviour and ourselves, precisely for fear that we should separate the two. The sacred text passes from one to the other without indicating any change of person, and Christ Himself, after speaking of His body, begins suddenly and without warning to speak of Himself. Where Unity itself points to perfect union, why should language introduce division?

Though absent from our eyes, Christ our Head is bound to

[420]

us by love. Since the whole Christ is Head and body, let us so listen to the voice of the Head that we may also hear the body speak.

He no more wished to speak alone than He wished to exist alone, since He says: "Behold, I am with you all days, unto the consummation of the world" (Matt. 28:20). If He is with us, then He speaks in us, He speaks of us, and He speaks through us; and we too speak in Him.[20]

Christ speaks as if He were ourselves; He assumes our part and transfigures us into Himself, says Augustine.

He who disdained not to assume us unto Himself, did not disdain to take our place and speak our words, in order that we might speak His words.[21]

So, too, Christ speaks for us when He says: "O My God, I shall cry by day, and Thou wilt not hear" (Ps. 21:3).

Certainly He says this for me, for thee, for this other man, since He bears His body, the Church. Unless you imagine, brethren, that when He said: "My Father, if it be possible, let this cup pass away from Me" (Matt. 26:39), it was the Lord that feared to die. . . . But Paul longed to die, that he might be with Christ. What? The Apostle desires to die, and Christ Himself should fear death? What can this mean, except that He bore our infirmity in Himself, and uttered these words for those who are in His body and still fear death? It is from these that the voice came; it was the voice of His members, not of the Head.[22]

When He said, "My soul is sorrowful unto death" (Matt. 26:38), He manifested Himself in thee, and thee in Himself.[23]

And when He said, "My God, My God, why hast Thou forsaken Me?" (Matt. 27:46), the words He uttered on the Cross were not His own, but ours.[24]

Such great mercy moves Augustine's soul to cry out:

O Lord Mediator, God above us, man for our sakes, I acknowledge Thy mercy. For the fact that Thou, who art so great, should will to be troubled so profoundly for love of us, brings comfort to many members of Thy body who are harassed by the weakness of their nature, and saves them from despair and perdition.[25]

How can we continue to be proud in the presence of such condescension? How can we pretend to be free from misery and sin when Christ Himself confesses them in our stead?

[421]

Why does He speak thus, if not because we are in Him and because the Church is the body of Christ? . . .

Why does He say "the words of My sins" (Ps. 21:2)? Is it not because He Himself is praying for our sins, and because He has made our sins His sins, that He might make His justice our justice?[26]

Augustine addresses the same question directly to Christ:

Why, Lord, dost Thou ask pardon for Thy sins? Why prayest Thou in this way? What sins hast Thou to expiate? And He replies: "Each time that one of My members prays thus, it is I who pray." Has He not said, "Inasmuch as ye did it to one of the least of these My brethren, ye did it to Me"? (Matt. 25:40.)[27]

A good lesson for the Pelagians — and for the faithful as well.

Therefore, on hearing His words let no one say either: "These are not Christ's words," or "These are not my words." On the contrary, if he knows that he is in the body of Christ, let him say: "These are both Christ's words and my words." Say nothing without Him, and He will say nothing without thee.[28]

We must not consider ourselves as strangers to Christ, or look upon ourselves as other than Himself.[29]

III. § 1

His prayer is our prayer, and our prayer is His, provided that we do not cut ourselves off from Him.

Therefore as soon as our Head begins to pray, let us understand that we are in Him, that we may unite our prayer with His as we share in His tribulation.[30]

From these and other like passages one might build up a complete treatise on Christian prayer. Let us listen as he begins his explanation of the eighty-fifth Psalm.

No greater gift could God bestow on men than to give them as their Head His Word, by whom He made all things, and to unite them as members to that Head. Thus the Word became both Son of God and Son of man: one God with the Father, one Man with men.

Hence, when we offer our petitions to God, let us not separate ourselves from the Son; and when the body of the

Son prays, let it not detach itself from its Head. Let it be He, the sole Saviour of His body, our Lord Jesus Christ, the Son of God, who prays for us, who prays in us, and who is prayed to by us.

He prays for us as our Priest; He prays in us as our Head; He is prayed to by us as our God. Let us therefore hear both our words in Him and His words in us. . . .

We pray to Him in the form of God; He prays in the form of the slave. There He is the Creator; here He is in the creature. He changes not, but takes the creature and transforms it into Himself, making us one man, head and body, with Himself.

We pray therefore to Him, and through Him, and in Him. We pray with Him, and He with us; we recite this prayer of the Psalm in Him, and He recites it in us.[31]

Just as the Scriptures are the authentic expression of our most interior prayer, so, too, are they the expression of the catholic life of the whole Church, because they are the expression of Christ's thought and because the same Christ who prays in each one, prays in all. So each of us can say: "To Thee have I cried from the ends of the earth" (Ps. 60:3).

Who is this that cries from the ends of the earth? Who is this one man who reaches to the extremities of the universe?[32]

He is one, but that one is unity. He is one, not one in a single place, but the cry of this one man comes from the remotest ends of the earth. But how can this one man cry out from the ends of the earth, unless he be one in all?[33]

This cry that rises from the entire face of the earth will not be stilled until the end of time.

Christ's whole body groans in pain. Until the end of the world, when pain will pass away, this man groans and cries to God. And each one of us has part in the cry of that whole body. Thou didst cry out in thy day, and thy days have passed away; another took thy place and cried out in his day. Thou here, he there, and another there. The body of Christ ceases not to cry out all the day, one member replacing the other whose voice is hushed.

Thus there is but one man who reaches unto the end of time, and those that cry are always His members.[34]

His prayer ascends to God without interruption: "O Lord, in the day when I am in trouble, incline Thy ear to me" (Ps. 103:3). This is Christ that prays, for He is the unity of the body. If one member suffers, all the members suffer with it. "Thou art troubled today," He says, "and it is I that am troubled. Tomorrow another is troubled, again it is I that am troubled. After this generation will come others and yet others. They will be troubled, and it is I that am troubled. Until the end of time, whenever anyone in My body is in tribulation, it is I that am in tribulation."[35]

All Christendom, throughout all space and in all ages, is one vast and perpetual suppliant. One may perhaps neither see nor feel this vision of catholicity; it is enough to believe. Even when we are alone our prayer ascends to God from Christ and from the Church. When we pray in Christ, a "mounting canticle" (*cantica graduum*), a hymn of all humanity, rises to God.

Let him rise up, this one chanter; let this man sing from the heart of each of us, and let each one of us be in this man. When each of you sings a verse, it is still this one man that sings, since you are all one in Christ. We do not say, "To Thee, O Lord, have we lifted up our eyes," but "To Thee have I lifted up my eyes" (Ps. 122:1). You should of course consider that each of you is speaking, but that primarily this one man is speaking who reaches to the ends of the earth.[36]

§ 2

In this one man the Saviour continues His Passion, just as in him He prolongs His prayer. The blood of the Agony still flows through the wounds of the martyrs.

The Apostle says: "I make up in my flesh what is lacking to the sufferings of Christ" (Col. 1:24). "I make up," he tells us, "not what is lacking to my sufferings, but what is lacking to the sufferings of Christ; not in Christ's flesh, but in mine. Christ is still suffering, not in His own flesh which He took with Him into heaven, but in my flesh, which is still suffering on earth."[37]

Yet these sufferings remain Christ's sufferings. The sole difference is that when His sufferings pass into the Church they take on, so to speak, a catholic extension. "You all kill Me," says the Psalm (Ps. 61:4).

What does the Scripture mean when it tells us of the body of one man so extended in space that all can kill him? We must understand these words of ourselves, of our Church, of the body of Christ. For Jesus Christ is one man, having a Head and a body. The Saviour of the body and the members of the body are two in one flesh, and in one voice, and in one passion, and, when iniquity shall have passed away, in one repose.

And so the passion of Christ is not in Christ alone; and yet the passion of Christ is in Christ alone. For if in Christ you consider both the Head and the body, then Christ's passion is in Christ alone; but if by Christ you mean only the Head, then Christ's passion is not in Christ alone. . . . Hence if you are in the members of Christ, all you who hear me, and even you who hear me not (though you do hear me, if you are united with the members of Christ), whatever you suffer at the hands of those who are not among the members of Christ, was lacking to the sufferings of Christ. It is added precisely because it was lacking. You fill up the measure, you do not cause it to overflow. You will suffer just so much as must be added of your sufferings to the complete passion of Christ, who suffered as our Head and who continues still to suffer in His members, that is, in us. Into this common treasury each pays what he owes, and according to each one's ability we all contribute our share of suffering. The full measure of the Passion will not be attained until the end of the world.[38]

For Christians, suffering is not an accident but an obligation of their profession. Life for them means death to a previous life; it means incorporation in a Saviour who wills to continue in them His expiatory sufferings and His struggle against sin. He Himself was hated by the world because He was a contradiction to the world; hence His body, too, must endure persecution and contempt.

When the Head and members are despised, then the whole Christ is despised, for the whole Christ, Head and body, is that just man against whom deceitful lips speak iniquity (Ps. 30:19).[39]

The life of the Head was the beginning of the life of the members. All that took place during Jesus' earthly existence, each event of His history, has a deep meaning for, and a profound action upon, Christian life.

All that occurred on the Cross, at His burial, in His resurrection on the third day, in His ascent into heaven, and when He took His place at the right hand of the Father — all this

[425]

happened in such a way as to prefigure, not in mysterious words only, but in very reality, the Christian life that we are leading today.[40]

In the passage last quoted Augustine is explaining how we receive life through baptism in the death of Christ. In a similar development he shows that the Mass is the continuation of the sacrifice of the Cross.

Like the Passion, so, too, the sacrifice, which is the culmination of the Passion, is prolonged in the Church. For, as Augustine tells us often, the Mass is the immolation of the Saviour being completed in His members, or again, expressing the same thought in a different way, it is the oblation of the Church, considered as the effect and the plenitude of the oblation of Christ. According to this view the Eucharist is not simply the sacrament of the Real Presence, but it also has a necessary connection with ecclesiastical unity. It is the sacred sign or sacrament of the unity of the Church; it is the sacrament of the Mystical Body. Protestant critics conclude, from the Saint's familiar use of the term *sacrament* in this connection, that according to Augustine the Host did not contain the physical body of Christ at all, but rather the Mystical Body. The inference is evidently false, for the Eucharist can be the source of the life and unity of the Church only because it is the very substance of the Saviour. Yet the error does indicate how vigorously Augustine inculcates our incorporation in Christ whenever he comes to speak of the Eucharist. We can see this for ourselves from the following passage, in which the Saint explains the mystery of the altar to his neophytes.

If thou wilt understand what the body of Christ is, hear what the Apostle says to the faithful: "You are the body of Christ, and severally His members" (1 Cor. 12:27). Since then you are the body of Christ and His members, it is your mystery that is placed on the Lord's Table; it is your mystery that you receive. To words that tell you what you are, you answer "Amen," and in answering you subscribe to the statement. For you hear the words: "The body of Christ," and you answer "Amen." Be therefore members of Christ, that your "Amen" may be true.

But why is this mystery accomplished with bread? Let us

offer no reason of our own invention, but listen to the Apostle speak of this sacrament: "We many are one bread, one body" (1 Cor. 10:17). Understand this and rejoice. Unity, truth, piety, charity. "One bread." What is this one bread? It is one body formed of many. Remember that bread is not made of one grain, but of many. During the exorcisms you were ground like wheat; at baptism water was poured over you, as flour is mingled with water, and the Holy Spirit entered into you like the fire which bakes the bread. Be what you see, and receive what you are.

This is what the Apostle teaches concerning the bread. Though he does not say what we are to understand of the chalice, his meaning is easily seen. . . . Recall, my brothers, how wine is made. Many grapes hang from the vine, but the juice of all the grapes is fused into unity.

Thus did the Lord Christ manifest us in Himself. He willed that we should belong to Him, and He has consecrated on His altar the mystery of our peace and unity.[41]

This passage, as well as the Saint's doctrine of the Mass, contains a very profound view concerning the essence of the Holy Sacrifice and the purpose of the Eucharist. However, an adequate explanation of this view would require a long development. We simply wish to remark here how the holy Doctor continues the teaching of Tradition on this point by uniting in one and the same realism his doctrine of the Real Presence and of the Holy Sacrifice with his doctrine of the Mystical Body.

§ 3

For Augustine the Church is so truly the continuation of Christ that all Christian morality consists in reproducing in ourselves, or rather in permitting the diffusion in ourselves of the dispositions of the Saviour by means of His grace and our own efforts. We have a new life, which must be allowed to grow, in strength and in joy.

O sons of peace, sons of the One Catholic [Church], walk in your way, and sing as you walk. Travelers do this in order to keep up their spirits. Do you also sing on the way. I beseech you, by the very road on which you walk, sing on this road; sing the new canticle. Let no one sing old songs, but sing the songs of love of your country; let none sing the old. For the way is new, the traveler new, and the song new.[42]

[427]

In these renewed souls, new and youthful virtues must spring from a new source. As members of the Saviour Christians are obliged to develop in themselves Christ's meekness, His humility, His boundless tenderness toward the afflicted, His patience, and in a word, His holiness. They must do their good works not in their way but in His, so that they may be more truly His works than their own.

Their holiness will be essentially collective, since even when it is within them all, it will still be His holiness; the virtues of one will bring honor to the others, and all things will be common to all in unity. Again, this holiness will shine resplendent in them all, because in them all it will be part of the complete holiness of Christ. This the Psalmist declares: "Preserve my soul, O Lord, for I am holy" (Ps. 85:2).

"For I am holy." When I hear these words I recognize the voice of the Saviour. But shall I take away my own? Certainly when He speaks thus He speaks in inseparable union with His body. But can I say, "I am holy"? If I mean a holiness that I have not received, I should be proud and a liar; but if I mean a holiness that I have received — as it is written: "Be ye holy, because I the Lord your God am holy" (Lev. 19:2) — then let the body of Christ say these words. And let this one man, who cries from the ends of the earth, say with his Head and united with his Head: "I am holy." . . . That is not foolish pride, but an expression of gratitude. If you were to say that you are holy of yourselves, that would be pride; but if, as one of Christ's faithful and as a member of Christ, you say that you are not holy, you are ungrateful. . . .
Since then all Christians, all the faithful who are baptized in Christ have put on Christ, as the Apostle says: "All of you who were baptized into Christ, have put on Christ" (Gal. 3:27), and since they are become members of His body, they offer insult to their Head if they say they are not holy; for then His members would not be holy. See where thou art, and from thy Head accept thy dignity.[43]

Human frailty will not destroy this holiness; little by little our infirmities will be consumed by it.

"Ye were sometime darkness," as it is written (Eph. 5:8); but did you remain darkness? Did He who is Light come for this, that you should remain darkness, or that you should become light in Him?

[428]

Therefore let every Christian, yea, let the whole body of Christ everywhere cry out, despite the tribulations it endures, despite temptations and countless scandals, saying: "Preserve my soul, for I am holy; save Thy servant, O my God, that trusteth in Thee" (Ps. 85:2). No, this holy one is not proud, for he trusts in God.[44]

Nor on the other hand will this holiness in Christ destroy our own poor individuality. Were not the hearts of each one of us so fashioned, one by one, by God's hand, as the Psalmist says (Ps. 32:15), that we might have life in the one Christ?

With the hand of His grace, with the hand of His mercy, He has fashioned and modeled our hearts, modeled them one by one, giving us each a heart, but without destroying their unity. For as the members are formed singly and each has its particular function, and yet all live in the unity of the body; as the hand does what the eye cannot do, and as the ear can do what neither eye nor hand can do, yet all work together in unity, and as, though hand and eye and ear have different functions there is no discord between them, so it is in the body of Christ. Each man, as an individual member, has his own proper gifts, since He who chose the people for His inheritance has fashioned their hearts one by one. "Are all apostles? Are all prophets? Are all teachers? Have all gifts of healing? Do all speak with tongues? Do all interpret? To one through the Spirit is granted utterance of wisdom; to another utterance of knowledge; to another faith, in the same Spirit; and to another gifts of healings" (1 Cor. 12:29,30,8,9). Why? Because God has fashioned their hearts one by one. And just as in our members there is diversity of functions but unity of strength, so in all Christ's members there is a diversity of graces, but one charity.[45]

§ 4

This continuation of Christ's virtues and holiness in His members does not impair His unity. On the contrary, it is because Christ remains one that the faithful are included in His unity and share His holiness. God made the unity of Christ firm enough to contain us all:

He is one, we are many; He is one, and we are one in Him.[46]
We are one, because Christ is one and we are His members.[47]
Say not that He is one and we are many, but say that we many are one in Him who is one.[48]

[429]

Like Paul, Augustine cannot conceive the Church as a mere multitude made up of disparate elements.

> The members of Christ, many though they be, are bound to one another by the ties of charity and peace under the one Head, who is our Saviour Himself, and form one man. Often their voice is heard in the Psalms as the voice of one man; the cry of one is as the cry of all, for all are one in One.[49]
> And because we are many, the Scripture says that we praise God all together (*collaudamus*); and because we are one, it says that we each praise Him (*laudamus*). The same who are many are one; for He is ever one, in whom we are one.[50]

This one man is he that God draws to Himself. "Blessed is he whom Thou hast chosen and taken to Thee" (Ps. 64:5). We should observe, says St. Augustine, that here the Scripture speaks in the singular and not in the plural.

> The Word takes to Himself one man, for He takes unity. He does not take schisms to Himself, nor does He take heresies; these form but a multitude, not a unity that can be assumed. . . . So it is one man who is taken, and his Head is Christ. . . . This is that "blessed man who hath not walked in the counsel of the ungodly" (Ps. 1:1); this is he that is assumed. He is not outside of us. . . . Let us be in Him, and we shall be assumed; let us be in Him, and we shall be chosen. . . . Therefore this one man that is taken to become the temple of God, is at once many and one.[51]

Although Christ contains a multitude, yet His unity is so perfect that even when He bears the whole Church in Himself, He is still one.

> Our Lord Jesus Christ Himself has said: "No man hath ascended into heaven but he that descended from heaven, the Son of man who is in heaven" (John 3:13, D.V.). He seems to have spoken only of Himself. If then He alone ascends who alone hath descended from heaven, have the others been left behind? What must these others do? They must be united with His body, that there may be one Christ who descends and ascends. The Head has descended, and He ascends with the body, clothed with His Church that He has presented to Himself, without spot or wrinkle (Eph. 5:27). Thus He still ascends alone. But when we are so united with Him as to be His members, then even with us He is alone, and hence one, and always one.

[430]

It is unity that joins us to this One, and only they ascend not with Him who refuse to become one with Him.[52]

In like manner Scripture tells us that only the Good Shepherd gives His life for His sheep. That is to say, that all the other pastors who sacrifice themselves for their flock are in reality but one Shepherd with Christ. So again, though they are many who pray and who cry out to God, yet the Church is one petitioner, one suppliant. All Christians are one priest, as they are but one sheep; all are like so many stones resting on the one cornerstone and making up a single stone. Thus we see that the union of the faithful with the Saviour borders on identity. Augustine even dares to affirm that they are taken up in the Ego of the Saviour — or rather, it is our Lord Himself who refers to the faithful as "I."

§ 5

Let us listen to Augustine as he tells us this most astounding mystery of all. The passage repeats certain thoughts that we have already seen, but it deserves to be quoted in full because of the new light which it brings to the doctrine. The theme is once more the holiness which the Saviour communicates to His members.

Since He is the Mediator of God and men, the man Christ Jesus has been made Head of the Church, and the faithful are His members. Wherefore He says: "For them I hallow Myself" (John 17:19). But when He says, "For them I hallow Myself," what else can He mean but this: "I sanctify them in Myself, since truly they are Myself"? For, as I have remarked, they of whom He speaks are His members, and the Head and the body are one Christ. . . .

That He signifies this unity is certain from the remainder of the same verse. For having said, "For them I hallow Myself," He immediately adds, "in order that they too may be hallowed in truth," to show that He refers to the holiness that we are to receive in Him. Now the words "in truth" can only mean "in Me," since Truth is the Word who in the beginning was God.

The Son of man was Himself sanctified in the Word at the moment of His creation, when the Word was made flesh, for Word and man became one Person. It was therefore in that

[431]

instant that He hallowed Himself in Himself; that is, He hallowed Himself as man, in Himself as the Word. For there is but one Christ, Word and man, sanctifying the man in the Word.

But now it is on behalf of His members that He adds: "and for them I hallow Myself." That is to say, that since they too are Myself, so they too may profit by this sanctification just as I profited by it as man without them. "And for them I hallow Myself"; that is, I sanctify them in Myself as Myself, since in Me they too are Myself. "In order that they too may be hallowed in truth." What do the words "they too" mean, if not that they may be sanctified as I am sanctified; that is to say, "in truth," which is I Myself?[53]

Quia et ipsi sunt ego: "since they too are Myself." Only the real unity that they express can match the daring of the words. Christians are not intruders in the inner unity or in the personal life of Jesus, or even in what is most strictly His own, His very Ego. They are "He," and it is Jesus Himself who says so.

Quia et ipsi sunt ego. They are sanctified in Him because He is the Holy One of God and because they are He. This is exactly the same theology of grace, now expressed in the form of a contemplation, that Augustine proposed against the Pelagians.[54] Grace is the flow, into us members, of that perfect holiness which the Incarnation confers upon our Head; for we are in Him, and we are mystically He.

In a later passage of the same commentary of St. John, Augustine reiterates the statement that we are He. The Saint is explaining the closing words of Jesus' discourse after the Last Supper: "In order that the love wherewith Thou hast loved Me may be in them, and I in them" (John 17:26). "What is this presence of Christ in us?" demands Augustine; and he answers:

> His presence in us as in His temple is quite different from the presence that He has within us because we are Himself (*quia et nos ipse sumus*). We are He, since we are His body and since He was made man in order to be our Head.[55]

In another passage, which is rather subtle, Augustine repeats the same idea with emphasis. He explains that Christ could rightly say: "I go not up to this festival day" (John

7:8, D.V.), since He was speaking only of us who are His body, and who no longer observe the Jewish feasts. The exegesis is strained, as our Saint admits, but we are interested less in the exegesis itself than on the principle on which it is based. Let us hear Augustine explain this principle:

> If we consider ourselves, if we think of His body, we shall see that He is ourselves. For if we were not He, it would not be true that "inasmuch as ye did it to one of the least of these My brethren, ye did it to Me" (Matt. 25:40). If we were not He, these words would not be true: "Saul, Saul, why dost thou persecute Me?" (Acts 9:4.) Therefore we too are He, because we are His members, because we are His body, because He is our Head, because the whole Christ is Head and body.[56]

Ergo et nos ipse: "therefore we too are He." Such a union must needs make us all precious in the eyes of God and men.

What the Head has must pass into the members: the glory that is His cannot but become their own, and since He is God, they too must be made divine. Was it not in order to make them partakers of His divinity that the Word willed to share their humanity? Was it not in order to make them one with Himself that He became one with them, so truly one that in a mystical sense He is they?

> We are members of this Head, and this body cannot be decapitated. If the Head is in glory forever, so too are the members in glory forever, that Christ may be undivided forever.[57]
> Although He was God with the Father who made us, He became one of us by means of His flesh, that we might be the body of this Head.[58]

Thus is wrought the divinization of the Christians, a divinization as real as their incorporation in Christ. The only Son of God, the whole Christ, is the Word Incarnate plus themselves. And, to mention that other marvelous fact, so delicately human, so too the Son of Mary, taken in His entirety, is Jesus of Nazareth plus themselves.

So truly is the Saviour's divinity united with the divinization of the elect that the one helps us to understand the other; and the glories of the Sacred Humanity, which is one with the Word of God, illustrate, against the Pelagians, the nature of the grace that incorporates the faithful in that Humanity.

[433]

This assumption of the whole human race, which takes place in the Church and which will be perfected in heaven, is the culmination of that assumption whereby He alone of all the children of men was consecrated the only Son of God.

> In this one man, the whole Church has been assumed by the Word.[59]
> She has been taken from amongst men, in order that her Head might be the very flesh that is united with the Word, and that the faithful might be the members of that Head.[60]
> Let us therefore be in Him, and we shall be assumed . . . for this one man that is taken to become the temple of God is at once one and many.[61]

In the Incarnate Word, therefore, it is not Christ alone that is deserving of love, but Christ and ourselves; or rather, it is not Christ alone, but the whole Christ. This point merits a separate treatment.

§ 6

This is the mystery of charity in the mystery of unity. We recall how intimately these two heavenly realities are united in the Gospel of St. John. Augustine, who has been styled "the Doctor of divine love," follows the example of "the disciple whom Jesus loved." He repeats over and over again that charity is something essential to the Mystical Body. Charity is its first principle, for it owes its very existence to the divine love that has united us all with His Incarnate Son. Charity is also its first consequence, for our union with God and with our fellow men gives rise in us to both the exigency and the power to love God and our brethren with a new, theological love. When this love meets and unites with the divine love, which is ever desirous to enfold us more tightly in its embrace, it becomes the principle of a more intimate union. This latter union now calls for and excites a more intense love, which in turn leads to a union still more profound. In this way do charity and unity beget and intensify each other. But the two are not of the same order: of first importance in the entire work is the divine Charity, while of first importance in us is the unity that joins us to God and to one another.

[434]

So real is this unity that God Himself cannot separate these two that He has joined together; in order to love Christ completely, so to speak, He must love all of us together with our Head.

God, who loves His Son, cannot do otherwise than love the members of His Son. Nor has He any other reason for loving them except that He loves the Son. He loves the Son according to His divinity, since He has begotten the Son equal to Himself; but He loves the Son also in His human nature, because the Only-begotten Word became flesh, and because of the Word the flesh of the Word is dear to Him. Us He loves because we are the members of His well-beloved Son. And, that we might become members, He loved us before we came into existence.

Incomprehensible and immutable is the love wherewith God loves. He did not begin to love us only on the day we were reconciled to Him by the blood of His Son; He loved us before the world was made, that we too might become His sons together with His Only-begotten Son, long before we had any existence. . . .

And since God hates none of the things that He has made, who can adequately describe how dearly He loves the members of His Only-begotten Son? And how much greater is His love for the Only-begotten Himself?

Thus the love wherewith the Father loves the Son is also in us. It is in us because we are the members of the Son; we are loved in Him, because the Son is loved wholly, Head and body.[62]

These words are indeed but a faint echo of Christ's supreme prayer as recorded by St. John: "That the love wherewith Thou hast loved Me may be in them, and I in them" (John 17:26), but at least they express the same broadness and catholicity of outlook.

This all-inclusive catholicity must enter into our own charity, as Augustine teaches in certain beautiful pages that we should like to quote in full. This space will not permit, but we shall cite a few of the more characteristic passages, reserving the most decisive statements until last, for the sake of emphasis.

Charity, says the holy Doctor, should be vast as the world; it should be extended to all, as the grace of God is extended to all; it should be offered not only to those who are already our brothers, but to others as well, even to our enemies, that they too may become our brothers.

> Love all men, even your enemies; love them, not because they are your brothers, but that they may become your brothers. Thus you will ever burn with fraternal love, both for him who is already your brother and for your enemy, that he may by loving become your brother. . . .
> Even he that does not as yet believe in Christ . . . love him, and love him with fraternal love. He is not yet thy brother, but love him precisely that he may be thy brother.
> Thus all our charity is brotherly love, and includes all the members of Christ.[63]

This love, therefore, is generous, as all-embracing as the Church and as international as the Church. See how Augustine brings home this ever-needed lesson of catholic charity:

> Let us therefore run, brothers; let us run toward our heavenly country, and let us love Christ. What Christ? Jesus Christ. Who is He? The Word of God. And how came He to the sick? "The Word was made flesh and dwelt amongst us" (John 1:14). All is therefore accomplished that the Scripture foretold: "that the Christ should suffer, and should rise from the dead on the third day" (Luke 24:46). And where is His body? It is where His members are suffering. Where then shouldst thou be, that thou mayest be under thy Head? "And that in His name should be preached repentance unto forgiveness of sins unto all the nations, beginning from Jerusalem" (Luke 24:47). There let thy love pour itself out. Christ tells us this, and also the Psalm, that is, the Spirit of God, saying: "Thy commandment is exceeding broad" (Ps. 118:96).

Then, in sharp contrast, comes the cry:

> Yet some would limit charity to the land of Africa!

Only too often had Augustine come in contact with the narrow bigotry of schism. And, as always, he protests:

> Extend thy charity over the entire earth if thou wilt love Christ, for the members of Christ are to be found everywhere in the world. If thou lovest only a part, thou art divided; if thou art divided, thou art not in the body; if thou art not in the body, thou art not under the Head.
> What is the use of believing, if thou dost blaspheme? Thou adorest Him as Head, and dost blaspheme Him in His body. He loves His body. Thou canst cut thyself off from the body,

but the Head does not detach itself from its body. "Thou dost honor Me in vain," He cries from heaven, "thou dost honor Me in vain!" If someone wished to kiss thy cheek, but insisted at the same time on trampling thy feet; if with his nailed boots he were to crush thy feet as he tries to hold thy head and kiss thee, wouldst thou not interrupt his expressions of respect and cry out: "What art thou doing, man? Thou art trampling upon me!" . . .

It is for this reason that before He ascended into heaven our Lord Jesus Christ recommended to us His body, by which He was to remain upon earth. For He foresaw that many would pay Him homage because of His glory in heaven, but that their homage would be vain, so long as they despise His members on earth.[64]

Thus we are forced to love our brothers if we are to love Christ. Augustine repeats the same thought with even greater force in another passage of the same homily. This capital text we shall quote by way of conclusion. There is question of one of the closing verses of the first Epistle of St. John:

"Herein we know that we love the children of God, when we love God" (1 John 5:2). What does this mean, my brothers? The preceding verse referred only to the Son of God, not to the children of God. It presented one Christ to us, and told us: "Whoso believeth that Jesus is the Christ, is begotten of God; and whoso loveth the begetter (that is, the Father), loveth also the begotten of Him" (that is, the Son, our Lord Jesus Christ). Then John continues: "herein we know that we love the children of God." . . . He had just said "the Son of God," and now he says "the children of God."

The reason is that the children of God are the body of the only Son of God, and, since He is the Head and we the members, there is but one Son of God. Therefore he that loves the children of God loves the Son of God, and he that loves the Son of God loves the Father. Nor can anyone love the Father unless he love the Son; and he that loves the Son loves also the children of God. What children of God? The members of the Son of God. And by loving he too becomes a member; through love he enters into the unity of the body of Christ, and there shall be one Christ, loving Himself (*et erit unus Christus amans seipsum*).

For when the members love one another, the body loves itself.[65]

This continuity, unity, and interiority of charity are developed at length by Augustine. He finds them treated in St. Paul: it is in order to inculcate these qualities of charity that after saying, "If one member suffereth, all the members suffer therewith; if a member be honored, all the members rejoice therewith," the Apostle immediately adds:

> "Now you are the body of Christ, and severally His members" (1 Cor. 12:26,27). Similar too is the teaching of St. John on the subject of brotherly love: "He that loveth not his brother whom he hath seen, cannot love God whom he hath not seen" (1 John 4:20). But when thou lovest thy brother, perhaps thou lovest him alone, and not Christ? How can that be, when thou lovest the members of Christ? Hence when thou lovest the members of Christ, it is Christ that thou lovest; in loving Christ, thou lovest the Son of God; in loving the Son of God, thou lovest the Father. Therefore love cannot be divided.
>
> Choose to love whomsoever thou wilt: all else will follow. Thou mayest say, "I love only God, God the Father." Wrong! If Thou lovest Him, thou dost not love Him alone; but if thou lovest the Father, thou lovest also the Son. Or thou mayest say, "I love the Father and I love the Son, but these alone: God the Father and God the Son, our Lord Jesus Christ who ascended into heaven and sitteth at the right hand of the Father, the Word by whom all things were made, the Word who was made flesh and dwelt amongst us; only these do I love." Wrong again! If thou lovest the Head, thou lovest also the members; if thou lovest not the members, neither dost thou love the Head.[66]

IV

These passages present in its full force what we may call Augustine's psychological conception of the Mystical Body. Fundamentally it is the same doctrine as that which the Saint proposed against the Donatists and against the Pelagians: it concerns the divine life which is communicated to us in the unity of the Christ Mediator, and the prolongation of the mystery of the Incarnation in the whole Church by means of grace and the divinization of the faithful.

Furthermore, it is the same teaching which we saw in the writings of the Greek Fathers; namely, that in Christianity there is only Christ, who is all things in all men; that therefore Christianity consists in a single doctrine, but a complete ⌣ doctrine, of the whole Christ, God and man, Head and members. All the life of the Church has its source in the Incarnation, the virtue of which extends to all men.

The Greek Fathers, however, and particularly Cyril of Alexandria, have in view rather the divine origin of this unity, while Augustine insists more upon its interior aspects. The Greeks explain more clearly the reason why this unity can take possession of our souls; Augustine helps us to understand better how deeply it penetrates our inmost souls. We have seen that in speaking of this mystical function of Christ neither Augustine nor the Greek Fathers lose sight of the individual personality of the Saviour. On the contrary, the very intensity of His personal life is the necessary condition of His full mystical life. And since the members conform in all things to the condition of their Head, their own individual life, far from suffering any diminution, is rather made more full and complete by reason of its inclusion in so perfect an immanence.

Hence the life of each is a catholic and transcendent reality. All men, even sinners, are our members, or at least should be our members, and our love must include them all, just as they are all included in the design of God.

How pitiful are the clear but restricted views of Donatists and Pelagians in comparison with this immense universalism! The conception of the Mystical Body which Augustine opposed to these errors itself appears stifled and dwarfed in such an unfavorable atmosphere; it cannot represent the full extent and vitality of the Mystical Body.

But here, in the absence of any controversy, these limitations vanish in the distant mists. Not of course that sin no longer exists or that its traces have been effaced. No, but we have something much better, for these things have also been included in the work of God. Suffering, humiliation, and penance, all the consequences of our faults remain in the Mystical Body of which we are the members. But in this body, because of the Christ who is its Head, they become a healing remedy; far from impeding the full development of the organism and the free exercise of all its powers, they help both to extend and to strengthen it.

On such occasions Augustine's doctrine has perhaps less exactitude of expression and more of imagery and enthusiasm. But how well it expresses what is innermost in his own life, in the life of the Church, and in the very life of Christian dogma! It is human, yet most exacting; it is most universal and most psychological; it loses touch neither with the true interior of the soul nor with the interior life of Christ, since it is in Christ that we, the members of the Church, have our inner life.

The doctrine is not, of course, his own invention, nor does he enrich it with any new elements. All he does is to quote the Scriptures, to meditate on what has been said before him by Paul and by John, by Jesus, by Tradition. But God had so fashioned his soul and had so guided his life as to give him a clearer perception of certain treasures concealed within the changeless deposit of revealed truth. In Augustine we see Tradition developing, and Christ continuing His teaching through His saints.

Et erit unus Christus amans seipsum. Probably no words more beautiful ever came from the pen of Augustine. For Christians, there is only Christ. The love of God for us, our love for Him, the love of each for all and of all for each; in short, the very plenitude of charity: not one of these is outside the fullness of Christ. All the effusion of the divinity into our humanity, every real good that is done in the depths of the individual soul, throughout the whole expanse of the earth and down all the ages: all this is one life, immanent as all true life is immanent, and as limitless as eternal Life; one Christ, who builds up His own Body; one Christ, who knows Himself and who loves Himself wholly and entirely. *Et erit unus Christus amans seipsum.*

Chapter V

The Early Middle Ages

⊱⊰

I. *Echoes of St. Augustine.* Early medieval theology was greatly influenced by the doctrine of the Mystical Body as explained in Augustine's sermons. Decline of this influence in later centuries. Two examples:

a) Doctrine of the Eucharist. The relation of the Blessed Sacrament to the Mystical Body of the Saviour. The theology of the *res sacramenti:* its progressive development and general acceptance; then its decline, particularly during the controversy with the Protestant Reformers.

b) Exegesis of the Psalms: "The theme of the Psalter is the whole Christ, Head and members." This is for long the commonly accepted teaching, but it begins to suffer neglect in the sixteenth century.

II. *Some outstanding personalities:* The School of St. Bernard, and more especially William of Saint-Thierry and Isaac of Stella.

a) William of Saint-Thierry. Charity described as a theological love that makes us like to the Man-God.

b) Isaac of Stella. Love of our neighbor; loving the whole Christ. Christ remits sin through the Church. As members of Christ, Christians are sons of the Blessed Virgin and of the Church.

I

THE SERMONS of St. Augustine mark one of the high points in the development of the doctrine of the Mystical Body. After him there comes a period of slow decline. Not that there was any lack of great personalities or of original thinking, however; on the contrary, the more carefully one studies the Middle Ages, the more complex and diversified they appear, while beneath the seeming uniformity of authors who copy

[441]

one from the other, one perceives minds that are keenly tempered and capable of effecting a renewal.

For this reason we do not propose to say all that might be said, or even to study all the principal features of the period. Our sole aim is to unite, by a slender thread if need be, the age of the Fathers with that of the Schoolmen. Hence it will be sufficient to show, by means of a few examples, that St. Augustine continues during the Middle Ages to exert a notable influence upon the doctrine of the Mystical Body as well as upon theology in general, and that at the same time other important developments are being set on foot.

The survival of Augustine's teaching is particularly evident in the theology of the Eucharist and in the interpretation of the Psalms. We shall limit our consideration to these two points.

It was the common and emphatic teaching of the time that the Eucharist is the sacrament of ecclesiastical unity, and that its object is to incorporate us in Christ and with one another. Other doctrinal points relating to the Blessed Sacrament were treated much less adequately. We may mention, for instance, the lack of an exact formula of the dogma of the Real Presence. Authors hesitate or adopt different opinions as to the best way of expressing the relation of the physical body of Christ to the sacred species. Yet all of them, those who accentuate the spiritual aspect of the Presence as well as those who emphasize its realism, are in perfect accord on its relation to the Mystical Body.

In the eleventh century, Adelmann of Liège (c. 1050) and Hildebertus of Lavardin (c. 1100) endeavor to account for the Real Presence by means of a kind of communication of properties in virtue of which Christ's humanity, though limited in itself, is by the divinity rendered omnipresent. The idea calls for correction and clearer explanation, of course, but we mention it here because it has some relation, remote, it is true, with the theory of the Mystical Body.[1]

At the same time, about the eleventh century, begins the gradual elaboration of the Scholastic formula that was to render possible a clear distinction of the rather complex relationships, which, as St. Augustine had already pointed out, exist between the sacramental species, the physical body of Christ, and the Mystical Body. This development was due in great part, it would seem, to the School of Chartres. The formula was outlined by St. Fulbert (d. 1029), who was the founder of the school, and supplemented by one of his disciples, Alger of Liège (d. 1131), in the treatise *De sacramento corporis et sanguinis dominici,* which, with that of Paschasius Radbertus, surpasses in beauty all other works written on the Blessed Sacrament during this period. Guitmond (c. 1075), another disciple of Fulbert, likewise deserves to be mentioned in this connection. At last the classic formula is expressed by Peter the Lombard (c. 1150). All who write after him agree in saying that the Eucharist is at once a sacred sign [sacrament] and a sacred reality. Hence a distinction is drawn between what is the mere sign, what is both sign and sacred reality, and what is the sacred reality alone: *sacramentum tantum, sacramentum et res, res tantum.* The sacrament considered as sign consists of the species of bread and wine; the sacrament which is also the sacred reality is Christ present beneath the species; and lastly, the sacred reality, represented by the symbolism of the species and produced by the very body of Christ, is the unity of the Church.

When it had once been proposed, this teaching becomes common property, and is handed on from one author to another. With the passage of time, however, it receives less and less attention. The doctrine is stated once more, and emphatically, by the Council of Trent. But from this time forward the controversy against the Protestants leads writers to treat the subject with great caution. Generally speaking, the mystical symbolism of the Eucharist was about all that the heretics would admit; hence this particular point, which they do not deny, and which their exaggerations have rendered almost suspect, is passed over without comment, while every effort is concentrated on the study and proof of the fact of the Real Presence, which they do deny.

Much the same may be said of the interpretation of the Psalms, which we mentioned as a further instance of the survival of Augustine's teaching. The Saint's statement that

[443]

the entire Psalter speaks only of Christ, of Christ united with His body, or in other words, of Christ and His Church, is a familiar saying during the early Middle Ages. The subject matter of the Psalms is declared to be the whole Christ, Head and members. In the Golden Age of Scholasticism it is maintained by St. Thomas (d. 1274), Hugh of Saint-Cher (c. 1234), William of Saint-Amour (d. 1272), and later on by Michael Aiguani (d. 1400), James Parez of Valencia (d. 1490), Catharinus (1487–1553), John Baptist Folengo (1490–1559), Bottens (d. 1717), and others, who continue to say that the Psalter never speaks of anything but Christ, Head and body, and that it is of little importance to know whether this or that verse refers to Christ or to the Church, since the two are one and the same thing.

But in the sixteenth and seventeenth centuries this interpretation is gradually abandoned. The pressing needs of the controversy against Protestantism impel exegetes to substitute the historical and philological methods in its stead.

II

One might naturally expect the name of St. Bernard (1090–1153) to figure prominently among the commentators of whom we have been speaking. The truth is that the holy abbot seldom introduces the idea of our incorporation in Christ in his explanation of Scripture. As a general rule he and his school have little to say of the Mystical Body. Union with Christ they conceive primarily under the aspect of love. Of this love, intense and personal, for the Saviour and for His Virgin Mother, they speak with a depth of feeling that is unparalleled in earlier writings.

But, though St. Bernard did not personally contribute to the development of the doctrine of the Mystical Body, he made it possible for certain of his disciples to do so. We refer to William of Saint-Thierry and Isaac of Stella.

William of Saint-Thierry, a native of Liège and later abbot of Saint-Thierry near Rheims, was a friend and admirer of St. Bernard. He is almost the latter's equal for intense spirituality, profound contemplation and unction of language, while he discourses on the subject of divine love with an ardor which surpasses even that of his master. His treatise *De contemplando Deo*, one of the most beautiful works of the Middle Ages, is one long cry of love. He shows how charity is the action of God within us, penetrating and sustaining us, drawing our activity into the divine activity and fusing the two into one. What he expresses in these terms is not precisely our incorporation in Christ, but a consequence of this incorporation and of the divinization which it produces in us. It is the new love that corresponds to our new being. Since this consequence is so characteristic, and since the passage in which William explains it provides a remarkable complement to the texts we have already cited on the subject of charity, we shall quote it here.

Love is nothing else than an ardent and well-disposed will (*vehemens et bene ordinata voluntas*).

Thou therefore dost love Thyself in Thyself, O lovable God, when from the Father and from the Son proceeds the Holy Spirit, the love of the Father for the Son and the love of the Son for the Father. So intense is this love that it is unity; and so great is this unity that it is consubstantiality.

And Thou lovest Thyself in us, when Thou sendest the Spirit of Thy Son into our hearts; in the sweetness of love and the ardent good will that Thou inspirest in us, He cries: "Abba, Father" (Rom. 8:15). Thus dost Thou make us love Thee; or rather, it is thus that Thou lovest Thyself in us. We could only hope before . . . but now, through the inspiration of Thy grace and by the Spirit of adoption, we have confidence that whatever the Father has is ours; and through the grace of our adoption we invoke Thee by the very name with which He addresses Thee who is Thy only Son by nature. . . .

Thou dost love us, because Thou makest us love Thee; and we love Thee because we receive from Thee Thy Spirit . . . who transforms us into the purity of Thy truth and into the truth of Thy purity, in perfect conformity with Thy love. This produces so great an attachment and union, such enjoyment of Thy sweetness, that our Lord, Thy Son, called it Unity, saying: "That they may be one in Us," and so great a dignity and glory that He immediately added: "as I and Thou are one" (John 17:21,22). O joy, O glory, O riches, O pride! For wisdom too has a special kind of pride. . . .

We love Thee, or Thou lovest Thyself in us; we by our affections, Thou by Thy power. And Thou dost make us one by

[445]

Thy unity, that is, by Thy Holy Spirit, whom Thou hast given to us.

Just as for the Father, to know the Son is nothing else than to be what the Son is; and as for the Son, to know the Father is nothing else than to be what the Father is . . . and as for the Holy Spirit, to know and to comprehend the Father and the Son is nothing else than to be what the Father is and what the Son is, so too for us (who were created to Thy image, who have seen that image disfigured by Adam, and who see it renewed each day by Christ), so for us who love God, to love and fear God and to observe His commandments is nothing else than to be with God and to be one spirit with God. For to fear God and keep His commandments is the whole man (Eccles. 12:13).

O adorable, awful, and most blessed God, give us this Spirit. "Send forth Thy Spirit and they shall be created, and Thou shalt renew the face of the earth" (Ps. 103:30). . . . Long enough has this cataclysm continued, long enough has been the punishment of the sons of Adam. Bring Thy Spirit upon the earth. . . . Let us be sanctified by Thy holiness, and let us be united by Thy unity.[2]

The deep emotion that pulsates throughout the passage illustrates the fact that despite their seeming uniformity, many writers of the period were gifted with a very distinctive individuality. The lines we have quoted bear comparison with the finest pages of St. Augustine. What is more, they supplement what he taught. In the charity that unites God, Christ, and men, the bishop of Hippo showed us "one Christ, loving Himself." The Abbot of Saint-Thierry takes a further step: insisting upon the divinization that we receive in Christ, he represents Christian charity as an operation in which God's activity and our own are fused and united in one theandric reality. We love God through God, and all supernatural love constitutes, so to speak, one God, loving Himself in Jesus Christ.

This formula is more "theological" than Augustine's "one Christ loving Himself." It is also a forceful expression of one of the consequences of our incorporation in the Word made flesh, namely, the divinization of our activity in Christ, which follows from the divinization of our being in Christ.

Isaac of Stella was an English Cistercian. He had come from

England to France and been made abbot of l'Etoile, near Poitiers. Isaac, too, is a great admirer of St. Bernard. He is less emotional than William of Saint-Thierry and more given to complex speculative developments; but, because of his calmer tone and his intimate acquaintance with the works of St. Augustine his teaching is more like that of the great Doctor. In addition, he is thoroughly grounded in the doctrine of St. Bernard, and has a very personal and interesting manner of presentation. It is strange that so remarkable a man should have been studied so little. Although our treatment of this period must necessarily be brief, we feel that a few quotations from his works will not be out of place.

The following passage on the love of the neighbor will serve as a complement of the text we have just quoted from William of Saint-Thierry:

> Therefore, my brothers, let this be your manner of life (for this is the true training for holy living): to converse in thought and desire with Christ in our heavenly country, and in our earthly pilgrimage to refuse no service of charity for the sake of Christ. Let us follow the Lord Christ in heaven in our dealings with the Father, by attenuating ourselves, simplifying ourselves, uniting ourselves with Him in the quiet of contemplation. And let us follow Christ here below in our dealings with our neighbor, by extending our activity, multiplying ourselves, by making ourselves all to all (*actione distendi, multifariam dividi, omnibus omnia fieri*). Let us despise nothing that is done for Christ; let us thirst for one alone, and be occupied with one alone, where Christ is one; and let us be ready to serve all, where Christ is many.

The service of all men, we are told, is primarily the work of the body, and the contemplation of Christ is the occupation of the soul.

> The soul must tend upwards, the flesh downwards, in order that the whole man may follow the whole Christ, and that the whole man may serve the whole Christ. . . .
> If therefore the flesh sees its image [a poor man] in infirmity beneath itself, let it not shrink away; let it not refuse its service or withdraw, but let it touch reverently. Never does the soul more truly merit to see its image [Christ] which is above in truth, than when the flesh bends down in charity to its own image [the afflicted] which is beneath it.[3]

[447]

The development is a bit awkward but how strikingly it illustrates true Christian charity and the mystical identity of the Saviour with the poor!

We shall quote two other passages, in which the Abbot represents the Church as the Mystical Body and the prolongation of Christ. The first, which refers to the sacrament of Penance, may be compared with the texts in which St. Augustine declares that even with us Christ still remains one. Christ alone forgives sins, remarks Isaac of Stella. How then can we say that the Church forgives sins, unless the Church, when united with Christ, is still Christ, Christ alone, but the whole Christ?

The Bridegroom, who is one nature (*unum*) with the Father, is one person (*unus*) with His Bride. He has cast out and nailed to the Cross every foreign element that He found in her. He bore her sins upon the wood and destroyed them by the wood. What was natural and proper to her He took unto Himself, and what was proper to Himself and divine He has given to her. Therefore He has cast out the diabolical, assumed the human, and given the divine, in order that whatever belongs to the Bride may belong also to the Bridegroom, and that whatever belongs to the Bridegroom may belong also to the Bride.

This interchange accounts for the dignity of confession and for the power to remit sins. Christ has said: "Get thee hence and show thyself to the priest" (Luke 5:14). This power becomes no less truly and solely Christ's by belonging to the Church; nay, it would not belong to the whole Christ unless it did belong to the Church. In like manner this power is no less truly and solely God's power by being Christ's, and would not belong to the whole God, so to speak, if it were not Christ's.

Hence let no sinner consider himself healed after he has groaned in his heart, where sin is forgiven by Christ alone, but not by the whole Christ. If he neglects to present himself to the priest, to whom is given the power of remitting sin, and to whom, therefore, is due the homage of confession, the leprosy will return. . . .

Thus the Church can forgive no sin without Christ, and Christ wills to forgive none without the Church. . . . Strictly speaking, Christ the all-powerful can do all things: He can baptize, consecrate the Eucharist, ordain, remit sin. But this humble and faithful Bridegroom wills to do none of these things without the Bride. "What God hath joined together let no man put asunder" (Matt. 19:6). . . . Christ did not will to be decapitated, but to be laid upon the Cross, to be stretched upon it and to hang from it, in order to unite all things, the low and the high, and those between. Do not therefore take away the Head, for then the whole Christ would exist nowhere. For nowhere is Christ complete without the Church, just as the Church can nowhere be whole and entire without Christ. The whole Christ, the complete Christ, is the Head and body. . . .

This is the one Man who alone can forgive sins. First He touches the sinner inwardly, to arouse repentance in his heart; then He sends him to the priest, outwardly, for oral confession; lastly, the priest sends him to God, to perform works of satisfaction.[4]

Certain points mentioned in the passage, and particularly what concerns the proper efficacy of absolution, call for a more accurate explanation at the hands of later theologians. Complete and perfect formulas had not yet been developed for every detail of the doctrine of penance. But few authors give evidence of so profound an appreciation of the necessity for the Church's intervention in obtaining the divine pardon for sin. In order to have the whole Christ, to have Christ as He is, we must take Him in the Church; and to have Christ's pardon totally and really, we must seek it in the Church's pardon.

To this passage concerning the theology of the sacraments, we may join the following, which treats of Mariology. In a sermon on the Assumption of our Lady, the author uses the idea of the Mystical Body to explain the divine Motherhood of the Blessed Virgin.

The First-born of many brothers, who was the only Son by nature, has by grace taken to Himself many brothers, who are one with Him. . . .

Of themselves, by reason of their birth according to the flesh, these are many; but by their new, divine birth they are one with Him. The one and complete and sole Christ is the Head and the body. This One is the only Son of one God in heaven and of one Mother on earth. There are many sons, and there is but one Son.

And, as the Head and members are one Son and many sons, so Mary and the Church are one Mother and two mothers, one Virgin and two virgins. Both are mothers, both virgins. Both have conceived, by the power of the same Holy Spirit, without concupiscence; both have brought forth children to God the Father without sin. The first, without any sin, has given the body its Head; the other, by the remission of all sins, has given the Head its body. Both are Mothers of Christ; but neither has given birth to the whole Christ without the other. Hence in the divinely inspired Scriptures, what is said in general of the virgin mother Church is true of the Virgin Mother Mary in particular; and what is said of the Virgin Mother Mary in particular is to be understood also of the virgin mother Church in general, so that whatever is said of the one may ordinarily be applied equally to the other.[5]

As we see, Isaac of Stella is a theologian. In this brief passage he links up ecclesiology, Mariology, Christology, and the doctrine of grace. Mary is the Mother of Christians for the same reason that God is their Father: that is to say, because of their mystical identity with the Incarnate Word, who is the Son of God and of the Virgin Mother of God. And the Church, which is ever bringing forth children to God, is typified by the Mother of Jesus, since the faithful are Christ continued.

Chapter VI

The Scholastics — 1. "The Grace of Headship"

>—<

I. 1. *The Scholastics.* Apparent regression of the doctrine of the Mystical Body. The causes of the regression. Nevertheless some progress is made, mainly during the two great epochs of Scholasticism: the thirteenth and sixteenth centuries.

2. The Schoolmen complete the doctrine of the Mystical Body as proposed by Augustine in answer to the Pelagians. The treatise on the "Grace of Head" in Christ; development and general plan of the treatise. We shall consider one by one the different parts of the Mystical Body.

II. *"Gratia capitis."* 1. Christ possesses the "grace of Head."

2. This Headship consists principally in a real, physical power to communicate (*influere*) grace to us. Christ is Head according to His human nature.

III. 1. He is Head according to the whole substance, and in every act of this human nature. Physical influence of His Passion and Resurrection upon the entire Church; the divinization of our whole life, and even of our ills.

2. A theory of the Redemption based upon Christ's Headship; historical significance of the theory.

I. § 1

THE AUGUSTINIAN tradition that had been so characteristic a feature of the early Middle Ages suffers a gradual decline during the age of the Scholastics. One notices at the first contact with their works that the doctrine of the Mystical Body no longer occupies its position of prominence; rarely is it mentioned, and even then it is spoken of with great moderation.

There is a reason for this reserve: it is the natural consequence of the providential role assigned to the Schoolmen. Theirs was the task of "summing up" the revealed truth, of expressing the dogmas of faith with the greatest clarity, in the most logical order, and with the greatest coherence possible. A formidable task indeed, but with God's help they brought it to a successful conclusion. Because of their efforts, fuller light is thrown on Christian thought and mistakes are more readily avoided.

It was only natural that these men of precision should devote little study to a truth so mysterious as our incorporation in Christ. The doctrine always and necessarily retains a certain vagueness which, to judge from the mentality of many of the Scholastics, was scarcely calculated to win their sympathy.

A further cause of neglect lay in the circumstances, favorable and unfavorable, of which Providence made use in directing the thought of the age. Platonism was steadily giving way to the system of Aristotle. Rigorously defined concepts were the order of the day, and there was a fashion, almost a fever, for dialectics. On the other hand, much of what the Fathers had said of the Mystical Body was suggested by Platonist ideas, and it was no easy matter to define the Mystical Body in the precise formulas required for syllogistic argumentation.

At this period, too, the old Roman Law was again gaining the ascendancy in the nascent States and in the minds of men; it even invaded the domain of theology. Not that the Scholastics were all jurists; such a conclusion would be exaggerated and misleading. But they were men of their time. Not a few took pride in showing that Christian doctrine could be expressed *ad apices iuris*, quite as well as any other science, in terms of contracts, divine decrees, promises, etc. As a matter of fact these concepts had been introduced into theology long before, nor do we see any solid reason that would warrant their exclusion. Law is too human a thing, and Christianity likewise is too human a thing, in the sense that God has adapted it perfectly to our nature; hence it is not only possible, but legitimate and even desirable that the two should go hand in hand. Unquestionably the union was at times carried to excessive lengths, but the abuse of a thing is no argument against its use. We wish to make it quite clear that in our opinion a juridical interpretation of the Gospel is perfectly justifiable in principle, and, provided it be kept within reasonable limits, it may even contribute to doctrinal progress.

At the same time one must admit the fact, evident in itself, that the coincidence between law and Christianity is far from perfect, and that not all the truths of our religion can be adequately expressed in legal terms. In particular, our union with Christ, this prodigy of love and mercy, is distinctly opposed to the cold rigidity of legal codes, and a juridical turn of mind would scarcely predispose a man to speak either at length or with enthusiasm upon such a subject.

A similar phenomenon accompanied the rise of the Protestant controversies in the sixteenth century. It is true that a new impetus was then given to the study of theology: new weapons had to be prepared and new treatises developed; we witness the appearance of controversial works, of studies made on the sources of theology, on the Church, on indulgences, on justification. The treatment of these matters becomes more positive and more historical. But, with a few exceptions which we shall indicate, the doctrine of the Mystical Body receives little benefit from this renewal. It does not appear, on first sight at any rate, to be connected with the points at issue, and, precisely because of its mysteriousness, it does not readily lend itself to the purposes of controversy and disputation.

Thus the principal factors that influenced the development of Scholastic theology: the Aristotelian revival, the passion for dialectics, the favor enjoyed by juridicism, and the struggle with the Reformers — all these tended to hamper the growth of the doctrine of the Mystical Body. Such is the law of things human: progress rarely takes the form of an advance along the entire front; the army must feel its way forward, with a local success here and a temporary delay there. But when the movement is viewed as a whole, these delays are only apparent; each division of the army profits by the advance of the others, and the brave men who hold the penetrating wedge are preparing the way for a movement all along the line. So, too, it is with Christian teaching. The truth of the Mystical Body cannot be dissociated from the other truths. Despite an apparent stagnation, despite the superficial and unconscious suspicion that it engendered, the doctrine actually receives new perfection at the hands of the Schoolmen. Most important of all, it is made ready for further progress.

We are not in a position to indicate the various stages of its development in medieval history. For, although this field of research is fully as vast as any other, it has probably received the least attention of all. We can only say that the most marked progress takes place during the two most glorious periods of Scholastic theology itself: the thirteenth and sixteenth centuries. The thirteenth witnesses the reaction of Christian thought to the philosophy of Aristotle; the sixteenth beholds the composition of the great defensive works against the Protestant heresy. During the first period, which is the formative stage, so to speak, of Scholasticism, the treatise on the Mystical Body also receives its structure and its essential content; while during the second, a time of rehabilitation and of progress for Scholasticism in general, our treatise takes on renewed vigor and is enriched with new elements.

But this historical progress, though real, is not well enough defined to furnish a clear-cut plan of study. Indeed, from its first beginnings down to our own day — for it still lives — the Scholastic doctrine of the Mystical Body has remained sufficiently the same, and its development has been sufficiently continuous to make it impossible to discern any interruptions or divisions.

Hence in our present study we shall depart from the chronological order and adopt the logical. The Schoolmen have left us a systematic treatise of the Mystical Body. The plan of that treatise shall be ours; we shall consider each of its parts in succession, and in connection with each part we shall call attention to views that are peculiar to certain authors, and we shall indicate the new contributions that are made in the course of the centuries. This method will bring us back again, in a certain sense, to the chronological order. The first three chapters will be concerned chiefly with the earlier period, while the fourth chapter and the end of the second chapter will be devoted mainly to the later epoch.

§ 2

As is usual for medieval theology, the point of departure of the entire movement is found in St. Augustine. In the pre-

Scholastic age we saw that the Latin doctrine of the Mystical Body was in large part a survival of the teaching of the Doctor of Grace. Authors repeat the Saint's statements concerning the unity of the Head and body, and concerning the one man who is Christ plus the Christians. While these formulas are full of theological significance, they are rather devotional than technical, and lose their force of connotation with the passage of time. We likewise observed that the tradition grows weaker in proportion to its distance from Augustine. Yet at this very time, when Augustine's influence is lessening in one direction, it is being accentuated in another. The Scholastics preserve but little of the doctrine of the Mystical Body as proposed by the Saint in his sermons to the faithful. Meanwhile, however, without intending to do so, perhaps — but what does that matter? — they take up and complete the teaching as expressed in his anti-Pelagian writings. This is a doctrine less rich in applications, in references to the interior life, in energy and directness, but it is also clearer, more systematic, and better suited to the dialectic mind.

We studied this doctrine in the third chapter of this part of our work. It consists in a general tableau of the economy of redemption, representing the whole life of grace in the members of the Mystical Body as a prolongation of that supreme grace whereby the Head of the body is constituted the very Son of God and the Holy of holies.

This teaching is adopted by the Scholastics when they come to speak of the grace which is given to Christ. It is here that they describe the dignity which belongs to Christ as the source of grace for all humankind and as Head of a body of regenerated members.

The development of which we speak begins at a very early date. The works that should be consulted, if we were to trace its very first beginnings, have either never been published, or are now lost. The few indications that can be gleaned from the *De sacramentis christianae fidei* of Hugh of St. Victor, from the anonymous *Sententiae divinitatis* (c. 1148), and from the *Elucidarium* of Honorius of Autun, already contain certain elements, though not co-ordinated, of what was to become the treatise on Christ, the Head of the Mystical Body.

[455]

But these are only preliminary efforts. What actually started the movement, a movement that was to suffer no interruption until it had run its full course, was the *Sententiarum libri quattuor* of Peter the Lombard, composed about 1150 or 1152. Hence we are already in the middle of the twelfth century.

The author opens his third book with a treatise on the Incarnation. At the thirteenth distinction he asks the question: "Was it possible for Christ in His human nature to grow in wisdom and grace, and did He actually make such progress?" The answer is long, and there is no need of considering it in full. Certain remarks, however, are connected with our subject. The "Master of the Sentences" states that Christ's human nature possesses wisdom and grace: first, because it has become one Person with the Word; secondly, because it has been sanctified intrinsically; and lastly, because it has been made the principle of sanctification for all Christians. Thus there are in Christ three distinct kinds of holiness, three distinct graces: the grace of the hypostatic union, His personal grace, and the grace of Mystical Head. This last is the point that interests us. The Lombard himself is very brief in his treatment of it, but fortunately his commentators present a fuller explanation, so that the study of the "Grace of Head," or the grace which Christ possesses as Head of the Mystical Body, becomes a little treatise by itself.

The first of these commentators to be mentioned is Peter of Poitiers, who wrote twenty or thirty years after the Lombard. One of his works, the *Sententiarum libri quinque,* has come down to us. In content and general plan the book is very similar to the *Sentences,* and in almost the same place, the author includes a treatise on the grace of Christ, in which he speaks of the grace of Headship. He asks a question which already presupposes a rather advanced theological development on this point: "Is Christ Head of the Church according to His human nature, or according to His divine nature?" He replies at great length, considering the matter from a variety of viewpoints, with many deductions and arguments, and touches upon all the points that were soon to be embodied in the treatise on the grace of Head. However, the treatise itself does not yet appear.

[456]

Twenty or thirty years later we see it beginning to take definite shape in the *Summa aurea* of William of Auxerre. Now the principal divisions of the treatise are discernible. Shortly afterwards, Alexander of Hales takes up the same treatise and develops it at length in his *Universa theologiae summa*. For the time being we shall merely take note of an interesting expression which occurs in his work and in that of William of Auxerre. This statement shows clearly that the consideration of the Mystical Body does not cause these men to lose sight of the concrete and visible aspect of our religion: the physical body of Christ, they tell us, is the sacred sign, the "sacrament," of the Mystical Body.

Now come the very greatest of the Schoolmen: first, St. Albert the Great treats the question in his *Commentarii in libros sententiarum* and *Quaestiones de Incarnatione;* then St. Bonaventure, in his *Commentarius in quattuor libros sententiarum Petri Lombardi* and in his *Breviloquium;* finally, St. Thomas takes it up in the *Scriptum super sententiis magistri Petri Lombardi,* develops it further in *De veritate* and in the *Compendium theologiae ad Reginaldum,* and at last gives it its definitive form in the *Summa theologica.*

Little more is added by the successors and commentators of St. Thomas. Generally speaking, the Thomists are particularly faithful in treating of the grace of Headship. The Scotists, following the example of the *Doctor Subtilis,* often say nothing about it. The Jesuits, who appear on the scene later on, are likewise brief in their consideration of the subject, at least until the nineteenth century. We refer only to Jesuit theologians; the exegetes, such as Maldonatus, Giustiniani, and Cornelius à Lapide have more to say.

One may, therefore, take almost any commentary on the *Sentences* or on the *Summa,* and he will find, almost always in the same section (the thirteenth distinction of the third book of the *Sentences,* or the eighth question of the third part of the *Summa*), a short treatise arranged in the following order:

Firstly, Christ possesses the "Grace of Head," because He is "Head" of the Church and because He communicates (*in-*

fluit) supernatural life to the whole Church which is His body.

Secondly, the members of this Head are all men in general, at least all those who can still save their souls. At this point our authors frequently propose questions such as these: "Are pagans and infidels members of Christ? Are heretics? The just of the Old Testament? The angels? Or again, are men members of Christ by reason of their souls only, or also by reason of their bodies?"

Finally, they examine the relation that exists, in Christ Himself, between His grace of Headship, the grace that sanctifies Him personally, and the grace which consists in His union with the Word. They ask, too, whether this Headship is proper to Christ alone, or whether, and in what manner, He shares it with ecclesiastical superiors.

To these are often added certain considerations regarding the "body of the damned," whose head is Satan. These latter articles however, are of slight importance; since they are but the remnants of speculations on the "body of the devil," which Ticonius long before had set up in contrast to the body of Christ, they receive little attention from the Scholastics. Despite all that has been said of the Middle Ages, demonology never invaded the field of theology, and we are quite content to imitate the silence of our masters on this subject.

It is to be noted that the Scholastics, in writing of the grace of Headship, have produced a veritable treatise on the Church. Incidentally, this is the principal treatise on the Church that is to be found in their works; ecclesiology had not as yet been assigned a definite place in their systematic exposition. Yet so intimate is the union of Head and body that when they treat of the Head and discuss His most personal gifts, that is, the graces whereby His human nature is sanctified, the Schoolmen are naturally led to speak of the organism to which this grace is communicated for the sanctification of all Christians.

Later on, it is true, this bond of union between Head and members seems to become less intimate, as we shall see in the eighteenth century and later. The treatise on the grace of Head is by many authors removed from its position at the center of Christology, and even its name is changed. It becomes a study of Christ's title of Head, and is joined with other similar considerations of Christ as King, Christ as Priest, Christ as Mediator. Together these form a kind of appendix to Christology, devoted to the study of the Saviour's glory and dignity. Where this method is adopted, the grace of Head usually receives a rather brief treatment.

This arrangement, however, was destined to be only temporary. The treatise is taken out of Christology only to become a part of ecclesiology, where, as a matter of fact, we find it today. When modern Scholastics wish to show the nature of the Church's hidden life, and how she unites souls to the one Saviour, they explain that she is the Mystical Body of Christ, through which Christ communicates (*influit*) grace to men.

Thus the moderns speak of the Head by describing the body, while the older Scholastics argued to the nature of the body from the nature of the Head. Again and always, the members and the Head are inseparable.

II. § 1

Now that we have an idea of the general content and history of the treatise on the "grace of Head," we must now consider each of its elements in greater detail. In this and the following chapter we shall study those that have to do with the Head; in the last two chapters we shall examine those that refer to the members.

The questions that are proposed on the subject of the Head may be divided into two classes: the first refers directly to the grace of Headship itself, and the second deals with the relation of this grace to the two other graces of the Saviour, the grace of union and His individual grace. We shall divide the subject matter of these first two chapters in the same way.

First of all, the Scholastics set out to prove the existence of this grace of Headship. On this point no references are necessary, since it is admitted by all who write on this matter. Many even add that it is a truth of faith, because it is frequently and clearly expressed in the Scriptures. The proofs that they adduce in support of this view are ordinarily limited to the well-known texts in which St. Paul expresses the relationship of the Head and members (Eph. 4:15, 1:12; Col. 1:18, 2:10; 1 Cor. c. 12; Rom. 12:5). Other passages of St. Paul and St. John, which describe the Church as the continuation of Christ (Gal. 3:27; Col. 3:11; John cc. 15 and 17, etc.), appear far less frequently. The absence of the latter texts accounts partially for the fact that certain of the elements of the doctrine of the Mystical Body are not so well brought out by our authors.

Now, what is meant by the grace of Head? The term itself, say the Scholastics, is a metaphor suggested by the human body. They note with St. Augustine that while the head is of the same nature as the other members, it is nevertheless superior to them. It alone possesses all the senses, whereas the rest of the body has only the sense of touch; and besides, it communicates life and direction to the entire organism. The same is true of Christ. Though He is consubstantial with us, He is superior to us by reason of the hypostatic union; He possesses in Himself the fullness of supernatural life, of which we receive only a limited share, and it is from Him that this life flows into each Christian.

Therefore, the Scholastics conclude, Christ is truly Head, in the sense that He truly has the same relation to the Church as the head has to the body. According to this explanation it is clear that when our authors state that the term "Head" is a metaphor, they do not by any means intend to deny the vital unity that attaches us to Him, but simply to prevent anyone from understanding this unity in a crude sense.

They are likewise very careful to explain that Christ is "Head" of the Church in an infinitely higher sense than that in which the superior part of the human body is the head of the rest of the organism. Christ has absolutely no need of the other members; He receives from them neither assistance nor holiness, whereas the head cannot live without the organism. Furthermore, it is He who builds up His own body and who makes His own members. These two prerogatives, commonly proposed by the Scholastics, lead many of them to compare the role of Head with that of the heart, or even with that of the soul. Moreover, it is the universal teaching, at least after the time of St. Thomas, that Christ is not a member of the Church in any strict sense. The contrary view had occasionally been defended before St. Thomas, but always with qualifications, and it appears even in the writings of the Angelic Doctor. The reason for this was the Vulgate reading: "You are all the body of Christ, and members of member" (1 Cor. 12:27, D.V.). This last phrase, "members of member," it was argued, could mean only "members of Christ." Therefore Christ, too, is a member of the body.

This exegesis and this opinion did not enjoy favor for long. As time goes on the Scholastics speak of it more and more reservedly, and often the opposite view is considered so certain that it is made the basis of the following objection: "How can Christ be the Head of the Church, since He is not a member?" The answer consists of a series of distinctions between the divinity and the humanity of Christ, between the "body" of Christ considered in the widest possible sense and the "body" of Christ in the strict sense, between the term "member," as connoting the imperfection of being only a part (*partialitas*), and "member" inasmuch as it signifies merely union with the organism.

Keeping all due proportion, of course, and remembering that the humanity of Christ derives all its excellence from the divine nature, one may say that the relation between the faithful and Christ is like that which exists between creatures and God. Just as the world, which after all is something, adds nothing to God's perfection, so with all due proportion, we repeat, it may be said that the members confer no new holiness upon Christ when they are joined to Him or when they receive a closer union with Him. In the words of Cardinal de Torquemada, there is no more grace in the Mystical Body, Head and members combined, than there is in Christ alone.

And just as the transcendence of God, which makes it impossible for Him to receive any perfection from us, is at the same time the reason why He contains our whole being supereminently in Himself; so, too, the elevation of Christ, which precludes His being a part of the body, nevertheless brings Him into even closer union with the entire organism, since it makes Him its very unity and totality. Hence, if the Scholas-

[461]

tics refuse to consider Christ as a member like the others, it is not that they wish to separate Him from us; rather, they do so in order to unite Him still more intimately with all. Thus our authors have their own way of expressing a thought which is less often explicitly stated in their writings than in the works of their predecessors; namely, that Christ is not only the "Head" of the Church, but that He is also, mystically, the whole Church.

§ 2

As Head of the Church, Christ "pours" life (*influit sensum et motum*) into the entire organism. *Influit:* He diffuses, causes to flow, communicates life. Let us note the word. It is traditional: it was in embryo in the Church from the beginning. It is a consecrated word: the Schoolmen have made it the technical expression of our relation to Christ. Lastly, it is a significant word: if the masters of medieval theology, with all their fondness for clear concepts, unanimously adopt at this point a term so indefinite as the verb *influere*, in preference to the Aristotelian concept of causes and even of instrumental cause — an idea which was so suited to their mentality and which they employ so regularly elsewhere — there must be some good reason. The reality of a mysterious organism and of a supernatural life flow must needs have struck them with compelling force.

It is true that when the time comes for further explanation of this vital flow and of this organism, many turn to more definite concepts; as might have been expected, some even strip the term of its natural meaning, and speak only of a system of juridical relationships. Especially is this tendency noticeable in the sixteenth and seventeenth centuries, when monarchy was enjoying its greatest prestige. Such theologians are pleased to explain "Head" in the sense of "king," and they readily represent the Head of the Mystical Body as a plenary, uncontested authority exercised in a society.

But they who thus translate theology into politics are few. The majority are content with certain comparisons borrowed from the administration of kingdoms and which do not nullify the special significance of the term "Head." Some go even further, and openly reject this minimizing interpretation. St. Thomas had already noted that Christ is Head in an entirely higher sense than are human, and even ecclesiastical superiors, for the reason that His "influence" consists not in external direction merely, but in the infusion of a most immanent life. Quite naturally, this distinction receives greatest emphasis in the disputes with the Reformers. Catholic controversialists explain that while the Church has visible superiors in addition to the one invisible Superior, nevertheless she has only one Head, since the invisible Head is the sole source of the interior and mysterious life that sustains the entire organism.

The influx of Christ is unlike any other. Thus, according to the explanation proposed by Driedo of Turnhout, we enjoy with our Head, Christ, a communion that we can never have with any king.

When we become members under the Head who is Christ, we are united to Him by the ineffable operation of the Holy Spirit, and we pass into Christ. We put on Christ, we are engrafted upon Him by means of an incorporation and a union that make us divine.[1]

Elsewhere in their works, and especially when they treat of the power of Christ, our authors state clearly that this influx is not simply a moral entity, not a mere juridical communication of merits and satisfaction. St. Thomas and his school, along with many other Scholastics, declare that it is an activity of the physical order, *per efficientiam*. In fact, certain passages seem to imply that there is question here of a physiological causality, exerted by means of a vital continuity. There is today much discussion of this notion of physical influx on the part of Christ's humanity, and it is interesting to observe how the idea is related to the more central truth of our incorporation in Christ.

Furthermore, this power is at work in a vast field of activity. According to our authors it enters not only into the bestowal of grace, but into every supernatural transformation that conduces to the fulfillment of the purpose of the Incarnation, which is to recapitulate all things in Christ. Zumel writes:

It is according to Christian philosophy that, as the Father

[463]

has done all things in the natural order through the Word, so too He has done all things in the supernatural order through the merits of Christ. And just as in the order of nature God acts as a rule only through secondary causes, so in the order of supernature and of grace He acts only through the humanity of Christ, which is hypostatically united with the Word. In it are contained, as in a fountain head (*arca fontalis*), all the spiritual goods and gifts that are conferred on men, and from it they flow into us. Therefore Christ's humanity is the universal cause of spiritual gifts.[2]

Immense though this activity be, it is exercised, not by the divinity of Christ, but by His humanity. On this point all the Scholastics, with very few exceptions, are agreed: Christ is Head of mankind in His human nature. As God, of course, He is the Lord and principle of all things; but as God He is neither the first-born of our race nor the organism of grace in whose fullness we are saved.

This view had already been expressed by the Fathers in explaining the very similar doctrine of the mediation of the Saviour. It is Christ's humanity that unites the human race to the divinity. The same is true in the conferring of grace: it is because Christ is of the same nature as ourselves and because He is in contact with us that He can communicate life to us.

III. § 1

Just as Christ is Mediator by reason of His entire humanity, so is He Head by reason of His entire humanity. His flesh and blood, as well as His intellect and His soul, are the source of our divine life.

> Even what is corporal in Christ has a spiritual power, on account of the divinity that is united with it; and for this reason it acts in us by means of a spiritual contact.[3]

Not only the Saviour's whole humanity, but every act of that humanity exercises this influx upon us. When our authors speak in this strain, they do not mean mere moral causality by way of intercession and merit, but a physical and efficient causality. St. Thomas and many of his disciples are quite definite on this point. As a matter of fact, in so doing they simply continue the ancient tradition. They repeat with the Fathers that all the actions of the Saviour, especially His passion and death, His resurrection and ascension, affect us directly. The importance which they attribute to these last two events indicates clearly that there can be no question of moral causality, since after His death Christ was no longer capable of merit in the strict sense of the word.

This is unquestionably a profound mystery, but it does not discourage the Schoolmen; instead, it rather rejoices the hearts of these men of faith. The idea is proposed by St. Thomas as calmly as if it were the most ordinary thing in the world.

> Christ's passion was in a sense a universal cause of salvation for the living as well as for the dead. But a universal cause is applied to particular effects by some special means. Hence it is that just as the virtue of His passion is applied to the living by means of the sacraments, so it was applied to the dead by His descent into Limbo.[4]

In the following passage, which is a magnificent combination of Aristotelian metaphysics and Pauline theology, Thomas explains that Christ's resurrection is the cause of the resurrection of our bodies.

> What is first in any genus is also the cause of whatever comes after it in the same genus, as we have said in the second book of the *Metaphysica*. But we have shown that the resurrection of Christ was first in the genus of true resurrection. Therefore Christ's resurrection must be the cause of our resurrection. This is the teaching of the Apostle: "Christ is risen from the dead, the first-fruits of them that sleep. For since by a man came death, by a man also cometh resurrection from the dead" (1 Cor. 15:20,21). It is reasonable, too, for according to the Psalmist (Ps. 25:10) and St. John (John 5:21), the principle of the vivification of men is the Word of God. Now it is the natural order of things, established by God, that every cause should act first upon what is nearest itself, and by this means act upon things that are more remote; as fire heats first the surrounding air by means of which it then heats distant objects, and so God Himself first illuminates the substances nearest Himself, and by their means gives light to those that are more distant, according to Dionysius (*Cael. Hierarch.*, c. 13). Hence the Word of God first gives immortal life to the body which is united naturally to Himself, and through that body He effects the resurrection in all the others.[5]

In another passage the Saint is more explicit:

> Christ's ascension is the cause of our salvation, not by way of merit, but by way of efficiency.
>
> Christ's passion removes the obstacles; His ascension is directly the cause of our ascension, by beginning it in our Head, to which the members must be united.[6]

The disciples of St. Thomas call attention to the forcefulness of this doctrine. Thus, Father Capponi della Porretta observes in a marginal note:

> It is as if the Saint had said explicitly: Christ rose from the dead not only in order that we might live for Him, but also that, by an efficient and exemplary causality, His resurrection might cause us to live for Him.[7]

And, explains Noël Alexandre,

> We are all therefore risen in the Saviour; we have all been restored to life in Him; we have entered heaven before being born on earth.[8]

All of human life is transformed by this mystical contact with the life of the Saviour. Even suffering has a value — a divine value, says Cajetan, whose opinion is followed by Bartholomew of Medina, Suarez, and Nazarius.

> Christ has taken in Himself all suffering, in order to divinize all the ills of the universe. For just as the Word of God has in a sense assumed all the good in the universe by taking a human nature — that is, inasmuch as all creatures are to be found in man, as we have said in the beginning of this book — so by assuming the miseries of men in all the pains of His passion, He has divinized all the ills of the universe, for these ills are in some manner included in the ills of men.

Cajetan allows himself to be carried away by this idea. Christ, he tells us, has even divinized that evil which is sin.

> As a sign of this [divinization of all ills], He even willed that His flesh should be subject to the evil of sin in the fathers [of the Old Testament], in order that by taking a body from a sinful mass, He might, so to speak, divinize the evil of sin.[9]

Consoling though it may appear, the formula has never found acceptance, and neither Medina nor Nazarius transcribe this sentence. Suarez considers it untenable. And rightly so, for Christ has in no way taken sin to Himself. It is precisely by reason of its perfect innocence that His humanity differs from our own. Therefore we, too, shall pass over this unfortunate expression, which Cajetan himself would certainly have sacrificed with good grace. But let us hear the rest of the holy cardinal's explanation, in which he is once more followed by Medina:

Thus was fulfilled the word: "God so loved the world" (that is, both the good and the evil that it contains), "that He gave His only-begotten Son" (John 3:16). This great dignity which is conferred upon the world's ills is very helpful to the human race. For since the sin of Adam such things are inevitable; they who walk in the path of virtue toward the heavenly country cannot escape them. These evils are by their very nature hateful and repulsive; hence the path of this life is called narrow and difficult.

But now that they are assumed by the Word of God in His own Person, these miseries have unquestionably been divinized. They are therefore more to be desired than gold and precious stones when we have them not, and sweeter than honey when we have them (Ps. 18:11). This is confirmed by the Acts of the Martyrs, who say: "This is what I have always desired; I have always hoped for such a feast; I seem to be walking on roses," etc. Thus too, even when it is painful, the path of virtue is become lovable and desirable for the human race. It is become even delightful. But the animal man does not perceive the things of God; to a sick palate bread is a torture, though it has a pleasant taste for one who is in good health, and the same light which causes pain to diseased eyes is a joy to eyes that are healthy.[10]

§ 2

So real is this mystical efficacy of the Saviour's sufferings that St. Thomas makes it the center of his treatise on the Redemption in the *Summa theologica* (III, qq. 48, 49). The treatise itself is of great importance; and in the opinion of those who were in the best position to judge, this is one of the treatises in which St. Thomas appears at his best. Moreover, it marks an epoch in the history of the dogma of the Redemption, for it effects a synthesis of the two principal theories

[467]

which had previously been proposed in an effort to explain this point of our faith. The first we may call the "real" or "mystical" theory, according to which, on account of our mystical solidarity with Christ, our whole nature was transformed by the very fact of the Incarnation; we were all, in principle, sanctified in the Man-God, while the expiation of Calvary has merely done away with the obstacles that still prevented the Incarnation from producing its total effect. The other theory, more "moral" and more juridical, is the theory of vicarious satisfaction which had been brought to the fore a short time previously by St. Anselm. According to this second view we are born anew unto justice in virtue of the decree by which God applies to us the superabundant merits acquired for us by the Saviour during His passion. In our study we have often met with both of these conceptions; both are orthodox, and neither is exclusive. St. Thomas admits both, and makes each perfect the other in a splendid synthesis.

It is certainly true, he declares, that Christ atones in our stead by vicarious satisfaction; but the reason why He can expiate sin in our place and make His satisfaction our own, without a purely arbitrary disposition on God's part, is His real and mystical unity with us. On the other hand, this unity cannot be established unless the obstacle of sin, which is opposed to unity in us, be destroyed. And it is precisely the Saviour's vicarious satisfaction that performs this work of destruction. The Angelic Doctor outlines his position in the opening lines of the treatise.

Did the passion of Christ cause our salvation by way of merit?

I answer that, as we have said above, grace has been given to Christ, not only as an individual, but as Head of the Church; that is to say, in order that it might flow from Him into His members. Thus the actions of Christ have the same relation both to Himself and to His members, as the actions of a man in the state of grace have to the man himself. But it is evident that any man in the state of grace who suffers for justice' sake, by that very fact merits his own salvation, according to the text of St. Matthew: "Blessed are they that suffer persecution for justice' sake" (Matt. 5:10, D.V.). Wherefore by His passion Christ has merited salvation not only for Himself, but also for all His members.[11]

[468]

It is scarcely necessary to call attention to the force of the Saint's statement: "Christ's actions have the same relation to His members as one's own actions have to oneself."

> The Head and the members are as one mystical person, and therefore Christ's satisfaction belongs to all the faithful as His members.[12]

In the remaining articles of the same question and in the following question, the holy Doctor explains other truths related to the Redemption: its modalities, its superabundance, and its effects. But as soon as he touches upon the central point, the same explanation always returns:

> The members and the Head are but one person. Therefore, since Christ is our Head by reason of His divinity and His superabundant fullness of grace, and since we are His members, His merit is not something outside us (*extraneum*), but it flows into us on account of the unity of the Mystical Body.[13]

Thus far we have the realistic and mystical part of his doctrine of the Redemption, and we see how forcibly it is expressed. Now let us turn to the moral part. The Saint tells us that sin prevented the diffusion of Christ's justice in our souls. Hence it was necessary that sin be destroyed, that Christ satisfy for our sins, and that He redeem us from perdition. His sufferings possessed the power to do all this.

But, in order to have this efficacy, Christ's sufferings had to possess a certain immensity. This character of immensity is strongly emphasized by our Saint, and adds a mystical element to the moral part of his system, which is concerned with satisfaction and with the divine decrees.

For Thomas, therefore, the Saviour's passion was universal. By this he means not only that the sacred humanity suffered in its every part, not only that it bore every kind of torture inflicted by every kind of executioner, but also that it contained in itself the universality of suffering. It had to expiate all the sins of all men. In that case, declares the Angelic Doctor, the humanity alone, even considered as distinct from the divinity, had to possess an immensity equal to so immense a satisfaction. Furthermore, it had to render possible and efficacious all our own satisfactory acts; hence it had in some way to contain them all in itself.

Therefore it was not the suffering of an ordinary man, but the suffering of Him who is Head, of Him who contains all men mystically in Himself. We might even add that the passion was precisely the means by which He became the Head of all men *in actu*, for it was the means He used to destroy the obstacles to union that sin had placed in men. As He is mystical, so the passion, too, had to have a mystical character, an immense and mysterious character, in order to correspond in the order of expiation and of suffering, to that other mysterious immensity, which, in the order of supernatural sanctification, is the grace of Head.

Thus the sufferings of the Head were by their very nature fitted to effect the purification and salvation of all the members. St. Thomas repeats: when Christ suffers, all humanity is redeeming itself in Him.

> The passion of Christ causes the remission of sins by way of redemption. . . . The passion which He endured through charity and obedience is as it were a price; for by it He, as Head, delivered us, His members, from our sins; just as a man, by a meritorious work done with his hands, might redeem himself from a sin he had committed with his feet. For, just as a natural body is one whole, composed of many members, so the whole Church, which is the Mystical Body of Christ, is one person with its Head, who is Christ (*computatur quasi una persona cum suo capite quod est Christus*).[14]

Not a word of explanation! Some may find the ideas wanting in precision, but St. Thomas is satisfied. Christ and we are one; He possesses supernatural life in order to communicate it to all. What more is needed to account for our redemption in Him?

This theory of the Redemption, based upon Christ's Headship, has had only a faint echo in Tradition. With the exception of a few great Thomists, most of the Scholastics have accorded it scant attention. Many even omit all comment on the questions of the *Summa* in which these passages appear. Since these questions were devoted to considerations on the life of Christ, they were left to the exegetes, while the theologians turned to problems in which they took a deeper interest, such as, for instance, whether the Redemption was carried out according to the full rigor of law. And even those who follow the holy Doctor into the discussion of these questions often stopped at mere details. All eyes are not the eyes of an eagle; these men composed learned historical dissertations on the exact date of the Crucifixion and on the number of the nails, but they were less concerned about our mystical solidarity in the Saviour.

Nevertheless the doctrine which the Saint proposed was not lost. Like an obstructed stream, it finds another course. We shall see it reappear at another point, in conjunction not with the Head, but with the members, and in answer to a question which had its day of celebrity and of which we shall speak again in Chapter IX: "What is the satisfactory and redemptive value of Christian good works?"

Chapter VII

The Scholastics — 2. The Humanity of Christ, Instrument of the Divinity

✂

I. *The Grace of Headship is Christ's individual grace*, rendered excellent by the hypostatic union. Relation of the three graces in Christ.
II. *Christ is Head, because His human nature is the instrument of the divinity.* For the sole reason that it is united with the Word, the sacred humanity is capable of acting upon all souls. The nature of this intrinsic elevation. The humanity of the Word is an instrument of a very special order; it operates *virtute propria*, and even after the manner of a principal cause.
III. The Scholastics present a very complete doctrinal synthesis. Comparison with the doctrine of the Mystical Body as proposed by the Greek Fathers and by St. Augustine. Some progress has been made, but further development is necessary on certain points.

I

AS WE have seen, grace is present in the humanity of Christ under three aspects: as the grace of union, as His personal grace, and as the grace of Head. The next question concerns the relation that exists between the grace of Head and the other two graces. It will be observed that the answer to this question consists in a study of the nature and origin of the power to "infuse" (*influere*).

According to St. Thomas and most of the other theologians, the grace of Head is the same as the individual grace of the Saviour. The same holiness which makes Christ's human nature pleasing to God likewise gives it the power to act upon us and to sanctify us. Let us hear the intrepid Doctor propose his opinion:

[472]

Every being acts according as it is a being in act. Hence the act whereby it is in act must necessarily be the same as that whereby it acts. Yet not every act that suffices to actuate a being is sufficient to make it a principle of action with regard to others. For, since the "agent" is more perfect than the "patient," as both Augustine and the Philosopher tell us, the being which acts upon others must possess the act in an eminent degree. But we have said above that the soul of Christ has received grace in the most eminent degree possible. This eminence of grace that He has received enables Him to confer grace upon others, and this power pertains to the nature of Head. Therefore the individual grace which justifies the soul of Christ is essentially the same as the grace whereby He is Head of the Church, justifying the others. There is merely a distinction of reason between the two graces.[1]

The exact sense of the proposition is clear. There is no question of identifying the grace which Christ possesses as an individual with the grace which is communicated to the Mystical Body and which sanctifies the Church. That would be heresy. St. Thomas is speaking only of Christ, and he means that His personal holiness and that pre-eminence whereby He is able to justify all souls by His merits, by His Redemption, and by His action, are one and the same thing. To determine the precise relation that exists between His own grace — which is at once His individual grace and the grace of Head — and the grace that sanctifies the individual Christian, is an entirely different question, which the Scholastics discuss in another treatise. As we observed in the preceding chapter, our authors indicate the continuity of these two graces, when they show how the unity of the Head and members accounts for Christ's action in us and our sanctification in Christ.

But whence does Christ's individual grace derive this special pre-eminence that makes it the grace of Head? "From the grace of union," says St. Thomas, and he repeats the same answer several times. The first principle of the whole supernatural order is the assumption of human nature by the Word. In Christ this assumption is a grace, a gift; it is not a quality in the strict sense, of course, but it is a relationship, the closest possible relationship with the Word, since it gives to the human nature the personality of the Word, and a dignity that is strictly infinite.

[473]

St. Thomas goes on to explain that the grace of union produces in the Saviour's human nature a created holiness, without which it could not act, or know, or will in a manner befitting the only Son of God. This holiness, which as it were adapts the humanity to the hypostatic union, is the individual grace of Christ. Since it is a quality inherent in a human nature, it is essentially finite, as the nature itself is finite. But in its finite order it is infinite, in the sense that it corresponds to an infinite dignity; that it proceeds from the closest possible union with God; that it can, therefore, have no equal in its own order; that it possesses within itself all that belongs to the nature of grace (*quidquid pertinet ad rationem gratiae*), without limit or measure. Just as fire, the cause of all heat, may be said to contain heat to the absolute degree, and just as the sun possesses in itself the fullness of light, so too, according to St. Thomas, Christ's humanity is endowed with a totality of grace that is limitless. By its very immensity this individual grace is designed to "influence" (*influere*); and the Schoolmen set out to prove its immensity precisely because they see the necessity of such an influx. Now, inasmuch as this grace "influences," it is the grace of Head. Therefore the grace of Head is formally the individual grace of the Saviour, in the sense that the hypostatic union has rendered it perfect enough, near enough to the first principle, and hence superabundant enough so that it can act upon us. Let us read the explanation which the Saint proposes at the end of his *Quaestiones disputatae de veritate:*

> As the Damascene tells us, Christ's humanity was in some manner the instrument of the divinity, and hence its actions were capable of being salutary for us. Therefore, inasmuch as it was a special instrument of the divinity, it had to have a special union with the divinity. But the more closely a substance approaches to the divine Goodness, the more it partakes of the divine Goodness, as is clear from what Dionysius says.
>
> Consequently, for the very reason that it is united to the divinity in a closer and more special way, the humanity of Christ, through the gift of grace, also shares in the divine Goodness to a more excellent degree. Thereby it is made capable not only of possessing grace, but even of transmitting grace to others, just as the light of the sun reaches all the other planets by means of the more luminous bodies. Therefore,

[474]

since Christ in some way transmits (*influit*) the effects of grace to all rational creatures, He becomes in this way the principle of all grace according to His humanity, just as God is the principle of all being. And, as all perfection of being is united in God, so in Christ is found the fullness of grace and virtue. By this fullness He is able not only to perform works of grace, but also to lead others to grace. This power is what gives Him the quality of Head. For in nature the head has not only the sensitive faculties, so that it can perceive by means of the sight, the hearing, the touch, and the other senses, but it may be said to possess the very root of this power, whence the senses go forth to the other members. In the same manner there is in Christ one and the same habitual grace, which is called the grace of union, inasmuch as it befits a nature that is united with the divinity; the grace of Head, inasmuch as it overflows (*refusio fit*) into others for their salvation; and personal grace, inasmuch as it gave Christ the power to perform meritorious actions.[2]

Such is the theory of St. Thomas and the common opinion. However, we must note that it was not universally accepted. A certain number of theologians make the grace of Head consist in the grace of union or in some special relation to the divinity. Some regard it merely as a particular disposition or investiture, whereby God appointed Christ the Lord of the whole supernatural order. They are plainly inclined to view this dignity rather as an authority to command than as a power to "infuse" (*influere*). However, such writers are the exception. As a rule, when theologians associate the grace of Head with the grace of union, they mean primarily to imply that the first principle of this "power of influence" is the hypostatic union. It is true that they do not lay much stress upon the mystical solidarity that binds the Head to the members. But they do not teach a doctrine different from that of St. Thomas; they simply insist upon another point of the doctrine. What they emphasize is the first principle, whereas St. Thomas' prime concern was with the intrinsic nature of the "power of influence."

In all essential points the doctrine of the Scholastics is almost unanimous; and the whole of it is a corollary of the Incarnation. The Incarnation is the grace of union, inasmuch as it makes the humanity of the Saviour one with the Word.

[475]

This union in turn gives the humanity an intrinsic holiness (the individual grace), so abundant that it naturally tends to overflow and to "influence," to act upon us (the grace of Head).

II

Our masters propose the same doctrine elsewhere and in other terms, when they explain how, by the power of the Word, the Saviour's humanity becomes the instrument of our salvation. Their teaching on this point explains too well and too clearly the passages we have just read, and the whole of it is too important to be passed over unnoticed. We shall therefore present it here, adding a few comments to indicate how their explanation fits in with what we have already seen of their doctrine. In the following paraphrase the reader can easily distinguish between what is historical exposition and what is our own commentary.

According to the Scholastics, the humanity of the Saviour has of course no power to sanctify, if we prescind from the hypostatic union. Any such power comes to it from the Word who has assumed that human nature, and God alone is always the principal cause of whatever supernatural activity it exercises.

But this humanity was assumed by the Word for our salvation; it is the instrument of which the Word deigned to make use in order to unite us to Himself and to adapt His activity to our nature. Now, when God takes an instrument, He does not do so with the intention of leaving it impotent. If it was taken for the sanctification of souls, Christ's humanity must be capable of giving grace to all the faithful. It is in this that its instrumental causality consists. As the bearer of the divine life and as the means of sanctification, the humanity of Christ is what the sacraments were to become: it is the sign, the efficacious sign of a deifying operation. However, it is so in a pre-eminent way, *per ministerium excellentiae,* which means that all other sources of grace derive their institution and their virtue from it; that they have no value except in its name; and that it so surpasses all these other means of grace that it can produce all their proper effects without their intervention.

The sacred humanity receives its instrumentality and its pre-eminent power from the divine personality in which it subsists. *Instrumentum excellens et coniunctum,* say the Scholastics. Nothing else is required: the sole and sufficient reason for its power is the fact of its assumption by the Word.

Thus the Schoolmen reaffirm, in a different way, the privileges that we have already studied. Since it was wholly assumed for our sanctification, Christ's humanity must be fully and wholly capable of producing this effect. Therefore its most material element has the power to act upon souls and to produce spiritual effects within them. Its most transitory element, the events of its life, exercises a perpetual action upon the souls of men. Its most personal element, its individual grace, is adapted to "influence" our whole race. Its most humble element, its sufferings and its passion, is great enough to expiate all crimes, and to contain and render efficacious all our works of satisfaction.

Yet, in spite of these privileges it would still remain a useless instrument, so long as it lacked a contact with men close enough so that it could communicate the gifts which it has received for them. In order to complete the Scholastic formula, we should say: *"Instrumentum excellens et excellenter coniunctum operi, quia excellenter coniunctum operanti:* a pre-eminent instrument, pre-eminently united with the effect, because of its pre-eminent union with the cause." Since the human nature of the Saviour was assumed for the purpose of applying the action of the divinity to men, the hypostatic union with the Word of God must also have given it a real union with men. In the economy of the Redemption there is ever the same principle and the same continuity: by the mere fact that the Word takes up an instrument. He adapts it to His purpose. But His humanity is to communicate and adapt God's action to us. Therefore it, too, must be adapted to us; it must reach us and touch us. To suppose that the divinity supplies here for the lack of contact and itself transmits to creatures the operation of the sacred humanity would be to reverse the proper order of things. In Christ it is not the divinity that is mediator and instrument, but the humanity; of course, all proceeds from the first, but all comes to us through the second.

We do not recall having found this last consideration proposed by the Scholastics in connection with the present subject. But it is, we may say, implicitly present. So much is certain, that, as St. Thomas expresses it, they consider Christ as man to be the first principle, not *of* the order of grace, but *in* the order of grace, and that He produces whatever takes place in that order. This doctrine is one of the gems of Thomistic theology. St. Thomas alone, declares Medina, was capable of explaining how the sacraments are efficient causes of grace.

> He alone could explain this mystery, on account of the profound esteem which he had for the humanity of Christ, which God has so loved and exalted as to unite it to Himself in unity of person. He teaches therefore that the humanity of the Lord Christ is the efficient cause of our justification and sanctification, of all the miracles that took place during the lifetime of Christ, and of all those that will take place until the end of the world; and he teaches that it is through this humanity that the restoration and renovation of the whole world will be effected. This truly divine doctrine is very often repeated in his writings.[3]

We find the most forceful affirmation of this view in the passage which follows. The Angelic Doctor is speaking of the resurrection of Christ, which, he explains, is the cause of our own resurrection.

> Christ's resurrection is the efficient cause of our resurrection, inasmuch as the humanity, with which He rose from the dead, is in some manner the instrument of His divinity, and operates in virtue of that divinity, as we have said above. And therefore, just as all that Christ did or suffered in His humanity is salutary for us by virtue of His divinity, so also the resurrection of Christ is the efficient cause of our resurrection by the divine power, the proper function of which is to give life to the dead. This divine virtue is present to all places and all times (*praesentialiter attingit omnia loca et tempora*). Such a virtual contact suffices for this efficient causality.[4]

The Saint's thought is evidently this: the divine causality,

[478]

which alone is by its nature present at all times and in all places, communicates something of its excellence to the instrument that it employs, and to the degree in which it employs that instrument. Otherwise the operation would be exclusively its own, and in no sense that of the instrument. For this reason, then, we can and must say that Christ's humanity, in virtue of the divinity, has taken an active part, always, everywhere, in every salutary work.

It was left to the Thomists of the sixteenth century, to Cajetan and the School of Salamanca, to give the finishing touches to this doctrine. They clearly perceived the difficulty: to act, there must be contact; if Christ's humanity, the instrument of the Word, is to act upon the entire human race, it must have contact with the entire human race, and that contact must be as real as its operation is real. But, since it is not the divinity, how can its presence be said to extend to all times and all places?

Of course the sacred humanity is not everywhere, and since our masters already had their hands full with the controversy against the Protestants, they were as careful as anyone not to attribute anything like omnipresence to the human nature of the Saviour. They confuse neither the two natures in Christ, nor the operations of the two natures; but they do remember that in the hypostatic union Christ's humanity is elevated, and that the two natures act in perfect harmony with each other. Therefore, they say, inasmuch as, and only inasmuch as the human nature is one with the Word, it is not distant from anything; rather, distance no longer exists, or at least ceases to be a hindrance when there is question of the activity of Christ's human nature in the conferring of grace; for in it, and for it, and through it, the entire order of grace is one, one single body.

Of course, so realistic a treatment of the mystery was not to everyone's taste. Some do not even wish to hear it, while even its proponents hesitate and essay different solutions when they come to define the exact nature of this power. Some have recourse to the "obediential potency" of creatures with respect to the Creator, while others account for it by the simple fact that the humanity is an instrument in the hands of God; some consider it a permanent quality, giving Christ the permanent power to sanctify, while many speak of a momentary elevation or virtue, existing in the humanity only when the divinity wills to make use of it.

On this last point, therefore, it appears that the teaching of the Scholastics is still unsettled. Perhaps, however, it can be made clearer by means of a comparison with their doctrine concerning the grace of Head. We have just seen that it helps to explain that grace; hence it is but just that it should receive some light from the latter.

The power in question may be conceived as the power of the Mystical Head, since it consists in the ability to produce all the effects that are included in the purpose of the Incarnation, which is to build up the Mystical Body. And what is this power which Christ has to build up a Mystical Body for Himself, if it is not the power of the Mystical Head as such?

But we have seen that the grace of Head is a quality intrinsic to the humanity of the Saviour. Hence, since in the order of activity the power of Head corresponds to what grace is in the order of being, it seems that this pre-eminence must likewise be an inherent quality of the Saviour.

It seems also that this pre-eminence must be permanent, since the quality of Head is permanent. Always Christ's humanity is the instrument of the divinity; always, therefore, it should possess a power proportionate to the work for which it was chosen.

Upon us, habitual grace confers a certain permanent power and obligation to act as befits a member of the Mystical Body; in other words, it gives us the power to concur in the building of that body. Thus again, it would seem that Christ's habitual grace should give Him the power to cause the growth of the entire organism.

But the habitual grace which He possesses receives such excellence and perfection by reason of the hypostatic union that it is the grace of Head and the universal principle in the order of grace. It ought, therefore, to confer a proportionate power, a power which, by virtue of the hypostatic union — *instrumentum excellens quia coniunctum* — is great enough to be the power of Head and of universal agent in the order of grace.

Now, while it is true that men in the state of grace have the power to perform good works, this power does not pass into act except by means of an actual grace. May we not apply the same principle to the power of Christ? In order to act, this power would require a special impulse on the part of the divine nature. Thus we might explain the opinion of certain authors, already referred to, who make this power consist in a momentary elevation of the sacred humanity by the Word.

At the same time, it would not necessarily follow that the power as such does not reside in Christ radically and permanently; for the power and the obligation to do good works remains radically present in the just, even outside those moments during which they are actually being aided by grace in performing these good works.

If all this is true, there would be a perfect parallel between the power of Head and the grace of Head. However, we shall not insist further upon the parallel. To give all the necessary precisions would take us too far afield; we simply wished to point out the great similarity of the two prerogatives, and we think we have said enough for that purpose.

Let us now return to the explanations which the Scholastic theologians propose on the subject of this instrument of grace. Irrespective of their theory as to how Christ's humanity derives its instrumental power, all agree that it possesses that power in a unique and unparalleled manner. It is indeed so excellent that some are led to wonder whether it should still be classed as an instrumental cause.

Bartholomew of Medina, whom we have already mentioned several times, is to our knowledge the first to formulate the question. He declares that in the work of salvation Christ's humanity acts after the manner of a principal cause. It works miracles and sanctifies souls in its own name. That which it communicates to souls is not only the likeness willed by the First Cause, but its own image, a communication of its own union with God. Therefore it operates by its own proper form. Thus, according to Medina, one might say:

[481]

Christ as man is, after God [*secundum Deum,* an expression which Medina's successors find almost unintelligible], the principal cause of our justification; but as such He is a secondary, dependent cause. For God has conferred this grace and privilege on the humanity of Christ, that in it and by it all things may be restored and renewed.[5]

Such is Medina's carefully considered conclusion. He retains the traditional vocabulary, but he is inclined in this particular instance to conceive instrumental causality as something very closely approximating principal causality. Nevertheless his opinion was viewed with suspicion, and Suarez even calls it temerarious. But then Suarez himself was accused of exaggeration by the Thomists of his time. Nor do the latter adopt Medina's idea; it is sustained only by Pedro de Cabrera and a few others.

To us, too, the view seems untenable. In spite of all its excellence, or rather, in its very excellence, the Saviour's humanity has neither subsistence nor salutary activity apart from the Word. Therefore it lacks that character of completeness and independence which is necessary for principal causality.

But it is an instrument in a manner all its own, which is only analogous to the action of an ordinary instrument. It forms but one divine Person with Him who makes use of it, and one mystical person with those in whom it operates; and its activity consists in communicating to others, in "infusing" into others, by means of a certain vital contact, that which it possesses in plenitude. It is, therefore, instrument of grace, just as it is Head of the Mystical Body, in a manner that is unique and proper to itself alone. When these two functions are studied more closely, they are seen to coincide, and it is quite natural that one should be explained by means of comparisons drawn from the other. Our sole purpose in mentioning Medina's peculiar opinion was to bring out this identity more strikingly.

III

Such is the synthesis which Scholastic theology has produced. It is an important synthesis, and one that requires further examination. It marks an epoch in the history of the Mystical Body, for it not only completes the doctrine of Augustine, but also makes the latter more like the teaching of the Greek Fathers.

In our study of St. Augustine we remarked that certain points had been left incomplete in the theology of grace and of the Mystical Body which he proposed against the Pelagians. He was more concerned with the infirmities of the members than he was with the dignity of the Head, and while he explained clearly that all supernatural life comes to us from the Incarnation, he did not show how the Incarnation makes it possible for Christ's humanity to diffuse the divine life in us.

The Schoolmen go further. Here their dialectic turn of mind is of great value, for it induces them to consider the Christ-life, as they do everything else, in its causes and principles. Therefore they begin with the first principle of all grace and of all union with God, which is the Incarnation, the hypostatic union of Christ's human nature with the divinity. By itself, without any new decree of God and without any further privilege, so they tell us, this union explains all, because it makes the sacred humanity of Jesus Christ the source of all supernatural influx and of all union with God. The entire economy of salvation consists henceforth in diffusing and communicating to the members what the Head possesses in plenitude. And the union of the members with the Head, that makes this communication possible, is the result of the Incarnation, which has likewise produced the very life that is to be communicated. By the mere fact that the Word has taken it as an instrument, the humanity of the Saviour receives what is essential to an instrument; that is, contact with the object upon which it is to work.

Here, be it noted in passing, is a splendid instance of authentic doctrinal progress. We have been able to see how direct and how continuous the development has been; now let us observe how perfectly it corresponds to the first beginnings of the doctrine. The synthesis reached by the Scholastics is in substance exactly the same as that formulated eight hundred years earlier by St. Cyril of Alexandria, in which he summed up his own teaching and completed that of the Greek Fathers

[483]

in general. The words he used are almost the same: Christ's humanity, he said, is made the life-giving Head of a Mystical Body by its very union with the Word of Life. Cyril's style is more homiletic, and that of the Scholastics is more deductive, but the system is exactly the same. Yet how great were the differences of milieu, of philosophical formation, of speculative and practical interests, and of intellectual development! So many factors appear to have been forcing these two currents of thought in opposite directions. But no; they simply follow different channels toward the same destination. Such a perfect coincidence of doctrine, maintained despite the great diversity of writers, is proof of the profound unity of inspiration that binds them together; it reveals the one Master who lives in His doctrine and who guides His faithful.

Coincidence it is, but not a mere superposition of lifeless formulas. Christian dogma is a living thing, and hence, even when two lines of development converge, certain new features appear, to indicate that progress has been realized, while the indefiniteness of other points shows where further progress has still to be made.

From the standpoint of unity and simplicity, the Scholastic synthesis is a pronounced improvement over the teaching of the Greek Fathers. St. Cyril of Alexandria had indeed shown that Christ's Headship proceeded from the hypostatic union alone. But when he came to define this Headship, he had recourse to such extraordinary powers as that of raising the dead to life and of restoring sight to the blind. While it is true that these powers also follow from the union of Christ's human nature with the Word of Life, they complicated the system unduly, and in the face of Monophysitism they proved to be a weakness. They do not enter into the Scholastic synthesis; here it is the Incarnation itself, which by its very nature confers upon the humanity of the Word the closest possible union with God, and makes it the instrument of the entire order of grace. The whole economy of salvation is represented as a single continuous line.

Yet, though the picture is more distinct, it is also less vivid. The Scholastics indicate more clearly the nature of the mystery, but they do not describe it with vigor and forcefulness. Their doctrine possesses neither the amplitude and richness in which St. Cyril had clothed it, nor the depth of interior life that characterized it in the writings of Augustine.

Here, then, is the point at which theological progress must be continued.

Chapter VIII

The Scholastics — 3. Who are Members of Christ?

⋈

I. 1. In general and *de iure,* all men are members of Christ.
2. *Different classes of men:* the saints, the faithful, infidels,
the damned. Particular cases: Adam in the state of original justice? the angels? In what sense are the latter members of the
Saviour?
II. *The material universe?* According to the common view,
it is not a member of Christ, although the contrary opinion is
proposed by a few authors. But certain concessions are made by
all: (*a*) on account of its union with man, the universe is bene-
fited and ennobled by the Incarnation; (*b*) it too will be glorified
on the Last Day; (*c*) it too has the Incarnate Word for its end
and as the goal of its aspirations; (*d*) it is used by Christ for
the good of the elect. In this sense, it is part of the Mystical
Body, but only because of its relation to men.

I. § 1

AFTER the Head we must consider the members. According
to St. Thomas, the members are all men, body and soul: the
soul first, and then the body.

Speaking in general of the entire duration of the world,
Christ is Head of all men, but in varying degrees. First and
principally, He is Head of those who are actually united with
Him in glory; secondly, of those who are actually united with
Him by charity; thirdly, of those who are actually united with
Him by faith; fourthly, of those who as yet are only capable
(*in potentia*) of being united with Him, but who, in the divine
predestination, will eventually be united with Him; fifthly, of
those who are still capable of being united with Him, but will
never actually attain this union, as are those men living in the
world who are not predestined.[1] These latter at their death
cease altogether to be members of Christ, since they are no
longer even capable of being united with Him.[2]

As a matter of fact, there is some difference of opinion

[486]

among the Schoolmen as to who belongs to the Mystical Body. The reason is that, although they agree on basic principles, not all speak of the Mystical Body in the same sense. St. Thomas, and many other theologians with him, usually consider the question from the standpoint of the plenitude of grace possessed by Christ, and teach that the Mystical Body includes all those who are capable of receiving life from Him. Therefore, they maintain, the "body of Christ" embraces all men and all the angels, and excludes only the damned. For others, the "body of Christ" signifies all those who actually receive the influx of grace from the Head. If we accept this definition, the "body" coincides more or less with the "soul" of the Church; that is, it includes the saints and all men who possess the virtue of charity, or at least faith. Finally, and especially at the time of the Protestant controversies regarding the nature of the Church, the "body of Christ" is by many theologians identified with the "body" of the Church. According to this opinion, one is united with the Mystical Body by the same bonds that unite him to the *magisterium* of the Church. However, these writers seldom follow out this principle to all its consequences. We do not recall, for instance, that any one of them excludes the fervent catechumen from the body of Christ, although, since he lacks the baptismal character, he is not a member of the visible Church. Indeed, our theologians are quite willing to admit that on this point the principal difference is one of terminology. They agree unanimously that in some sense at least the quality of "member of Christ" belongs to the entire human race; that it concerns all men, body and soul; that it depends upon union with Christ, and that, like this union, it admits of varying degrees, the most important of which are enumerated by St. Thomas in the passage quoted at the beginning of the present chapter. We shall now consider these degrees in greater detail.

§ 2

First, it is to be noted that men are members of Christ both as to their souls and as to their bodies. Primarily the influx of grace affects the soul, which is the act and the form of the

[487]

body, but it extends also to the body, taking possession of our members in order to make them instruments of justice, and giving them supernatural life.

Of all men, the saints are the most perfect members of the Saviour; they are united with Him in the most complete and most inseparable union possible. Theologians usually rank the souls in Purgatory together with the saints, since they, too, are forever united with Christ, though of course their union is less perfect.

Next in order come the faithful in the state of grace; they are members of Christ in a manner that is actual and complete, but not definitive. If they lose grace, but keep faith, the common opinion is that they remain members of Christ, but imperfectly, like sick or dying or dead members. If they lose faith itself, and keep up only the external profession of religion, then, according to most authors, they are still members of Christ, but "more remotely." If they give up this external profession or fall into schism or are excommunicated, this "remoteness" is further increased. Many authors even hold that such men are no longer members of Christ.

The majority of theologians exclude notorious and obdurate heretics from the "body of Christ." Infidels and pagans are not members of Christ except potentially. Of course, Christ possesses abundant grace with which to vivify them supernaturally, but certain obstacles, either exterior or interior, prevent the ministers of the Gospel from reaching them. This, however, must not be taken to mean that they are wholly cut off from the "influence" of the Saviour; Scholastic theology proposes, rather late, to be sure, the idea of an immense effusion of actual graces, emanating from Christ and extending to the entire universe, in order that souls may everywhere be prepared supernaturally for the gift of faith.

Last of all, there are the damned, who are totally excluded from the body of Christ. The supernatural character which some of these may bear, and which they have received solely through Christ, does not make them members of His body in any sense; the character remains only for their shame and punishment, not for their vivification. Even if one admits that the divine mercy mitigates the chastisement of the damned, this alleviation is attributable only to God's goodness, and not, properly speaking, to the merits of Christ. In no case would it be the life-giving influx that constitutes one a member of the Saviour.

With the damned are reckoned infants who die without baptism or before birth. As long as they are alive, these infants are at least potentially members of Christ; some have even been sanctified in their mother's womb. But if they die without receiving grace, they go to Limbo. There, whether their lot be mitigated suffering, a neutral state, or natural beatitude, they are outside the economy of redemption and cannot be reckoned as members of Christ.

It was also in Limbo, but in "the Limbo of the Fathers," that the souls of the just of the Old Testament awaited the coming of Christ. It is commonly taught that while there they were members of Christ. Besides, these saints of the Old Law were already actual members of Christ during their lifetime. Their faith in the promised Messias, their hope, their charity, their supernatural life already constituted a bond of union with Christ, in virtue of the future merits of the Saviour. However, the influx of the Head was less perfect then than it is now; therefore they were members of Christ in a lesser degree than are we.

The same may be said of Adam after his sin. He, like other men, is redeemed and attains salvation through incorporation in the new Adam. But what of Adam before the fall? Was his grace of innocence due to the influx of Christ? The question is often discussed, and generally answered in the negative. We shall not enter into the details of the controversy, since the views expressed on this point are the same as those proposed in reply to a very similar question which we shall consider here: Are the angels members of Christ?

Certain it is, as all the Scholastics admit, that like Adam before the fall, and independently of the Redemption, of which they had no need, the angels received grace. Nevertheless it is also the common and certain teaching — a doctrine of faith, according to some — that Christ in His humanity is Head of the angels as well as of men. Here some explanation is

[489]

necessary. It is given by St. Thomas in the following quotation, but the reader will observe that in doing so the Saint adopts a much more general definition of the Mystical Body.

> Where there is one body there must be one head. Now, by analogy we may call a multitude a body, when it is organized according to a diversity of functions for the attainment of a particular end. But it is evident that both men and angels are ordained for one and the same end, which is the possession of God in glory. Hence the Mystical Body of the Church consists not only of men, but also of the angels. Christ is Head of this whole multitude, because He is nearest to God, whose gifts He shares more perfectly than either men or angels, and because His "influence" extends not to men alone, but also to the angels. For it is said in the Epistle to the Ephesians (1:21): "[The Father] hath seated Christ at His right hand in the heavenly places, above every principality and power and virtue and domination, above every name that is named not only in this world but also in that which is to come."[3]

This is a minimized conception of the Mystical Body: a mere multitude, organized according to different functions for the pursuit of a common end. It looks at first as if Thomas were speaking of an ordinary society. But soon he reintroduces its essential and unique characteristic, which is the vital and organic influx emanating from the Head.

The whole School is at one in recognizing that the angels are not members of Christ in as full a sense as men are. They have not the same identity of species and the same solidarity with Him, in virtue of which grace flows, as it were, naturally from Him into us. But, although the bond of union is less close, it is no less real. The angels are not of the same species as Christ's humanity and men, but at least they belong to the same genus: they are creatures, and the distance between them and God is just as infinite. And, since Christ bridges this gap between the Creator and creation, He can be Mediator and source of grace for the angels as well as for men.

A further difference between angels and men is the fact that the former receive less abundantly of the influx of Christ. Since they are not sinners, they had no need of redemption; they were given grace independently of original sin and of the expiation of the Saviour. Therefore what they receive from

Christ is not supernatural life itself, but certain accidental perfections added to that life: new illuminations, an increase of beatitude, a new bond of union with God, and joy that the vacancies, which were left in their ranks by the defection of the devils, are to be filled with men.

It may be noted, however, that a considerable number of representative theologians take a further step, affirming that the angels owe all their grace to the influx of Christ. This view is defended, first, by those who say that the Incarnation would have taken place even if Adam had not sinned. Christ, they maintain, is not only the crowning glory of creation, but its very purpose. God has made all things in order that He might unite them all to Himself, by recapitulating them all in His well-beloved Son. All the graces that have been conferred on angels, on men, on Adam himself, were given in view of Christ and through His mediation, past or foreseen.

While this opinion has never enjoyed wide acceptance, it has never ceased to have its defenders. But some other theologians there are, who, without making this first view their own, nevertheless declare that the angels, and Adam in the state of original justice, received their essential grace from the "influence" of Christ. We shall indicate their theory here.

In the divine plan, original sin was foreseen from all eternity, and in consequence of this sin, the Incarnation, too, was decreed from all eternity. Once it had been determined upon, the Incarnation was made, by reason of its unparalleled excellence, the center of the whole order of Providence. Henceforth, at least in all His supernatural works, God willed nothing and saw nothing except in His well-beloved Son. His eternal decrees were carried out solely in view of Christ; in Him are God's elect and loved ones chosen and loved. Therefore the grace of the angels, like that of men, has Christ, and Christ alone as its type, its glory, and its *raison d'être*. In them all there is but one holiness, which is Christ's.

II

After the angels, the theologians turn their attention to the opposite extremity of creation; namely, to material creatures.

[491]

Have these Christ as their Head, and are they members of His body?

At first sight the answer appears quite evident: since material things cannot be in the state of grace, they are incapable of receiving any sanctifying influx. It is so hard to see how Christ could be their Head that most authors do not even ask the question, or if they do ask it, they answer with a brief "No." Christ, they declare, may well be called "Master" and "Lord" of all things, but not "Head."

In reality, however, the matter is not quite so simple, and it demands a few moments' consideration. First let us mention two authors who oppose the unanimous opinion and reply in the affirmative. This answer has made them traditional "adversaries" on this point, which means that their opinions are handed down from one author to another, each time in a more simplified form, to be refuted by each generation.

The first is Peter Galatinus, who, in an apologetical work entitled *De arcanis catholicae veritatis,* undertakes to prove the truth of the Catholic religion from rabbinical traditions. Now, according to one of these traditions, when the Eternal Father foresaw original sin, He abandoned His plan of creating the world. But the Son intervened, promising to become man in order to restore all. Then, in view of the Incarnation, God created all things. Therefore, since they were created for the sake of Christ, all things belong to the Mystical Body by the very fact of their existence.

The other "adversary," more brilliant but quite as daring, is Ambrosio Lancellotto de' Politi, better known as Catharinus. He was a writer of no mean importance, an implacable foe of Protestantism, and one of the most active influences at the Council of Trent. Unfortunately, however, his impetuous zeal often carried him into uncharted seas; in the words of Moreri, he did not scruple to part company with St. Augustine, St. Thomas, and the other theologians. He made a special study of predestination, and, as was his wont, elaborated certain rather eccentric theories on the subject. One of these concerns Christ's relation to the universe. So excellent is the predestination of Christ, he tells us, that it includes God's whole plan with regard to the universe. God willed His Incarnate Son before all things; hence He created and ordained all things for Him, so that Christ and the recapitulation of all things in Christ constitute the sole purpose and the sole *raison d'être* of the order of nature as well as of the order of grace.

The names of a few more obscure authors might be added to those of Catharinus and Galatinus, but to our knowledge none of the great theologians ever subscribed to this view. It is still the unanimous opinion that Christ is not "Head of all things."

However, it is instructive to note certain qualifying remarks made on this subject by other writers. Peter de Lorca, for instance, who, in concert with all the other theologians, warns us "not to say that all things are members of Christ,"[4] nevertheless admits that the statement might be strictly true, but adds that according to the Scriptures the Church alone is the Body of Christ, and only her members are members of Christ.

To the name of Lorca may be joined one still more famous, that of Suarez. While the *Doctor eximius* also manifests great reserve, he speaks somewhat more freely. He tells us that Christ may be called the Head of all creatures, but not in the same sense that He is Head of mankind. He argues, first, from the text of the Epistle to the Colossians (1:15), where Christ is called the first-born of every creature; and secondly, from Christ's pre-eminent dignity and His incomparable nearness to God. Still, whatever influx He can exercise upon material things must belong exclusively to the supernatural order; it would be difficult to establish any activity on the part of Christ in the conferring of natural existence, and even then nothing could be proved from such activity.

> Christ may be said to "influence" all things and to be their "Head," because He is the Lord of all, or because all things receive a certain dignity or nobility from the Incarnation, as we have said above; or certainly in this sense, that He can use them all for the salvation of the elect, particularly since after Judgment Day all things will be renewed by Christ and will receive a certain splendor and incorruptibility. Hence it is stated in the Epistle to the Romans (8:19): "Creation awaiteth the manifestation of the children of God."[5]

In these few lines Suarez sums up perfectly all that can be

[493]

said in favor of the thesis. He himself, however, is still not fully decided, and he concludes the article with the remark that even if Christ is Head of all things, one may not say that the universe is part of His Mystical Body.

The theologians do not follow Suarez. The point is evidently of slight interest to them, and they do not even examine the reasons that he gives. This does not mean that they are ignorant of the truths which he uses as arguments, for elsewhere in their works they develop these same truths at length. But they do not even think of introducing them here.

One of the most interesting of these truths enters regularly into their study of the Incarnation. In the very beginning of the treatise the Schoolmen always ask whether the Incarnation was fitting, and one of the points treated in the response is precisely that "ennobling of the entire universe by the Incarnate Word," of which Suarez speaks in the passage just quoted. The Incarnation, to cite the daring expression of Cajetan, is the assumption of the whole universe to a divine Person; that is, as Medina explains, the communication of God, not to men only, but to all creatures.

The anthropology of the School naturally leads to this conception. Once the principle is laid down that man is a rational animal, it follows that by reason of his body he is a part of the universe; hence whatever affects him must have a reaction upon the entire world. The assumption of a human nature by the Word, and the elevation of all humanity by grace, must ultimately concern all creatures. Medina illustrates the idea very well by means of a figure that had been employed in the same sense by Athanasius: "All creatures are intimately related with one another, like the strings of a zither. Hence the divine Goodness need touch only one of them in order to set them all in motion."[6] The divine influx extends, as if by successive waves, from the Word to the humanity of Jesus, from His humanity to our own, from our humanity to the universe. In this way the grace of the Incarnation reaches to the limits of creation, by a kind of continuity which becomes less perfect and flows less abundantly at each level. In the lowest plane, that of material things, what is infused is not moral sanctity as such, but only a certain supernatural dignity: the sacred honor of being that whole of which the children of God and the very Son of God Himself are part.

A further indication of this intimate connection of the universe with the Mystical Body is the fact that the glorification of the elect will bring with it the exaltation of the entire world. At the resurrection, as Suarez tells us, "all things will be renewed by Christ, and will receive a certain splendor and incorruptibility." This is also the common teaching of the Scholastics, although they speak of it, not when treating of Christ as Head, but in relation to the last end or the final judgment. At the end of time, according to the Apocalypse, there will be "a new heaven and a new earth" (Apoc. 21:1). Therefore, with their sound and supernatural common sense, they conclude that God will not annihilate anything that is capable of lasting forever: this world, created by God and in which the Incarnate Son has deigned to live, will likewise have an appropriate eternal life. In one of the splendid passages so frequent in the *Summa contra gentes,* the Angel of the Schools expresses this thought in the following terms:

> Once the Last Judgment has taken place, all human nature will be permanently established in its final state. But since all corporal things were made for man, it is fitting that at this time the condition of all material creation should also be transformed, to correspond with the new state of mankind.

Then all things will pass, together with man, from mutability to eternity:

> The movement of the heavens will cease, as well as all generation and corruption in the elements. But the substance of things will remain, sustained by the immutability of the divine Goodness (*ex immobilitate divinae bonitatis*). God created them that they might exist; therefore the things that have an aptitude to continue in existence without end will do so . . . God's power will supply for their weakness.[7]

This amelioration is necessary, in order that all nature may continue to fulfill its providential role in man's regard. The universe was created in order to manifest God to our senses and our minds; such it will remain, but in a more perfect manner, for all eternity.

The eye of the flesh cannot attain to the vision of the divine essence. Therefore, in order that it too may receive from the vision of the divinity a consolation proportionate to its powers, it will contemplate the divinity in its corporal effects. In these will appear evident manifestations of the divine majesty, first and foremost in the flesh of Christ, then in the bodies of the blessed, and lastly in all other bodies. Hence all these other bodies must then receive a greater "influence" from the divine Goodness than now; their species will not be changed, but they will have a certain increase of perfection and glory. This will be the renewal of the world. Thus, in the same instant, the world will be made new and man will be glorified.[8]

The reader will have remarked how St. Thomas brings all creatures into one synthesis: "In the flesh of Christ, in the bodies of the blessed, and in all other bodies, will appear evident manifestations of the divine majesty." Thus, if we may use the expression, "God's visibility in man," which is realized most perfectly of all in Christ, and which is realized by grace also in the saints, will extend even to our material universe. Faint it is during this life, and it makes little impression upon our eyes of flesh, but when Christ shall appear in His glory, it, too, will shine forth in splendor. There will be in the universe a mystical prolongation and influx, remote, of course, and of lesser degree, but still magnificent, of the divine beauty of the Saviour. The beatific vision will be accompanied by the contemplation, esthetic but ineffably pure, of the whole Christ, Head and body, humanity and the universe.

Once more St. Thomas expresses this continuity between the Mystical Christ and the material universe, at the end of the passage from which the above quotation is taken:

Since men will be not only delivered from corruption, but also clothed in glory, and since material creation will ultimately be disposed in conformity with the state of men, it is fitting that material creation should likewise receive a certain splendor and glory. Hence it is written: "I beheld a new heaven and a new earth" (Apoc. 21:1), and again: "Behold I create new heavens and a new earth; and the former things shall not be in remembrance, and they shall not come upon the heart. But you shall be glad and rejoice forever" (Isa. 65:17,18). Amen.[9]

This "Amen" concludes the *Summa contra gentes*. An eternal and immense perspective is opened before our eyes. In Christ all creation receives that supreme perfection, that union with God as total as possible, to which, as St. Paul tells us, it so ardently aspires. We recall the text of the Epistle to the Romans, referred to above in the text of Suarez. Although we have already quoted the passage in our study of the writings of St. Paul, it will be well to repeat it here, since the Scholastics often mention this text in explaining the final glorification of material things in Christ.

> Creation with eager straining awaiteth the manifestation of the children of God. For creation was made subject to vanity — not of its own will, but by reason of him who subjected it — yet with hope that creation itself shall be freed from its slavery to corruption unto the freedom of the glory of the children of God. For we know that all creation doth groan and travail together to this hour. And not only so, but ourselves, too, who have the first-fruits of the Spirit — we ourselves groan within ourselves while awaiting adoption.[10]

The text is clear enough, but Augustine had given an interpretation which greatly minimized its significance. Through fear of Manichaeism and Origenism he declared that "all creation" refers in reality only to man, since man contains in himself all the elements of creation, which are spirit, life, and matter. So, when man alone cries to God in his agony of suspense, we may say that in him the whole universe is crying to God. For a time Augustine's authority prevailed in the exegesis of the passage, but finally the evidence carried the day. Forced, so to speak, by Scripture itself, the Scholastics at last find the courage to paint the grandiose but vague vision of a universe breathless with expectancy and straining after the divine adoption. To account for this restlessness of material things they have recourse to the union that exists between man and the world, and tell us that since the universe is destined to have a share in the glory of the saints, it is figuratively represented as being filled with hope.

But the world does not have to wait until the Last Judgment, in order to be included in the economy of salvation. Even now Christ makes use of it for the good of His elect. We have quoted Suarez' words: "He is Lord of all things." This universal dominion is unanimously admitted by the Scholastics, although all do not understand it in exactly the same sense. Christ as man is Lord of all, because all things enter into His work of redemption.

The same formula may also serve as our conclusion. By reason of their continuity with man, material things receive a certain prolongation of the influx of grace, while at the same time they serve in their own way to transmit that influx. Christ, therefore, is their Head, inasmuch as they fulfill this role in the economy of redemption. The whole Christ is the Saviour, together with the whole of humanity; but the whole of humanity is man, together with the entire universe. Therefore, the whole Christ is Christ together with all men and the whole world.

Understood in this sense, the thesis has never been questioned, as far as we know, by any Scholastic theologian. Nuñez Cabezudo, a Thomist, and Frassen, a Scotist, even assert that it is the common teaching of the School. This is evidently an overstatement; generally speaking, the Scholastics are more concerned with clear distinctions than with such elusive relationships, and hence they do not view the question from this particular angle.

Chapter IX

The Scholastics — 4. The Dignity of the Members of Christ

><

I. What the Scholastics have to say concerning the dignity of the members of Christ is contained principally in their refutation of the Reformers. *The Protestant doctrine of the Mystical Body;* its presuppositions and deficiencies.
II. *The teaching of the Council of Trent.* Quotations from the Council; the theory that they imply.
III. 1. How Providence prepared the way for this teaching. *The merits and satisfactory works of the members of Christ.* Cajetan: Christ lives, merits, and satisfies in us.
2. Views expressed at the Council itself.
3. Hosius; the School of Salamanca. Our satisfaction as members is inseparable from the satisfaction of Christ. The consequent value of our satisfactory works. Christ is the *hypostasis* of His Mystical Body. Objections proposed against the theory; it enjoys a period of favor, then loses popularity among theologians.
IV. *Union of the members among themselves.* On this point we find only a few passages, mostly drawn from the Scholastic explanation of Indulgences and their teaching on the Communion of Saints.
V. *General conclusion.*

I

IT IS not enough to know who possess the dignity of members of Christ; we must also know in what this dignity consists. On this point the Scholastics have left no systematic development; their views can be ascertained only by means of indications gleaned from various parts of their works, and these very indications do not become particularly significant until the time of the Reformation.

Indeed, the Protestant doctrine of grace also implies a doctrine of the Mystical Body and of the dignity conferred upon those who are incorporated into it. Naturally, in order to combat the false view, the Schoolmen were obliged to explain the Catholic teaching, not only on the subject of the Mystical Body in general, but also concerning the dignity of the individual member. For the reasons which we gave at the beginning of our study of the Scholastics, these explanations are not marked by any great emphasis. Naturally, too, they are formulated in terms of the doctrinal system which they were intended to refute. Therefore, in order to make our own exposition clear, we must call to mind, at least briefly, the gist of that system. This is all the more necessary, since later on we shall have to consider certain theories of the Mystical Body which are not wholly unrelated to the Protestant doctrine. The short summary given here will help to place the entire question in its proper setting.

For the present we shall endeavor to study the inner logic of the heretical system rather than its historical causes. Our aim is to find the central, essential, and specifically Protestant element of this new doctrine of the Mystical Body; we wish to trace its philosophical genealogy and its logical consequences. Therefore we shall ignore the many differences between sects, differences that necessarily manifest themselves in a great variety of ways of understanding the point in which we are interested. We shall confine our attention to the primordial thesis, the sole thesis of the Reformation, which is the thesis of justification by extrinsic imputation. The question is this: What doctrine does this thesis imply with regard to our union with Christ? Doubtless such a simplification masks the complex nature of the reality; but it is an excellent means of discovering the very soul of the system. And this is our only purpose at the moment.

But in order to take the tree at its very root, far below the point where the branches separate, we must go more deeply. We believe that at the source, not only of Protestantism, but also of the other heresies and errors of which we shall have to speak, there lies a latent presupposition. It is with this that we wish to begin our search.

The presupposition in question belongs to the metaphysical

order. Indeed, it is almost a general rule that theological aberrations begin with metaphysics, even when at first sight their roots do not appear to penetrate so far.

This time, the presupposition has to do with the relation of creatures to God. The point, clearly, is of vital concern for any religious doctrine, since religion is nothing else than the sum total of our relations with God. It is of vital concern, too, for the concept of Christianity, which is the sum total of the new relations that God has established between Himself and us through the Saviour. Need we add, finally, that it is of vital concern for the truth of the Mystical Body, which is in a higher sense, so to speak, the sum total of the relations that go to make up Christianity, for it is the union of all men with God, in the Man-God. And, insofar as the knowledge of this relation between the world and God is attainable by natural reason, it pertains to the metaphysical order.

On the other hand, few periods in history have been so ill prepared for the study of metaphysics as was the age that gave birth to Protestantism. It was the time when Nominalism was invading the Schools. Now, as we know, Nominalism consists in an attitude of distrust in *a priori* cognition and in the power of reason to make any real contribution to human knowledge; at the same time it consists in an attitude of confidence in sensible perception and experience. Such a disposition is excellent in the field of experimental science, but in the domain of pure thought it is abominable. If a man is concerned solely with the data of experience, what must be his reaction to spiritual realities, particularly on the subject of God and the relations of the world with God?

In the golden age of Scholasticism, in the years when the metaphysics of Thomism was being molded into a system, the philosophical doctrine on this question was simple and easy. God was described as *Ipsum Esse*, the Pure Act of Existence, or simply "Being," without further restriction or determination. This perfect simplicity was itself an adequate definition; this one note distinguishes God from all else, expressing both His absolute transcendence and the relation of all things to Him. Since He is the Pure Act of Being, He has nothing in common with what is limited and finite; this constitutes His

[501]

transcendence. At the same time, since He is Being in Pure Act, His nature is such that all must be like Him, in order to belong to the category of being. This necessary resemblance despite the total absence of any common element, this analogy and participation should, of course, receive a more thorough study, were it our intention to show these concepts in all their richness. However, the little we have said will suffice for our present purpose. The reader can see how easy it was in the great Scholastic system to define precisely both the essence of the Infinite and the relations of the finite to the Infinite; but he can likewise appreciate the mental effort that is constantly necessary in order to keep these subtle notions intact and in order to see beyond sensation and even beyond the concept itself. It is not so easy to rise above self, to the Being who is superior to all things and to us.

Nor is it strange that men should soon tire of the effort, and, finding the road too steep, begin to experiment with more accessible concepts. They come to say that God is the Supreme Being, the Infinite Being, the perfect Being, the all-powerful Being, the Being that rules all things. There is nothing wrong with these determinations as such; they are used by the greatest theologians, and are excellent so long as they are employed only as a means of rendering the idea of Pure Act more tangible.

But right here is the deviation that can lead to Protestantism. One is tempted to substitute these determinations, more concrete and easier to conceive, in the place of the abstract metaphysical idea which they are calculated to clarify. The temptation proved too strong for the Nominalists, and they took these determinations for perfect definitions. God, they said, is the perfect Being; hence the creature is imperfect being. God is the supreme Being, and the creature is the lowest being. They are two extremes, and the sole relation between them is the distance that separates them.

That *separates* them? Yes, for once God is placed in any category, the only way to save something of His transcendence is to insist upon His remoteness: religion must consist in fleeing from Him. Thus, apart from other consequences, the dualism that marked the beginning becomes quite naturally an attitude of contempt for our nature, and an attitude of pessimism with regard to man.

This attitude toward man is all the more natural, as this "finite-infinite," philosophical dualism is bound up with another dualism, which is moral and theological: this is the "God-sin" and "grace-nature" dualism. To the distance that already separated us from God, we have added a new and culpable remoteness; to our insignificance we have added our sins. Then, in the name of piety — and also, by reason of the deplorable state into which Christendom had fallen — these sins were rather exaggerated than minimized. As a result, the work of salvation was made to appear as essentially a struggle and an opposition: our concupiscence as opposed to the holiness of God, and our pride as opposed to grace.

Now the question arises: if men are so despicable, both by nature and by their crimes, how can they become just and holy? The only way, according to the Protestants, is through a justice and holiness which God puts in them without their having anything to do with it. At best they can be mere receptacles of goodness, or rather, they can be no more than a foil: their ignominy can only accentuate the contrast between the purity and excellence of the gift and the depravity of the recipient. At all events they cannot be collaborators in the work; they cannot be truly united with the gift, blended with it, transformed into it. To associate God, in this way, with our abject nothingness would be a profanation of the divine. Hence, until death has destroyed everything that is in man, until it has suppressed all of his natural life, he is totally incapable of possessing any intrinsic justice or of placing any salutary act.

This is the Protestant theory, which makes justification something external to ourselves. One sees how logically it follows from the dualism and Nominalism to which we have referred. Whether or not this was its historical origin is a question which, we have said, does not concern us here.

As we shall see, this heretical theory of justification is at the same time a heretical theory of the Mystical Body. In order to have the latter, one has only to substitute the term, "incorporation in Christ" for "justification."

[503]

What meaning can incorporation in Christ, the Son of God, have for such miserable, insignificant beings as we are? It can mean nothing else, reply the Protestants, than the entrance into us of the very life of the Saviour, over and above our own sinful life. Just as Christ justifies us by casting the cloak of His holiness over our incurable malice, so He vivifies us by covering our diseases and our death with His own eternal life.

On occasion, Protestants have been known to speak with vigor and insistence of this entrance of the life of the divine Head into us, the members. At such times they appear to differ from the Catholic teaching on this point only by a more lively and more keenly felt persuasion; since they have not the Eucharist or the *magisterium* of the Church to bind them to the Saviour, they seem to concentrate all their attention on the thought of the invisible bond that joins them with the Mystical Body.

The impression is quite false, however; Christian faith is one indivisible whole. In rejecting one part of it, they have deprived themselves of all, and the incorporation in Christ which they prize so highly becomes a nonentity. It seems to be everything; it seems to give us the whole life of Christ: for He alone is holy; He alone lives, with an eternal life; we have no life but His, and we have all of that life. Yes, indeed. But according to their doctrine this life does not vivify. Like justification, of which it is one aspect, this life remains external to us; the Mystical Body as they describe it possesses life, to be sure, but a life that is outside the body itself. The body is dead; it lies in closest proximity to the Living One, but it is a corpse, nonetheless. It is just as inert and impotent as it ever was, despite the flow of energy that rises beside it, and even within it, but not from it. It is like a lighted lamp: the flame is hot, it lights the lamp, and through the lamp it illumines everything round about; but the lamp itself does not cease to be opaque metal and hard glass. One cannot help wondering whether this flow of energy is so powerful after all, since it does not produce any activity; and whether the humanity of Christ can still be called Life, if it cannot truly vivify us.

[504]

Certain Lutheran theologians go more deeply into the systematic explanation of the Mystical Body, but since all they do is to push this same theory of extrinsic imputation to greater lengths, their exposition makes no better sense.

We refer particularly to the *Formula of Concord,* which was added in 1576 to the *Confession of Augsburg.* After considering various other doctrinal points, the Protestant divines who signed the document finally ask how the Saviour's humanity vivifies us in itself, and how it is the Head of a body of regenerated men. Their answer applies to the concept of Mystical Head the same extrinsicism that characterizes the Protestant concept of membership in the Mystical Body. Hence we may say that their system is very specifically Protestant. They teach that Christ's Headship is just as external to His humanity as our justification is external to our humanity. Human nature, they continue, is finite wherever it is, in Christ as well as in other men. To say that it is divinized, and especially to say that it is a universal principle of divinization, is to attribute to it a perfection of which it is absolutely incapable. If it had the power to confer eternal life, it would cease to be finite; it would cease to be itself.

They admit that Scripture states plainly and repeatedly that Christ's humanity possesses power to confer eternal life. But, they warn us, these expressions must be properly understood. For, in a finite nature like ours, such a power cannot be an inherent quality or an intrinsic mode of being or acting. Hence it must be a kind of extrinsic exaltation, something like legal possession. A very tiny man may be the lawful proprietor of a vast region. In some similar fashion, Christ's humanity can be said to possess the power of giving life. Of itself, despite its union with the Word, that humanity is absolutely finite, and wholly devoid of any power to divinize, which power is by its very nature infinite. But precisely because it is united with the Word, it possesses the Word, and through the Word it possesses all the powers of the Word. Since the Word can give light, vivify, and save, it too can do these things; not that it exercises any virtue of its own in these works, but it has the power of the Word; it uses this power as it wills and as much

[505]

as it wills, because ever and always this power is its own as truly as the Word is its own.

But what has become of the doctrine of the Mystical Body in this system? The Saviour's humanity is no longer mystical in any sense. Gone is that mysterious fullness, the *pleroma*, that made it the source of all supernatural life and the Head of a body of regenerated men. God makes use of it, but without transforming it; He applies it to a marvelous work, but without giving it any proportion to the wondrous gifts that it communicates. It acts, but this activity makes no change in the instrument; it is no more productive of divine life in the sacred humanity of the Saviour than it is in us. In other words, God holds Himself aloof from that humanity, even when He assumes it to Himself in a personal union, just as He keeps us at a distance, even when He makes us His adoptive sons. But in that case, what is left of our adoptive sonship and of the hypostatic union? And where is the excessive bounty of our God?

How far we have come from the vast syntheses of Cyril and Augustine! There, too, we saw only God, but a God who truly gives Himself to us in Christ; a God who makes Christ's humanity truly capable of making us truly divine. There, too, we saw only one doctrine, the Incarnation; but a doctrine that attains an immense expansion, without losing aught of its unity; a doctrine that includes, in the union of the two natures which constitutes the Head, that other union of nature and grace which constitutes the members. Here, on the contrary, the heretics have abandoned the Light of life, and everything falls into darkness and death; they have broken away from unity, and the whole mosaic is shattered into fragments.

Protestantism is a principle of division, not only in the ranks of its adherents, but in its very doctrine. It set out to prove that Christ was everything; it succeeds only in proving Him impotent. It meant to attribute everything to grace; but by despoiling human nature it succeeds in eliminating grace entirely. It promised to lead us to the presence of God alone; but by destroying everything that God has made to lead us to Him, it makes Him inaccessible. Incorporation in Christ was to be our whole life; yet it leaves us corpses.

At first sight the Protestant doctrine of the Mystical Body seems to be a miracle of simplicity. God wills to see us in His Son; He wills that His Son's humanity should possess the deifying power that is proper to the Word. And that is all. The mystery of the Head and members is reduced to a few divine decrees, such as we ourselves might have issued if we were powerful enough. There is no longer any divinization, or any instrument capable of making us divine. What difficulty can the mind discover in this man-made system?

None, of course. But the elimination of these few difficulties has destroyed the mystery: it is easy enough to understand now, but the object to be understood no longer exists! If the members have no life in them, how can they be members? And if the Head has nothing that He can communicate, how can He be Head?

Strictly speaking, there is nothing left, either in ourselves or in Christ, that can constitute a true organism. Therefore the Mystical Body does not exist in itself. It exists only in God, and it consists of divine decrees. God acts *as if* the humanity of Christ could divinize us, *as if* we really received eternal life through that humanity, and *as if* there were a Mystical Body. But there is none!

Everything is drawn, so to speak, into God. But then God Himself withdraws into the unknowable. He is infinite; what proportion can He have with our finite intellects? He is holiness; what can He have in common with our weakness? Inasmuch as He is everything in Himself, He is nothing to us who are nothingness. Thus everything vanishes: God Himself, His gifts, the union He offers us, just when we hoped to obtain all.

The result was inevitable: since Protestantism has broken away from the Church, which is the Mystical Body of Christ, its doctrine of the Mystical Body must necessarily disintegrate and be lost.

The foregoing remarks are very general, and, we repeat, they have been developed from the standpoint of logic rather than from that of history. Nevertheless we believe that they are correct, and that they bring out clearly what is essential to the Protestant doctrine. We wished to call attention to this

[507]

example of "regressive evolution," and to contrast it with the progress that we have witnessed. Unfortunately, we shall meet the same regression again, though on a reduced scale. In the seventeenth century, the Jansenists follow the same path to ruin. Others, some of them fervent Catholics, venture upon it, only to be restrained and saved by their attachment to the Church, and retrace their steps to the way of truth. Although foreshadowed here, these doctrinal aberrations do not take place until later. They will form the subject matter of another chapter.

Throughout the above exposition, there is question of Protestantism only in its original form. Were we to study the doctrine of the Mystical Body as it is understood by the Protestants of today, we should find that far greater emphasis is laid upon interior union with Christ than upon extrinsic justification. For the modern Protestant, the Mystical Body is a kind of mystic soul, a common spirit, a union with Christ in the mysterious depths of the soul. But does this interior renewal consist in an intrinsic transformation of the Christian? Does it sanctify him, divinize him, or does it leave him just as he was? Is it a mere imputation of juridical holiness? Rarely do we find forceful, or even clear, answers to these questions. Apparently the matter is not considered important. The point insisted upon is that this new life is something wholly spiritual, wholly personal, and has no need of any external union with the Saviour, no need of a visible *magisterium*, no need of a Church to sanctify the soul. The Mystical Body, be it repeated, is primarily a soul, a soul without a body; as if man, and as if the God-Man too, were not necessarily, though of course secondarily, a body.

II

Let us now leave these errors aside. It will be necessary to return to them again, but for the present we are concerned with the doctrine of the Mystical Body which the Church proposed against the Reformers. At the beginning of the preceding chapter we said that the discussions had scarcely touched upon this subject. The statement is true, but there are exceptions.

Amid all the argumentation and citing of texts, almost lost in the bustle of controversy, we do find some traces of the doctrine. We shall study the most important of these.

The intrinsic dignity that the members of Christ receive through their incorporation in Christ, and concerning which we have just recalled the Protestant views, was made the object of the Church's definitions at the Council of Trent. In the magnificent chapters on justification, the Fathers affirm that Christ is indeed our only life and our only strength. But, they continue, He is all this in reality: His holiness is great enough to make us truly holy, and His power is great enough to enable us, poor sinners though we are, to become in strict truth causes of salutary works, once we have been united with Him and have been made members of His body.[1] Therefore each of us receives a justice that is his own, yet which is at the same time the justice of God — not the justice by which God Himself is holy, but the justice that is communicated by God to our souls and which makes us, as members of Christ, intrinsically holy.[2]

> Christ Jesus Himself constantly "infuses" His power into those that have been justified, as the head infuses power into its members and the vine into its branches. This power precedes, accompanies, and follows their good works; without it these works can in no manner be pleasing to God.[3]

Christ "infuses" (*influit*); note that the word has been officially accepted. And, though this influx leaves our holiness really distinct from that of our Head, there is no separation of the two.

> For that justice, which is called ours because we are justified by its inherence in our souls (*per eam nobis inhaerentem*), is also the justice of God, since it is infused into us by God in consideration of the merits of Christ.[4]

If our good works were ours alone, they would be worthless, but since they are united with God and with His Christ, they also become the works of Christ, and therefore something sacred.

This teaching is defined by the Council during its fourteenth session, in which it speaks of the sacrament of penance and explains how the pardoned sinner must unite his own satis-

[509]

factory works with the satisfaction of Christ. Far from minimizing the efficacy of the passion and redemption, this doctrine only brings out more clearly the true immensity of
Christ's satisfaction: it is a principle capable of giving satisfactory value even to the poor actions of men.

> A further proof [for the satisfactory value of good works]
> is that when we suffer to satisfy for our sins, we become like to
> Christ, who satisfied for our sins, and from whom alone is our
> sufficiency. Hence we have the certain assurance that if we
> suffer with Him, we shall likewise be glorified with Him. For
> the satisfaction which we make for our sins is not our own to
> such an extent that it does not come through Christ. We can
> do nothing of ourselves by our own unaided strength; but with
> His co-operation we can do all things in Him that strengtheneth
> us. Man therefore has nothing in which he has reason to glory;
> all our glory is in Christ, in whom we live, in whom we move,
> in whom we make satisfaction, bringing forth worthy fruits of
> penance which have their virtue from Him, which by Him are
> offered to the Father, and which because of Him are accepted
> by the Father.[5]

We have cited this last passage principally because of its
resemblance to the texts that are to follow, and which indicate, we think, the very realistic sense in which the words of
the definition should be taken. We readily grant that neither
this text nor the other texts of the Council speak with great
emphasis of the Mystical Body. But they do speak of it, and it
is instructive to hear the Church formulate her faith in these
particular terms, at the very moment when, in her most solemn
assembly, she condemns most explicitly one of the most vicious
heretical attacks upon that faith.

Let us dwell briefly on the doctrine expressed in these texts,
and let us note carefully its entire content. The Church teaches
that there are two aspects to membership in the Saviour. First,
the member of Christ possesses a true interior life. This the
Council establishes before all else, when it defines the intrinsic
character of justification. But, it continues, the member has
this life only through union with the Head. This is clearly
stated in the texts which we have just read. To sum up this
doctrine, and to explain the whole in terms of the Mystical
Body, we may say that the Council teaches both that the

members have life in themselves, and that they have life only by their incorporation in the organism. Does this not mean that to possess life and to be in the organism, are one and the same thing?

Therefore certain Scholastics were wrong, when shortly before and even during the Council, they spoke of a twofold justification. In their opinion, Christians have two kinds of holiness: one their own, which is the grace inherent in their souls, and another, which is the holiness of Christ imputed to them by God.

As if a member could have two lives, its own and that of the organism! As if the union of Head and members were an extrinsic imputation, a kind of legal fiction. It is perfectly right, indeed necessary to distinguish between cause and effect, between Christ's personal grace and the grace that is infused into us. But one cannot separate the ray from the sun, and then hope to obtain a better view of its brightness! The error of Protestantism lies precisely in the idea of an extrinsic justification and vivification. Repeating a false view can never correct it, even if the contradictory view is added; this is simply introducing the germ of the disease into the remedy.

Another point to be noted here is that the error of Protestantism consists much more in mutilating the truth than in introducing false ideas. There is no sin in stating that God sees us clothed in the life and holiness of Christ, or that God unites us with the eternal life that is in Christ; all this is true in a certain sense. The error lies in the claim that this divine action is no more than an extrinsic decree, a juridical fiction, in virtue of which we are considered as living in the Saviour without having life in ourselves. The Mystical Body has been robbed of the life whereby it lived; our union with Christ is stripped of all that entered into the very being of Christ and of Christians. Such an external and superficial vivification differs from true incorporation in Christ, not as a sick man differs from one in good health, but as a headless man differs from a living man; it differs by an absence, which, we may say, is the absence of everything.

No complex argumentation is needed to prove the inadequacy of this truncated system. A comparison with the Catholic teaching is enough. When placed side by side with the truth, its utter poverty is only too apparent.

The Church herself has drawn this comparison in her solemn reply to the innovators. The members of Christ, she teaches, are united with the Head by the very life they have within them. This is no superficial attachment, as the heretics would have it; it is essential and intrinsic. That this union may be total, it is not necessary that we be absolute nothingness; on the contrary, our attachment to Christ will be all the closer in proportion to the intensity of our own personal life, since it is this life that makes us His members, and since we belong to Him precisely by that which makes us our individual selves.

When there is question of Him who is the soul of our soul and the light of our eyes, the words *without* and *within, exterior* and *interior* cease to apply. They are perfect for expressing spatial realities, but they are wholly unsuited to describe the operations of grace. Their use involves paradoxes that are eloquent witness of the higher plane to which we have been raised. We must say, for instance, that Christians are outside themselves, since they live in Christ. And yet we must add that this wondrous exteriority gives them a more truly interior, personal life than any natural means can give, since it confers on them a supernatural depth of life. On the other hand, we must say that, while Christ is exterior to them by His divine transcendence, He is nevertheless interior to them, since He lives in them. To be even more exact, we must say that He is more truly within them than they are within themselves, since He is the source of the life by which they live. In short, we must affirm that, while the life which superabounds in Him is of course distinct from the life that flows into us — for to deny this would be to destroy one or the other — yet the two are inseparable, since the members can live only by their union with the Head.[6]

Such is the mystery of unity, the mystery of the Head and members, the mystery of Christ and the Church. It shines with a luminousness and a marvelousness far surpassing the petty system of clear concepts which heretics would substitute in its place. No one who has tasted the pure wine can feel any desire for the water that has been extracted from it.

Now that we have considered all that is implied in the Catholic teaching, we have still to study the explanations and commentaries added by the Fathers and theologians of the Council, as well as by other Scholastic writers.

III. § 1

In preparation for the task that was to face the Council, divine Providence had inaugurated an important work in the Schools. Naturally this was focused on the point which was being assailed by the Reformers: the value of good works performed by the just, and the value of satisfactory works in particular.

According to the certain and unanimous doctrine, the good works of a Christian in the state of grace possess an immense value, and give him, *ex condigno*, a right to eternal life, in the sense that God's free promises and the merits of Jesus Christ make it impossible for Him to refuse an eternal reward. It is likewise certain, continue our masters, that the works are far inferior in dignity to the satisfaction of Jesus Christ. He alone, they repeat, has made satisfaction in full rigor of justice, since He alone was in a position to offer God a reparation which was proportionate to the offense and which did not consist of goods already belonging to God. Lastly, He alone by His grace can render our satisfaction acceptable to God.

Many theologians say a little more. Christ's works of satisfaction are so excellent, that by union with them our own satisfactory works receive a certain accidental increase of dignity. However, they add, our works are of themselves still incapable of meriting heaven in strict justice; they are still finite, and something infinite is necessary.

Still others, of whom we shall speak here, take even a further step. They find that the systems which we have already mentioned ascribe either too much value to our merits or too little: too much, if these merits are considered outside of Christ, and too little, if they are considered in Christ. Such a manner of speaking, they say, would be correct if grace were something separate from our incorporation in Christ; it would then be purely and simply finite, and could confer only a finite

[513]

value on our acts. But if grace is merely the influx of the Man-God in us, there is no need of another divine decree, or even of an additional intention on God's part, in order that both grace and our acts may be united with that infinite value which is in Christ. The Incarnation has already done all this, by making Christ our Head and us His members; in him, therefore, we can in strict justice make satisfaction for our sins.

As a matter of fact, when there is question of such a mystery of love and unity, rigid juridical formalities are out of place. But it is the doctrine itself, not the vocabulary, that interests us. This doctrine is a continuation of the opinion of St. Thomas, to which we referred in the sixth chapter, and according to which Christ's satisfaction is ours by virtue of His real and mystical unity with us. This explains the entire economy of the Redemption. Now the theologians invoke the same principle to explain how the Redemption is continued in our own satisfactory works: because of our real and mystical unity with Christ, our satisfaction is His; in Him, therefore, it possesses an infinite value, and is, in strict justice, an adequate atonement for our sins. And this doctrine explains all Christian merit.

From the beginning Christian tradition has affirmed that Christ's passion is twofold: the sufferings of the Head and the sufferings of the members. Therefore, the Scholastics conclude, the satisfaction of Christ is likewise twofold: the satisfaction offered by the Head and the satisfaction offered by the members. Just as the sufferings of both have the same dignity, since the Head and members are one body, so too they possess the same satisfactory value, since Christ and the Christians make up one Mystical Christ. Both have the same value, but not in the same manner: it is in Christ principally, and in us only secondarily and by way of participation. Hence, while there is a certain equality between Head and members, this does not at all mean that the members are as great as the Head, but only that they are one with Him. If they are placed beside Him, then of course they are nothing; but they are not beside Him! They are in Him, and, being in Him, they are everything, since He is everything, and since, even when joined with them, He is still one. It is on account of this unity of the Mystical Body, as St. Thomas says, that the merits of the Head flow into the members. The first writer to give clear expression to this teaching is Cardinal Cajetan.

> Christ and ourselves, His members, make up one mystical person. Therefore my satisfaction, when joined to the satisfaction of Christ and considered as the satisfaction of one mystical person, becomes strictly equal to the offense, and at times even superabundant.[7]

However, as the Cardinal explains in another passage:

> This does not mean that we merit eternal life by our works inasmuch as they proceed from us, but inasmuch as they come, in us and through us, from Christ.[8]

Cajetan expresses the thought best in his commentary on the text of St. Paul to the Galatians (2:20, D.V.): "I live, now not I, but Christ liveth in me."

> Note how the Apostle explains the words he has just written [in the preceding verse]: "that I may live to God." He does so by correcting the use of the first person, "that *I* may live." "No," he continues, "it is not I that live, but it is Christ that lives in me. Hence all my vital acts, such as to know and to think, to love, to rejoice or to be sad, to desire, to labor, are mine no longer; they no longer come from me, but from Christ within me." For he who is crucified with Christ has Christ as the reason for all his actions; Christ so directs, disposes, and uses his internal and external faculties that he can justly say: "Christ lives in me."[9]

In his opusculum *De fide et operibus adversus lutheranos*, the Cardinal interprets the same verse in exactly the same sense, but in terms which are more forceful and which made a greater impression upon his contemporaries. We shall quote a long text from it for the sake of the beautiful thoughts it contains on the subject of the Mystical Body. The exegesis to which we refer occurs toward the middle of the passage.

> Theologians assign three reasons why our works have merit for eternal life: first, they proceed from charity; secondly, they proceed from sanctifying grace; and thirdly, they proceed from the Holy Spirit who dwells within us.

But Cajetan is not satisfied with these reasons. He prefers another explanation, which he considers "clearer and more persuasive" (*clarior et persuasibilior*). We cannot forego the pleasure of repeating these two words, especially the first. The quotation continues:

> But a clearer and more persuasive way to explain this merit is to show that it is not so much our work as the work of Christ our Head, acting in us and through us.
>
> For we must suppose, as the Apostle does when he writes to the Romans (12:5), to the Ephesians (4:12–16), and to the Colossians (2:9–11), that men in the state of grace are the living members of Christ. We must also suppose that the union of Christ our Head with those men who are His living members is not like that of a political body (such, for instance, as the body of citizens in a well-ordered republic), but that the Head and members form one body, as in a natural body. Christ the Head vivifies the members by His spirit, and, as St. Paul plainly teaches, He unites them together by means of spiritual joints and bonds. Again, we must suppose, as the Scripture teaches, that the sufferings and actions of Christ's living members are the sufferings and actions of Christ, their Head. On the subject of their sufferings, we have Christ's own words: "Saul, Saul, why dost thou persecute Me?" (Acts 9:4.) Yet Paul was persecuting only His members. And Paul reminds the Galatians (Gal. 3:1) that Christ was crucified in them, by which he clearly means, in the sufferings they have endured for Christ. On the subject of their actions, St. Paul writes to the Corinthians (2 Cor. 13:3): "Seek ye a proof of Christ who speaketh in me?" Finally, speaking in general, he tells the Galatians (2:20, D.V.): "I live, now not I, but Christ liveth in me."
>
> From all this, I conclude that it is perfectly true for me to say: "I merit; no, it is not I who merit, but Christ who merits in me. I fast; now not I, for it is Christ that fasts within me," and so of all the free actions that the living members of Christ perform for God.

This is the exegesis of which we spoke; its significance is evident enough. But the rest of the passage is too interesting to pass over:

> In this way the merit of eternal life is not attributed so much to our own works as to the works which Christ, our Head, performs in us and through us.

This it is that distinguishes the merit of eternal life, as it is found in infants [from the merit of adults]. In infants, eternal life is due solely to the merit of Christ; that is, to the merits that Christ acquired when He led our mortal life, through His sufferings and death. But adults who grow in grace have a double claim to eternal life: first, in virtue of the merit which Christ acquired in His own person, and secondly, in virtue of the merit which Christ gains when, as Head, He acts in and through the adult. It is fitting that the divine liberality should communicate this twofold merit of eternal life to the adults who are the children of God. For, as it is written in the Epistle to the Romans (8:29, D.V.): "He predestinated them to be made conformable to the image of His Son." But they are made more conformable to Christ by having this twofold merit of eternal life. For Christ also possesses eternal life [by a two-fold title]: first, in virtue of the grace of personal union whereby the Word became flesh, and herein Christ possesses eternal life without any merit on His part; secondly, however, He merited the same glory by His obedience unto death, as St. Paul tells the Philippians (2:8–11): "He humbled Himself by obedience unto death, yea, unto death upon a cross. Wherefore God hath exalted Him," etc. Thus, we are made more conformable to this Christ who has a twofold right to glory, when we likewise have a twofold claim to eternal life: the first we have, not by any merit of our own, but through the merit acquired by Christ in His own person; the second we have with merit on our part, through the merit which Christ acquires in us and through us. And, just as Christ's glory is enhanced by the fact that He has also, by His own merit, deserved the eternal life of His body and the exaltation of His name, etc., so too the dignity of the members of Christ is greater if they can co-operate with their Head in gaining eternal life. For, as Dionysius says, there is nothing more divine than to become God's collaborator. From this it also follows that our merit is not superfluous, since through it eternal life is due us in a new way and by a new title, just as Christ merited His own exaltation by making it His due in virtue of a new title.[10]

Note how carefully Cajetan rejects every semblance of a separation between Christ and us. The merits of Christ that are applied to us at baptism, and those which we ourselves acquire with the help of His grace, are both our own, and both constitute our intrinsic holiness; similarly, the merits Christ acquired during His mortal life and those that He acquires now in His mystical life in the Church, are equally the merits of Christ. As Cajetan repeats, whether Christ acts

[517]

in His own person, or whether He acts in us and through us, it is ever the same Christ.

Nor was Cajetan the only one to formulate these thoughts. In 1542, about eight years after the Cardinal's death, they were reiterated, by a theologian who wished his name withheld, in a memorial drawn up for Pope Paul III in view of the coming Council. The doctrine of the Mystical Body, writes this author, furnishes the Catholics with an excellent means of refuting the Protestant heresy. The Reformers claimed that whatever efficacy is attributed to the merits of the Christian detracts from the merits of Christ. On this point the memorial remarks:

> To this objection, Catholics have an easy answer: It is Christ Himself who merits and offers satisfaction in us. . . . Christ gives the first and intrinsic impulse, and we contribute our co-operation and our obedience.[11]

Then the author goes on to repeat, almost word for word, Cajetan's commentary on the text of the Galatians. The same ideas are stressed in another anonymous memorial composed under like circumstances:

> Our works are meritorious and satisfactory, not because of any deficiency or inadequacy on the part of the merits of Jesus Christ, but because of the perfection and affluence (*affluentia*) of those very merits. By His grace He communicates to His members the virtue of His own infinite merit.[12]

In other words, as Sylvester Maurus writes at a later date, the glory of the vine consists not in producing grapes by itself, but in communicating this power to its branches. In like manner, the Saviour's glory consists not in reserving to Himself alone the power to perform holy and meritorious acts, but in infusing into us, His members, the power to do good and to acquire true merit.

§ 2

The Council itself took up the doctrine, first in the sixth session, which dealt with the subject of justification, and again in the fourteenth session, which had to do with satisfactory works. We have already quoted, in their proper place at the beginning of this exposition, the official definitions that touch upon our subject. It is now time to say a few words concerning the manner in which these texts were explained, defended, and understood by the Fathers and theologians of Trent.

At the beginning of the sixth session, when there was question only of determining the exact nature, the causes, and the gratuitousness of justification, very little was said of the Mystical Body. The chief concern at the moment was to prove that Christian holiness is something intrinsic to us, and that it consists neither in faith alone nor in an imputation to us of the merits of Christ.

It was only later on, when the Council came to discuss the value of the good works performed by the just, that attention was focused on our incorporation in Christ. The following problem was proposed: When a man dies in the state of grace, does he possess all that is necessary in order to enter heaven, or must God make some further application of Christ's justice to the soul? During the hearings devoted to the examination of this question, which began in October, 1546, the theologian who spoke most emphatically of the Mystical Body was Jerome Seripandus. But he was not alone; both before and after him many others expressed the same ideas.

One expression in particular is constantly on their lips. We have already seen it formulated by Cajetan: "We live, says St. Paul, or rather, it is not we that live, but it is Jesus Christ that lives in us; in the same way, we merit and offer satisfaction, or rather, it is not we that merit and offer satisfaction, but it is Christ who merits and offers satisfaction in us."

Fewer documents are available concerning the fourteenth session than concerning the sixth; the *Acta* of this session and the doctrinal treatises which go with them have not yet been published in the huge collection of documents undertaken by the Görresgesellschaft. However, the indications furnished by Le Plat and Theiner are sufficient to show that the same ideas and the same manner of speaking were maintained in the later session. Thus, on November 10, 1551, the bishop of Coutances addressed the Council:

[519]

It may be said that even now Christ offers satisfaction in us. For Christ has satisfied before, He is satisfying now, and He will continue to satisfy forever. Therefore, even with us, it is always He that satisfies; we cannot say that we satisfy of ourselves, but that it is Christ who satisfies together with us.[13]

The very next day, the bishop of Chioggia returned to the same thought:

Though what we do be little, yet since we are incorporated in Christ, it is something great that we do. Therefore when we make satisfaction we can say: "Christ is making satisfaction," as St. Paul writes: "I live, now not I, but Christ liveth in me."[14]

And on the following day, the bishop of Tuy observed:

When we satisfy, Christ too makes satisfaction, as universal efficient cause.[15]

These are not isolated expressions; many bishops and theologians spoke in a similar strain. But to quote every such statement is out of the question; many are not available, and those which we have are too numerous and too much alike. We shall mention only one name, that of Ruard Tapper, Chancellor of the University of Louvain. Both in the treatises he prepared for this session of the Council, where he played a prominent part, and in his other writings he insists strongly upon the life and activity that Christ continues in us and through us.

Enough has been said, we think, to show in what sense we should interpret the ninth chapter of the doctrinal decree on the sacrament of penance which we quoted above.[16] When the Council states that our satisfaction makes us conformable to Christ who has satisfied for us; that through it we shall, by suffering with Him, be glorified with Him; that it is not our satisfaction to such an extent that it is not also His, and that it is in Christ that we live and move and make satisfaction, we easily see what is meant by this life, this movement, and this satisfaction which we possess within us, or rather, which Christ possesses in us and through us. The Council means that in the order of grace we have a true activity, or rather, it is not we who act, but Christ who acts in us and through us. The words of Cajetan could receive no more solemn approval.

§ 3

Nor were these words to fall into oblivion. About a year after the fourteenth session of the Council, they are repeated by Hosius in his famous *Confessio fidei catholicae* (1552–1553). Hosius, who was then bishop of Ermeland in Poland, was made cardinal in 1561, and Papal Legate to the Council of Trent from 1561 to 1563. His work created a sensation, and ran into many editions. He writes:

> If Christ lives in us, He cannot do so without acting in us. . . . What we do in this manner must necessarily be worthy of eternal life, not because of the merit of the works themselves, but because of the merit of Him who lives and acts within us.

The merits of Christ and the merits of Christians are all one, as the Head and the members are one.

> Why do they [the Protestants] not see that when they speak of the actions of Christians, they belittle, not our works, but our Lord Jesus Christ, from whom we receive them and to whom we refer them. If He is taken out of our good works, then indeed they are no better than filthy rags.[17]

In speaking thus, the great theologian felt that he was in full accord with the doctrine of the Schoolmen and with the belief of all the faithful. He appeals to the testimony of all Tradition, and it is interesting to note that he appeals even to the little prayer books that form and nourish the piety of the simple faithful. Everywhere he finds this teaching: the excellence of our works is due to Christ, to Christ who lives with us.

Needless to say, such theologians as Cajetan, Hosius, and Tapper saw as well as we that these expressions border on an abyss. This transfer into our souls of the satisfaction of Christ recalls the heretical doctrine of justification through an extrinsic imputation of the holiness of Christ. This they knew; but they likewise knew that truth extends as far as error exclusively, and they knew that to place any further restriction upon truth, even under the pretext of more surely avoiding an error, is simply to fall into another error. They knew, too, that the only way to refute error is to win back the shreds of truth

[521]

that have been stolen and disfigured, to vindicate their true meaning, and to restore them to their only authentic context. There is, perhaps, a superficial resemblance; but what an enormous difference exists between their system and that of the heretics! One is extrinsic imputation, the other an intrinsic compenetration and incorporation; according to one, the satisfaction of Christ is merely cast over us like a cloak, while according to the other, our poor acts proceed from our inmost selves and have a true satisfactory value, because in our inmost selves we live by our attachment to Christ.

After Hosius, and after the Council of Trent, which closed in 1563, the idea lives on. Among the Scholastics, it is to be found especially in the studious atmosphere of the schools of Spain. Influenced perhaps by Cajetan, whom he held in high esteem, Father Francis de Victoria (1480–1546) introduced the system into the famous Dominican school which he had founded at Salamanca. This school exerted a powerful influence in the field of theology; placed in so advantageous a position, the doctrine was assured of wide diffusion. It is quite likely that many who proposed these ideas in the Council had imbibed them here.

The question under discussion is always the same, and it is the question that was examined at Trent: What is the intrinsic value of the good works and satisfaction of Christians, if we prescind from any divine promise? Let us quote, for instance, the declaration of Bartholomew of Medina:

> Each time a man does a good and meritorious work, Christ performs the work in him, and gives him the power to perform it.[18]

To Medina, the principle seems so fundamental and so clearly expressed in Scripture that he considers it a matter of faith. The very union of Head and members is at stake. Therefore there can no longer be any doubt: not only are our merits the prolongation of the merits of Christ, but our merits also share in the value of His merits.

The same thought is expressed in the following passage, taken from another theologian, John Paul Nazarius. He does not belong to the School of Salamanca, and he wrote more than half a century after Medina. But, as we shall see, the ideas which he develops are those of the famous school. He even repeats and commentates the expressions, now become classical, of Cajetan. We hope the reader will excuse these repetitions, for they are instructive.

Christ is in a sense the very person (*hypostasis*) of His Mystical Body, which is the Church. This Cajetan tells us in his commentary on the following words: "For, as . . . all the members of the body, whereas they are many, yet are one body, so also is Christ" (1 Cor. 12:12, D.V.). This is how he explains the text. Just as when a man says, "So am I," he means his whole body together with its members, since the pronoun *I* expresses the whole person; in like manner, when Paul says, "So is Christ," he is speaking of Christ's Mystical Body together with all its members. For Christ is as it were the personality (*tenet locum hypostasis*) of His Mystical Body. But it is evident that the actions of both head and members are to be attributed to that one person to whom both head and members belong.[19]

Nazarius can find no better example to illustrate this personal unity than that of the hypostatic union itself. Just as Christ's two natures subsist in one Person, he says,

so Christ in His Mystical Body is one mystical person, having two modes of existence: the first He has in Himself as Head; the other He has in the faithful who receive grace and charity from Him. Inasmuch as He subsists in Himself, He is one individual person; but inasmuch as He subsists mystically in His members, He acts as the personality, not only of each of those who are His living members, but of many together, or even of all together.

Thus united with us, Christ gives His own dignity to our actions through a sort of communication of properties, analogous to that which exists between His two natures.

We therefore attribute to Him as to one person, not only what is true of His divine nature and of His human nature, but also the actions and sufferings of His members. . . .
St. Paul says, "Christ liveth in me." The words "in me" indicate a mystical mode of existence whereby Christ lives and speaks in Paul. In like manner, declares Cajetan,[20] I too can say: "I merit, now not I, but Christ merits in me; I make satisfaction, now not I, but Christ makes satisfaction in me;

[523]

I fast, now not I, but Christ fasts in me." And so of all the free actions that the living members of Christ perform for God. Thereby the merit of eternal life is attributed not so much to our works as to the works of Christ our Head, our mystical personality, who subsists mystically in us and acts through us.

These expressions may seem vague, but they were the delight of the Scholastics in question, who were quite as fond of clear concepts as anyone else. We may say that during the closing years of the sixteenth century and throughout the seventeenth, this was the common teaching, at least among the Thomists. It is, declares De la Parra, "a true and mystical doctrine." We like to see this association of the two adjectives.

Not only did the doctrine invade the Schools, but it is found in works dealing with the spiritual life. At about the same time that Nazarius wrote, St. Francis de Sales was developing the same thought, with his inimitable charm, in the *Traité de l'amour de Dieu:*

> Scarlet and purple or deep crimson is a most precious and princely material, not because of the wool, but because of the color. The works of good Christians possess so great a value that in return for them we obtain heaven; yet, Theotime, it is not because they proceed from us, and are the wool of our hearts, but because they are reddened with the blood of the Son of God, or in other words, because the Lord sanctifies our works by the merits of His blood. The branch, united and joined to the vine, bears fruit, not by its own power, but by the power of the vine. Now we are united through charity to our Redeemer, as the members are united with the head; hence it is that our fruits and good works draw their virtue from Him, and so merit eternal life.[21]

However, such a doctrine could not enjoy favor for very long; it was too "mystical" and too difficult of expression in abstract terms, and so failed to win a permanent place in the Schools. Many theologians reject it; many others, significantly enough, confess their total inability to understand it. After a time all avoided it, as mariners steer clear of a rocky coast.

Its adversaries always advance the same objection: In order to speak accurately, we must accept the principle that we are finite beings, and that in consequence whatever proceeds from us is likewise finite. Grace itself cannot take away our limitations, since essentially and intrinsically it is an accidental quality of our soul. Therefore it is finite, as the soul itself is finite. It is true, they continue, that the title of member of the Saviour confers a sublime dignity upon us; nevertheless, since it is in us who are finite, it cannot be anything else than finite. On the other hand, to make satisfaction means to compensate for an infinite offense: *iniuria est in iniuriato, satisfactio in satisfaciente.* Nothing that we possess can have any proportion with the infinite; hence no expiation of ours can be equal in strict justice to the sin that is to be atoned for, or to the possession of God that is to be merited. If, then, our good works are capable of producing this result, it is not because of any intrinsic value that they have of themselves, but because of the promises that God has made, because of the merits of Jesus Christ which God takes into consideration, and because of the entire supernatural economy.

The defenders of the doctrine always answer in the same way; namely, by denying the supposition. The objectors take for granted that the Christians are separated from Christ, that the members are divorced from the Head, and that they are considered merely as they are in themselves. But this would be a contradiction: the members are intrinsically constituted members by their intrinsic attachment to the body; if they are considered apart from the body, they cease to be members. The dignity that we have as members of Christ is not a quality that resides in ourselves alone; it resides in our very union with the Saviour. One must be blind to look upon that dignity without seeing Him at the same time.

One might take a further step in the same direction, and say that the grace whereby each Christian is intrinsically sanctified is inseparable from the grace whereby he is a member of the Saviour. This would be merely to apply to Christians what the Schoolmen say of Christ and of the relation between His personal grace and His grace as Head. But as far as we know none of the Scholastics make the application. The nearest approach to it is the opinion we have just recorded concerning the satisfactory value of good works performed in the state of grace.

IV

Now, turning our attention from the dignity proper to each member of Christ, we can gather some observations from the same masters relative to the union of the individual member with the other members. Our search need not be long, for in the same passages which we have quoted, our authors are always careful to say that the good works of Christians have their value, not only from their union with Christ, but also from their union with the rest of the faithful. But to find the frequent, common, and traditional expression of this truth, it is necessary to consult the treatise on Indulgences, which occurs at the nineteenth distinction of the fourth book, in commentaries on the *Sentences,* and at the twenty-fifth question of the *Supplement* to the third part, in commentaries on the *Summa.* Other developments may be found in the treatises on the sacraments, especially on the Eucharist and baptism, on penance and the power of the keys, or again, on the Communion of Saints, on the value of suffrages for the souls in Purgatory, and on the effects of excommunication.

Each of these treatises should receive a thorough explanation at this point. That, of course, is impossible. We shall only note that according to St. Thomas, the unity of the Mystical Body explains how it is that the treasury of the Church consists of the satisfaction of the saints, as well as of the satisfaction of Christ, and how this satisfaction is applicable to all the faithful. Even though they may have been unaware of the fact, the saints have expiated for the whole Church. For, as Cajetan observes:

It was Christ's intention to suffer for the whole Church in general, for the passion of Christ is a universal cause of salvation. Similarly, the intention of the saints was to suffer for the whole Church, over and above their own expiation. For the passion of the saints and the passion of Christ are alike common to all, since the passion of the saints is the completion (*consummatio*) of the passion of Christ.[22]

Moreover, it is the traditional teaching that a Christian in the state of grace can make satisfaction for another, because we are all one in Christ. And, as the merits of the members have a universal value in Christ, so too they have an inexhaustible value in Christ.

The merit of the passion and death of Christ and of the saints, in whom Christ suffers and will continue to suffer until the consummation of the world, has been and is far greater than all the crimes of the world have been or ever can be; for a single drop of Christ's blood would have sufficed to wash away all sins.[23]

Again, always, and in all things, Christians are as Christ is, but only in Christ and with Christ. For are not Head and members one whole? Therefore, since Christ is unity, we are all one with all the others in Him; and here we have the dogma of the Communion of Saints. We shall not repeat all that the Scholastics have said on this subject; that would require too much time and space, but we shall indicate a few passages, so as not to pass over the point in total silence.

The goods of the entire organism belong to each member, as had already been remarked by Alexander of Hales; the goods which each member possesses, he possesses not for himself alone, but for the good of the whole, since in unity all things are common to all; and even when he shares them with all, they remain his, since in unity "all" are still "himself." This catholic force of expansion is no accidental quality superadded to the good works of Christians; it requires neither an explicit intention nor a new intervention of grace. It is present in the work itself, and proceeds from the very principle that makes the work possible; for the same principle that gives life to the member also causes the member to live in the unity of all the members. No matter what their function may be, they are attached intrinsically to all the other members, or, to quote the beautiful words of St. Thomas, they communicate, through a common root, with all the other members.

For the action of him who is one with me, is in some sense my own work.[24]

Only in good, and especially in supernatural good, is such a communication possible. Evil does not proceed from unity, but from a want of unity; hence sinners harm only themselves.

[527]

Mere natural goodness benefits only the individual who practices it, but in the order of grace every good is a common good, and is beneficial to the entire body.

> Just as in a living body the operation of one member promotes the welfare of the whole body, so it is in the spiritual body, which is the Church. Since all the faithful are one body, the good of each is communicated to the others. . . . Whence it follows that whoever possesses charity, shares in all the good that is done in the whole world.[25]

To be with the members of Christ, again and always, is to be with Christ; the idea is beautifully expressed in the form of a prayer by St. Peter Canisius in his *Confessions:*

> O Lord, I ask Thy help, and I beg Thee to sustain me, not only by the merits of Christ, who is our Head and the Holy of holies, but also by the merits of His most noble members and of His whole body, which is the Church, that I may have part, not only in general but also in particular, with all those who fear Thee and who keep Thy commandments in heaven and on earth. I beseech Thee, Father of all majesty, that they who serve Thee may serve Thee also for me, that for me they may make intercession, adore, love, and glorify Thy holy name, which is rightly honored in the humblest of Thy creatures. May this name be glorified in Thy elect, whom from eternity Thou hast loved and predestined to be made conformable to the image of Thy Son, who is and ever will be the first-born of His brethren. And I beseech Thee that they may praise this Thy glorious and adorable name in me, and that they may supplicate Thy glory for me.[26]

A mystery of life, a mystery of union in life; such is the mystery of the Church in Christ.

V

We have seen what the Scholastics have to say of this mystery. Despite all the circumstances that might have deterred them, many have spoken of it, and often with emphasis. The most illustrious of their number are also the most outspoken on the subject, for the names which figure most prominently in this study are likewise the most famous. We have also seen that the Scholastics, like the Fathers, speak of the Mystical

Body in connection with a great many dogmas: in treating of Christ, of the Redemption, of the Eucharist, of the Communion of Saints.

But they do all this in their own way, in accordance with a strictly organized plan, in which each point is deduced from some first truth. Let us recall, for instance, the procedure of St. Thomas. What is first in any order, he says, is the cause of everything in that order. But Christ is first in the order of those that have grace, and His resurrection is first in the order of true resurrection. Therefore, since He possesses union with God and divine life in the supreme degree, He has the power to infuse life into all. The treatise is built up accordingly: first it speaks of the Head, then of the members, carefully developing every point and following a strictly logical order.

This systematic arrangement, which is their contribution to the traditional doctrine, gave them a better understanding of certain elements of that doctrine; their teaching continues and perfects that of the Fathers. They show, both more clearly and more simply, how the life of the faithful is a flow, a participation of the life of Christ, and how the grace of justification is a prolongation, in the members, of that grace which, in the Head, is the hypostatic union.

In conclusion, however, we must say that while they have perfected the patristic teaching on these points — or rather, while God has used them as a means to bring the deposit of revealed truth nearer to its full explanation — on other points there has been a regression. All in all, they have spoken little, and with little emphasis, of the Mystical Body; the Fathers gave us a much more vigorous doctrine. Indeed, it would be a mistake to judge the Scholastic teaching solely from the quotations that we have given. When they are taken together, supporting one another as they do in these pages, they seem to constitute a very considerable part of the doctrine of the School. But as soon as they are restored to their context, scattered in huge tomes and lost in developments from which the idea of our incorporation in Christ is absent, they by no means possess the same significance. The very authors who have furnished the most vigorous statements — St. Thomas, Cajetan, Medina, Nazarius, speak forcefully of the Mystical

Body only when they recognize it as a decisive argument. Soon they cease to think about it, or else they are content merely to repeat the trite phrases that are handed down from author to author. This remark is necessary, and the correction must be made, for the sake of the accuracy of our exposition. But this does not impair the content of our chapters in any way, for the doctrinal tradition of the Mystical Body meets with no interruption at the hands of the Scholastics. It may have lost some of its vividness, but it still lives; and so great is its vitality that even amid these unfavorable conditions we can see evidences of progress along certain lines.

Chapter X

The French School. The Mystical Body and the Spiritual Life

><

I. *The theology of our incorporation in Christ.* Pierre de Bérulle. Religion is the center of all, and the heart of religion is Jesus Christ. Comparison with the Greek Fathers. Christ is the life of souls, "a divine capacity for souls." The Eucharist. The mysteries of Christ's life are present and perpetual.

II. *Spirituality based on this theology.* The ideal: to be in the same relation to the humanity of Jesus as His humanity is to the Word: that is, we should be without subsistence of our own, continuing in Him the divine mission of the Word. Obedience, contemplation, adherence to God.

III. *Rigorism of the doctrine,* especially as proposed by Condren and Olier. The sternness of Bérulle's teaching. The Jansenist theory of grace and of the Mystical Body. Sources and characteristics of the theory of the Mystical Body as taught by Condren; by Olier. Both manifest a certain disdain for human nature. We are loathsome in the eyes of God, and even in the eyes of Jesus Christ. We ought to feel a like detestation for ourselves. To lose and to annihilate self.

IV. This rigorism is belied by their true spirit of Christian charity.

I

THE ENERGY and richness which the doctrine of the Mystical Body loses at the hands of the Schoolmen is restored by the masters of the French Oratory and of St. Sulpice. These are Cardinal Pierre de Bérulle, founder and first general of the Congregation of the Oratory of Jesus Christ, Père Charles de Condren, disciple and successor of Bérulle in the office of general, and Jean-Jacques ("Monsieur") Olier, the founder of St. Sulpice. It is not our purpose here to tell the story of their lives,

[531]

but simply to discover what they have to say of the Mystical Body in their doctrine of the spiritual life; for all three, and especially Condren and Olier, must be classed as spiritual writers rather than as theologians. Our task will be easy and fruitful, for the doctrine of the Mystical Body occupies a prominent place in their writings; it will be a simple task as well, since the teaching of all three is very much the same, and may be studied as one. Consequently we shall restrict ourselves to a summary of the doctrine of Bérulle, who is first both in time and in theological importance. Toward the end of the chapter, when we shall have to turn our attention to a secondary though important feature, the rigorism and the negative side of the doctrine, we shall also quote from Condren and Olier, in whose writings this tendency is more pronounced. In this way we shall have an opportunity to indicate the characteristics proper to these two masters.

In speaking of Bérulle, we should first consider the reasons which led him to take a special interest in the truth of the Mystical Body. Unfortunately, however, we can make only conjectures on this point. His method of prayer, together with the assistance of grace, seems to have been one of his sources of information concerning our incorporation in the Incarnate Word. But his biographers have so crowded their accounts with other developments that it is impossible to determine the exact nature of the spiritual lights which he thus received. These were probably only the first germ of the doctrine which he was to develop through profound meditation and laborious study. His teaching is marked by a blend of deep sincerity and bookish profusion that appears to indicate some such combination of divine light, personal work, and dogged assimilation at the beginning. Moreover, he had excellent opportunity to improve his knowledge of the subject, by reason of his association with several mystics, with various theories of mysticism, and perhaps also with the masters of the School of Salamanca on the occasion of his visits to Spain. We know that he went to Spain in order to make arrangements for bringing the Carmelites of St. Theresa to France. And, as a matter of fact, St. Theresa lays much stress upon our incorporation in Christ. Not that she makes use either of the idea or of the expression as such, but she frequently speaks of the life of Christ in the soul, which is a corollary of our incorporation in Him. However, we are not told whether or not Bérulle was impressed by this aspect of Teresian spirituality.

Though the contributing influences are not so easily distinguishable as we might wish, the doctrine is sufficiently complete to explain itself. We shall indicate its principal elements here.

The summit of all is God; the foundation of all our duties is religion, worship, the adoration of God. The center and bond of all is Christ, God like the Father and man like ourselves, who unites heaven and earth in Himself and who is Himself our religion. To adore God in Christ and through Christ is, we may say, the sole preoccupation of the founder of the Oratory, and the résumé of his spirituality.

Personally, he would have wished to count for naught in his own works, and let Jesus be everything in them. He would have preferred to remain silent and not to write, in order that the one Master should speak to souls. According to the testimony of Père Bourgoing, he sought to have no sentiment or thought or activity outside of Jesus; he united himself with Jesus in every undertaking, and, after transacting the most important business, he could return within himself to Jesus, the sole object of his life, with as much ease and tranquillity as if he had spent the entire time in contemplation.

As he lived it and as he presents it to his readers, the Christ-life is a limitless dependence; he loved to call it his "slavery"; often he speaks of it as an attachment, a belonging to Christ, an incorporation. This life comes to us wholly from the Incarnate Word, since according to the idea and the explanation that he borrows from the Greek Fathers, the Incarnation has stored up in Christ the life of all humanity.

> Jesus is Life in a threefold manner: in His eternal nature, in His divine Person, and in His new nature, which is His humanity. In His eternal nature, for the divinity is not simply the source of life, but Life itself; in His Person, for to be Life is His proper and personal prerogative. by virtue of His eternal generation; in His humanity, since He vivifies it and makes it the plenitude and inexhaustible source of life.[1]

The Father is the principle of all life, the First Principle. The Word is likewise a principle of life, but He is a principle generated by the Father. The human nature assumed by the Word is also a principle by reason of its assumption, but it is a dependent principle. It is the principle in the order of grace and of the second creation, as God is the Principle of the first creation. It was made such by God, of course; it was even created for this purpose. As Bérulle tells us, it was created to be our very own:

> Christ is ours by reason of His office (*par état*), and not merely because of certain actions; He is ours by birth, and not simply in virtue of His office: "He was born for us" (Isa. 9:6). He is ours forever, and not merely for a time; He is ours for all our needs and for all our uses; He is ours by the same power whereby the Father generates Him in Himself.[2]

At the same time that the Word places His humanity in an order apart and draws it to the Father, He also makes that humanity our life, and causes it to reach out toward men; it becomes a universal Life, of which we are all "begotten and derived,"[3] and in which we are all vivified. The Saviour, declares Bérulle, is "a divine capacity for souls."

> *Jesus is a divine capacity for souls, and He is the source of the life whereby they live in Him.*
> There are in Jesus two wonderful capacities. By the one He is rendered capable of divinity, capable of the fullness of the divinity and of equality with God, though with dependence. The second is a capacity for souls; this He possesses in Himself, in His authority, in His power. For, if He has a capacity for the divinity, there is all the more reason why He should have a capacity for creatures. Our Lord receives this second capacity from the fullness of the divinity that is in Him; it makes Him a capacity for souls just as God is a capacity for His creatures: a capacity that contains, preserves, protects, and places souls in a continual and profound dependence upon Jesus and upon God. And it pleased Jesus Christ to institute the sacrament of His body in order to bind our souls to Himself, and to draw them into the plenitude of the divinity that abides in Him, by means of His lovable and adorable capacity to contain them and to give them life and subsistence in Himself. Thus we have a representation of that wondrous chain composed of three links, of which the Fathers speak. The first link binds the only Son to the eternal Father by the bond of

consubstantiality and unity of essence. The second binds the Son to our nature by the unity of His sacred Person. The third binds this deified humanity, this Man-God, to the person of each of us, by the efficacious and singular virtue of the Sacrament of His body, which incorporates us in His sacred humanity and causes us to live in Him, to share His life as His members, and to live with Him in His Father. Thus man ascends to this deified flesh and even to God, while God descends to the flesh and even to us.[4]

These limitless perspectives are the joy of the founder of the Oratory.

Jesus is all, and He must be all in us. And we must be nothing, treat ourselves as nothing, be nothing in ourselves, and be only in Him. . . . This is the work that we must begin on earth, and which will be consummated in heaven, where Jesus shall be all in all.[5]

We must quote Bérulle's rather lengthy development of this thought, entitled, *Of the life of the Christian in Jesus,* and addressed "to the Carmelites of the Convent of N."

Jesus is the crowning perfection (*accomplissement*) of our being; we subsist in Him alone, more truly than the body has its life and its perfection only in the soul, and the branch in the vine, and the part in the whole. For we are part of Jesus, and He is our all; all our good is to be in Him, as the branch exists and draws life and fruit from the vine. The truth is more real and more important than the reality of the branch in the vine; the latter is but a shadow and figure of the true reality.

We must regard our being as something defective and imperfect, as an empty space that needs to be filled, as a part that needs to be completed, as a piece of silver that awaits the stamp of the mint, or as a painting that has yet to receive the final life-like touches from the brush of a great artist.

Bérulle's sentences are labored and heavy, to be sure, but how insistent he is!

We should look upon Jesus as our consummation (*accomplissement*). This He is, and this He wills to be, as the Word is the consummation of the human nature that subsists in Him. . . .

Jesus alone is our consummation. We must attach ourselves to Him, who by His divinity is the foundation of our being, and who by His humanity is the bond that unites our being to God. He is the life of our life, the fullness of our capacity.

Our first lesson should be a realization of our incomplete and imperfect condition, and our first step should be toward Jesus, who is our consummation. In this search for Jesus, in this adherence to Jesus, in this continual and profound dependence upon Jesus, lie our life, our rest, our strength, and all our power of action. Never must we act except united with Him, directed by Him, and drawing life from Him.

Since He was created Head of human nature, we have a relationship with Him, a proportion with Him, an aptitude for Him; we wait to be actuated by Him and to be filled by Him. . . . We are a capacity, a pure capacity for Him; none can actuate and fill it but He. . . .

We must not suffer ourselves to be in ourselves, except to see to it that Jesus Christ be living in us, and that He may use and enjoy possession of all that is within us.[6]

Echoing the words of St. Cyril of Alexandria, Bérulle explains that Jesus exercises this possession of us by means of the Eucharist. Through this sacrament,

we are joined to this divine substance in a real and substantial union, which approaches very nearly to the unity of the divine Persons, and which is a perfect imitation of that unity. This union I ought to recognize as a masterpiece of the divinity, a masterpiece which is itself divine. This union I ought to contemplate as a portrait drawn from life by a great Master, Jesus Christ, according to a model as divine, as perfect, and as incomparable as is the union, or rather, the unity, of the divine Persons of the Most Holy Trinity.[7]

Not only the Person of Jesus, but, as Bérulle says in concert with the Fathers and the Scholastics, all His mysteries, all His dispositions, and all His sentiments affect us and vivify us. Past though they are in execution, His acts and His virtues are "perpetual" in their effects. One of his treatises bears the title:

Of the perpetuity of the mysteries of Jesus Christ.

We must consider the infinity which is communicated to these mysteries by the infinite Person who performs them in His human nature. We must weigh, as it were, the perpetuity of these mysteries. They took place under certain circumstances in the past, yet they continue and are present and perpetual in a new manner.

They are past in execution, but present by their virtue. . . . The Spirit of God by whom this mystery was wrought, the interior disposition of the outward mystery, the efficacy and virtue whereby this mystery lives and acts in us, this virtuous state and disposition, the merit by which He acquired us for the Father and merited heaven, His life, and His very self, the actual taste and sentiments He experienced when He accomplished the mystery — all this is ever living, actual, and present to Jesus. So that, if it were necessary or pleasing to God His Father, He would be ready to suffer anew and to accomplish once more this work, this action, this mystery. Therefore we must treat the things of Jesus and His mysteries, not as things that are past and dead, but as things that are living and present, yea eternal, from which we too should reap fruit that is present and eternal.[8]

Perpetually then, according to Bérulle, "the Incarnation is a mystery binding God to man and man to God, a mystery to which we must bind ourselves";[9] perpetually the childhood of Jesus confers the grace of innocence and of docile obedience to direction, and the wound of the Sacred Side of the Crucified is an eternal mark of love. We cannot forego the pleasure of quoting the beautiful page which Bérulle devotes to this "Eternal Wound."

Let us note that the living Heart of Jesus is already wounded deeply enough by love. Therefore the blow of the lance is reserved for His dead Heart; it is as if the wound of love was so great that the steel could inflict no deeper wound until He was dead. His Heart is eternally open, eternally wounded; His glory does not efface this wound, for it is a wound of love; the mark of the lance is but the symbol of the true and eternal wound of His Heart. This wound of the Side belongs to Jesus alone; it is proper neither to crucifixion nor to other men that are crucified; it is an eternal wound. It is a torment or wound inflicted upon a dead man, but it will endure unto eternal life, a wound that began in death but remains in life. This is not the case for others who are wounded, for their wounds do not survive death and will not be permanent in the resurrection. Give thanks to the eternal Father, who in decreeing the torment of the Cross for His humiliation, also decreed for Him this wound which is not proper to crucifixion, in order that we may abide in His Heart for all eternity.[10]

Christ willed all the mysteries and all the events of His life, in order that He might thus elevate and "deify" in Himself all the conditions in which men may find themselves.

In Jesus, childhood is deified; death is deified; even penance, shame, and sorrow are deified. For, as the cardinal explains:

> The Incarnation of the Word is the basis and foundation of the supreme dignity, which is not only the sanctification, but also the deification of all the dispositions and mysteries that enter into the life and pilgrimage of the Son of God on earth. All these dispositions and mysteries are deified. Therefore they have a divine dignity, a supreme power, a holy operation; and they are accomplished for the glory of God and for our particular good. . . . It is God's plan that all these dispositions should be honored, appropriated, and applied to our souls. As He distributes His gifts and graces, so also He distributes His dispositions and His mysteries among men and even among the angels.[11]

It is the duty of each Christian to fulfill his own proper part in these mysteries. One is made partaker of His humiliations, another of His authority; but always and through all, it is the Incarnation that acts upon the faithful.

> In all these various states and conditions He gives Himself to all. He gives us His Heart, His grace, His Spirit. He incorporates us in Himself. He makes Himself our own, and appropriates us to Himself. He communicates Himself to us and incorporates us in Himself. He makes us His own, living in Him, of Him, and by Him, as forming part of His body, of His Spirit, and of Himself, in a manner that is far more efficacious and important than that whereby our members form part of our own body and of ourselves.[12]

When the true nature of our Christ-life is represented in such a light, one immediately sees what rules of conduct it must impose upon us.

II

The Holy Scriptures and the earliest of the Fathers had already represented our incorporation in Christ as a first principle that should govern all our conduct. We recall, for instance, how Paul drew from it exhortations to charity, union, chastity, patience. This concern for practical applications is more characteristic of Latin than of oriental theology, but with the masters of the French School it attains its highest development. Their doctrine of the Mystical Body is primarily spiritual. Others use it merely on occasion, but with these writers it becomes a sort of system of spirituality.

The general principle, sometimes called "the fundamental equation," is that Christ our Head, who gives us life and movement, is likewise the norm of our activity, and that our relations with Him and with God are similar to those which unite His humanity to the divinity.

Thus, explains Bérulle, since Christ's human nature lacked a human personality, we too must cease to be a complete and self-sufficient whole. Christ's humanity subsists only in the personal existence of the Word; therefore we must live and act in total dependence upon Christ, placing ourselves in the same relation to Him as His humanity is in relation to, and dependent upon His divinity.

Such a manner of existence demands, first of all, a total abnegation. However, for the sake of better order, we shall reserve this particular point until later in the chapter. Another consequence is the supernatural nobility and dignity that is conferred upon the flesh and the soul of Christ by the hypostatic union. Christ's humanity becomes strictly divine and the source of supernatural life, while we are divinized and animated with a new life. And, just as all holiness is given to the humanity of Christ by its union with the divinity, so our new life obliges us to supernatural goodness, purity, and virtue.

The humanity of Christ was the instrument of the Word in working out the salvation of the world. In like manner, we too must be docile instruments in the hands of Christ for the sanctification of the world. However, it is not often that the cardinal speaks of this nobility and of our function as instruments of God; he sees the entrance of God into us, rather than our assimilation and transfiguration at His hands.

By its personal union with the Word, the activity of the sacred humanity of Jesus shares in the mission on which the Father still continues to send His Incarnate Son. So it is also with the Christians, when they act as Christians. Their activity is a prolongation of Christ's activity; therefore it unites them with the same mission, which emanates from the Father and which sends forth the only-begotten Son.

[539]

This divine mission is fundamental to all other missions. All others must adore it, depend upon it, and imitate it particularly in this point: that as the Son of God did not come into this world to do the work of the Father, worthy and important as that work was, without being sent by His Father, so no one must enter into the field of Jesus Christ, which is His Church, without justifying His mission and proving that it originates from that first mission.[13]

But the mission of the Word is itself united with His eternal procession from the Father. So, too, for the Christians: whatever they do in Christ has a connection and a relation, through Christ, with the eternal generation of the Second Person of the Trinity.

The divine action whereby, without any change, the Father generates His Son, is the origin of the mystery of the Incarnation, in which He gives His Son to human nature and begets Him anew in this second nature. The same divine action is also the origin of the union of the Son, in His twofold nature, with us all, uniting us to Him, giving us life in Him, and making us part of Him as the branch is part of the vine.[14]

Thus we are brought back to the Trinity; the masters of the Oratory refuse to stop short of this goal. Since our life and activity as Christians is the prolongation of the Incarnation, it is joined through Christ to the eternal generation of the Word, who is the sole principle of the personality of the indivisible Christ. Therefore our actions have God, not only as their first beginning, but also as their first exemplar and ultimate norm. To know what the conduct of a Christian should be, we must in the first place consider, not the Christian himself — he is merely a participation — nor the relation between the two natures in Christ — this is simply a mediation indicating a higher principle — instead, we must first study the relations that unite the three divine Persons in the inner life of the Trinity.

So, our authors tell us, the prime reason for all obedience is the bond that unites the Son to the Father. Since the Son is only a subsistent relation, the Christian must have no existence, no will, no tendency except toward God. This Christian obedience must be wholly transformed into love, free of all servility, just as the term of the union between the Father and the Son is the Spirit of Love. In the Trinity there is order and love, but no domination. Hence our authors require that superiors exercise authority only for the sake of charity and never for their selfish ends.

Another conclusion which they draw from the generation of the Word is this: every Christian is essentially consecrated to the contemplative life, through faith and prayer here below and through the beatific vision in heaven.

> I say that the Christians are called to contemplation, not only by [a special] inspiration, but by the very state and condition of life and of grace that they have received in baptism. This grace elevates them and binds them to God through Jesus Christ His Son, who is His Word, His Thought, His Contemplation.[15]

Again, as the Person of Christ united with the Father is the sole principle of the Holy Spirit, so the faithful must be principles of holy and spiritual works. This they cannot be except through union with God, through adherence to Him and dependence upon Him.

> We must adhere to Jesus. In this adherence to His divine Person — which is continually active in the production of the Holy Spirit who proceeds from Him — and in imitation of Him, we must be constantly occupied with spiritual and eternal things, directing our every act to God. The Son of God is ever acting with God His Father in the production of the Holy Spirit; He operates with His Father in such a manner that He is one and the same Principle with the Father. This model we must both adore and imitate in our own activity, never acting alone, but conjointly with God our Father, in dependence upon Him yet in a union so intimate that we may be one principle and one spirit with Him. "He that cleaveth to the Lord is one spirit with Him" (1 Cor. 6:17).[16]

Comparisons and arguments of this kind are very frequent in the writings of our masters, and most of all in the works of Cardinal de Bérulle. We know of no other author who has drawn so calmly and intrepidly the last consequences of our incorporation in the Incarnate Word. Especially in the matter of practical applications, none other has given us so sublime and so faithful a commentary of the words of Jesus Christ recorded by St. John: "Thou in Me, and I in Thee, that they may be one in Us, as We are one" (John 17:21,23). Small wonder that at these lofty heights Bérulle's thought and vocabulary betray a certain hesitancy; the more finely the point is drawn, the more flexible it becomes. Not a few of the cardinal's expressions demand explanation. The same remark is even more true of Père de Condren and Monsieur Olier. But the explanation is not hard to find; the context itself is usually a sufficient indication of the orthodox sense in which the passage should be understood.

Their teaching is extremely rich, as the reader will have been able to judge; it constitutes a considerable contribution to the doctrine of the Mystical Body. We believe that they have been more successful than others in effecting the synthesis between Christology and spirituality, and in proposing the truth of our incorporation in Christ as a code of perfection; they have also been more successful than anyone else in the Latin Church, in bringing out the divine and transcendent aspect of the life that is given us in Christ, and the elevation of soul that is demanded of us in consequence.

They have restored to the Latin doctrine of the Mystical Body the vigor of expression that it had lost in the works of the Schoolmen. No longer has it any reason to envy the teaching of the Greek Fathers, except for one thing: it lacks a certain supernatural optimism. We must now turn our attention to this last point.

III

The reader will have observed that the holy cardinal proposes a most exacting spirituality. His constant refrain is "adherence, dependence, a manner of acting derived from Jesus,"[17] a complete stripping off of self in order to be a capacity, a pure capacity for Jesus, distrust of self in order to experience to the full the influence of Jesus. The supernatural life comes to us, not from a living God, but from a dying God — what the author means is clear; it is therefore a grace of self-annihilation, a spirit of death, an operation wherein God "confiscates" our whole being.

This note of sternness is presented even more vividly by

Père Charles de Condren and Monsieur Jean-Jacques Olier. However, in order to understand their teaching properly, we must first of all consider the circumstances of the period in which they wrote.

In this seventeenth century a chill breath of rigorism reaches even to the highest summits of spirituality. Protestantism had been condemned, it is true, together with its doctrine of contempt for our nature and for our liberty, while the Church, aided here and hampered there by the secular power, was laboring to win back souls from heresy. Yet, so deep seated was the poison that it now gave rise, within the Church, to errors and heresies that were simply new manifestations, less virulent but even more dangerous, of the same morbid disease. What was worse, the new heretics were obstinate in their determination to remain in the Church. We need mention only a few names: Baius, who died in 1589; Jansenius, in 1638; Saint-Cyran, in 1643; Molinos, in 1697; and Quesnel, in 1719; and we may recall the long survival of Jansenism. One is struck by the profound resemblance that exists between these several errors, despite their many differences. Each is a different way of professing the same contempt for human nature. All teach that man's part in the work of salvation is to abstain from acting, to withdraw, to do nothing. They look upon all human love, all natural spontaneity, all affection for creatures, all joy and all gaiety, all seeking for personal happiness, and even all initiative, as sins, or at least as shortcomings and deviations from virtue; all these things appear to them as so many encroachments of man upon the universal domain of God.

True, they do not adopt the attitude of the Protestants, but there is a strong resemblance. They do not say with the Reformers that sin has vitiated the very substance of our nature; in fact, they consider this nature to be capable of true sanctification. But they do agree with the Reformers, when they maintain that this holiness cannot be the effect of our own acts, except insofar as these are acts of abstention; the less we have to do with our sanctification the better it will succeed. Their chief anxiety, it would seem, is to keep the human element at the greatest possible distance from the divine. Was not this also the chief anxiety of the Protestants?

What had man done during those centuries to deserve this treatment? How explain such contemptuousness? Was it an infiltration of Protestant ideas? Possibly it was; but, in our opinion, the reasons for the spread of the contagion lay rather in the general unhealthy condition and the intellectual decadence of the period. In speaking of Protestantism, we noted how the great metaphysical tradition had lost much of its vigor and breadth; many minds had chosen the simplest, and at the same time the most misleading concept of God and creature, representing them as two extremities of the same category. Consequently, the only way now remaining to exalt the Infinite was to annihilate the finite.

Had the monarchist conceptions of the day anything to do with this mentality? We are rather inclined to believe so. Absolute monarchy and enlightened despotism were beginning to assert themselves in politics; the deference and self-effacement of courtiers in the presence of human majesties offered a convenient illustration of the proper attitude to be taken before the King of Kings. At all events, rigorism was in vogue; nature had to be degraded, all but crushed, lest it spoil God's work.

Quite naturally, it was impossible for the doctrine of the Mystical Body to develop freely in this atmosphere of constraint. Before we return to the masters of the French School, let us give one example. The truth of the Mystical Body is not, of course, quite so open a contradiction in the Jansenist doctrine as it is in Protestantism; nevertheless it still suffers from the same internal opposition. It could be prominent enough on occasion, as happened at the time of the Reformation, to compromise the Mystical Body in the eyes of many, and even to give heresy an appearance of piety. But the truth has been misrepresented in such cases. The whole Mystical Body is indeed described as really living, for according to the Jansenist doctrine human nature is truly sanctified and vivified by grace, at least in the few fortunate souls that are chosen by God. Yet it is only half alive. Though they are sanctified, the just remain passive under the impulses and delectations that they receive from God. There is no spontaneity, no initiative, no life proceeding from ourselves. We are like spectators, looking on while another acts within our own being. In this doctrine, grace leaves our natural activity just as tightly bound up in its insignificant nothingness as grace itself is distributed with a miserly hand. Grace enters into us, but only to drive out our will, our liberty, our natural love for ourselves, all that is most personal to us. It enters like a sword, not like the root which, while absorbing, also transforms us. So inseparable are the physical body of the Saviour and His Mystical Body that this conception of the action of grace reminds us of that style of crucifix in which the immense appeal of the outstretched arms of Christ is reduced to a gesture of rejection.

This brief sketch is necessary, not simply to give one more example of a false and heretical theory of the Mystical Body, but to throw proper light on the pages that follow. We shall be obliged to emphasize deficiencies and to point out certain unfortunate resemblances to these false ideas in the theology of the masters of the Oratory and of St. Sulpice. The first part of this chapter should make it clear that these deficiencies are by no means their own doing, but rather the invasion of a disease proper to their time. In fact, they themselves, less seriously infected than others, have helped to eliminate the evil from Christian thought.

With Père Charles de Condren the doctrine of the French School takes on a special character. Cardinal de Bérulle had made the virtue of religion the center of all, and had synthesized all Christian life in the religion of Christ. His disciple and successor introduces still greater unity into the doctrine by centering all that pertains to the religion of Christ round the immolation of Golgotha, the final act in which He offered His entire self to the glory of His Father. Thus the Cross and the Mass, rather than the person of the Man-God, make up the essence of Christianity, for it is in these that the person of the Man-God is found in its fullest actuality. Hence the chief Christian virtue is not religion, since this is merely a general disposition, but rather the spirit of oblation, of mortification, of sacrifice. One feels at once that this is an austere and exacting doctrine; nor is that first impression altered by what is to follow.

What was it that led Père de Condren to insist on this aspect of the spiritual life? To judge from the remarks of his biographer and confidant, Père Denis Amelotte, the answer is to be sought in his ardent piety, and also in his character and intellectual preoccupations. The following incident is significant. When he was about twelve years of age, writes Père Amelotte,

> It happened that one day, while studying in his chamber and keeping watch at the door of wisdom, as he was wont ever to do in a spirit of sacrifice, converting all his reading into motives of adoration —

One moment. Condren, we notice, does not appear before God as a *tabula rasa;* he will naturally interpret the grace he is now to receive in the light of his previous dispositions. So, while he was studying and reflecting, in a spirit of sacrifice and adoration,

> his spirit was suddenly surrounded with an extraordinary light, in which the divine majesty appeared to him, so immense and so infinite that it seemed this pure Being alone could subsist, and that the entire universe must be immolated to His glory. He saw that God had no need of any of His creatures, and that even His Son, who was all His joy, had to sacrifice His life; that only the annihilation of ourselves and of all things with the dying Christ can give honor to the divine infinity, and that our love for Him is not great enough unless we have the desire to be consumed together with His Son in proof of our love.
>
> So pure and powerful was this light that it made an impression as of death in his soul, never to be effaced. He gave himself whole-heartedly to God, to be reduced to nothingness in His presence and to live henceforth in a spirit of death. Then he knew that the whole world was condemned to the flames for the sins of men, in which all creatures are accomplices, and that the holy, pure, just God feels an utter aversion toward them. . . . He saw that almost all men, even Christians, were filled with sentiments and affections opposed to those of God; that they loved passionately what He condemns and that there was scarcely one who was not possessed by the spirit of the world, which is an abomination in the eyes of God.

This is the negative side. Now, in growing contrast, appears the positive side of the doctrine.

As he was in the abyss of his nothingness in presence of the divine holiness, ardently desiring to be sacrificed to His glory, he experienced an incomparable joy in the reflection that the Son of God is ever offering Himself to His Father as Victim, and that the saints in heaven and the priests on earth likewise offer Him up incessantly in honor of the holiness and all the perfections of God. He understood that the sacrifice of Jesus Christ is both the consummation and the supplement of the zeal of those who, passionately desirous of immolating themselves, feel that their own sacrifice is wholly incapable of giving due honor to God. He understood that infinite praise is offered to God's holiness, to His justice, to His essential and absolute independence, in a word, to His infinity, when we present His dead Son to Him, protesting that not only the universe but even this Son had to be destroyed in His divine presence. He understood that nothing is worthy of God except this unique sacrifice of Jesus Christ, that it is the foundation and support of the new creation, the bond of union between heaven and earth, the accomplishment of all that God desires for Himself and for His children, the refuge of all the saints in their helplessness, the perfection of all virtues and the inexhaustible source of eternal life.[18]

This is indeed a wonderful vision, and yet — perhaps the reader may have a different impression — there is something frightening about it, like an immense desert landscape. The constant repetition of our nothingness, but most of all the peculiar glory that God is said to take in the fact that His Son is offered to Him dead, are depressing details. If I may venture an opinion, these elements do not appear quite wholesome; in this complex vision they seem to proceed from Condren's previous disposition rather than from the grace itself. In reading the masters of the French School, true men of God though they are, it is often necessary to draw this same distinction between the Christian piety that they profess, and the way in which, owing to the evils of their times, they sometimes conceive this piety. We wished to make the point very clear before examining this phase of their doctrine. With the reader's permission, we shall not repeat the caution each time that the circumstances might warrant it; we shall mention it again at the end of the chapter, adding the necessary explanations.

Much the same criticism may be made concerning Monsieur Olier. He, too, had his attention drawn by certain interior experiences, though less tragic, to our union with Christ. One of these made a profound impression upon him, and certainly exerted considerable influence on his doctrine. He heard our Lord Himself say: "I am really present to souls." Père de Condren, who was his spiritual director at the time, urged him to make this assurance the center of his spiritual life. The mention of Père de Condren is significant: grace was not acting wholly alone in Olier, either.

At all events, these words do give the distinctive note of his spirituality. For Olier, as for Bérulle and Condren, the religion of Christ and the sacrifice of Christ are the center of Christianity; but since Olier is more directly intent upon showing how this religion and this sacrifice are ever present to us, he considers them where they are perpetuated; namely, in the Host that prolongs the Sacrifice of the Mass and where Christ remains always at the center of His religion. Therefore he sees the Christ-life primarily as a union with the Eucharistic Christ, as a sacramental and spiritual communion by which the religion and the sacrifice of Christ pass into us. He is quite as exacting as Condren, except that he speaks rather of effacement than of immolation: one is reminded more of a candle burning itself out than of a victim being slaughtered. Apart from this, his doctrine presents exactly the same rigor as that of Condren, and we explain the two as one doctrine. We prefer to quote Olier. His developments are less strained and less brief than Condren's, and less cumbersome than Bérulle's; of the masters of the French School, he is not the greatest theologian, for that is Bérulle; nor the most vigorous, for that is Condren; but he is the most readable and the most classical. In his writings the tradition of the School is clear and calm.

Here again the point of departure is a too contemptuous view of human nature. We repeat that it is not the Protestant or the Jansenistic view. Our masters declare that our nature is capable of true sanctity and of efficacious co-operation with grace. But they do say that our nature is so despicable, so wounded by sin, that its activity must always remain suspect and that the wisest course is to limit, as much as possible, its sphere of operation. In the words of Père de Condren:

> Were God to treat us as we deserve, we should have no other thoughts but those of the devils and of sin, like the damned, for we should be in the same condition as they.[19]

By "sin," Monsieur Olier tells us, he means the whole life of the flesh.

> Originally God had formed man in a perfect state; He had imprinted in him His own image and resemblance, and had made him a partaker of His nature and of all His perfections. When sin came, this pure and holy likeness of God within us was effaced, and man became so perverted and corrupt that now he has almost nothing of what he had received from God. True, the image of the divinity is still there, but its chief beauty is spoiled and stained. . . . [The soul still possesses its natural being.] But, before it is restored through baptism, it is in sorry disorder and in total opposition to God, since in itself, in its interior and exterior faculties it is wholly covered with sin. It seems we may say that in a sense it has lost even its natural being, for, whereas it was once a most pure spirit, it has become flesh by entering into an alliance with the body and by plunging into the abyss of fleshy sentiments.[20]

Such pessimism cannot be truly Christian. In fact, as we shall see, it prevents one from viewing either the Incarnation in all its truth, or the Christ-life in all its hopeful assurance.

At the sight of our ignoble nature, God in His holiness can feel only an infinite revulsion. All this revulsion has passed into the God-Man. To show this, our authors recall how human nature is treated in Him. The Incarnation leaves it without a subsistence of its own; in the redemption it is crushed with opprobrium; finally, in its very glorification it is forever annihilated, so to speak, since it is all but absorbed in the divine splendor. Even now in the Eucharist it disappears beneath the Sacred Species, and comes upon the altar only to be a victim for the sacrifice. Thus, in the Incarnate Word, God is quite as remote from the world as ever, and when Christ comes to dwell in our souls in Holy Communion, "He lives in us with horror of us, and with condemnation for us."[21] Therefore we, too, must feel a like revulsion toward ourselves; human holiness must consist, like the holiness of God and Christ, in fleeing from human nature.

Our principal function in the work of our perfection is to withdraw from ourselves. Bérulle had described asceticism not as a matter of prudent strategy and sustained effort, though he admitted the necessity of these, but as an adherence and attachment to Christ, to His mysteries and His dispositions. The source of all virtues is Christ; hence the essential thing is to attach ourselves to that source, in order that the life stream may flow into us. Condren and Olier likewise insist upon this self-abdication. Our first act in prayer should be to renounce ourselves and our own intentions. If we are to grow in the eyes of God, we must first annihilate ourselves and "have a tendency and an inclination to nothingness."

> Death must always precede life. This is nothing else than the entire ruin of our whole selves, in order that whatever is opposed to God in us may be destroyed, and that His Spirit may abide within us in the purity and holiness of His ways.[22]

Once we shall have wholly emptied ourselves of ourselves, God can at last be all in us; the gentlest breath of the Spirit can instantly elevate the soul that is no longer weighed down by anything of earth. We shall then be a pure capacity, where Jesus fills all and does all; we shall be true Christians:

> There is nothing greater, nothing more august, nothing more glorious; such a soul is Jesus Christ, living on earth.[23]

The conclusions are magnificent and beautifully expressed. But, since we have already explained these in the first part of the chapter, we need not dwell upon them here. What interests us at present is the path by which our masters arrive at these conclusions. In order to indicate the route with greater completeness, we think it best to quote a lengthy passage from Monsieur Olier's *Catéchisme de la vie intérieure:*

> *In order to be a Christian, is it enough to have the dispositions that you have explained to me thus far?*
> No. Christians must also take part in all the mysteries of

Jesus Christ; for our lovable Redeemer performed them in His person precisely in order that they might be the source of the most abundant and most special graces in His Church.

Did each mystery obtain a special grace for the Church?

Yes. Each mystery obtained for the Church sanctifying grace and a variety of dispositions and special graces which God confers upon purified souls when He pleases, but particularly at the times when the mysteries are solemnly commemorated. . . .

What grace is wrought in us by the mystery of the Incarnation?

The grace of annihilation to all self-interest and all self-love.

What is meant by annihilation to all self-interest and self-love?

It means that, as by the sacred mystery of the Incarnation our Lord's sacred humanity was annihilated in its own person,[24] in such wise that it no longer sought itself, no longer had any interest of its own, no longer acted for itself, since for its own personality another Person had been substituted, namely, the personality of the Son of God, who sought only the interests of His Father whom He saw always and in all things — so we too must be annihilated to all our own designs, to all our own interests, and entertain only those of Jesus Christ, who is present within us in order to live in us for His Father. "Just as My Father, in sending Me to earth, cut away every root of self-seeking, when instead of giving Me a human personality, He united Me to a divine Person in order to make Me live for Him; so when you eat Me, you will live wholly for Me and not for yourselves, for I shall live in you. I shall fill your souls with My desires and My life, which will consume and annihilate in you all that is your own, so that it will be I, not you, that live and desire all things in you; and, thus annihilated in yourselves, you will be wholly clothed in Me."

Is this putting on of Christ another grace of the Incarnation?

Yes, for besides the fact that the mystery of the Incarnation, properly speaking, effects in us a complete stripping off and renunciation of ourselves, it likewise clothes us with our Lord, by a total consecration to God; just as on the day of the Incarnation our Lord wholly consecrated Himself and all His members to His Father, thereby sanctifying in advance each individual occasion which He and His members should ever have of serving and glorifying God.

On the most holy day of the Incarnation, did our Lord Jesus Christ offer His life and the lives of all His members to God His Father?

Yes, He offered them, and He still continues to make the same offering. He is still living in the same dispositions that

[551]

He had during His whole life. He never interrupts them, and He is ever offering Himself to God, in Himself and in all His members, in all the occasions that they have to serve, honor, and glorify Him. Our Lord in His divine Person is an altar, upon which all men are offered to God with all their actions and all their sufferings. This is that golden altar (Apoc. 8:3), on which every perfect sacrifice is consummated. The human nature of Jesus Christ and of all the faithful is the victim, His spirit is the fire, and the offering is made to God the Father, who is thus adored in spirit and in truth.[25]

Certainly there exists no easier road to such sublime heights of spirituality. But at this altitude, how far man is left behind, and how little he matters! And yet Olier is speaking here only of the dignity which grace confers on our nature. What would he say if he were expressly treating of our misery and sinfulness?

We wish to make ourselves perfectly clear. It is not the precepts of renunciation and of austerity that we find too severe; one who follows a crucified Head can never practice too much abnegation. We find fault only with the manner in which these precepts are laid down, and which, we repeat, betrays a certain contempt for human nature — not a Protestant or Jansenistic contempt, certainly, as we have already observed. Thanks be to God, our authors have themselves helped to counteract the malady. But human nature is a very essential part of Christianity, and too great a contempt of the part must inevitably influence one's attitude toward the whole.

After all, human nature is also present, truly and fully, in Christ. One who has little esteem for that nature will be inclined to belittle it even in Him. Yet Christ is Head precisely in His human nature, a fact that is difficult to explain in such a view. Our authors have much to say in praise of the humanity of the Saviour, and in what they say we perceive a new tone which at once betrays their intense love and their profound meditation on the subject. But unfortunately, all that is purely human in Christ appears to them so despicable that even in these moments their chief care is to represent the humanity of Christ, not as humanity, but as the subsistent religion of men, as a holocaust offered to God, or as a total annihilation before the Most High. The abasement of the

Incarnation, the ignominy of Calvary, the very glory of heaven, and the mystery of the tabernacle are all regarded as a kind of sacred annihilation, obscuring their vision of the most sweet humanity and gentle goodness through which the Word has made Himself accessible to the children of men. They have little to say of His life, of His human actions, of the wonderful yet familiar proximity that He ever sought to have with us. Lastly, the hypostatic union, as they conceive it, does not make Christ's humanity human, more human even than it would otherwise have been, but rather absorbs that humanity, so to speak, into a glory and a function that are divine.

These are delicate points, and we regret that we have had to express them in a way that makes them appear more serious than they actually are. But as we see, the very idea of the Mystical Body is here at stake. The Saviour's humanity is raised to the Headship of our race precisely because of its supernatural and mysterious proximity to us, and because of its extremely perfect manner of being man, true man. Once this fact is lost sight of, the very concept of the Mystical Christ must suffer.

Once more, what we have said of the Head is true of the members, so great is their solidarity. The same concept of our nature makes it impossible for our authors to explain clearly the supernatural dignity which makes us the body of Christ. What nobility can there be in poor nothings and poor sinners such as we are? Out of respect for the dignity of God and for the holiness of Christ, out of respect for the very justification that we are to receive, they tell us that our activity must be restricted. Their most beautiful pages are marred by the idea, which amounts almost to an obsession, of annihilation; the word is ever on their lips, and they keep repeating that our worship must consist essentially in offering to God His lifeless Son; our prayer must consist in renouncing our own desires, and our virtue must consist in stripping ourselves entirely of ourselves and of our acts. As with the Head, so with the members, the part of human nature in the supernatural life is certainly not denied, but it is minimized.

One cannot help thinking of the great Scholastics. For all

their seeming abstraction, they were more human and also, we believe, more Christian. They saw nothing in mere annihilation that could give honor to Him who is. Therefore, out of respect for the Creator and out of love for the Word made flesh, they refuse to admit that the least of even material creatures will return to nothingness, if it is capable of lasting forever.

We must remember that the great metaphysical tradition has meanwhile lost much of its early vigor. Upon the systems of philosophy and theology there has fallen a certain pessimism; this it is that prevents the free development of the doctrine of the Mystical Body in the works of the founders of the French School. Its effects, alas, were far more disastrous in other instances.

IV

However, this pessimism did not succeed in conquering the spirit that inspired them. We have read many beautiful thoughts in the preceding pages, and, in order not to leave an unfavorable and false impression of our authors, we wish to conclude with a brief consideration of one of the most human and most Christian aspects of their doctrine; namely, their teaching concerning charity toward the neighbor. We do not mean their systematic teaching, for that is poor; their slight esteem for human nature was not apt to induce them to assign a prominent place in their system of spirituality to a humble and devoted love for men. But it is to their living teaching, their practical counsels, and their example that we refer; in these they continue the urgent precept of the Gospel to love one's brethren before all else. This doctrine is forcibly expressed in manuscripts that were discovered among Monsieur Olier's papers after his death.

> We must hold as certain that Jesus Christ abides in the Church of God, and therefore in the faithful, by His spirit, His graces, His gifts, His virtues. All that is of Jesus Christ is holy, great, divine, and hence it merits our adoration and our homage. The duty of a Christian toward the whole Church and toward each of her members is in consequence a duty of cult and of honor. . . .

The vow of servitude obliges us so to love all the members of Jesus Christ that we enter into their interests, and even prefer their interests to our own. . . . We shall make it our study to please them in all things . . . and lastly, we shall treat them as a servant treats his master.[26]

These are not empty words. "I give myself to God, that I may belong to all who come to me," said Père de Condren in his "vow of servitude."[27] And, for fear of taking back that offering, he dared not send away the most exasperating visitor. "Since I am the servant of all," he explained, "everyone has the right to order me about." His very office as general he regarded as "a universal servitude that obliges me to serve all my subjects," so that, when harassed by the importunate, by disappointments and humiliations, he would say with a smile: "I haven't a chance to do my own will in this world."[28]

Such perfect graciousness is the most eloquent commentary on any rigidity of doctrine. Their attitude is somewhat passive perhaps; but so human, so deferential, and so supernatural a love for the neighbor is the best possible recognition of the incorporation of men in Christ and of the dignity which God has conferred upon our nature.

For such heroes of charity, rigoristic formulas can be only superficial and incidental, traces of an evil to which their Christian souls are opposed and which their disciples succeed in eliminating, simply by remaining faithful to their teaching.

But they themselves remain inimitable. Now that the Church has spoken clearly, it is easy to avoid certain errors that were less perceptible in their day. Yet there are some things concerning our incorporation in Christ that can be learned best only from their lips. Too great a gap would have been left in our studies if we had not examined their doctrine rather carefully.

Chapter XI

The Doctrine of the Mystical Body Today

⋊⋉

I. Resurgence of the doctrine of the Mystical Body, freed from the pessimism of the masters of the French School; this progress is apparently due to the influence of the same French School and to the advance of positive theology.

II. *Naturalism and the doctrine of the Mystical Body.* Cardinal Pie. Human nature united with God in Christ. All creation supernaturalized. The life of Christ prolonged in men, and even in material things. The doctrine of the Mystical Body as compared with naturalistic pantheism.

III. *The Vatican Council.* According to the *Schema De Ecclesia,* the Church is essentially the Mystical Body of Christ. From this principle the document deduces the Church's visibility, necessity, and unfailing unity. Generally favorable reception of this *Schema.*

IV. *The Popes.* Leo XIII repeats the doctrine of the Church as the Mystical Body of Christ, which had been formulated in the *Schema De Ecclesia.* Pius X points out that the Blessed Virgin Mary is the Mother of the members of the Mystical Body. Catholic Action and the Mystical Body. In the encyclical *Miserentissimus Redemptor,* His Holiness Pope Pius XI explains how our works of expiation and satisfaction have their value: through their union with the expiation and satisfaction of Christ. Redemption in the Mystical Body.

V. *The antidote for modern heresies,* especially for Modernism.

I

IN OUR own day, the doctrine of the Mystical Body is making rapid progress. Indeed, one of the distinctive notes of present-day theology is a tendency to broaden more and more the scope of our doctrine. We cannot ignore the part which the French School has taken in this progress. The Congregation of the Oratory, and to an even greater extent the

Congregation of St. Sulpice, have devoted themselves to the formation of the clergy. It was inevitable that their spiritual teaching, which insists so strongly on our incorporation in Christ, should have made a profound impression on the minds of the many eminent bishops and priests who were trained in their seminaries.

Another factor contributing to this growth was the development of positive theology. The inspired writers and the Fathers are not studied merely as sources whence arguments may be drawn in support of a thesis; they are being read more and more for the sake of becoming familiar with their way of thinking and with their concept of Christianity. But since these sources speak forcibly of the Mystical Body, as is abundantly clear from the foregoing studies, it is quite natural that a more objective exposition of Scriptural and patristic theology should lead to a more realistic doctrine of the Mystical Body.

Whatever may have been the causes, the effect is visible enough. Not only is the doctrine more widely accepted, but it has been set free from the pessimism that enshrouded it in the teaching of the French School. It retains its note of austerity, to be sure, but it has taken on a more optimistic and cheerful spirit.

So many theologians are now teaching it that we shall make no attempt to enumerate them, much less to class them into schools. Again, its proponents are so recent that it is as yet too early to devote a historical study to them. We intend here only to examine a few documents which appear to possess greater authority.

II

Let us mention in the first place Cardinal Pie, bishop of Poitiers, friend of Pius IX, and one of the most influential among the Fathers of the Vatican Council. He has written with vigor and eloquence of our unity in Christ, for he recognized this doctrine as the providential remedy for the error of his day — and alas, of our own as well; that error is Naturalism.

Naturalism claims that man is sufficient unto himself; he has neither need nor knowledge of any higher reality that transcends his own sphere. This pride in human nature and this assumption of man's ability to do without supernatural assistance are, after all, only a perversion of a moral attitude which is in itself quite legitimate; namely, respect for human nature. Hence the error can be best refuted, not so much by lowering man in his own eyes as by letting him see his true dignity. Realizing this, the bishop of Poitiers chose the doctrine of the Mystical Body as the means of showing the inadequacy of the teachings of naturalism. They tell us man is sufficient unto himself. That might be true, answers our author, if there were question of his being simply a man. But other perspectives open before our eyes: God invites us to a union with His only Son, so intimate that one is almost tempted to call it identification. This, he observes, is an error to be avoided, but

> keeping this necessary qualification in mind, our deification in Jesus Christ is one of the fundamental truths of Christianity. In it are our title to nobility for the present and our assurance of happiness and glory for the future. And, since this doctrine reaches to the inmost depths of our being, since it is bound up with our whole destiny, present and future, since it is at once our charter of rights and our code of duty, this article of our faith can never be impressed deeply enough on the minds of the faithful; it must often be presented to them and explained from every possible point of view. The deeper the darkness in which naturalism envelops the sphere of profane knowledge, the greater the light which sacred theology must throw upon the whole Christ, that is, upon that mystery in which human nature is deified hypostatically in the individual person of Jesus Christ, and deified by adoption in all the elect, who are the members of the body of Jesus Christ. This deification affects the whole of creation, angelic and terrestrial, of which man is the center and the bond of union; it is an obligatory deification, commanded by God, so that he who presents himself without this supernatural gift and without this divine supplement will be found wanting in the heavenly balance.[1]

This deification is obligatory, not simply because God desires its presence in all His works, but also because of the dignity of our human nature; when man voluntarily rejects the supernatural nobility that is offered him, he sins against his own nature.

> The Word of God has descended into the very heart of His work; He assumed our humanity, and by means of this nature, which, being at once spiritual and corporal, reaches to both extremities of creation, He has communicated Himself to every part of that creation, vivifying the angelic spirits as well as inferior beings, extending the divine activity to all things in heaven and on earth, bringing to all nature a supernatural consecration and elevating it from its base and profane condition. . . . The Word has come unto His own; can it be optional for them to receive Him or to reject Him as they please? . . . Still more important is this question: if Jesus Christ has been given us by God, in order to raise us up to a glory and a beatitude that transcend all the exigencies and all the ambitions of our nature, can we be free to select a more humble destiny and propose to ourselves a purely natural end? Ah, it is here that the Scriptures break down the very foundations of naturalism.[2]

Far from belittling our human nature, this doctrine is a message of respect. Human nature was made to be united to God in Christ, because the humanity of Christ was made that it might penetrate all things, *ut impleret omnia* (Eph. 4:10). For, as the bishop of Poitiers observes, with careful precision:

> There is no question here of His presence as God, for as God He has always been present, but of His presence both as God and as man.

This presence embraces our whole nature:

> The history of humanity, the history of nations, of peace and of war, and especially the history of the Church, is but the history of the life of Jesus filling all things, *ut impleret omnia*.[3]

Over and above the life that Jesus led in Judea, there is another life, mystical and real, written by each of the faithful, not on pages of parchment but on the living tables of the heart; "in all that goes to make up what we may call the equipment or the organism of the Christ-life, the divine Youth of Nazareth is still living and growing on this earth."[4]

Nor is this all. It is not to our nature alone that this theandric dignity is offered. The entire universe is likewise destined for this glory, because of its relation to us. Naturalism would cut it off from God, set it up as a self-sufficient whole, and make of it a kind of god. This is naturalistic pantheism, a more subtle error, yet allied with the first. But the doctrine of the Mystical Body confutes and destroys this theory also. They tell us of a God striving to be God, of an immense "becoming" that is destined to produce something divine.

> Indeed, yes! All that is true, provided it is understood not of the eternal and changeless God who is God by nature and essence, but of this God who is united in Jesus Christ with the very heart of the divinity, and yet extends throughout the world in time and space. These sacrilegious counterfeiters, these instruments of him whom Tertullian calls "the ape of truth," have merely put a horrible blasphemy in the place of an adorable truth; they have substituted the absurd and the impossible for the masterpiece of the wisdom and power and love of the heavenly Father who has called us to His eternal glory in Jesus Christ, and who, having discovered a way to make men partakers of His divine nature, has caused this deification to flow into every part of the universe in greater or less abundance according as each part concurs more or less directly in the operations of the supernatural order, as St. Paul writes to the early Christians: "All things are yours, and you are Christ's, and Christ is God's" (1 Cor. 3:23).[5]

As grace transcends nature, so this teaching transcends that of naturalism, and it expresses in addition the full and expansive optimism of the doctrine of the Mystical Body.

III

Cardinal Pie was not the only one who looked on this doctrine as the remedy for the religious ills of the present time. The entire episcopate shared his view, as may be seen from what the Fathers of the Vatican Council have to say on the subject of our incorporation in Christ. The *Schema De Ecclesia Christi* which was distributed to the bishops on January 21, 1870, states that the primary characteristic, the very essence of the Church is her quality as the Mystical Body of the Saviour.

[560]

Times have changed: heresy no longer strikes at the visibility of the Church, as it did in the days of the Reformers. Naturalism takes a bolder step, and denies the hidden life and mystical presence of Christ which makes His supernatural society an organism of salvation. These, therefore, are the truths that must now be insisted upon; from them, if possible, must be deduced the chief prerogatives of the Church: her holiness, her indefectibility, her necessity, and even her visible unity. The *Schema* does just this; in its opening lines, it states that the whole of Christ's work on earth and the entire economy of salvation consist in the building up of the Mystical Body.

> *That the Church is the Mystical Body of Christ.*
> The only-begotten Son of God, who enlighteneth every man that cometh into the world (John 1:9), and who has never failed to come to the aid of the unfortunate children of Adam, did, in the fullness of time appointed by the eternal decree, become like unto men. Assuming the form of our body, He appeared in visible guise in order that earthly and carnal men, putting on the new man who is created according to God in justness and holiness of truth (Eph. 4:24), might make up a Mystical Body of which He Himself should be the Head. To effect this union of the Mystical Body the Lord Christ instituted the sacred waters of regeneration and renewal, whereby the sons of men, once so sadly divided among themselves and especially corrupted by sin, might be purified from every stain of their sins and so become members one of the other, and that being united to their divine Head by faith, hope, and charity, they might all be vivified by the one Spirit and filled with heavenly graces and spiritual gifts. We can never commend too highly to the consideration of the faithful, or impress too deeply on their minds this remarkable [visible] feature (*species*) of the Church, whereby she has as her Head Christ, "from whom the whole body, welded and compacted together throughout every joint of the system, part working in harmony with part, deriveth its increase, unto the upbuilding of itself in charity" (Eph. 4:16).[6]

From such a principle it is easy to deduce the other properties of the Church. The *Schema* begins with her visibility.

> Since such is the nature of the true Church of Christ, we declare that the visible and perceptible society whereof we speak is the very same as that Church of the divine promises

and mercies which Christ was pleased to distinguish and enrich with so many prerogatives and privileges.

Her constitution is so clearly determined that none of those societies which have withdrawn from the unity and communion of her body can in any sense be called a part or a member. She is not divided or dismembered by the different societies that call themselves "Christian"; she is one whole, gathered together and closely united within herself (*totam in se collectam penitusque cohaerentem*), and her conspicuous unity is the outward manifestation of that undivided and indivisible body which is the Mystical Body of Christ Himself.[7]

The same principle explains why membership in the Church is a necessary means of salvation.

> Hence let all understand how necessary for salvation is this society, this Church of Christ. She is as necessary as attachment to and union with Christ and the Mystical Body are necessary. . . . This is why we teach that membership in the Church is not a matter of option, as if it made no difference whether one knows the Church or not, whether he enters her or not, as far as salvation is concerned, but that it is a matter of necessity, not only in virtue of the precept whereby the Lord commanded every nation to enter the Church, but also as a means. For in the economy of salvation which Providence has established, none can receive the communication of the Holy Spirit, and none can partake of truth and of life except in the Church and through the Church, whose Head is Christ.[8]

The Church's vitality, her perpetuity, all her prerogatives become just as evident when one considers her as the body of Christ.

> Although the Church grows — and God grant that she may ever continue to grow in faith and charity in order that the body of Christ may be built up! — and although her development varies in different ages and according to the changing circumstances in which she leads her ever militant existence, she always remains intrinsically the same, adhering immutably to the constitution given her by Christ. Therefore the Church of Christ can never lose her attributes and her qualities, her sacred *magisterium*, her ministry, and her power of jurisdiction, for Christ must remain forever and for all men, by means of His visible body, the way, the truth, and the life.[9]

Lastly, we are told that even the Church's right to possess property follows from the same general principle.

This right is more sacred and more sublime in the Church than elsewhere, since the goods in question belong to the Mystical Body of Christ, and are therefore consecrated in a more special manner to Christ.[10]

The *Schema* is not a definition, of course; it was not even publicly discussed at the Council. Its framers were not bishops but theologians, consultors of the theologico-dogmatic Commission. Nevertheless it does indicate what these scholars regarded as definable doctrine. Nor were these men ordinary theologians; they were the most eminent of their time, selected by the central commission of the Council, and their appointment was approved by the Pope.

They were unanimous in making the truth of the Mystical Body the first principle of the doctrine concerning the Church. The records of their discussions indicate no divergence of view on this subject.

While the Council itself passed no final judgment on the *Schema,* the motivated opinions of a considerable number of its members are on record. Copies of the *Schema* had been distributed to all beforehand, in order to give them an opportunity to examine it and to hand in their comments and criticisms before March 4, as was requested. There were about 639 Fathers in Rome at the time of the Council; this was the number that assisted at the general session of March 18. About 230, or a little better than a third, presented their written opinions either on the *Schema* as a whole or on those parts that have the most direct reference to the Mystical Body; namely, the beginning and the first chapter. Of this number only four expressed regret at the mention of the Mystical Body in such a document. They considered that the doctrine was vague, ill understood, too mystical. Of the twenty-five others who objected, though less vigorously, to its mention, about twenty wished to substitute the term "kingdom of God" or "society"; in short, they desired a simpler, more practical definition of the Church. A good hundred approved the manner in which the doctrine was presented, some making certain reservations, some suggesting slight modifications, some openly expressing their satisfaction. Seventy of the Fathers fail to mention the Mystical Body in their comments.

[563]

If, as is frequently the case, we may presume that those who are satisfied deem it unnecessary to say so, we might count these seventy, as well as the four hundred who gave no opinion, with the hundred who said they approved of the *Schema*. The resulting majority of six sevenths in favor of the mention of the Mystical Body would of course be an exaggeration, and we cannot base any argument upon it. But this tabulation at least shows that a majority of the bishops, the greater part of the ordinariy *magisterium*, did not object to centering the treatise on the Church round the doctrine of the Mystical Body.

The reservations that were made cannot be said to concern the doctrine as such. The most unsympathetic did not say that this manner of presentation was false, but that it was too complicated, obscure, vague. Most of the criticisms deal with certain inadequacies, some of which are undeniable, in the way the doctrine was expressed. The following are the most common objections. First, it is certain that the concept of the Mystical Body does not coincide perfectly with that of the Church. This point is important. It may be disputed, for instance, whether sinners and fervent catechumens are members of the Mystical Body; yet it is beyond doubt that the former are members of the Church, while the latter are not. One may also regret, with certain bishops, that the *Schema* fails to state clearly that this "body" of Christ possesses both a visible and an invisible character, corresponding to what are termed "the body of the Church" and "the soul of the Church." He may likewise regret the absence of a complete and accurate Scholastic definition of the Church. The fact that so prominent a place was accorded to the idea of the Mystical Body was no excuse for this omission; on the contrary it made a positive and scientific explanation all the more necessary.

Accordingly a second project was drawn up by Father Kleutgen, S.J., in which the suggestions offered by the Fathers were taken into account. The principle now becomes a scientific definition of the Church, and the idea of the Mystical Body passes into the background. However, the latter still remains very much in evidence, for, as Father Kleutgen observes, "not only is the Mystical Body very frequently and very explicitly spoken of in Scripture, but it also helps very much to an understanding of the properties of the Church."[11]

It is impossible to say whether this new *Schema* would have satisfied the Council. It was not examined by the Fathers of the deputation whose business it was to pass on questions concerning the faith, nor was it submitted to the bishops. We think that some, perhaps many, of the latter would have regretted the summary treatment of a concept which in the first *Schema* they had considered so useful and so true. Is it not significant that almost all the other projects proposed by bishops to take the place of the original formula give far greater prominence to the Mystical Body than does the project of Father Kleutgen?

Whether these suppositions be true or false, we may note, in summing up what we have said of the Council, that the majority of the bishops and the most noted theologians have rendered an important testimony to the doctrine of our incorporation in Christ.

IV

After the suspension of the Council, the doctrine was not hidden away in the archives along with the documents that contained it. Within a few short years, we find it expressed in solemn ecclesiastical pronouncements.

Leo XIII, who had assisted as cardinal at the sessions of the Council, formulates the doctrine in his famous encyclical *Satis Cognitum,* in which he speaks of the Church. It is interesting to note the resemblance between the words of the encyclical and the teaching contained in the *Schema De Ecclesia Christi.* The Pope declares, as the *Schema* had done, that the doctrine of the Mystical Body is the résumé of all that can be said of the Church.

It is because of all these reasons that in Scripture the Church is so often called a body, or the body of Christ: "You are all the body of Christ" (1 Cor. 12:27). Because it is a body, it is visible to the eyes of men; because it is the body of Christ, it is a living body, active and growing, for it is sustained and animated by the power which Jesus Christ communicates to it, almost as the vine nourishes and renders fruitful the branches that are united with it.

In living beings the vital principle is itself something mysterious and hidden, but it manifests its presence in the movement and activity of the members; in like manner the principle of the supernatural life which animates the Church is made known to all by the effects which it produces.[12]

Again like the *Schema De Ecclesia*, the Pope proceeds to show, from what Christ is, what the Church must be, and what Christ Himself must, therefore, be in His Mystical Body.

The Church is not a dead thing; she is the body of Christ, alive with His supernatural life. Christ, her Head and Model, is not complete if we regard either His visible nature alone, as the Photinians and Nestorians do, or His invisible nature alone, as the Monophysites are wont to do; He is one by the union of both natures, visible and invisible. In the same way, His Mystical Body is the true Church simply because her parts derive their life and strength from supernatural gifts and other invisible sources.[13]

Hence there can be but one Church.

Moreover, the Son of God decreed that the Church should be His Mystical Body, and He willed to be united with it as Head, as His human head is joined naturally with the human body which He took in the Incarnation. Therefore, just as He assumed only one mortal body, to be delivered up to torment and death in order to pay the price of man's redemption, so too He has but one Mystical Body, in which and by means of which He makes men partakers of sanctification and of eternal salvation: "[God] hath made Him Head over all the Church, which is His body" (Eph. 1:22,23, D.V.).

Members that are isolated and dispersed cannot be united to one and the same head, or form a single body. . . . Members that withdraw from the other members cannot be attached to the same head. . . . To make the unicity of the Church more manifest, God presents it in the form of a living body, whose members can have life only on condition that they be attached to the head, and draw their vital energy (*vim vitalem*) from it. . . .[14]

He, therefore, who thinks that there can be any other Church besides that which is the body of Christ, must look for some other head like Christ; he must look for some other Christ.[15]

The Christ who willed that there should be but one Church,

willed also that it should possess unity, in order that all who are destined to be its members should together form a single body. . . . Nay, He desired His disciples to be so intimately and so perfectly united that their union might be the very image, so to speak, of His own unity with the Father: "I pray . . . that they all may be one, even as Thou, Father, art in Me, and I in Thee" (John 17:21).[16]

Many other statements of Leo XIII might be cited concerning the function of the Holy Ghost or the special significance of the Eucharist with regard to the Mystical Body.

The Eucharist, according to the testimony of the holy Fathers, is to be considered as a continuation and extension of the Incarnation. For through this sacrament the substance of the Incarnate Word is united with each individual man.[17]

Our whole life as Christians centers round the Eucharist, just as the Incarnation is the center toward which God directs everything that pertains to the supernatural order.

But if the Incarnation is continued in the Mystical Body, it follows that the Virgin Mother of God, who served as the instrument of God in the Incarnation, is also used by God as Mediatrix in the prolongation of the Incarnation, the purpose of which is to form Christ in us. This truth was proclaimed by Pius X, early in his pontificate. On February 2, 1904, fifty years after the definition of the dogma of the Immaculate Conception, the Pope wrote of Mary, the Mother of divine grace:

All must accept this principle, that Jesus, the Word made flesh, is also the Saviour of the human race. As the God-Man, He possesses a human body like other men; as the Restorer of our race, He has a spiritual, or mystical body, as it is called, which is the society of those who believe in Christ: "We many are one body in Christ" (Rom. 12:5). But the Virgin did not conceive the Son of God solely in order that, by receiving human nature from her, He should become man, but also that, through the nature which He received from her, He might become the Saviour of men. This is the reason why the angel told the shepherds: "There hath been born to you this day a Saviour, who is Christ the Lord" (Luke 2:11).

Consequently, in the same womb of this most pure Mother, Christ assumed not only mortal flesh but a spiritual body as well, consisting of all those who were to believe in Him. Thus we may say that Mary bore within her womb, not Christ

[567]

only, but also all those whose life was contained in the life of the Saviour.

Therefore, since we are all united with Christ, and since, as the Apostle says, "we are members of His body, of His flesh, and of His bones" (Eph. 5:30, D.V.), we too have all been born of the womb of the Virgin, as a body united with its head.

Hence it is that in a spiritual and mystical sense we are called children of Mary, and she is called the Mother of us all. "She is spiritually and truly the Mother of us who are the members of Christ."[18] If then the most Blessed Virgin is Mother both of God and of men, who can doubt but that she exerts all her influence with Christ, who is Head of His body, the Church, in order that He may infuse His gifts into us His members, and first of all, in order that we may come to know Him and live by Him?

. . . The source of all these gifts, of course, is Christ, "of whose fullness we have all received" (John 1:16), and "from whom the whole body, welded and compacted together throughout every joint of the system . . . deriveth its increase, unto the upbuilding of itself in charity" (Eph. 4:16). But, as St. Bernard aptly observes, Mary is the channel, or the neck, whereby the body is joined to the Head and through which the Head transmits its virtue and power to the body. "For she is the neck of our Head, through which all spiritual gifts are communicated to His Mystical Body."[19]

While the following words of Pius X do not say much of the Mystical Body as such, they are important and interesting because they appear in one of the first great papal pronouncements on the subject of Catholic Action. From the very beginning of the encyclical, in which he recommends Catholic Action to the bishops of Italy, the Sovereign Pontiff links up the lay apostolate with the doctrine of the Mystical Body:

All of us in God's Church are called to make up that one body whose Head is Christ; as the Apostle teaches, this body is closely knit and co-ordinated in all its parts by virtue of the functions proper to each member, and thus derives its increase, building itself up little by little in the bond of charity (cf. Eph. 4:16).

And if, in this work of building up the body of Christ, it is Our first duty to teach, to point out the methods to be followed and the means to be taken, to urge and to exhort as a father, it is also the duty of all Our beloved sons everywhere in the world to receive Our words, to put them into execution first in themselves, and then to co-operate effectively in making others

[568]

put them into practice, each one according to the grace he has received from God, according to his state and office, and according to the zeal that burns in his heart.

Here We wish simply to mention the many works of zeal that are being carried out for the good of the Church, of society, and of individuals, and which are commonly referred to as "Catholic Action."[20]

The history of the Church, the Mystical Body of Christ, reproduces the very history of the Saviour. In the words of Pius X:

Must not the Church become daily more like Christ? Must she not become the living image of Him who bore so much and such bitter suffering?[21]

Not only the Incarnation, but the Redemption as well is being continued in the Church. This doctrine, which has the authority of all Tradition behind it, had been expressed, like that of the Church as the Mystical Body, in the documents drawn up in preparation for the Vatican Council. The proposed decrees *De doctrina christiana*, which were submitted to the Fathers, gives the union of the members with the Head as the reason why Christ's satisfaction is one with the satisfactory works of Christians.

We shall not quote this text, however, since we possess a more solemn and more recent pronouncement on a very similar subject. This is the encyclical *Miserentissimus Redemptor* of His Holiness Pope Pius XI. The doctrine of the Mystical Body is not here treated *ex professo*, for the Pope is speaking directly of devotion to the Sacred Heart of Jesus. However, in developing this theme he is led to mention our union with the Saviour, just when he is denouncing naturalistic rationalism, to which we have made frequent reference in the foregoing pages. In answer to this rationalism, Pius XI lays emphasis upon two truths: the fallen state of our nature and the duty of reparation that is incumbent upon us. He then takes a further step, and exalts the dignity which belongs to our works of reparation by reason of their union with Christ's passion.

For there exists a wonderful and intimate union of all the faithful with Christ, like to that which joins the head to the

[569]

other members of the body. Moreover, through the mysterious communion of saints which our Catholic faith professes, all men and all peoples are united not only with one another but also with Him who is the Head, Christ. . . . This is the unity that the Mediator of God and men, Jesus Christ Himself, asked of the Father a few hours before His death: "I in them and Thou in Me, that they may be perfected in unity" (John 17:23).[22]

It is this unity that gives value to our acts of reparation, acts that would otherwise be worthless.

The passion of Christ is renewed, and in some way continued and consummated in His Mystical Body, which is the Church. . . . Therefore Christ, who is still suffering in His Mystical Body, asks us to be His companions in expiation. For that matter, our very union with Him demands this: "You are the body of Christ, and members of member" (1 Cor. 12:27, D.V.). Whatever the Head suffers, the members too must suffer with Him.[23]

This, declares the Pope, is a most timely doctrine for our day, when sin abounds and when society seems to be in rebellion against Christ and His Church.

V

We wish to close our studies with these words, in which Pius XI repeats with his pontifical authority what we have read in the *Schema* of the Vatican Council: the doctrine of the Mystical Body, which the Pope calls "this most beautiful doctrine" (*haec pulcherrima mystici Iesu Christi corporis doctrina*),[24] is peculiarly suited to our modern age.

It is a remedy for the naturalism that is chilling the Christ-life in too many souls and in too many peoples, weakening faith and blinding men's eyes to the true nature of the Church.

May we not generalize the statement, and say that this same truth is the remedy for all the many errors that are rife today?

It is a remedy for the liberal individualism which still isolates the lives and thoughts of so many of the faithful. No one lives alone; the member must be mindful of the good of the other members. A true Christian must be, in spirit at least, a missionary.

It is a remedy for that other still more dangerous and more aggressive egoism which is known as nationalism. "There is neither Jew nor Greek," writes St. Paul, "for ye are all one person in Christ Jesus" (Gal. 3:28). If this catholic concept were only realized, what a transformation it would accomplish! A Christ who unites the men of every tongue and nation and color in the same love and in the same supernatural dignity! What joy and security and good will would then reign, instead of the barbed-wire entanglements and the engines of war that mark our frontiers!

It is a remedy, too, for that false conception of society, be it economic, social, or political, which seeks to strengthen the unity of groups at the sacrifice of the rights, at times even the most essential rights, of the individual. That there should be progress in the unification of human societies, as there is in all things human, we cannot doubt. It is quite natural that this progress should be more rapid in an age such as ours, when a spirit of revolt, engendered by the evils of a system of unbridled economic liberalism, is driving nations into the hands of dictators, and when the necessary interdependence of individuals in human society is making itself felt with unprecedented force. Experience is proving more conclusively each day that a union of all with all, in work and in study, in every enterprise, scientific and moral included, is now more indispensable than ever before. Even the apostolate is taking on a more collective aspect, through the many groups that are being formed in response to the call of Catholic Action. But if social unity must progress more rapidly in our day, there is all the greater need for a careful direction of this advance. Whoever imagines that a greater group unity can be attained by weakening the internal unity that makes each member a person, is evidently pursuing a false course. For how can an attempt on the lives of the members be conducive to the good of the organism?

In its own way the doctrine of the Mystical Body warns men against making such a mistake; it shows them a God-made society, a supernaturally perfect society. This is, of course, an ideal society, unattainable by natural groups, but very instructive nevertheless. In it they can see how the unity

[571]

of the group goes hand in hand with the intensity of each member's personal life. The same attachment to Christ which reinforces supernaturally the personal unity of each member, unites him at the same time with all the other members in the unity of the whole. Here men can learn an important lesson on the necessity of reconciling the inalienable rights of the individual with the needs of the whole: the two must be united, not so that one destroys the other, but so that each perfects the other. Nor should we be surprised that a supernatural reality should teach a lesson that applies to the natural order. Grace is made to perfect nature, and there seems to be no danger that men will ever exhaust even the social and economic lessons that are contained in the doctrine of the Mystical Body.

It is, lastly and chiefly, a remedy for the heresy of Modernism, for its false views on religion, and for its false doctrine of immanence. Modernism, as we know, is an attempt to make all religion, or at least whatever we can know of religion, something purely subjective. The rest is the Unknowable. Of God, of His nature, even of our immortal soul, we can know nothing. *A fortiori*, the divinity of Christ and the transcendent character of the Christ-life and of the Church are wholly beyond the range of our intelligence. The most that we can attain is something subjective, an interior sentiment, an attraction for the divine, the need for an ideal; these alone can give meaning to religious formulas, and especially to the dogmas and facts of Christianity. Venerable and wonderful as these latter are, all their beauty comes from the light that we bear in our own souls: all that man can discover in them is himself, only himself and his vague but persistent longing for an ideal that is unknowable and perhaps nonexistent.

It takes only a moment to see that such a system is not so much a heresy as the sum total of all heresies. It does away with the very notion of the supernatural, and even of the suprasensible.

That aspiration toward a more interior religion, with which it has tempted certain minds in our present age, will ever appear false, even painfully commonplace to those who have come to know the doctrine of the Mystical Body. What a poor immanence is this, that imprisons man in himself, and how sad this cry that loses itself in the darkness!

Immanence? Certainly. Why abandon a word that heresy has stolen from Truth? But we will have no immanence that robs us of our most precious personal treasure. All life is immanent; the life of man is immanent. But this immanence does not consist in man's isolating himself in himself, but in his aspiring to the supreme Life and Immanence, to the God who is immanent Life. The Christ-life, too, is immanent, but with an immanence far superior to that of unaided man. Since we are all taken up in Christ, we are all united in God. It is the eternal Life, which by vivifying the sacred humanity of the Saviour, vivifies us all in Him. It is a catholic life, universally human as it is eternal and divine. And because it is life, it is an immanence. But what an immanence! It is the presence within us of the Mystical Christ, the intimacy of all that is catholic, the union within the individual, in Christ and through Christ, with all of regenerated humanity and with God.

Each Christian has his own personal grace; yet in all who possess grace, all these individual graces remain united in their common source, which is Christ, the Head of the Church. In the supernatural order there is but one living organism in Christ. This organism grows and develops through the ages and it extends itself to all peoples over the entire face of the earth; yet all of this, all this life, all the good that is wrought in heaven by the saints and by men here on earth, in the whole universe and throughout all time — all this is one Christ, Head and members, *unus Christus amans seipsum.*

GENERAL CONCLUSION

General Conclusion

THE DOCTRINE of the Mystical Body has been the remedy for the principal heresies of history, as it is today for Modernism. In the course of this study we saw how it was employed by the Fathers and the theologians to refute Gnosticism, Arianism, Apollinarism, Nestorianism, Donatism, Pelagianism, and later on Protestantism and Naturalism.

The very nature of the doctrine makes it both the center of resistance against error and the heart of the Church's positive teaching. As we have seen, it develops as the revelation develops, gradually becoming more distinct in proportion as the Scriptures describe more and more clearly their essential object, which is Christ. Like the Saviour, it is prefigured in the Old Testament and revealed explicitly in the New. And even here it is like the Saviour, for at least in the earlier books of the New Testament it is still veiled. The Spirit who inspired the Scriptures did not will that these writings should contain a systematic exposition or complete expression of this mystery of Christ and the Church, just as He did not will that they should contain a ready-made and scientific explanation of the mystery of Christ Himself. As a rule, Christ is revealed in them by means of signs that are easily visible but whose meaning is not immediately evident, and by means of brief statements that demand reflection. The Mystical Body is described in a similar fashion, in the very shadow of the Master so to speak, by signs that are brimful of meaning and by expressions that are brief yet vivid as flashes of lightning.

St. Paul is the first to proclaim and explain the doctrine that he has learned. Even while he is yet engaged in the task of laying the foundations of the Church, we hear him telling his neophytes that the Church is the body of Christ. Thus the externals of the doctrine change, but the substance remains the same, for the works of God are without repentance. Hence-

[577]

forth it is no longer Christ that we see, but the Church. Be not deceived, however: the Church is not a mere multitude of isolated individuals. The Church is Christ: there is neither Greek nor barbarian, neither Jew nor Gentile, but only Christ, who is all things in all men.

·Then comes St. John, through whom the Spirit teaches most clearly and emphatically the divinity of Christ. The Scripture has now completed its message concerning the Saviour. But it has not done so without giving at the same time its message concerning the Mystical Body of that Saviour. For in the same passages and in the very same words which tell us that Christ is God, that He is Life, Light, and eternal Son, John also states that He is the new life that is infused into men, the unfailing light that is kindled in their souls, and the divine gift whereby all receive the power to become sons of God. In the same breath he describes the divinity of the Saviour and the divinization of the Mystical Body; the two are disclosed together, one within the other. Christ is fully revealed only when the nature of the Church is revealed, for the fullness of Christ is the Church.

Therefore the Church cannot live the life of grace that she has received, without manifesting herself to others and to herself as the Mystical Body of the Saviour. She cannot believe and meditate upon the truths entrusted to her keeping, she cannot foster the love infused into her, she cannot know herself, without finding herself in the presence of Christ, of the Christ who wills to live, to know Himself, and to love Himself in His members.

This perennial vitality, this perpetual growth, this unfailing influx of Christ and of His truth in the Church, constitutes Catholic Tradition. Hence, insofar as we have been able to trace its successive stages, we have seen that the development of Tradition corresponds to the development of the Scriptural revelation.

Beginning with the Eastern Church, we recognize in the history of oriental theology a reproduction of the doctrinal progress which we saw in the Scriptures. This theology opens with the statement that the Church is the organism in which Christ continues to act, and it closes with the declaration that since this organism is the mystical prolongation of the Saviour, it lives in Him with a divine life. In reality, of course, these two stages of development are not separable, for in the unity of life all growth is one; there is simply a shifting of emphasis, a greater or lesser insistence upon particular points. First Ignatius of Antioch, then Irenaeus insist upon the unity of the Church, upon the necessity of union with the *magisterium* and with Tradition, in order to be united with God. This idea of union with God through Christ in the Church continues to grow more perfect and complete until Athanasius, Hilary, and particularly Cyril of Alexandria come to explain more fully the nature of this unity, and to show how it enables creatures to share the very life of God in Christ. They teach that the very fact of the Incarnation, which makes Christ the Man-God and the common Saviour of men, has bestowed such abundance of divine life upon His sacred humanity that it becomes the source and principle of all life, possessing in itself sufficient grace to make us all sons of adoption and deified men.

This point marks the end of one stage in the development of the theology of the Mystical Body. Here is repeated what was taught in the last books of the Scriptures. In their refutation of the Christological heresies the Greek Fathers, speaking like St. John in his testimony to the Word made flesh, declare that the Mystical Body is constituted by the union of human nature with eternal Life, just as the union of two natures in the one Person of the Son constitutes Christ.

Latin theology follows the same procedure. In Augustine especially, then in the Scholastics and in subsequent writers, we have seen the progressive development of a concept of the supernatural order, according to which all the grace that the members receive is regarded as the prolongation, the connatural prolongation of the unlimited grace which the Incarnation has wrought in the Head. Here, as in the Scriptures and in the Eastern Tradition, Christ and the Church are always treated as one; the final word is always that the life of the "body" is at once human and divine; in short, that it is theandric as the life of the Head is theandric, for the life of the body is but the continuation of the life of the Head.

Since it is inseparable from the dogma of Christology, the

[579]

doctrine of the Mystical Body is one with the central truth of Christianity. Yet, despite the important position that it occupies, it is seldom explained for its own sake and *ex professo*. We confess — why not? — that our first researches in the field of ecclesiastical tradition were disappointing. We had expected the doctrine to be very much in evidence, but found it for the most part only dimly visible.

However, what we discovered was far better than we had hoped for. Life is not something juxtaposed to what it animates; it lies within. Similarly, the truth of the Mystical Body is not restricted to any one part of Christian teaching; it is everywhere. Just as the Christ of whom it speaks is present in all the faithful in order to communicate light and strength to all, so the Mystical Body is somehow present in every dogma, giving each truth a new meaning for the interior life and a new lesson to guide the actions, thoughts, and affections of men.

If at first sight one fails to recognize the doctrine, the reason is not that it is absent, but that it is within. To discover its presence a superficial glance is not sufficient; one must study, even meditate upon the innermost meaning of Christian dogmas.

All this we have been able to observe in the course of our study: the Fathers taught the truth of our incorporation in Christ in connection with practically every dogma of our faith; or rather, they presupposed this truth in their explanations of dogma. They proclaimed the dogma of the Trinity, but in teaching and defending it they spoke of the mysterious union whereby Christians are made divine and become sons of adoption through grace, in Christ. They did battle for the dogma of Christology, but in order to illustrate this truth of two natures in the one Person of Christ they spoke of the two elements, divine and human, grace and nature, that are united in the members of the Saviour. They fought for the dogmas of ecclesiology, of grace, of the Real Presence, of the value of good works; and each time, in order to give these truths a better expression, they have mentioned the Mystical Body. They all followed this method. That they did so without previous agreement is evident; that they did so unconsciously, at least on occasion, is very likely. It would appear that the very internal unity of these truths made any such explicit intention unnecessary; else the use of the doctrine could not have been either so universal or so constant. At the heart of the Christian teaching is Christ, who is with the faithful all days. If we regard that teaching with the eyes of faith, we shall find Him without having to seek for Him.

We might now make a more general application of what has been said concerning the Fathers. We might speak, not merely of the few dogmas that have been mentioned, but of all dogmas. All are objects of theological faith, since they come from God and tell us of God; they are objects of faith for men and essential to their personal supernatural life, since they speak of the union that we have with God in Christ, or in other words, because they manifest one or other aspect of the Mystical Body of Christ. In this sense Christ is present in these truths as He is present in the faithful; He is present in them, hidden to superficial investigation just as His presence in men is invisible to the eyes of flesh. He abides in the faithful as the source of their actions and of their life, and He abides in Christian dogmas as the principle whence they derive all their light and virtue.

As long as we perceive only the conceptual expression of these truths, they will doubtless appear abstract and unattractive. But this is because we see them alone and isolated. In them, as in all the truths that proceed from Him who is Truth, we must see Him who is Truth. Once we catch even a glimpse of Him, the dogmas become full of interest, meaning, and beauty, brimful of life. They are the truth of God, and the God of truth communicating Himself to men through faith.

If then we were to show what it is that makes Christian truth the light of all Christian souls, we should have to point out how that truth speaks to men, always and everywhere, of the union with God that they all receive in Christ. We should have to make a kind of synthesis of Catholic teaching, embracing two points of view: that of Christ and that of the Christian. Such a task is, of course, too vast to be given here, even in outline form; but with God's help we hope to undertake it later on.

[581]

However, these remarks have not carried us away from our subject, for such a synthesis would explain what the Mystical Body really is. Beginning with the Scriptural and patristic formulas that we have seen, following each of these until they all unite in a common affirmation, and synthesizing what may be said of the Mystical Body in connection with all the dogmas and all the truths of our faith, it would furnish a complete description of the Mystical Body, not merely from a historico-theological, but from a purely theological viewpoint. But we repeat, an attempt to sketch this further development would take too much space in this conclusion.

Our present task is now ended. Of course, all has not been said, and many rich sources have been left unexplored. We have drawn little or nothing from the collections of conciliar documents, from the books of the liturgy or the lives of the saints; we have scarcely opened the works of asceticism or mysticism, and even to the Scriptures and to the works of the Fathers, Scholastics, and other theologians which we have considered, we have been able to devote only a most summary treatment. But we hope that we have at least paved the way for more detailed studies which will make possible a more complete, more accurate, and more beautiful exposition.

However, with all its limitations, this general study indicates sufficiently the important place which the truth of the Mystical Body occupies in Catholic teaching. It also suffices, we think, to show how real is the unity of that body. The image of the Head and the members, of the Vine and the branches, the idea of incorporation, of life-giving inclusion, of mystical identity are too much in evidence and too often repeated in Scripture and Tradition to permit one to regard them only as figures of speech and rhetorical exaggerations.

If there were question merely of explaining that Christ is the Redeemer and the Model of men, and that the grace which sanctifies them intrinsically is due to His grace and similar to His grace, why should Scripture and Tradition be so constantly insisting on "unity," so emphatic in telling us of the "mystery," assuring us that we are in Christ, that mystically we are Christ? We might with justice echo the cry of Bossuet, in his commentary of Christ's discourse at Capharnaum:

[582]

"Why all these fine words, if we must so weaken their meaning and finally reduce them to so simple a statement?"

It is well to bear in mind, moreover, that the most forceful affirmations of this unity have come down to us, not from the ordinary run of authors, but from the very greatest among the inspired writers, among the Fathers, saints, and doctors of the Church, from the Holy of holies Himself, who is the sole Master. We have recorded what He says in the Synoptic Gospels and in St. John, what He said to St. Paul, and what He has promised to tell us on the Last Day.

Of the ecclesiastical authors it may almost be said that their doctrinal importance is in direct proportion to the energy with which they speak of the Mystical Body. There are, of course, certain exceptions, like St. Basil and St. Bernard. But as a rule the names that occur most frequently in our studies are likewise the most famous: Ignatius of Antioch, Irenaeus, Athanasius, Hilary, Cyril of Alexandria, Cyprian, Augustine, Thomas Aquinas. Moreover, these glorious sons of the Church give their most explicit testimony on the subject of the Mystical Body precisely at those moments when they are at their best, when they are, so to speak, the very incarnation of Tradition, whether it be in refuting heresy or in proposing dogmas of the faith. Once more we ask, is it likely that divine Providence would have permitted a mere metaphor, an inexact expression, to retain so prominent a place in the tradition of Truth?

Such might possibly be the case if the doctrine of the Mystical Body appeared in only a few remote parts of Christian teaching. But it penetrates everywhere; one by one all our dogmas have been linked by Scripture or by Tradition to this central truth. It is as it were the principle supporting the arguments of the Fathers, the refutation of heresies, the proofs of dogmas; upon it the inspired writers and the witnesses of the faith have based their ascetical counsels and their rules for Christian living. What a flimsy structure all this would be, if the truth of the Mystical Body were just a metaphor, or a vague, inaptly expressed idea!

We readily concede that this truth is not easy either to conceive or to define. Philosophy meets with difficulties as soon

[583]

as it tries to understand the supernatural solidarity that makes Christians members one of the other. But why should this difficulty surprise us? Is it the part of human speculation to set limits to the gift of God? Is it not intended rather that reason should lead us, first to faith, with the help of God's grace, and then to a search for certain more or less perfect analogies, certain more or less clear indications that may aid us in understanding the mystery?

It would indeed be interesting to gather up such few halting phrases as unaided human reason could utter on the subject of this mystery of unity, but that was not our intention in these pages. We wished to listen solely to the voice of God, to hear only the message of union which He Himself addresses to us in the whole of Scripture and in the whole of Tradition.

The message is this: in the Church, which is the continuation of Christ, there exists between the Incarnate Word and each Christian more than any bond of love, however ardent, more than a relation of resemblance, however close, more than the bond of total dependence that binds to their one Saviour all men who have received the grace of pardon and sanctification. There is something more than the union of subjects to any king, more than the insecure incorporation of members in an organism, more than the closest possible moral union. There is a "physical" union, we should say, if the very term itself did not appear to place this bond in the category of mere natural unions. At all events it is a real, ontological union, or, since the traditional names are still the best, it is a mystical, transcendent, supernatural union whose unity and reality exceed our powers of expression; it is a union that God alone can make us understand, as He alone was able to bring it into being.

Notes

PART ONE

CHAPTER I

[1] Eph. 1:1–5.
[2] Gal. 3:8,9,15,16.
[3] Isa. 5:1 ff. (Private translation.)
[4] Isa. 63:14. (Private translation.)
[5] Isa. 62:5. (Private translation.)
[6] Zach. 8:2. (Private translation.)
[7] Ezech. 16:3,5,8,7,13.
[8] Isa. 54:7 ff.
[9] *Ibid.*
[10] Cant. 1:1; 2:2,8; 4:8,9.

[11] Isa. 60:1,4.
[12] Isa. 41:8–14.
[13] Exod. 4:22,23.
[14] Jer. 31:8,9.
[15] Jer. 31:20.
[16] Ps. 73:22.
[17] Jer. 51:36.
[18] Ezech. 25:8,9.
[19] Ezech. 39:6,7,25.
[20] Levit. 11:44–46.

CHAPTER II

[1] Acts 28:23,31.
[2] The history of the Passion occupies about one ninth of the Synoptic narrative, and about one third of the Gospel of St. John, including the discourse after the Last Supper.
[3] Mark 3:6.
[4] Mark 1:1.
[5] Mark 8:27–30; Matt. 16:15.
[6] Luke 1:45.
[7] St. Augustine, *In Ps.* 118, *sermo* 17, Migne, *Patrologiae cursus completus, series latina* (P.L.), Vol. 37, 1547.
[8] St. Augustine, *Tract. in Johannem*, 24:2, Migne, P. L., Vol. 35, 1593.
[9] Mark 1:14,15.
[10] Luke 10:9.
[11] Mark 4:26–32.
[12] Matt. 5:44,45,48.

[13] Matt. 5:23.
[14] Matt. 28:20.
[15] Matt. 18:2–7; 10–35.
[16] Matt. 18:19,20.
[17] Matt. 16:19.
[18] Luke 10:16.
[19] Matt. 23:8–10.
[20] Matt. 18:5.
[21] Matt. 10:40–42.
[22] Mark 9:36; Luke 9:48.
[23] Matt. 6:14,15.
[24] Matt. 28:18,19; Luke 10:16.
[25] Matt. 25:31–46.
[26] *Jésus-Christ*, Vol. 1, p. 380 (Paris 1928); English translation by Dom Basil Whelan, O.S.B., and Ada Lane (New York, 1934), Vol. 2, pp. 78, 79.
[27] *Ibid.*, Vol. 1, p. 388; Eng. trans., Vol. 2, p. 86.
[28] Acts 1:1.

NOTES

Chapter III

[1] Acts 28:23,31.
[2] Acts 1:5,8.
[3] Luke 24:49.
[4] Acts 1:1.
[5] Luke 1:35.
[6] Acts 2:1–4.
[7] Acts 1:5.
[8] Luke 4:1, D.V.
[9] Acts 15:28.

[10] Acts 3:6; 9:34.
[11] *Méditations sur l'Evangile, la cène*, I, 88.
[12] Acts 7:54 ff.
[13] Acts 7:59,60.
[14] Acts 9:4,5; cf. 22:3 ff.; 26:9 ff.
[15] Gal. 1:13–17.
[16] Gal. 2:20.
[17] Acts 9:6.

Chapter IV

[1] Chronological order of St. Paul's Epistles:
1. The two Epistles to the Thessalonians.
2. The "Great Epistles": 1, 2 Corinthians, Galatians, Romans.
3. The "Epistles of the Captivity": Philemon, Colossians, Ephesians, Philippians.
4. The Epistle to the Hebrews, and the Pastoral Epistles.

The Epistles to the Ephesians and to the Colossians are often called the "Christological Epistles," since in them the author is more particularly concerned with the divinity of Christ.
[2] Acts 9:5.
[3] Gal. 2:20.

[4] 1 Tim. 2:5.
[5] In *Act. Apost.*, 27. *Opera*, Vol. 10 (Antwerp, 1662), p. 16.
[6] *Sermon I pour le samedi saint*, in *Oeuvres oratoires*, Vol. 1 (Paris, 1914), p. 106.
[7] Eph. 3:1–9.
[8] Prat, *la Théologie de saint Paul*, Vol. 1, 15th edition (Paris, 1927), p. 369.
[9] 1 Thess. 5:18–23.
[10] 1 Cor. 1:4,5,9.
[11] 1 Cor. 1:28–30.
[12] 1 Cor. 2:6,7.
[13] 1 Cor. 2:16.
[14] Rom. 3:21–26.
[15] Rom. 6:23.
[16] Rom. 8:1.
[17] Rom. 8:39.
[18] Rom. 16:25–27.
[19] Eph. 1:3,7–10.

Chapter V

[1] 1 Thess. 1:1.
[2] 2 Cor. 13:5.
[3] Rom. 16:3,8,12,21.
[4] Rom. 16:22.
[5] St. Augustine, *De Trinitate*, 13:24, P. L., Vol. 42, 1034.
[6] Eph. 1:3–14.
[7] "According to the theory of the Mystical Body, we become an integral part of Christ, we put on Christ, we are plunged into Christ; Christ is in us, and we are in Him. Such is the usual, and as it were, the technical sense of the formula *in Christo* as used by St. Paul, especially when there is question of the supernatural life of the Christian, or of the union of the faithful among themselves." Prat, *la Théologie de saint Paul*, Vol. 2, 6th edition (Paris, 1923), p. 478.
[8] Rom. 6:3–5.

[9] Gal. 3:27.
[10] Prat, *op. cit.*, Vol. 2, p. 361.
[11] 2 Cor. 3:17.
[12] 2 Thess. 1:12.

Chapter VI

[1] 1 Cor. 6:15–18.
[2] 1 Cor. 10:15–21.
[3] 1 Cor. 12:12–29.
[4] 1 Cor. 12:27,12.
[5] Rom. 12:3–8.
[6] Eph. 1:18,19.
[7] Eph. 1:20–23.
[8] Eph. 4:10–16.
[9] Col. 2:19.
[10] Eph. 5:21–32.
[11] Col. 2:9–11.
[12] Eph. 2:16.
[13] Eph. 4:1–6.
[14] Col. 1:24.
[15] Col. 3:15.
[16] In Gal. 3:29, *Opera*, Vol. 9 (Antwerp, 1556), p. 40.
[17] Col. 1:18,20.
[18] Eph. 5:23.
[19] Col. 2:10,12.
[20] Eph. 1:20–22.
[21] Col. 2:9,10.
[22] Col. 1:15,17–19.
[23] Gal. 3:26,29.

Chapter VII

[1] Gal. 2:19–21.
[2] Rom. 8:29.
[3] 2 Tim. 2:12.
[4] Eph. 3:6.
[5] Rom. 8:17.
[6] Col. 2:12,13.
[7] Acts 2:42; Phil. 2:1; 2 Cor. 13:13; 1 Cor. 1:9.
[8] Col. 1:24.
[9] Gal. 5:24; 1 Cor. 15:23; 3:23, etc.
[10] Phil. 2:5.
[11] 1 Cor. 2:16.
[12] Phil. 1:20,21.
[13] Col. 3:4.
[14] 2 Cor. 5:14–20.
[15] Gal. 6:14,15.
[16] Eph. 2:8–10.
[17] 2 Cor. 4:6.
[18] Gal. 3:28.
[19] Eph. 2:11–19.
[20] Eph. 4:10–13.
[21] 1 Cor. 1:10–13.
[22] 1 Cor. 12:12.
[23] Col. 3:9–11.
[24] Col. 2:9,10.
[25] Col. 1:15–19.
[26] Eph. 1:3–10.
[27] Col. 3:3,4.
[28] Rom. 6:10,11.
[29] Col. 3:15.
[30] Eph. 5:19,20.
[31] Col. 3:17.
[32] Rom. 8:18–23.
[33] Gal. 3:25–29.
[34] Tit. 3:5,6. D.V.
[35] 1 Cor. 12:4–13.
[36] Eph. 4:3,4.
[37] Eph. 2:12,13,17–20.
[38] Eph. 4:4–6.
[39] Rom. 8:14–17.
[40] Eph. 3:14–17.
[41] 2 Cor. 1:21,22.
[42] Eph. 2:22, D.V.
[43] Rom. 8:9–11.
[44] 1 Cor. 6:15–20.
[45] 2 Cor. 13:13.

Chapter VIII

[1] Matt. 25:40.
[2] Apoc. 1:7,8.
[3] Apoc. 22:17,20,21.
[4] Apoc. 1:9.
[5] Apoc. 21:1–5.
[6] Apoc. 21:22.
[7] Apoc. 21:23.
[8] Apoc. 22:1,2.

[9] Apoc. 3:19–22.
[10] John 1:35–39.
[11] John 20:31.
[12] 1 John 5:11–13,14,19–21.
[13] 1 John 1:1–4.

[14] John 1:14,16,17.
[15] John 1:1–3.
[16] John 1:4–13.
[17] John 1:14.

Chapter IX

[1] John 4:16.
[2] John 3:10.
[3] John 7:19.
[4] John 13:13; 15:15.
[5] St. Augustine, *Tract. in Johannem*, 24:2, P. L., Vol. 35, 1593.
[6] John 3:2,3.
[7] John 3:5,6,8.
[8] John 3:15,16,18,19,36.
[9] John 5:21–24.
[10] John 6:32,33,35,40.
[11] John 6:49,51,53,54,56,58.
[12] 1 John 3:9.

[13] John 11:25,26; 8:12; 1:4.
[14] John 7:37–39.
[15] John 8:12.
[16] John 12:46.
[17] John 9:4,5.
[18] John 9:39.
[19] John 12:36.
[20] John 10:3,4,14.
[21] John 10:10,15,27,28.
[22] John 11:25.
[23] John 6:56.
[24] Isa. 5:7. (Private translation.)
[25] John 15:1–8.

Chapter X

[1] John 1:12,14.
[2] John 5:26,21.
[3] John 6:57.
[4] John 17:1–5.
[5] John 17:6–9.
[6] John 17:10,11.
[7] John 17:12–20.
[8] John 17:20–23.
[9] John 17:24–26.
[10] John 17:11,21–23.

[11] John 17:21,23.
[12] John 13:25.
[13] John 17:23,25.
[14] John 13:35.
[15] 1 John 3:14.
[16] John 4:7,8; 9–11; 12,16.
[17] Matt. 12:34.
[18] John 13:31.
[19] John 17:26.
[20] John 11:52.

Chapter XI

[1] Hebr. 4:12.
[2] 1 Cor. 16:21,22.

[3] Apoc. 22:17,20.

PART TWO

Chapter I

[1] 1 Clementis, 40.
[2] *Didache,* 9:3, 4.
[3] *Ibid.,* 10:2.
[4] *Ibid.,* 10:5, 6.
[5] Rom. 4:1,2.

[6] Rom. 7:2.
[7] Rom. 6:2.
[8] Philad. 7:1 — 8:1.
[9] Trall. 7:2.
[0] Sm. 8:1.

NOTES

NOTES

¹¹ Philad. 4.
¹² Magn. 2.
¹³ Magn. 6:2 — 7:1.
¹⁴ Trall. 3:1.
¹⁵ Sm. 8:1.
¹⁶ Epistle of Barnabas, 16:8–10, Migne, *Patrologiae cursus completus, series graeca* (P.G.), Vol.

2, 773.
¹⁷ *Ibid.*, 6:11–13, P. G., 741.
¹⁸ 2 Clementis, 14:1–5.
¹⁹ Cf. Eph. 5:32; Apoc. 21:2 ff.; 19:7.
²⁰ Cureton, *Spicilegium Syriacum* (London, 1855), p. 47.
²¹ 1 Apol. 32:8, P. G., Vol. 6, 380.

CHAPTER II

¹ *Adv. Haer.*, I, 10, 1, P. G., Vol. 7, 550–552.
² *Epideixis*, 6, from the French translation of the Armenian mss., by Père Barthoulot, in *Recherches de science religieuse*, Vol. 6 (1916), p. 372.
³ *Adv. Haer.*, IV, 38, 1 and 2, P. G., Vol. 7, 1105, 1107.
⁴ *A. H.*, III, 16, 6, P. G., 925.
⁵ *A. H.*, IV, 33, 10, P. G., 1079.
⁶ *A. H.*, V, 14, 1, P. G., 1161.
⁷ *A. H.*, IV, 22, 2, P. G., 1047.
⁸ *A. H.*, III, 17, 1, P. G., 929. Cf. *infra*, p. 236.
⁹ *A. H.*, IV, 34, 1, P. G., 1083.
¹⁰ *A. H.*, III, 16, 6, P. G., 925, 926.
¹¹ *A. H.*, IV, 33, 7 and 8, P. G., 1077, 1078.

¹² *A. H.*, III, 17, 1 and 2, P. G., 929, 930.
¹³ *A. H.*, III, 24, 1, P. G., 966.
¹⁴ *A. H.*, V, 1, 1–3, P. G., 1121 ff.
¹⁵ *A. H.*, IV, 39, 2, P. G., 1110.
¹⁶ *A. H.*, IV, 13, 1, P. G., 1007.
¹⁷ *A. H.*, V, 16, 2, P. G., 1167.
¹⁸ *A. H.*, III, 18, 7, P. G., 937.
¹⁹ *A. H.*, III, 19, 1 and 3, P. G., 938–941.
²⁰ Otto, *Corpus apologetarum*, IX, 419, fragm. 13.
²¹ *Convivium*, 3:4, P. G., Vol. 18, 54, C. B., Vol. 27, Methodius, p. 30.
²² *A. H.*, IV, 6, 2, and I, 10, 1, P. G., Vol. 7, 987 and 549.

CHAPTER III

¹ Clement, *Stromata*, 6:1, P. G., Vol. 9, 209, Berlin, *Corpus of Greek Christian Writers of the First Three Centuries*, (C. B.), Clement, II, 423.
² *De principiis*, 4:29, P. G., Vol. 11, 403, 404, C. B., Origen, V, 351.
³ *In Rom.*, 5:10, P. G., Vol. 14, 1056.
⁴ *In Joh.*, 1:39, P. G., Vol. 14, 89, C. B., Origen, IV, 43.
⁵ *De principiis*, 4:31, P. G., Vol. 11, 406, C. B., Origen, V, 355.
⁶ Clement, *Protrepticus*, I, 8, 4, P. G., Vol. 8, 64, C. B., Clement I, 9.
⁷ *Comment. in Joh.*, 1, P. G., Vol. 14, 37, C. B., Origen, IV, 13.
⁸ *In Gen.*, 4, P. G., Vol. 12, 185.

⁹ *Comment. in Joh.*, 10:20, P. G., Vol. 14, 372, 373, C. B., Origen, IV, 210.
¹⁰ *Comment. in epist. ad Rom.*, 4:7, P. G., Vol. 14, 985.
¹¹ *In Jer. hom.*, 9:4, P. G., Vol. 13, 356, 357, C. B., Origen, III, 70.
¹² *Comment. in Joh.*, preface, P. G., Vol. 14, 32.
¹³ 1 Cor. 15:27,28.
¹⁴ *In Levit. hom.*, 7:2, P. G., Vol. 12, 478, 479, C. B., Origen, VI, 374–376.
¹⁵ *Ibid.*, P. G., 480, C. B., 376.
¹⁶ *Ibid.*, P. G., 481, 482, C. B., 379, 380.
¹⁷ *Contra Celsum*, 6:48, P. G., Vol. 11, 1373, C. B., Origen, II, 119.

[589]

Chapter IV

[1] *Oratio de incarnatione Verbi*, 41, P. G., Vol. 25, 168.

[2] *Oratio contra gentes*, 42, P. G., Vol. 25, 84.

[3] *Oratio de incarnatione*, 47, P. G., Vol. 25, 180, 181.

[4] *Ibid.*, 48, P. G., 181.

[5] *Ibid.*, 27, 28, P. G., 141–145.

[6] *Ibid.*, 48, P. G., 181.

[7] *Ibid.*, 30, P. G., 148.

[8] Eccles. 1:9; Prov. 8:22; Matt. 24:36; John 17:19; Rom. 1:4; 1 Cor. 15:27,28; John 17, *passim*.

[9] *Histoire ancienne de l'Eglise*, Vol. 2, p. 168.

[10] *I Contra arianos*, 39, P. G., Vol. 26, 93.

[11] *II Contra arianos*, 69, 70, P. G., Vol. 26, 293–296.

[12] *Ibid.*, P. G., 296.

[13] *II Contra arianos*, 59, P. G., Vol. 26, 273.

[14] *III Contra arianos*, 57, P. G., Vol. 26, 444.

[15] *Ibid.*, 58, P. G., 444, 445.

[16] *III Contra arianos*, 33, P. G., Vol. 26, 393.

[17] *Ibid.*, 34, P. G., 397.

[18] *I Contra arianos*, 43, P. G., Vol. 26, 100.

[19] *III Contra arianos*, 22, P. G., Vol. 26, 368, 369.

[20] *Ibid.*, P. G., 368.

[21] *Apologia pro fuga sua*, 13, P. G., Vol. 25, 661.

[22] *I Contra arianos*, 21, P. G., Vol. 26, 96, 97.

[23] *Ibid.*, 46, 47, P. G., 108, 109.

[24] Prov. 8:22. The Vulgate reading is *possedit me*.

[25] *II Contra arianos*, 55, 56, P. G., Vol. 26, 264, 265.

[26] *Ibid.*, P. G., 265.

[27] *De incarnatione et contra arianos*, 5, P. G., Vol. 26, 992.

[28] *Ibid.*, 12, P. G., 1004.

[29] *Ibid.*

[30] *Ibid.*, 21, P. G., 1022.

[31] *Ibid.*

[32] *Ibid.*, 8, P. G., 996, 997.

[33] Moehler, *Athanasius der Grosse und die Kirche seiner Zeit* (Mainz, 1827), p. 122.

Chapter V

[1] *De Trinitate*, 2, P. L., Vol. 10, 33.

[2] *Ibid.*, 1:13, P. G., 35.

[3] *Comment. in Mt.*, 2:5, P. L., Vol. 9, 927.

[4] *Ibid.*, 28:1, P. L., 1063.

[5] *Ibid.*, 19:5, P. L., 1025.

[6] *Ibid.*, 4:12, P. L., 935.

[7] *In Ps.* 91, 9, P. L., Vol. 9, 499, Vienna, *Corpus of Latin Ecclesiastical Writers* (C. V.), Vol. 22, 353.

[8] *In Ps.* 125, 6, P. L., Vol. 9, 688, C. V., Vol. 22, 609.

[9] *In Ps.* 14, 5, P. L., Vol. 9, 302, C. V., Vol. 22, 87.

[10] N. 95, P. L., Vol. 9, 95 ff.

[11] *De Trinitate*, 2:24, P. L., Vol. 10, 66.

[12] *Ibid.*, 2:25, P. L., 66.

[13] *Ibid.*, 9:3, P. L., 282.

[14] *Ibid.*, 9:4, P. L., 284.

[15] *Ibid.*, 9:7, P. L., 286.

[16] *Ibid.*, 9:8, P. L., 287.

[17] *Ibid.*, 9:9, P. L., 288.

[18] *De Trinitate*, 8:6, P. L., Vol. 10, 241.

[19] *Ibid.*, 8:7, P. L., 241.

[20] *Ibid.*, 8:8, P. L., 242.

[21] *Ibid.*, 8:11, P. L., 243.

[22] *Ibid.*, 8:12, P. L., 245.

[23] *Ibid.*, 8:13, P. L., 246.

[24] *De Trinitate*, 8:15, P. L., Vol. 10, 247, 248.

[25] *Ibid.*, 8:16, P. L., 248.

[26] *Ibid.*, 8:17, P. L., 249.

NOTES

CHAPTER VI

[1] *Oratio,* 7:23, P. G., Vol. 35, 785.
[2] *Oratio,* 38:16, 17, 18, P. G., Vol. 36, 329 and 332.
[3] *Ibid.,* 18, P. G., 332, 333.
[4] *Oratio,* 37:2, P. G., Vol. 36, 284.
[5] *Oratio,* 2:25, P. G., Vol. 35, 433.
[6] *Oratio,* 38:15, P. G., Vol. 36, 329.
[7] *Oratio,* 19:12, 13, P. G., Vol. 35, 1057.
[8] *Oratio,* 1:4, 5, P. G., Vol. 35, 397.
[9] *Oratio,* 30:14, P. G., Vol. 36, 121.
[10] *Oratio,* 40:45, P. G., Vol. 36, 424.
[11] *Oratio,* 30:6, P. G., Vol. 36, 109.
[12] *Epistola ad Cledonium,* P. G., Vol. 37, 181.
[13] *Ibid.,* 185.
[14] *Ibid.,* 188.
[15] μίξις, κρᾶσις, σύγκρασις, meaning "mixture," "fusion," "a mingling," are terms frequently used by the Greek Fathers to denote the intimacy of the union that exists between the two natures of Christ in the hypostatic union, and the intimacy of the union which men have with Christ by reason of their incorporation in Him.
[16] *Contra Apollinarem,* 53, P. G., Vol. 45, 1252.
[17] *Ibid.,* 16, P. G., 1153.
[18] *Epistola* II, fragm. II, P. L., Vol. 13, 352.
[19] *Ibid.,* 353.
[20] *In illud: Tunc ipse Filius subjicietur,* P. G., Vol. 44, 1317.
[21] *Ibid.,* 1317–1320.
[22] *Ibid.,* 1320.
[23] *Ibid.,* 1324.
[24] *Oratio catechetica,* 25, P. G., Vol. 45, 65.

CHAPTER VII

[1] *In Gal. comment.,* cap. 3, P. G., Vol. 61, 656.
[2] These expressions must be properly understood. Christ in the Eucharist is impassible; it is not He, but the species, that are broken at the Communion of the Mass.
[3] *In Joh. hom.* 46, P. G., Vol. 59, 260.
[4] *In I Cor. hom.* 24, P. G., Vol. 61, 200.
[5] *In I Tim. hom.* 15, P. G., Vol. 62, 586.
[6] *In Mt. hom.* 83, P. G., Vol. 58, 743 ff.
[7] Like the other writers of the school of Antioch, St. John Chrysostom insists upon, and at times overemphasizes, the role of human liberty in the work of our salvation.
[8] *In Mt. hom.* 88, P. G., Vol. 58, 778.
[9] *In Mt. hom.* 50, P. G., Vol. 58, 509.
[10] *In II Joh. hom.* 27, P. G., Vol. 59, 161.
[11] *In Mt. hom.* 49, P. G., Vol. 58, 502.
[12] *In II Cor. hom.* 17, P. G., Vol. 61, 522.
[13] *In Act hom.* 45, P. G., Vol. 60, 318, 319.
[14] *In Rom. hom.* 15, P. G., Vol. 60, 547, 548.
[15] *In II Cor. hom.* 20, P. G., Vol. 61, 540.
[16] *In Joh. hom.* 14, P. G., Vol. 59, 9.

CHAPTER VIII

[1] One of the expressions which the Saint was later to reject as inadequate. It recurs several times in the rest of the passage.

[591]

NOTES

2 *In Joh.*, 4, P. G., Vol., 73, 601.
3 *Ibid.*, P. G., 604.
4 This, too, is an inaccuracy of expression, which was to be eliminated by the development of theology. If taken strictly, the statement expresses the Monothelete heresy that in Christ there is no human will, but only the divine will. What Cyril means is that although Christ possesses two "energies," two operations, just as He possesses two distinct natures and two principles of operation, yet there is but one *operans*, one person who acts.
5 *In Joh.*, 4, P. G., Vol. 73, 577.
6 *In Joh.*, 6, P. G., Vol. 73, 964.
7 *In Joh.*, 12, P. G., Vol. 74, 628.
8 *In Joh.*, 4:2, P. G., Vol. 73, 577.
9 *Ibid.*, P. G., 584.
10 *Epist. oecumenica*, II, P. G., Vol. 77, 121.
11 *Adv. Nestorium*, 4, P. G., Vol. 76, 193.
12 *Ibid.*, P. G., 197.
13 *In Joh.*, 11:11, P. G., Vol. 74, 557.
14 *Ibid.*, P. G., 560.

15 *Ibid.*, 561.
16 *In Joh.*, 11:11, P. G., Vol. 74, 561.
17 *In Joh.*, 11:12, P. G., Vol. 74, 564, 565.
18 *In Joh.*, 5:2, P. G., Vol. 73, 753–756.
19 *In Joh.*, 10:2, P. G., Vol. 74, 432.
20 *In Joh.*, 1:9, P. G., Vol. 73, 161–164.
21 *In Joh.*, 12:1, P. G., Vol. 74, 700.
22 *De recta fide ad Theodosium*, P. G., Vol. 76, 1177.
23 *In Joh.*, 1:9, P. G., Vol. 73, 153.
24 *Hom. pasch.*, 10, P. G., Vol. 77, 617.
25 *Glaphyra in Genesim*, 3, P. G., Vol. 69, 148.
26 *In Joh.*, 11:10, P. G., Vol. 74, 541.
27 *Ibid.*, P. G., 545.
28 *De nostris rectis dogmatibus veritatis*, *Oratio*, III, 10, 11, P. G., Vol. 89, 1340.
29 *De fide orthodoxa*, 3:25, P. G., Vol. 94, 1093.
30 *De duabus in Christo voluntatibus*, 44, P. G., Vol. 95, 184.
31 *De fide orthodoxa*, 4:13, P. G., Vol. 94, 1154.

PART THREE

CHAPTER I

1 *De paenitentia*, 10, P. L., Vol. 1, col. 1245.
2 *Epistolae*, 1:4, P. L., Vol. 4, 200.
3 *Ibid.*, 1:5, P. L., Vol. 4, 203.
4 *De catholica Ecclesiae unitate*, 5, P. L., Vol. 4, 501, C. V., Vol. 3, 213.
5 *Ibid.*, 6, P. L., Vol. 4, 503, C. V., Vol. 3, p. 214.
6 *Ibid.*, 23, P. L., Vol. 4, 517.

7 Cf. *supra*, Part I, p. 233.
8 *De oratione dominica*, 8, P. L., Vol. 4, 523, 524.
9 *Ibid.*, 3, P. L., Vol. 4, 521.
10 *Epistolae*, 76, P. L., Vol. 3, 1142.
11 *Epistolae*, 43, P. L., Vol. 4, 383.
12 *Epistolae*, 59, P. L., Vol. 4, 406.
13 *Epistolae*, 40, P. L., Vol. 4, 336.
14 *Epistolae*, 71, P. L., Vol. 3, 1116.
15 *Epistolae*, 57, P. L., Vol. 3, 996.

CHAPTER II

1 *Confessiones*, 3:6, P. L., Vol. 32, 687, C. V., Vol. 33, 51.
2 *Ibid.*, 7:10, P. L., Vol. 32, 742, C. V., Vol. 33, 157.

3 Rom. 13:13, 14. Cf. *supra*, Part I, p. 108 ff.
4 *Confessiones*, 8:12, P. L., Vol. 32, 762, C. V., 33, 195.

⁵ *Ibid.*, 9:1, P. L., Vol. 32, 763, C. V., Vol. 33, 197.
⁶ *Ibid.*, 10:28, P. L., 32, 795, C. V., Vol. 33, 255.
⁷ *In Ps.* 54, P. L., Vol. 36, 643.
⁸ *Sermo* cxxix, P. L., Vol. 38, 722.
⁹ *Ibid.*
¹⁰ *Ibid.*, 722, 723.
¹¹ *Contra epist. Parm.*, 3:4, P. L., Vol. 43, 101, C. V., Vol. 51, 131.

¹² *Psalmus contra partem Donati,* P. L., Vol. 43, 30, C. V., Vol. 51, 12.
¹³ *Epistolae,* 128, P. L., Vol. 33, 490, C. V., Vol. 44, 33.
¹⁴ Cf. *infra,* Chapter IV, for texts which express this idea.
¹⁵ *Contra litteras Petiliani,* 3:9, P. L., Vol. 43, 353, C. V., Vol. 52, 171.

Chapter III

¹ *De civitate Dei,* 14:28, P. L., Vol. 41, 436, C. V., Vol. 40, 56.
² *De gratia Christi et de peccato originali,* 2:24, P. L., Vol. 44, 398, C. V., Vol. 42, 187.
³ John 15:5.
⁴ Rom. 5:5.

⁵ *De praedest. sanctorum,* 15, P. L., Vol. 44, 981.
⁶ *Ibid.*, 982.
⁷ *Ibid.*, 982, 983.
⁸ *De dono perseverantiae,* 24, P. L., Vol. 45, 1033.
⁹ *Ibid.*, 1034.

Chapter IV

¹ *Sermo* 45, P. L., Vol. 38, 265, 266.
² *In Ps.* 39, *enarratio* 2ᵃ, P. L., Vol. 36, 219.
³ *In Ps.* 127, P. L., Vol. 37, 1686.
⁴ *In. Ps.* 34, *sermo* 1, P. L., Vol. 36, 331.
⁵ *In Ps.* 136, P. L., Vol. 37, 1768.
⁶ *In Ps.* 91, P. L., Vol. 37, 1683.
⁷ *In Ps.* 127, P. L., Vol. 37, 1683.
⁸ *In Ps.* 103, *sermo* 3, P. L., Vol. 37, 1376.
⁹ *In Ps.* 74, P. L., Vol. 36, 948.
¹⁰ *In Ps.* 90, *sermo* 2, P. L., Vol. 37, 1159.
¹¹ *In Joh.*, 21, P. L., Vol. 35, 1568.
¹² G. Morin, *Sermones post maurinos reperti* (Morin, IX), pp. 620, 621.
¹³ Acts 9:4.
¹⁴ Ticonius, *Regulae,* P. L., Vol. 18, 18.
¹⁵ *In Ps.* 37, P. L., Vol. 36, 399.
¹⁶ *Ibid.*, 400.
¹⁷ Compare this text with that of St. Gregory of Nyssa, quoted above, p. 316.

¹⁸ *In Ps.* 26, *enarratio* 2ᵃ, P. L., Vol. 36, 199.
¹⁹ *Sermo* 138, P. L., Vol. 37, 1797.
²⁰ *In Ps.* 56, P. L., Vol. 36, 662.
²¹ *In Ps.* 30, *enarr.* 2ᵃ, P. L., Vol. 36, 230.
²² *In Ps.* 21, *enarr.* 2ᵃ, P. L., Vol. 36, 172.
²³ Morin, *Sermones,* 27, p. 107.
²⁴ *In Ps.* 43, P. L., Vol. 36, 483.
²⁵ *In Joh.*, 52, P. L., Vol. 35, 1769, 1770.
²⁶ *In Ps.* 21, *enarr.* 2ᵃ, P. L., Vol. 36, 172.
²⁷ *In Ps.* 140, P. L., Vol. 37, 1819.
²⁸ *In Ps.* 85, P. L., Vol. 37, 1082.
²⁹ *In Ps.* 54, P. L., Vol. 36, 629.
³⁰ *Ibid.*, 630.
³¹ *In Ps.* 85, P. L., Vol. 37, 1081.
³² *In Ps.* 122, P. L., Vol. 37, 1630.
³³ *In Ps.* 54, P. L., Vol. 36, 640.
³⁴ *In Ps.* 85, P. L., Vol. 37, 1085.
³⁵ *In Ps.* 101, *sermo* 1, P. L., Vol. 37, 1296.
³⁶ *In Ps.* 142, P. L., Vol. 37, 1630.
³⁷ *In Ps.* 142, P. L., Vol. 37, 1846.
³⁸ *In Ps.* 61, P. L., Vol. 36, 730.

³⁹ *In Ps.* 30, *sermo 3*, P. L., Vol. 36, 250.
⁴⁰ *Enchiridion*, 53, P. L., Vol. 40, 257.
⁴¹ *Sermo* 272, P. L., Vol. 38, 1247.
⁴² *In Ps.* 66, P. L., Vol. 36, 807.
⁴³ *In Ps.* 85, P. L., Vol. 37, 1084.
⁴⁴ *Ibid.*, 1085.
⁴⁵ *In Ps.* 32, *sermo 2*, P. L., Vol. 36, 296.
⁴⁶ *In Ps.* 88, *sermo 1*, P. L., Vol. 37, 1124.
⁴⁷ *In Ps.* 60, P. L., Vol. 36, 724.
⁴⁸ *In Ps.* 127, P. L., Vol. 37, 1679.
⁴⁹ *In Ps.* 69, P. L., Vol. 36, 866.
⁵⁰ *In Ps.* 147, P. L., Vol. 37, 1919.
⁵¹ *In Ps.* 64, P. L., Vol. 36, 779.
⁵² *In Ps.* 122, P. L., Vol. 37, 1630.

⁵³ *In Joh.*, 108, P. L., Vol. 35, 1916.
⁵⁴ Cf. *supra*, pp. 403 ff.
⁵⁵ *In Joh.*, 109, P. L., Vol. 35, 1929.
⁵⁶ *Sermo* 133, P. L., Vol. 38, 742.
⁵⁷ *In Ps.* 88, *sermo 1*, P. L., Vol. 37, 1122.
⁵⁸ *Contra Faustum manichaeum*, 12:8, P. L., Vol. 42, 258.
⁵⁹ *In Ps.* 3, P. L., Vol. 36, 77.
⁶⁰ *In Ps.* 44, P. L., Vol. 36, 495.
⁶¹ *In Ps.* 64, P. L., Vol. 36, 779, 780.
⁶² *In Joh.*, 110, 111, P. L., Vol. 35, 1923, 1929.
⁶³ *In epist. ad Parthos*, 10, P. L., Vol. 35, 2059.
⁶⁴ *Ibid.*, 2060, 2061.
⁶⁵ *Ibid.*, 2055.
⁶⁶ *Ibid.*, 2055, 2056.

CHAPTER V

¹ This is another way of expressing the idea, familiar to St. Cyril of Alexandria, that the body of the Word is rendered life-giving by reason of its union with Life.
² *De contemplando Deo*, P. L., Vol. 184, 375–377.
³ *Sermo* 11, P. L., 194, 1731.
⁴ *Ibid.*, 1728.
⁵ *Sermo* 51, P. L., Vol. 194, 1863.

CHAPTER VI

¹ *De captivitate et redemptione generis humani, pars III, tract. II*, cap. 2, art. 5 (Louvain, 1572), p. 50.
² *In I divi Thomae partem commentaria*, I, q. 23, art. 5, disp. 2 (Venice, 1597), p. 577.
³ St. Thomas, III, q. 48, art. 6, ad 2.
⁴ III, q. 52, art. 1, ad 2.
⁵ III, q. 56, art. 1, c.
⁶ III, q. 57, art. 6, ad 1 et ad 2.
⁷ *Comment. in III partem*, q. 56, art. 2, in *Summa* (Padua, 1698), Vol. 4, p. 412.
⁸ *De symbolo*, art. 6, c. 5, in *Theologia dogmatica et moralis*, Vol. 1, p. 127.
⁹ *Comment. in III partem*, q. 46, art. 5, annot. 2, in *Summa* (Padua, 1698), Vol. 4, p. 247.
¹⁰ *Ibid.*
¹¹ III, q. 48, art. 1, c.
¹² *Ibid.*, art. 2, ad 1.
¹³ *In III Sent.*, dist. 18, art. 6, solutio 1, ad 2.
¹⁴ III, q. 49, art. 1, c.

CHAPTER VII

¹ III, q. 8, art. 5, c.
² *De veritate*, q. 29, art. 5, c.
³ *In III partem*, q. 13, art. 2 (Venice, 1582), p. 193.
⁴ III, q. 56, art. 1, ad 3.
⁵ *In III partem*, q. 13, art. 2 (Venice, 1582), p. 197.

Chapter VIII

[1] And who, as is evident from the context, are not in the state of sanctifying grace.

[2] III, q. 8, art. 3, c.

[3] *Ibid.*, art. 4, c.

[4] *Commentaria et disputationes in III partem* (Alcala, 1616), disp. 45, p. 334.

[5] *De incarnatione*, disp. 23, sect. 1,

9, 10 (Paris, 1860), p. 649.

[6] *In III partem*, q. 48, art. 6, p. 571.

[7] *Contra Gentes*, lib. 4, cap. 97.

[8] *Supplementum ad III partem*, q. 91, art. 1, c.

[9] *Contra Gentes*, lib. 4, cap. 97, ad finem.

[10] Rom. 8:19–23.

Chapter IX

[1] Session VI, cap. 7, in *Enchiridion Symbolorum* (Denzinger-Umberg), 800.

[2] *Ibid.*, Denzinger, 799.

[3] Session VI, cap. 16, Denzinger, 809.

[4] *Ibid.*

[5] Session XIV, cap. 8, Denzinger, 904. Cf. infra, p. 519.

[6] *Conc. Trid.*, Session XIII, cap. 2, Denzinger, 875.

[7] *Comment. in Summam Sti. Thomae*, III, q. 1, art. 2 (Padua, 1698), Vol. 4, p. 7.

[8] *Tractatus (undecimus) de fide et operibus adversus lutheranos ad Clementem VII, Pont. Max.*, Vol. 3, tract. 11, cap. 12, p. 292.

[9] *Epistolae Pauli juxta sensum literalem enarratae*, in Gal. 2:19, 20 (Paris, 1542), p. 238.

[10] *Tractatus de fide et operibus adversus lutheranos*, etc., cap. 9, pp. 290, 291. The cardinal's meaning is clear, although greater accuracy might be desired for certain formulas.

[11] *Brevis annotatio ex SS. Litteris de praedestinatione, justificatione et merito ad Paulum III*, in *Concilium Tridentinum*, Vol. 12, Opusculum 92, p. 336, line 40 ff.

[12] *De necessitate bonorum operum et eorum merito, Ibid.*, Opus-

culum 43, pp. 341, line 47, and 342, line 33.

[13] Aug. Theiner, *Acta genuina S. Oec. Concilii Tridentini* (Zagreb, 1874), Vol. 1, p. 571.

[14] *Ibid.*, p. 572.

[15] *Ibid.*, p. 575.

[16] Cf. *supra*, p. 510.

[17] *Confessio fidei catholicae*, in *Opera omnia in 2 tomos divisa* (Cologne, 1584), Vol. 1, pp. 282, 283.

[18] *In III partem*, q. 19, art. 4 (Venice, 1582), p. 270.

[19] *Commentaria et controversiae in III partem Sti. Thomae*, q. 1, art. 2, controv. 7 (Bologna, 1519), Vol. 1, p. 111.

[20] *Epistolae Pauli juxta sensum litteralem enarratae*, in 1 Cor. 12 (Paris, 1542), folio 149.

[21] *Traité de l'amour de Dieu* (1616), livre 11, ch. 6 (Annecy, 1894), (*Oeuvres*, Vol. 5), p. 253.

[22] Tract. 15, cap. 8, in *Opuscula omnia* (Lyons, 1588), Vol. 1, p. 95.

[23] Hosius, *Confessio fidei catholicae*, Vol. 1, cap. 48, p. 160.

[24] *In IV Sent.*, dist. 45, q. 2, art. 1, solutio 1, c. et ad 2.

[25] St. Thomas, *Expositio super symbolo apostolorum*, art. 10.

[26] *Confessiones*, I, 6, Braunsberger edition (Freiburg, 1896), Vol. 1, p. 28.

Chapter X

¹ *Oeuvres de pieté* (Paris, 1657), Vol. 33, p. 530.
² *Ibid.*, p. 528.
³ *Ibid.*, 111, p. 634.
⁴ *Ibid.*, 33, p. 529.
⁵ *Ibid.*, 142, p. 664.
⁶ *Ibid.*, 43, pp. 665–668.
⁷ *Discours de l'eucharistie*, I, 8, p. 457.
⁸ *Oeuvres de pieté*, 76, p. 582.
⁹ *Ibid.*, 5, p. 494.
¹⁰ *Ibid.*, 68, p. 578.
¹¹ *Ibid.*, 17, p. 511.
¹² *Ibid.*
¹³ *Ibid.*, 15, p. 508.
¹⁴ *Ibid.*, 143, p. 666.
¹⁵ *Ibid.*, 7, p. 497.
¹⁶ *Ibid.*, 30, p. 525.
¹⁷ *Ibid.*, 190, p. 722.
¹⁸ Denis Amelotte, *la Vie du P. Charles de Condren* (Paris, 1657), p. 42.
¹⁹ *Lettre* 42, p. 449.
²⁰ *Journée chrétienne*, preface, col. 167.
²¹ *Ibid.*, ch. 1, col. 174.
²² *Introduction à la vie et aux vertus chrétiennes*, ch. 3, col. 59.
²³ *Catéchisme chrétien*, ch. 1, lesson 3, col. 458.
²⁴ Certainly M. Olier does not intend the phrase in the sense of the Monotheletes. He means simply that the Saviour's sacred humanity existed, but without a human personality of its own. However, that humanity was possessed of all the constitutive elements of a complete human nature; in particular, it acted and willed in a human way. Hence it also possessed the love which every man has naturally for himself and for his own life, but in Christ this natural love of self, this human will, was in perfect harmony with the divine will.
²⁵ *Catéchisme de la vie intérieure*, ch. 1, lesson 20, col. 477–479.
²⁶ *Mémoires manuscrits*, V, 11, col. 1102.
²⁷ Amelotte, *Vie du P. Charles de Condren*, II, 21, p. 605.
²⁸ *Ibid.*, II, 33, 29, 34, pp. 617, 592, 623.

Chapter XI

¹ *Troisième instruction synodale sur les principales erreurs du temps présent*, in *Oeuvres de Msgr. l'évêque de Poitiers* (Poitiers, 1867), Vol. 5, p. 135.
² *Ibid.*, p. 150.
³ *Ibid.*, p. 166.
⁴ *Ibid.*, p. 168.
⁵ *Ibid.*, p. 169.
⁶ Mansi, *SS. Conciliorum amplissima collectio*, Vol. 51, col. 539.
⁷ *Ibid.*, cap. 5, col. 541.
⁸ *Ibid.*, cap. 6.
⁹ *Ibid.*, cap. 8, col. 542.
¹⁰ *Ibid.*, cap. 15, col. 551.
¹¹ Mansi, Vol. 53, col. 319.
¹² Leo XIII, Encyclical *Satis Cogni-* tum, June 25, 1896, in *Acta Sanctae Sedis*, Vol. 28 (1895–1896), p. 710.
¹³ *Ibid.*
¹⁴ *Ibid.*, p. 713.
¹⁵ *Ibid.*, p. 714.
¹⁶ *Ibid.*, p. 715.
¹⁷ Encycl. *Mirae caritatis*, May 28, 1902, in *Acta Sanctae Sedis*, Vol. 34, 1902, p. 645.
¹⁸ St. Augustine, *De sancta virginitate*, 6, P. L., Vol. 40, col. 399.
¹⁹ Encycl. *Ad diem illum*, Feb. 2, 1904, in *Acta Sanctae Sedis*, Vol. 36 (1904), pp. 452–454.
²⁰ Encycl. *Il firmo proposito*, June

15, 1905, in *Acta Sanctae Sedis,* Vol. 37, p. 742.

[21] Encycl. *Communium rerum,* April 21, 1909, in *Acta Apostolicae Sedis,* Vol. 1 (1909), p. 363.

[22] Encycl. *Miserentissimus Redemptor,* June 6, 1928, in *Acta Apos-* *tolicae Sedis,* Vol. 20 (1928), p. 171.

[23] *Ibid.,* pp. 174, 175.

[24] Encycl. *De sacerdotio Christi,* in *Acta Apostolicae Sedis,* Vol. 27 (1936), p. 12.

Index

NOTE: Most of the abbreviations used are self-explanatory. We shall indicate only a few, by way of example: M.B. (Mystical Body), Pre-Schol. (Pre-Scholastics), Syn. (Synoptic Gospels), Wm. of St. Th. (William of Saint-Thierry).

came gradually into being: 36, *199–201*, 233, 577–578

F. *History of the revelation of the M.B.:*

a) God's use of visions: Syn., 67–68; Paul, 79–82, 86, 88, 101, 150, 197, 200, 291; John, 153–155, 157, 197, 291; Hilary, 290–291; Cyprian, 374; Aug., 386–389; French School, 546–548. His use of words and idioms: 25–26, 130. His use of the natural temperament of the human writer: *81* ff., 157–158, 308–309, 385, 413, 419. Cf. Psychology, Understanding

b) Principal stages of this history; in general, 577–580; in Scripture: 36, 80, 81 ff., 199–203, 577–578; Old Test., 21, 23–25, 27–28; New Test., 36, 56–57, 200; Syn., 40 ff. (Cf. Gospels); Acts, 71–72, 75–76, 79, 81; Paul, 85–88, 98, 112, 149–150; John, 152, 155–156, 158, 166, 169–170, 199. Comparison between Script. and Trad.: *203–204, 209–212, 220–221*, 267, 290–291, 294, 306, 309–310, 324–325, 345, 377, 387–388, 419, 435, 440, 459–460, 465, 538, 577–580; between East and West: 367–370, 578–579. Principal stages in Trad.: 267, 357–358, 577–580; Apost. Fathers, 214–216, 220–222; Iren., 228–231; Asia Minor, 246–247; Clem. and Orig., 250, 256–257; Ath., 267–270, 274–277; Hilary, 292, 304–306; Naz., 308, 316–317; Nyssa, 318, 320, 321; Chrys., 324, 336; Cyril Alex., 337–339, 342–343, 345, 348–349, 354 ff.; Western Fathers, 367, 373, 379; Aug., 385, 391–392, 396, 397, 399, 407–409, 411, 413, 416–417, 440; Pre-Schol., 441–442; Schol., 451–455, 459, 484–485, 499–500, 528–529; French School, 531–532, 538–539, 542; Moderns, 556, 557

c) Each writer expresses the doctrine in his own way (rarely *ex professo;* cf. below, G): see Gospels (esp. 167–168); Paul, 87–88, 90–93 ff., 104–105, 113, 114, 119, 123, 129, 133, 137–139, 149–150, *196* ff.; John, 156–158, 167–168, 196 ff.; Trad., 210–211, 247; Latin writers, 367–369; Clem. Rom., 214; Ign., 216–221; Iren., 228–230, 241; Asia Minor, 246–247; Clem. and Orig., 249–250, 255–256; Ath., 267, 269; Naz., 308; Nyssa, 321; Chrys., 324–326, 330, 336; Cyril Alex., 338–342; Tert., 371–372; Cyprian, 373, 381–383; Aug., 385, 408–411, 413, 416, 419, 439; Pre-Schol., 441–442; Isaac of Stella, 447; Schol., 451–453, 484–485, 528–529; French School, 532, 538–539. Cf. Progress, Style

G. a) Importance of this doctrine: 5–6, 12, 14, 168–169, 204–205, 221, 572, 577, 580; Scripture, *202–203;* Syn., 40, 44–45, 47–49, 50–55, 70; Paul, 86, 88–90, 104, 117, 130–131; John, 152, 154, 156, 160, 163–164, 168, 182–188; Ign., 216–217; Iren., 232, 239–240; Ath., 264–266, 269, 270, 277–278, 284–285; Hilary, 293; Chrys., 336; Cyril Alex., 338, 345; Cyprian, 376, 382–383; Aug., 384, 390–392, 399, 408, 419, 440; Schol., 463, 467, 468, 479, 521, 528–529; Trent, 510; Card. Pie, 558; Vatican, 562–564; Leo XIII, 565; Pius X, 567–569

b) Mentioned in symbols of faith: 577; Iren., 231–232; Orig., 262 (Ath., 272–274, 285); Naz., 312; Cyril Alex., 342, 352; Aug., 416, 420, 422–425, 431–432; Schol., 522–523; Vatican, 561, 564–565

c) Implied in many other dogmas: 5, 10–11, 40 ff., 50 ff., 55–56, 112, 152, 222, 240, 263–264, 285, 382–383, 390, 455, 506–507, 525–529, 570, 579–581. Cf. Dogmas

d) Often not explicit, but presupposed: 6, 317, 577–581; John, 152; Ign., 222; Iren., 240; Ath., 285; Aug., 391–392, 399

e) As an answer to errors and heresies: 570–572, 577, 583; Paul, 87, 88, 123–124, 149, 198 (cf. 93–

94, 112–113) ; Docetism, 218, 229–232 ; Gnosticism, 228–232, 236–239 ; Arianism, 188, 268–287, 299 ff., 317–318, 345 ; Apollinarism, 313–317 ; Nestorianism, 339, 344 ; Aphthartodocetism and Monotheletism, 361–362 ; Donatism, 389, 390 ff., 396–397, 410, 420, 436, 439 ; Pelagianism, 399 ff., 410, 422, 433, 439, 484 ; Protestantism, 463, 499–527 ; Naturalism, 557–561 ff., 569, 570 ; Pantheism, 560 ; Rationalism, 569

f) This doctrine to be preached of̩ten: (Aug., 416) ; Card. Pie, 558 ; Vatican, 561 (cf. 164, 188). Cf. Soteriological Argument, Exegesis, Heresy, Schism

H. *"A spiritual body"*: Tert., 372 ; Pius X, 566. Cf. 253, 256. The "body" of the devil: Schol., 458 (cf. Paul, 113)

BODY, physical, of Christ, and M.B.: Paul, 113–114 ; Ath., 271–276, 278, 282–283 ; Hilary, 293, 296, 299, 304 ; Naz., 310–311 ; Nyssa, 319, 321 ; Chrys., 330 ff., 335 ; Cyril Alex., 339 ff., 343 ff., 345, 346–347 ; French School, 534. It is the "sacrament" of the M.B.: 457 ; it constitutes the dignity of our bodies: 276 ; it is a mute intercession for us: 276, 312. "Christ places us in the body of His flesh": 296. Cf. Christ (A,B), Eucharist, Flesh

BONAVENTURE, St.: 457

BORNE. We are "borne" in Christ: Iren., 233 ; Ath., 276, 279, 280, 284 ; Hilary, 300 ; Naz., 312 ; Nyssa, 315 ; Cyril Alex., 349, 350 ; Anast. of Antioch, 359 ; Cyprian, *377–379;* Aug., 421

BOSSUET, J. B.: 79, 89, 582

BOTTENS, F.: 444

BRIDEGROOM and Bride, Christ and the Church: Old Test., 29–30 ; Paul, 112, *119–120;* John, 154 ; Aug., 414, 419–420 ; Isaac of Stella, 448. Cf. Voice

CABEZUDO, Didacus Nunno: 498

CABRERA, Peter de: 483

CAJETAN, T. de Vio Cardinal: *446–467,* 480, 494, *515–516,* 519 520, 529

CANISIUS, Peter, St.: 528

CANTICLE, The new: Orig., 260 ; Ign., 219 ; Aug., 424, 427. Cf. Paul, 143. Cf. Mystical Body (C), New, Thanksgiving

CAPPONI DELLA PORETTA, Seraphino: 466

CATHARINUS (Ambrosio Lancellotto de' Politi): 492, 493

CATHOLICITY, necessity of: New Test., 200–202 ; Paul, 90, 139 ; Aug., 423, 435–436. It is an intrinsic bond: 5, 202 ; Cyprian, 377 ; Aug., 408, 423, 439 ; French School, 534–535. Cf. Members, Mystery (A), Prayer, Universal

CAUSALITY exercised by the mysteries of Christ's life upon our lives: 4 ; Paul, 124–125, 129 ff.; John, 166 ff., 194 ; Iren., 234, 239, 241 ; Melito, 244 ; Ath., 282, 286 ; Hilary, 297–299 ; Naz., 309–311 ; Cyril Alex., 341–342 ; Damascene, 361 ; Aug., 425–426 ; Schol., 464–466, 476–479, 517 ; French School, 534–538, 551. Cf. the individual mysteries of Christ's life, and Mystery (B)

CELSUS: 261

CHARITY, necessity of: 192. It cannot be divided: John, 193–194 ; Aug., 435–438. Cf. 393, 440. It is universal: John, 192 ; Aug., 435, *436;* French school, 554–555 ; it proceeds from God and from Christ: Paul, 144, 148 ; John, 192–193 ; Ign., 219–220 ; Aug., 434 ; Wm. of St. Th., *445–446.* Cf. Honor, Love

CHASTITY and the M.B.: Paul, *112–113,* 131, 148 ; Ign., 219 ; 2 *Clementis,* 224

CHOSEN by God in Christ: Old Test., 23 ; Acts, 81 ; Paul, 89–90, 93, 94, 97, 107, 110, 121, 142, 198 ; John, 198 ; Hilary, 296, 297 ; Aug., 430 ; Schol., 491

GRACE. Creation is a grace: 22. The M.B. is a grace: Paul, 23, 97, 99, 141–142, 148; John, 162; Hilary, 302. Knowledge of the M.B. is a grace: 11–12, 16; Paul, 82, 95, 99, 117–118, 141–142; John, 157, 159, 160. Grace and the M.B.: 4, 580; Paul, 88, 93, 99–100; John, 162; Iren., 240; Clem. and Orig., 254; Chrys., 335–336; Latin Fathers, 369; Aug., 396–397, *402–411*, 455; Schol., 456–529; Prot., 503–508; French School, 541; Card. Pie, 559

GRANDMAISON, Léonce de: 70

GREGORY I, Pope St.: 359

GREGORY Nazianzen: *303–314* ff., 320, 359, 369

GREGORY of Nyssa: 245, *314–322*, 359

GUITMOND: 443

HARNACK, Adolph von: 101

HEAD. Christ, Head of the M.B.: Paul, 118–120, 122, 124 ff.; Schol., 455–512. He is truly Head: 460, 468 ff. Cf. Christ (B, C, D), Strength

HEADSHIP, Grace of. History of the treatise: 455–456 ff. Its place in theology: 458–459. Universality of grace in Christ: 404–405, 460–464, 468 ff., 472–474. Solidarity of doctrines of grace and of the M.B.: Iren., 238–239; Clem. and Orig., 254; Aug. and Cyril Alex., 408–409; Aug., 403–408; Schol., 455, 472 ff.; Prot., 499–508. Cf. Adoption, Influx, and headings there indicated

HEAVEN. The M.B. comes from heaven: 24. Heaven will reveal the full meaning of the M.B.: Syn., 68; John, 158; French School, 535. Cf. 494 ff. Our life is already in heaven: Paul, 142; Ath., 279; Chrys., 328; Isaac of Stella, 447

HERESY bears witness, despite itself, to the M.B.: 218; refuted by the very truths that it has stolen: 573; Ath., 269–270; Schol.,

522; Card. Pie, 558; refuted by a mere exposition of the truth: 8, 510–512, 522; often an obstacle to doctrinal progress: 96, 112–114, 188, 306, 382, 409, 439, 444, 497, 507, 511, 544, 553–554, 560. Cf. Mystical Body (F), Progress (C)

HERETICS, members of the M.B.: Aug., 430; Schol., 488

HERMAS of Rome: 214, 215, 367

HILARY, St.: 245, 277, 286, *288–306*, 307, 320, 324, 326, 336, 338, 342, 345, 349, 367, 377, 379, 579, 583

HILDEBERT of Lavardin: 442

HISTORY. All human history is the development of the M.B.: Old Test., 23, 24; New Test., 204; Syn., 67, 68; Paul, 90; John, 156, 162, 166 ff., 176, 195; Iren., 233–235, 242; Cyril Alex., 357; Schol., 491. Christ's history is twofold: in Him and in us: 203–205; Syn., 44–45, 53, 54, 72; Acts, 76, 132; Paul, *125, 129,* 130–133; John, 152, 166; Clem. and Orig., 255; Naz., 310, 311; Aug., 423–425; Isaac of Stella, 449–450; Card. Pie, 559; Pius XI, 570. Twofold, in both Old and New Test.: Iren., 233–234. Cf. Twofold

HOLINESS, collective: Aug., 428. Holiness (of God, of Christ, our own) implies revulsion from ourselves: French School, 549–550. Cf. Annihilation, Nature

HONOR due to members of the M.B. (cf. 174): Ign., 220; Ath., 275–276, 282–284, 286; Chrys., 328, 334–335; Ticonius, 418; Aug., 436–437; Pre-Schol., 445–446; French School, 554. Cf. Adoption, Dignity, and headings there indicated

HONORIUS of Autun: 455

HOPE and the M.B.: 106, 107, 121, 133, 147, 200, 204, 219

HOSIUS, S. Cardinal: 499, *521–522*

HUET, Pierre-Daniel: 258

HUGH of Saint-Cher: 444

HUGH of Saint Victor: 455